ISBN 0198692021

OXFORD ENGLISH

A Guide to the Language

COMPILED BY
I.C.B. DEAR

SPECIAL EDITION
FOR
IBM
IBM UNITED KINGDOM LIMITED

Oxford New York
OXFORD UNIVERSITY PRESS

First published by Oxford University Press in 1986

This edition specially published 1989 by
Oxford University Press
for IBM United Kingdom Limited
Registered Office: PO Box 41
North Harbour, Portsmouth
Hampshire PO6 3AU

Oxford is a trade mark of Oxford University Press

Printed in Great Britain by
Richard Clay Ltd.
Bungay, Suffolk

ABOUT IBM

The IBM Corporation

In the early years of its life in the USA, IBM was known as the Computing-Tabulating-Recording Company, manufacturing commercial scales and tabulating and time-recording equipment. Thomas J. Watson Senior joined as General Manager in 1914 and became its first President ten years later, when the company changed its name to IBM—International Business Machines Corporation. Watson continued to serve the company, eventually as Chairman of the Board, until his death in 1956 at the age of 82. By then IBM had expanded around the world and now operates in 132 countries.

Today the company develops, manufactures, and markets information-handling products and provides associated services and supplies. Products include electronic typewriters, telecommunications systems and services, and information processors ranging from the IBM Personal System/2 to the largest mainframe systems.

Since the earliest days, IBM's basic aim has never changed: to provide products which will improve the customer's efficiency. This has meant a heavy investment in research and development over the years, and a continuing drive for improved productivity within IBM. Much of the credit for IBM's growth and success can be attributed to the approach to business and the wider community practised by the IBM Corporation world-wide. The Corporation is founded on three basic business beliefs: respect for the individual, service to the customer, and the pursuit of excellence.

In addition to the three basic beliefs, IBM has five business goals:

- to enhance our customer partnerships;
- to be the leader in products and services—excelling in quality and innovation;
- to grow with the industry;
- to be the most efficient in everything we do;
- to sustain our profitability, which funds our growth.

In recent years there has been a growing recognition that there are five stakeholder groups to whom the Corporation has a responsibility. They are: shareholders, employees, customers, business associates, and the community at large. IBM's reputation as an employer has been built on the concept of partnership between managers and their employees, whilst commercial and financial success have grown from the very strong links forged with customers and with business associates such as suppliers, dealers, agents, and consultants. IBM practises good corporate citizenship through its active participation in, and contribution to, the communities in which it operates.

IBM IN THE UK

IBM opened a London office in 1951, and in the same year started manufacturing typewriters in temporary premises in Greenock, Strathclyde. Now, there are more than sixty IBM locations in the UK, including a research and development laboratory, a scientific centre, and two manufacturing plants. IBM has over 18,500 employees in the UK. Its employment practices include open communications, payment according to merit, single status, and equal opportunity.

Research and Development

Hursley, near Winchester in Hampshire, is the home of the IBM United Kingdom Development Laboratory, whose reputation for innovation is strongly supported by a constant flow of patents and technical publications. Among Hursley's 'firsts' was the IBM 9335 Direct Access Storage Device, which broke new ground in the field of disk storage capacity and won IBM the Queen's Award for Technological Achievement in 1988, Hursley's thirtieth anniversary year. The 9335 disk file has been incorporated into the top models of IBM's newest mid-range product line, the AS/400.

IBM's UK Scientific Centre in Winchester carries out scientific research, the general theme of which is to improve human interaction with computer systems. Recent projects have focused on natural language understanding, data visualization, and parallel processing. The Scientific Centre's work is carried out in collaboration with other research organizations, covering a number of disciplines.

The Centre's work on its WINSOM solid modelling programme for engineering applications, which has also been used in computer archaeology and sculpture, received the British Computer Society's 1988 Award for Innovative Applications. The Scientific Centre also hosts a resident artist from the Royal College of Art, William Latham, who uses modelling and graphics systems including WINSOM to bridge the gap between fine art and science by producing incredibly complex images on IBM computers.

The Academic Community

IBM has educational links with schools, universities, polytechnics, and other educational establishments, sponsoring projects that in many cases pioneer advanced computer techniques, benefiting IBM, the academic world, and the scientific, engineering, and technical community. The IBM Institute, for example, provides sponsorship for a number of major projects at universities and polytechnics around the country, including: economics at the University of Oxford; computer-aided engineering at Cambridge; and personal computer networks at Durham and Southampton Universities.

Manufacturing

IBM has two manufacturing plants in the UK, at Greenock in Strathclyde and at Havant in Hampshire. The Greenock plant uses some of the world's most advanced manufacturing techniques in the production of the IBM Personal System/2, the Personal Computer range, keyboards, and information display terminals. Greenock was honoured by the visit in April 1988 of the Prime Minister, Margaret Thatcher, who activated production of the plant's two millionth personal computer. The Prime Minister expressed warm and enthusiastic appreciation of IBM's growing contribution to the UK economy.

Havant began production in 1967, and is now responsible for manufacturing large and medium-sized processors, communications products, and cash-issuing terminals for the finance industry. Havant is the world-wide single source for the IBM 9335 disk file and was named one of *Management Today*'s best six production plants in 1988.

Over 80 per cent of the products from both plants are exported and the company won the Queen's Award for Export Achievement in 1986 and 1987.

Marketing

Often the first contact customers have with IBM is through its branch offices, through sales representatives, systems and customer engineers, and branch administrators. Enhancing partnerships with customers is their primary goal, and they provide services ranging from initial identification of customers' needs to installation and future maintenance of IBM systems.

Dealers and Agents

Since the successful launch of the IBM Personal Computer, IBM has relied on Authorized Dealers to market its small systems. They are the primary outlet for the IBM PS/2. In addition, mid-range systems are now being marketed by IBM Agents.

IBM Agents and Authorized Dealers offer the kind of sales and service a customer would expect from IBM itself, and IBM values its partnership with them very highly.

Marketing and Demonstration Centres

Customers can see IBM products in action and discuss specific needs at one of the Marketing Centres, located in Manchester, Warwick, and London's South Bank. IBM Warwick also houses a custom-built Computer Integrated Manufacturing (CIM) demonstration centre, with an actual working production line demonstrating the benefits of CIM to customers.

Customer Education

IBM's own education and training facilities are available to customers so that they can benefit from IBM's business experience and resources. Customer education is offered at two levels: to customer executives and to customer staff. Some 1,200 senior executives from approximately 250 companies participate in the Customer Executive Education programme held each year at Hursley and at the IBM UK headquarters at North Harbour in Portsmouth. Customer staff are hosted at IBM's three education centres: St John's Wood and North Harrow in London and Basingstoke in Hampshire, as well as at twelve learning centres around the country. Over 20,000 students attended courses during 1988.

The Community

Community support takes the form of long-term, planned, and carefully implemented programmes embracing education, job creation, sports and arts sponsorship, and the secondment of IBM employees. Typical programmes include: support to Enterprise Agencies; the donation of equipment to 'ChildLine', the national telephone helpline for children in trouble or danger; sponsorship of sixty-one contemporary British artists called 'The Self Portrait—A Modern View'; and education and training for many voluntary and educational organizations.

A major sponsorship activity by IBM in early 1989 was the exhibition of the greatest range of Leonardo da Vinci drawings to be gathered together for thirty years under one roof. The exhibition was held at the Hayward Gallery on London's South Bank.

IBM also donated equipment, software, and specialist staff to the Oxford University Press to assist in the task of combining *The Oxford English Dictionary* and its *Supplement*, in the preparation of the Second Edition, published in the Spring of 1989. The 20-volume edition contains 21,728 pages defining more than half a million words and weighs almost 140 lbs.

Excellence

The pursuit of excellence is a way of life in IBM. Throughout the Corporation, the objective of development and manufacturing is to ensure that IBM products are superior to any others currently available. The entire company is orientated to the customer's needs—analysing them, understanding them, and meeting them.

CONTENTS

CONTRIBUTORS

DR ROBERT BURCHFIELD, editor of *A Supplement to the Oxford English Dictionary*

PROFESSOR STANLEY HUSSEY, University of Lancaster

PROFESSOR BRAJ B. KACHRU, University of Illinois

ROBERT LAWRENCE, examiner for the London Academy of Music and Dramatic Art

MICHAEL MABE, scientific editor/writer with the British Standards Institution

SIR PETER MEDAWAR, formerly Visiting Scientific Worker, Transplantation Biology Section, Medical Research Council Research Centre, Harrow

PROFESSOR PAT ROGERS, University of South Florida, Tampa

DR ANDREW SANDERS, University of London

LESLIE SHEPARD, author of *The History of Street Literature*

JOHN SIMPSON, author of *The Concise Oxford Dictionary of Proverbs*

E. S. C. WEINER, editor of the *New Oxford English Dictionary*

AUDREY WHITING, author of *The Kents*

PETER WILBY, Education Correspondent, *Sunday Times*

DR LISE WINER, Southern Illinois University

Acknowledgements

The publishers would like to express their gratitude to Stan Remington and Book Club Associates for their special interest and encouragement.

'Famous Writers and their Works' (pp. 412–510) is abridged and adapted from *The Oxford Companion to English Literature* 5th edition edited by Margaret Drabble (© Margaret Drabble and OUP 1985) by permission of A D Peters & Co. Ltd.

'Everyday Scientific and Medical Terms' (pp. 616–62) is adapted from the *Concise Science Dictionary* (OUP 1984; © Market House Books 1984) and from the *Concise Medical Dictionary* (2nd edition OUP 1985; © Laurence Urdang Associates Limited 1980, 1985) by permission of Market House Books Limited.

ABBREVIATIONS
USED IN THIS BOOK

a.	(*ante*) before
abbrev.	abbreviation
abl.	ablative (case)
Amer.	American
attr.	attributed
Aust.	Australian
bk.	book
c.	(*circa*) around
c.	century
ch.	chapter
COD	*The Concise Oxford Dictionary* (edn. 7, Oxford, 1982)
colloq.	colloquial
Dict.	Dictionary
edn.	edition
EETS	Early English Text Society
esp.	especially
et al.	(*et alii*) and others
f.	from
Fr.	French
Ger.	German
Gr.	Greek
Hart's Rules	*Hart's Rules for Compositors and Readers* (edn. 39, Oxford, 1983)
hist.	with historical reference
It.	Italian
Jap.	Japanese
l.	line
L.	Latin
ME	Middle English
medL	medieval Latin
MEU	H. W. Fowler, *A Dictionary of Modern English Usage* (edn. 2, revised by Sir Ernest Gowers, Oxford, 1965)
modE	modern English
modF	modern French
MS	manuscript
NEB	*The New English Bible* (Oxford and Cambridge, 1970)
NY	New York
obs.	obsolete
ODWE	*The Oxford Dictionary for Writers and Editors* (Oxford, 1981)
OE	Old English
OED	*The Oxford English Dictionary* (Oxford, 1933) and its supplementary volumes, A–G (1972); H–N (1976); O–Scz (1982)
OF	Old French
ON	Old Norse
orig.	originally
p.	page
pa.t.	past tense
perf.	performed
pl.	plate
Port.	Portuguese
pt.	part
pub.	published
rev.	revised
Ser.	Series
Sp.	Spanish
TLS	*The Times Literary Supplement*
tr.	translation of, translated by
US	United States
usu.	usually
vol.	volume
*	See entry for this word or name.

GRAMMATICAL TERMS
USED IN THIS BOOK

WHERE an example is partly in italics and partly in roman type, it is the words in roman that exemplify the term being defined.

absolute used independently of its customary grammatical relationship or construction, e.g. Weather permitting, *I will come*.

acronym a word formed from the initial letters of other words, e.g. *NATO*.

active applied to a verb whose subject is also the source of the action of the verb, e.g. *We* saw *him*; opposite of **passive**.

adjective a word that names an attribute, used to describe a noun or pronoun, e.g. small *child*, *it is* small.

adverb a word that modifies an adjective, verb, or another adverb, expressing a relation of place, time circumstance, manner, cause, degree, etc., e.g. *gently*, *accordingly*, *now*, *here*, *why*.

agent noun a noun denoting the doer of an action, e.g. *builder*.

agent suffix a suffix added to a verb to form an agent noun, e.g. *-er*.

agree to have the same grammatical number, gender, case, or person as another word.

analogy the formation of a word, derivative, or construction in imitation of an existing word or pattern.

animate denoting a living being.

antecedent a noun or phrase to which a relative pronoun refers back.

antepenultimate last but two.

antonym a word of contrary meaning to another.

apposition the placing of a word, especially a noun, syntactically parallel to another, e.g. *William the Conqueror*.

article *a*|*an* (**indefinite** article) or *the* (**definite** article).

attributive designating a noun, adjective, or phrase expressing an attribute, characteristically preceding the word it qualifies, e.g. *old* in *the old dog*; opposite of **predicative**.

auxiliary verb a verb used in forming tenses, moods, and voices of other verbs.

case the form (**subjective**, **objective**, or **possessive**) of a noun or pronoun, expressing relation to some other word.

clause a distinct part of a sentence including a **subject** (sometimes by implication) and **predicate**.

collective noun a singular noun denoting many individuals; see pp. 106 f.

collocation an expression consisting of two (or more) words frequently juxtaposed, especially adjective + noun.

comparative the form of an adjective or adverb expressing a higher degree of a quality, e.g. *braver*, *worse*.

comparison the differentiation of the **comparative** and **superlative** degrees from the positive (basic) form of an adjective or adverb.

complement a word or words necessary to complete a grammatical construction: the complement of a clause, e.g. *John is* (a) thoughtful (man), *Solitude makes John* thoughtful; of an adjective, e.g. *John is glad* of your help; of a preposition, e.g. *I thought of* John.

compound preposition a preposition made up of more than one word, e.g. *with regard to*.

concord agreement between words in gender, number, or person, e.g. *the girl* who is *here*, *you who* are *alive*, Those *men* work.

conditional designating (1) a clause which expresses a condition, or (2) a mood of the verb used in the consequential clause of a conditional sentence, e.g. (1) *If he had come*, (2) *I* should have seen *him*.

consonant (1) a speech sound in which breath is at least partly obstructed, combining with a **vowel** to form a syllable; (2) a letter usually used to represent (1); e.g. *ewe* is written with vowel + consonant + vowel, but is pronounced as consonant (y) + vowel (oo).

co-ordination the linking of two or more parts of a compound sentence that are equal in importance, e.g. *Adam delved and Eve span*.

correlative co-ordination co-ordination by means of pairs of corresponding words regularly used together, e.g. *either . . . or*.

countable designating a noun that refers in the singular to one and in the plural to more than one, and can be qualified by *a*, *one*, *every*, etc. and *many*, *two*, *three*, etc.; opposite of **mass (noun)**.

diminutive denoting a word describing a small, liked, or despised specimen of the thing denoted by the corresponding root word, e.g. *ringlet*, *Johnny*, *princeling*.

diphthong: see **digraph**, p. 66.

direct object the **object** that expresses the primary object of the action of the verb, e.g. *He sent* a present *to his son*.

disyllabic having two syllables.

double passive: see pp. 112 f.

elide to omit by **elision**.
elision the omission of a vowel or syllable in pronouncing, e.g. *let's*.
ellipsis the omission from a sentence of words needed to complete a construction or sense.
elliptical involving **ellipsis**.
feminine the gender proper to female beings.
finite designating (part of) a verb limited by person and number, e.g. *I* am, *He* comes.
formal designating the type of English used publicly for some serious purpose, either in writing or in public speeches.
future the tense of a verb referring to an event yet to happen: **simple future**, e.g. *I shall go*; **future in the past**, referring to an event that was yet to happen at a time prior to the time of speaking, e.g. *He said he* would go.
gerund the part of the verb which can be used like a noun, ending in *-ing*, e.g. *What is the use of my* scolding *him?*
govern (said of a verb or preposition) to have (a noun or pronoun, or a case) dependent on it.
group possessive: see p. 115.
hard designating a letter, chiefly *c* or *g*, that indicates a guttural sound, as in *cot* or *got*.
***if*-clause** a clause introduced by *if*.
imperative the mood of a verb expressing command, e.g. Come *here!*
inanimate opposite of **animate**.
indirect object the person or thing affected by the action of the verb but not primarily acted upon, e.g. *I gave* him *the book*.
infinitive the basic form of a verb that does not indicate a particular tense or number or person; the ***to*-infinitive**, used with preceding *to*, e.g. *I want* to know; the **bare infinitive**, without preceding *to*, e.g. *Help me* pack.
inflexion a part of a word, usually a suffix, that expresses grammatical relationship, such as number, person, tense, etc.
informal designating the type of English used in private conversation, personal letters, and popular public communication.
intransitive designating a verb that does not take a direct object, e.g. *I must* think.
intrusive *r*: see pp. 241 f.
linking *r*: see pp. 240 f.
loan-word a word adopted by one language from another.
main clause the principal clause of a sentence.
masculine the gender proper to male beings.

mass noun a noun that refers to something regarded as grammatically indivisible, treated only as singular, and never qualified by *those*, *many*, *two*, *three*, etc.; opposite of **countable** noun.
modal relating to the **mood** of a verb; used to express mood.
mood form of a verb serving to indicate whether it is to express fact, command, permission, wish, etc.
monosyllabic having one syllable.
nominal designating a phrase or clause that is used like a noun, e.g. What you need *is a drink*.
nonce-word a word coined for one occasion.
non-finite designating (a part of) a verb not limited by person and number, e.g. the infinitive, gerund, or participle.
non-restrictive: see p. 134.
noun a word used to denote a person, place, or thing.
noun phrase a phrase functioning within the sentence as a noun, e.g. The one over there *is mine*.
object a noun or its equivalent governed by an active transitive verb, e.g. *I will take* that one.
objective the case of a pronoun typically used when the pronoun is the object of a verb or governed by a preposition, e.g. *me*, *him*.
paradigm the complete pattern of inflexion of a noun, verb, etc.
participle the part of a verb used like an adjective but retaining some verbal qualities (tense and government of an object) and also used to form compound verb forms: the **present participle** ends in *-ing*, the **past participle** of regular verbs in *-ed*, e.g. *While* doing *her work she had* kept *the baby* amused.
passive designating a form of the verb by which the verbal action is attributed to the person or thing to whom it is actually directed (i.e. the logical object is the grammatical subject), e.g. *He* was seen *by us*; opposite of **active**.
past a tense expressing past action or state, e.g. *I* arrived *yesterday*.
past perfect a tense expressing action already completed prior to the time of speaking, e.g. *I* had arrived *by then*.
pejorative disparaging, depreciatory.
penultimate last but one.
perfect a tense denoting completed action or action viewed in relation to the present, e.g. *I* have finished *now*; **perfect infinitive**, e.g. *He seems* to have finished *now*.
periphrasis a roundabout way of expressing something.
person one of the three classes of personal pronouns or verb-forms, denoting the person speaking **(first person)**, the person spoken

to (**second person**), and the person or thing spoken about (**third person**).

phrasal verb an expression consisting of a verb and an adverb (and preposition), e.g. *break down*, *look forward to*.

phrase a group of words without a predicate, functioning like an adjective, adverb, or noun.

plural denoting more than one.

polysyllabic having more than one syllable.

possessive the case of a noun or a pronoun indicating possession, e.g. *John's*; **possessive pronoun**, e.g. *my*, *his*.

predicate the part of a clause consisting of what is said of the subject, including verb + complement or object.

predicative designating (especially) an adjective that forms part or the whole of the predicate, e.g. *The dog is* old.

prefix a verbal element placed at the beginning of a word to qualify its meaning, e.g. *ex-*, *non-*.

preposition a word governing a noun or pronoun, expressing the relation of the latter to other words, e.g. *seated* at *the table*.

prepositional phrase a phrase consisting of a preposition and its complement, e.g. *I am surprised* at your reaction.

present a tense expressing action now going on or habitually performed in past and future, e.g. *He* commutes *daily*.

pronoun a word used instead of a noun to designate (without naming) a person or thing already known or indefinite, e.g. *I*, *you*, *he*, etc., *anyone*, *something*, etc.

proper name a name used to designate an individual person, animal, town, ship, etc.

qualify (of an adjective or adverb) to attribute some quality to (a noun or adjective/verb).

reflexive implying the subject's action on himself or itself; **reflexive pronoun**, e.g. *myself*, *yourself*, *etc.*

relative: see pp. 133ff.

restrictive: see p. 134.

semivowel a sound intermediate between vowel and consonant, e.g. the sound of *y* and *w*.

sentence adverb an adverb that qualifies or comments on the whole sentence, not one of the elements in it, e.g. Unfortunately, *he missed his train*.

simple future: see **future**.

singular denoting a single person or thing.

soft designating a letter, chiefly *c* or *g*, that indicates a sibilant sound, as in *city* or *germ*.

split infinitive: see pp. 138 ff.

stem the essential part of a word to which inflexions and other suffixes are added, e.g. *un*limit*ed*.

stress the especially heavy vocal emphasis falling on one (the **stressed**) syllable of a word more than on the others.

subject the element in a clause (usually a noun or its equivalent) about which something is predicated (the latter is the **predicate**).

subjective the case of a pronoun typically used when the pronoun is the subject of a clause.

subjunctive the mood of a verb denoting what is imagined, wished, or possible, e.g. *I insist that it* be *finished*.

subordinate clause a clause dependent on the main clause and functioning like a noun, adjective, or adverb within the sentence, e.g. *He said* that you had gone.

substitute verb the verb *do* used in place of another verb, e.g. '*He likes chocolate*.' 'Does *he?*'

suffix a verbal element added at the end of a word to form a derivative, e.g. *-ation*, *-ing*, *-itis*, *-ize*.

superlative the form of an adjective or adverb expressing the highest or a very high degree of a quality, e.g. *brave*, *worst*.

synonym a word identical in sense and use with another.

transitive designating a verb that takes a direct object, e.g. *I* said *nothing*.

unreal condition (especially in a **conditional** sentence) a condition which will not be or has not been fulfilled.

unstressed designating a word, syllable, or vowel not having **stress**.

variant a form of a word etc. that differs in spelling or pronunciation from another (often the main or usual) form.

verb a part of speech that predicates.

vowel (1) an open speech sound made without audible friction and capable of forming a syllable with or without a consonant; (2) a letter usually used to represent (1), e.g. *a*, *e*, *i*, *o*, *u*.

***wh*-question word** a convenient term for the interrogative and relative words, most beginning with *wh*: *what*, *when*, *where*, *whether*, *which*, *who*, *whom*, *whose*, *how*.

PART ONE
THE WRITTEN WORD

THE STORY OF THE ENGLISH LANGUAGE

1. *Old English:* c.*740* AD *to 1066*

THE English language began its life in the speech of Germanic tribesmen living in Frisia and neighbouring territories. In the fifth century AD some of these tribes, all speaking closely related but not identical dialects, came to the British Isles. They spread out over much of the country, driving the Celtic-speaking Britons back to the western and northern fringes. From Celtic speakers they adopted many place-names and place-name elements (e.g. *cumb* valley, *torr* rocky peak), but only a handful of general words (e.g. *bannoc* a piece (of cake or loaf), *brocc* badger, *dunn* dun).

Most of the Germanic newcomers were illiterate but their rune-masters brought with them an alphabet called the runic alphabet or *futhorc* (named from the first six characters, *feorh* wealth, *ur* aurochs, *thorn* thorn, *os* ?mouth, *rad* riding, and *cen* torch). The runes were scratched or carved on many objects as indications of ownership or of fabrication, or for some other practical or ornamental purpose.

These runic characters gave way to the Roman alphabet when Christian missionaries arrived at the end of the sixth century, and the language of the dominant Anglo-Saxon tribes was forced into this new alphabet. Only the thorn (the Old English version of *th*), wynn (= *w*), and ash (written *æ*, the vowel equivalent to that in modern English *cat*) survived from the runic alphabet.

The earliest English written in the Roman alphabet is found in a manuscript of *c.*737 AD. One of the poems in the manuscript, a Northumbrian version of Caedmon's *Hymn*, shows common Old English words in their earliest form (e.g. *uard* later *weard* 'guardian', *eci dryctin* later *ece dryhten* 'eternal lord').

By coming to Britain, the newcomers, who at an early stage called themselves 'English', separated themselves in nationality and language from their European counterparts for ever, though it could not have been evident to them at the time. The first great severance of the western Germanic languages had occurred. At some point between the fifth and the eleventh centuries an independent language called English became clearly distinguishable—independent, that is, from the other Germanic tribal languages, those that later came to be called Dutch, German, Danish, Icelandic, and so on.

The vocabulary of Old English is almost entirely Germanic. Nouns, which fell clearly into numerous demonstrably different declensions, also possessed grammatical gender (masculine, feminine, or neuter) and were inflected according to case (nominative, accusative, genitive, and dative) and number. Nouns in the dative case were sometimes, but not always, preceded by a preposition. Verbs, then as now, fell into three main classes, called by modern grammarians strong (in which the past tense is formed by a change of internal vowel, for example, OE *rīdan*, *rād*, modE *ride*, *rode*); weak (in which the past tense is formed in modE by the addition of *-ed*, for example, OE *cyssan*, *cyssede*, modE *kiss*, *kissed*); and irregular (OE *bēon*, *gān*, etc., modE *be*, *go*, etc.). Adjectives and most of the numbers were inflected according to certain obligatory rules. The numbering system changed after the number 60 (*þrītig* 30, *fēowertig* 40, *fiftig* 50, *siextig* 60, but *hundseofontig* 70, *hundeahtatig* 80). The subjunctive mood and impersonal constructions were obligatory in many more circumstances than they are now. There was no future tense. Periphrastic verbal forms of the type 'he was coming' were exceedingly rare. Dialectal variation was extremely complicated. Nearly all of the written work that has survived is literary (especially alliterative poetry), documentary (charters, wills, etc.), or religious (homilies): in other words formal in content and elevated in style. The form of English used in the daily conversations of Anglo-Saxons has not survived.

After the arrival of St Augustine in Canterbury in AD 597, and the gradual adoption of Christianity in most parts of the country, the language began to absorb some Latin words. A few Latin words had even made their way into the tribal homelands of the Germanic peoples before our ancestors moved to Britain, among them *mint* (OE *mynet* coin), *pound* (OE *pund*), and *street* (OE *strǣt*). In the Christian period a much larger group of Latin words appeared in the language for the first time, among them *cook* (OE *cōc*), *font* (OE *font*), *pope* (OE *pāpa*), and *school* (OE *scōl*, from medL *scōla*, L. *schola*).

In the later part of the Anglo-Saxon period, Old English also acquired many expressions from Scandinavian sources when Danish soldiers, and later settlers, crossed the North Sea to this country. The poems and chronicles of the later Anglo-Saxon period show words of Scandinavian origin like *dreng* 'warrior', *niðing* 'villain', *cnearr* 'a small ship', and *scegð* 'a light ship'. The settling down of the Danes is reflected in other loan-words—*husbonda* 'householder, husband', *feolaga* 'fellow', *griþ* 'peace', and, perhaps most important of all, *lagu* 'law'. Three of the commonest Old English verbs were gradually superseded by their Scandinavian equivalents: as time went on *call* (late OE *ceallian*, ON *kalla*) slowly displaced OE *hātan* and *clipian*; *take* (late OE *tacan*, ON *taka*) superseded OE *niman* in its main senses, leaving *nim* only in the restricted sense 'steal'; and *cast* (early ME *casten*, ON *kasta*) slowly displaced OE *weorpan* in the sense 'throw'.

2. *Middle English: 1066 to 1476*

The dates are somewhat arbitrary: 1066 is the year of the Battle of Hastings and the arrival of the Normans, and 1476 is chosen as the year in which printing was introduced in England by William Caxton.

From 1066 for nearly three hundred years the official language of the British Isles was French, though English remained the ordinary spoken language of the majority of the population.

During this period the influence of Norman French was strong enough for it to bring an ordinal numeral (*second*) into English to replace the traditional Old English one (*other*, OE *ōþer*). The phonetic contribution was somewhat more substantial. For example, numerous words came into English with the diphthong *-oi-* (or *-oy*), a very rare combination in the system developed from native Old English words. Many such words, for example *choice, cloister, coy, employ, exploit, joy, loyal, noise, poise, royal*, and *voyage*, came into English then.

But the main development was the replacement of a large number of Old English words by more or less synonymous French words. The old patterns of behaviour and of social codification of the Anglo-Saxons were replaced by new Gallic ones, and in consequence new vocabulary drove out the old. In the space of two or three hundred years English vocabulary was revolutionized by the acquisition of such words.

Obsolete OE words	*Replaced by OF words*
æþeling	prince
ēam	uncle
fulluht	baptism
hǣland	saviour

Obsolete OE words	*Replaced by OF words*
milts	mercy
rǣdbora	counsellor
sige	victory
stōw	place
wuldor	glory

The radical nature of the change is underlined by the fact that whereas the words *king* and *queen* are English, *advise, command, commons, country, court, govern, parliament, peer, people, Privy Council, realm, reign, royalty, rule*, and *sovereign* are all French. As with the terms for government and power, so too with the old concepts for poor and poverty. Thus OE *earm* miserable, *þearfa* destitute, *wǣdl* poverty, and *wǣdla* pauper gave way to *miserable, poor, destitute, poverty, pauper, mendicant*, etc. And most of the Old English words for war (*gūþ, wīg, tohte*, etc.) were replaced by *battle, conflict, strife, war*, etc., all of French derivation.

Some Romance words, borrowed at different periods, produced doublets in English:

cadence/chance both ultimately descended from L. cadere 'to fall'	
compute/count	computāre
dignity/dainty	dignitās

In most of these the longer form came more or less directly from Latin, and the shorter one from a reduced form produced by phonetic change in France.

Some of these early loan-words show features subsequently changed or abandoned in the French language itself. English retains, for example, the *s* that the French have abandoned in such words as *beast* and *feast* (*bête* and *fête* in modern French). Similarly the initial *ch-* in many French loan-words came to be pronounced like native words that in Anglo-Saxon were spelt *c-* but pronounced /tʃ/: so *chain, charity* (from French, cf. Latin *catēna*, *cāritās*) were Anglicized with initial /tʃ/ to accord with the initial sound of the native words *chaff* (OE *cæf, ceaf*), *chalk* (OE. *cælc, cealc*). In other cases words which had /k/ in Norman French but not in Parisian French came to us in their Norman French form, for example *caitiff* (cf. modF *chétif*), *catch* (cf. modF *chasser*), and *carrion* (cf. modF *charogne*). Anyone considering the nature of the indebtedness of English to French must always keep in mind that most of the loan-words did not come from the central repository of received or standard French but from that variety which happened to be spoken by the Norman conquerors.

From the Conquest until the fourteenth century a French dialect, or 'Anglo-French' as scholars call it, was the accredited language of the Court and of the Law. As a result, many legal terms which came into English from Norman French during this period still remain as part of the central terminology of English law, for example *embezzle*, *judge* (Lat. *jūdex*, *jūdicem* as noun, *jūdicāre* as verb), *jury*, *larceny*, *lease* (related to modF *laisser* and modE *lax*), *perjury*.

Orthographical changes brought to the language by Norman scribes were very remarkable. The scribes assessed the language they found before them and in general respelt it to accord with their own conventions. They also, in a quite straightforward way, set down the language as it was *used*, without the embellishments and anachronisms employed and preserved by the Anglo-Saxon scribes during the reigns of Edward the Confessor and of Harold.

Among their adventurous innovations was the adoption of the spelling *qu*, especially familiar to them from Latin pronouns, as a replacement for the 'foreign-looking' *cw* of the Anglo-Saxons.

OE	cwealm	→	qualm (modE qualm)
	cwellen	→	quelen (modE quell)
	cwēn	→	queen (modE queen)
	cwic	→	quik (modE quick)

At a stroke this change caused English to take on the outward appearance of a Romance language: *queen* and *quest, quick* and *quit, quell* and *quiet* were made to look like members of the same linguistic family by the scholarly clerks as they copied their manuscripts.

It is worthy of note that many words of French origin became thoroughly acclimatized as time went on, and in particular those adopted before the middle of the seventeenth century. French words that have come into English since the Restoration have often retained at any rate some of the phonetic or intonational features of the original language. Thus, for example, old borrowings like *baron* (XIII, i.e. thirteenth century), *button* (XIII), and *mutton* (XIII) have fallen into the English dominant pattern, and are always stressed on the first syllable; by contrast the later loanwords *balloon* (XVIII), *bassoon* (XVIII), *cartoon* (XIX), and *platoon* (XVII) are invariably stressed on the second syllable. Similarly *baggage* (XV), *cabbage* (XIV), *homage* (XIII), and *language* (XIII) show the primary accent on the first syllable, and a fully Anglicized /dʒ/ in the unstressed second syllable; whereas *badinage* (XVII), *camouflage* (XX), *entourage* (XIX), and *sabotage* (XX) remain at a kind of half-way house with the main stress on the first syllable but with the last syllable pronounced /ɑːʒ/.

At the end of the Middle English period the English language remained a recognizable branch of the Germanic family, but by the 1470s firmly severed from its western European analogues and not intelligible to them without interpreters. Spoken English continued to diversify but the printers and typesetters, wherever they worked, soon began to set the language down in one spelling system, that of London.

3. *Early Modern English: 1476 to 1776*

The period 1476 to 1776 was characterized by the establishment of a standard form of written English. It was nevertheless a period of radical change. Writing was no longer restricted to a special few. Pens came into the hands of merchants, artisans, yeomen, and scientists, and they all brought their own linguistic patterns with them, and a preference for the vernacular.

One major feature of the period is that writers of the time took sides and waged battles about Latin neologisms (like *condisciple* fellow-student and *obtestate* to beseech) or 'inkhorn' terms as they came to be called. Writers like Edward Hall and Sir Thomas Elyot were on the side of the new learning, while Sir Thomas More, Sir John Cheke, Thomas Wilson, and others attacked these novelties.

During this period the ceremonial language of Parliament and the Law, and of the Bible and the Book of Common Prayer, settled into a form resembling permanence. It was tinged with Latinity and other elements of antiquity, but was firmly presented in the vernacular. Sheer practical needs also led to the preparation of dictionaries and grammars of English for foreigners seeking refuge in this country from religious oppression in Europe, and then of lexicons and grammatical works for the use of native speakers themselves.

Caxton and the early printers in England broadly accepted the spelling patterns of the late Middle English period and rendered them relatively immobile, though they tolerated more, fairly trivial, variation in detail than is allowed today. For example:

> There was a *damoyselle* that had a pye in a cage.
> This *daymosell* was after moche scorned.
> And it happed that the lord of the *hows* . . .
> And in the *hous* therfore was grete sorowe.

The scribes in slightly earlier manuscripts had been much less thorough in the avoidance of casual variation.

Similarly, the spelling of Shakespeare's words in the First Folio (1623) is less rigidly fixed than in modernized systems:

> LEO. for she was as tender
> As Infancie, and Grace. But yet (*Paulina*)
> *Hermione* was not so much wrinckled, nothing
> So aged as this seemes.
>
> (*The Winter's Tale*, Act v)

Some of the detailed spelling changes of the period substantially affected the appearance of the language: for example, initial *fn* (ME *fnēsen*, modE *sneeze*) and *wl* (ME *wlatsom* loathsome) disappeared from the language; *gh* or *f* took the place of earlier *h* or *ȝ* (yogh), pronounced /x/ in final position or before another consonant, as in *cough* (ME *coȝe*), *enough* (OE *genōh*), *fight* (OE *feoht*), and *plight* (OE *pliht*). The old runic letter *thorn* (*þ*) drifted in the way it was written until it so resembled the letter *y* that it had to be abandoned in favour of *th*. Final *s* and *f* after a short vowel passed through periods of great uncertainty (*blis*/*bliss*, *witnes*/*witness*; *bailif*/*bailiff*, *mastif*/*mastiff*) but finally settled down in doubled form. The spelling *-ick* (for earlier *-ic* or *-ik*(*e*)), as in *academick, authentick, musick, publick, stoick*, and so on, adorned the great literary works of the period, and remained as the spelling preferred by Dr Johnson in his *Dictionary* (1755) but not much beyond. The letters *u* and *v*, largely interchangeable or used as mere positional variants in such words as *vnder* (under), *vse* (use), *saue* (save), and *vniuersal* (universal) for much of the period, had divided themselves into their present-day functions by about 1630. So too had *i* and *j* (and *g*): the earlier consonantal use of *i* in words like *ientyl* (gentle), *Iob* (Job), *iudge* (judge), and *reioyce* (rejoice) was abandoned in the early part of the seventeenth century, as was the earlier occasional vocalic use of *j*, as in *jn* (in) and *jngeniously* (ingeniously).

When one turns to vocabulary one cannot but be impressed by the hospitality of the English language. Wave after wave of words entered the language from French, Latin, and Italian, and were for the most part made to conform to the vernacular patterns of spelling and pronunciation. The Renaissance, with its renewed interest in antiquity, also brought a solid vein of Greek words into the language. Smaller clusters of words were adopted from other European countries, especially the Netherlands, and also from much further afield—from Japan, China, and the Dutch East Indies (now Malaysia, Singapore, and Indonesia). Not all the loan-words entered the general language: many of them eked out a temporary existence in literary or scientific works and were then abandoned. Others came to stay and became so thoroughly acclimatized that their original foreignness is no longer evident.

The extent of the French element can be gauged from the following tables, which show the period of first record in each case:

1476–1576	abeyance, colonel, compatible, entertain, grotesque, minion, pioneer, portrait, trophy, vogue
1577–1676	adroit, bayonet, chocolate, fanfare, minuet, moustache, portmanteau, reveille, tube, vehicle
1677–1776	boulevard, brochure, cohesion, envelope, glacier, meringue, précis, salon, vaudeville

In a great many cases it cannot be determined whether a particular word entered English from French or directly from Latin, for example *conclusion* (OF *conclusion*, L. *conclūsiōnem*) and *genitive* (OF *génitif*, fem. *-ive*, L. *genetīvus*).

Italian loan-words of the period include *balcony*, *ballot*, *carnival*, *cupola*, *lottery*, *macaroni*, and *squadron*, as well as numerous musical words, for example *cantata*, *concerto*, *oratorio*, and *soprano*.

Words from the Netherlands mainly reflect the trade and shipping contacts of the two countries, for example *cruise*, *freebooter*, *hawker*, *keelhaul*, and *yacht*.

Words adopted from more distant countries are usually self-evidently exotic, and many reached English by an indirect route, transmitted through French, Spanish, or medieval Latin. A few examples: *harem*, *hashish*, *mufti* (Arabic); *mikado*, *soy* (Japanese); *kapok*, *sago* (Malay); *bazaar*, *shawl* (Persian); and *caviare*, *kiosk* (Turkish).

Changes in accidence and syntax in the received standard language during the period 1476 to 1776 are important.

The third person present indicative in *-eth* (*he runneth*, *he liveth*) gave way to *-s* (*he runs*, *he lives*). In 1476 many nouns had normal plurals in -(*e*)*n* (*eyen*, *hosen*, *housen*, *shoon*, etc.). By 1776 they had dwindled to the few that still remain in the language: *brethren*, *children*, *oxen*, and the archaic *kine*.

The pronominal system developed in various ways. By 1476 the main modern English pronouns (*I*, *he*, *she*, *it*, *we*, *us*, *they*, etc.) existed in the standard language, though some of them were relative newcomers (*she*, *they*, *their*, *them*). *It* lacked a possessive form: *his* (the traditional genitive of (*h*)*it*) or *her* were called on as the context required, as well as such devices as *thereof*:

Yf salt have loste hyr saltnes what shall be seasoned ther with?
Vnto the riuer of Egypt and the great sea and the border thereof.

The missing link *its* came into general use in the 1590s.

In 1476 *thou* was the regular form of the singular second-person pronoun and *ye* the normal plural one. From about 1600 *thou* became reserved for special uses (as in the Bible) and *you* became widely used as the normal form in speech when addressing a single person.

The possessive pronouns *mine*, *ours*, *yours*, etc., developed new uses, especially of the type *this house of ours*. The forms *my*, *our*, *your*, etc., became gradually restricted to the position immediately before the governed noun (*my book*, *our children*, *your grief*).

The most striking changes of all are found in the development of the verbs. The so-called 'strong' verbs—those which changed their stem vowels when used in the past tense, like *ride/rode* (OE *rīdan*, *rād*)—receded sharply. Many now became established as 'weak': *reap*/pa.t. *rope* (OE *rīpan/rāp*) became *reap/reaped*; *bow*/pa.t. *beh* (OE *būgan/bēag*) became *bow/bowed*. Others fell out of use altogether or retreated into dialectal use: the Middle English descendants of OE *hrīnan* touch, *snīþan* cut, *stīgan* ascend, *brēotan* break, and many others. The weak verbs became the dominant class, those which for the most part form their past tense in *-ed*. Nearly all new verbs, whether formed within English or directly adopted from other languages (*contend*, *elect*, *fuse*, *suggest*), were fashioned in the mould of the old 'weak' class. There were a few exceptions, for example *strive* (OF *estriver*), taken over at an earlier date into the native conjugation of *drive*, etc.; and *dig*, originally conjugated weak (*digged*), as always in Shakespeare, the Authorized Version, and Milton, but drawn into the class of strong verbs in the seventeenth century under the influence of verbs like *stick/stuck*. But these were rare.

The third class of older verbs, the irregular or anomalous ones, changed unsystematically as new needs arose, especially the ones traditionally known as 'preterite-present' verbs, the descendants of OE *witan* to know (*wāt* knows, pa.t. *wiste*), *āgan* to own (*āh* owns, pa.t. *āhte*), *cunnan* to know (*cann* knows, pa.t. *cūþe*); (without infinitive) *mæg* be able (pa.t. *mihte*), *sceal* be obliged (pa.t. *scolde*), *dearr* dares (pa.t. *dorste*), *mōt* may (pa.t. *mōste*); and also the descendants of the OE verbs *wesan*, *bēon* to be, *willan* to be willing, *dōn* to do, and *gān* to go.

From this group the language acquired a range of ways of forming the future tense. Wyclif rendered the Latin future tense of verbs in the Bible by *shall* and the present tense of Latin *volo* by *will*. Throughout the period, and in the standard language in Britain to this day, a distinction between *shall* and *will* remained, though it is now fast falling away.

May, *might*, *can*, *could*, *ought*, and *do* spread their wings and had an extraordinarily complex history between the Old English period and about 1700, by which time most of their present-day functions had been established. For example, *may* started out (in Anglo-Saxon) as a verb of complete predication: OE *ic mæg wel* I am in good health; ME (1398) *Shepe that haue longe taylles may worse* (are less hardy) *wyth wynter than those that haue brode taylles*. It was also a mere, but yet very powerful, auxiliary of predication: *No man may separate me from thee* (1582); *when thou comest there . . . thou maist see to the Gate* (Bunyan, 1678). The first use disappeared before 1476. Meanwhile *may* acquired the power to express permission or sanction: *Justice did but (if I may so speak) play and sport together in the businesse* (1653). The intermediate steps, and other uses of *may* before 1776, cannot be briefly described. And so it is with the other auxiliaries.

The old anomalous verbs branched out to enable the language to express periphrastic tenses of commanding usefulness and naturalness to the native speaker, and of equally striking difficulty for foreigners learning the language, expressions of the type *is beaten*, *is being beaten*, *will be beaten*, *has been beaten*; *am eating*, *will be eating*, *have been eating*; *will have been shown*; *are you reading?*; *do you believe?*; *I do not believe*, and so on. The virtual absence of such constructions is a striking feature of the language at an earlier stage.

Two other features of the period call for brief mention. As in Old and Middle English, negation continued to be cumulative and not self-cancelling, at least until late in the seventeenth century:

1154 Þe erthe ne bar nan corn.
1411 He knoweth wel that . . . he ne hath noght born hym as he sholde hav doon.
1568 They should not neede no more to feare him then his shadowe.
1632 Rauenna, which for antiquity will not bow her top to none in Italy.

Finally, the particle *to* followed by an infinitive continued to appear in all the customary circumstances, the so-called 'split' infinitive among them. The construction shades off into antiquity:

*c.*1400 To enserche sciences, and to perfitly knowe alle manere of Naturels þinges.
1606 To quite rid himselfe out of thraldome.

Just after the secession of the American colonies, Dr Johnson wrote his 'Lives of the Poets', and in the life of Milton he wrote 'Milton was too busy to much miss his wife'.

4. *Modern English: 1776 to the Present Day*

In 1776 and for some time afterwards the main body of English speakers still lived in the British Isles. English was indisputably a language with its centre of gravity in London. Give or take a few words, George Washington used the same kind of vocabulary as his political equivalent in England. William Cobbett's *Grammar of the English Language*, first published in 1818 in New York, made no formal distinctions between American and British English.

The history of the language during the last two hundred years is one of growth and dissemination on an unprecedented scale. In 1776 there were perhaps 15 million speakers of English, under two million of them in the United States. Now there are estimated to be more than 300 million people whose first language is English, and of these easily the largest number live in the United States. Substantial numbers of English speakers are to be found in Australia, Canada, New Zealand, South Africa, the West Indies, and elsewhere.

Lexical changes in the period from 1776 to the present day are very numerous.

Almost all the normal methods of word formation have been drawn on generously in the modern period. The prefixes *a-*, *de-*, *meta-*, *micro-*, *mini-*, *multi-*, *neo-*, *non-*, *retro-*, and *ultra-* (as well as many others) have been especially prolific, as in *apolitical* (first recorded in 1952), *decaffeinate* (1934), *metastable* (1897), *microcosmic* (1783), *minibus* (1845), *multistorey* (1918), *neo-grammarian* (1885), *non-event* (1962), *retroflexion* (1845), and *ultrasonic* (1923).

Similarly old suffixes like *-ize*, *-less*, *-like*, *-ness*, *-some*, and *-y* have lost none of their formative power, for example *privatize* (1969), *carless* (1927), *pianola-like* (1945), *pushiness* (1920), *chillsome* (1927), and *jazzy* (1919).

Somewhat more complicated formations, though still containing familiar elements, are commonplace, for example *demythologize* (1950), *denazify* (1944), *paraphrasability* (1965), *post-doctoral* (1939), *prepsychotically* (1941), *renormalization* (1948), and *rubbernecker* (1934).

New suffixes of the nineteenth and twentieth centuries include *-burger*, as in *beefburger* (1940) and *cheeseburger* (1938); *-ette*, denoting a female, as in *majorette* (1941), *suffragette* (1909), and *usherette* (1925); *-in*, signifying a large gathering, as in *love-in* (1967), *sit-in* (1937), and *teach-in* (1965); and *-nik* (from Russian or Yiddish), as in *beatnik* (1958), *peacenik* (1965), and *sputnik* (1957).

Back-formations are very numerous, as *reminisce* (verb) (1829) from *reminiscence*, and *window-shop* (verb) from *window-shopping*. So too are shortened or clipped formations like *exam* (1877), *gym* (1871), and *lab* (1895).

Blended words abound, for example *brunch* (breakfast + lunch, 1896), *chortle* (chuckle + snort, 1872), *octopush* (octopus + push, 1970, a kind of underwater hockey), *rurban* (rural + urban, 1918), *savagerous* (savage + dangerous, 1932), Joyce's *scribbledehobble* (scribble + hobbledehoy, 1922), *smaze* (smoke + haze, 1953), and *smog* (smoke + fog, 1903). Closely related are humorous perversions of similarly sounding words, for example *screwmatics* (after *rheumatics*, 1895) and *slimnastics* (after *gymnastics*, 1970).

Rhyming slang has produced a crop of interesting expressions, for example, *apple(s) and pears* (= stairs, 1857), *half-inch* (= to 'pinch', steal, 1925), and *butcher's* (short for *butcher's hook* = look, 1936). Rhyming combinations like *brain-drain* (1963), *fuddy-duddy* (1904), *hanky-panky* (1841), and *walkie-talkie* (1939) continue an old tradition, as do near-rhyming combinations like *ping-pong* (1900).

Newly coined words as such are comparatively rare in the modern period and they tend to look rather unimportant, for example *Oerlikon* (1944), *oomph* (1937), and *oracy* (1965). One of the largest classes of new words at the present time is that which gives us acronyms, that is words formed from the initial letters of (usually) separate words. This technique of word formation seems to be political and military in origin, to judge from the types *Ogpu* (Russ. *Ob"edinënnoe Gosudárstvennoe Politícheskoe Upravlénie*, United State Political Directorate), first recorded in 1923, and *Anzac* (Australian and New Zealand Army Corps), first recorded in 1915. In more recent times they have become very numerous, especially in the period since 1945, and are now admitted to general dictionaries only on a very selective basis. Well-known acronyms include *Nato* (*N*orth *A*tlantic *T*reaty *O*rganization, set up in 1949) and *radar* (*ra*dio *d*etection *a*nd *r*anging, 1941). But organizations of every kind cast around for a set of initials pronounceable as a word: typical examples of trade union acronyms, for example, are *Aslef*

(*A*ssociated *S*ociety of *L*ocomotive *E*ngineers and *F*iremen), COHSE /'kəuzɪ/ (*C*onfederation *o*f *H*ealth *S*ervice *E*mployees), and SOGAT /'səugæt/ (*S*ociety *o*f *G*raphical and *A*llied *T*rades). The great majority of them have no other meaning than the name of the organization itself, and there are no derivatives. Thus **Aslefer* does not exist in the sense 'a member of Aslef', nor is there a verb *to *aslef*, 'to become a member of Aslef, to act in the manner of members of Aslef', though it seems likely that such derivatives will in due course occur. Many acronyms are so skilfully contrived that they seem to presuppose the existence of genuine Latin, Greek, or Old English words: thus *Nato* has distant echoes of L. *natāre* to swim; *thalidomide* (a near relation of an acronym in that it is formed from ph*thali*m*ido*glutar*imide*) misleadingly suggests some kind of connection with Greek *θάλαμος*, Latin *thalamus*, an inner chamber; and *rurp* (*r*ealized *u*ltimate *r*eality *p*iton), first recorded in 1968, sounds like an imitative word of native origin (cf. *burp*, *slurp*). Others are made as homonyms of ordinary English words, for example DARE (*D*ictionary of *A*merican *R*egional *E*nglish), *Sarah* (*s*earch *a*nd *r*escue *a*nd *h*oming), the name of a portable radio transmitter, and OWLS, the *O*xford *W*ord and *L*anguage *S*ervice (launched in 1983).

The period since 1776 has witnessed a slowing-down of the rate of absorption of loan-words from foreign languages, though such words are still quite common. By contrast there has been an enormous increase in the outflow of English words to foreign languages—hence the phenomena of *franglais*, Japlish, Spanglish, etc.

The adoption of foreign loan-words is a direct result of culture contact, whether by imperialist conquest, by tourism, or by the receiving of new fashions of food, clothing, entertainment, or the like, in one's own country from abroad. French expressions of varying degrees of naturalization (*blasé*, *femme de chambre*, *jeune fille*, *pendule*, *porte-cochère*, etc.) abound in nineteenth-century novels. But modern writers tend to look further afield. Travel, war, and politics have brought into our language a great many expressions from all the major languages of the world, many of them awkwardly pronounced and only half understood. A few examples must suffice: from Arabic, *Hadith* (body of traditions relating to Muhammad), *naskhi* (cursive script), *qasida* (elegiac poem), and *rafik* (companion); Chinese, *Lapsang Souchong*, *mah-jong*, *Pinyin* (alphabet), *putonghua* (standard spoken language), *qi* (life-force), and loan-translations like *capitalist-roader*, *running dog*, and *scorched earth*; German, *Bildungsroman*, *Gestalt*, *Gestapo*, *gesundheit* (expression to wish good health), *hausfrau*, and *langlauf* (cross-country skiing); Hebrew, *mazel tov* (good luck!), *Mizpah* (expression of association), *Mizrach* (Judaic practice of turning towards Israel in prayer), *pilpul* (rabbinical argumentation), and *Sabra* (Israeli Jew); Japanese, *happi(coat)*, *Noh*, *origami* (paper-folding), *pachinko* (kind of pin-ball), and *sashimi* (strips of raw fish); Malay, *langsat* (edible fruit), *merdeka* (freedom), *nasi* (cooked rice), *ronggeng* (popular dance), and *satay* (skewered meat); Russian, *nekulturny* (boorish person), *samizdat*, *sastruga*, and *sputnik*; and Yiddish, *lox*, *mazuma*, *pastrami*, *schlemiel* (blunderer), and *schmuck* (idiot).

In grammar and syntax the period since 1776 has been characterized, as in earlier periods, by innovation, by new freedoms from traditional constraints, and by numerous other developments. Perhaps the most important development is the incursion of the noun modifier into the traditional territory of the adjective.

From earliest times most adjectives could be used both before the nouns they qualified (OE *strang rāp*, modE *strong rope*) and after, in what is called the predicative position (OE *sē rāp is strang*, modE *the rope is strong*). A few adjectives can be used only in the attributive position (*the utter absurdity of his views*) and some only in the predicative position (*her reply was tantamount to a flat refusal*). But in the last two hundred years, and especially in the present century, there has been a seemingly ungovernable growth in the use of attributive *nouns*, that is of nouns (frequently more than one) used in a position normally occupied by adjectives at an earlier date. A typical example is *Greenham Common peace women*, where the word *women* is preceded by three nouns. It would be possible to construct even longer strings of nouns without wrecking intelligibility. (An acount of the rise of noun modifiers is given in my book *The English Language*, pp. 48–50.)

There has also been a substantial increase in the use of the word *one* as what Henry Sweet called a 'prop-word':

Examples: He rents a house, but I own one.
Two checked shirts and a blue one.

Important developments by the standards of the eighteenth century have also come about in the way verbs are used, especially in the emergence of new periphrastic forms and in the use of the passive. None of the following constructions could have been used before 1800:

We were having a nice time before you arrived.
He is having to give up smoking.
With a view to preventing waste.
He has been known to be rude to his neighbours.

Another important development in this period has been the virtual demise of the subjunctive mood in modern British English except in formulaic expressions (e.g. *come what may*, *suffice it to say*, *be that as it may*) and in an optional use of *were* instead of *was* in expressions like *I wish I were/was dead*.

Despite the remarkable and irreversible changes that have come upon the English language since the Anglo-Saxon period, it has not yet reached a point of perfection and stability such as we sometimes associate with Latin of the Golden Age, the language of Virgil, Horace, and others. Equally it is not entering a period of decline. From earliest times, linguistic radicals have looked at fashionable change and liked it or have not objected to it. Linguistic conservatives have fought to preserve old ways of speaking and writing. The battle continues unabated. The issue is one of sovereignty. Who decides whether it is right to confuse *infer* and *imply*, *disinterested* and *uninterested*, or *refute* and *deny*? Is *hopefully*, in its new use as a sentence adverb, acceptable, and to whom? Should we all say *kílometre* and condemn *kilómetre*? Is *privatization* to be admitted to the language without dissent?

Battles like these have been fought for centuries. Grievous alterations to the structure of the language, and to individual words, have occurred. These old ambuscades and assaults on the language have been forgotten, but the new ones, here and now, are once more seen by many people as subversive and destructive.

Yet is it not true that our language, far from bleeding to death, still lies ready to hand as a flexible and noble instrument of majesty and strength? The works of modern writers like Virginia Woolf, Iris Murdoch, and T. S. Eliot are as linguistically potent as those of great writers of the past. The oratory of Winston Churchill was not inferior to that of Edmund Burke or Thomas Babington Macaulay. And everyday English, as it is spoken and written by ordinary people, looks like remaining an effective communicative force, though existing in many varieties each of which is subject to perpetual change, for many centuries to come.

WORD FORMATION

THIS section is concerned with the ways in which the forms of English words and word elements change or vary. It deals primarily with their written form, but in many cases the choice between two or more possible written forms is also a choice between the corresponding spoken forms. What follows is therefore more than merely a guide to spelling, although it is that too. A great part is taken up with guidance on the way in which words change when they are inflected (e.g. the possessive case and plural of nouns, the past tense and past participle of verbs) or when derivational prefixes and suffixes are added (e.g. the adjectival *-able* and *-ible* suffixes, the adverbial *-ly* suffix). Because this is intended as a very basic outline, little space has been given to the description of the meanings and uses of the inflected and compounded forms of words. Instead, the emphasis is on the identification of the correct, or most widely acceptable, written form. Particular attention is given to the dropping, doubling, and alteration of letters when derivatives are formed. Space has also been given to problems of spelling that are not caused by derivation, especially the different ways of spelling the same sound in different words (e.g. *y* or *i* in *cider*, *cipher*, *gypsy*, *pygmy*, etc.). A comprehensive coverage of all words requiring hyphens or capitals would require more space than is available here. The entries for these two subjects attempt only to offer guidelines in certain difficult but identifiable cases. For a fuller treatment the reader is referred to the *Oxford Dictionary for Writers and Editors* and *Hart's Rules for Compositors and Readers*. Wherever possible, notes are added to indicate where the conventions of American spelling differ from those recommended here.

In cases where there is widespread variation in the spelling of a particular word or form, the spelling recommended here is that preferred (as its 'house style') by the Oxford University Press.

abbreviations

It is usual to indicate an abbreviation by placing a point (full stop) after it, e.g.

H. G. Wells, *five miles S.* (= south), *B.Litt.*, *Kt.*, *Sun.* (= Sunday), *Jan.* (= January), *p. 7* (= page 7), *ft.*, *in.*, *lb.*, *cm.*

However, no point is necessary:

1. With a sequence of capitals alone, e.g. *BBC*, *MA*, *QC*, *NNE*, BC, AD, *PLC* (and not, of course, with acronyms, e.g. *Aslef*, *Naafi*).

2. With the numerical abbreviations *1st*, *2nd*, etc.

3. *C*, *F* (of temperature), chemical symbols, and measures of length, weight, time, etc. in scientific and technical use.

4. *Dr*, *Revd*, *Mr*, *Mrs*, *Ms*, *Mme*, *Mlle*, *St*, *Hants*, *Northants*, *p* (= penny or pence).

5. In words that are colloquial abbreviations, e.g. *co-op*, *demo*, *recap*, *trad*, *vac*.

-ability* and *-ibility

Nouns ending in these suffixes undergo the same changes in the stem as adjectives in *-able* and *-ible* (see next entry).

-able* and *-ible

Words ending in *-able* generally owe their form to the Latin termination *-abilis* or the Old French *-able* (or both), and words in *-ible* to the Latin *-ibilis*. The suffix *-able* is also added to words of 'distinctly French or English origin' (*OED*, s.v. *-ble*), and as a living element to English roots.

A. Words ending in *-able*. The following alterations are made to the stem:

1. Silent final *-e* is dropped (see pp. 26ff).

Exceptions: words whose stem ends in *-ce*, *-ee*, *-ge*, *-le*, and the following:

blameable	*rateable*
dyeable	*ropeable*
giveable (but *forgivable*)	*saleable*
hireable	*shareable*
holeable	*sizeable*
likeable	*tameable*
liveable	*tuneable*
nameable	*unshakeable*

● Amer. spelling tends to omit *-e-* in the words above.

2. Final *-y* becomes *-i-* (see p. 51).

Exception: *flyable*.

3. A final consonant may be doubled (see pp. 25 f.)

Exceptions:

inferable	*referable*
preferable	*transferable*
(but *conferrable*)	

4. Most verbs of more than two syllables ending in *-ate* drop this ending when forming adjectives in *-able*, e.g. *alienable*, *calculable*, *demonstrable*, etc. Verbs of two syllables ending in *-ate* form adjectives in *-able* regularly, e.g. *creatable*, *debatable*, *dictatable*, etc.

   For a list of *-able* words, see *Hart's Rules*, pp. 83–4.

B. Words ending in *-ible*. These are fewer, since *-ible* is not a living suffix. Below is a list of the commonest. Almost all form their negative in *in-*, *il-*, etc., so that the negative form can be inferred from the positive in the list below; the exceptions are indicated by (*un*).

accessible	*edible*	*perfectible*
adducible	*eligible*	*permissible*
admissible	*exhaustible*	*persuasible*
audible	*expressible*	*plausible*
avertible	*extensible*	*possible*
collapsible	*fallible*	*reducible*
combustible	(*un*)*feasible*	*repressible*
compatible	*flexible*	*reproducible*
comprehensible	*forcible*	*resistible*
contemptible	*fusible*	*responsible*
corrigible	*gullible*	*reversible*
corruptible	*indelible*	*risible*
credible	(*un*)*intelligible*	*sensible*
defensible	*irascible*	(*un*)*susceptible*
destructible	*legible*	*tangible*
digestible	*negligible*	*vendible*
dirigible	*ostensible*	*vincible*
discernible	*perceptible*	*visible*
divisible		

ae and oe

In words derived from Latin and Greek, these are now always written as separate letters, not as the ligatures *æ*, *œ*, e.g. *aeon*, *Caesar*, *gynaecology*; *diarrhoea*, *homoeopathy*, *Oedipus*. The simple *e* is preferable in several words once commonly spelt with *ae*, *oe*, especially *medieval* (formerly with *ae*) and *ecology*, *ecumenical* (formerly with initial *oe*).

• In Amer. spelling, *e* replaces *ae*, *oe* in many words, e.g. *gynecology*, *diarrhea*.

American spelling

Differences between Amer. and British spelling are mentioned at the following places: ***-able* and *-ible*** (p. 19); ***ae* and *oe*** (p. 21); ***-ce* or *-se*** (p. 24); **doubling of final consonant** (p. 26); **dropping of silent *-e*** (p. 28); **hyphens** (p. 34); ***l* and *ll*** (p. 37); ***-oul-*** (p. 39); ***-our* or *-or*** (p. 39); **past of verbs, formation of** (pp. 40f.); ***-re* or *-er*** (pp. 47 f.); ***-xion* or *-ction*** (p. 49); ***-yse* or *-yze*** (p. 51).

See also 'Words Commonly Misspelt' (pp. 201ff.) passim.

ante-* and *anti-

ante- (from Latin) = 'before'; *anti-* (from Greek) = 'against, opposite to'. Note especially *antechamber* and *antitype*.

-ant* or *-ent

-ant is the noun ending, *-ent* the adjective ending in the following:

dependant	*dependent*
descendant	*descendent*
pendant	*pendent*
propellant	*propellent*

independent is both adjective and noun; *dependence*, *independence* are the abstract nouns.

The following are correct spellings:

ascendant, -nce, -ncy	*relevant, -nce*
attendant, -nce	*repellent*
expellent	*superintendent, -ncy*
impellent	*tendency*
intendant, -ncy	*transcendent, -nce*

a* or *an

A. Before *h*.

1. Where *h* is aspirated, use *a*, e.g. *a harvest, hero, hope*.

2. Where *h* is silent, use *an*, e.g. *an heir*, *honour*, *honorarium*.
3. In words in which the first syllable is unstressed, use *a*, e.g. *a historic occasion*, *a hotel*.

• The older usage was not to pronounce *h* and to write *an*, but this is now almost obsolete.

B. Before capital letter abbreviations.

Be guided by the pronunciation.

1. Where the abbreviation is pronounced as one or more letter-names, e.g.

a B road	*a UN resolution*
a PS	*a VIP*

but

an A road	*an MP*
an H-bomb	*an SOS*

2. Where the abbreviation is pronounced as a word (an acronym), e.g.

a RADA student *a SABENA airline typist*

but

an ACAS official *an OPEC minister*

But where the abbreviation would in speech be expanded to the full word, use *a* or *an* as appropriate to the latter, e.g. *a MS* 'a manuscript'.

-ative or *-ive*

Correct are:

(*a*)	*authoritative*	*qualitative*
	interpretative	*quantitative*
(*b*)	*assertive*	*preventive*
	exploitive	

by- prefix

'Tending to form one word with the following noun, but a hyphen is still frequently found' (*ODWE*).

One word: *bygone*, *byline*, *byname*, *bypass*, *bypath*, *bystander*, *byway*, *byword*; the others (e.g. *by-election*, *by-road*) are hyphened.

• *Bye* (noun) in sport, *bye-bye* (= good-bye) are the chief words with final *-e*.

c and ck

Words ending in *-c* interpose *k* before suffixes which otherwise would indicate a soft *c*, chiefly *-ed*, *-er*, *-ing*, *-y*, e.g.:

bivouacker, -ing	*panicky*
colicky	*picnicked, -er, -ing*
frolicked, -ing	*plasticky*
mimicked, -ing	*trafficked, -ing*

Exceptions: *arced, -ing, zinced, zincify, zincing.*

Before *-ism*, *-ist*, *-ity*, and *-ize c* (chiefly occurring in the suffix *-ic*) remains and is pronounced soft, e.g. *Anglicism, physicist, domesticity, italicize.*

capital or small initials

There are four classes of word that especially give trouble.

A. Compass points. Use capitals:

1. When abbreviated, e.g. *NNE* for *north-north-east.*
2. When denoting a region, e.g. *unemployment in the North.*
3. When part of a geographical name with recognized status, e.g. *Northern Ireland, East Africa, Western Australia.*
4. In Bridge.

Otherwise use small initials, e.g. *facing (the) south, the wind was south, southbound, a southeaster.*

B. Parties, denominations, and organizations.

'The general rule is: capitalization makes a word more specific and limited in its reference: contrast a Christian scientist (man of science) and a Christian Scientist (member of the Church of Christ Scientist).' (*Hart's Rules*, pp. 10–11.)

So, for example, *Conservative*, *Socialist*, *Democratic* (names of parties); *Roman Catholic*, *Orthodox*, *Congregational*; but *conservative*, *socialist*, *democratic* (as normal adjectives), *catholic sympathies*, *orthodox views*, *congregational singing.*

C. Words derived from proper names.

When connection with the proper name is indirect (the meaning associated with or suggested by the proper name), use a small initial letter, e.g.

(nouns) *boycott*, *jersey*, *mackintosh*, *quisling*;
(adjectives) *herculean* (*labours*), *platonic* (*love*), *quixotic* (*temperament*);
(verbs) *blarney*, *bowdlerize*, *pasteurize*.

When the connection of a derived adjective or verb with a proper name is immediate and alive, use a capital, e.g.

Christian, *Platonic* (*philosophy*), *Rembrandtesque*, *Roman*;
Anglicize, *Christianize*, *Russify*.

• Adjectives of nationality usually retain the capital even when used in transferred senses, e.g. *Dutch courage*, *go Dutch*, *Russian salad*, *Turkish delight*. The chief exceptions are *arabic* (*numeral*), *roman* (*numeral*, *type*).

D. Proprietary names.

The name of a product or process, if registered as a trade mark, is a proprietary name, and should be given a capital initial, e.g. *Araldite*, *Coca-Cola*, *Marmite*, *Olivetti*, *Pyrex*, *Quaker Oats*, *Vaseline*, *Xerox*.

-cede or -ceed

Exceed, *proceed*, *succeed*; the other verbs similarly formed have *-cede*, e.g. *concede*, *intercede*, *recede*. Note also *supersede*.

-ce or -se

Advice, *device*, *licence*, and *practice* are nouns; the related verbs are spelt with *-se*: *advise*, *devise*, *license*, *practise*. Similarly *prophecy* (noun), *prophesy* (verb).

• Amer. spelling favours *licence*, *practice* for both noun and verb; but the nouns *defence*, *offence*, *pretence* are spelt with *c* in Britain, *s* in America.

***co-* prefix**

Most words with this prefix have no hyphen (even if a vowel, other than *o*, follows the prefix). Those that have a hyphen are:

1. Words with *o* following, e.g. *co-operate* (and derivatives; but *uncooperative*), *co-opt*, *co-ordinate* (often *coordinate* in Mathematics; also *uncoordinated*).

2. Words in which the hyphen preserves correct syllabication, so

aiding recognition, e.g. *co-latitude*, *co-religionist*, *co-respondent* (distinguished from *correspondent*).

3. Words, especially recent or nonce coinages, in which *co-* is a living prefix meaning 'fellow-', e.g. *co-author*, *co-pilot*, *co-wife*.

doubling of final consonant

1. When certain suffixes beginning with a vowel are added to nouns, adjectives, adverbs, and verbs, the final consonant of the stem word is doubled before the suffix:

(*a*) if the preceding vowel is written with a single letter (or single letter preceded by *qu*) and

(*b*) if that vowel bears the main stress (hence all monosyllables are included).

So *bed*, *bedding* but *head*, *heading*; *occúr*, *occúrred* but *óffer*, *óffered*; *befít*, *befítted* but *bénefit*, *bénefited*.

Suffixes which cause this doubling include:

(*a*) The verb inflexions *-ed*, *-ing*, e.g

begged, *begging* | *revved*, *revving*
equipped, *equipping* | *trek*, *trekking*

(*b*) The adjective and adverb suffixes *-er*, *-est*, e.g. *sadder*, *saddest*.

(*c*) Various derivational suffixes, especially *-able*, *-age*, *-en*, *-er*, *-ery*, *-ish*, *-y*, e.g.

clubbable | *waggery*
tonnage | *priggish*
sadden | *shrubby*
trapper

Exception: *bus* makes *bused*, *busing*.

2. Words of more than one syllable, not stressed on the last syllable, do not double the final consonant, unless it is *l*, when a suffix beginning with a vowel is added, e.g.

biased | *gossipy* | *wainscoted*
blossoming | *lettered* | *wickedest*
combated | *pilotage* | *womanish*
focusing

Exception: *worship* makes *worshipped*, *-ing*.

Note that some other words in which the final syllable has a full vowel (not obscure *e* or *i*), some of which are compounds, also double the final consonant, e.g.

handicap	*kidnap*	*periwig*
hobnob	*leapfrog*	*sandbag*
horsewhip	*nonplus*	*zigzag*
humbug		

• Amer. sometimes *kidnaped, kidnaping, worshiped, worshiping.*

3. Consonants that are never doubled are *h, w, x, y.*

4. When endings beginning with a vowel are added, *l* is *always* doubled after a single vowel wherever the stress falls, e.g.

controllable	*jeweller*
flannelled	*panelling*

Note also *woollen, woolly.*

Exceptions: *parallel* makes *paralleled, -ing*; *devil* makes *devilish*; some (rare) superlatives such as *brutalest, loyalest, civil(l)est.*

• In Amer. spelling *l* obeys the same rules as the other consonants (except *h, w, x, y*), e.g. *traveler, marvelous,* but *compelling, pally.*

Note also Amer. *woolen* (but *woolly*).

5. A silent final consonant is not doubled. Endings are added as if the consonant were pronounced, e.g.

crocheted, -ing	*rendezvouses* (third person singular)
précised	*rendezvousing*

dropping of silent -*e*

A. When a suffix beginning with a vowel (including *-y*) is added to a word ending in silent *-e* (including *e* following another vowel), the *-e* is dropped.

So:

1. Before suffixes beginning with *e-* (i.e. *-ed, -er, -ery, -est*), e.g.

braver, bravery, bravest	*hoed*
dyed, dyer	*issued*
eeriest	*manœuvred*
freer, freest	*queued*

2. Before *-able*, e.g.

adorable	*bribable*	*manœuvrable*
analysable	*imaginable*	*usable*

Exceptions:

(*a*) Words ending in *-ce* and *-ge* retain the *e* to indicate the softness of the consonant, e.g. *bridgeable*, *peaceable*.
(*b*) In a number of *-able* adjectives, *e* is retained in order to make the root word more easily recognizable. See list on p. 19.
(*c*) *ee* is retained, e.g. *agreeable*, *feeable*, *foreseeable*.
(*d*) The few adjectives formed on verbs ending in consonant + *-le*; e.g. *handleable*.

3. Before *-age*, e.g. *cleavage*, *dotage*, *linage* (number of lines).

Exceptions: *acreage*, *mileage*.

4. Before *-ing*, e.g. *centring*, *fatiguing*, *housing*, *manœuvring*. With change of *i* to *y*: *dying*, *lying*, etc. (see p. 36).

Exceptions:

(*a*) *ee*, *oe*, and *ye* remain, e.g.

agreeing	*eyeing*	*shoeing*
canoeing	*fleeing*	*tiptoeing*
dyeing	*hoeing*	

(*b*) *blueing*, *cueing* (*gluing*, *issuing*, *queuing*, etc. are regular).
(*c*) *ageing* (*raging*, *staging*, etc. are regular).
(*d*) *routeing*, *singeing*, *swingeing*, *tingeing* are distinguished from *routing* 'putting to flight', *singing*, *swinging*, and *tinging* 'tinkling'.

5. Before *-ish*, e.g.

bluish	*nicish*	*roguish*
latish	*purplish*	*whitish*

Exception: *moreish*.

6. Before *-y*, e.g.

bony	*chancy*	*mousy*
caky	*cliquy*	*stagy*

Exceptions: see **-y or -ey adjectives,** p. 50.

B. When a suffix beginning with a consonant (e.g. *-ful*, *-ling*, *-ly*, *-ment*, *-ness*, *-some*) is added to a word ending in silent *-e*, the *-e* is retained, e.g.

abridgement	*definitely*	*judgement* (*judgment* often in legal works)
acknowledgement	*fledgeling*	
amazement	*houseful*	*useful*
awesome		*whiteness*

Exceptions: *argument*, *awful*, *duly*, *eerily*, *eeriness*, *truly*, *wholly*.

• In Amer. spelling *e* is dropped after *dg* and before a suffix beginning with a consonant, e.g. *fledgling*, *judgment*.

C. Final silent *-e* is omitted in Amer. spelling in several words in which it is found in British spelling, and so often is final silent *-ue* in the endings *-gogue*, *-logue*, e.g.

ax	*adz*	*program*
analog	*epilog*	*pedagog*

-efy or -ify

The chief words with *-efy* (*-efied*, *-efication*, etc.) are:

liquefy	*rarefy*	*torrefy*
obstupefy	*rubefy*	*tumefy*
putrefy	*stupefy*	

All the others have *-ify* etc. See also **-ified or -yfied**, p. 34.

-ei- or -ie-

The rule '*i* before *e* except after *c*' holds good for nearly all words in which the vowel-sound is *ee*, as *Aries*, *hygienic*, *yield*.

Exceptions where *ie* follows *c* are: *prima facie*, *specie*, *species*, *superficies*.

Note also *friend*, *adieu*, *review*, *view*.

The following words which are, or can be, pronounced with the *ee*-sound have *ei*:

caffeine	*either*	*protein*
casein	*forfeit*	*receipt*
ceiling	*heinous*	*receive*
codeine	*inveigle*	*seise*
conceit	*Madeira*	*seize*
conceive	*neither*	*seizure*
counterfeit	*perceive*	*surfeit*
deceit	*peripeteia*	*weir*
deceive	*plebeian*	*weird*

en- or in-

The following pairs of words can give trouble:

encrust (verb)	*incrustation*
engrain (verb) to dye in the raw state	*ingrain* (adjective) dyed in the yarn
	ingrained deeply rooted

enquire ask	*inquire* undertake a formal investigation
enquiry question	*inquiry* official investigation
ensure make sure	*insure* take out insurance (against risk: note *assurance* of life)

-er and -est

These suffixes of comparison may require the following changes in spelling:

1. Doubling of final consonant (see p. 25).
2. Dropping of silent *-e* (see p. 26).
3. *Y* to *i* (see p. 51).

-erous or -rous

The ending *-erous* is normal in adjectives related to nouns ending in *-er*, e.g. *murderous, slanderous, thunderous*. The exceptions are:

ambidextrous	*disastrous*	*monstrous*
cumbrous	*leprous*	*slumbrous*
dextrous	*meandrous*	*wondrous*

final vowels before suffixes

A. For treatment of final *-e* and *-y* before suffixes, see **dropping of silent -e,** pp. 26ff., and ***y* to *i*,** pp. 51f.

B. For treatment of final *-o* before *-s* (suffix), see **plural formation,** p. 42, and **-*s* suffix,** p. 48.

C. In nearly all other cases, the final vowels *-a*, *-i*, *-o*, and *-u* are unaffected by the addition of suffixes and do not themselves affect the suffixes. So:

bikinied (*girls*)	*mascaraed*	(*they*) *rumbaed*
echoed	*mustachioed*	*taxied*
hennaed	*radioed*	
echoer	*skier*	*vetoer*
areas	*emus*	(*he*) *skis*
cameras	*gnus*	*taxis*
corgis	(*he*) *rumbas*	
echoing	*scubaing*	*taxiing*
radioing	*skiing*	*vetoing*

Exceptions: *idea'd* (having ideas); past *ski'd* from *ski* (contrast *skied* from *sky*).

D. Final *-é* in words taken from French is retained before all suffixes; the *e* of *-ed* is dropped after it, e.g.

appliquéd	*canapés*	*communiqués*
appliquéing	*chasséing*	*émigrés*
attachés	*clichéd*	*soufflés*
cafés		

for- and *fore-*

The prefix *for-* 'means away, out, completely, or implies prohibition or abstention' (*MEU*). *Fore-* is the same as the ordinary word so spelt, = 'beforehand, in front'.

Note especially:

forbear refrain	*forebear* ancestor
forgather	*foreclose*
forgo abstain from	*forego* (esp. in *foregoing* (*list*), *foregone* (*conclusion*)
forfeit	

f to *v*

Certain nouns that end in *f* or *f* followed by silent *e* change this *f* to *v* in some derivatives. Most are familiar, but with a few derivatives there is variation between *f* and *v* or uncertainty about which consonant is correct; only these are dealt with below.

beef: plural *beeves* oxen, *beefs* kinds of beef.
calf (young bovine animal): *calfish* calflike; *calves-foot jelly*.
calf (of leg): (*enormously*) *calved* having (enormous) calves.
corf (basket): plural *corves*.
dwarf: plural *dwarfs*. ● *Dwarves* only in J. R. R. Tolkien's writings.
elf: *elfish* and *elvish* are both acceptable; *elfin* but *elven*.
handkerchief: plural *handkerchiefs*.
hoof: plural usually *hoofs*, but *hooves* is commonly found, e.g. *The useless tool for horses' hooves* (Graham Greene); *Listening for Sebastian's retreating hooves* (Evelyn Waugh); adjective *hoofed* or *hooved*.
knife: verb *knife*.
leaf: *leaved* having leaves (*broad-leaved*, etc.) but *leafed* as past of *leaf* (*through a book*, etc.).

life: *lifelong* lasting a lifetime; *livelong* (*day*, etc., poetic: the *i* is short); the plural of *still life* is *still lifes*.
oaf: plural *oafs*.
roof: plural *roofs*. • *Rooves* is commonly heard and sometimes written, e.g. *Several acres of bright red rooves* (George Orwell). Its written use should be avoided.
scarf (garment): plural *scarves*; *scarfed* wearing a scarf.
scarf (joint): plural and verb keep *f*.
sheaf: plural *sheaves*; verb *sheaf* or *sheave*; *sheaved* made into a sheaf.
shelf: plural *shelves*; *shelvy* having sandbanks.
staff: plural *staffs* but archaic and musical *staves*.
turf: plural *turfs* or *turves*; verb *turf*; *turfy*.
wharf: plural *wharfs* or *wharves*.
wolf: *wolfish* of a wolf.

-*ful* suffix

The adjectival suffix *-ful* may require the following changes in spelling:

1. Change of *y* to *i* (see p. 52)
2. Simplification of *-ll* (see ***l* and *ll***, p. 37).

hyphens

A. Hyphens are used to connect words that are more closely linked to each other than to the surrounding syntax. Unfortunately their use is not consistent. Some pairs or groups of words are written as a single word (e.g. *motorway*, *railwayman*), others, despite their equally close bond, as separate words (e.g. *motor cycle*, *pay phone*); very similar pairs may be found with a hyphen (e.g. *motor-cyclist*, *pay-bed*). There are no hard and fast rules that will predict in every case whether a group of words should be written as one, with a hyphen, or separately. Useful lists can be found in *Hart's Rules*, pp. 76–81; numerous individual items are entered in *ODWE*.

1. Groups consisting of attributive noun + noun are probably the most unpredictable. It is the nature of English syntax to produce limitless numbers of groups of this kind. Such a group generally remains written as separate words until it is recognized as a lexical item with a special meaning, when it may receive a hyphen. Eventually it may be written as one word, but this usually happens when the two nouns are monosyllabic and there is no

clash between the final letter of the first and the first letter of the second.

This generalization is, however, a very weak guide to what happens in practice. Compare, for example, *coal tar*, *coal-face*, *coalfield*; *oil well*, *oil-painting*, *oilfield*; *blood cell*, *blood-pressure*, *bloodstream*.

2. Nouns derived from phrasal verbs, consisting of verb + adverb, are slightly more predictable. They are never written as two words, frequently hyphened, and sometimes written as one, e.g. *fall-out*, *play-off*, *set-back*, *turn-out*; *feedback*, *layout*, *runoff*, *turnover*. Phrases consisting of agent-noun in *-er* + adverb are usually hyphened, e.g. *picker-up*, *runner-up*; those consisting of gerund in *-ing* + adverb are usually left as two words, e.g. *Your coming back so soon surprised me*, unless they have become a unit with a special meaning, e.g. *Gave him a going-over*.

3. Various collocations which are not hyphened when they play their normal part in the sentence are given hyphens when they are transferred to attributive position before a noun, e.g.

   (*a*) adjective + noun: *a common-sense argument* (but *This is common sense*), *an open-air restaurant* (but *eating in the open air*).

   (*b*) preposition + noun: *an out-of-date aircraft* (but *This is out of date*), *an in-depth interview* (but *interviewing him in depth*).

   (*c*) participle + adverb: *The longed-for departure* and *Tugged-at leaves and whirling branches* (Iris Murdoch) (but *the departure greatly longed for*; *leaves tugged at by the wind*).

   (*d*) other syntactic groups used attributively, e.g. *A tremendous wrapping-up-and-throwing-away gesture* (J. B. Priestley); *An all-but-unbearable mixture* (Lynne Reid Banks).

4. Collocations of adverb + adjective (or participle) are usually written as two words when attributive as well as when predicative, e.g. *a less interesting topic*, *an amazingly good performance*, but may very occasionally take a hyphen to avoid misunderstanding, e.g. *Sir Edgar, who had heard one or two more-sophisticated rumours* (Angus Wilson) (this does not mean 'one or two additional sophisticated rumours').

   See also **well,** p. 99.

5. When two words that form a close collocation but are not normally joined by a hyphen enter into combination with another

word that requires a hyphen, it may be necessary to join them with a hyphen as well in order to avoid an awkward or even absurd result, e.g. *natural gas* needs no hyphen in *natural gas pipeline*, but *natural-gas-producer* may be preferred to the ambiguous *natural gas-producer*; *crushed ice* + *-making* looks odd in *crushed ice-making machine*, and so *crushed-ice-making machine* may be preferred. Occasionally a real distinction in meaning may be indicated, e.g. *The non-German-speakers at the conference used interpreters* versus *The non-German speakers at the conference were all Austrians*. Many people, however, prefer to avoid the use of long series of hyphened words.

6. A group of words that has been turned into a syntactic unit, often behaving as a different part of speech from the words of which it is composed, normally has hyphens, e.g. *court-martial* (verb), *happy-go-lucky* (adjective), *good-for-nothing*, *stick-in-the-mud*, *ne'er-do-well* (nouns).

7. A hyphen is used to indicate a common second element in all but the last word of a list, e.g. *two-*, *three-*, or *fourfold*.

B. Hyphens are also used within the word to connect a prefix or suffix to the stem. With most prefixes and suffixes it is normal to write the whole compound as a single word; the use of the hyphen is exceptional, and the writing of prefix or suffix and stem as two words virtually unknown.

The hyphen is used in the following cases:

1. After a number of prefixes that are considered to be living formative elements, i.e. prefixes that can be freely used to form new compounds:

   ex- (= formerly), e.g. *ex-President*; *neo-* (denoting a revived movement), e.g. *neo-Nazism*; *non-*, e.g. *non-stick*; *pro-* (= in favour of), e.g. *pro-marketeer*; *self-*, e.g. *self-destructive*.

   Exceptions: *Neoplatonism* (*-ic*, etc.); *selfsame*, *unselfconscious*.

2. After a number of prefixes to aid recognition of the second element, e.g. *anti-g*, or to distinguish the compound from another word identically spelt, e.g. *un-ionized* (as against *unionized*); see also ***co-* prefix, *re-* prefix**.

3. Between a prefix ending with a vowel and a stem beginning with the same vowel, e.g. *de-escalate*, *pre-empt*; see also ***co-* prefix**, ***re-* prefix**.

4. Between a prefix and a stem beginning with a capital letter, e.g. *anti-Darwinian*, *hyper-Calvinism*, *Pre-Raphaelite*.

5. With some living suffixes forming specially coined compounds, e.g. *Mickey Mouse-like*; or still regarded to some extent as full words, such as *-wise* (= as regards ——), e.g. *Weather-wise we have had a good summer*.

6. With suffixes in irregularly formed compounds, e.g. *unget-at-able*.

7. With the suffix *-like* after a stem ending in *-l*, e.g. *eel-like*, when attached to a word of two or more syllables, e.g. *cabbage-like*, and with the suffix *-less* after a stem ending in double *-l*, e.g. *bell-less*, *will-lessness*.

Note. In Amer. spelling there is a greater tendency than in British spelling to write compounds as one word, rather than hyphened, e.g. *nonplaying*, *nonprofit*, *roundhouse*, *runback*, *sandlot*.

-ified or -yfied

-ified is usual, whatever the stem of the preceding element, e.g.

citified	*dandified*	*townified*
countrified	*Frenchified*	*whiskified*

But *ladyfied*.

in- or un-

There is no comprehensive set of rules governing the choice between these two negative prefixes. The following guidelines are offered. Note that *in-* takes the form of *il-*, *im-*, or *ir-* before initial *l*, *m*, or *r*.

1. *in-* is from Latin and properly belongs to words derived from Latin, whereas *un-*, as a native prefix, has a natural ability to combine with any English word. Hence

(*a*) *un-* may be expected to spread to words originally having *in-*. This has happened when the *in-* word has developed a sense more specific than merely the negative of the stem word:

unapt	*inept*
unartistic	*inartistic*
unhuman	*inhuman*
unmaterial	*immaterial*
unmoral	*immoral*
unreligious	*irreligious*
unsanitary	*insanitary*
unsolvable	*insoluble*

(*b*) It is always possible, for the sake of a particular effect, for a writer to coin a nonce-word with *un-*:

A small bullied-looking woman with unabundant brown hair (Kingsley Amis)
Joyce's arithmetic is solid and unnonsensical (Anthony Burgess)

2. Adjectives ending in *-ed* and *-ing* rarely accept *in-* (while participles can of course be formed from verbs like *inactivate*, *indispose*, etc.).

Exception: *inexperienced*.

3. *in-* seems to be preferred before the prefixes *ad-*, *co-* (*col-*, *com-*, *con-*, *cor-*), *de-*, *di*(*s*)-, *ex-*, *per-*.

Important exceptions are:

unadventurous	*uncooperative*	*undevout*
uncommunicative	*undemonstrative*	*unexceptionable*
unconditional	*undeniable*	*unexceptional*
unconscionable	*undesirable*	*unpersuasive*
unconscious	*undetectable*	

4. *un-* is preferred before the prefixes *em-*, *en-*, *im-*, *in-*, *inte*(*r*)-.

5. Adjectives ending in *-able* usually take *in-* if the stem preceding the suffix *-able* is not, by itself, an English word:

educable, stem *educ-*, negative *in-*
palpable, stem *palp-*, negative *im-*

Exceptions: *unamenable*, *unamiable*, *unconscionable*.

They usually take *un-* if the stem has only one syllable and is an English word:

unbridgeable	*unreadable*
unlovable	*unsaleable*

Exceptions: *incurable*, *immovable*, *impassable* (that cannot be traversed: *impassible* = unfeeling).

But no generalization covers those with a polysyllabic English stem:

illimitable	*undeniable*
invariable	*unmistakable*

Note: Rule 2 overrides rule 3 (e.g. *uncomplaining*, *undisputed*, *unperturbed*); rule 3 overrides rule 5 (*unconscionable*); rule 4 overrides rule 5 (*unimpressible*).

_i_ to _y_

When the suffix *-ing* is added to words (chiefly verbs) that end in *-ie*, *e* is dropped (see **dropping of silent -e,** p. 26), and *i* becomes *y*, e.g.

dying	*lying*	*tying*	*vying*

Exceptions: *hie*, *sortie*, *stymie* make *hieing*, *sortieing*, *stymieing*.

-ize and _-ise_

-ize should be preferred to *-ise* as a verbal ending in words in which both are in use.

1. The choice arises only where the ending is pronounced *eyes*, not where it is *ice*, *iss* or *eez*. So: *precise*, *promise*, *expertise*, *remise*.

2. The choice applies only to the verbal suffix (of Greek origin), added to nouns and adjectives with the sense 'make into, treat with, or act in the way of (that which is indicated by the stem word)'.

Hence are eliminated

(*a*) nouns in *-ise*:

compromise	*exercise*	*revise*
demise	*franchise*	*surmise*
disguise	*merchandise*	*surprise*
enterprise		

(*b*) verbs corresponding to a noun which has *-is-* as a part of the stem (e.g. in the syllables *-vis-*, *-cis-*, *-mis-*), or identical with a noun in *-ise*. Some of the more common verbs in *-ise* are:

advertise	*despise*	*incise*
advise	*devise*	*merchandise*
apprise	*disguise*	*premise*
arise	*emprise*	*prise* (*open*)
chastise	*enfranchise*	*revise*
circumcise	*enterprise*	*supervise*
comprise	*excise*	*surmise*
compromise	*exercise*	*surprise*
demise	*improvise*	*televise*

3. In most cases, *-ize* verbs are formed on familiar English stems, e.g. *authorize*, *familiarize*, *symbolize*; or with a slight alteration to the stem, e.g. *agonize*, *dogmatize*, *sterilize*. A few words have no such immediate stem: *aggrandize* (cf. *aggrandizement*), *appetize*

(cf. *appetite*), *baptize* (cf. *baptism*), *catechize* (cf. *catechism*), *recognize* (cf. *recognition*); and *capsize*.

l* and *ll

Whether to write a single or double *l* can be a problem in the following cases:

1. Where a suffix is added to single final *l*: see **doubling of final consonant,** p. 26.

2. *l* is single when it is the last letter of the following verbs:

annul	*enrol*	*fulfil*
appal	*enthral*	*instil*
distil	*extol*	

These double the *l* before suffixes beginning with a vowel (see p. 26), but not before *-ment*:

annulment	*enthralment*	*distillation*
enrolment	*fulfilment*	*enthralling*

• In Amer. spelling *l* is usually double in all these words except *annul(ment)*, *extol*.

3. Final *-ll* is usually simplified to *l* before suffixes or word elements that begin with a consonant, e.g.

almighty, *almost*, etc.	*fulfil*	*skilful*
chilblain	*gratefully*	*thraldom*
dully	*instalment*	*wilful*

Exception: Before *-ness*, *-ll* remains in *dullness*, *fullness*.

• In Amer. spelling *ll* is usual in *skillful*, *thralldom*, *willful*.

-ly

The suffix *-ly* is added to words (mainly nouns and adjectives) to form adjectives and adverbs, e.g. *earth*, *earthly*; *part*, *partly*; *sad*, *sadly*. With certain words one of the following spelling changes may be required:

1. If the word ends in double *ll*, add only *-y*, e.g. *fully*, *shrilly*.

2. If the word ends in consonant + *le*, change *e* to *y*, e.g. *ably*, *singly*, *terribly*.

Exception: *supplely* (distinguished from the noun and verb *supply*).

3. If the word ends in consonant + *y*, change *y* to *i* and add *-ly*, e.g. *drily*, *happily*.

Exceptions: *shyly*, *slyly*, *spryly*, *wryly*.

4. If the word ends in unstressed *-ey*, change *ey* to *i* and add *-ly*, e.g. *matily*.

5. If the word has more than one syllable and ends in *-ic*, add *-ally*, even if there is no corresponding adjective in *-ical*, e.g. *basically*, *scientifically*.

Exceptions: *politicly* (from the adjective *politic*, distinguished from *politically*, from the adjective *political*), *publicly* (● not *publically*).

6. Final *-e* is exceptionally dropped before *-ly* in *duly*, *eerily*, *truly*, *wholly* (*palely*, *puerilely*, *vilely*, etc., are regular).

7. Final *-y* is exceptionally changed to *i* before *-ly* in *daily*, *gaily* (*greyly*, *coyly* are regular).

-ness

As a suffix added to adjectives, it may require the change of *y* to *i*: see p. 52

-or* and *-er

These two suffixes, denoting 'one who or that which performs (the action of the verb)', are from Latin (through French) and Old English respectively, but their origin is not a sure guide to their distribution.

1. *-er* is the living suffix, forming most newly-coined agent nouns; but *-or* is frequently used with words of Latin origin to coin technical terms.

2. *-er* is usual after doubled consonants (except *-ss-*), after soft *c* and *g*, after *-i-*, after *ch* and *sh*, and after *-er*, *-graph*, *-ion*, and *-iz-*, e.g.

chopper, *producer*, *avenger*, *qualifier*, *launcher*, *furnisher*, *discoverer*, *photographer*, *executioner*, *organizer*.

Principal exceptions: *counsellor*, *carburettor*, *conqueror*.

3. *-or* follows *-at-* to form a suffix *-ator*, often but not always in words related to verbs in *-ate*, e.g. *duplicator*, *incubator*.

Exception: *debater*.

Note: nouns in *-olater*, as *idolater*, do not contain the agent suffix.

4. No rule can predict whether a given word having *-s-*, *-ss-*, or *-t-* (apart from *-at-*) before the suffix requires *-or* or *-er*. So *supervisor*, *compressor*, *prospector*, but *adviser*, *presser*, *perfecter*. *-tor* usually follows *-c*, unstressed *i*, and *u*, e.g. *actor*, *compositor*, *executor*; *-ter* usually follows *f*, *gh*, *l*, *r*, and *s*, e.g. *drifter*, *fighter*, *defaulter*, *exporter*, *protester*; but there are numerous exceptions.

5. A functional distinction is made between *-or* and *-er* in the following:

accepter one who accepts	*acceptor* (in scientific use)
adapter one who adapts	*adaptor* electrical device
caster one who casts, casting machine	*castor* beaver; plant giving oil; sugar (sprinkler); wheel
censer vessel for incense	*censor* official
conveyer one who conveys	*conveyor* device
resister one who resists	*resistor* electrical device
sailer ship of specified power	*sailor* seaman

6. A number of words have *-er* in normal use but *-or* in Law:

abetter	*mortgager* (*mortgagor*)
accepter	*settler*
granter	

-oul-

In the words *mould*, *moulder*, *moult*, and *smoulder*, Amer. spelling favours *o* alone instead of *ou*.

-our or -or

1. In agent nouns, only *-or* occurs as the ending (cf. **-or and -er**), e.g. *actor*, *counsellor*.

Exception: *saviour*.

2. In abstract nouns, *-our* is usual, e.g. *colour*, *favour*, *humour*. Only the following end in *-or*:

error	*pallor*	*terror*
horror	*squalor*	*torpor*
languor	*stupor*	*tremor*
liquor		

• In Amer. English *-or* is usual in nearly all words in which British English has *-our* (*glamour* and *saviour* are the main exceptions).

3. Nouns in *-our* change this to *-or* before the suffixes *-ation*, *-iferous*, *-ific*, *-ize*, and *-ous*, e.g.

> *coloration, humorous, odoriferous, soporific, vaporize, vigorous.*

But *-our* keeps the *u* before *-able*, *-er*, *-ful*, *-ism*, *-ist*, *-ite*, and *-less*, e.g.

> *armourer, behaviourism, colourful, favourite, honourable, labourite, odourless, rigourist.*

past of verbs, formation of

A. Regular verbs add *-ed* for the past tense and past participle, and may make the following spelling changes:

1. Doubling of final consonant (see pp. 25f.).
2. Dropping of silent *-e* (see p. 26).
3. Change of *y* to *i* (see p. 51).

Note *laid*, *paid*, and *said* from *lay*, *pay*, and *say*.

B. A number of verbs vary in their past tense and past participle between a regular form and a form with *-t* (and in some cases a different vowel-sound in the stem):

burn	*kneel*	*leap*	*smell*	*spill*
dream	*lean*	*learn*	*spell*	*spoil*

The *-t* form is usual in Received Pronunciation* and should be written by those who pronounce it. The regular form is usual in Amer. English.

Bereave is regular when the reference is to the loss of relatives by death; *bereft* is used when to loss of immaterial possessions.

Cleave is a rare word with two opposite meanings: (i) = stick; *A man .. shall cleave unto his wife* (Genesis 2: 24) (regular). (ii) = split; past tense *clave* is archaic; *clove*, *cleft*, and regular *cleaved* are all permissible, but *cleaved* is usual in scientific and technical contexts; past participle, in fixed expressions, *cloven-footed*, *cloven hoof*, *cleft palate*, *cleft stick*; *cleaved* is technical, but probably also best used outside the fixed expressions.

• *Earn* is regular. There is no form *earnt*.

C. A number of verbs vary in the past participle only between the regular form and one ending in *-(e)n*:

> *hew, mow, saw, sew, shear, show, sow, strew, swell.*

* See p. 227.

In most of these the latter form is to be preferred; in British English it is obligatory when the participle is used attributively as an adjective. So *new-mown hay*, *a sawn-off* (Amer. *sawed-off*) *shotgun*, *shorn* (not *sheared*) *of one's strength*, *a swollen gland*; *swollen* or *swelled head* (= conceit) is a colloquial exception.

D. The past tense has *-a-*, the past participle *-u-*, in

begin	*shrink*	*stink*
drink	*sing*	*swim*
ring	*sink*	

● It is an error to use *begun*, *drunk*, etc. for the past tense, as if they followed *clung*, *flung*, *spun*, etc.

E. The past tense and past participle of the following verbs can cause difficulty:

abide (*by*) makes *abided*
alight makes *alighted*
bet: *betted* is increasingly common beside *bet*
bid (make a bid): *bid*
bid (command; say (goodnight, etc.)): *bid* is usual (*bade*, *bidden* are archaic)
broadcast unchanged in past tense and past participle
chide: *chided* is now usual (older *chid*)
forecast unchanged in past tense and past participle
hang: *hanged* is frequent for the capital punishment; otherwise only *hung*
knit: *knitted* is usual, but *knit* is common in metaphorical use (*he knit his brows*)
light makes past *lit*, past participle *lit* in predicative use (*a fire was lit*) but *lighted* attributively (*a lighted match*)
quit makes *quitted* ● Amer. *quit*
reeve (nautical) makes *rove*
rid unchanged in past tense and past participle
speed makes *sped*, but *speeded* in the senses 'cause to go at (a certain) speed' and 'travel at illegal or dangerous speed'
spit makes *spat* ● Amer. *spit*
stave (to dent) *staved* or *stove*; (to ward off) *staved*
sweat makes *sweated* ● Amer. *sweat*
thrive: *thrived* is increasingly common beside *throve*, *thriven*

plural formation

Most nouns simply add *-s*, e.g. *cats*, *dogs*, *horses*, *cameras*.

A. The regular plural suffix *-s* is preceded by *-e-*:

1. After sibilant consonants, where ease of pronunciation requires a separating vowel, i.e. after

   ch: e.g. *benches*, *coaches*, *matches* (but not *conchs*, *lochs*, *stomachs* where the *ch* has a different sound)
   s: e.g. *buses*, *gases*, *pluses*, *yeses* (note that single *s* is not doubled)
   sh: e.g. *ashes*, *bushes*
   ss: e.g. *grasses*, *successes*
   x: e.g. *boxes*, *sphinxes*
   z: e.g. *buzzes*, *waltzes* (note *quizzes* with doubling of *z*)

Proper names follow the same rule, e.g. *the Joneses*, *the Rogerses*, *the two Charleses*.

- *-es* should not be replaced by an apostrophe, as *the Jones'*.

2. After *-y* (not preceded by a vowel), which changes to *i*, e.g. *ladies*, *soliloquies*, *spies*.

Exceptions: proper names, e.g. *the Willoughbys*, *the three Marys*; also *trilbys*, *lay-bys*, *standbys*, *zlotys* (Polish currency).

3. After *-o* in certain words:

bravoes (= ruffians; *bravos* = shouts of 'bravo!')
buffaloes
calicoes
cargoes
dingoes
dominoes
echoes
embargoes
goes
grottoes
haloes
heroes
innuendoes
mangoes
mementoes
mosquitoes
mottoes
Negroes
noes
peccadilloes
porticoes
potatoes
salvoes (= discharges; *salvos* = reservations, excuses)
stuccoes
tomatoes
tornadoes
torpedoes
vetoes
volcanoes

Words not in this list add only *-s*.

It is helpful to remember that *-e-* is never inserted:

(*a*) when the *o* is preceded by another vowel, e.g. *cuckoos*, *embryos*, *ratios*.
(*b*) when the word is an abbreviation, e.g. *hippos*, *kilos*.
(*c*) with proper names, e.g. *Lotharios*, *Figaros*, *the Munros*.

4. With words which change final *f* to *v* (see pp. 30 f.), e.g. *calves*, *scarves*.

B. Plural of compound nouns.

1. Compounds made up of a noun followed by an adjective, a prepositional phrase, or an adverb attach *-s* to the noun, e.g.

(*a*) *courts martial* *heirs presumptive*
cousins-german *poets laureate*

But *brigadier-generals*, *lieutenant-colonels*, *sergeant-majors*.

(*b*) *men-of-war* *tugs of war*
sons-in-law

(*c*) *hangers-on* *whippers-in*
runners-up

Note: In informal usage *-s* is not infrequently transferred to the second element of compounds of type (*a*).

2. Compounds which contain no noun, or in which the noun element is now disguised, add *-s* at the end. So also do nouns formed from phrasal verbs and compounds ending in *-ful*, e.g.

(*a*) *ne'er-do-wells* *will-o'-the-wisps*
forget-me-nots

(*b*) *pullovers* *set-ups*
run-throughs

(*c*) *handfuls* *spoonfuls*

3. Compounds containing *man* or *woman* make both elements plural, as usually do those made up of two words linked by *and*, e.g.

(*a*) *gentlemen ushers* *women doctors*
menservants

(*b*) *pros and cons* *ups and downs*

C. The plural of the following nouns with a singular in *-s* is unchanged:

biceps *means* *species*
congeries *mews* *superficies*
forceps *series* *thrips*
innings

The following are mass nouns, not plurals:

bona fides (= 'good faith'), *kudos*

● The singulars *bona-fide* (as a noun; there is an adjective *bona-fide*), *congery*, *kudo*, sometimes seen, are erroneous.

D. Plural of nouns of foreign origin. The terminations that may form their plurals according to a foreign pattern are given in alphabetical order below; to each is added a list of the words that normally follow this pattern. It is recommended that the regular plural (in *-s*) should be used for all the other words with these terminations, even though some are found with either type of plural.

1. *-a* (Latin and Greek) becomes *-ae*:

alga	*lamina*	*nebula*
alumna	*larva*	*papilla*

Note: *formula* has *-ae* in mathematical and scientific use.

2. *-eau*, *-eu* (French) add *-x*:

beau	*château*	*plateau*
bureau	*milieu*	*tableau*

3. *-ex*, *-ix* (Latin) become *-ices*:

appendix	*cortex*	*matrix*
calix	*helix*	*radix*

Note: *index*, *vortex* have *-ices* in mathematical and scientific use (otherwise regular).

4. *-is* (Greek and Latin) becomes *-es* (pronounced *eez*):

amanuensis	*crisis*	*oasis*
analysis	*ellipsis*	*parenthesis*
antithesis	*hypothesis*	*synopsis*
axis	*metamorphosis*	*thesis*
basis		

5. *-o* (Italian) becomes *-i*:

concerto grosso (*concerti grossi*)

graffito	*ripieno*
maestro	*virtuoso*

Note: *solo* and *soprano* sometimes have *-i* in technical contexts (otherwise regular).

6. *-on* (Greek) becomes *-a*:

criterion	*parhelion*	*phenomenon*

Note: The plural of *automaton* is in *-a* when used collectively (otherwise regular).

7. *-s* (French) is unchanged in the plural (note: it is silent in the singular, but pronounced *-z* in the plural):

chamois	*corps*	*fracas*
chassis	*faux pas*	*patois*

Also (not a noun in French): *rendezvous*.

8. *-um* (Latin) becomes *-a*:

addendum	*datum*	*maximum*
bacterium	*desideratum*	*minimum*
candelabrum	*dictum*	*quantum*
compendium	*effluvium*	*scholium*
corrigendum	*emporium*	*spectrum*
cranium	*epithalamium*	*speculum*
crematorium	*erratum*	*stratum*
curriculum		

Note: *medium* in scientific use, and in the sense 'a means of communication' (as *mass medium*) has plural in *-a*; the collective plural of *memorandum* 'things to be noted' is in *-a*; *rostrum* has *-a* in technical use; otherwise these words are regular. In the technical sense 'starting-point' *datum* has a regular plural.

9. *-us* (Latin) becomes *-i*:

alumnus	*fungus*	*nucleus*
bacillus	*gladiolus*	*radius*
bronchus	*locus*	*stimulus*
cactus	*narcissus*	*terminus*
calculus		

Note: *focus* has plural in *-i* in scientific use, but otherwise is regular; *genius* has plural *genii* when used to mean 'guardian spirit', but in its usual sense is regular; *corpus*, *genus*, *opus* become *corpora*, *genera*, *opera*.

• The following words of foreign origin are plural nouns; they should normally not be construed as singulars (see also as separate entries in 'Vocabulary'):

bacteria	*graffiti*	*phenomena*
candelabra	*insignia*	*regalia*
criteria	*media*	*strata*
data		

E. There is no need to use an apostrophe before *-s*:

1. After figures: *the 1890s*.
2. After abbreviations: *MPs*, *SOSs*.

But it is needed in: *dot the i's and cross the t's*, *fair do's*, *do's and don'ts*.

possessive case

To form the possessive:

1. Normally, add -'*s* in the singular and -*s*' (i.e. apostrophe following the plural suffix -*s*) in the plural, e.g.

Bill's book	*the Johnsons' dog*
his master's voice	*a girls' school*

Nouns that do not form plural in -*s* add -'*s* to the plural form, e.g.

children's books	*women's liberation*

2. Nouns ending in *s* add '*s* for the singular possessive, e.g.

boss's	*Hicks's*
Burns's	*St James's Square*
Charles's	*Tess's*
Father Christmas's	*Thomas's*

To form the plural possessive, they add an apostrophe to the *s* of the plural in the normal way, e.g.

bosses'	*the octopuses' tentacles*
the Joneses' dog	*the Thomases' dog*

French names ending in silent *s* or *x* add -'*s*, which is pronounced as *z*, e.g.

Dumas's (= Dumah's)	*Crémieux's*

Names ending in -*es* pronounced *iz* are treated like plurals and take only an apostrophe (following the pronunciation, which is *iz*, not *iziz*), e.g.

Bridges'	*Moses'*
Hodges'	*Riches'*

Polysyllables not accented on the last or second last syllable can take the apostrophe alone, but the form with -'*s* is equally acceptable, e.g.

Barnabas'	or	*Barnabas's*
Nicholas'	or	*Nicholas's*

It is the custom in classical works to use the apostrophe only, irrespective of pronunciation, for ancient classical names ending in -*s*, e.g.

Ceres'	*Herodotus'*	*Venus'*
Demosthenes'	*Mars'*	*Xerxes'*

Jesus' 'is an accepted liturgical archaism' (*Hart's Rules*, p. 31). But in non-liturgical use, *Jesus's* is acceptable (used, e.g., in the NEB, *John* 2: 3).

With the possessive preceding the word *sake*, be guided by the pronunciation, e.g.

for goodness' sake	but	*for God's sake*
for conscience' sake (!)		*for Charles's sake*

After *-x* and *-z*, use *-'s*, e.g. *Ajax's*, *Berlioz's music*, *Leibniz's law*, *Lenz's law*.

3. Expressions such as:

a fortnight's holiday	*two weeks' holiday*
a pound's worth	*two pounds' worth*
your money's worth	

contain possessives and should have apostrophes correctly placed.

4. In *I'm going to the butcher's, grocer's*, etc. there is a possessive with ellipsis of the word 'shop'. The same construction is used in *I'm going to Brown's, Green's*, etc., so that properly an apostrophe is called for. Where a business calls itself *Brown, Green*, or the like (e.g. *Marks and Spencer*, *J. Sainsbury*) the apostrophe would be expected before *-s*. But many businesses use the title *Browns*, *Greens*, etc., without an apostrophe (e.g. *Debenhams*, *Barclays Bank*). No apostrophe is necessary in *a Debenhams store* or in (*go to* or *take to*) *the cleaners*.

5. The apostrophe must not be used:

(*a*) with the plural non-possessive *-s*: notices such as *TEA'S* are often seen, but are wrong.

(*b*) with the possessive of pronouns: *hers*, *its*, *ours*, *theirs*, *yours*; the possessive of *who* is *whose*.

- *it's* = *it is*; *who's* = *who is*.
- There are no words *her's*, *our's*, *their's*, *your's*.

-re or -er

The principal words in which the ending *-re* (with the unstressed *er* sound—there are others with the sound *ruh*, e.g. *macabre*, or *ray*, e.g. *padre*) is found are:

accoutre	*centre*	*louvre*
* *acre*	* *euchre*	* *lucre*
amphitheatre	*fibre*	*lustre*
* *cadre*	*goitre*	*manœuvre*
calibre	*litre*	* *massacre*

* *meagre*	*ochre*	*sepulchre*
* *mediocre*	* *ogre*	*sombre*
metre (note *meter* the measuring device)	*philtre*	*spectre*
mitre	*reconnoitre*	*theatre*
nitre	*sabre*	*titre*
	sceptre	* *wiseacre*

- All but those marked * are spelt with *-er* in Amer. English.

re- prefix

This prefix is followed by a hyphen:

1. Before another *e*, e.g. *re-echo*, *re-entry*.
2. So as to distinguish the compound so formed from the more familiar identically spelt word written solid, e.g.

re-cover (put new cover on): *recover*
re-form (form again): *reform*
re-sign (sign again): *resign*

silent final consonants

Words borrowed from French having silent final consonants give difficulty when inflexions are added to them:

A. In the plural: see p. 45.

B. In the possessive: see p. 46.

C. With verbal inflexions: see p. 26.

-s suffix

A. As the inflexion of the plural of nouns: see **plural formation**.

B. As the inflexion of the third person singular present indicative of verbs, it requires the same changes in the stem as the plural ending, namely the insertion of *-e-*:

1. After sibilants (*ch*, *s*, *sh*, *x*, *z*), e.g. *catches*, *tosses*, *pushes*, *fixes*, *buzzes*; note that single *s* and *z* are subject to doubling of final consonant (see p. 25), though the forms in which they occur are rare, e.g. *gasses*, *nonplusses*, *quizzes*, *whizzes*.
2. After *y*, which is subject to the change of *y* to *i* (see p. 52), e.g. *cries*, *flies*, *carries*, *copies*.
3. After *o*: *echo*, *go*, *torpedo*, *veto*, like the corresponding nouns, insert *-e-* before *-s*; *crescendo*, *radio*, *solo*, *zero* should follow their nouns in having *-s*, but in practice there is variation.

-xion or *-ction*

Complexion, *crucifixion*, *effluxion*, *fluxion*, *genuflexion*, *inflexion* all have *-x-*; *connection*, *reflection* (which formerly sometimes had *-x-*) have *-ct-*; *deflexion* is increasingly being replaced by *deflection*.

• In Amer. spelling *-ction* is more usual in *connection*, *deflection*, *genuflection*, *inflection*, *reflection*.

-y, *-ey*, or *-ie* nouns

The diminutive or pet form of nouns can be spelt *-y*, *-ey*, or *-ie*. The majority of nouns which end in the sound of *-y* are so spelt (whether diminutives or of other origin), e.g.

aunty	*granny*	*nappy*
baby	*missy*	*potty*

The following are the main diminutives spelt with *-ey* (*-ey* nouns of other kinds are excluded from the list):

goosey	*lovey-dovey*	*Sawney*
housey-housey	*matey*	*slavey*
Limey	*nursey*	

The following list contains the diminutives in *-ie*, together with a number of similar nouns that are not in fact diminutives but do end in *-ie*. Note that most Scottish diminutives are spelt with *-ie*, e.g. *corbie*, *kiltie*.

beanie	*genie* (spirit; plural *genii*)	*movie*
birdie	*Geordie*	*nightie*
bookie	*gillie*	*oldie*
brownie	*girlie*	*pinkie* (little finger)
budgie	*goalie*	*pixie*
caddie (golf; *tea caddy*)	*hippie*	*quickie*
chappie	*junkie*	*rookie*
charlie	*Kewpie* (doll)	*sheltie*
clippie	*laddie*	*softie*
cookie	*lassie*	*Tin Lizzie*
coolie	*mealie* (maize; *mealy* adjective)	*walkie-talkie*
dearie	*mountie*	*zombie*
doggie (noun; *doggy* adjective)		

Note: *bogie* (wheeled undercarriage), *bogey* (golf), *bogy* (ghost).

-*y* or -*ey* adjectives

When -*y* is added to a word to form an adjective, the following changes in spelling occur:

1. Doubling of final consonant (see pp. 25f.).

2. Dropping of silent -*e* (see p. 27).

Exceptions:

(*a*) After *u*:

bluey *gluey* *tissuey*

(*b*) In words that are not well established in the written language, where the retention of -*e* helps to clarify the sense:

cagey *dikey* *pricey*
cottagey *matey* *villagey*
dicey *pacey*

Note also *holey* (distinguished from *holy*); *phoney* (of unknown origin).

3. Insertion of -*e*- when -*y* is also the final letter of the stem:

clayey *skyey* *sprayey* *wheyey*

Also in *gooey*.

4. Adjectives ending in unstressed -*ey* (2 (*a*) and (*b*) and 3 above) change this -*ey* to -*i*- before the comparative and superlative suffixes -*er* and -*est* and the adverbial suffix -*ly*, e.g.

cagey: *cagily* *matey*: *matily* *pricey*: *pricier*
dicey: *dicier* *pacey*: *pacier* *phoney*: *phonily*
gooey: *gooier*

Before -*ness* there is variation, e.g.

cagey: *cageyness* *matey*: *mateyness*, *matiness* *phoney*: *phoniness*
clayey: *clayeyness* *wheyey*: *wheyiness*

y* or *i

There is often uncertainty about whether *y* or *i* should be written in the following words:

Write *i* in:	Write *y* in:
cider	*gypsy*
cipher	*lyke-wake*
dike	*lynch law*

Write *i* in:	Write *y* in:
Libya	*pygmy*
lich-gate	*style* (manner)
linchpin	*stylus*
sibyl (classical)	*stymie*
sillabub	*Sybil* (frequently as Christian name)
silvan	*syrup*
siphon	*tyke*
siren	*tympanum* (ear-drum)
stile (in fence)	*tyre* (of wheel)
timpani (drums)	*wych-elm*
tiro	*wych-hazel*

-*yse* or -*yze*

This verbal ending (e.g. in *analyse*, *catalyse*, *paralyse*) is not a suffix but part of the Greek stem *-lyse*. It should not be written with *z* (though *z* is normally used in such words in America).

y* to *i

Words that end in *-y* change this to *-i-* before certain suffixes. The conditions are:

A. When the *-y* is not preceded by a vowel (except *-u-* in *-guy*, *-quy*).

-y does not change to *-i-* when preceded by a vowel (other than *u* in *-guy*, *-quy*). So *enjoyable*, *conveyed*, *parleyed*, *gayer*, *gayest*, *donkeys*, *buys*, *employer*, *joyful*, *coyly*, *enjoyment*, *greyness*.

Exceptions: *daily*, *gaily*, and adjectives ending in unstressed *-ey* (see p. 50).

B. When the suffix is:

1. *-able*, e.g. *deniable*, *justifiable*, *variable*.

Exception: *flyable*.

2. *-ed* (the past tense and past participle), e.g. *carried*, *denied*, *tried*.
3. *-er* (agent-noun suffix), e.g. *carrier*, *crier*, *supplier*.

Exceptions: *flyer*, *fryer*, *shyer* (one who, a horse which, shies), *skyer* (in cricket). Note that *drier*, *prier*, *trier* (one who tries) are regular.

4. *-er*, *-est* (comparative and superlative); e.g. *drier*, *driest*; *happier*, *happiest*.

5. *-es* (noun plural and third person singular present indicative), e.g. *ladies*, *soliloquies*, *spies*; *carries*, *denies*, *tries*.

Exceptions: see p. 42.

6. *-ful* (adjectives), e.g. *beautiful*, *fanciful*. (*Bellyful* is a noun, not an adjective.)

7. *-less* (adjectives), e.g. *merciless*, *remediless*.

Exceptions: some rare compounds, e.g. *countryless*, *hobbyless*, *partyless*.

8. *-ly* (adverbs), e.g. *drily*, *happily*, *plaguily*.

Exceptions: *shyly*, *slyly*, *spryly*, *wryly*.

9. *-ment* (nouns), e.g. *embodiment*, *merriment*.

10. *-ness* (nouns), e.g. *happiness*, *cliquiness*.

Exceptions: *dryness*, *flyness*, *shyness*, *slyness*, *spryness*, *wryness*; *busyness* (distinguished from *business*).

VOCABULARY

> The perfect use of language is that in which every word carries the meaning that it is intended to, no less and no more.
>
> (C. Connolly, *Enemies of Promise*)

THIS section is concerned with problems of meaning, construction, derivation, and diction, associated with individual words. The main aim is to recommend the meaning or construction most appropriate for serious writing or formal speaking, but some attention is paid to informal and American usage.

aboriginal (noun) should be used in formal contexts as the singular of *aborigines*; *Aboriginal, Aboriginals* (with capitals) are preferable for singular and plural when referring to the aboriginal inhabitants of Australia.

• *Aborigine* is informal only.

account, to reckon, consider, is not followed by *as*, e.g. *Mere morality . . was once accounted a shameful and cynical thing* (G. B. Shaw).

affect, to have an influence on, e.g. *Hugh was immensely affected by the way Randall had put it* (Iris Murdoch).

• Do not confuse with *effect* to accomplish, e.g. *He picked at the German's lapel, hoping to effect a closer relationship by touch* (Patrick White).

• There is a noun *effect* 'result, property', e.g. *to good effect, personal effects, sound effects*; but there is no noun *affect* except in the specialized language of Psychology.

affinity *between* or *with*, not *to* or *for*, since mutual relationship or attraction is meant, e.g. *Ann felt an affinity with them, as if she too were an old dusty object* (Iris Murdoch); *Points of affinity between Stephen and Bloom* (Anthony Burgess).

afflict: see **inflict**.

aftermath can be used of any after-effects, e.g. *The aftermath of the wedding seemed to mean different things to different people* (*The*

Times). It is pedantic to object to the sense 'unpleasant consequences' on the ground of derivation.

agenda (from a Latin plural) is usually a singular noun (with plural *agendas*), e.g. *It's a short agenda, by the way* (Edward Hyams). But it is occasionally found in its original use as a plural meaning 'things to be done' or 'items of business to be considered' (singular *agend*).

aggravate (1) To make worse, e.g. *The war . . simply aggravates the permanent human situation* (C. S. Lewis). (2) To annoy, exasperate.

• Sense (2) is regarded by some people as incorrect, but is common informally. The participial adjective *aggravating* is often used in sense (2) by good writers, e.g. *He had pronounced and aggravating views on what the United States was doing for the world* (Graham Greene).

ain't (= are not, is not, have not, has not) is not used in Standard English except in representations of dialect speech, or humorously. *Aren't* (= are not) is also a recognized colloquialism for *am not* in the interrogative construction *aren't I*.

alibi, a plea that when an alleged act took place one was elsewhere.

• The sense 'an excuse' is informal and to many people unacceptable, e.g. *Low spirits make you seem complaining . . I have an alibi because I'm going to have a baby* (L. P. Hartley).

all of (= the whole of, the entirety of, every one of) is usual before pronouns, e.g. *And so say all of us*, or emphatically, often paralleling *none of* etc., before nouns, e.g. *Marshall Stone has all of the problems but none of the attributes of a star* (Frederic Raphael). Otherwise *all* + noun is normal, e.g. *All the King's men*.

• The general use of *all of* before nouns is Amer. only.

all right. This phrase is popularly thought of as a unit, e.g. *an all-right bloke*, but its unitary nature has not yet been recognized in spelling by the standard language, probably because the expression remains largely an informal one.

• *Alright*, though widely seen in the popular press, remains nonstandard, even where the standard spelling is somewhat cumbersome, as in: *I just wanted to make sure it was all all right* (Iris Murdoch).

allude means 'refer indirectly'; an *allusion* is 'an indirect reference', e.g. *He would allude to her, and hear her discussed, but never mention her by name* (E. M. Forster).

• The words are not, except very informally, mere synonyms for *refer*, *reference*.

alternative (adjective and noun). The use of *alternative* with reference to more than two options, though sometimes criticized, is acceptable, e.g. *We have been driven to Proletarian Democracy by the failure of all the alternative systems* (G. B. Shaw).
● Do not confuse with *alternate* happening or following in turns, e.g. *Just as every sense is afflicted with a fitting torment so is every spiritual faculty; . . the sensitive faculty with alternate longing and rage* (James Joyce).

altogether. ● Beware of using this when *all* (adjective) *together* (adverb) is meant, e.g. *The dogs were now running, all together*. The reverse error, of using *all together* for the adverb *altogether*, should also be avoided; *altogether* is correct in *There's too much going on altogether at the moment* (Evelyn Waugh).

amend, to alter to something that sounds better, make improvements in; to make better, e.g. *If you consider my expression inadequate I am willing to amend it* (G. B. Shaw); *I have amended my life, have I not?* (James Joyce); noun *amendment*.
● Do not confuse with *emend* to remove errors from (something written), e.g. *An instance of how the dictionary may be emended or censored* (Frederic Raphael); noun *emendation*. An *emendation* will almost always be an *amendment*, but the converse is not true.

analogous means 'similar in certain respects'. It is not a mere synonym for *similar*.

anticipate (1) To be aware of (something) in advance and take suitable action, to deal with (a thing) or perform (an action) before someone else has had time to act so as to gain an advantage, to take action appropriate to (an event) before the due time, e.g. *His power to . . anticipate every change of volume and tempo* (C. Day Lewis); *I shall anticipate any such opposition by tendering my resignation now* (Angus Wilson); *She had anticipated execution by suicide* (Robert Graves); *Some unknown writer in the second century . . suddenly anticipated the whole technique of modern . . narrative* (C. S. Lewis).
(2) To take action before (another person) has had the opportunity to do so, e.g. *I'm sorry—do go on. I did not mean to anticipate you* (John le Carré).
(3) To expect (used only with an event as a direct object), e.g. *Serious writers . . anticipated that the detective story might supersede traditional fiction*; *Left-wing socialists really anticipated a Fascist dictatorship* (A. J. P. Taylor).
● Sense (3) is well established in informal use, but is regarded as incorrect by many people. Use *expect* in formal contexts. In any

case, *anticipate* cannot be followed, as *expect* can, by infinitive constructions (*I expect to see him* or *him to come*) or a personal object (*I expect him today*) and cannot mean 'expect as one's due' (*I expect good behaviour from pupils*).

antithetical to means 'characterized by direct opposition to'; it is not a mere synonym for *opposed to*.

approve (1) (Followed by direct object) authorize, e.g. *I will give letters of introduction to persons approved by you* (NEB).
(2) (Followed by *of*) consider good, e.g. *All the books approved of by young persons of cultivated taste* (C. P. Snow).
• *Approve* should not be used in sense (2) with a direct object, as (wrongly) in *Laziness, rudeness, and untidiness are not approved in this establishment* (correctly, *approved of*).

apt, followed by the *to*-infinitive, carries no implication that the state or action expressed by the infinitive is undesirable from the point of view of its grammatical subject (though it often is from that of the writer), e.g. *In weather like this he is apt to bowl at the batsman's head* (Robert Graves). It indicates that the subject of the sentence is habitually predisposed to doing what is expressed by the verb, e.g. *Time was apt to become confusing* (Muriel Spark). Compare **liable,** which, however, is not complementary to *apt to*, but overlaps with it; *apt to*, followed by a verb with undesirable overtones, = 'habitually or customarily liable to'.

aren't: see **ain't**.

Argentine, Argentinian can be both noun (= a native of Argentina) and adjective (= belonging to Argentina).
• Only the former is used in *Argentine Republic*, and it also has the advantage of brevity when used in other contexts. It rhymes with *turpentine*.

artiste, a professional singer, dancer, or similar public performer: used of persons of either sex.

as (1) = *that*, *which*, or *who* (relative) is now non-standard except after *same*, *such*, e.g. *Such comments as seem to be needed* (George Orwell); but not *I know somebody who knows this kid as went blind* (Alan Sillitoe, representing regional speech).
(2) = *that* (conjunction), introducing a noun clause, is now non-standard, e.g. in *I don't know as you'll like it*.

Asian is to be preferred when used of persons to *Asiatic*, which is now widely considered derogatory; the formation of *Asian* is in any case more closely parallel to that of *European*, *African*, etc. *Asiatic* is acceptable in other contexts, e.g. *Asiatic coastal regions*; *The Royal Asiatic Society*; *Asiatic cholera*.

as from is used in formal dating to mean 'from' or 'after' and followed by an actual date, e.g. *As from 10 p.m. on 15 October. As of*, originally Amer., has the same meaning and use.
● *As of now*, *yesterday*, and the like, are informal and humorous only.

aside from: Amer., = apart from, except for.

as if, as though (1) Followed by the past tense when the verb refers to an unreal possibility (i.e. when the statement introduced by *as if*, *as though* is untrue, or unlikely), e.g. *Every critic writes as if he were infallible* (Cyril Connolly); *It's not as though he lived like a Milord* (Evelyn Waugh). (2) Followed by the present tense when the statement is true, or might be true; this is especially common when the verbs *look* or *sound* precede, e.g. *I suppose you get on pretty well with your parents. You look as though you do* (Kingsley Amis); *He speaks as though even the rules which we freely invent are somehow suggested to us in virtue of their being right* (Mary Warnock).

attention. *Someone called it to my attention* (Alison Lurie) represents an illogical reversal of the idiom, not uncommon in speech; *someone called* (or *drew*) *my attention to it* or *someone brought it to my attention* would be better in formal contexts.

author (verb) is a rarely required synonym for *write*; *co-author*, however, is acceptable as a verb.

avenge: one avenges an injured person or oneself *on* (occasionally *against*) an offender, or a wrong *on* an offender; the noun is *vengeance* (*on*), and the idea is usually of justifiable retribution, as distinct from **revenge,** though the distinction is not absolute.

aware is normally a predicative adjective followed by an *of*-phrase or a *that*-clause, but can also be preceded by an adverb in the sense 'aware of, appreciative of (the subject indicated by the adverb)', a chiefly Amer. use, e.g. *The most intellectually ambitious and the most technically aware* (W. S. Graham).
● To use *aware* without any qualifying word at all is modish but meaningless, e.g. *Aware, provincial, intelligent, tall Englishman* (*New Statesman*).

bacteria is the plural of *bacterium*, not a singular noun.

baluster, a short pillar with a curving outline, especially in a balustrade; *banister*, an upright supporting a stair handrail (usually in the plural).

beg the question, to assume the truth of the thing which is to be proved, e.g. *I scoffed at that pompous question-begging word 'Evolution'* (H. G. Wells).

• It does not mean (1) to avoid giving a straight answer; or (2) to invite the obvious question (that . .).

behalf: *on behalf of X* (= in X's interest, as X's representative) should not be confused with *on the part of X* (= proceeding from or done by X); *behalf* cannot replace *part* in *His death was largely due to panic on his part.*

benign (in Medicine) has *malignant* as its antonym.

beside (preposition) is used of spatial relationships, or in figurative adaptations of these, e.g. *Beside oneself with joy*; *Quite beside the question*; *We all seemed children beside him* (Evelyn Waugh); *besides* = in addition to, other than, e.g. *Besides this I started my second year by joining the Ruskin School of Art* (Evelyn Waugh).

between. There are no grounds for objection to the use of *between* 'to express the relation of a thing to many surrounding things severally and collectively' (*OED*); *among* should not be substituted in, e.g., *Cordial relations between Britain, Greece, and Turkey.*

See also **choose between.**

bi- (prefix). *Biannual* = appearing (etc.) twice a year, half-yearly; *biennial* = recurring (etc.) every two years, two-yearly. *Bi-monthly*, *bi-weekly*, and *bi-yearly* are ambiguous in sense, meaning either 'twice a month (etc.)' or 'every two months (etc.)'; they are best avoided.

• Use *twice a month* or *semi-monthly*, *twice a week* or *semi-weekly*, and *twice a year* in the first sense, and *every two months*, *fortnightly* or *every two weeks*, and *every two years* in the second sense.

billion, etc. (1) Traditional British usage has a *billion* = a million million (1,000,000,000,000 = 10^{12}), a *trillion* = a million^3 (10^{18}), and a *quadrillion* = a million^4 (10^{24}); the logic is that the initial *bi-*, *tri-*, *quadri-*, etc. relate to the powers of a million.

(2) The US usage makes each 'step' from *million* to *quadrillion*, and beyond, a power of 1,000; i.e. *million* = 1000^2, *billion* = 1000^3, *trillion* = 1000^4, *quadrillion* = 1000^5.

(3) For the quantity 'thousand million' ($1000^3 = 10^9$), the older British term *milliard* is now rare. Many people who have frequent need to refer to the quantity, namely astronomers and economists, use the American *billion* for this. Most British national newspapers have officially adopted it too.

• In general contexts it is probably safer to use *thousand million* (X,000 m.). But where the sense is vague, e.g. *A billion miles away*, *Billions of stars*, the exact value is immaterial. Note that American *trillion* (10^{12}) = traditional British *billion*.

but = 'except', followed by a pronoun: see pp. 105 f.

candelabra is properly the plural of *candelabrum* and is best kept so in written English.

• *Candelabra* (singular), *candelabras* (plural) are frequent informally.

censure, to criticize harshly and unfavourably, e.g. *Laura censured his immoral marriage* (E. M. Forster).

• Do not confuse with *censor* to suppress (the whole or parts of books, plays, etc.).

centre about, (a)round, meaning (figuratively) 'to gather, revolve, or turn around' is criticized by many authorities, though used by good writers, e.g. *A rather restless, cultureless life, centring round tinned food,* Picture Post, *the radio and the internal combustion engine* (George Orwell). It can be avoided by using *to be centred in* or *on*, e.g. *My universe was still centred in my mother's fragrant person* (Richard Church).

century. Strictly, since the first century ran from the year 1 to the year 100, the first year of a given century should be that ending in the digits 01, and the last year of the preceding century should be the year before, ending in two noughts.

• In popular usage, understandably, the reference of these terms has been moved back one year, so that one will expect the twenty-first century to run from 2000 to 2099. Beware of ambiguity in their written use.

character. The use of this word after an adjective as a substitute for an abstract-noun termination (*-ness*, *-ty*, or the like), or for the word *kind*, devalues it and should be avoided, e.g. *the uniqueness and antiquity of the fabric*, not *the unique and ancient character of the fabric*.

charisma (1) Properly, a theological word (plural *charismata*) designating any of the gifts of the Holy Spirit (see I Corinthians 12). (2) In general use (usually as a mass noun, with no plural), a term (drawn from the works of the German sociologist Max Weber) for the capacity to inspire followers with devotion and enthusiasm.

charismatic (1) Designating a Christian movement that lays stress on the *charismata*. (2) Generally, 'having the capacity to inspire with devotion and enthusiasm', e.g. *A forcefully charismatic hero compensating in physical presence for what he politically lacks* (Terry Eagleton).

choose between: this construction, and *choice between*, are normally followed by *and* in written English; informally *or* is sometimes used, e.g. *The poorest girl alive may not be able to choose between being Queen of England or Principal of Newnham; but she can choose between ragpicking and flowerselling* (G. B. Shaw).

chronic is used of a disease that is long-lasting, though its manifestations may be intermittent (the opposite is *acute* 'coming sharply to a crisis'); it is used in much the same way of other conditions, e.g. *The chronic unemployment of the nineteen-twenties* (A. J. P. Taylor); *The commodities of which there is a chronic shortage* (George Orwell).

● The sense 'objectionable, bad, severe' is very informal.

comparable is followed by *with* in sense (1) of **compare** and by *to* in sense (2). The latter is much the more usual use, e.g. *The little wooden crib-figures . . were by no means comparable to the mass-produced figures* (Muriel Spark).

compare. In formal use, the following distinctions of sense are made:

(1) 'Make a comparison of x with y', followed by *with*, e.g. *You've got to compare method with method, and ideal with ideal* (John le Carré).

(2) 'Say to be similar to, liken to', followed by *to*, e.g. *To call a bishop a mitred fool and compare him to a mouse* (G. B. Shaw).

(3) Intransitively, = 'to be compared', followed by *with*, e.g. *None can compare with thee* (NEB).

● *Compare with* is loosely used in sense (2); the senses overlap, e.g. *How can you compare the Brigadier with my father?* (John Osborne). Conversely, in the separate clause (*as*) *compared with* or *to x*, only sense (1) is possible, but *to* occurs as well as *with*, e.g. *Tarzan . . bewails his human ugliness as compared to the beauty of the apes* (Tom Stoppard); *Earth is tractable stuff compared with coal* (George Orwell).

comparison is usually followed by *with*, especially in *by* or *in comparison with*. It is followed by *to* when the sense is 'the action of likening (to)', e.g. *The comparison of philosophy to a yelping she-dog* (Jowett).

complaisant, disposed to please others or comply with others' wishes; noun *complaisance*, e.g. *The indulgent complaisance which Horace did not bother to disguise* (Frederic Raphael).

● Do not confuse with *complacent* self-satisfied (noun *complacency*).

compose can be used to mean 'constitute, make up' with the constituents as subject and the whole as object, e.g. *The* *tribes which composed the German nation.* It is more commonly used in the passive with the whole as subject and the constituents as object, e.g. *His face was . . composed of little layers of flesh like pallid fungus* (Iris Murdoch).

comprise. The proper constructions with *comprise* are the converse of those used with **compose**. (1) In the active, meaning 'consist of', with the whole as subject and the constituents as objects, e.g. *The faculty comprises the following six departments.*

● In sense (1), *comprise* differs from *consist* in not being followed by *of*. Unlike *include*, *comprise* indicates a comprehensive statement of constituents.

(2) In the passive, meaning 'to be embraced or comprehended *in*', with the constituents as subject and the whole as object, e.g. *Fifty American dollars comprised in a single note* (Graham Greene).

● *Comprise* is often used as a synonym of **compose,** e.g. *The twenty-odd children who now comprise the school* (Miss Read). This is regarded as incorrect by many people. It is especially objectionable in the passive, since *comprise* is not followed by *of*; write *The faculty is composed* (not *comprised*) *of six departments.*

condole, to express sympathy, is always followed by *with*, e.g. *Many . . had come . . to condole with them on their brother's death* (NEB).

● Do not confuse with *console* 'to comfort', followed by direct object, e.g. *Console one another . . with these words* (NEB).

conduce, to lead or contribute (to a result), is always followed by *to*; similarly *conducive* (adjective); e.g. *The enterprise was popular, since it conduced to cut-price jobs* (J. I. M. Stewart).

conform may be followed by *to* or *with*, e.g. *The United Nations . . conformed to Anglo-American plans* (A. J. P. Taylor); *Having himself no particular opinions or tastes he relied upon whatever conformed with those of his companion* (John le Carré).

congeries, a collection of things massed together, is a singular noun, e.g. *A congeries of halls and inns on the site* (J. I. M. Stewart); it is unchanged in the plural.

● The form *congery*, formed in the misapprehension that *congeries* is plural only, is erroneous.

connote, denote. *Connote* means 'to imply in addition to the primary meaning, to imply as a consequence or condition', e.g. *Literature has needed to learn how to exploit all the connotations that lie latent in a word* (Anthony Burgess).

Denote means 'to be the sign of, indicate, signify', e.g. *A proper name . . will convey no information beyond the bare fact that it denotes a person* (Stephen Ullman).

● The two terms are kept rigidly distinct in Logic, but in popular usage *connote* is frequently used to mean 'convey to the mind', or 'mean in actual use' and hence verges on the sense of *denote*. *Denote* cannot be used in the senses of *connote*, e.g. in *His silence does not connote hesitation* (Iris Murdoch).

consequent, following as a result, adverb *consequently*, e.g. *Two engaged in a common pursuit do not consequently share personal identity* (Muriel Spark). These are nearly always to be used rather than *consequential* 'following as an indirect result' and *consequentially*, which are rarer and more specialized.

consist: *consist of* = be composed of, made up of; *consist in* = have as its essential quality, e.g. *All enjoyment consists in undetected sinning* (G. B. Shaw).

continual, always happening, very frequent and without cessation; *continuous*, connected, unbroken, uninterrupted; similarly the adverbs; e.g. *He was continually sending Tiberius not very helpful military advice* (Robert Graves); *There was a continuous rattle from the one-armed bandits* (Graham Greene).

continuance, continuation. The former relates mainly to the intransitive senses of *continue* (to be still in existence), the latter to its transitive senses (to keep up, to resume), e.g. *The great question of our continuance after death* (J. S. Huxley); *As if contemplating a continuation of her assault* (William Trevor).

cousin (1) The children of brothers or sisters are *first cousins* to each other. (2) The children of first cousins are *second cousins* to each other. (3) The child of one's first cousin, and the first cousin of one's parent, is one's *first cousin once removed.* (4) The grandchild of one's first cousin, or the first cousin of one's grandparent, is one's *first cousin twice removed*; and so on. (5) *Cousin-german* = first cousin.

credible, able to be believed.

● Do not confuse with *credulous*, too ready to believe things, as e.g. in *Even if one is credible* (correctly *credulous*) *enough to believe in their ability* (*Daily Telegraph*).

crescendo, used figuratively, means 'a progressive increase in force or effect'. Do not use it when *climax* is meant, e.g. in *The storm reached a crescendo* (correctly *a climax*) *at midnight.*

criteria is the plural of *criterion*, not a singular noun.

crucial, decisive, critical, e.g. *His medical studies were not merely an* *episode in the development of his persona but crucial to it* (Frederic Raphael).

• The weakened sense 'important' is informal only.

data (1) In scientific, philosophical, and general use, usually considered as a number of items and treated as plural, e.g. *Let us give the name of 'sense-data' to the things which are immediately known in sensation: such things as colours, sounds,* (etc.) (Bertrand Russell); *The optical data are incomplete* (*Nature*); the singular is *datum*, e.g. *Personality is not a datum from which we start* (C. S. Lewis).

(2) In computing and allied disciplines it is treated as a mass noun (i.e. a collective item), and used with words like *this*, *that*, and *much*, and with singular verbs; it is sometimes so treated in general use, e.g. *Useful data has been obtained* (Winston Churchill).

• Some people object to use (2).

• *Data* is not a singular countable noun and therefore cannot be preceded by *a*, *every*, *each*, *either*, *neither*, and cannot be given a plural form *datas*.

decidedly, decisively. *Decidedly*, definitely, undoubtedly, e.g. *The bungalow had a decidedly English appearance* (Muriel Spark). *Decisively* (1) conclusively, so as to decide the question, e.g. *The definition of 'capital' itself depends decisively on the level of technology employed* (E. F. Schumacher); (2) resolutely, unhesitatingly, e.g. *The young lady, whose taste has to be considered, decisively objected to him* (G. B. Shaw).

decimate, (originally) to kill or destroy one in every ten of; (now usually) to destroy or remove a large proportion of, e.g. *All my parents' friends, my friends' brothers were getting killed. Our circle was decimated* (Rosamond Lehmann).

• *Decimate* does not mean 'defeat utterly'.

decline (verb: to refuse an invitation) has no derived noun; we have to make do with *refusal* if *declining* cannot be used.

definitive, decisive, unconditional, final; (of an edition) authoritative; e.g. *The Gold Cup flat handicap, the official and definitive result of which he had read in the Evening Telegraph* (James Joyce).

• Do not use instead of *definite* (= having exact limits, distinct, precise); it cannot replace the latter in *We finally received a definite no*.

delusion, illusion. A general distinction can be drawn, though it is not absolute. *Delusion* would naturally occur in psychiatric contexts, and is used similarly outside them, to denote a false idea, impression, or belief held tenaciously, arising mainly from the internal workings of the mind; e.g. *delusions of grandeur*, and *He's been sent here for delusions. His most serious delusion is that he's a murderer* (Robert Graves).

Illusion denotes a false impression derived either from the external world, e.g. *optical illusion*, and *A partition making two tiny boxes, giving at least the illusion of privacy* (Doris Lessing), or from faulty thinking, e.g. *I still imagine I could live in Rome, but it may be an illusion* (Iris Murdoch).

It is in this second sense that *illusion* is almost equivalent to *delusion*; cf. *I hope to strike some small blows for what I believe to be right, but I have no delusions that knock-outs are likely* (Frederic Raphael). It should be remembered that *delusion* carries the sense of *being deluded* (by oneself or another), whereas no verb is implied in *illusion*; on the other hand, one can be said to be *disillusioned*, whereas *delusion* forms no such derivative.

demean (1) *Demean oneself* = conduct oneself (usually with adverbial expression), e.g. *Even on the scaffold he demeaned himself with dignity*. (2) *Demean* (*someone* or *something*) = lower in status, especially with *oneself*, e.g. *Their nobles would not demean themselves to serve their governor* (NEB).

denote: see **connote**.

depend, to be contingent on (a condition or cause), is followed by *on* or *upon*.

● The use of *it depends* followed, without *on* or *upon*, by an interrogative clause, is informal only, e.g. *It depends what you have . . in mind in forming a library of gramophone records whether you think it worth acquiring* (*The Times*).

depreciate, deprecate. *Depreciate* (1) to make or become lower in value; (2) to belittle, disparage, e.g. *To defend our record we seem forced to depreciate the Africans* (*Listener*); *To become a little more forthcoming and less self-depreciating* (Richard Adams).

Deprecate (1) (with a plan, proceeding, purpose, etc. as the object) to express a wish against or disapproval of, e.g. *I deprecate this extreme course, because it is good neither for my pocket nor for their own souls* (G. B. Shaw); *Polly . . patted her father's head in deprecation of such forcible metaphor* (Anthony Powell). (2) (with a person as the object) to express disapproval of, to reprove; to disparage, e.g. *Anyone who has reprinted his reviews is in no position to deprecate our reprinter* (Christopher Ricks).

● Sense (2) of *deprecate* tends to take on the sense of *depreciate* (2), especially in conjunction with *self*. This use is frequently found in good writers, e.g. *A humorous self-deprecation about one's own advancing senility* (Aldous Huxley); *The old, self-deprecating expression* (Susan Hill). It is, however, widely regarded as incorrect.

derisive = scoffing; *derisory* = (1) scoffing, (2) so small or unimportant as to be ridiculous (now the more usual sense), e.g. *A part . . once looked upon as discreditable and derisory* (Anthony Powell).

dialect (form of speech) forms *dialectal* as its adjective; *dialectic* (form of reasoning) can be adjective as well as noun, or can have *dialectical* as its adjective.

dice is the normal singular as well as the plural (*one dice, two dice*); the old singular, *die*, is found only in *the die is cast, straight* (or *true*) *as a die*, and in mathematical discussions, e.g. *Rolling a die will generate a stream of random numbers.*

dichotomy in non-technical use means 'differentiation into contrasting categories' and is frequently followed by *between*, e.g. *An absolute dichotomy between science and reason on the one hand and faith and poetry on the other.*

● It does not mean *dilemma* or *ambivalence.*

die (noun): see **dice**.

different can be followed by *from, to*, or *than.*

(1) *Different from* is the most usual expression in both written and spoken English; it is the most favoured by good writers, and is acceptable in all contexts, e.g. *It is also an 'important' book, in a sense different from the sense in which that word is generally used* (George Orwell).

(2) *Different to* is common informally. It sometimes sounds more natural than *different from*, and should then be used; e.g. when yoked with *similar* and followed by a phrase introduced by *to*: *His looks are neither especially similar nor markedly different to those of his twin brother.*

(3) *Different than* is an established idiom in American English, but is not uncommon in British use, e.g. *Both came from a different world than the housing estate outside London* (Doris Lessing). Both *different to* and *different than* are especially valuable as a means of avoiding the repetition and the relative construction required after *different from* in sentences like *I was a very different man in 1935 from what I was in 1916* (Joyce Cary). This could be recast as *I was a very different man in 1935 than I was in 1916* or *than in 1916*. Compare *The American theatre, which is suffering from a different malaise than ours*, which is

greatly preferable to *suffering from a different malaise from that which ours is suffering from.*
This construction is especially common when *different* is part of an adverbial clause (e.g. *in a different way*) or when the adverb *differently* is used, and has been employed by good writers since the seventeenth century, e.g. *Things were constructed very differently now than in former times* (Trollope); *Sebastian was a drunkard in quite a different sense to myself* (Evelyn Waugh); *Puts one in a different position to your own father* (John Osborne).

differential, a technical term in Mathematics, an abbreviation for *differential gear*, or a term for a maintained difference in wage between groups of workers.
• It is not a synonym for *difference.*

digraph = a group of two letters standing for a single sound, e.g. *ea* in *head*, *gh* in *cough*; *ligature* = a typographical symbol consisting of two letters joined together, e.g. fi, fl. The term *diphthong* is best restricted to the sense for which there is no synonym, namely 'a union of two vowels pronounced in one syllable', which is something primarily spoken and heard, not written; *i* in *find*, *ei* in *rein*, and *eau* in *bureau* all *represent* diphthongs. One cause of confusion is that Latin had two *diphthongs* (*ae* and *oe*) often printed as the *ligatures* æ and œ; in English words derived from Latin these are now *digraphs ae* and *oe* (sometimes modified into *e*: see pp. 20f.) representing single vowel sounds.

dilemma (1) A choice between two (or sometimes more than two) undesirable or awkward alternatives, e.g. *The unpleasant dilemma of being obliged either to kill the father or give up the daughter*. (2) More loosely, a perplexing situation in which a choice has to be made, e.g. *The dilemma of the 1960s about whether nice girls should sleep with men* (Alan Watkins).
• It is not merely a synonym for *problem.*

diphthong: see **digraph**.

direct is used as an adverb in two of the main senses of the adjective: (1) straight, e.g. *Another door led direct to the house* (Evelyn Waugh); (2) without intermediaries, e.g. *I appeal now, over your head, . . direct to the august oracle* (G. B. Shaw).

directly is used in most of the main senses of the adjective, e.g. *Why don't you deal directly with the wholesalers?* (G. B. Shaw); *The wind is blowing directly on shore*; *directly opposite, opposed.*
• It is not usually used to mean 'straight', since it has an extra sense, used in similar contexts, 'immediately, without delay', e.g. *Just a night in London—I'll be back directly* (Iris Murdoch).

discomfit, to thwart, disconcert; similarly *discomfiture*; e.g. *He discomfited his opponents by obliging them to disagree with a great logician* (Frederic Raphael).

● Do not confuse with *discomfort* (now rare as a verb, = make uneasy).

disinterest, lack of interest, indifference, e.g. *Buried the world under a heavy snowfall of disinterest* (Christopher Fry).

● The use of *disinterest* in this sense may be objected to on the same grounds as sense (2) of **disinterested**; but the word is rarely used in any other sense, and the possible alternative *uninterest* is very rare indeed.

disinterested (1) Impartial, unbiased, e.g. *Thanks to his scientific mind he understood—a proof of disinterested intelligence which had pleased her* (Virginia Woolf). The noun is *disinterestedness*. (2) Uninterested, indifferent, e.g. *It is not that we are disinterested in these subjects, but that we are better qualified to talk about our own interests* (*The Times*). The noun is **disinterest**.

● Sense (2) is common in informal use, but is widely regarded as incorrect and is avoided by careful writers, who prefer *uninterested.*

disposal is the noun from *dispose of* (get off one's hands, deal with); *disposition* is the noun from *dispose* (arrange, incline).

distinctive, serving to distinguish, characteristic, e.g. *It had smelled like this soap today, a light, entirely distinctive smell* (Susan Hill).

● Do not confuse with *distinct*, separate, individual, definite, e.g. *Trying to put into words an impression that was not distinct in my own mind* (W. Somerset Maugham).

drunk, drunken. In older and literary usage, the predicative and attributive forms respectively; now usually allocated to distinct senses, namely 'intoxicated' and 'given to drink', e.g. *They were lazy, irresponsible, and drunken; but on this occasion they were not drunk. Drunken* also means 'caused by or exhibiting drunkenness', e.g. *a drunken brawl.*

due to (1) That ought to be given to, e.g. *Pay Caesar what is due to Caesar* (NEB). (2) To be ascribed to, e.g. *Half the diseases of modern civilization are due to starvation of the affections in the young* (G. B. Shaw). *Due* is here an adjective with a complementary prepositional phrase, like *liable* (*to*), *subject* (*to*). As an adjective it needs to be attached to a noun as complement (see example above), or as part of a verbless adjective clause, e.g. *A few days' temporary absence of mind due to sunstroke was . . nothing to worry about* (Muriel Spark).

(3) = *owing to*. A sentence conforming to type (2) above like *He suffered a few days' absence of mind due to sunstroke* can be equated with *He suffered a few days' absence of mind, owing to sunstroke*. In this way *due to* has borrowed from *owing to* the status of independent compound preposition, a use not uncommon even with good writers, e.g. *It . . didn't begin until twenty past due to a hitch* (William Trevor); *Due to an unlikely run of nineteens and zeros, I gained the equivalent of three hundred pounds* (Graham Greene).

• The use of *due to* as a compound preposition is widely regarded as unacceptable. It can often be avoided by the addition of the verb *to be* and *that*, e.g. It is *due to your provident care* that . . *improvements are being made* (NEB).

effect: see **affect**.

e.g., i.e.: *E.g.* (short for Latin *exempli gratia*) = for example, for instance; it introduces one or more typical examples of what precedes it: *Many countries of Asia, e.g. India, Indonesia, and Malaysia, were once ruled by European powers. I.e.* (short for Latin *id est*) = that is; it introduces an amplification or explanation of what precedes it: *It was natural that the largest nation* (*i.e.* *India*) *should take the lead*; *The United States presence, i.e. the maintenance of American military personnel, in south-east Asia.*

egoism, -ist(ic), egotism, -ist(ic). *Egoism* is the term used in Philosophy and Psychology, and denotes self-interest (often contrasted with *altruism*), e.g. *Egoistic instincts concerned with self-preservation or the good of the Ego* (Gilbert Murray). *Egotism* is the practice of talking or thinking excessively about oneself, self-centredness, e.g. *He is petty, selfish, vain, egotistical; he is spoilt; he is a tyrant* (Virginia Woolf).

• In practice the senses tend to merge, e.g. *Human loves don't last, . . they are far too egoistic* (Iris Murdoch); *A complete egotist in all his dealings with women* (Joyce Cary).

egregious, remarkable in a bad sense; gross, outrageous; used mainly with words like *ass*, *impostor*, *liar*, *blunder*, *folly*, *waste*, e.g. *Wark tenderly forgives her most egregious clerical errors* (Martin Amis).

either (adjective and pronoun). (1) One or other of the two, e.g. *Simple explanations are for simple minds. I've no use for either* (Joe Orton). (2) Each of the two, e.g. *Every few kilometres on either side of the road, there were Haitian and Dominican guard-posts* (Graham Greene).

• *Either* is frequently used in sense (2), in preference to *each*, with reference to a thing that comes naturally in a pair, e.g. *end, hand, side.* This use is sometimes ignorantly condemned but is both the older sense of *either* and commonly found in good writers of all periods.

elder (adjective) the earlier-born (of two related or indicated persons), e.g. *The first and elder wife . . returned . . to Jericho* (Muriel Spark); *He is my elder by ten years. Eldest* first-born or oldest surviving (member of family, son, daughter, etc.).

elusive (rather than *elusory*) is the usual adjective related to *elude*; *illusory* (rather than *illusive*) is the usual adjective related to *illusion.*

enjoin: one can enjoin an action, etc., *on* someone, or enjoin someone *to* do something; the former is more usual; e.g. *To . . enjoin celibacy on its laity as well as on its clergy* and *That enables and enjoins the citizen to earn his own living* (G. B. Shaw).

enormity (1) Great wickedness (of something), e.g. *Hugh was made entirely speechless . . by the enormity of the proposal* (Iris Murdoch); a serious crime or offence, e.g. *They had met to pass sentence on Wingfield for his enormities* (David Garnett). (2) Enormousness, e.g. *The war in its entire magnitude did not exist for the average civilian . . The enormity of it was quite beyond most of us* (G. B. Shaw).

● Sense (2) is commonly found, but is regarded by many people as incorrect.

enthuse, to show or fill with enthusiasm, is chiefly informal.

● **equally as** (+ adjective) should not be used for *equally*, e.g. in *How to apply it in a calm, unruffled manner was equally as important* (G. F. Newman), or for *as*, e.g. *The Government are equally as guilty as the Opposition.*

event: *in the event of* is followed by a noun or gerund, e.g. *In the event of the earl's death, the title will lapse.*

● *In the event that*, treated as a compound conjunction, is ungainly and avoided by good writers; it is even worse with *that* omitted, e.g. *In the event the car overturns.*

ever. When placed after a *wh*-question word in order to intensify it, *ever* should be written separately, e.g. *Where ever have you been?, when ever is he coming?, who ever would have thought it?, why ever did you do it?, how ever shall I escape?* When used with a relative pronoun or adverb to give it indefinite or general force, *ever* is written as one word with it, e.g. *Wherever you go I'll follow*; *whenever he washes up he breaks something*; *there's a reward for whoever* (not *whomever*) *finds it*; *whatever else you do, don't get lost*; *however it's done, it's difficult.*

evidence, evince. *Evidence* (verb), to serve as evidence for the existence or truth of, e.g. *There was an innate refinement . . about Gerty which was unmistakably evidenced in her delicate hands* (James Joyce).

Evince, to show that one has a (hidden or unseen) quality, e.g. *Highly evolved sentiments and needs* (*sometimes said to be distinctively human, though birds and animals . . evince them*) (G. B. Shaw).

• *Evince* should not be confused with *evoke* to call up (a response, a feeling, etc.), e.g. *A timely and generous act which evoked a fresh outburst of emotion* (James Joyce).

exceedingly, extremely; *excessively*, beyond measure, immoderately, e.g. *The excessively rational terms employed by people with a secret panic* (Muriel Spark).

excepting (preposition) is only used after *not* and *always.*

exceptionable, to which exception may be taken; *unexceptionable* with which no fault may be found, e.g. *The opposite claim would seem to him unexceptionable even if he disagreed with it* (George Orwell).

• Do not confuse with (*un*)*exceptional*, that is (not) an exception, unusual.

excess. *In excess of* 'to a greater amount or degree than' forms an adverbial phrase.

• Prefer *more than* where the phrase qualified is the subject or object, e.g. in *The Data Centre, which processes in excess of 1200 jobs per week*.

expect (1) in the sense 'suppose, think' is informal; (2) see **anticipate**.

explicit, express. *Explicit*, distinctly expressing all that is meant, leaving nothing implied, e.g. *I had been too tactful, . . too vague . . But I now saw that I ought to have been more explicit* (Iris Murdoch); *express*, definite, unmistakable in import, e.g. *Idolatry fulsome enough to irritate Jonson into an express disavowal of it* (G. B. Shaw).

exposure (to) may be used figuratively to mean 'being made subject (to an influence, etc.)' but should not be used for *experience* (*of*), e.g. in *Candidates who have had exposure to North American markets*.

express (adjective): see **explicit**.

facility in the sense 'ease in doing something', e.g. *I knew that I had a facility with words* (George Orwell), should not be confused with a similar sense of *faculty*, viz. 'a particular kind of ability', e.g. *Hess . . had that odd faculty, peculiar to lunatics, of falling into strained positions* (Rebecca West).

factious: see **fractious.**

factitious, made for a special purpose; not natural; artificial; e.g. *Heroic tragedy is decadent because it is factitious; it substitutes violent emotionalism for emotion* (and) *the purple patch for poetry* (L. C. Knights); *fictitious*, feigned, simulated; imaginary, e.g. *Afraid of being suspected, he gave a fictitious account of his movements.*

farther, farthest: though originally interchangeable with *further, furthest*, these words are now only used where the sense of 'distance' is involved, e.g. *One whose actual dwelling lay presumably amid the farther mysteries of the cosmos* (J. I. M. Stewart).

● Even in this sense many people prefer *further, furthest.*

feasible, capable of being done, achieved, or dealt with, e.g. *Young people believing that niceness and innocence are politically as well as morally feasible* (J. I. M. Stewart).

● It is sometimes used to mean 'possible' or 'probable', but whichever of these two words is appropriate should be used instead.

fewer: see **less.**

fictitious: see **factitious.**

flammable, easily set on fire; preferable as a warning of danger to *inflammable*, which may be mistaken for a negative (= not easily set on fire). The real negatives are *non-flammable* and *non-inflammable.*

flaunt, to display proudly or ostentatiously, e.g. *The wicked flaunt themselves on every side* (NEB); *As though to defy reason, as though to flaunt a divine indestructibility, the question will not go away: is God?* (Tom Stoppard).

● Do not confuse with *flout* 'to disobey openly and scornfully', e.g. *His deliberate flouting of one still supposedly iron rule* (Frederic Raphael): *flout* should have been used by the public figure reported as having said *Those wanting to flaunt the policy would recognize that public opinion was not behind them.*

following, as a sequel to, consequent on, is used in two ways. (1) Properly, as an adjective, dependent on a preceding noun, e.g. *During demonstrations following the hanging of two British soldiers.* (2) By extension, as an independent quasi-preposition, e.g. *The prologue was written by the company following an incident witnessed by them.*

● Many people regard use (2) as erroneous (cf. **due to** (3)). It can also give rise to ambiguity, e.g. *Police arrested a man following* *the hunt*. In any case, *following* should not be used as a mere synonym for *after* (e.g. *Following supper they went to bed*).

for: The subject of a clause of which the verb is the *to*-infinitive is normally preceded by *for*, e.g. *For him to stay elsewhere is unthinkable* (contrast *that he should stay elsewhere* . .). But if the clause is a direct object in a main sentence, *for* is omitted: hence *I could not bear for him to stay elsewhere* (*Daily Mail*) is non-standard.

forensic (1) of or used in courts of law, e.g. *forensic medicine*, *forensic science*; (2) of or involving forensic science, e.g. *An object which has been sent for forensic examination*.

● Sense (2) is often deplored as an illogical extension, but is widespread.

former (latter). When referring to the first (last) of three or more, *the first* (*the last*) should be used, not *the former* (*the latter*).

fortuitous means 'happening by chance, accidental', e.g. *His presence is not fortuitous. He has a role to play* (André Brink).

● It does not mean either 'fortunate' or 'timely', as (incorrectly) in *He could not believe it. It was too fortuitous to be chance*.

fractious, unruly; peevish; e.g. *Block tackle and a strangling pully will bring your lion to heel, no matter how fractious* (James Joyce).

● Do not confuse with *factious* 'given to, or proceeding from, faction', e.g. *In spite of such a divisive past and a fractious* (correctly, *factious*) *present* (*New York Times*).

fruition, fulfilment, especially in the phrase *be brought to*, *come to*, *grow to*, *reach*, etc. *fruition*, once stigmatized as a misuse, is now standard.

fulsome is a pejorative term, applied to nouns such as *flattery*, *servility*, *affection*, etc., and means 'cloying, excessive, disgusting by excess', e.g. *They listened to fulsome speeches, doggedly translated by a wilting Olga Fiodorovna* (Beryl Bainbridge).

● *Fulsome* is not now regarded as a synonym of *copious*, though this was its original meaning.

further, furthest: see **farther, farthest.**

geriatric means 'pertaining to the health and welfare of the elderly'; it is incorrect to use it as a synonym of *senile* or *elderly*, or as a noun meaning 'elderly or senile person'.

gourmand, glutton; *gourmet*, connoisseur of good food.

graffiti is the plural of *graffito*; it is not a singular mass noun.

half. The use of *half* in expressions of time to mean *half-past* is indigenous to Britain and has been remarked on since the 1930s, e.g. *We'd easily get the half-five bus* (William Trevor); it is to be distinguished from the use of *half* + the succeeding hour (i.e. *half-nine* = half-past eight) in parts of Scotland and Ireland. It remains non-standard.

hardly. (1) *Hardly* is not used with negative constructions.
● Expressions like *Without hardly a word of comment* (substitute *with hardly* or *almost without a word*. .) and *I couldn't hardly tell what he meant* (substitute *I could hardly tell* . .) are non-standard.
(2) *Hardly* and *scarcely* are followed by *when* or *before*, not *than*, e.g. *Hardly had Grimes left the house when a tall young man . . presented himself at the front door* (Evelyn Waugh).

heir apparent, one whose right of inheritance cannot be superseded by the birth of another heir; as opposed to an *heir presumptive*, whose right can be so superseded.
● *Heir apparent* does not mean 'seeming heir'.

help. *More than*, or *as little as*, *one can help* are illogical but established idioms, e.g. *They will not respect more than they can help treaties extracted from them under duress* (Winston Churchill).

hoi polloi can be preceded by *the*, even though *hoi* represents the Greek definite article, e.g. *The screens with which working archaeologists baffle the* hoi polloi (Frederic Raphael).

● **homogenous** is a frequent error for *homogeneous*, and is probably due partly to the form of the related verb *homogenize*. A word *homogenous* exists, but has a technical meaning that is quite different and very restricted in its use. *Homogeneous* means 'of the same kind, uniform', e.g. *The style throughout was homogeneous but the authors' names were multiform* (Evelyn Waugh).

hopefully, thankfully. These adverbs are used in two ways: (1) As adverbs of manner = 'in a hopeful/thankful way', 'with hope/gratitude', e.g. *The prevailing mentality of that deluded time was still hopefully parliamentary* (G. B. Shaw); *When it thankfully dawned on her that the travel agency . . would be open* (Muriel Spark). (2) As sentence adverbs, outside the clause structure and conveying the speaker's comment on the statement, e.g. *Hopefully they will be available in the autumn* (*Guardian*); *The editor, thankfully, has left them as they were written* (TLS).
● Use (2) is widely regarded as unacceptable. The main reason is that other commenting sentence adverbs, such as *regrettably*, *fortunately*, etc., can be converted to the form *it is regrettable*, *fortunate*, etc., *that* —, but these are to be resolved as *it is to be hoped* or *one hopes that* — and *one is thankful that* —. (The same objection could be, but is not, made to *happily* and *unhappily*

which mean *one is (un)happy* not *it is (un)happy that —*, e.g. in *Unhappily children do hurt flies* (Jean Rhys).) A further objection is that absurdity or ambiguity can arise from the interplay of senses (1) and (2), e.g. *There is also a screen, hopefully forming a backdrop to the whole stage* (Tom Stoppard); *Any decision to trust Egypt . . and move forward hopefully toward peace . . in the Middle East* (*Guardian Weekly*). This use of *hopefully* probably arose as a translation of German *hoffentlich*, used in the same way, and first became popular in America in the late 1960s; the same American provenance, but not the German, holds good for *thankfully*. It is recommended that sense (2) should be restricted to informal contexts.

i.e.: see **e.g., i.e.**

if in certain constructions (usually linking two adjectives or adverbs that qualify the same noun or verb) can be ambiguous, e.g. *A great play, if not the greatest, by this author*.

● It is best to paraphrase such sentences as, e.g., either *A great play, though not the greatest by this author* or *A great play, perhaps* (or *very nearly*) *the greatest by this author*.

ignorant is better followed by *of* than by *about*, e.g. *Is this famous teacher of Israel ignorant of such things?* (NEB).

ilk. *Of that ilk* is a Scots term, meaning 'of the same place, territorial designation, or name', e.g. *Wemyss of that ilk* = Wemyss of Wemyss.

● By a misunderstanding *ilk* has come to mean 'sort, lot' (usually pejorative), e.g. *Joan Baez and other vocalists of that ilk* (David Lodge). This should be avoided in formal English.

ill used predicatively = 'unwell'; *sick* used predicatively = 'about to or likely to vomit, in the act of vomiting', e.g. *I felt sick*; *I was violently sick*; used attributively = 'unwell', e.g. *a sick man*, except in collocations like *sick bay, sick leave*.

● It is non-standard to use *ill* predicatively for 'in the act of vomiting' or *sick* predicatively for 'unwell' (though the latter is standard Amer.), except in the phrase *off sick* 'away on sick leave'.

illusion: see **delusion**.

illusory: see **elusive**.

impact, used figuratively, is best confined to contexts in which someone or something is imagined as striking another, e.g. *The most dynamic colour combination if used too often loses its impact* (i.e., on the eye). It is weakened if used as a mere synonym for *effect, impression*, or *influence*.

impedance. The total resistance of an electric circuit to the flow of alternating current.

● Do not confuse with *impediment*, a hindrance, a defect (in speech, etc.), e.g. *Convinced of the existence of a serious impediment to his marriage* (Evelyn Waugh).

imply, infer. *Imply* (1) to involve the truth or existence of; (2) to express indirectly, insinuate, hint at. *Infer* (1) to reach (an opinion), deduce, from facts and reasoning, e.g. *She left it to my intelligence to infer her meaning. I inferred it all right* (W. Somerset Maugham); *He is a philosopher's God, logically inferred from self-evident premises* (Tom Stoppard). (2) = *imply*, sense (2), e.g. *I have inferred once, and I repeat, that Limehouse is the most overrated excitement in London* (H. V. Morton).

● Sense (2) of *infer* is generally unacceptable, since it is the reverse of the primary sense of the verb.

imprimatur, official licence to print.

● Do not confuse with *imprint*, the name of the publisher/printer, place of publication/printing, etc., on the title-page or at the end of a book.

inapt, inept. *Inapt* = 'not apt', 'unsuitable'; *inept* = (1) without aptitude, unskilful, e.g. *Fox-trots and quicksteps, at which he had been so inept* (David Lodge); (2) inappropriate, e.g. *Not much less than famous for looking ineptly dressed* (Anthony Powell); (3) absurd, silly, e.g. *Here I was, awkward and tongue-tied, and all the time in danger of saying something inept or even rude* (Siegfried Sassoon).

inchoate means 'just begun, underdeveloped', e.g. *Trying to give his work a finished look—and all the time it's pathetically obvious . . that the stuff's fatally inchoate* (John Wain).

● It does not mean *chaotic* or *incoherent*.

include: see **comprise** (1).

industrial action is an imprecise, often inappropriate, and sometimes socially divisive expression. If possible, use *strike*, *work-to-rule*, *overtime ban*, etc., as appropriate.

infer: see **imply**.

inflammable: see **flammable**.

inflict, afflict. One *inflicts* something *on* someone or *afflicts* someone *with* something; something is *inflicted on* one, or one is *afflicted with* something.

● Do not use *inflict with* where *afflict with* is meant, e.g. in *The miners are still out, and industry is inflicted* (correctly, *afflicted*) *with a kind of creeping paralysis*.

ingenious, clever at inventing, etc.; noun *ingenuity*; *ingenuous* open, frank, innocent; noun *ingenuousness*.

insignia is a plural noun, e.g. *Fourteen different airline insignia* (David Lodge); its singular, rarely encountered, is *insigne*.

insinuendo, a blend of *insinuation* and *innuendo*, is at best only jocular.

intense, existing, having some quality, in a high degree, e.g. *The intense evening sunshine* (Iris Murdoch); *intensive* employing much effort, concentrated, e.g. *Intensive care*; *The intensive geological surveys of the Sahara* (Margaret Drabble).

interface (noun) (1) A surface forming a common boundary between two regions, e.g. *The concepts of surface tension apply to the interfaces between solid and solid, solid and liquid,* (etc.). (2) A piece of equipment in which interaction occurs between two systems, processes, etc., e.g. *Modular interfaces can easily be designed to adapt the general-purpose computer to the equipment*. (3) A point or area of interaction between two systems, organizations, or disciplines, e.g. *The interface between physics and music is of direct relevance to .. the psychological effects of hearing* (*Nature*).

● Sense (3) is widely regarded as unacceptable, since it is often debased into a high-sounding synonym for *boundary*, *meeting-point*, *interaction*, *liaison*, *link*, etc., e.g. *The need for the interface of lecturer and student will diminish*.

interface (verb), to connect (equipment) with (equipment) by means of an interface; (of equipment) to be connected by an interface; e.g. *A multiplexed analog-to-digital converter interfaced to a PDP 11-40 computer* (*Lancet*).

● *Interface* should not be used as a synonym for *interact* (*with*), as, e.g., in *The ideal candidate will have the ability to interface effectively with the heads of staff of various departments*.

internment, confinement (from verb *intern*).

● Do not confuse with *interment*, burial (from verb *inter*).

into: it is common informally, but incorrect in formal prose, to use *in* where *into* is required, especially after verbs of motion, e.g. *Practically knocked me over in his eagerness to get in the house* (David Lodge).

invite (noun = 'invitation'), although over three centuries old, remains informal (and somewhat non-standard) only.

ironic, ironical, ironically. The noun *irony* can mean (1) a way of speaking in which the intended meaning (for those with insight) is the opposite to, or very different from, that expressed by the words used (and apprehended by the victim of the irony); or (2) a condition of affairs or events that is the opposite of what might be expected, especially when the outcome of an action appears as if it is in mockery of the agent's intention.

The adjectives *ironic*, *ironical*, and the adverb *ironically* are commonly used in sense (1) of *irony*, e.g. *Ironical silent apology for the absence of naked women and tanks of gin from the amenities* (Kingsley Amis). They are also frequently found in sense (2), e.g. *The outcome was ironic. The expenditure of British treasure served to rearm the United States rather than to strengthen Great Britain* (A. J. P. Taylor); *The fact that after all she had been faithful to me was ironic* (Graham Greene).

● Some people object to this use, especially when *ironically* is used to introduce a trivial oddity, e.g. *It was ironic that he thought himself locked out when the key was in his pocket all the time.*

kind of, sort of (1) *A kind of*, *a sort of* should not be followed by *a* before the noun, e.g. *a kind of shock*, not *a kind of a shock*. (2) *Kind of*, *sort of*, etc., followed by a plural noun, are often treated as plural and qualified by plural words like *these*, *those*, or followed by a plural verb, e.g. *They would be on those sort of terms* (Anthony Powell). This is widely regarded as incorrect except in informal use: substitute *that* (etc.) *kind* (or *sort*) *of* or *of that kind* (or *sort*), e.g. *this kind of car is unpopular* or *cars of this kind are unpopular*. (3) *Kind of*, *sort of* used adverbially, e.g. *I kind of expected it*, are informal only.

kudos is a mass noun like *glory* or *fame*, e.g. *He's made a lot of kudos out of the strike* (Evelyn Waugh).

● It is not a plural noun and there is no singular *kudo*.

latter: see **former**.

laudable, praiseworthy, e.g. *The Opposition's abstention from criticism of the Government in this crisis was laudable*; *laudatory*, expressing praise, e.g. *One politician's remarks about another are not always laudatory*.

lay (verb), past *laid*, = 'put down, arrange', etc. is only transitive, e.g. *Lay her on the bed*; *They laid her on the bed*; (reflexive, somewhat archaic): *I will both lay me down in peace, and sleep* (Authorized Version).

● To use *lay* intransitively, to mean 'lie', e.g. *She wants to lay down*; *She was laying on the bed*, is non-standard, even though fairly common in spoken English. Cf. *lie*.

leading question, in Law, is a question so worded that it prompts a person to give the desired answer, e.g. *The solicitor . . at once asked me some leading questions . . I had to try to be both forthcoming and discreet* (C. P. Snow).

● It does not mean a 'principal' (or 'loaded' or 'searching') 'question'.

learn with a person as the object, = 'teach', is non-standard, or occasionally jocular as in *I'll learn you.*

less (adjective) is the comparative of (*a*) *little*, and, like the latter, is used with mass nouns, e.g. *I owe him little duty and less love* (Shakespeare); *fewer* is the comparative of (*a*) *few*, and both are used with plural countable nouns, e.g. *Few people have their houses broken into; and fewer still have them burnt* (G. B. Shaw).

● *Less* is quite often used informally as the comparative of *few*, probably on the analogy of *more*, which is the comparative both of *much* (with mass nouns) and *many* (with plural countable nouns), e.g. *I wish that they would send less delicacies and frills and some more plain and substantial things* (Susan Hill). This is regarded as incorrect in formal English.

● *Less* should not be used as the comparative of *small* (or some similar adjective such as *low*), e.g. *a lower price* not *a less price.*

lesser, not so great as the other or the rest, e.g. *He opened* The Times *with the rich crackle that drowns all lesser sounds* (John Galsworthy).

● *Lesser* should not be used when the meaning is 'not so big' or 'not so large': its opposition to *greater* is essential. It cannot replace *smaller* in *A smaller prize will probably be offered.*

lest is very formal (in ordinary English, *so that . . not* or *in case* is used); it is followed by *should* or (in exalted style) the subjunctive, e.g. *Lest the eye wander aimlessly, a Doric temple stood by the water's edge* (Evelyn Waugh); *Lest some too sudden gesture or burst of emotion should turn the petals brown* (Patrick White).

let, to allow (followed by the bare infinitive) is rarely used in the passive: the effect is usually unidiomatic, e.g. *Halfdan's two sons . . are let owe their lives to a trick* (Gwyn Jones). *Allowed to* is usual.

liable (1) can be followed by *to* + a noun or noun phrase in the sense 'subject to, likely to suffer from', or by an infinitive; (2) carries the implication that the action or experience expressed by the infinitive is undesirable, e.g. *Receiving in the bedroom is liable to get a woman talked about* (Tom Stoppard); (3) can indicate either the mere possibility, or the habituality, of what is expressed by the verb, e.g. *The cruellest question which a novelist is liable . . to be asked* (Frederic Raphael); *The kind of point that one is always liable to miss* (George Orwell).

• The sense 'likely to' is Amer., e.g. *Boston is liable to be the ultimate place for holding the convention.*
Contrast **apt**.

lie (verb) past *lay*, *lain*, = 'recline', 'be situated', is only intransitive, e.g. *Lie down on the bed; The ship lay at anchor until yesterday; Her left arm, on which she had lain all night, was numb.*
• To use *lie* transitively, to mean 'lay', e.g. *Lie her on the bed*, is non-standard. The past *lay* and participle *lain* are quite often wrongly used for *laid* out of over-correctness, e.g. *He had lain this peer's honour in the dust.* Cf. **lay**.

ligature: see **digraph**.

like, indicating resemblance between two things: (1) It is normally used as an adjective followed by a noun, noun phrase, or pronoun (in the objective case), e.g. *A man with human frailties like our own* (NEB); *He loathes people like you and me* (not . . *and I*). It can be used to mean 'such as' (introducing a particular example of a class about which something is said), e.g. *With a strongly patterned dress like that you shouldn't really wear any jewellery* (Iris Murdoch).
• In formal contexts some people prefer *such as* to be used if more than one example is mentioned, e.g. *British composers such as Elgar, Vaughan Williams, and Britten.*
(2) It is often used as a conjunction with a dependent clause, e.g. *Everything went wrong . . like it does in dreams* (Iris Murdoch); *Not with a starched apron like the others had* (Jean Rhys), or with an adverbial phrase, e.g. *With glossy hair, black, and a nose like on someone historical* (Patrick White); *It was as if I saw myself. Like in a looking-glass* (Jean Rhys).
• Although this is not uncommon in formal writing, it is often 'condemned as vulgar or slovenly' (*OED*), and is best avoided, except informally. Use *as*, e.g. *Are you going to kill me as you killed the Egyptian?* (NEB), or recast the sentence, e.g. *A costume like those that the others wore.*
(3) It is often informally used to mean 'as if', e.g. *The light at either end of the tunnel was like you were looking through a sheet of yellow cellophane* (Patrick White); *You wake like someone hit you on the head* (T. S. Eliot).
• This use is very informal.

likely (adverb), in the sense 'probably', must be preceded by *more*, *most*, or *very*, e.g. *Its inhabitants . . very likely do make that claim for it* (George Orwell).

• The use without the qualifying adverb is Amer., e.g. *They'll likely turn ugly* (Eugene O'Neill).

linguist means 'one whose subject is linguistics' as well as 'one skilled in the use of languages'; there is no other suitable term (*linguistician* is disfavoured).

literally. In very informal speech, *literally* is used as an intensifying adverb without meaning apart from its emotive force.

• This use should be avoided in writing or formal speech, since it almost invariably involves absurdity, e.g. *The dwarfs mentioned here are literally within a stone's throw of the Milky Way* (*New Scientist*). The appropriate use is seen in *She emerged, fully armed, from the head of Zeus who was suffering from a literally splitting headache* (Frederic Raphael).

loan (verb) has some justification where a businesslike loan is in question, e.g. *The gas industry is using a major part of its profits to benefit the PSBR by loaning money to Government* (*Observer*). Otherwise it is a needless variant for *lend*.

locate can mean 'discover the place where someone or somebody is', e.g. *She had located and could usefully excavate her Saharan highland emporium* (Margaret Drabble); it should not be used to mean merely 'find'.

lot. *A lot of*, though somewhat informal, is acceptable in serious writing; *lots of* is not.

luncheon is an especially formal variant of *lunch*; the latter should normally be used, except in fixed expressions like *luncheon voucher*.

luxuriant, growing profusely, prolific, profuse, exuberant, e.g. *His hair . . does not seem to have been luxuriant even in its best days* (G. B. Shaw).

• Do not confuse with *luxurious* (the adjective relating to *luxury*), e.g. *The food, which had always been good, was now luxurious* (C. P. Snow).

majority can mean 'the greater number of a countable set', and is then followed by the plural, e.g. *The majority of the plays produced were failures* (G. B. Shaw).

• *Great* (or *huge*, *vast*, etc.) can precede *majority* in this sense, e.g. *The first thing you gather from the vast majority of the speakers* (C. S. Lewis); but not *greater*, *greatest* (since 'more' is already contained in the word).

• *Majority* is not used to mean 'the greater part of an uncountable mass', e.g. *I was doing most* (or *the greater part*) *of the cooking* (not *the majority of the cooking*).

masterful, domineering, e.g. *People might say she was tyrannical, domineering, masterful* (Virginia Woolf).

● Do not confuse with *masterly*, very skilful, e.g. *A masterly compound of friendly argumentation and menace* (Iris Murdoch).

maximize, to make as great as possible.

● It should not be used for 'to make as good, easy, (etc). as possible' or 'to make the most of' as in *To maximize customer service*; *To maximize this situation.*

means (1) Money resources: a plural noun, e.g. *You might find out from Larry . . what his means are* (G. B. Shaw).

(2) That by which a result is brought about. It may be used either as a singular noun or as a plural one, without any change in form, e.g. (singular) *The press was, at this time, the only means . . of influencing opinion at home* (A. J. P. Taylor); (plural) *All the time-honoured means of meeting the opposite sex* (Frederic Raphael).

● Beware of mixing singular and plural, as in *The right to resist by every* (singular) *means that are* (plural) *consonant with the law of God.*

media, agency, means (of communication etc.), is a plural noun, e.g. *The communication media inflate language because they dare not be honest* (Anthony Burgess). Its singular is *medium* (rare except in *mass medium*).

● *Media* cannot be treated as a singular noun or form a plural *medias*. *Medium* (in Spiritualism) forms its plural in *-s*.

militate: see **mitigate**.

milliard: see **billion**.

minimize, to reduce to, or estimate at, the smallest possible amount or degree, e.g. *Each side was inclined to minimize its own losses in battle.*

● It does not mean *lessen* and therefore cannot be qualified by adverbs like *greatly*.

minority. *Large*, *vast*, etc. *minority* can mean either 'a considerable number who are yet less than half', or 'a number who are very much the minority': it is best to avoid the ambiguity.

mitigate, appease, alleviate, moderate (usually transitive), e.g. *Its heat mitigated by the strong sea-wind* (Anthony Burgess).

● Do not confuse with *militate* (intransitive) *against*, to serve as a strong influence against, e.g. *The very fact that Leamas was a professional could militate against his interests* (John le Carré): it is only the idea of countering that they have in common.

momentum, impetus.

● Do not confuse with *moment* 'importance', e.g. *He has marked his entrance with an error of some moment* (not *momentum*).

more than one is followed by a singular verb and is referred back to by singular pronouns, e.g. *More than one popular dancing man inquired anxiously at his bank* (Evelyn Waugh).

motivate, to cause (a person) to act in a particular way.

● It does not mean 'supply a motive, justify', e.g. (wrongly) in *The publisher motivates the slim size of these volumes by claiming it makes them more likely to be read.*

mutual (1) Felt, done, etc., by each to(wards) the other, e.g. *The mutual affection of father and son was rather touching* (W. Somerset Maugham).

(2) Standing in a (specified) relation to each other, e.g. *Kings and subjects, mutual foes* (Shelley). This sense is now rare.

(3) Common to two (or more) parties, e.g. *a mutual friend* or *acquaintance*.

● Sense (3) is acceptable in a small number of collocations, such as the two indicated, in which *common* might be ambiguous; cf. *They had already formed a small island of mutual Englishness* (Muriel Spark): *common Englishness* might imply vulgarity. Otherwise *common* is preferable, e.g. in *By common* (rather than *mutual*) *consent the Chinese meal had been abandoned.*

nature. ● Avoid using adjective + *nature* as a periphrasis for an abstract noun, e.g. write *The dangerousness of the spot*, not *The dangerous nature of the spot.*

need (*this needs changing*, etc.): see **want**.

neighbourhood. *In the neighbourhood of* is an unnecessarily cumbersome periphrasis for *round about*.

neither (adverb). ● It is non-standard to use it instead of *either* to strengthen a preceding negative, e.g. *There were no books either* (not *neither*).

non-flammable: see **flammable**.

normalcy is chiefly Amer.

● Prefer *normality*.

not only: see **only** (4).

no way (1) (Initially, followed by inversion of verb and subject) = 'not at all, by no means', e.g. *No way will you stop prices or unemployment going up again* (James Callaghan). ● Informal only. (2) (Emphatic) = 'certainly not', e.g. '*Did you go up in the elevator?*' '*No way.*' ● Chiefly Amer.; informal only.

number. *A number* (*of*) is constructed with the plural, *the number* (*of*) the singular, e.g. *Many of you are feeble and sick, and a number have died* (NEB); *The number of men who make a definite contribution to anything whatsoever is small* (Virginia Woolf).

obligate (verb) is in Britain only used in Law.

• There is no gain in using it (as often in Amer. usage) for *oblige*.

oblivious, in the sense 'unaware of, unconscious of', may be followed by *of* or *to*, e.g. '*When the summer comes,' said Lord Marchmain, oblivious of the deep corn and swelling fruit . . outside his windows* (Evelyn Waugh); *Rose seemed oblivious to individuals* (Angus Wilson).

• This sense, which developed from the older sense 'forgetful', is sometimes censured, but is now fully established in the language.

of used for *have*: see **of,** p. 208, and **have,** p. 116.

off of used for the preposition *off*, e.g. *Picked him off of the floor*, is non-standard.

one (pronoun) (1) = 'any person, the speaker or writer as representing people in general' has *one*, *one's*, and *oneself* as objective, possessive, and reflexive forms.

• These forms should be used to point back to a previous use of *one*, e.g. *One always did, in foreign parts, become friendly with one's fellow-countrymen more quickly than one did at home* (Muriel Spark). *One* should not be mixed with *he* (*him*, *his*, etc.) (acceptable Amer. usage) or *we*, *you*, etc.

(2) = single thing or person, following *any* and *every*; the resulting phrase is written as two words and is distinct from *anyone*, *everyone* (= anybody, everybody), e.g. *Any one* (*of these*) *will do*; *Perhaps every one of my conclusions would be negatived by other observers* (George Orwell).

ongoing has a valid use as an adjective meaning 'that goes on', i.e. 'that is happening and will continue' (just as *oncoming* means 'that comes on'), e.g. *The refugee problem in our time is an ongoing problem* (Robert Kee).

• The vague or tautologous use of *ongoing* should be avoided, as in the cliché *ongoing situation*, or in *We have an ongoing military relationship which we are continuing* (*Guardian*).

only (1) In spoken English, it is usual to place *only* between subject and verb, e.g. *He ònly saw Bill yesterday*: intonation is used to show whether *only* limits *he*, *saw*, *Bill*, or *yesterday*.

(2) It is an established idiom that, in a sentence containing *only* + verb + another item, in the absence of special intonation, *only* is understood as limiting, not the subject or verb, but the other item. *I only want some water* is the natural way of saying

I want only some water. If there is more than one item following the verb, *only* often limits the item nearest the end of the sentence, e.g. *A type of mind that can only accept ideas if they are put in the language he would use himself* (Doris Lessing) (= only if . .); but not always, e.g. *The captain was a thin unapproachable man . . who only appeared once at table* (Graham Greene) (= only once). This idiom is tacitly recognized by all good writers, e.g. *They only met on the most formal occasions* (C. P. Snow); *The contractors were only waiting for the final signature to start their work of destruction* (Evelyn Waugh); *The Nonconformist sects only influenced minorities* (George Orwell).

(3) Despite the idiom described under (2), there are often sentences in which confusion can arise, e.g. *Patrick only talked as much as he did, which was not as much as all that, to keep the ball in the air* (Kingsley Amis), where at first sight *only* might appear to limit *he* (referring to some other person) but really limits *to keep . . air*. If confusion or ambiguity is likely to arise, *only* should be placed before the item which it limits, e.g. *They sought to convert others only by the fervour of their sentiments and the earnestness of their example* (Frederic Raphael); *The coal-miner is second in importance only to the man who ploughs the soil* (George Orwell).

(4) *Not only* should always be placed next to the item which it qualifies, and not in the position before the verb. This is a fairly common slip, e.g. *Katherine's marriage not only kept her away, but at least two of Mr. March's cousins* (C. P. Snow); *kept not only her* would be better. If placing it before the verb is inevitable, the verb should be repeated after *but* (*also*), e.g. *It not only brings the coal out but brings the roof down as well* (George Orwell).

orient, orientate. In meaning the two words are virtually synonymous. In general, as opposed to technical, use, *orientate* seems to be predominant, but either is acceptable.

other than can be used where *other* is an adjective or pronoun, e.g. *He was no other than the rightful lord*; *The acts of any person other than myself*.

• *Other* cannot be treated as an adverb: *otherwise than* should be used instead, e.g. in *It is impossible to refer to them other than very cursorily*.

out used as a preposition instead of *out of*, e.g. *You should of* [sic] *pushed him out the nest long ago* (character in work by Muriel Spark), is non-standard.

outside of (1) = apart from (a sense *outside* cannot have) is informal only, e.g. *The need of some big belief outside of art* (Roger Fry, in a letter).

(2) = beyond the limits of, e.g. *The most important such facility outside of Japan* (*Gramophone*).

• In sense (2) *outside* alone is preferable: the *of* is redundant.

outstanding. • Do not use in the sense 'remaining undetermined, unpaid, etc.' in contexts where ambiguity with the sense 'eminent, striking' can arise, e.g. *The other outstanding result* (in sport).

overly, excessively, too, is still regarded as an unassimilated Americanism, e.g. *Those overly rationalistic readers* (TLS).

• Use *excessively, too,* or *over-* instead; for *not overly, not very* or *none too* make satisfactory replacements.

overseas (adjective and adverb) is now more usual than *oversea.*

overview is an Americanism that has not found acceptance in Britain: *survey, review,* or *outline* are adequate substitutes.

owing to, unlike **due to,** has for long been established as a compound preposition, e.g. *My rooms became uninhabitable, owing to a burst gas-pipe* (C. P. Snow).

• *Owing to the fact that* should be avoided: use a conjunction like *because.*

pace means 'despite (someone)'s opinion', e.g. *Our civilization,* pace *Chesterton, is founded on coal* (George Orwell).

• It does not mean 'according to (someone)' or 'notwithstanding (something)'.

parameter. (1) (In technical use, especially in Mathematics and Computing) (roughly) a quantity constant in the case considered, but varying between different cases.

(2) (In extended use) a defining characteristic, especially one that can be measured, e.g. *The three major parameters of colour—brightness, hue, and saturation.*

(3) (Loosely) a limit or boundary, e.g. *The considerable element of indeterminacy which exists within the parameters of the parole system* (*The Times*); an aspect or feature, e.g. *The main parameters of the problem.*

• Use (3) is a popular dilution of the word's meaning, probably influenced (at least in the first quotation) by *perimeter*; it should be avoided.

parricide refers to the killing of one's father, one's close relative, or a person regarded as sacred, or to treason; *patricide* only to the killing of one's father.

part (on the part of): see **behalf**.

partially, partly. Apart from the (rare) use of *partially* to mean 'in a partial or biased way', these two words are largely interchangeable. Note, however, that *partly . . partly* is more usual than *partially . . partially*, e.g. *Partly in verse and partly in prose.*

peer, as in *to have no peer*, means 'equal', not 'superior'.

pence is sometimes informally used as a singular, e.g. *How Fine Fare, on lard, is one pence up on Sainsbury's* (Malcolm Bradbury).

● This use is very informal. Normally *penny* should be used in the singular.

perquisite (informal abbreviation *perk*) a casual profit, incidental benefit attaching to an employment, thing to which a person has sole right, e.g. *Free travel by train was a perquisite of railway managerial staff.*

● Do not confuse with *prerequisite* 'something required as a previous condition (*for*, *of*, or *to* something)', e.g. *Her mere comforting presence beside me which was already a prerequisite to peaceful sleep* (Lynne Reid Banks).

persistency is limited in sense to 'the action of persisting in one's course', e.g. *They made repeated requests for compensation, but an official apology was the only reward for their persistency*; *persistence* is sometimes used in that sense, but more often for 'continued existence', e.g. *One of the more surprising things about the life-ways of primitive societies is their persistence* (Sean O'Faolain).

perspicuous, easily understood, clearly expressed; expressing things clearly; similarly *perspicuity*; e.g. *There is nothing more desirable in composition than perspicuity* (Southey).

● Do not confuse with *perspicacious*, having or showing insight, and *perspicacity*, e.g. *Her perspicacity at having guessed his passion* (Vita Sackville-West).

***petit* bourgeois, petty bourgeois.** The meaning (and with many people, the pronunciation) of these is the same. If the former is used, the correct French inflections should be added: *petits bourgeois* (plural), *petite*(*s*) *bourgeoise*(*s*) (feminine (plural)); also *petite bourgeoisie*. With *petty bourgeois* it should be remembered that the sense of the original French *petit* is not English *petty*, although that may be one of its main connotations.

phenomena is the plural of *phenomenon*.

● It cannot be used as a singular and cannot form a plural *phenomenas*.

picaresque (of a style of fiction) dealing with the adventures of rogues.

● It does not mean 'transitory' or 'roaming'.

pivotal, being that on which anything pivots or turns, e.g. *The pardon of Richard Nixon was pivotal to those who made up their minds at the last minute.*

• Do not use it merely to mean *vital.*

plaid, shawl-like garment; *tartan,* woollen cloth with distinctive pattern; the pattern itself.

• **plus** (conjunction), = 'and in addition', is an Amer. colloquialism of little acceptability, e.g. —— *have big names at big savings. Plus you get one year manufacturer's guarantee* (Advertisement).

polity, a form of civil government, e.g. *A republican polity*; a state.

• It does not mean *policy* or *politics.*

portentous can mean: (1) Like a portent, ominous, e.g. *Fiery-eyed with a sense of portentous utterance* (Muriel Spark). (2) Prodigious, e.g. *Every movement of his portentous frame* (James Joyce). (3) Solemn, ponderous, and somewhat pompous, e.g. *Our last conversation must have sounded to you rather portentous* (Iris Murdoch); *A portentous commentary on Holy Scripture* (Lord Hailsham).

• Sense (3) is sometimes criticized, but is an established, slightly jocular use.

• The form *portentious* (due to the influence of *pretentious*) is erroneous.

post, pre. Their use as full words (not prefixes) to mean 'after' and 'before' is unnecessary and disagreeable, e.g. in *Post the Geneva meeting of Opec* (*Daily Telegraph*); *Pre my being in office* (Henry Kissinger).

practicable, practical. When applied to things, *practicable* means 'able to be done', e.g. (with the negative *impracticable*), *Schemes which look very fine on paper, but which, as we well know, are impracticable* (C. S. Lewis); *practical* 'concerned with practice, suitable for use, suited to the conditions', e.g. *Having considered the problem, he came up with several practical suggestions*; *It is essential that the plan should cover all the practical details.*

pre: see **post, pre.**

precipitous, like a precipice, e.g. *Our rooms were . . reached by a precipitous marble staircase* (Evelyn Waugh).

• Do not confuse with *precipitate,* hasty, rash, e.g. *They were all a little out of breath from precipitate arrival* (Patrick White).

predicate (verb): (1) (Followed by *of*) to assert as a property of, e.g. *That easy Bohemianism—conventionally predicated of the 'artistic' temperament* (J. I. M. Stewart). (2) (Followed by *on*) to found or base (something) on, e.g. *A new conception* *of reality . . predicated on dissatisfaction with formalist literature* (TLS)

• Sense (2) tends to sound pretentious. Use *found*, or *base*, *on*.

pre-empt (1) To obtain beforehand, secure for oneself in advance, e.g. *Sound allows the mind an inventive role systematically pre-empted by the cinema* (Frederic Raphael). (2) To preclude, forestall, e.g. *The Nazi régime by its own grotesque vileness pre-empted fictional effort* (*Listener*).

• Sense (2) is better expressed by a verb such as *preclude* or *forestall*.

• *Pre-empt* is not a synonym for *prevent*.

prefer. The rejected alternative is introduced by *to*, e.g. *Men preferred darkness to light* (NEB). But when the rejected alternative is an infinitive, it is preceded by *rather than* (not *than* alone), e.g. *I'd prefer to be stung to death rather than to wake up . . with half of me shot away* (John Osborne).

preferable to means 'more desirable than' and is therefore intensified by *far*, *greatly*, or *much*, not *more*, e.g. *After a hundred and eighty* (skips) *an unclear head seemed much preferable to more skips* (Kingsley Amis).

preference. The alternatives are introduced by *for* and *over*, e.g. *The preference for a single word over a phrase or clause* (Anthony Burgess); but *in preference* is followed by *to*, e.g. *Both were sensitive to artistic impressions musical in preference to plastic or pictorial* (James Joyce).

prejudice (1) = bias, is followed by *against* or *in favour of*; (2) = detriment, is followed by *to*; (3) = injury, is followed by *of* (in the phrase *to the prejudice of*).

prepared: *to be prepared to*, to be willing to, has been criticized as officialese by some authorities, but is now established usage, e.g. *One should kill oneself, which, of course, I was not prepared to do* (Cyril Connolly).

prerequisite: see **perquisite**.

prescribe, to lay down as a rule to be followed; *proscribe*, to forbid by law.

presently (1) After a short time, e.g. *Presently we left the table and sat in the garden-room* (Evelyn Waugh). (2) At present, currently, e.g. *The praise presently being heaped upon him* (*The Economist*).

• Sense (2) (for long current in American English) is regarded as incorrect by some people but is widely used and often sounds more natural than *at present*.

prestigious (1) Characterized by juggling or magic, delusive, deceptive, e.g. *The prestigious balancing act which he was constantly obliged to perform* (TLS): now rare. (2) Having or showing prestige, e.g. *A career in pure science is still more socially prestigious . . than one in engineering* (*The Times*): a fully acceptable sense.

prevaricate, to speak or act evasively or misleadingly, e.g. *I never have told a lie . . On many occasions I have resorted to prevarication; but on great occasions I have always told the truth* (G. B. Shaw); *procrastinate*, to postpone action, e.g. *Hamlet . . pronounces himself a procrastinator, an undecided man, even a coward* (C. S. Lewis).

prevent is followed by the objective case and *from* + the gerund, or by the possessive case + the gerund, e.g. *prevent me from going* or *prevent my going*.

• *Prevent me going* is informal only.

• **pre-war** as an adverb, in, e.g., *Some time pre-war there was a large contract out for tender* (*Daily Telegraph*): prefer *before the war*.

pristine (1) Ancient, original, e.g. *Stone which faithfully reproduced its pristine alternations of milk and cream* (J. I. M. Stewart). (2) Having its original, unspoilt condition, e.g. *Pristine snow reflects about 90 per cent of incident sunlight* (Fred Hoyle).

• *Pristine* does not mean 'spotless', 'pure', or 'fresh'.

procrastinate: see **prevaricate**.

prone (followed by *to*) is used like, and means much the same as, **liable**, except that it usually qualifies a personal subject, e.g. *My literary temperament rendering me especially prone to 'all that kind of poisonous nonsense'* (Cyril Connolly).

proportion means 'a comparative part, share, or ratio'; it is not a mere synonym for *part*.

proscribe: see **prescribe**.

protagonist, the leading character in a story or incident.

• In Greek drama there was only one protagonist, but this is no reason to debar the use of the word in the plural, e.g. *We . . sometimes mistook a mere supernumerary in a fine dress for one of the protagonists* (C. S. Lewis).

• Do not confuse with *proponent*: the word contains the Greek prefix *prot-* 'first', not the prefix *pro-* 'in favour of', and does not mean 'champion, advocate'.

protest (verb, transitive) to affirm solemnly, e.g. *He barely attempted to protest his innocence* (George Orwell).

• The sense 'protest against', e.g. in *The residents have protested the sale*, is Amer. only.

proven. It is not standard to use this as the ordinary past participle of *prove* in British English (it is standard Scots and Amer.); it is, however, common attributively in certain expressions, such as *of proven ability*.

provenance, origin, place of origin, is used in Britain; the form *provenience* is its usual Amer. equivalent.

prudent, showing carefulness and foresight, e.g. *It seemed prudent to inform him of my plans rather than let him hear about them indirectly*; *prudential*, involving or marked by prudence, e.g. *The humble little outfit of prudential maxims which really underlay much of the talk about Shakespeare's characters* (C. S. Lewis).

pry, to prise (open, etc.): chiefly Amer., but occasionally in British literary use, e.g. *For her to pry his fingers open* (David Garnett). The normal sense is 'peer' or 'inquire'.

quadrillion: see **billion.**

question: (1) *No question that* (sometimes *but*), no doubt that, e.g. *There can be no question that the burning of Joan of Arc must have been a most instructive and interesting experiment* (G. B. Shaw); *There is no question but Leslie was an unusually handsome boy* (Anthony Powell).

(2) *No question of*, no possibility of, e.g. *There can be no question of tabulating successes and failures and trying to decide whether the successes are too numerous to be accounted for by chance* (C. S. Lewis). See also **beg the question, leading question.**

quote (noun = quotation) is informal only (except in Printing and Commerce).

• **re** (in the matter of, referring to) is better avoided and should not be used for 'about, concerning'.

reason. *The reason* (*why*) . . *is* . . should be followed by *that*, not *because*, e.g. *The reason why such a suggestion sounds hopeless . . is that few people are able to imagine the radio being used for the dissemination of anything except tripe* (George Orwell).

recoup (1) (transitive) to recompense (oneself or a person) *for* (a loss or expenditure), e.g. *Dixon felt he could recoup himself a little for the expensiveness of the drinks* (Kingsley Amis); also *to recoup one's losses*; (2) (intransitive) to make good one's loss, e.g. *I had . . acquired so many debts that if I didn't return to England to recoup, we might have to run for it* (Chaim Bermant).

• This word is not synonymous with *recuperate* except partly in sense (2) above ('to make good one's loss').

recuperate (1) (intransitive) to recover from exhaustion, ill-health, financial loss, etc., e.g. *I've got a good mind . . to put all my* *winnings on red and give him a chance to recuperate* (Graham Greene); (2) (transitive) to recover (health, a loss, material). In sense (2) *recover* is preferable.

redolent, smelling *of* something, e.g. *Corley's breath redolent of rotten cornjuice* (James Joyce); also used figuratively to mean 'strongly suggestive or reminiscent of', e.g. *The missive most redolent of money and sex* (Martin Amis).

referendum. • For the plural, *referendums* is preferable to *referenda.*

refute, to prove (a statement, opinion, accusation, etc.), to be false, e.g. *The case against most of them must have been so easily refuted that they could hardly rank as suspects* (Rebecca West); to prove (a person) to be in error, e.g. *One of those German scholars whose function is to be refuted in a footnote* (Frederic Raphael).

• *Refute* does not mean 'deny' or 'repudiate' (an allegation etc.).

regalia is a plural noun, meaning 'emblems of royalty or of an order'. It has no singular in ordinary English.

region: *in the region of*, an unwieldy periphrasis for *round about*, is better avoided.

register office is the official term for the institution informally often called the *registry office*.

regretfully, in a regretful manner; *regrettably*, it is to be regretted (that).

• *Regretfully* should not be used where *regrettably* is intended: *The investigators, who must regretfully remain anonymous* (TLS), reads as a guess at the investigators' feelings instead of an expression of the writer's opinion, which was what was intended. The influence of **hopefully** (2) may be discernible here.

renege (intransitive), to fail to fulfil an agreement or undertaking, is usually constructed with *on*, e.g. *It . . reneged on Britain's commitment to the East African Asians* (*The Times*).

resource is often confused with *recourse* and *resort*. *Resource* means (1) a reserve upon which one can draw (often used in the plural); (2) an action or procedure to which one can turn in difficulty, an expedient; (3) mental capabilities for amusing oneself, etc. (often used in the plural, e.g. *Left to his own resources*); (4) ability to deal with a crisis, e.g. *A man of infinite resource*. *Recourse* means the action of turning to a possible source of help; frequently in the phrases *have recourse to*, *without recourse to*. *Resort* means (1) the action of turning to a possible source of help (= *recourse*; but *resorting* is more usual than *resort* after *without*); frequently in the phrase *in the last resort*, as a last expedient, in the end; (2) a thing to which one can turn in difficulty.

responsible for (1) Liable to be called to account for, e.g. *I'm not responsible for what uncle Percy does* (E. M. Forster).

(2) Obliged to take care of or carry out, e.g. *Both they and the singers, who were responsible for their respective duties* (NEB).

(3) Being the cause of, e.g. *A war-criminal responsible for so many unidentified deaths* (Graham Greene).

• Beware of using senses (1) or (2) in expressions in which sense (3) can be understood, with absurd results, e.g. *Now, as Secretary for Trade, he is directly responsible for pollution* (*The Times*).

restive (1) Unmanageable, rejecting control, obstinate, e.g. *The I.L.P. . . had been increasingly restive during the second Labour government, and now, refusing to accept Labour-party discipline in the house of commons, voluntarily disaffiliated from the Labour party* (A. J. P. Taylor).

(2) Restless, fidgety, e.g. *The audiences were not bad, though apt to be restive and noisy at the back* (J. B. Priestley).

• Sense (2) is objected to by some authorities but is quite commonly used by good writers.

revenge: one revenges oneself or a wrong (*on* an offender); one is revenged (*for* a wrong): the noun is *revenge*, and the idea is usually of satisfaction of the offended party's resentment. Cf. **avenge**.

reverend, deserving reverence; *reverent*, showing reverence.

(*The*) *Revd*, plural *Revds*, is the abbreviation of *Reverend* as a clergy title (not *Rev.*).

reversal is the noun corresponding to the verb *reverse*; *reversion* is the noun corresponding to the verb *revert*.

same. • It is non-standard to use the phrase *same as* as a kind of conjunction meaning 'in the same way as, just as', e.g. *But I shouldn't be able to serve them personally, same as I do now* (L. P. Hartley).

• The phrase *same like*, used for *just like* or *in the same way as*, is illiterate, e.g. *I have rich friends, same like you* (Iris Murdoch).

sanction (verb) to give approval to, to authorize, e.g. *This council sanctioned the proclamation of a state of war with Germany from 11 p.m.* (A. J. P. Taylor).

• It does not mean 'impose sanctions on'.

sc. (short for Latin *scilicet* = *scire licet* one is permitted to know) introduces (1) a word to be supplied, e.g. *He asserted that he had met him* (*sc. the defendant*) *on that evening*, or (2) a word to be substituted for one already used, in order to render an expression intelligible, e.g. '*I wouldn't of* (*sc. have*) *done*' *was her answer*.

scabrous (1) (In Botany and Zoology) having a rough surface. (2) Encrusted with dirt, grimy, e.g. *The streaky green distempered walls and the scabrous wooden W.C. seat* (John Braine). (3) Risqué, salacious, indecent, e.g. *Silly and scabrous titters about Greek pederasty* (C. S. Lewis).

• *Scabrous* does not mean 'scathing, abusive, scurrilous'.

scarify, to loosen the surface of (soil, etc.); to make slight cuts in (skin, tissue) surgically.

• The verb *scarify* (pronounced scare-ify) 'scare, terrify', e.g. *To be on the brink of a great happiness is a scarifying feeling* (Noel Coward), is informal only.

scenario (1) An outline of the plot of a play. (2) A film script giving details of scenes, stage-directions, etc. (3) An outline of an imagined (usually future) sequence of events, e.g. *Several of the computer 'scenarios' include a catastrophic and sudden collapse of population* (*Observer*).

• Sense (3) is valid when a detailed narrative of events that might happen under certain conditions is denoted. The word should not be used as a loose synonym for *scene*, *situation*, *circumstance*, etc.

scilicet: see **sc**.

Scottish is now the usual adjective; *Scotch* is restricted to a fairly large number of fixed expressions, e.g. *Scotch broth*, *egg*, *whisky*; *Scots* is used mainly for the Scottish dialect of English, in the names of regiments, and in *Scotsman*, *Scotswoman* (*Scotchman*, *-woman* are old-fashioned). To designate the inhabitants of Scotland, the plural noun *Scots* is normal.

seasonable, suitable for the time of year, occurring at the right time or season, opportune; *unseasonable* occurring at the wrong time or season, e.g. *You are apt to be pressed to drink a glass of vinegary port at an unseasonable hour* (Somerset Maugham).

• Do not confuse with *seasonal*, occurring at or associated with a particular season, e.g. *There is a certain seasonal tendency to think better of the Government . . in spring* (*The Economist*).

senior, superior are followed by *to*. They contain the idea of 'more' (advanced in years, exalted in position, etc.) and so cannot be constructed with *more . . than*, e.g. *There are several officers senior*, or *superior in rank*, *to him*, not . . *more senior*, or *more superior in rank*, *than him*.

sensibility, ability to feel, sensitiveness, delicacy of feeling, e.g. *The* *man's moving fingers . . showed no sign of acute sensibility* (Graham Greene).

• *Sensibility* is not the noun corresponding to *sensible* meaning 'having good sense'; i.e. it does not mean 'possession of good sense'.

sensual, gratifying to the body; indulging oneself with physical pleasures, showing that one does this, e.g. *His sensual eye took in her slim feminine figure* (Angus Wilson); *sensuous*, affecting or appealing to the senses (without the pejorative implications of *sensual*), e.g. *I got up and ran about the . . meadow in my bare feet. I remember the sensuous pleasure of it* (C. Day Lewis).

serendipity, the making of pleasant discoveries by accident, or the knack or fact of doing this; the adjective (usually applied to a discovery, event, fact, etc.) is *serendipitous*.

• *Serendipitous* does not mean merely 'fortunate'.

sic (Latin for *thus*) is placed in brackets after a word that appears odd or erroneous to show that the word is quoted exactly as it stands in the original, e.g. *Daisy Ashford's novel* The Young Visiters (*sic*).

sick: see **ill**.

• **sit, stand.** The use of the past participle *sat*, *stood* with the verb *to be*, meaning *to be sitting*, *standing*, is non-standard, e.g. *No really, I'd be sat there falling asleep if I did come* (Kingsley Amis).

situation. A useful noun for expressing the sense 'position of affairs, combination of circumstances' which may validly be preceded by a defining adjective, e.g. *the financial*, *industrial*, *military*, *political*, *situation*.

• The substitution of an attributive noun for an adjective before *situation* should be carefully considered. It should not be used when the resulting phrase will be tautologous (e.g. *a crisis situation*, *people in work situations*: *crises* and *work* are themselves *situations*). The placing of an attributive phrase before *situation* is nearly always ugly and should be avoided, e.g. *The deep space situation, a balance-of-terror situation, a standing credit situation.*

• The combination of **ongoing** with *situation* is a cliché to be avoided.

sled is Amer. for *sledge*; *sleigh* is a sledge for passengers that is drawn by horses (or reindeer).

so used adverbially as a means of linking two clauses and meaning 'therefore' may be preceded by *and* but need not be; e.g. *Leopold Bloom is a modern Ulysses, so he has to encounter Sirens and* *a Cyclops* (Anthony Burgess); *I had received no word from Martha all day, so I was drawn back to the casino* (Graham Greene).

so-called (1) has long been used in the sense 'called by this term, but not entitled to it'; (2) is now often used quite neutrally, without implication of incorrectness, especially in Science.

sort of: see **kind of**.

specialty, except for its use in Law, is an equivalent of *speciality* restricted to North America.

spectate, to be a spectator, is at best informal.

● *Watch* is usually an adequate substitute, e.g. in *A spectating, as opposed to a reading, audience* (*Listener*).

strata is the plural of *stratum*.

● It is incorrect to treat it as a singular noun, e.g. in *The movement has . . sunk to a wider and more anonymous strata.*

style. (1) Adjective + *-style* used to qualify a noun, e.g. *European-style clothing, contemporary-style dancing*, is acceptable.

(2) Adjective or noun + *-style*, forming an adverb, is somewhat informal, e.g. *A revolution, British-style* (A. J. P. Taylor).

substantial, actually existing; of real value; of solid material; having much property; in essentials; e.g. *substantial damages, progress; a substantial house, yeoman; substantial agreement.*

● It is not merely a synonym of *large*.

substantive (adjective) is used mainly in technical senses; e.g. *substantive rank*, in the services, is permanent, not acting or temporary.

substitute (verb) to put (someone or something) in place of another: constructed with *for*; e.g. *Democracy substitutes election by the incompetent many for appointment by the corrupt few* (G. B. Shaw).

● The sense 'replace (someone or something) *by* or *with* another' is incorrect, or at best highly informal, e.g. in *Having substituted her hat with a steel safety helmet, she went on a tour of the site* (better, *Having replaced her hat with . .* or *Having substituted a steel safety helmet for . .*).

such as: see **like**.

superior: see **senior**.

suppositious, hypothetical, conjectural; *supposititious*, fraudulently substituted (especially of a child displacing a real heir), e.g. *Russia . . is the supposititious child of necessity in the household of theory* (H. G. Wells).

synchronize (transitive), to make to occur at the same time, e.g.

Everyday cordialities would be synchronized with gazes of rapt ardour (Martin Amis).

• It is not a synonym for *combine* or *co-ordinate*.

than: see **different, other than, prefer, senior.**

thankfully: see **hopefully.**

the (article). When a name like *The Times* or *The Hague* is used attributively, *The* is dropped, e.g. *A* Times *correspondent*, *Last year's Hague conference*. If *the* precedes the name in such a construction, it belongs to the succeeding noun, not to the name, and is therefore not given a capital initial (or italics), e.g. *A report from the* Times *correspondent*.

the (adverb) prefixed to a comparative means 'thereby' or 'by so much', e.g. *What student is the better for mastering these futile distinctions?* This combination can enter into the further construction seen in *The more the merrier* (i.e. 'by how much more, by that much merrier'). It cannot enter into a construction with *than*: the tendency to insert it before *more* and *less* (putting *any the more*, *none the less* for *any more*, *no less*) should be resisted, e.g. in *The intellectual release had been no less* (not *none the less*) *marked than the physical*.

then may be used as an adjective preceding a noun as a neat alternative to *at that time* or similar phrase, e.g. *Hearing that they were on personal terms with the then Prime Minister* (Frederic Raphael).

• It should not be placed before the noun if it would sound equally well in its usual position, e.g. *Harold Macmillan was the then Prime Minister* could equally well be . . *was then the Prime Minister*. The same applies to an adverbial use of *then* before attributive adjectives, e.g. *The then existing constitution*: write *The constitution then existing*.

there- adverbs, e.g. *therein*, *thereon*, *thereof*, etc., belong mainly to very formal diction and should be avoided in ordinary writing (apart from certain idiomatic adverbs, e.g. *thereabouts*, *thereby*, *thereupon*); e.g. *We did not question this reasoning, and there lay our mistake* (Evelyn Waugh): a lesser writer might have written *therein*. But such adverbs can be employed for special effectiveness, e.g. *This idea brought him rocketing back to earth. But he stood thereupon like a giant* (Iris Murdoch).

through, up to and including, e.g. *Friday through Tuesday*, though useful, is Amer. only.

too followed by an adjective used attributively should be confined to poetry or special effects in prose, e.g. *Metropolis, that too-great* *city* (W. H. Auden); *A small too-pretty house* (Graham Greene).

● In normal prose it is a clumsy construction, e.g. *The crash came during a too-tight loop.*

tooth-comb and *fine tooth-comb*, arising from a misapprehension of *fine-tooth comb*, are now established expressions whose illogicality it is pedantic to object to.

tortuous, torturous. Do not confuse: *tortuous* means (1) twisting, e.g. *Through tortuous lanes where the overhanging boughs whipped the windscreen* (Evelyn Waugh); (2) devious, e.g. *Control had his reasons; they were usually so bloody tortuous it took you a week to work them out* (John le Carré). *Torturous* means 'involving torture, excruciating', e.g. *Torturously original inlay-work* (TLS).

transcendent, surpassing (e.g. *Of transcendent importance*), (of God) above and distinct from the universe, e.g. *Such transcendent power does not come from us, but is God's alone* (NEB); *transcendental*, visionary, idealistic, beyond experience, etc., e.g. *Most of those who have been near death have also described some kind of mystical or transcendental experience* (*British Medical Journal*). (Other more technical senses of each word are ignored here.)

transpire (figuratively): (1) To leak out, come to be known, e.g. *What had transpired concerning that father was not so reassuring* (John Galsworthy). (2) To come about, take place, e.g. *What transpired between them is unknown* (David Cecil).

● Sense (2), probably arising from the misunderstanding of sentences like 'What had transpired during his absence he did not know', is chiefly informal. It is regarded by many people as unacceptable, especially if the idea of something emerging from ignorance is absent: it should therefore not be used in sentences like *A storm transpired.*

trillion: see **billion**.

triumphal, of or celebrating a triumph, e.g. *A triumphal arch*; *triumphant*, conquering, exultant.

try (verb) in writing normally followed by the *to*-infinitive: *try and* + bare infinitive is informal.

turbid (1) thick, dense; (2) confused, disordered, e.g. *In an access of despair had sought death in the turbid Seine* (W. Somerset Maugham).

turgid (1) swollen; (2) (of language) inflated, grandiloquent, e.g. *Some of them are turgid, swollen with that kind of intellectual bombast which never rises to gusto* (G. H. Vallins).

underlay (verb) (past *underlaid*) to lay something under (a thing), e.g. *Underlaid the tiles with felt*: a somewhat rare verb; *underlie* (past tense *underlay*, past participle *underlain*) to lie under; to be the basis of; to exist beneath the surface of, e.g. *The arrogance that underlay their cool good manners* (Doris Lessing).

unequivocal, not ambiguous, unmistakable; similarly *unequivocally* adverb, e.g. *Made her intentions unequivocally clear*.

• The forms *unequivocable*, *-ably*, sometimes seen, are erroneous.

unexceptionable, -al: see **exceptionable**.

unique: (1) Being the only one of its kind, e.g. *The fighting quality that gives war its unique power over the imagination* (G. B. Shaw): in this sense *unique* cannot be qualified by adverbs like *absolutely*, *most*, *quite*, *so*, *thoroughly*, etc. (2) Unusual, remarkable, singular, e.g. *A passionate human insight so unique in her experience that she felt it to be unique in human experience* (Muriel Spark).

• Sense (2) is regarded by many people as incorrect. Substitute one of the synonyms given above, or whatever other adjective is appropriate.

unlike (adverb) may govern a noun, noun phrase, or pronoun, just as *like* may, e.g. *A sarcasm unlike ordinary sarcasm* (V. S. Pritchett).

• It may not govern a clause with or without ellipsis of the verb, e.g. *He was unlike he had ever been*; *Unlike in countries of lesser economic importance*.

• **various** cannot be used as a pronoun followed by *of* (as, for example, *several* can), as (wrongly) in *The two ministers concerned . . have been paying private visits to various of the Commonwealth representatives*.

venal, able to be bribed, influenced by bribery; *venial*, pardonable.

vengeance: see **avenge**.

verbal (1) of or in words; (2) of a verb; (3) spoken rather than written.

• Some people reject sense (3) as illogical and prefer *oral*. However, *verbal* is the usual term in a number of idioms, such as *verbal communication*, *contract*, *evidence*.

verge (verb) in *verge on*, *upon*, to border on, e.g. *He told two or three stories verging on the improper* (John Galsworthy), is in origin a different word from *verge* in *verge to*, *towards* to incline towards, approach, e.g. *The London docks, where industrial disputes always verged towards violence* (A. J. P. Taylor). Both are acceptable.

vermin is usually treated as plural, e.g. *A lot of parasites, vermin who feed on God's love and charity* (Joyce Cary).

via (1) By way of (a place), e.g. *To London via Reading*. (2) By means of, through the agency of, e.g. *Other things can . . be taught . . via the air, via television, via teaching machines, and so on* (E. F. Schumacher); *I sent it via my secretary*.

• Sense (2) is sometimes criticized, but is certainly acceptable in informal use.

waive to refrain from using or insisting on, to forgo or dispense with, e.g. *The satisfaction . . of waiving the rights which my preaching gives me* (NEB).

• Do not confuse this with *wave*, chiefly in conjunction with *aside*, *away*, as (wrongly) in *But the Earl simply waived the subject away with his hand* (Trollope).

want, need (verbs) in the sense 'require' can be followed (1) by a gerund as object, e.g. *Your hair needs* or *wants cutting* or (2) by an object and a past participle as complement to the object (with the verb 'to be' omitted), e.g. *We want* or *need this changed*.

• The idiom *We want* or *need this changing* (perhaps a mixture of the two constructions, but having the sense of (2)) is informal only.

well is joined by a hyphen to a following participle when the combination is used attributively, e.g. *A well-worn argument*. Predicatively a hyphen is not necessary unless the combination is to be distinguished in meaning from the two words written separately, e.g. *He is well-spoken* but *The words were well spoken*.

what ever, when ever, where ever: see **ever**.

whence meaning 'from where', does not need to be preceded by *from*.

who ever: see **ever**.

whoever, any one who, no matter who: use *whoever* for the objective case as well as the subjective, rather than *whomever*, which is rather stilted.

-wise (suffix) added to nouns (1) forming adverbs of manner, is very well established, but is now, except in fixed expressions like *clockwise*, rather literary or poetic, e.g. *The Saint wears tight yellow trousers . . and is silkily shaven Romanwise* (TLS); (2) forming viewpoint adverbs (meaning 'as regards —'), e.g. *I can eat only Cox's Orange Pippins, and am in mourning applewise from April to October* (Iris Murdoch).

• (2) is widely regarded as unacceptable in formal usage.

• Adverbs of type (2) are formed on nouns only, not on adjectives: hence sentences like *The rate-payers would have to shoulder an extra burden financial-wise* are incorrect (substitute . . *burden finance-wise* or *financial burden*).

• **without** = 'unless' is illiterate, e.g. *Without you have a bit of class already, your town gets no new theatre* (*Listener*).
See also **hardly**.

womankind is better than *womenkind* (cf. *mankind*).

worth while is usually written as two words predicatively, but as one attributively, e.g. *He thought it worth while*, or *a worthwhile undertaking, to publish the method.*

write (to compose a letter) with indirect personal object, e.g. *I will write you about it*, is not acceptable British English (but is good Amer. English).

GRAMMAR

> Language is an instrument for communication. The language which can with the greatest ease make the finest and most numerous distinctions of meaning is the best.
>
> (C. S. Lewis, *Studies in Words*)

THIS section deals with specific problems of grammar; it makes no attempt at a systematic exposition of English syntax.

It is notoriously difficult to find convenient labels for many of the topics on which guidance is needed. Wherever possible, the headings chosen for the entries are, or include, the words which actually cause grammatical problems (e.g. *as*, *may* or *might*). Some headings include the grammatical endings involved (e.g. *-ing*). But inevitably many entries have had to be given abstract labels (e.g. *double passive*, *subjunctive*). To compensate for this, a number of cross-references are included, by which the user can find a way to the required entry. The aim throughout is to tackle a particular problem immediately and to give a recommendation as soon as the problem has been identified. Explanations entailing wider grammatical principles are postponed or even omitted.

adverbial relative clauses

A relative clause, expressing time, manner, or place, can follow a noun governed by a preposition (*on the day* in the example below):

On the day that you eat from it, *you will certainly die* (NEB)

It is possible for the relative clause to begin with the same preposition and *which*, e.g.

On the day on which this occurred, *I was away*

But it is a perfectly acceptable idiom to use a relative clause introduced by *that* without repetition of the preposition, especially after the nouns *day*, *morning*, *night*, *time*, *year*, etc., *manner*, *sense*, *way* (see p. 147), *place*, e.g.

Envy in the consuming sense that certain persons display *the trait* (Anthony Powell)

It is, if anything, even more usual for *that* to be omitted:

He cannot have been more than thirty at the time we met him (Evelyn Waugh)
If he would take it in the sense she meant it (L. P. Hartley)
On the day you pass over the Jordan (NEB)

adverbs without *-ly*

Most adverbs consist of an adjective + the ending *-ly*, e.g. *badly*, *differently*. For the changes in spelling that the addition of *-ly* may require, see pp. 37 f.

Normally the use of the ordinary adjective as an adverb, without *-ly*, is non-standard, e.g.

I was sent for special
The Americans speak different *from us*
They just put down their tools sudden *and cut and run*

There are, however, a number of words which are both adjective and adverb and cannot add the adverbial ending *-ly*:

early	*fast*	*much*
enough	*little*	*straight*
far	*low*	

Some other adjectives can be used as adverbs both with and without *-ly*. The two forms have different meanings:

deep	*high*	*near*
hard	*late*	

The forms without *-ly* are the adverbs more closely similar in meaning to the adjectives, as the following examples illustrate:

deep: *Still waters run deep*
He read deep into the night

hard: *They hit me hard in the chest*
He lost his hard-earned money
We will be hard put to it to be ready by Christmas

high: *It soared high above us*
Don't fix your hopes too high

late: *I will stay up late to finish it*
A drawing dated as late as 1960

near: *He won't come near me*
As near as makes no difference
Near-famine conditions

The forms with *-ly* have meanings more remote from those of the adjectives:

deeply is chiefly figurative, e.g. *Deeply in love*
hardly = 'scarcely', e.g. *He hardly earned his money*
highly is chiefly figurative, e.g. *Don't value possessions too highly*
lately = 'recently', e.g. *I have been very tired lately*
nearly = 'almost', e.g. *The conditions were nearly those of a famine*

• The forms with and without *-ly* are not interchangeable and should not be confused.

See also ***-lily* adverbs**.

article, omission of

To omit, or not to omit, *a* (*an*) and *the*?

Omission of the definite or indefinite article before a noun or noun phrase in apposition to a name is a journalistic device, e.g.

Clarissa, American business woman, comes to England (*Radio Times*)
Nansen, hero and humanitarian, moves among them (*The Times*)

It is more natural to write *an American business woman, the hero and humanitarian*.

Similarly, when the name is in apposition to the noun or noun phrase, and the article is omitted, the effect is of journalistic style, e.g.

NUM President Arthur Scargill
Best-selling novelist Barbara Cartland
Unemployed labourer William Smith

Preferably write: *The NUM President*, *The best-selling novelist*, *An unemployed labourer* (with a comma before and after the name which follows).

After *as* it is possible to omit *a* or *the*, e.g.

As manipulator of words, the author reminded me of X.Y.
The Soviet system could no longer be regarded as sole model for Communism everywhere

It is preferable not to omit these words, however, except where the noun or noun phrase following is treated as a kind of generic mass noun, e.g.

> *The vivid relation between himself, as man, and the sunflower, as sunflower* (D. H. Lawrence)

as, case following

In the following sentences, formal usage requires the *subjective* case (*I*, *he*, *she*, *we*, *they*) because the pronoun would be the subject if a verb were supplied:

> *You are just as intelligent as* he (in full, *as he is*)
> *Widmerpool . . might not have heard the motif so often as* I (Anthony Powell) (in full, *as I had*)

Informal usage permits *You are just as intelligent as* him.

Formal English uses the *objective* case (*me*, *him*, *her*, *us*, *them*) only when the pronoun would be the object if a verb were supplied:

> *I thought you preferred John to Mary, but I see that you like her just as much as* him (which means . . *just as much as you like him*)

In real usage, sentences like this are rare and not very natural. It is more usual for the verb to be included in the sentence or for the thought to be expressed in a different construction.

as if, as though

For the tense following these see p. 57.

auxiliary verbs

There are sixteen auxiliary verbs in English, three primary auxiliaries (used in the compounding of ordinary verbs) and thirteen modal auxiliaries (used to express mood, and, to some extent, tense).

Primary: *be*, *do*, *have*

Modal:	*can*	*ought* (*to*)
	could	*shall*
	dare	*should*
	may	*used* (*to*)
	might	*will*
	must	*would*
	need	

Auxiliaries differ from regular verbs in the following ways:

(1) They can precede the negative *not*, instead of taking the *do not* construction, e.g. *I cannot* but *I do not know*;
(2) They can precede the subject in questions, instead of taking the *do* construction, e.g. *Can you hear* but *Do you know*.

The modal auxiliaries additionally differ from regular verbs in the following ways:

(3) They are invariable: they do not add *-s* for the third person present, and do not form a separate past tense in *-ed*; e.g. *He must go*; *he must have seen it*.
(4) They are usually followed by the bare infinitive; e.g. *He will go, he can go* (not 'to go' as with other verbs, e.g. *He intends to go, he is able to go*).

Use of auxiliaries
In reported speech and some other *that*-clauses *can*, *may*, *shall*, and *will* become *could*, *might*, *should*, and *would* for the past tense:

He said that he could *do it straight away*
I told you that I might *arrive unexpectedly*
I knew that when I grew up I should *be a writer* (George Orwell)
Did you think that the money you brought would *be enough?*

In clauses of this kind, the auxiliaries *must*, *need*, and *ought*, which normally refer to the present tense, can also be used for the past tense:

I had meant to return direct to Paris, but this business . . meant that I must *go to London* (Evelyn Waugh)
To go to church had made her feel she need *not reproach herself for impropriety* (V. S. Pritchett)
She was quite aware that she ought *not to quarter Freddy there* (G. B. Shaw)

Note that this use is restricted to *that*-clauses. It would not be permissible to use *must*, *need*, or *ought* for the past tense in a main sentence; for example, one could not say: *Yesterday I must go*.

Further discussion of the use of auxiliary verbs will be found under ***can* and *may*, *dare*, *have*, *need*, *ought*, *shall* and *will*, *should* and *would*, *used to*, *were* or *was*.**

***but*, case following**

The personal pronoun following *but* (= 'except') should be in the case it would have if a verb were supplied.

I walked through the mud of the main street. Who but I? (Kipling)
Our uneducated brethren who have, under God, no defence but us (C. S. Lewis)

In the Kipling example *I* is used because it would be the subject of *I walked.* In the Lewis example *us* is used because it would be the object of *who have* (i.e. 'who have *us* as their only defence').

can and may

The auxiliary verbs *can* and *may* are both used to express permission, but *may* is more formal and polite:

I'm going to come and see you some time—may I? (Evelyn Waugh)

collective nouns

Collective nouns are singular words that denote many individuals, e.g.

army
audience
board (of directors, examiners, etc.)
choir
clan
class
club
committee
company
congregation
crowd
family
fleet
flock
gang
government
group
herd
jury
majority
militia
navy
orchestra
parliament
party (i.e. body of persons)
squad
swarm
team
tribe
union (i.e. trade union)

the aristocracy
the bourgeoisie
the Cabinet
the clergy
the élite
the gentry
the intelligentsia
the laity
the nobility
the proletariat
the public
the upper class
the working class

It is normal for collective nouns, being singular, to be followed by singular verbs and pronouns (*is*, *has*, *consists*, and *it* in the examples below):

The Government is *determined to beat inflation, as* it has *promised*
Their family is *huge:* it consists *of five boys and three girls*
The bourgeoisie is *despised for not being proletarian* (C. S. Lewis)

The singular verb and pronouns are preferable unless the collective is clearly and unmistakably used to refer to separate individuals rather than to a united body, e.g.

The Cabinet has made its *decision*, but
The Cabinet are *resuming* their *places around the table at Number 10 Downing Street*
The Brigade of Guards is *on parade*, but
The Brigade of Guards are *above average height*

The singular should always be used if the collective noun is qualified by a singular word like *this*, *that*, *every*, etc.:

This family is *divided*
Every team has its *chance to win*

If a relative clause follows, it must be *which* + singular verb or *who* + plural verb, e.g.

It was not the intelligentsia, but just intellectual society, which was *gathered there* (John Galsworthy)
The working party who *had been preparing the decorations* (Evelyn Waugh)

• Do not mix singular and plural, as (wrongly) in

The congregation were *now dispersing*. It *tended to form knots and groups*

comparison of adjectives and adverbs

Whether to use *-er*, *-est* or *more*, *most*.

The two ways of forming the comparative and superlative of adjectives and adverbs are:

(*a*) The addition of the comparative and superlative suffixes *-er* and *-est* (for spelling changes that may be required see pp. 25, 26, 51). Monosyllabic adjectives and adverbs almost always require these suffixes, e.g. *big* (*bigger, biggest*), *soon* (*sooner*, *soonest*), and so normally do many adjectives of two syllables, e.g. *narrow* (*narrower*, *narrowest*), *silly* (*sillier*, *silliest*).

(*b*) The placing of the comparative and superlative adverbs *more* and *most* before the adjective or adverb. These are used with adjectives of three syllables or more (e.g. *difficult*, *memorable*), participles (e.g. *bored*, *boring*), many adjectives of two syllables (e.g. *afraid*, *awful*, *childish*, *harmless*, *static*), and adverbs ending in *-ly* (e.g. *highly*, *slowly*).

Adjectives with two syllables vary between the use of the suffixes and of the adverbs.

There are many which never take the suffixes, e.g.

antique	*breathless*	*futile*
bizarre	*constant*	*steadfast*

There is also a large class which is acceptable with either, e.g.

clever	*handsome*	*polite*
common	*honest*	*solemn*
cruel	*pleasant*	*tranquil*
extreme		

The choice is largely a matter of style. Some examples will show how much variation there is in literary English.

With the suffixes:

An attitude of completest *indifference* (George Orwell)
The extremest *forms of anti-Semitism* (Lewis Namier)
You are so much honester *than I am* (Iris Murdoch)
Now the stupidest *of us knows* (C. S. Lewis)

With the adverbs:

I was a bit more clever *than the other lads* (Angus Wilson)
The most solemn *of Jane Austen's beaux* (Iris Murdoch)
Those periods which we think most tranquil (C. S. Lewis)

With a mixture in one sentence:

Only the dirtiest *and* most tipsy *of cooks* (Evelyn Waugh)

Even monosyllabic adjectives can sometimes take *more* and *most*:

(i) When two adjectives are compared with each other, e.g.

More dead than alive
More good than bad
More well-known than popular

This is standard (we would not say 'better than bad' or 'better-known than popular').

(ii) Occasionally, for stylistic reasons, e.g.

I am the more bad because I realize where my badness lies (L. P. Hartley)
This was never more true than at present

(iii) Thoughtlessly, e.g.

Facts that should be more well known
The most well-dressed man in town
Wimbledon will be yet more hot tomorrow

• These are not acceptable: substitute *better known*, *best-dressed*, and *hotter*.

comparisons

Comparisons between two persons or things require the comparative (*-er* or *more*) in constructions like the following:

I cannot tell which of the two is the elder (not *eldest*)
Of the two teams, they are the slower-moving (not *slowest-moving*)

The superlative is of course used when more than two are compared.

compound subject

A subject consisting of two singular nouns or noun phrases joined by *and* normally takes a plural verb:

My son and daughter are *twins*
Where to go and what to see were *my main concern*

If one half of the subject is the pronoun *I* or the pronoun *you*, and the other is a noun or third person singular pronoun (*he*, *she*, or *it*), or if the subject is *you and I*, the verb must be plural.

He and I are *good friends*
Do *my sister and I look alike?*
You and your mother have *similar talents*
You and I are *hardly acquainted*

But if the phrase containing *and* represents a single item, it is followed by a singular verb:

The bread and butter was *scattered on the floor* (W. Somerset Maugham)

And similarly if the two parts of the subject refer to a single individual:

His friend and legal adviser, John Smith, was *present*
My son and heir is *safe!*

See also ***neither . . nor*** and **subjects joined by (*either . .*) *or*.**

co-ordination

The linking of two main clauses by a comma alone, without any connecting conjunction, is sometimes said to be incorrect. It is on occasion used by good writers, however, as the examples show. It should be regarded as acceptable if used sparingly.

The peasants possess no harrows, they merely plough the soil several times over (George Orwell)

Charles carried a mackintosh over his arm, he was stooping a little (C. P. Snow)

I began to wonder when the Presidential Candidate would appear, he must have had a heavy handicap (Graham Greene)

correlative conjunctions

The correct placing of the pairs

both . . and	*neither . . nor*
either . . or	*not only . . but* (*also*)

A sentence containing any of these pairs must be so constructed that the part of the sentence introduced by the first member of the pair (*both*, *either*, *neither*, or *not only*) is parallel in structure to the part introduced by the second member (*and*, *or*, *neither*, or *but* (*also*)).

The rule is that if one covers up the two correlative words and all the words between them, the remaining sentence should still be grammatical.

The following sentence from a typical newspaper advertisement illustrates this rule:

Candidates will have a background in either commercial electronics or *university research*

Because *in* precedes *either*, it need not be repeated after *or*. If it had followed *either*, it would have had to be inserted after *or* as well. But the sentence as given is the most economical structure possible.

In the following example the preposition *of* comes after *either* and must therefore be repeated after *or*:

He did not wish to pay the price either *of peace* or *of war* (George Orwell)

This conforms with the rule stated above, while perhaps sounding better than *of either peace or war* (which would be as good grammatically).

It is, however, not uncommon for the conjunctions to be placed so that the two halves are not quite parallel, even in the writings of careful authors, e.g.

I end neither *with a death* nor *a marriage* (W. Somerset Maugham)
People who either *hadn't been asked to pay* or *who were simply not troubling themselves* (V. S. Pritchett)

In the first example, *with* belongs to both halves and needs to be repeated after *nor*. In the second, *who* precedes *either* and strictly need not be repeated after *or*.

These sentences exhibit fairly trivial slips that rarely cause difficulty (except in the case of *not only*: see p. 84).

• A more serious error is the placing of the first correlative conjunction too late, so that words belonging only to the first half are carried over to the second, resulting in a grammatical muddle, e.g.

The other Exocet was either destroyed or blew up (BBC News)

This should be carefully avoided.

dare

The verb *to dare* can be used either like a regular verb or like an auxiliary verb. Either use is entirely acceptable (though in a particular context, one may sound better than the other).

As an ordinary verb it forms such parts as:

I dare	*I do not dare*	*do I dare?*
he dares	*he does not dare*	*does he dare?*
he dared	*he did not dare*	*did he dare?*
I would dare	*I have dared*	

As an auxiliary verb it forms:

I dare not	*he dared not*
he dare not	*dared he?*
dare he?	

The first use, as an ordinary verb, is always acceptably followed by the *to*-infinitive, e.g.

I knew what I would find if I dared to look (Jean Rhys)
James did not dare to carry out the sentence (Frederic Raphael)

But many of the forms can also be followed by the bare infinitive. This sometimes sounds more natural:

None of which they'd dare go near (John Osborne)
Don't you dare put that light on (Shelagh Delaney)

The second use, as an auxiliary verb, normally requires the bare infinitive, e.g.

How dare he keep secrets from me? (G. B. Shaw)
He dared not risk being carried past his destination (C. S. Forester)

double passive

The construction whereby a passive infinitive directly follows a passive verb is correctly used in the following:

The prisoners were ordered to be shot
This music is intended to be played on a piano

The rule is that if the subject and the first passive verb can be changed into the active, leaving the passive infinitive intact, the sentence is correctly formed. The examples above (if a subject, say *he*, is supplied) can be changed back to:

He ordered the prisoners *to be shot*
He intends this music *to be played on a piano*

In other words, the passive infinitive is not part of the passive construction. An active infinitive could equally well be part of the sentence, e.g.

The prisoners were ordered to march

The examples below violate the rule because both the passive verb and the passive infinitive have to be made active in order to form a grammatical sentence:

The order was attempted to be carried out
(active: *He attempted to carry out the order*)
A new definition was sought to be inserted in the Bill
(active: *He sought to insert a new definition in the Bill*)

This 'double passive' construction is unacceptable.

The passive of the verbs *to fear* and *to say* can be followed by either an active or a passive infinitive, e.g.

(i) *The passengers are feared* to have drowned
The escaped prisoner is said to be very dangerous

or

(ii) *The passengers are feared* to have been killed
The escaped prisoner is said to have been sighted

The construction at (ii) is not the double passive and is entirely acceptable. Both constructions are sometimes found with other verbs of saying (e.g. *to allege, to assert, to imply*):

Morris demonstrated that Mr Elton was obviously implied to be impotent (David Lodge)

either . . or: see **subjects joined by (*either . .*) *or*.**

***either* (pronoun)**

Either is a singular pronoun and should be followed by a singular verb:

Enormous evils, either of which depends on *somebody else's voice* (Louis MacNeice)

In the following example the plural verb accords with the notional meaning 'both parents were not'.

It was improbable that either of our parents were *giving thought to the matter* (J. I. M. Stewart)

This is quite common in informal usage, but should not be carried over into formal prose.

gender of indefinite expressions

It is often uncertain what personal pronoun should be used to refer back to the indefinite pronouns and adjectives in the following list:

any	*no* (+ noun)
anybody	*nobody*
anyone	*none*
each	*no one*
every (+ noun)	*some* (+ noun)
everybody	*somebody*
everyone	*someone*

and also to refer back to (*a*) *person*, used indefinitely, or a male and female noun linked by (*either . .*) *or* or *neither . . nor*, e.g.

Has anybody eaten his/their *lunch yet?*
A person who is upset may vent his/their *feelings on* his/their *family*
Neither John nor Mary has a home of their/his or her *own*

If it is known that the individuals referred to are all of the same sex, there is no difficulty; use *he* or *she* as appropriate:

Everyone in the women's movement has had her *own experience of sexual discrimination*

If, however, the sex of those referred to is unknown or deliberately left indefinite, or if the reference is to a mixed group, the difficulty arises that English has no singular pronoun to denote common gender.

The grammarians' recommendation, during the past two centuries, has been that *he* (*him*, *himself*, *his*) should be used. Many good writers follow this:

Everyone talked at the top of his *voice* (W. Somerset Maugham)
Everyone took his *place in a half-circle about the fire* (Malcolm Bradbury)
(The context of each shows that the company was mixed.)

The long street in which nobody knows his *neighbour* (G. B. Shaw)
Each person should give as he *has decided for* himself (NEB)

Popular usage, however, has for at least five centuries favoured the plural pronoun *they* (*them*, *themselves*, *their*).

This is entirely acceptable in informal speech:

Nobody would ever marry if they *thought it over* (G. B. Shaw)
It's the sort of thing any of us would dislike, wouldn't they*?* (C. P. Snow)

It is by no means uncommon in more formal contexts:

Nobody stopped to stare, everyone had themselves *to think about* (Susan Hill)
His own family were occupied, each with their *particular guests* (Evelyn Waugh)
Delavacquerie allowed everyone to examine the proofs as long as they *wished* (Anthony Powell)

(The context of the second and third example shows that the company was mixed.)

Many people regard it as inequitable that the masculine pronoun *he* should be used to include both sexes, and therefore prefer to use *they*.

One can avoid the difficulty from time to time by writing *he or she*, as many writers do on awkward occasions:

Nobody has room in his or her *life for more than one such relationship at a time* (G. B. Shaw)

But this grows unwieldy with repetition:

If I ever wished to disconcert anyone, all I had to do was to ask him (or her) *how many friends* he/she *had* (Frederic Raphael)

There are some contexts in which neither *he* nor *they* will seem objectionable. In others, where *he* and *they* both seem inappropriate for the reasons given, it may be necessary simply to recast the sentence.

group possessive

The group possessive is the construction by which the ending *-'s* of the possessive case can be added to the last word of a noun phrase, which is regarded as a single unit, e.g.

The king of Spain's daughter
John and Mary's baby
Somebody else's umbrella
A quarter of an hour's drive

Expressions like these are natural and acceptable.

Informal language, however, permits the extension of the construction to long and complicated phrases:

The people in the house opposite's geraniums
The woman I told you about on the phone yesterday's name is Thompson
The man who called last week's umbrella is still in the hall

In these, the connection between the words forming the group possessive is much looser and more complicated than in the earlier examples. The effect is often somewhat ludicrous.

• Expressions of this sort should not be used in serious prose. Substitute:

The geraniums of the people in the house opposite
The name of the woman I told you about on the phone yesterday is Thompson
The umbrella of the man who called last week is still in the hall

have

1. The verb *to have*, in some of its uses, can form its interrogative and negative either with or without the verb *to do*, e.g. *Do you have/have you?*, *You don't have/you haven't.*

In sentences like those below, *have* is a verb of event, meaning 'experience'. The interrogative (in the first example) and the negative (in the second example) are always formed in the regular way, using the verb *do*:

Do you *ever* have *nightmares?*
We did not have *an easy time getting here*

In the next pair of sentences, *have* is a verb of state, meaning 'possess'. When used in this sense, the interrogative (in the first example) and negative (in the second example) can be formed in the manner of an auxiliary verb, without the verb *do*:

What have you *in common with the child of five whose photograph your mother keeps?* (George Orwell)
The truth was that he hadn't *the answer* (Joyce Cary)

In more informal language, the verb *got* is added, e.g. *What have you got*, *He hadn't got the answer*. This is not usually suitable for formal usage.

It was formerly usual to distinguish the sense 'experience' from the sense 'possess' by using the *do*-formation for the first and the auxiliary formation for the second (but only in the present tense). Hence *I don't have indigestion* (as a rule) was kept distinct from *I haven't* (*got*) *indigestion* (at the moment). The use of the *do*-construction when the meaning was 'possess' was an Americanism, but it is now generally acceptable.

• However, the use of *do* as a substitute verb for *have*, common informally, is not acceptable in formal prose:

I had stronger feelings than she did (substitute *than she had*)
Some have money, *some* don't (substitute *some haven't*)

2. *Have* is often wrongly inserted after *I'd* in sentences like:

If I'd have *known she'd be here I don't suppose I'd have come* (Character in play by John Osborne)

This is common, and hardly noticed, in speech, but should not occur in formal writing. The correct construction is:

If I'd known *she'd be here* . .

Without the contraction, the clause would read: *If I had known*, with the past perfect, which is the correct form in this kind of *if*-clause. The only expression that the mistaken *If I'd have known* could stand for is *If I would have known*, which is impossible in this context.

he who, she who

He who and *she who* are correctly used when *he* and *she* are the subject of the main clause, and *who* is the subject of the relative clause:

He who *hesitates is lost*
She who *was a star in the old play may find herself a super in the new* (C. S. Lewis)

In these examples *he* and *she* are the subjects of *is lost* and *may find* respectively; *who* is the subject of *hesitates* and *was*.

He who and *she who* should not be treated as invariable. They should change to *him who* and *her who* if the personal pronouns are not the subject of the main clause:

The distinction between the man who gives with conviction and him (not *he*) *who is simply buying a title*

Similarly *who* must become *whom* if it is not the subject of the relative clause:

I sought him whom *my soul loveth* (Authorized Version)

See also ***who* and *whom* (interrogative and relative pronouns)**.

-*ics*, nouns in

Nouns ending in -*ics* denoting subjects or disciplines are sometimes treated as singular and sometimes as plural. Examples are:

apologetics	*genetics*	*optics*
classics (as a study)	*linguistics*	*phonetics*
dynamics	*mathematics*	*physics*
economics	*mechanics*	*politics*
electronics	*metaphysics*	*statistics*
ethics	*obstetrics*	*tactics*

When used strictly as the name of a discipline they are treated as singular:

Psychometrics is *unable to investigate the nature of intelligence* (*Guardian*)
The quest for a *hermeneutics* (TLS)

So also when the complement is singular:

Mathematics is *his strong point*

When used more loosely, to denote a manifestation of qualities, often accompanied by a possessive, they are treated as plural:

His politics were *a mixture of fear, greed and envy* (Joyce Cary)
I don't understand the mathematics of it, which are *complicated*
The acoustics in this hall are *dreadful*
Their tactics were *cowardly*

So also when they denote a set of activities or pattern of behaviour, as commonly with words like

acrobatics	*dramatics*	*heroics*
athletics	*gymnastics*	*hysterics*
callisthenics		

E.g. *The mental gymnastics required to believe this* are *beyond me*

These words usually retain a plural verb even with a singular complement:

The acrobatics are *just the social side* (Tom Stoppard)

infinitive, present or perfect

The perfect infinitive is correctly used when it refers to a state or action earlier in time than that referred to by the verb on which it depends, e.g.

If it were real life and not a play, that is the part it would be best to have acted (C. S. Lewis)
Someone seems to have been making *a beast of himself here* (Evelyn Waugh)

In the above examples, the infinitives *to have acted* and *to have been making* relate to actions earlier in time than the verbs *would be best* and *seems*.

Only if the first verb relates to the past and the infinitive relates to a state or action prior to that should a perfect infinitive follow a past or perfect verb, forming a sort of 'double past', e.g.

When discussing sales with him yesterday, I should have liked to have seen *the figures beforehand*

In this example *I should have liked* denotes the speaker's feelings during the discussion and *to have seen* denotes an action imagined as occurring before the discussion.

If the state or action denoted by the infinitive is thought of as occurring at the same time as the verb on which it depends, then the present infinitive should be used:

She would have liked to see *what was on the television* (Kingsley Amis)

The 'double past' is often accidentally used in this kind of sentence informally, e.g.

I should have liked to have gone to the party

A literary example is:

Mr. McGregor threw down the sack on the stone floor in a way that would have been extremely painful to the Flopsy Bunnies, if they had happened to have been *inside it* (Beatrix Potter)

This should be avoided.

-*ing* (gerund and participle)

1. The *-ing* form of a verb can in some contexts be used in either of two constructions:

(i) as a gerund (verbal noun) with a noun or pronoun in the possessive standing before it, e.g.

In the event of Randall's not going (Iris Murdoch)
She did not like his being *High Church* (L. P. Hartley)

(ii) as a participle with a noun in its ordinary form or a pronoun in the objective case standing before it, e.g.

What further need would there have been to speak of another priest arising*?* (NEB)
Dixon did not like him doing *that* (Kingsley Amis)

The option of using either arises only when the word before the *-ing* form is a proper or personal noun (e.g. *John*, *father*, *teacher*) or a personal pronoun.

It is sometimes said that the construction with the possessive (as in (i) above) is obligatory. This rule, in its strict form, should be disregarded. Instead one should, in formal usage, try to employ the possessive construction wherever it is possible and natural:

To whom, without its being *ordered, the waiter immediately brought a plate of eggs and bacon* (Evelyn Waugh)

The danger of Joyce's turning *them into epigrams* (Anthony Burgess)

But it is certainly not wrong to use the non-possessive construction if it sounds more natural, as in the New English Bible quotation above. Moreover, there is sometimes a nuance of meaning. *She did not like his being High Church* suggests that she did not like the fact that he was High Church, and need not imply personal antipathy, whereas *Dixon did not like him doing that* suggests an element of repugnance to the person as well as to his action.

When using most non-personal nouns (e.g. *luggage*, *meaning*, *permission*), groups of nouns (e.g. *father and mother*, *surface area*), non-personal pronouns (e.g. *anything*, *something*), and groups of pronouns (e.g. *some of them*), there is no choice of construction: the possessive would not sound idiomatic at all. Examples are:

Travellers in Italy could depend on their luggage *not* being *stolen* (G. B. Shaw)

Altogether removing possibility of its meaning being *driven home* (Anthony Powell)

His lines were cited . . without his permission having *been asked* (*The Times*)

Due to her father and mother being *married* (Compton Mackenzie)

Owing to its surface area being *so large relative to its weight* (George Orwell)

The air of something *unusual* having *happened* (Arthur Conan Doyle)

He had no objection to some of them listening (Arnold Bennett)

When the word preceding the *-ing* form is a regular plural noun ending in *-s*, there is no spoken distinction between the possessive and the non-possessive form. It is unnecessary to write an apostrophe:

If she knew about her daughters *attending the party* (Anthony Powell)

2. There is also variation between the gerundial and the participial uses of the *-ing* form after nouns like *difficulty*, *point*, *trouble*, and *use*.

Formal English requires the gerundial use, the gerund being introduced by *in* (or *of* after *use*):

There was . . no difficulty in finding *parking space* (David Lodge)
There doesn't seem much point in trying *to explain everything* (John Osborne)

Informal usage permits the placing of the *-ing* form immediately after the noun, forming a participial construction, e.g.

He had some trouble convincing *Theo Craven* (Lynne Reid Banks)
The chairman had difficulty concealing *his irritation*

• This is not acceptable in formal usage.

***I* or *me, we* or *us,* etc.**

There is often confusion about which case of a personal pronoun to use when the pronoun stands alone or follows the verb *to be*.

1. When the personal pronoun stands alone, as when it forms the answer to a question, formal usage requires it to have the case it would have if the verb were supplied:

Who killed Cock Robin?—I (in full, *I killed him*)
Which of you did he approach?—Me (in full, *he approached me*)

Informal usage permits the objective case in both kinds of sentence, but this is not acceptable in formal style. It so happens that the subjective case often sounds stilted. It is then best to avoid the problem by providing the substitute verb *do*, or, if the preceding sentence contains an auxiliary, by repeating the auxiliary, e.g.

Who likes cooking?—I do
Who can cook?—I can

2. When a personal pronoun follows *it is*, *it was*, *it may be*, *it could have been*, etc., it should always have the subjective case:

Nobody could suspect that it was *she* (Agatha Christie)
We are given no clue as to what it must have felt like to be he (C. S. Lewis)

Informal usage favours the objective case:

I thought it might have been him *at the door*
Don't tell me it's them *again!*

• This is not acceptable in formal usage.

When *who* or *whom* follows, the subjective case is obligatory in formal usage and quite usual informally:

It was I *who painted the back door purple*
It's they *whom I shall be staying with in London*

The informal use of the objective case often sounds substandard:

It was her *who would get the blood off* (Character in work by Patrick White)

(For agreement between the personal pronoun antecedent and the verb in *It is I who* etc., see ***I who, you who,* etc.**)

In constructions which have the form *I am* + noun or noun phrase + *who*, the verb following *who* agrees with the noun (the antecedent of *who*) and is therefore always in the third person (singular or plural):

I am the sort of person who likes *peace and quiet*
You are the fourth of my colleagues who's *told me that* (Character in work by Angus Wilson) (*'s* = *has*, agreeing with *the fourth*)

The following is not standard, but must be explained by the uniqueness of the person denoted by the subject:

How then canst thou be a god that hidest thyself*?* (NEB)

I should or *I would*

There is often uncertainty whether to use *should* or *would* in the first person singular and plural before verbs such as *like* or *think* and before the adverbs *rather* and *sooner*.

1. *Should* is correct before verbs of liking, e.g. *be glad, be inclined, care, like*, and *prefer*:

Would you like a beer?—I should prefer *a cup of coffee, if you don't mind*
The very occasions on which we should *most like to write a slashing review* (C. S. Lewis)

2. *Should* is correct in tentative statements of opinion, with verbs such as *guess, imagine, say*, and *think*:

I should imagine *that you are right*
I should say *so*
I should*n't have* thought *it was difficult*

3. *Would* is correct before the adverbs *rather* and *sooner*, e.g.

I would *truly* rather *be in the middle of this than sitting in that church in a tight collar* (Susan Hill)

Would is always correct with persons other than the first person singular and plural.

See also ***should* and *would***.

I who, you who, etc.

The verb following a personal pronoun (*I*, *you*, *he*, etc.) + *who* should agree with the pronoun and should not be in the third person singular unless the third person singular pronoun precedes *who*:

I, who have *no savings to speak of, had to pay for the work*

This remains so even if the personal pronoun is in the objective case:

They made me, who have *no savings at all, pay for the work* (not *who has*)

When *it is* (*it was*, etc.) precedes *I who*, etc., the same rule applies: the verb agrees with the personal pronoun:

It's I who have *done it*
It could have been we who were *mistaken*

Informal usage sometimes permits the third person to be used (especially when the verb *to be* follows *who*):

You who's *supposed to be so practical!*
Is it me who's *supposed to be keeping an eye on you?* (Character in work by David Lodge)

• This is not acceptable in formal usage.

like

The objective case of personal pronouns is always used after the adjectives *like* and *unlike*:

Unlike my mother and me, *my sister is fair-haired* (not *Unlike my mother and I*)

-lily adverbs

When the adverbial suffix *-ly* is added to an adjective which already ends in *-ly*, the resulting adverb tends to have an unpleasant jingling sound, e.g. *friendlily*.

Adverbs of this kind are divided into three groups, here arranged in order of decreasing acceptability:

(i) Those formed from adjectives in which the final *-ly* is an integral part of the word, not a suffix, e.g. *holily*, *jollily*, *sillily*. These are the least objectionable and are quite often used.

(ii) Those of three syllables formed from adjectives in which the final *-ly* is itself a suffix, e.g. *friendlily*, *ghastlily*, *statelily*, *uglily*. These are occasionally found.

(iii) Those of four (or more) syllables formed from adjectives in which the final *-ly* is itself a suffix, e.g. *heavenlily*, *scholarlily*. Such words have been recorded but are deservedly rare.

The adverbs of groups (ii) and (iii) should be avoided if possible, by using the adjective with a noun like *manner* or *way*, e.g. *In a scholarly manner*.

A few adjectives in *-ly* can be used adverbially to qualify other adjectives, e.g. *beastly cold*, *ghastly pale*. Occasionally, to avoid the use of an adverb in *-lily*, the plain adjective has been used to qualify a verb, e.g.

> *Then I strolled* leisurely *along those dear, dingy streets* (W. Somerset Maugham)

This does not usually sound natural. It is recommended that *in a leisurely* (etc.) *way* should be used instead.

may* or *might

There is sometimes confusion about whether to use *may* or *might* with the perfect infinitive referring to a past event, e.g. *He may have done* or *He might have done*.

1. If uncertainty about the action or state denoted by the perfect infinitive remains, i.e. at the time of speaking or writing the truth of the event is still unknown, then either *may* or *might* is acceptable:

> *As they all wore so many different clothes of identically the same kind . . , there* may *have been several more or several less* (Evelyn Waugh)
>
> *For all we knew we were both bastards, although of course there* might *have been a ceremony* (Graham Greene)

2. If there is no longer uncertainty about the event, or the matter

was never put to the test, and therefore the event did not in fact occur, use *might*:

If that had come ten days ago my whole life might *have been different* (Evelyn Waugh)
You should not have let him come home alone; he might *have got lost*

• It is a common error to use *may* instead of *might* in these circumstances:

If he (President Galtieri) *had not invaded, then eventually the islands* may *have fallen into their lap*
I am grateful for his intervention without which they may *have remained in the refugee camp indefinitely*
Schoenberg may *never have gone atonal but for the break-up of his marriage*

(These are all from recent newspaper articles. *Might* should be substituted for *may* in each.)

measurement, nouns of

There is some uncertainty about when to use the singular form, and when the plural, of nouns of measurement.

1. All nouns of measurement remain in the singular form when compounded with a numeral and used attributively before another noun:

A six-foot *wall* *A five*-pound *note*
A three-mile *walk* *A 1,000*-megaton *bomb*

This rule includes metric measurements:

A ten-hectare *field* *A three*-litre *bottle*

2. *Foot* remains in the singular form in expressions such as:

I am six foot *She is five foot two*

But *feet* is used where an adjective, or the word *inches*, follows, e.g.

I am six feet tall *She is five feet three inches*
It is ten feet long

Stone and *hundredweight* remain in the singular form in plural expressions, e.g.

I weigh eleven stone *Three hundredweight of coal*

Metric measurements always take the plural form when not used attributively:

This measures three metres by two metres
Two kilos of sugar

Informally, some other nouns of measurement are used in the singular form in plural expressions, e.g.

That will be two pound fifty, please

• This is non-standard.

See also **quantity, nouns of**.

need

The verb *to need*, when followed by an infinitive, can be used either like an ordinary verb or like an auxiliary.

1. *Need* is used like an ordinary verb, and followed by thc *to*-infinitive, in the present tense when the sentence is neither negative nor interrogative, in the past tense always, and in all compound tenses (e.g. the future and perfect):

One needs friends, one needs to *be a friend* (Susan Hill)
One did not need to *be a clairvoyant to see that war . . was coming* (George Orwell)

2. *Need* can be used like an auxiliary verb in the present tense in negative and interrogative sentences. This means that:

(*a*) The third person singular need not add *-s*:

I do not think one need *look farther than this* (George Orwell)

(*b*) For the negative, *need not* can replace *does not need*:

One need not *be an advocate of censorship to recommend the cautious use of poison* (Frederic Raphael)

(*c*) For the interrogative, *need I* (*you*, etc.) can replace *do I need*:

Need I *add that she is my bitterest enemy?* (G. B. Shaw)

(*d*) The bare infinitive can follow instead of the *to*-infinitive:

Company that keeps them smaller than they need be (*Bookseller*) (This is negative in sense, for it implies *They need not be as small as this*)

This auxiliary verb use is optional, not obligatory. The regular constructions are equally correct:

I do not think one needs to look . .
One does not need to be . .
Do I need to add . .
Smaller than they need to be . .

One should choose whichever sounds more natural. It is important, however, to avoid mixing the two kinds of construction, as in the two following examples:

One needs not be *told that* (etc.)
What proved vexing, it needs be *said, was* (etc.)

neither . . nor

Two singular subjects linked by *neither . . nor* can be constructed with either a singular or a plural verb. Strictly and logically a singular verb is required (since both subjects are not thought of as governing the verb at the same time). When the two subjects are straightforward third person pronouns or nouns, it is best to follow this rule:

Neither he nor his wife has *arrived*
There is *neither a book nor a picture in the house*

Informal usage permits the plural and it has been common in the writings of good authors for a long time:

Neither painting nor fighting feed *men* (Ruskin)

When one of the two subjects is plural and the other singular, the verb should be made plural and the plural subject placed nearer to it:

Neither the teacher nor the pupils understand *the problem*

When one of the subjects is *I* or *you* and the other is a third person pronoun or a noun, or when one is *I* and the other *you*, the verb can be made to agree with the subject that is nearer to it. However, this does not always sound natural, e.g.

Neither my son nor I am *good at figures*

One can recast the sentence, but this can spoil the effect intended by using *neither . . nor*. It is often better to use the plural, as good writers do:

Neither Isabel nor I are *timid people* (H. G. Wells)

Neither Emily nor I were *quite prepared for the title* (Anthony Powell)

This is not illogical if *neither . . nor* is regarded as the negative of *both . . and.*

***neither* (pronoun)**

Neither is a singular pronoun and strictly requires a singular verb:

Neither of us likes *to be told what to do*

Informal usage permits not only a plural verb, but also a plural complement:

Neither of us like *tennis*
Neither of us are good players

Although this is widely regarded as incorrect, it has been an established construction for three or four centuries:

Thersites' body is as good as Ajax', When neither are *alive* (Shakespeare)
Neither were great inventors (Dryden)

It is recommended that one should follow the rule requiring the singular unless it leads to awkwardness, as when neither *he* nor *she* is appropriate:

John and Mary will have to walk. Neither of them have *brought* their *cars*

***none* (pronoun)**

The pronoun *none* can be followed either by singular verb and singular pronouns, or by plural ones. Either is acceptable, although the plural tends to be more common.

Singular: *None of them* was *allowed to forget for a moment* (Anthony Powell)
Plural: *None of the fountains ever* play (Evelyn Waugh)
None of the authors expected their *books to become best-sellers* (Cyril Connolly)

ought

Oughtn't or *didn't ought*?

The standard form of the negative of *ought* is *ought not* or *oughtn't*:

A look from Claudia showed me I ought not *to have begun it* (V. S. Pritchett)

Being an auxiliary verb, *ought* can precede *not* and does not require the verb *do*. It is non-standard to form the negative with *do* (*didn't ought*):

I hope that none here will say I did anything I didn't ought. *For I only done my duty* (Character in work by Michael Innes)

When the negative is used to reinforce a question in a short extra clause or 'question tag', the negative should be formed according to the rule above:

You ought to be pleased, oughtn't you*?* (not *didn't you?*)

In the same way *do* should not be used as a substitute verb for *ought*, e.g.

Ought he to go?—Yes, he ought (not *he did*)
You ought not to be pleased, ought *you?* (not *did you?*)

participles

A participle used in place of a verb in a subordinate clause must have an explicit subject to qualify. If no subject precedes the participle within the clause, the participle is understood to qualify the subject of the main sentence. In the following sentences the participles *running* and *propped* qualify the subjects *she* and *we*:

Running *to catch a bus, she just missed it* (Anthony Powell)
We both lay there, propped *on our elbows* (Lynne Reid Banks)

It is a frequent error to begin a sentence with a participial clause, with no subject expressed, and to continue it with a main clause in which the subject is not the word which the participle qualifies:

Driving *along the road*, the church *appeared on our left*
(*We*, not *the church*, is the subject of *driving*)

Having been relieved *of his portfolio in 1976*, the scheme *was left to his successor at the Ministry to complete*
(*He*, or a proper name, is the subject of *having been relieved*)

In sentences like these one must either recast the main clause so that its subject is the same as that of the subordinate clause, or recast the subordinate clause using a finite verb:

Driving along the road, we saw *the church* appear *on our left*
As we were *driving along the road, the church appeared on our left*

Sometimes a subject can be supplied in the participial clause, the clause remaining otherwise unchanged. This is usually only possible when the participle is *being* or *having*:

Jones *having been relieved of his portfolio in 1976, the scheme was left to his successor at the Ministry to complete*

If the subject supplied in accordance with this rule is a personal pronoun it should be in the subjective case:

He being *such a liar, no one will believe him when he tells the truth*
He rose bearing her, she *still weeping, and the others formed a procession behind* (Iris Murdoch)

When the participial clause includes a subject it should not be separated by a comma from the participle:

Bernadette being her niece, *she feels responsible for the girl's moral welfare* (David Lodge) (Not: *Bernadette, being her niece, she* . .)

This is in contrast with the punctuation of the other kind of participial clause, in which the participle qualifies the subject of the main sentence. If this type of participial clause follows the subject, it is either marked off by a pair of commas or not marked off at all:

The man, hoping to escape, *jumped on to a bus*
A man carrying a parcel *jumped on to the bus*

The rule that a participle must have an explicit subject does not apply to participial clauses whose subject is indefinite (= 'one' or 'people'). In these the clause is used adverbially, standing apart from and commenting on the content of the sentence:

Judging *from his appearance, he has had a night out*
Taking *everything into consideration, you were lucky to escape*
Roughly speaking, *this is how it went*

The participial clauses here are equivalent to 'If one judges . .', 'If one takes . .', 'If one speaks . .' Expressions of this kind are entirely acceptable.

preposition at end

It is a natural feature of the English language that many sentences and clauses end with a preposition, and has been since the earliest times. The alleged rule that forbids the placing of the preposition at the end of a clause or sentence should be disregarded.

The preposition *cannot* be moved to an earlier place in many sentences, e.g.

What did you do that for?
What a mess this room is in!
The bed had not been slept in
She was good to look at *and easy to talk* to (W. Somerset Maugham)

There are other kinds of construction which, generally speaking, allow a choice between placing the preposition at the end or placing it earlier—principally relative clauses, in which the preposition can stand before the relative pronoun if it is not placed finally. The choice is very often a matter of style. The preposition has been placed before the relative pronoun in:

The present is the only time in which *any duty can be done* (C. S. Lewis)
The . . veteran for whom *nothing has been real since the Big Push* (David Lodge)

But it stands at or near the end in:

Harold's Philistine outlook, which she had acquiesced in *for ten years* (L. P. Hartley)
The sort of attentive memory . . that I should have become accustomed to (C. P. Snow)

But notice that some prepositions cannot come at the end:

An annual sum, in return for *which she agreed to give me house room* (William Trevor)
During *which week will the festival be held?*

It would be unnatural to write *Which she agreed to give me house room in* return for, and *Which week will the festival be held* during?

Conversely, some relative clauses will not allow the preposition to stand before the relative pronoun:

The opposition (*that*) *I ran up* against *was fierce*
A sort of world apart which one can quite easily go through life without ever hearing about (George Orwell)

These cannot be changed to:

The opposition against *which I ran up . .*
A sort of world apart without ever hearing about *which . .*

One should be guided by what sounds natural. There is no need to alter the position of the preposition merely in deference to the alleged rule.

quantity, nouns of

The numerals *hundred*, *thousand*, *million*, *billion*, *trillion*, and the words *dozen* and *score* are sometimes used in the singular and sometimes in the plural.

1. They always have the singular form if they are qualified by a preceding word, whether it is singular (e.g. *a*, *one*) or plural (e.g. *many*, *several*, *two*, *three*, etc.), and whether or not they are used attributively before a noun or with nothing following:

A hundred days
Three hundred will be enough
I will take two dozen
Two dozen eggs

• The use of the plural form after a plural qualifier and when nothing follows is incorrect:

The population is now three millions (correctly *three million*)

Although they have the singular form, they always take plural verbs, even after the indefinite article:

There were *about a dozen of them approaching* (Anthony Powell)
There were *a score of them at a table apart* (J. I. M. Stewart)

2. They take the plural form when they denote indefinite quantities. Usually they are followed by *of* or stand alone:

Are there any errors?—Yes, hundreds
He has dozens of friends
Many thousands of people are homeless

reflexive pronouns

The reflexive pronouns are normally used to refer back to the subject of the clause or sentence in which they occur, e.g.

I *congratulated* myself *on outwitting everyone else*
Can't you *do anything for* yourself?

Sometimes it is permissible to use a reflexive pronoun to refer to someone who is not the subject. Very often the person referred to may be the subject of a preceding or following clause, e.g.

It was their success, both with myself *and others, that confirmed* me *in what has since been my career* (Evelyn Waugh)

You *have the feeling that all their adventures have happened to* yourself (George Orwell)

He *was furious with the woman, with a rancorous anger that surprised* himself (Joyce Cary)

In each of the above, there is a nearby *me*, *you*, or *he* to which the reflexive refers, but to have written *me*, *you*, and *him* respectively in these sentences would not have been grammatically incorrect.

A reflexive pronoun is often used after such words as

as	*but for*	*like*
as for	*except*	*than*
but	*except for*	

E.g. *For those who*, like himself, *felt it indelicate to raise an umbrella in the presence of death* (Iris Murdoch)

It can be a very useful way to avoid the difficult choice between *I*, *he*, *she*, etc. (which often sounds stilted) and *me*, *him*, *her*, etc. (which are grammatically incorrect) after the words *as*, *but*, and *than*, e.g.

None of them was more surprised than myself *that I'd spoken* (Lynne Reid Banks)

Here *than I* would be strictly correct, while *than me* would be informal.

Naturally a reflexive pronoun cannot be used in the ways outlined above if confusion would result. One would not write:

John was as surprised as himself *that he had been appointed*

but would substitute the person's name, or *he himself was*, for *himself*, or recast the sentence.

relative clauses

A relative clause is a clause introduced by a relative pronoun and used to qualify a preceding noun or pronoun (called its antecedent), e.g. *The visitor* (antecedent) *whom* (relative pronoun) *you were expecting* (remainder of relative clause) *has arrived*; *He* who hesitates *is lost*.

Exceptionally, there are nominal relative clauses in which the antecedent and relative pronoun are combined in one *wh*-pronoun, e.g. What you need *is a drink*: see **what (relative pronoun)**.

Relative clauses can be either restrictive or non-restrictive. A restrictive relative clause serves to restrict the reference of the antecedent, e.g. *A suitcase* which has lost its handle *is useless*. Here the antecedent *suitcase* is defined or restricted by the clause.

A non-restrictive relative clause is used not to narrow the reference of the antecedent, but to add further information, e.g. *He carried the suitcase*, which had lost its handle, *on one shoulder*. Here the suitcase is already identified, and the relative clause adds explanatory information.

Notice that no commas are used to mark off a restrictive relative clause from the rest of the sentence, but when, as above, a non-restrictive relative clause comes in the middle of the sentence, it is marked off by a comma at each end.

There are two kinds of relative pronouns:

(i) The *wh*-type: *who*, *whom*, *whose*, *which*, and, in nominal relative clauses only, *what*.

(ii) The pronoun *that* (which can be omitted in some circumstances: see ***that* (relative pronoun), omission of**).

When one relative clause is followed by another, the second relative pronoun

(*a*) may or may not be preceded by a conjunction; and

(*b*) may or may not be omitted.

(*a*) A conjunction is not required if the second relative clause qualifies an antecedent which is a word inside the first relative clause:

I found a firm which *had a large quantity of components* for which *they had no use*

Here *for which . . use* qualifies *components* which is part of the relative clause qualifying *firm*. *And* or *but* should not be inserted before *for which*.

But if the two clauses are parallel, both qualifying the same antecedent, a conjunction is required:

Help me with these shelves which I have to take home but *which will not fit in my car*

(*b*) The second relative pronoun can be omitted if (i) it qualifies the same antecedent as the first, and (ii) it plays the same part in its clause as the first (i.e. subject or object):

George, who *takes infinite pains and* (who) *never cuts corners, is our most dependable worker*

Here the second *who* qualifies the same antecedent (*George*) as the first *who*, and, like it, is the subject of its clause. It can therefore be omitted.

But if the second relative pronoun plays a different part in its clause, it cannot be omitted:

George, whom *everybody likes but* who *rarely goes to a party, is shy*

Here the first relative pronoun, *whom*, is the object, the second, *who*, is the subject, in their clauses. The second relative pronoun must be kept. This rule applies even if the two pronouns have the same form; it is the function that counts:

Like a child spelling out the letters of a word which *he cannot read and* which *if he could would have no meaning* (Jean Rhys)

The second *which* cannot be omitted.

See also **preposition at end, *that* (relative pronoun), omission of, *what* (relative pronoun), *which* or *that* (relative pronouns), *who* and *whom* (interrogative and relative pronouns), *who* or *which* (relative pronouns), *whose* or *of which* in relative clauses, *who/whom* or *that* (relative pronouns)**.

shall* and *will

'*The horror of that moment*', *the King went on*, '*I shall never*, never *forget!*' '*You will, though,*' *the Queen said*, '*if you don't make a memorandum of it.*' (Lewis Carroll)

There is considerable confusion about when to use *shall* and *will*. Put simply, the traditional rule in standard British English is:

1. In the first person, singular and plural.

(*a*) *I shall, we shall* express the simple future, e.g.

I am not a manual worker and please God I never shall *be one* (George Orwell)

In the following pages we shall *see good words . . losing their edge* (C. S. Lewis)

(*b*) *I will, we will* express intention or determination on the part of the speaker (especially a promise made by him or her), e.g.

I will *take you to see her tomorrow morning* (P. G. Wodehouse)

I will *no longer accept responsibility for the fruitless loss of life* (Susan Hill)
'*I don't think we* will *ask Mr. Fraser's opinion*', *she said coldly* (V. S. Pritchett)

2. For the second and third persons, singular and plural, the rule is exactly the converse.

(*a*) *You, he, she, it,* or *they will* express the simple future, e.g.

Will *it disturb you if I keep the lamp on for a bit?* (Susan Hill)
Seraphina will *last much longer than a car. She'll probably last longer than you* will (Graham Greene)

(*b*) *You, he, she, it,* or *they shall* express intention or determination on the part of the speaker or someone other than the actual subject of the verb, especially a promise made by the speaker to or about the subject, e.g.

Today you shall *be with me in Paradise* (NEB)
One day you shall *know my full story* (Evelyn Waugh)
Shall *the common man be pushed back into the mud, or* shall *he not?* (George Orwell)

The two uses of *will*, and one of those of *shall*, are well illustrated by:

'*I* will *follow you to the ends of the earth,' replied Susan, passionately.* '*It* will *not be necessary,' said George.* '*I am only going down to the coal-cellar. I* shall *spend the next half-hour or so there.*' (P. G. Wodehouse)

In informal usage *I will* and *we will* are quite often used for the simple future, e.g.

I will *be a different person when I live in England* (Character in work by Jean Rhys)

More often the distinction is covered up by the contracted form *'ll*, e.g.

I don't quite know when I'll *get the time to write again* (Susan Hill)

• The use of *will* for *shall* in the first person is not regarded as fully acceptable in formal usage.

should* and *would

When used for (*a*) the future in the past or (*b*) the conditional,

should goes with *I* and *we*
would goes with *you, he, she, it,* and *they*

(*a*) The future in the past.

First person:

I had supposed these to be the last . . I should *ever set eyes on* (Anthony Powell)
Julia and I, who had left . . , thinking we should *not return* (Evelyn Waugh)

The person's imagined statement or thought at the time was:

These are the last I shall *ever set eyes on*
We shall *not return*

with *shall*, not *will* (see ***shall* and *will***).

Second and third persons:

I told you that you would *find Russian difficult to learn*
He was there. Later, he would *not be there* (Susan Hill)

The person's statement or thought at the time was

You will *find Russian difficult to learn*
He will *not be there*

(*b*) The conditional.

First person:

I should *view with the strongest disapproval any proposal to abolish manhood suffrage* (C. S. Lewis)
If we had not hurried we should *never have got a seat*

Second and third persons:

If you cared about your work, you would *make more effort*
Isobel would *almost certainly have gone in any case* (Anthony Powell)

In informal usage, *I would* and *we would* are very common in both kinds of sentence:

I wondered whether I would *have to wear a black suit*
I would *have been content, I would never have repeated it* (Both examples from Graham Greene)

The use of *would* with the first person is understandable, because *should* (in all persons) has a number of uses which can clash with the conditional and the future in the past; sometimes the context does not make it clear, for example, whether *I should do* means 'it would be the case that I did' or 'I ought to do', e.g.

I wondered whether, when I was cross-examined, I should *admit that I knew the defendant*

• This use of *I would* and *we would* is not, however, regarded as fully acceptable in formal language.

See also ***I should* or *I would*.**

singular or plural

1. When subject and complement are different in number (i.e. one is singular, the other plural), the verb normally agrees with the subject, e.g.

(Plural subject)

Ships are *his chief interest*
Their wages were *a mere pittance*
Liqueur chocolates are *our speciality*

The Biblical *The wages of sin* is *death* reflects an obsolete idiom by which *wages* took a singular verb.

(Singular subject)

The ruling passion of his life was *social relationships*
What we need is *customers*
Our speciality is *liqueur chocolates*

2. A plural word or phrase used as a name, title, or quotation counts as singular, e.g.

Sons and Lovers has *always been one of Lawrence's most popular novels*
Coloured persons is *the term applied to those of mixed white and native blood*

3. A singular phrase that happens to end with a plural word should nevertheless be followed by a singular verb, e.g.

Everyone except the French wants (not *want*) *Britain to join*
One in six has (not *have*) *this problem*

See also ***-ics*, nouns in, quantity, nouns of, *-s* plural or singular, *what* (relative pronoun)**.

split infinitive

The split infinitive is the name given to the separation of *to* from the infinitive by means of an adverb (or sometimes an adverbial phrase), e.g. *He used* to continually refer *to the subject*. In this the adverb *continually* splits the infinitive *to refer* into two parts.

It is often said that an infinitive should never be split. This is an artificial rule that can produce unnecessarily contorted sentences. Rather, it is recommended that a split infinitive should be avoided by placing the adverb before or after the infinitive, unless this leads to clumsiness or ambiguity. If it does, one should either allow the split infinitive to stand, or recast the sentence.

1. Good writers usually avoid splitting the infinitive by placing the adverb before the infinitive:

I am not able, and I do not want, completely to abandon *the world-view that I acquired in childhood* (George Orwell)
One meets people who have learned actually to prefer *the tinned fruit to the fresh* (C. S. Lewis)
He did not want positively to suggest *that she was dominant* (Iris Murdoch)

On the other hand, it is quite natural in speech, and permissible in writing, to say:

What could it be like to actually live *in France?*
To really let *the fact that these mothers were mothers sink in*
(Both examples from Kingsley Amis)
Only one thing stops me from jumping up and screaming . . , it is to deliberately think *myself back into that hot light* (Doris Lessing)

2. Avoidance of ambiguity.

When an adverb closely qualifies the infinitive verb it may often be better to split the infinitive than to move the adverb to another position. The following example is ambiguous in writing, though in speech stress on certain words would make the meaning clear:

It fails completely to carry conviction

Either it means 'It totally fails . .', in which case *completely* should precede *fails*, or it means 'It fails to carry complete conviction', in which case that should be written, or the infinitive should be split.

3. Avoidance of clumsiness.

It took more than an excited elderly man . . socially to discompose *him . .* (Anthony Powell)

In this example *socially* belongs closely with *discompose*: it is not 'to discompose in a social way' but 'to cause social discomposure' or 'to destroy social composure'. There are quite a number of adverb + verb collocations of this kind. When they occur in the infinitive, it may be better either to split the infinitive or to recast the sentence than to separate the adverb from the verb.

4. Unavoidable split infinitive.

There are certain adverbial constructions which must immediately precede the verb and therefore split the infinitive, e.g. *more than*:

> *Enough new ships are delivered* to more than make up *for the old ones being retired*

And a writer may have sound stylistic reasons for allowing a parenthetic expression to split an infinitive:

> *It would be an act of gratuitous folly* to, as he had put it to Mildred, make *trouble for himself at this stage* (Iris Murdoch)

-*s* plural or singular

Some nouns, though they have the plural ending -*s*, are nevertheless treated as singulars, taking singular verbs and pronouns referring back to them.

1. *News*

2. Diseases:

measles *mumps* *rickets* *shingles*

Measles and *rickets* can also be treated as ordinary plural nouns.

3. Games:

billiards *dominoes* *ninepins*
bowls *draughts* *skittles*
darts *fives*

4. Countries:

the Bahamas *the Philippines*
the Netherlands *the United States*

These are treated as singular when considered as a unit, which they commonly are in a political context, or when the complement is singular, e.g.

> *The Philippines* is *a predominantly agricultural country*
> *The United States* has *withdrawn its ambassador*

The Bahamas and *the Philippines* are also the geographical names of the groups of islands which the two nations comprise, and in this use can be treated as plurals, e.g.

The Bahamas were *settled by British subjects*

Flanders and *Wales* are always singular. So are the city names *Athens*, *Brussels*, *Naples*, etc.

See also ***-ics*, nouns in**.

subjects joined by (*either* . .) *or*

When two singular subjects (either may be a noun, a pronoun, or a noun phrase) are joined by *or* or *either* . . *or*, the strict rule is that they require a singular verb and singular pronouns, since *or* (or *either* . . *or*) indicates that only one of them is the logical subject:

Either Peter or John has *had* his *breakfast already*
A traffic warden or a policeman is *always on the watch in this street*

However, 'at all times there has been a tendency to use the plural with two or more singular subjects when their mutual exclusion is not emphasized' (*OED*), e.g.

On which rage or wantonness vented themselves (George Eliot)

When one of the subjects joined by *or* is plural, it is best to put the verb in the plural, and place the plural subject nearer to the verb:

Either the child or the parents are *to blame*

When one subject is *I*, *we*, or *you*, and the other is a noun or a third person pronoun, or when the subjects are *you* and *I*, the verb is usually made to agree with the nearer of the two subjects:

Either he or I am *going to win*
Either he or you have *got to give in*
Either you or your teacher has *made a mistake*

This form of expression very often sounds awkward, especially when the sentence is a question:

Am *I or he going to win?*
Is *he or we wrong?*

It is usually best to recast the sentence by adding another verb:

Am I going to win, or is he?
Is he wrong, or are we?
Either he has got to give in, or you have

subjunctive

The subjunctive mood is indicated by the basic form of the verb, a form that is identical with the bare infinitive and imperative. In most verbs, e.g. *do*, *give*, and *make*, this will be the same as all the persons of the present tense except the third, which ends in *-s*. In the verb *to be*, however, the subjunctive is *be*, whereas the present tense is *am*, *are*, or *is*. For the past subjunctive of *to be* (*were*) see **were or was**.

The subjunctive is normal, and quite familiar, in a number of fixed expressions which cause no problems:

Be *that as it may*
Come *what may*
God bless *you*
God save *the Queen*
Heaven forbid
Heaven help *us*
Long live *the Queen*
So be *it*
Suffice *it to say that*

There are two other uses of the subjunctive that may cause difficulty, but they are entirely optional. This means that the ordinary user of English need not be troubled by the use of the subjunctive, apart from the past subjunctive *were*.

1. In *that*-clauses after words expressing command, hope, intention, wish, etc. Typical introducing words are

be adamant that
demand that
insist that
be insistent that
insistence that
propose that
proposal that
resolve that
suggest that
suggestion that

Typical examples are:

He had been insisting that they keep *the night of the twenty-second free* (C. P. Snow)

Joseph was insistent that his wishes be *carried out* (W. Somerset Maugham)

Chance . . dictated that I be *reading Sterne when . . Bellow's new novel arrived* (Frederic Raphael)

Your suggestion that I fly *out* (David Lodge)

Until recently this use of the subjunctive was restricted to very formal language, where it is still usual, e.g.

The Lord Chancellor put the motion that the House go *into Committee*

It is, however, a usual American idiom, and is now quite acceptable in British English, but there is no necessity to use the subjunctive in such contexts. *Should* or *may* with the infinitive, or (especially in informal use) the ordinary indicative, depending on the context, will do equally well:

Your demand that he should *pay the money back surprised him*
I insist that the boy goes *to school this minute*

• Beware of constructions in which the sense hangs on a fine distinction between subjunctive and indicative, e.g.

The most important thing for Argentina is that Britain recognize *her sovereignty over the Falklands*

The implication is that Britain does not recognize it. A small slip that changed *recognize* to *recognizes* would disastrously reverse this implication. The use of *should recognize* would render the sense quite unmistakable.

2. In certain concessive and conditional clauses, i.e. clauses introduced by *though* and *if*, the subjunctive can be used to express reserve on the part of the speaker about an action or state which is contemplated or in prospect, e.g.

Though he be *the devil himself he shall do as I say*
Though your sins be *as scarlet, they shall be as white as snow* (Authorized Version)
It is a fine thing if a man endure *the pain of undeserved suffering* (NEB)
The University is a place where a poor man, if he be *virtuous, may live a life of dignity and simplicity* (A. C. Benson)
If this be *true, then we are all to blame*

As the examples show, this is restricted to very formal and exalted language. It should not be used in ordinary prose, where sometimes the indicative and sometimes an auxiliary such as *may* are entirely acceptable, e.g.

Though he may be *an expert, he should listen to advice*
If this is *the case, then I am in error*

than, case following

A personal pronoun following *than* should have the case that it would have if a verb were supplied. In the following sentences, the subjective case is required because the personal pronoun would be the subject:

Other people have failed to grasp this, people much cleverer than I (in full, *than I am*)
We pay more rent than they (in full, *than they do*)

In the sentence below, the objective case is used, because the pronoun would be the object if there were a verb:

Jones treated his wife badly. I think that he liked his dog better than her (in full, *than he liked her*)

Informal English permits the objective case to be used, no matter what case the pronoun would have if a verb were supplied:

You do it very well. Much better than me

This is unacceptable in formal usage. The preferred alternative, with the subjective, often sounds stilted. When this is so, it can be avoided by supplying the verb:

We pay more rent than they do

The interrogative and relative pronoun *whom* is always used after *than*, rather than the subjective form *who*:

Professor Smith, than whom *there is scarcely anyone better qualified to judge, believes it to be pre-Roman*

that (conjunction), omission of

1. The conjunction *that* introducing a noun clause and used after verbs of saying, thinking, knowing, etc., can often be omitted in informal usage:

I told him (that) *he was wrong*
He knew (that) *I was right*
Are you sure (that) *this is the place?*

Generally speaking, the omission of *that* confers a familiar tone on the sentence, and is not usually appropriate in formal prose.

That should never be omitted if other parts of the sentence (apart from the indirect object) intervene:

I told him, as I have told everyone, that *he was wrong*
Are you sure in your own mind that *this is the place?*

The omission of *that* makes it difficult, in written prose, to follow the sense.

2. When the conjunction *that* is part of the correlative pairs of conjunctions *so . . that* and *such . . that*, or of the compound conjunctions *so that*, *now that*, it can be omitted in informal usage.

• It should not be omitted in formal style:

He walked so fast (or *at such a speed*) that *I could not keep up*
I'll move my car so that *you can park in the drive*
Are you lonely now that *your children have left home?*

that **(relative pronoun), omission of**

The relative pronoun *that* can often be omitted. Its omission is much more usual informally than formally.

In formal contexts the omission of *that* is best limited to relative clauses which are fairly short and which stand next to their antecedents:

The best thing (that) *you can do is make up for lost time*
None of the cars (that) *I saw had been damaged*
Nothing (that) *I could say made any difference*

That cannot be omitted when it is the subject of the relative clause, e.g.

Nothing that *occurred to me made any difference*
None of the cars that *were under cover had been damaged*

See also **adverbial relative clauses** and ***way*, relative clause following**.

there is **or** ***there are***

In a sentence introduced by *there* + part of the verb *to be*, the latter agrees in number with the noun, noun phrase, or pronoun which follows:

There was *a great deal to be said for this scheme*
There are *many advantages in doing it this way*

In very informal language *there is* or *there was* is often heard before a plural:

There's *two coloured-glass windows in the chapel* (Character in work by Evelyn Waugh)

• This is non-standard.

to

The preposition *to* can stand at the end of a clause or sentence as a substitute for an omitted *to*-infinitive, e.g.

He had tried not to think about Emma . . , but of course it was impossible not to (Iris Murdoch)
I gave him her message, as I should have been obliged to *if she had died* (C. P. Snow)

This is standard usage.

unattached phrases

An adjectival or adverbial phrase, introducing a sentence, must qualify the subject of the sentence, e.g.

While not entirely in agreement with the plan, *he had no serious objections to it*
After two days on a life-raft, *the survivors were rescued by helicopter*

The introductory phrases *While . . plan* and *After . . life-raft* qualify the subjects *he* and *the survivors* respectively.

It is a common error to begin a sentence with a phrase of this kind, anticipating a suitable subject, and then to continue the sentence with a quite different subject, e.g.

After six hours without food in a plane on the perimeter at Heathrow, *the flight was cancelled*

The phrase *After . . Heathrow* anticipates a subject like *the passengers*: a flight cannot spend six hours without food in a plane on an airport perimeter. Such a sentence should either have a new beginning, e.g.

After the passengers had spent *six hours . .*

or a new main clause, e.g.

After six hours . . Heathrow, the passengers learnt that *the flight had been cancelled*

used to

The negative and interrogative of *used to* can be formed in two ways:

(i) Negative: *used not to*
Interrogative: *used X to?*

This formation follows the pattern of the other auxiliary verbs.

Examples:

Used you to beat your mother? (G. B. Shaw)
You used not to have a moustache, used you? (Evelyn Waugh)

(ii) Negative: *did not use to, didn't use to*
Interrogative: *did X use to?*

This formation is the same as that used with regular verbs.

Examples:

She didn't use to find sex revolting (John Braine)
Did you use to be a flirt? (Eleanor Farjeon)

□ Either form is acceptable. On the whole *used you to*, *used he to*, etc. tend to sound rather stilted.

● The correct spellings of the negative forms are:
usedn't to and *didn't use to*

not:
usen't to and *didn't used to*

way, relative clause following

(*The*) *way* can be followed by a relative clause with or without *that*. There is no need for the relative clause to contain the preposition *in*:

It may have been the way he smiled (Jean Rhys)
Whatever way they happened *would be an ugly way* (Iris Murdoch)
She couldn't give a dinner party the way the young lad's mother could (William Trevor)

were or was

There is often confusion about whether to use the past subjunctive *were* or the past indicative *was*.

Formal usage requires *were*

1. In conditional sentences where the condition is 'unreal', e.g.

It would probably be more marked if the subject were *more dangerous* (George Orwell)
(The condition is unreal because 'the subject' is not very 'dangerous' in fact)

If anyone were *to try to save me, I would refuse* (Jean Rhys)
(The condition is regarded as unlikely)

2. Following *as if* and *as though*, e.g.

He wore it with an air of melancholy, as though it were *court mourning* (Evelyn Waugh)
(For a permissible exception see p. 57)

3. In *that*-clauses after *to wish*, e.g.

I wish I were *going instead of you*

4. In the fixed expressions *As it were, If I were you*

Notice that in all these constructions the clause with *were* refers to something unreal, something that in fact is not or will not be the case.

Were may also be used in dependent questions, where there is doubt of the answer, e.g.

Hilliard wondered whether Barton were *not right after all* (Susan Hill)

Her mother suddenly demanded to know if she were *pregnant* (Joyce Cary)

□ This is not obligatory even in very formal prose. *Was* is acceptable instead.

we (with phrase following)

Expressions consisting of *we* or *us* followed by a qualifying word or phrase, e.g. *we English, us English*, are often misused with the wrong case of the first person plural pronoun. In fact the rules are exactly the same as for *we* or *us* standing alone.

If the expression is the subject, *we* should be used:

(Correct) *Not always laughing as heartily as* we English *are supposed to do* (J. B. Priestley)

(Incorrect) *We all make mistakes, even* us anarchists (Character in work by Alison Lurie) (Substitute *we anarchists*)

If the expression is the object or the complement of a preposition, *us* should be used:

(Correct) *To* us English, *Europe is not a very vivid conception*

(Incorrect) *The Manchester Guardian has said some nice things about* we in the North-East

what (relative pronoun)

What can be used as a relative pronoun only when introducing nominal relative clauses, e.g.

> *So much of* what you tell me *is strange, different from* what I was led to expect (Jean Rhys)

In this kind of relative clause, the antecedent and relative pronoun are combined in the one word *what*, which can be regarded as equivalent to *that which* or *the thing(s) which.*

• *What* cannot act as a relative pronoun qualifying an antecedent in standard English. This use is found only in non-standard speech, e.g.

> *The young gentleman* what'*s arranged everything* (Character in work by Evelyn Waugh)

A *what*-clause used as the subject of a sentence almost always takes a singular verb, even if there is a plural complement, e.g.

> *What one first became aware of* was *the pictures* (J. I. M. Stewart)
> *What interests him* is *less events . . than the reverberations they set up* (Frederic Raphael)

Very occasionally the form of the sentence may render the plural more natural, e.g.

> *What once were great houses* are *now petty offices*
> *I have few books, and what there are* do *not help me*

which or _that_ (relative pronouns)

There is a degree of uncertainty about whether to use *which* or *that* as the relative pronoun qualifying a non-personal antecedent (for personal antecedents see **_who/whom_ or _that_**).

The general rule is that *which* is used in relative clauses to which the reader's attention is to be drawn, while *that* is used in clauses which mention what is already known or does not need special emphasis.

Which is almost always used in non-restrictive clauses, i.e. those that add further information about an antecedent already defined by other words or the context. Examples:

> *The men are getting rum issue*, which they deserve (Susan Hill)
> *Narrow iron beds with blue rugs on them*, which *Miss Fanshawe has to see are all kept tidy* (William Trevor)

• The use of *that* in non-restrictive clauses should be avoided. It is not uncommon in informal speech, and is sometimes employed by good writers to suggest a tone of familiarity, e.g.

> *Getting out of Alec's battered old car* that *looked as if it had been in collision with many rocks, Harold had a feeling of relief* (L. P. Hartley)

It should not, however, be used in ordinary prose.

Both *which* and *that* can be used in restrictive relative clauses, i.e. clauses that limit or define the antecedent.

There is no infallible rule to determine which should be used. Some guidelines follow:

1. *Which* preferred.

(*a*) Clauses which add significant information often sound better with *which*, e.g.

> *Was I counting on Israel to work some miracle* which *would give me the strength?* (Lynne Reid Banks)
>
> *Not nearly enough for the social position* which *they had to keep up* (D. H. Lawrence)

(*b*) Clauses which are separated from their antecedent, especially when separated by another noun, sound better with *which*, e.g.

> *Larry told her the story of the young airman* which *I narrated at the beginning of this book* (W. Somerset Maugham)

(*c*) When a preposition governs the relative pronoun, *which* preceded by the preposition is often a better choice than *that* with the preposition at the end of the sentence (see also **preposition at end**), e.g.

> *I'm telling you about a dream* in which *ordinary things are marvellous* (William Trevor)
>
> (*A dream that ordinary things are marvellous in* would not sound natural)
>
> *The inheritance* to which *we are born is one that nothing can destroy* (NEB)
>
> (*The inheritance that we are born to* would sound very informal and unsuited to the context)

2. *That* preferred.

In clauses that do not fall into the above categories *that* can usually be used. There is no reason to reject *that* if

(*a*) the antecedent is impersonal,
(*b*) the clause is restrictive,
(*c*) no preposition precedes the relative pronoun, and
(*d*) the sentencc does not sound strained or excessively colloquial.

Examples:

I read the letters, none of them very revealing, that *littered his writing table* (Evelyn Waugh)

He fell back on the old English courtesy that *he had consciously perfected to combat the increasing irritability* that *came with old age and arthritis* (Angus Wilson)

In these examples, *which* would be acceptable, but is not necessary.

When the antecedent is an indefinite pronoun (e.g. *anything*, *everything*, *nothing*, *something*) or contains a superlative adjective qualifying the impersonal antecedent (e.g. *the biggest car*, *the most expensive hat*) English idiom tends to prefer *that* to *which*:

Is there nothing small that *the children could buy you for Christmas?*

This is the most expensive hat that *you could have bought*

Note that *that* can sometimes be used when one is not sure whether to use *who* or *which*:

This was the creature, neither child nor woman, that *drove me through the dusk that summer evening* (Evelyn Waugh)

who and *whom* (interrogative and relative pronouns)

1. Formal usage restricts the use of the interrogative and relative pronoun *who* to the subject of the clause only, e.g.

I who'*d never read anything before but the newspaper* (W. Somerset Maugham)

When the pronoun is the object or the complement of a preposition, *whom* must be used:

Why are we being served by a man whom *neither of us likes?* (William Trevor)

The real question is food (*or freedom*) *for* whom (C. S. Lewis)

A midget nobleman to whom *all doors were open* (Evelyn Waugh)

• The use of *who* as object or prepositional complement is acceptable informally, but should not be carried over into serious prose, e.g.

Who *are you looking for?*
The person who *I'm looking for is rather elusive*

See also ***than*, case following**.

2. *Whom* for *who*.

Whom is sometimes mistakenly used for *who* because the writer believes it to be the object, or the complement of a preposition.

(*a*) For the interrogative pronoun the rule is: the case of the pronoun *who/whom* is determined by its role in the interrogative clause, not by any word in the main clause:

He never had any doubt about who *was the real credit to the family* (J. I. M. Stewart)

Who here is the subject of *was*. One should not be confused by *about*, which governs the whole clause, not *who* alone.

The error is seen in:

Whom *among our poets . . could be called one of the interior decorators of the 1950s?*
(Read *Who* . . because it is the subject of the passive verb *be called*)

Whom is correct in:

He knew whom *it was from* (L. P. Hartley)
(Here *whom* is governed by *from*)

Whom *he was supposed to be fooling, he couldn't imagine* (David Lodge)
(Here *whom* is the object of *fooling*)

(*b*) For the relative pronoun, when followed by a parenthetic clause such as *they say*, *he thinks*, *I believe*, etc., the rule is: the case of the pronoun *who/whom* is determined by the part it plays in the relative clause if the parenthetic statement is omitted:

Sheikh Yamani who they say *is the richest man in the Middle East*
(Not *whom they say* since *who* is the subject of *is*, not the object of *say*)

But *whom* is correct in:

Sheikh Yamani whom they believe to be *the richest man in the Middle East*

Here *they believe* is not parenthetic, since it could not be removed leaving the sentence intact. *Whom* is its object: the simple clause would be *They believe* him to be *the richest man.*

See also ***I who, you who,* etc.**

who or _which_ (relative pronouns)

If a *wh*-pronoun is used to introduce a relative clause it must be *who* (*whom*) if the antecedent is personal, e.g.

> *Suzanne was a woman* who *had no notion of reticence* (W. Somerset Maugham)

But it must be *which* if the antecedent is non-personal. e.g.

> *There was a suppressed tension about her* which *made me nervous* (Lynne Reid Banks)

If the relative clause is non-restrictive, i.e. it adds significant new information about an antecedent already defined, the *wh*-type of pronoun *must* be used (as above).

If the relative clause is restrictive, i.e. it defines or limits the reference of the antecedent, one can use either the appropriate *wh*-pronoun (as indicated above), or the non-variable pronoun *that*. For guidance about this choice see ***which* or *that* (relative pronouns)** and ***who/whom* or *that* (relative pronouns).**

whose or _of which_ in relative clauses

The relative pronoun *whose* can be used as the possessive of *which*, i.e. with reference to a non-personal antecedent, just as much as it can as the possessive of *who*. The rule sometimes enunciated that *of which* must always be used after a non-personal antecedent should be ignored, as it is by good writers, e.g.

> *The little book* whose *yellowish pages she knew* (Virginia Woolf)
>
> *A robe* whose *weight and stiff folds expressed her repose* (Evelyn Waugh)
>
> *A narrow side street*, whose *windows had flower boxes and painted shutters* (Doris Lessing)

In some sentences, *of which* would be almost impossible, e.g.

> *The lawns about* whose *closeness of cut his father worried the gardener daily* (Susan Hill)

There is, of course, no rule prohibiting *of which* if it sounds natural, e.g.

A little town the name of which *I have forgotten* (W. Somerset Maugham)

Whose can only be used as the non-personal possessive in *relative* clauses. Interrogative *whose* refers only to persons, as in *Whose book is this?*

who/whom or that (relative pronouns)

In formal usage, *who/whom* is always acceptable as the relative pronoun following an antecedent that denotes a person. (For the choice between *who* and *whom* see **who and whom (interrogative and relative pronouns).**

In non-restrictive relative clauses, i.e. those which add significant new information about an antecedent already defined, *who/whom* is obligatory, e.g.

It was not like Coulter, who *was a cheerful man* (Susan Hill)

In restrictive relative clauses, i.e those which define or limit the reference of the antecedent, *who/whom* is usually quite acceptable:

The masters who *taught me Divinity told me that biblical texts were highly untrustworthy* (Evelyn Waugh)

It is generally felt that the relative pronoun *that* is more impersonal than *who/whom*, and is therefore slightly depreciatory if applied to a person. Hence it tends to be avoided in formal usage.

However, if

(i) the relative pronoun is the object, and
(ii) the personality of the antecedent is suppressed

that may well be appropriate, e.g.

Then the woman that *they actually caught and pinned down would not have been Margot* (Evelyn Waugh)
They looked now just like the GIs that *one saw in Viet Nam* (David Lodge)

Informally *that* is acceptable with any personal antecedent, e.g.

You got it from the man that *stole the horse* (G. B. Shaw)
Honey, it's me that *should apologize* (David Lodge)

● This should be avoided in formal style.

you* and *I* or *you* and *me

When a personal pronoun is linked by *and* or *or* to a noun or another pronoun there is often confusion about which case to put the pronoun in. In fact the rule is exactly as it would be for the pronoun standing alone.

1. If the two words linked by *and* or *or* constitute the subject, the pronoun should be in the subjective case, e.g.

Only she *and her mother cared for the old house*
That's what we would do, that is, John and I
Who could go?—Either you or he

The use of the objective case is quite common in informal speech, but it is non-standard, e.g. (examples from the speech of characters in novels)

Perhaps only her *and Mrs Natwick had stuck to the christened name* (Patrick White)
That's how we look at it, me *and Martha* (Kingsley Amis)
Either Mary had to leave or me (David Lodge)

2. If the two words linked by *and* or *or* constitute the object of the verb, or the complement of a preposition, the objective case must be used:

The afternoon would suit her *and John better*
It was time for Sebastian and me *to go down to the drawing-room* (Evelyn Waugh)

The use of the subjective case is very common informally. It probably arises from an exaggerated fear of the error indicated under 1 above.

● It remains, however, non-standard, e.g.

It was this that set Charles and I *talking of old times*
Why is it that people like you and I *are so unpopular?* (Character in work by William Trevor)
Between you and I

This last expression is very commonly heard. *Between you and me* should always be substituted.

PRINCIPLES OF PUNCTUATION

apostrophe

1. Used to indicate the possessive case: see pp. 46 f.

2. Used to mark an omission, e.g. *e'er*, *we'll*, *he's*, *'69*.

• Sometimes written, but unnecessary, in a number of curtailed words, e.g. *bus*, *cello*, *flu*, *phone*, *plane* (not *'bus*, etc.). See also p. 45.

brackets

See: 1. **parentheses.**
2. **square brackets.**

colon

1. Links two grammatically complete clauses, but marks a step forward, from introduction to main theme, from cause to effect, or from premiss to conclusion, e.g. *To commit sin is to break God's law: sin, in fact, is lawlessness.*

2. Introduces a list of items (a dash should not be added), e.g. *The following were present: J. Smith, J. Brown, P. Thompson, M. Jones.*
It is used after such expressions as *for example*, *namely*, *the following*, *to resume*, *to sum up*.

comma

The least emphatic separating mark of punctuation, used:

1. Between adjectives which each qualify a noun in the same way, e.g. *A cautious, eloquent man.*

But when adjectives qualify the noun in different ways, or when one adjective qualifies another, no comma is used, e.g. *A distinguished foreign author*, *a bright red tie.*

2. To separate items (including the last) in a list of more than two

items, e.g. *Potatoes, peas, and carrots*; *Potatoes, peas, or carrots*; *Potatoes, peas, etc.*; *Red, white, and blue*.

• But *A black and white TV set*.

3. To separate co-ordinated main clauses, e.g. *Cars will turn here, and coaches will go straight on*. But not when they are closely linked, e.g. *Do as I tell you and you'll never regret it*.

4. To mark the beginning and end of a parenthetical word or phrase, e.g. *I am sure, however, that it will not happen*; *Fred, who is bald, complained of the cold*.

• Not with restrictive relative clauses, e.g. *Men who are bald should wear hats*.

5. After a participial or verbless clause, a salutation, or a vocative, e.g. *Having had breakfast, I went for a walk*; *The sermon over, the congregation filed out* or *The sermon being over*, (etc.); *My son, give me thy heart*.

• Not *The sermon, being over*, (etc.)

• No comma with expressions like *My friend Lord X* or *My son John*.

6. To separate a phrase or subordinate clause from the main clause so as to avoid misunderstanding, e.g. *In the valley below, the villages looked very small*; *He did not go to church, because he was playing golf*; *In 1982, 1918 seemed a long time ago*.

• A comma should not be used to separate a phrasal subject from its predicate, or a verb from an object that is a clause: *A car with such a high-powered engine, should not let you down* and *They believed, that nothing could go wrong* are both incorrect.

7. Following words introducing direct speech, e.g. *They answered, 'Here we are.'*

8. Following *Dear Sir*, *Dear John*, etc., in letters, and after *Yours sincerely*, etc.

• No comma is needed between month and year in dates, e.g. *In December 1982* or between number and road in addresses, e.g. *12 Acacia Avenue*.

dash

1. The *en rule* is distinct (in print) from the **hyphen** (see pp. 31 ff.) and is used to join pairs or groups of words wherever movement or

tension, rather than co-operation or unity, is felt: it is often equivalent to *to* or *versus*, e.g. *The 1914–18 war*; *current–voltage characteristic*; *The London–Horsham–Brighton route*; *The Fischer–Spassky match*; *The Marxist–Trotskyite split*.

• Note *The Marxist-Leninist position*; *The Franco-Prussian war* with hyphens.

It is also used for joint authors, e.g. *The Lloyd–Jones hypothesis* (two men), distinct from *The Lloyd-Jones hypothesis* (one man with double-barrelled name).

2. The *em rule* (the familiar dash) is used to mark an interruption in the structure of a sentence. A pair of them can be used to enclose a parenthetic remark or to make the ending and resumption of a statement interrupted by an interlocutor; e.g. *He was not—you may disagree with me, Henry—much of an artist*; '*I didn't—*' '*Speak up, boy!*' '*—hear anything; I was just standing near by*.' It can be used informally to replace the **colon** (use 1).

exclamation mark

Used after an exclamatory word, phrase, or sentence. It usually counts as the concluding full stop, but need not, e.g. *Hail source of Being! universal Soul!* It may also be used within square brackets, after a quotation, to express the editor's amusement, dissent, or surprise.

full stop

1. Used at the end of all sentences which are not questions or exclamations. The next word should normally begin with a capital letter.

2. Used after **abbreviations**: see pp. 18f. If a point making an abbreviation comes at the end of a sentence, it also serves as the closing full stop, e.g. *She also kept dogs, cats, birds, etc.* but *She also kept pets* (*dogs, cats, birds, etc.*).

3. When a sentence concludes with a quotation which itself ends with a full stop, question mark, or exclamation mark, no further full stop is needed, e.g. He cried '*Be off!*' *But the child would not move*. But if the quotation is a short statement, and the introducing sentence has much greater weight, the full stop is put outside the quotation marks, e.g. *Over the entrance to the temple at Delphi were written the words* '*Know thyself*'.

hyphen: see pp. 31 ff.

parentheses

Enclose:

1. Interpolations and remarks made by the writer of the text himself, e.g. *Mr X (as I shall call him) now spoke*.

2. An authority, definition, explanation, reference, or translation.

3. In the report of a speech, interruptions by the audience.

4. Reference letters or figures (which do not then need a full stop), e.g. (1), (*a*).

period: see **full stop**.

question mark

1. Follows every question which expects a separate answer. The next word should begin with a capital letter.

• Not used after indirect questions, e.g. *He asked me why I was there*.

2. May be placed before a word, etc., whose accuracy is doubted, e.g. *T. Tallis ?1505–85*.

quotation marks

1. Single quotation marks are used for a first quotation; double for a quotation within this; single again for a further quotation inside that.

2. The closing quotation mark should come before all punctuation marks unless these form part of the quotation itself, e.g. *Did Nelson really say* '*Kiss me, Hardy*'? but *Then she asked* '*What is your name?*' (see also **full stop,** 3).

The comma at the end of a quotation, when words such as *he said* follow, is regarded as equivalent to the final full stop of the speaker's utterance, and is kept inside the quotation, e.g. '*That is nonsense*,' *he said*. The commas on either side of *he said*, etc., when these words interrupt the quotation, should be outside the quotation marks, e.g. '*That*', *he said*, '*is nonsense*.' But the first comma goes inside the quotation marks if it would be part of the utterance even if there were no interruption, e.g. '*That, my dear fellow*,' *he said*, '*is nonsense*.'

3. Quotation marks (and roman type) are used when citing titles of articles in magazines, chapters of books, poems not published separately, and songs.

• Not for titles of books of the Bible; nor for any passage that represents only the substance of an extract, or has any grammatical alterations, and is not a verbatim quotation.

Titles of books and magazines are usually printed in italic.

semicolon

Separates those parts of a sentence between which there is a more distinct break than would call for a comma, but which are too closely connected to be made into separate sentences. Typically these will be clauses of similar importance and grammatical construction, e.g. *To err is human; to forgive, divine.*

square brackets

Enclose comments, corrections, explanations, interpolations, notes, or translations, which were not in the original text, but have been added by subsequent authors, editors, or others, e.g. *My right honourable friend* [*John Smith*] *is mistaken.*

GENERAL ABBREVIATIONS AND ACRONYMS

See also: Computer Terms, Commercial and Legal Terms, and Scientific and Medical Terms. The full point after units of measurement is omitted in scientific writing.

A: ampere(s).
Å: ångstrom(s).
AA: Advertising Association; Alcoholics Anonymous; anti-aircraft; Architectural Association; Associate in Arts; Automobile Association; film-censorship classification.
AAA: Amateur Athletic Association; American Automobile Association.
AB: able-bodied seaman; *Artium Baccalaureus* (US Bachelor of Arts).
ABA: Amateur Boxing Association.
abb.: abbess; abbey; abbot.
ABM: anti-ballistic-missile missile
a/c: account (*account current*).
ACAS: Advisory, Conciliation, and Arbitration Service.
ACT: Australian Capital Territory.
AD: of the Christian era (L. *anno Domini*).
ad: advertisement.
a.d.: after date.
***a.d.*:** *ante diem* (before the date).
ADC: aide-de-camp.
Adm.: Admiralty.
AF: audio frequency.
AFC: Air Force Cross.
AFM: Air Force Medal.
AGM: Annual General Meeting.
AID: artificial insemination by donor.
AIH: artificial insemination by husband.
a.k.a.: also known as.
ALCM: Associate of the London College of Music.
AM: amplitude modulation; Albert Medal; Air Ministry; *Artium Magister* (US Master of Arts); Member of the Order of Australia.
a.m.: before noon (L. *ante meridiem*).
ARAM: Associate of the Royal Academy of Music.
ARCM: Associate of the Royal College of Music.
ARIBA: Associate of the Royal Institute of British Architects.
a.s.a.p.: as soon as possible.
ass.: assistant.
AV: Authorized Version (of Bible).

Ave.: avenue.
AVM: Air Vice-Marshal.
AWOL: absent without leave.
B: black (pencil-lead).
b.: born.
BA: Bachelor of Arts.
b. & b.: bed and breakfast.
BAOR: British Army of the Rhine.
BBC: British Broadcasting Corporation.
BC: before Christ.
BCE: Bachelor of Civil Engineering; before Christian (*or* Common) Era.
BD: Bachelor of Divinity.
BEM: British Empire Medal.
Benelux: the customs union between Belgium, Netherlands, and Luxembourg which started in 1948. Complete economic union followed in 1960.
BHP: Broken Hill Proprietary Company Ltd. (Aust.).
b.h.p.: brake horsepower.
BMA: British Medical Association.
B.Mus.: Bachelor of Music.
BP: British Petroleum; boiling-point.
BR: British Rail.
BS: British Standard; Bachelor of Surgery.
B.Sc.: Bachelor of Science.
BSI: British Standards Institution.
BST: British Summer Time.
Bt.: Baronet.
BTU: British Thermal Unit.
BUPA: British United Provident Association.
C: centigrade; Celsius.
c.: century; chapter; cent.
c. or ***ca.***: *circa*.
Cantab.: Cantabrigian, of Cambridge or Cambridge University.
CAP: Common Agricultural Policy.
Capt.: Captain.
CB: Companion (of the Order) of the Bath; citizens' band.
CBE: Commander (of the Order) of the British Empire.
CBI: Confederation of British Industry.
CBS: Columbia Broadcasting System (US).
CCCP: Union of Soviet Socialist Republics (initials of *Soyuz Sovietskikh Sotsialisticheskikh Respublik* in the Russian alphabet).
CD: *Corps Diplomatique*.
Cdr.: Commander.
cf.: compare (L. *confer*).
cg.: centigram(s).
CGM: Conspicuous Gallantry Medal.
CH: Companion of Honour.
CI: Channel Islands.
CIA: Central Intelligence Agency.
CID: Criminal Investigation Department.
cm.: centimetre(s).
CMG: Companion (of the Order) of St Michael and St George.
CND: Campaign for Nuclear Disarmament.
CO: Commanding Officer.
Co.: company; county.

c/o: care of.
COD: cash (US, collect) on delivery.
C. of E.: Church of England.
COI: Central Office of Information.
c.p.: candlepower.
Cpl.: Corporal.
c.p.s. or **c/s:** cycles per second.
CSE: Certificate of Secondary Education.
CSIRO: Commonwealth Scientific and Industrial Research Organization (Aust.).
cu.: cubic.
CVO: Commander of the Royal Victorian Order.
DAA & QMG: Deputy Assistant Adjutant and Quartermaster-General.
DAQMG: Deputy Assistant Quartermaster-General.
dB: decibel(s).
DBE: Dame Commander (of the Order) of the British Empire.
DC: direct current; District of Columbia.
DCM: Distinguished Conduct Medal.
DCVO: Dame Commander of the Royal Victorian Order.
DD: Doctor of Divinity (L. *Divinitatis Doctor*).
DDR: German Democratic Republic (Ger. *Deutsche Demokratische Republik*).
derv: *d*iesel-*e*ngined *r*oad *v*ehicle: fuel oil for heavy vehicles.
DFC: Distinguished Flying Cross.
DFM: Distinguished Flying Medal.
DHSS: Department of Health and Social Security.
Dip.Ed.: Diploma in Education.
DIY: do-it-yourself.
DJ: disc jockey; dinner-jacket.
dl: decilitre(s).
D.Litt.: Doctor of Letters (L. *Doctor Litterarum*).
dm: decimetre(s).
D.Mus.: Doctor of Music.
DOE: Department of the Environment.
D.Phil.: Doctor of Philosophy.
DPP: Director of Public Prosecutions.
Dr: doctor.
DSC: Distinguished Service Cross.
D.Sc.: Doctor of Science.
DSM: Distinguished Service Medal.
DSO: Distinguished Service Order.
d.t., d.t.'s: delirium tremens.
E.: east(ern).
EEC: European Economic Community.
EET: Eastern European Time.
EFTA: European Free Trade Association.
e.g.: for example (L. *exempli gratia*).
e.m.f.: electromotive force.
ENE: east-north-east.
ENT: ear, nose, and throat.
EPNS: electroplated nickel silver.
ER: Queen Elizabeth (II) (L. *Elizabetha Regina*); King Edward (L. *Edwardus Rex*).

ERNIE: Electronic Random Number Indicator Equipment.

ESE: east-south-east.

ESP: extra-sensory perception.

Esq.: Esquire.

ETA: estimated time of arrival; Basque separatist movement.

***et al.*:** and others (L. *et alii*).

etc.: et cetera (and the rest, and so on).

ETD: estimated time of departure.

et seq.: and the following (pages, matter, etc.). (L. *et sequentia*).

F: Fahrenheit; farad(s); Fellow of; fine (pencil-head).

f.: female; feminine; focal length; folio; following page etc.

***f*:** forte (in music, loud).

FA: Football Association.

FBA: Fellow of the British Academy.

FBI: (US) Federal Bureau of Investigation.

ff.: following pages etc.

***ff*:** fortissimo (music).

FM: Field Marshal; frequency modulation.

FO: Flying Officer; *hist*. Foreign Office.

F.R.Ae.S.: Fellow of the Royal Aeronautical Society.

FRAM: Fellow of the Royal Academy of Music.

FRCS: Fellow of the Royal College of Surgeons.

FRGS: Fellow of the Royal Geographical Society.

FRIBA: Fellow of the Royal Institute of British Architects.

FRS: Fellow of the Royal Society.

Ft.: fort.

FZS: Fellow of the Zoological Society.

g.: gram(s); gravity, acceleration due to gravity.

GATT: General Agreement on Tariffs and Trade.

GB: Great Britain.

GC: George Cross.

GCB: Knight Grand Cross of the Order of the Bath.

GCE: General Certificate of Education.

GCHQ: Government Communications Headquarters.

GCMG: Knight *or* Dame Grand Cross of the Order of St Michael and St George.

GCVO: Knight *or* Dame Grand Cross of the Royal Victorian Order.

GDP: gross domestic product.

GDR: German Democratic Republic.

Gen.: General.

GHQ: General Headquarters.

GM: George Medal; Grand Master.

GmbH: limited liability company (Ger. *Gesellschaft mit beschränkter Haftung*).

GMT: Greenwich Mean Time.

GNP: gross national product.

GOC: General Officer Commanding.

GP: general practitioner.

GPO: General Post Office.

gr.: grain(s); gross.

GT: high-performance car (It. *gran turismo*).
H: hard (pencil-lead).
h: hecto-.
h.: hour(s); hot.
h. & c.: hot and cold (water).
HCF: highest common factor.
HE: high explosive; His or Her Excellency; His Eminence.
HF: high frequency.
hg: hectogram(s).
HGV: heavy goods vehicle.
HH: double-hard (pencil-lead); *also* 2H.
HHH: triple-hard (pencil-lead); *also* 3H.
HIH: His *or* Her Imperial Highness.
HM: Her *or* His Majesty('s).
HMS: Her *or* His Majesty's Ship.
HMSO: Her *or* His Majesty's Stationery Office.
HNC: Higher National Certificate.
HND: Higher National Diploma.
HSH: His *or* Her Serene Highness.
h.t.: *hoc tempore* (at this time); *hoc titulo* (in, *or* under, this title); high tension (in electricity).
Hz: hertz.
I.: Island(s); Isle(s).
IBA: Independent Broadcasting Authority.
ICI: Imperial Chemical Industries.
ILS: instrument landing system.
IMF: International Monetary Fund.
in.: inch(es).
INC: *in nomine Christi* (in Christ's name).
Inc.: (US) Incorporated.
IND: *in nomine Dei* (in God's name).
***infra dig.*:** undignified, unbecoming (L. *infra dignitatem*).
INI: *in nomine Iesu* (in the name of Jesus).
INRI: *Iesus Nazarenus, Rex Iudaeorum* (Jesus of Nazareth, King of the Jews).
INST: *in nomine Sanctae Trinitatis* (in the name of the Holy Trinity).
IOM: Isle of Man.
IOW: Isle of Wight.
IPA: International Phonetic Alphabet.
i.p.s.: inches per second.
IQ: intelligence quotient.
i.q.: *idem quod* (the same as).
IRA: Irish Republican Army.
IRBM: intermediate range ballistic missile.
ISBN: international standard book number.
ISC: Imperial Service College.
ITV: independent television.
IUD: intra-uterine (contraceptive) device.
J: joule(s).
K: kelvin; king (in chess).
K.: carat; King('s); Köchel (catalogue of Mozart's works).
k: kilo-.
K2: the second highest mountain in the world, in the Karakoram mountains.
KBE: Knight Commander of

the Order of the British Empire.

KCB: Knight Commander of the Order of the Bath.

KCMG: Knight Commander of the Order of St Michael and St George.

KCVO: Knight Commander of the Royal Victorian Order.

KG: Knight of the Order of the Garter.

kg.: kilogram(s).

KGB: (USSR) 'Committee of State Security'.

kHz: kilohertz.

KKK: Ku-Klux-Klan.

KO: knock-out.

KOSB: King's Own Scottish Borderers.

k.p.h.: kilometres per hour.

kV: kilovolt(s).

kW: kilowatt(s).

kWh: kilowatt-hour(s).

L: learner (driver).

L.: Lake; Liberal; Licenciate of.

l.: left; line; litre(s).

Lab.: Labour.

LAC: Leading Aircraftman; Licentiate of the Apothecaries' Company; London Athletic Club.

lb.: pound(s) weight (L. *libra*).

lbw.: leg before wicket.

l.c.: in the passage etc. cited (L. *loco citato*); lower case.

LCM: lowest common multiple.

L/Cpl.: Lance-Corporal.

Ld.: Lord.

LEA: Local Education Authority.

LF: low frequency.

l.h.: left hand.

Lib.: Liberal.

Litt.D.: Doctor of Letters (L. *Litterarum Doctor*).

LJ: (pl. L JJ) Lord Justice.

LL B: Bachelor of Laws (L. *Legum Baccalaureus*).

LL D: Doctor of Laws (L. *Legum Doctor*).

LL M: Master of Laws (L. *Legum Magister*).

LP: long-playing (record).

LRAM: Licentiate of the Royal Academy of Music.

LSD: lysergic acid diethylamide.

LSE: London School of Economics.

Lt.: Lieutenant; light.

l.t.: low tension.

LTA: Lawn Tennis Association.

Ltd.: Limited.

LV: luncheon voucher.

LXX: Septuagint.

M: mega-; motorway.

M.: Master; Monsieur.

m: milli-.

m.: metre(s); mile(s); million(s); minute(s); masculine; married; male.

MA: Master of Arts.

Maj.: Major.

MB: Bachelor of Medicine (L. *Medicinae Baccalaureus*).

MBE: Member of the Order of the British Empire.

MC: Master of Ceremonies; Military Cross.

MCC: Marylebone Cricket Club.

MCP: male chauvinist pig.

MD: Doctor of Medicine (L.

Medicinae Doctor); managing director.
MEP: Member of the European Parliament.
***mf*:** *mezzo forte* (in music, fairly loud).
MFH: Master of Foxhounds.
mfr.: manufacturer, manufacture.
mg.: milligram(s).
Mgr.: Monsignor; Monseigneur.
MHz: megahertz.
M.I.5.: Secret Service Division.
M.I.6.: Espionage Department.
MIRV: multiple independently targeted re-entry vehicle.
MIT: Massachusetts Institute of Technology.
ml.: millilitre(s); mile(s).
Mlle(s): Mademoiselle, Mesdemoiselles.
MLR: minimum lending rate.
MM: Messieurs; Military Medal.
mm.: millimetre(s).
Mme(s): Madame, Mesdames.
MO: Medical Officer; money order.
MP: Member of Parliament.
***mp*:** *mezzo piano* (in music, fairly soft).
m.p.g.: miles per gallon.
m.p.h.: miles per hour.
MRINA: Member of the Royal Institution of Naval Architects.
MS: manuscript; multiple sclerosis.
M.Sc.: Master of Science.
MSM: Meritorious Service Medal.
MSS: manuscripts.
Mt.: Mount.
MTB: motor torpedo-boat.
MVO: Member (of fourth or fifth class) of the Royal Victorian Order.
MW: megawatt(s).
N: knight (in chess); newton(s).
N.: New; north(ern).
n.: name; neuter; note.
n/a: (banking), no account; not applicable, not available.
NAAFI: Navy, Army, and Air Force Institutes (canteen for servicemen).
NASA: National Aeronautics and Space Administration.
NATO: North Atlantic Treaty Organization.
NB: note well (L. *nota bene*).
NCB: National Coal Board.
NCO: non-commissioned officer.
n.d.: no date.
NE: north-east(ern).
NHS: National Health Service.
NI: National Insurance; Northern Ireland.
NNE: north-north-east.
NNW: north-north-west.
no.: number (L. *numero*, ablative case of *numerus* number).
nr.: near.
NS: new style.
NSPCC: National Society for the Prevention of Cruelty to Children.
NSW: New South Wales.
NT: New Testament; Northern Territory (Australia).
NW: north-west(ern).

NY: New York.
NZ: New Zealand.
O.: Old.
OAP: old age pension(er).
OAU: Organization of African Unity.
OBE: (Officer of the) Order of the British Empire.
OC: Officer Commanding.
OECD: Organization for Economic Co-operation and Development.
***OED*:** *Oxford English Dictionary*.
OHMS: On Her *or* His Majesty's Service.
OM: Order of Merit.
ONC: Ordinary National Certificate.
OND: Ordinary National Diploma.
o.n.o.: or near offer.
OPEC: Organization of Petroleum Exporting Countries.
OS: old style; ordinary seaman; Ordnance Survey; outsize.
OT: Old Testament.
Oxon.: of Oxford University (L. *Oxoniensis*); Oxfordshire.
oz.: ounce(s) (It. *onza* ounce).
P: pawn (in chess).
p: penny, pence.
p.: page.
PA: personal assistant; public address.
p.a.: per annum.
P. & O.: Peninsular and Oriental Steamship Company.
p. and p.: postage and packing.
PAYE: pay-as-you-earn.
PBI: poor bloody infantry (man).
PC: police constable; Privy Counsellor.
p.c.: per cent.
pd.: paid.
p.d.q.: pretty damn quick.
PE: physical education.
PEI: Prince Edward Island.
PG: paying guest.
Ph.D.: Doctor of Philosophy (L. *Philosophiae Doctor*).
pl.: place; plate; plural.
PLO: Palestine Liberation Organization.
PLR: Public Lending Right.
PM: Prime Minister; post-mortem.
p.m.: after noon (L. *post meridiem*).
PO: Post Office; postal order; Petty Officer; Pilot Officer.
POW: prisoner of war.
pp.: pages.
p.p.: *per pro.* (by proxy, through an agent; L. *per procurationem*).
***pp*:** pianissimo (in music, very softly).
p.p.m.: parts per million.
PPS: Parliamentary Private Secretary; additional postscript.
PR: proportional representation; public relations.
pr.: pair.
Prof.: Professor.
PS: postscript.
PSV: public service vehicle.
PT: physical training.
pt.: part; pint(s); point; port.
PTA: parent–teacher association.
Pte.: Private.
PTO: please turn over.

Pty.: proprietary (Australia, New Zealand, South Africa).
PVC: polyvinyl chloride.
Q.: Queen('s); question.
QARANC: Queen Alexandra's Royal Army Nursing Corps.
QARNNS: Queen Alexandra's Royal Naval Nursing Service.
QC: Queen's Counsel.
QED: which was to be demonstrated (L. *quod erat demonstrandum*).
QM: quartermaster.
qr.: quarter(s).
qt.: quart(s).
q.t.: (colloq.), (on the) quiet.
q.v.: which see (in references) (L. *quod vide*).
qy: query.
RA: Rear-Admiral; Royal Academy; Royal Academician; Royal Artillery.
RAC: Royal Automobile Club.
RADA: Royal Academy of Dramatic Art.
RAF: Royal Air Force.
RAM: Royal Academy of Music.
RAMC: Royal Army Medical Corps.
RAOC: Royal Army Ordnance Corps.
RC: Roman Catholic.
RCA: Royal College of Art.
RCM: Royal College of Music.
RCP: Royal College of Physicians.
RCS: Royal College of Science; Royal College of Surgeons; Royal Corps of Signals.
Rd.: road.
RE: Royal Engineers.
REME: Royal Electrical and Mechanical Engineers.
Revd: Reverend.
r.h.: right hand.
RIP: rest in peace (L. *requiesca(n)t in pace*).
RM: Royal Marines.
RMA: Royal Military Academy.
RN: Royal Navy.
RNIB: Royal National Institute for the Blind.
RNLI: Royal National Life-boat Institution.
RoSPA: Royal Society for the Prevention of Accidents.
r.p.m.: revolutions per minute.
RSM: Regimental Sergeant-Major.
RSPCA: Royal Society for the Prevention of Cruelty to Animals.
RSV: Revised Standard Version (of Bible).
RSVP: (in invitation etc.) please answer (Fr. *répondez s'il vous plaît*).
rt.: right.
Rt. Hon.: Right Honourable.
Rt. Revd: Right Reverend.
RV: Revised Version (of Bible).
S.: south(ern).
s.: second(s); (former) shilling(s); singular; son.
SA: Salvation Army; sex appeal; South Africa; South Australia.
***s.a.*:** without date (L. *sine anno*).
SAC: Senior Aircraftman.
s.a.e.: stamped addressed envelope.

SALT: Strategic Arms Limitation Talks.
SAM: surface-to-air missile.
SAS: Special Air Service.
SAYE: save-as-you-earn.
sc.: scilicet (that is to say).
s.c.: small capitals.
Sc.D.: Doctor of Science (L. *Scientiae Doctor*).
SDP: Social Democratic Party.
SE: south-east(ern).
SEATO: South-East Asia Treaty Organization.
Sec.: Secretary.
sec.: second(s).
SEN: State Enrolled Nurse.
Sen.: Senator; senior.
SF: science fiction.
***sf*:** sforzando (in music, with sudden emphasis).
Sgt.: Sergeant.
SJ: Society of Jesus.
SNP: Scottish National Party.
Soc.: Socialist; Society.
SOS: International code-signal of extreme distress; urgent appeal for help etc.
***s.p.*:** *sine prole* (without issue).
SPCK: Society for Promoting Christian Knowledge.
SPQR: small profits and quick returns; L. *Senatus Populusque Romanus* = the Senate and Roman People.
sq.: square.
Sqn. Ldr.: Squadron Leader.
Sr.: Señor.
SRN: State Registered Nurse.
SS: Saints; steamship; *hist.* Nazi special police force (Ger. *Schutz-Staffel*).
SSE: south-south-east.
SSW: south-south-west.
St: Saint.
St.: street.
st.: stone.
STD: subscriber trunk dialling.
STOL: short take-off and landing.
s.v.: under a specified word (L. *sub voce* or *sub verbo*).
SW: south-west(ern).
t.: ton(s); tonne(s).
TA: Territorial Army.
TAM: television audience measurement.
TB: tubercle bacillus.
TD: Territorial Decoration.
TIR: international road transport (Fr. *Transport International Routier*).
TNT: trinitrotoluene.
TRH: Their Royal Highnesses.
TT: Tourist Trophy; tuberculin-tested; teetotal; teetotaller.
TUC: Trades Union Congress.
TV: television.
UCCA: Universities Central Council on Admissions.
UDI: unilateral declaration of independence.
UFO: unidentified flying object.
UHF: ultra-high frequency.
UHT: ultra heat treated (of milk, for long keeping).
UK: United Kingdom.
UN: United Nations.
UNESCO: United Nations Educational, Scientific, and Cultural Organization.
UNICEF: United Nations Children's (orig. Emergency) Fund.

UNO: United Nations Organization.
US: United States.
USA: United States of America.
USSR: Union of Soviet Socialist Republics.
UV: ultraviolet.
V: volt(s).
v.: verse; versus; very; *vide* (see, consult).
V. & A.: Victoria and Albert Museum.
VAT: value added tax.
VC: Victoria Cross.
VD: venereal disease; Volunteer Decoration.
VDU: visual display unit.
VHF: very high frequency.
VIP: very important person.
VRD: Royal Naval Volunteer Reserve Officers' Decoration.
vs.: versus.
VSO: Voluntary Service Overseas.
VTO: vertical take-off.
VTOL: vertical take-off and landing.
vv.: verses; volumes.
W: watt(s).
W.: west(ern).
w.: wicket(s); wide(s); with.
WASP: (US) White Anglo-Saxon Protestant.
WC: water-closet; West Central.
W/Cdr.: Wing Commander.
w.e.f.: with effect from.
WHO: World Health Organization.
WNW: west-north-west.
WPC: woman police constable.
w.p.m.: words per minute.
WRAC: Women's Royal Army Corps.
WRAF: Women's Royal Air Force.
WRNS: Women's Royal Naval Service.
WRVS: Women's Royal Voluntary Service.
WSW: west-south-west.
YMCA: Young Men's Christian Association.
YWCA: Young Women's Christian Association.

FOREIGN WORDS AND PHRASES

ab initio: from the beginning (L.).

ad hoc: for this (purpose), special (L.).

ad infinitum: without limit, for ever (L.).

ad lib: to speak without formal preparation, improvise (L. = *ad libitum*).

ad nauseam: to an excessive or sickening degree (L.).

aficionado: enthusiast for sport or hobby (Sp.).

a fortiori: with stronger reason (than a conclusion already accepted) (L.).

agent provocateur: person employed to detect suspected offenders by tempting them to overt action (Fr.).

aide-mémoire: aid to memory (Fr.).

à la carte: ordered as separate items from menu (Fr.).

al dente: cooked but not soft (It.).

alma mater: one's school or university (L. = bounteous mother).

alter ego: intimate friend; other aspect of oneself (L.).

amour propre: self-respect, proper pride (Fr.).

ancien régime: the old order of things (Fr.).

annus mirabilis: remarkable year (L.).

a posteriori: from effects to causes; involving reasoning thus (L.).

après-ski: done or worn after skiing (Fr.).

a priori: (reasoning) from causes to effects (L.).

arriviste: person ruthlessly and obsessively aspiring to advancement (Fr.).

au courant: fully acquainted (Fr.).

au fait: well acquainted with subject (Fr.).

au fond: at bottom, basically (Fr.).

au gratin: cooked with a crust of breadcrumbs or grated cheese (Fr.).

auto-da-fé: ceremonial judgement of heretics by Spanish inquisition; execution of heretics by public burning (Port. = act of faith).

autre temps, autres mœurs: other times, other manners (Fr.).

avant-garde: leading group of innovators, esp. in art and literature (Fr. = vanguard).

belles-lettres: writings or studies of a literary nature (Fr. = fine letters).
bête noire: person or thing particularly disliked (Fr. = black beast).
bonhomie: good nature (Fr.).
bon mot: a witticism (Fr.).
bonne-bouche: dainty morsel (Fr.).
bon ton: good style (Fr.).
cantatrice: professional woman singer (Fr. and It.).
carte blanche: full discretionary power given to person (Fr. = blank paper).
casus belli: the cause of war (L.).
cause célèbre: lawsuit that attracts much interest (Fr.).
caveat emptor: let the buyer beware (L.).
ceteris paribus: other things being equal, other conditions corresponding (L.).
chacun à son goût: everyone to his taste (Fr.).
chaise longue: long low chair able to support sitter's legs (Fr.).
chez: at the house or home of (Fr.).
chutzpah: shameless audacity (Yiddish).
circa: about (a specified date or number) (Fr.).
cognoscente: connoisseur (It.).
coiffure: hair-style (Fr.).
comme ci, comme ça: so-so, indifferently (Fr.).
comme il faut: as it should be (Fr.).
compos mentis: in one's right mind (L.).
confrère: fellow member of profession, etc. (Fr.).
congé: unceremonious dismissal; leave-taking (Fr.).
cordon bleu: of highest class in cookery; cook of this class (Fr.).
corps de ballet: a company of ballet dancers (Fr.).
corps diplomatique: diplomatic corps (Fr.).
corpus delicti: in law, the facts constituting an alleged offence (L.).
coup de foudre: stroke of lightning (Fr.).
coup de grâce: a finishing stroke (Fr.).
coup d'état: sudden or violent change in government (Fr.).
coup d'œil: a glance, wink (Fr.).
crème de la crème: the very best (Fr.).
cri de cœur: passionate appeal (Fr.).
crime passionnel: crime caused by sexual passion (Fr.).
crû: growth (wine) (Fr.).
cui bono?: who gains by it? (L.).
culottes: woman's divided skirt (Fr. = knee-breeches).
cum laude: Used in the US where it is sometimes added to a degree (or similar qualification) when the degree is above average. *Cum laude* is the lowest such award, *summa cum laude* being the highest and *magna cum laude* the next highest (L. = with

praise, with the utmost praise, with great praise).

currente calamo: extempore; without deliberation or hesitation (L.).

décolletage: (wearing of) low neck of dress (Fr.).

de facto: in actual fact (L.).

Dei gratia: by the grace of God (L.).

déjà vu: illusory feeling of having already experienced a present situation; something tediously familiar (Fr. = already seen).

de jure: by right (L.).

demi-monde: women of doubtful repute in society; group behaving with doubtful legality etc. (Fr. = half-world).

de profundis: out of the depths (L.).

de rigueur: required by custom or etiquette (Fr.).

déshabillé: state of being only partly dressed (Fr. = undressed).

de trop: not wanted, in the way (Fr. = excessive).

deus ex machina: unexpected power or event saving seemingly impossible situation, esp. in play or novel (L. = god from the machinery).

Dieu et mon droit: God and my right (English royal motto) (Fr.).

distrait: absent-minded (Fr.).

doppelgänger: wraith of living person (Ger. = double-goer).

double entendre: phrase affording two meanings, one usu. indecent (obs. Fr.).

dramatis personae: (list of) characters in a play (L.).

ecce homo: behold the man (L.).

émigré: emigrant, esp. political exile (Fr.).

éminence grise: one who exercises power or influence without holding office (Fr. = grey cardinal [orig. of Richelieu's secretary]).

en bloc: in a block, all at the same time (Fr.).

enfant terrible: person who causes embarrassment by indiscreet behaviour; unruly child (Fr. = terrible child).

en masse: all together (Fr.).

en passant: by the way (Fr. = in passing).

en route: on the way (Fr.).

entente cordiale: cordial understanding, that between Britain and France, 1904 onwards (Fr.).

esprit de corps: devotion and loyalty to body by its members (Fr.).

esprit de l'escalier: an inspiration or thought that comes too late to be of use (Fr.).

et cetera: and the rest, and so on (L.).

ex animo: from the mind, earnestly (L.).

ex cathedra: from the Pope's, professor's, chair, with authority (L.).

exceptis excipiendis: with the necessary exceptions (L.).

ex gratia: voluntary (L.).

ex hypothesi: according to the hypothesis proposed (L.).
ex officio: by virtue of one's office (L.).
ex parte: one-sided(ly) (L.).
ex post facto: retrospective(ly) (L. = from what is done afterwards).
fait accompli: thing that has been done and is past arguing against (Fr.).
faux pas: tactless mistake, blunder (Fr. = false step).
femme fatale: dangerously attractive woman (Fr.).
feu de joie: a salute (Fr.).
fin de siècle: end of the (nineteenth) century; decadent (Fr.).
fines herbes: mixed herbs used in cooking (Fr. = fine herbs).
flambé: (of food) covered with spirit and served alight (Fr.).
force majeure: irresistible force; unforeseen circumstances excusing from fulfilment of contract (Fr.).
frappé: iced, chilled (esp. of wine) (Fr.).
frisson: emotional thrill, a shudder (Fr.).
genius loci: the pervading spirit of the place (L.).
gestalt: a shape, the whole as more than the sum of its parts (Ger.).
grand mal: epilepsy with loss of consciousness (Fr. = great sickness).
gros-point: cross-stitch embroidery on canvas (Fr.).
habeas corpus: writ to produce a person before court (L. = have the body).
habitué: resident or frequent visitor (Fr.).
hara-kiri: suicide (Jap.).
haute couture: elegance inspired by the high-fashion houses (Fr.).
haut monde: fashionable society (Fr.).
hoi polloi: the masses (Gr.).
homo sapiens: modern man regarded as a species (L. = wise man).
Honi soit qui mal y pense: shamed be he who thinks evil of it (motto of the Order of the Garter) (Fr.).
hors de combat: disabled (Fr. = out of battle).
ich dien: I serve (motto of the Prince of Wales) (Ger.).
idée fixe: recurrent or dominating idea (Fr. = fixed idea).
in absentia: in (his or her or their) absence (L.).
in extenso: at full length (L.).
in extremis: at point of death; in great difficulties (L.).
in flagrante delicto: in the very act of committing an offence (L. = in blazing crime).
ingénue: artless young woman esp. as stage role (Fr.).
in loco parentis: in place of a parent (L.).
in memoriam: in memory of (L.).
in re: re (L.).
in situ: in its original place (L.).
inter alia: among other things (L.).

in toto: completely (L.).

intra vires: within one's powers (L.).

in vacuo: in a vacuum (L.).

in vino veritas: a drunken man speaks the truth (L.).

in vitro: describing biological phenomena that are made to occur outside the living body (traditionally in a test-tube) (L.).

in vivo: describing biological phenomena that occur within the bodies of living organisms (L.).

ipso facto: by the fact itself (L.).

jeunesse dorée: gilded youth (Fr.).

joie de vivre: feeling of exuberant enjoyment of life; high spirits (Fr. = joy of living).

laissez-faire: policy of non-interference (Fr. = let act).

lapsus linguae: a slip of the tongue (L.).

leitmotiv: theme, in music, associated with person, situation, or sentiment (Ger.).

lèse-majesté: any offence against the sovereign authority, esp. treason; presumptuous behaviour (Fr.).

lettre de cachet: warrant for imprisonment, bearing the royal seal (Fr.).

lex talionis: 'an eye for an eye' (L.).

lied (pl. *lieder*): German song, esp. of Romantic period (Ger.).

lingua franca: language used by speakers whose native languages are different; system for mutual understanding (It. = Frankish tongue).

locum tenens: a substitute (L.).

locus classicus: best-known or most authoritative passage on a subject (L.).

locus standi: recognized position (L. = place of standing).

Madame: title used of or to French-speaking woman, corresponding to Mrs or madam (Fr. *ma dame* = my lady).

Mademoiselle: title used of or to unmarried French-speaking woman, corresponding to Miss or madam (Fr. *ma demoiselle* = my damsel).

magna cum laude: see *cum laude*.

magnum opus: an author's chief work (L.).

mañana: tomorrow (as symbol of easy-going procrastination); indefinite future (Sp.).

manège: riding-school; horsemanship; movements of trained horse (Fr. f. It. = manage).

manqué: that might have been but which is not (Fr. *manquer* = to fall short of).

matériel: available means, esp. materials and equipment in warfare (Fr.).

mauvais quart d'heure: a short period of time which is embarrassing and unnerving; a brief but unpleasant experience (Fr. = bad quarter of an hour).

mélange: medley (Fr. *mêler* = to mix).

memento mori: a reminder of death, like a skull (L. = remember that you have to die).

mésalliance: a marriage with a person of inferior social position.

métier: one's trade, profession, or field of activity; one's forte (Fr.).

mezzo: half, moderately (It.).

modus operandi: a plan of working (L.).

modus vivendi: a way of living, a temporary compromise (L.).

mot: witty saying (Fr.).

mot juste: exactly appropriate expression (Fr.).

mutatis mutandis: with due alteration of details (in comparing cases) (L.).

ne plus ultra: furthest attainable point; acme, perfection (L. = not further beyond).

nil desperandum: despair of nothing, *not* never despair (L.).

noblesse oblige: privilege entails responsibility (Fr.).

noli me tangere: don't touch me (L.).

nom de guerre: assumed name (Fr.).

nom de plume: pseudonym (not in Fr. usage).

non plus ultra: perfection (L.).

non sequitur: conclusion that does not follow logically from the premisses (L.).

nouveau riche: one who has recently acquired (usu. ostentatious) wealth (Fr. = new rich).

nouvelle vague: new wave (Fr.).

nuit blanche: sleepless night (Fr. = white night).

obiter dictum: something said as an aside (L.).

objet d'art: small decorative object (Fr. = object of art).

œuvre: work, esp. writer's or artist's work taken as a whole (Fr.).

olla podrida: a mixture, mishmash (Sp. = a putrid pot).

pace: with due respect to (one holding a different view) (L.).

par excellence: above all others that may be so called (Fr.).

pari passu: at the same rate (L.).

parti pris: foregone conclusion, prejudice (Fr.).

pas: step in dancing; *pas de deux* is dance for two persons (Fr. = step).

passé: behind the times; past the prime (Fr.).

passim: throughout, at several points in, book or article etc. (L.).

penchant: inclination or liking for (Fr.).

per annum: for each year (L.).

per caput: (also *per capita*) for each person (L.).

perpetuum mobile: something never at rest (L.).

per se: by or in itself, intrinsically (L.).

persona (non) grata: person (not) acceptable to certain others (L.).

petit bourgeois: member of lower middle classes (Fr.).

petit mal: mild form of epilepsy (Fr. = small sickness).

petit point: embroidery on canvas using small stitches (Fr.).

pièce de résistance: the most important or remarkable item; main dish at meal (Fr.).

pied-à-terre: an occasional residence (Fr.).

pis aller: a second best (Fr.).

point d'appui: a base for operations (Fr.).

post hoc: after this (L.).

poste restante: the department in some post offices in which letters for visitors or travellers are kept till applied for (Fr. = letter(s) remaining).

pourboire: gratuity, tip (Fr.).

prima facie: at first sight; (of evidence) based on the first impression (L.).

pro bono publico: for the public good (L.).

pro patria: for one's country (L.).

propter hoc: because of this (L.).

pro rata: in proportion (L.).

pro tem: colloq., for the time being (L. *pro tempore*).

putsch: a revolutionary attempt (Ger.).

qua: in the capacity of (L. = [in the way] in which).

quasi-: prefix with sense 'seeming(ly)', 'almost' (L.).

quid pro quo: thing given as compensation (L. = something for something).

qui vive (on the): on the alert (L.).

raison d'être: purpose or reason that accounts for or justifies or originally caused thing's existence (Fr.).

rapprochement: resumption of harmonious relations esp. between States (Fr.).

rara avis: a phenomenon, prodigy (L. = rare bird).

realpolitik: practical politics (Ger.).

reductio ad absurdum: proof of falsity by showing absurd logical consequence; carrying of principle to unpractical lengths (L. = reduction to the absurd).

Regina: reigning queen (in titles of lawsuits, e.g. *Regina* v. *Jones*) (L. = queen).

rentier: person living on income from property or investments (Fr.).

Rex: reigning king (used as **Regina*) (L. = king).

roman-à-clef: novel about real people under disguised identities (Fr.).

roman-fleuve: sequence of novels about same characters over a period (Fr.).

sang-froid: composure (Fr. = cold blood).

sans pareil: unequalled (Fr.).

sauve qui peut: let him save himself who can (Fr.).

savoir faire: quickness to know and do the right thing, tact (Fr.).

schadenfreude: malicious enjoyment of others' misfortunes (Ger. = damage-joy).

sec: (of wine) dry (Fr.).

semper fidelis: always faithful (L.).

semper idem: always the same (L.).

señor: title used of or to Spanish-speaking man (Sp. f. L. *senior*).

señora: title used of or to Spanish-speaking married woman (Sp.).

señorita: title used of or to Spanish-speaking unmarried woman (Sp.).

sic: thus, so (printed usu. in brackets, as parenthetical comment on quoted words) (L.).

sine die: (of business adjourned indefinitely) with no appointed date (L.).

sine qua non: indispensable condition or qualification (L. = without which not).

soi-disant: self-styled (Fr.).

soigné: carefully finished or arranged, well-groomed (Fr.).

son et lumière: entertainment by night at historic building etc. with recorded sound and lighting effects to give dramatic narrative of its history (Fr. = sound and light).

sotto voce: in an undertone (It.).

status quo: the same state as now (L.).

sub judice: under consideration (L.).

sub rosa: in confidence or secretly (L. = under the rose).

succès d'estime: success with more honour than profit (Fr.).

sui generis: of its own kind, unique (L.).

summa cum laude: see *cum laude*.

summum bonum: chief or supreme good (L.).

table d'hôte: meal at fixed time and price in hotel etc., with less choice of dishes than **à la carte* (Fr. = host's table).

terra incognita: unexplored region (L.).

tour de force: a feat of strength or skill (Fr.).

trompe-l'œil: an illusion, esp. in still-life painting or plaster ornament (Fr.).

ultima Thule: distant unknown region, the end of the world. The ancient Greek and Latin name for a land six days' sail north of Britain.

ultra vires: beyond one's legal power (L.).

vade mecum: handbook etc. carried constantly for use (L. = go with me).

verboten: forbidden (Ger.).

vide: (as instruction in reference to passage in book etc.) see, consult (L. *videre* = to see).

viva voce: oral examination; to examine orally (L.).

vis-à-vis: in relation to; opposite to (Fr.).

vox populi: public opinion, general verdict, popular

belief (L. = the people's voice).

weltanschauung: world-philosophy (Ger.).

weltschmerz: world-sorrow (Ger.).

Zeitgeist: the spirit of the time (Ger.).

WRITTEN FORMS OF ADDRESS

KARL KRAUS, the Viennese satirist, once wrote that 'you should always write as if you were writing for the first and last time, say as much as if you were saying farewell, and say it as well as if it were your début.' Writing good letters should be a matter of personal pride, like dressing well for an evening out or keeping the front garden in good trim. Nowadays, few people write letters as an art form. Business and political negotiations, love affairs, and arrangements for meetings are most often conducted by telephone. That makes it all the more important that people should take trouble over letters. We usually write letters because more direct forms of approach are inappropriate: because we are approaching a stranger or lodging a formal complaint or asking for a favour.

Personal letters are most frequently written to people—relatives, lovers, or old friends—who live (temporarily or permanently) too far away to permit meetings or phone calls. But they may also be written—particularly when we wish to express strong feelings, perhaps after a row—because it is easier to order thoughts and emotions on paper, when we have time to reflect and revise.

In all these cases, the fundamental point about a letter is that it gives the recipient an impression of the writer. Very often, it is a first impression—and a potential employer, for example, may reject a sloppily-written application letter on sight. Often, too, it is the only impression—complaints, for example, are often pursued entirely by correspondence. It is a lasting impression, too—the recipient may well keep your letter for future reference.

Above all, the style of a letter is important because the writer cannot modify the impression created, by using other forms of communication, such as tone of voice, touch, or gesture. Irony, for example, is always a dangerous device in a letter, or any other form of writing. This is because irony depends on the audience understanding that we are not entirely serious. In conversation, we can communicate this by a laugh or a twinkle in the eye—significantly, we use a visual image ('tongue in cheek') as a metaphor for irony. In a letter, on the other hand, none of these devices are available and the reader may well take us literally. Which explains why, when people use irony in writing, they often add something like '(joke!)' or 'seriously, though'.

This is just one instance of the pitfalls involved in writing letters. Nevertheless, the first rule is not to worry too much. Many people are inhibited from writing letters because they fear getting 'the form' wrong. How should the letter start? How should they sign off? Should they address it to 'Mr John Brown' or 'John Brown, Esq.'? Should the address on the envelope be indented or not? Nowadays, most people rarely worry about these details and, in any case, there are differences of opinion in what they consider appropriate. Letter-writing manners have become more informal and easygoing in the same way as other social manners. If people look down on you because you have some piffling formality wrong, their etiquette is wrong, not yours.

The important rules are the following:

1. Modern letters nearly always have a specific function. A letter, therefore, should be written in the way appropriate to that function. Just as you would not write to your mother 'thank you for your letter of the 7th inst., which is receiving attention', so you would not make observations about the weather when writing a business letter to your solicitor.

2. A good letter, like a good story, has a beginning, a middle and an end. You should start by indicating the main point and purpose of the letter. In a job application, start by stating the position you are seeking. If you are making a complaint, start by saying so and explaining what it is you are complaining about. If you are replying to a letter, start with 'Thank you for your letter of 28th June'. You should end by indicating what you expect to happen next. 'I shall be free to attend an interview at any date over the next month, except Friday 15 May.' 'I expect the cost of the goods to be refunded in full.' 'I look forward to seeing you next Wednesday.'

3. Letters, like all other forms of writing, should avoid jargon, repetition, stilted language, and pomposity. Do not use long words where short ones would be just as good. Do not write over-long sentences. Say what you mean, simply and straightforwardly but courteously. Letter-writing has developed a curiously pompous language of its own, used particularly by professional people. 'We beg to acknowledge receipt of your letter of the 7th inst.' for example, is an abomination which should be replaced by 'Thank

you for your letter of 7th June'. 'I await the pleasure of a reply' is often unnecessary. If a letter needs a reply, it should be self-evident. But, if you want to end in this way, 'I look forward to your reply' or 'I look forward to hearing from you' is preferable.

4. Check what you have written before sending a letter. Ensure that you have enclosed anything you say you have enclosed. Above all, ensure that you are putting the right letter in the right envelope. A prominent Fleet Street writer once wrote simultaneously to her editor, giving details of features she intended to write, and to the company chairman, setting out several serious criticisms of the editor. She put the two letters in the wrong envelopes. Her career, naturally, came to an abrupt end.

Writing-paper

Letters should be written on good quality, plain, preferably white, writing-paper. Lines, coloured borders and pictures should always be avoided; folded writing-paper or notelets should be confined to personal correspondence. Business letters should be typed if possible, and may well have printed heads. Personal letters should ideally be handwritten, though this rule is not universally followed nowadays, partly because people so often write in haste, partly because many are aware that their handwriting would be illegible anyway. For business letters, you should *always* keep a copy.

Headings

The sender's address (unless there are printed headings) should be written in the top right-hand corner of the letter. After leaving a space immediately below, you should write the date. Then leave another space before writing the address of the recipient on the opposite side of the sheet:-

36 Blair Avenue,
Orwell,
Lancashire,
OR8 2EJ

4th April 1984

Mr W. Smith,
17, Victory Mansions,
London
SW3 7BD

Children used to be taught in school to indent the sender's address (as above), as well as 'stepping' the address on the envelope. This custom has declined, largely because of the growing use of the electric typewriter. For similar reasons, many modern letter-writers (particularly for business letters) do not indent paragraphs. As a general rule, indentation—in both the address and the text—looks more natural if the letter is handwritten. If you use the alternative 'blocked' style for the address (see below), you should also use it in the letter. It is then essential to leave a line between each paragraph.

The 'blocked' style is also, by some people, combined with 'open punctuation'—which means no punctuation at all—in the two addresses. If punctuation is used, there should be no full stop after the post code (it may confuse the Post Office computers) nor after the date.

The recipient's address, which is always written in the 'blocked' style, is a good example of how letter-writing form depends on the letter's function. Business letters are often typed and sent in batches by clerks or secretaries. At the other end, they may well be opened by a secretary working for several different people. The recipient's address, therefore, is essential to avoid confusion at either end; it is also needed for the sender's copy of a business letter. A personal letter, on the other hand, will not normally be handled by anyone else and the recipient's address can, therefore, be omitted.

A business letter may also include a reference number—yours, theirs, or both—among the headings and this should be written, after leaving a line, below the date. There may also be a heading, referring to the subject of the letter, written after the opening greeting and underlined:

36 Blair Avenue
Orwell,
Lancashire,
OR8 2EJ

4th April 1984

Your ref. E/345/WS

W. Smith, Esq.
Records Department,
Ministry of Truth,
Whitehall,
London
SW1 5AA

Dear Mr Smith,

Newsspeak Dictionary

Beginning a letter

Nearly all letters nowadays begin with 'Dear'. The peremptory 'Sir' or 'Madam' is used only as a formal mode of address to a complete stranger whom you never expect to meet or even to identify by name. Most often, you are addressing such a letter to a position rather than to its individual incumbent, and there is little expectation that the individual will even read the letter. Examples include letters for publication addressed to newspaper editors (which are, in fact, handled by a separate letters editor) and letters to government ministers.

At the other extreme, 'my dear', 'my dearest', 'my darling', and so on are only for the most intimate letters. Older people may still use the first, even for friends of the same sex, but, except between lovers, these forms are now likely to cause embarrassment.

The main problem is what follows the 'Dear'. You can best tackle this by following two simple rules. First, address people as you think they would wish to be addressed. Second, the formality of the address should reflect the extent and nature of your acquaintance—or, put more simply, start writing to the recipient as you would start speaking to him. Thus:

1. 'Dear Sir' is usual for formal business letters, particularly when you have never met the recipient or had any previous correspondence. Unless you are absolutely certain of the sex of the recipient, it is now essential to write 'Dear Sir or Madam' or 'Dear Sir/Madam'. If a letter is addressed to a company—Messrs Smith and Brown, say—you may begin 'Dear Sirs'.

2. 'Dear Mr Smith' is used when you have had, at least, some correspondence. If you would call him 'Mr Smith' when you met him, call him 'Mr Smith' in your letter.

3. 'Dear Winston'. The same rule. If you know Smith well enough to call him 'Winston' in conversation, use the same form of address here, even if it is a business letter.

4. 'Dear Miss/Mrs/Ms Brown'. This problem is often exaggerated. It is really quite simple. Address her as she wants to be addressed. If there is no previous correspondence or acquaintance (and you

could not be expected to know her marital status), 'Dear Madam' (*not* Madame, which has a quite different meaning in English). If you have previous correspondence, how does she sign herself? 'Jane Brown (Mrs)' clearly wishes to be addressed as 'Dear Mrs Brown'. 'Jane Brown' may be called 'Ms Brown' without hesitation. If she is old-fashioned enough to dislike this innovation, she should have added '(Mrs)' or '(Miss)' in order to avoid it.

5. 'Dear Winston Smith' or 'Dear Jane Brown'. This form is an American import. Though it is now widely accepted, it does not have much to commend it. It often signifies indecision between 'Dear Mr Smith' and 'Dear Winston' or between 'Dear Mrs Brown' and 'Dear Ms Brown' and, therefore, creates a bad impression. Since you would not normally address someone as 'Winston Smith' in speech—except in a roll-call—there is no real justification for doing so in writing. It can be useful, though, where there is genuine uncertainty about the recipient's sex—Alex Jones, for example, could be Alexander Jones or Alexandra Jones.

6. 'Dear Smith'. This form is virtually obsolete and best avoided. The surname only used to be a form of address between close male friends. More often, it was used for familiar male subordinates, such as pupils, employees or tenants. This latter form is still sometimes used by the over-60s and, if you receive a letter beginning in this way, *your* reply should begin 'Dear Mr —'. From anyone younger, 'Dear Smith' would probably cause offence but, again, it is acceptable if that is how you address Smith in speech.

Closing a letter

The forms here are less important than they used to be and, since first impressions count more than last, less important than the beginning of a letter.

The general rules are that where you begin 'Dear Sir' or 'Dear Madam', you should end 'yours faithfully'. Where you begin 'Dear Mr Smith' or 'Dear Mrs Brown', you should end 'yours sincerely'. 'Yours truly', 'yours affectionately', 'yours respectfully' have generally fallen into disuse. Where a business letter begins 'Dear Winston', 'yours sincerely' is an adequate conclusion.

'Best wishes' is now commonly used for personal letters with 'yours ever' reserved for fairly close friends. 'Love', of course, is traditionally for lovers and relatives but is now used in almost any personal letter to a member of the opposite sex or between women friends. A more exclusive affection is therefore signified by 'all my love'. 'Yours fraternally' was once widely used in correspondence between trade union members but, in these equality-conscious days, is best avoided.

The envelope

The address on the envelope—like the sender's address on the letter—can be indented or blocked. The important thing is to address it clearly and legibly, including the post code, and writing or typing the town in capitals. Some addresses include two place-names—Danbury, Chelmsford, for example. In these cases, the second name is the main post town, to which post is sent, and this should be in capitals.

The address should always start half-way down the envelope (otherwise it may be obscured by the postmark) as well as towards the middle.

The main problem on the envelope—and on the address inside the letter—is the name of the recipient. There are three simple rules:

1. A man may be addressed as Mr W. Smith or as W. Smith, Esq. but *not* 'Mr W. Smith, Esq.'. 'Esq.' is more formal and more often used when the letter begins 'Dear Sir'. If in doubt, use 'Esq.' since some sheltered traditionalists still find the 'Mr' rudely familiar. If you do not know the initials, however, write 'Mr Smith' not 'Smith Esq.'

2. Most married women now prefer to use their own initials or Christian names (Mrs June Simpson), though some use their husband's (Mrs Peter Simpson). A widow or divorcee should always be addressed by her own initials.

3. Unmarried women, no matter how young, have always been 'Miss Brown'. Boys are traditionally 'Master Peter Smith', but the age at which this is acceptable has fallen in recent years. Any boy in his teens now considers himself grown-up, so is best dubbed 'Mr Peter Smith'. 'Peter Smith, Esq.' sounds a false note for anyone under 18.

Envelopes are sometimes marked 'personal', 'confidential', 'private', or a combination of these. 'Personal' is normally used when a personal letter, about personal matters, is sent to the recipient's place of work. 'Private and confidential' suggests a business letter of a sensitive nature, and should be used sparingly. Very often, it excites interest from office colleagues, where none previously existed.

Formal business letters are sometimes addressed to a company but 'for the attention of Mr John Smith' is put above the address and underlined. This is acceptable practice, where your main relationship is with the company, not with the individual. John Smith just happens to be dealing with your affairs at the moment but they could be passed to someone else.

Use of titles

Since the titles of peers, baronets, knights, and members of the Royal Family are governed by somewhat complex rules, it is best to consult a current reference book, such as *Debrett*, before addressing envelopes to these people. You should not, in any case, write directly to the Queen, the Duke of Edinburgh, or the Queen Mother. All correspondence (unless you are a personal friend) should be addressed to their private secretaries.

The rules for opening a letter are similar to those for the untitled: use a formal style for a first approach, a more informal style once a relationship has been established.

Members of the Royal Family should be addressed formally as 'Sir' or 'Madam', more informally as 'Your Royal Highness'. Dukes are formally 'My Lord Duke', while other peers are 'My Lord'. Once acquainted, you can begin simply with 'Dear Duke of Wigan' (or 'Dear Duke') or, for other peers (such as a Marquess of Wigan), 'Dear Lord Wigan'.

The title itself is the guide to how the letter begins. The Earl of Cromer, the Marchioness of Cromer, the Viscount Cromer, the Lord Cromer, the Lady Cromer (wife of a baron or life peer), and Lady Cromer (wife of a baronet or knight), are all addressed as 'Dear Lord Cromer' or 'Dear Lady Cromer'. 'Lord Hugh Cromer' or 'Lady Sarah Cromer' (the children of peers) are addressed as 'Dear Lord Hugh' or 'Dear Lady Sarah'.

Those children of peers who bear the title 'The Hon.' (short for The Honourable) should be addressed as 'Dear Mr Ash', 'Dear Mrs Ash', or 'Dear Miss Ash', though the envelope will carry 'The Hon. Philip Ash', 'The Hon. Philippa Ash', or, in the case of Ash's wife, 'The Hon. Mrs Philip Ash'.

Knights and baronets—Sir William Evans or Sir James Evans, Bt.—are addressed as 'Dear Sir William' or 'Dear Sir James'. On the envelope a baronet and his wife are formally 'Sir James Evans,

Bt., and Lady Evans', but informally 'Sir James and Lady Evans' is enough.

Churchmen

In the Church of England, you should write to:

The Most Reverend and Rt. Hon. the Lord Archbishop of —
The Right Reverend and Rt. Hon. the Lord Bishop of London
The Right Reverend the Lord Bishop of —
(all except London)
The Very Reverend the Dean (or the Provost) of —
The Venerable the Archdeacon of —
The Reverend Canon David Wilson

You should then write to 'Dear Archbishop', 'Dear Bishop', and so on. Envelopes to vicars and rectors should be addressed to 'The Revd Patrick Johnson', but letters should start 'Dear Mr Johnson'. Wives — even archbishops' wives — have no titles and should be addressed as other wives are. For example, 'Dear Mrs Runcie', *not* 'Dear Mrs Canterbury', still less 'Dear Mrs Archbishop'.

In the Roman Catholic Church, you should write to:

His Eminence the Cardinal Archbishop of —
His Eminence Cardinal Jones

Either should be addressed as 'My Lord Cardinal' or 'Your Eminence'. His Grace the Archbishop of Neasden is addressed as 'Your Grace' or, if you happen to know his own surname, 'Dear Archbishop McDonald'. The Right Reverend Richard Price, Bishop of Surbiton is addressed as 'My Lord Bishop' or 'Dear Bishop Price'. The Reverend Monsignor George Lamont is addressed as 'Dear Monsignor Lamont'. Letters to other priests should, as in the Church of England, be addressed to 'The Revd William O'Donnell', but letters should begin 'Dear Father O'Donnell'.

Armed services

In all three services, the rule is to address the higher ranks by their military titles—'Dear Admiral Watson' or 'Dear General Bates'; 'Dear Admiral' or 'Dear General' is rather more informal. However, if Watson or Bates have other titles, these take precedence. 'Admiral Sir Rodney Watson' on the envelope becomes 'Dear Sir Rodney'.

The lowest ranks — Naval sub-lieutenants and below, RAF flying and pilot officers, and Army lieutenants and below — are 'Dear Mr

Jones'. 'RN' may be added after the names of all ranks below Rear-Admiral in the Royal Navy, 'RM' for Lt.-Col. and below in the Royal Marines. This has the simple practical point of distinguishing similarly-titled officers in the different services.

Government and Parliament

In ordinary social life, members of the government are addressed by their own names. In their official capacities, they are often addressed, particularly by their civil servants, as 'Secretary of State'. This practice is reflected in letters. An official letter to the Chancellor of the Exchequer is addressed to 'The Chancellor of the Exchequer' and the incumbent's name is used only if the letter is personal. Official letters should begin 'Sir' or 'Dear Sir' if you do not know the recipient, 'Dear Chancellor of the Exchequer' if you do know him.

Mayors' titles depend on the city. Some are 'The Rt. Hon. the Lord Mayor of —'; others 'The Rt. Worshipful Lord Mayor of —'; others again are 'The Rt. Worshipful Mayor of —'. All mayors of towns are 'The Worshipful Mayor of —'. Letters should begin 'Dear Lord Mayor' or 'Dear Mr Mayor' depending on the title.

Councillors and Aldermen are called 'Councillor Jones' or 'Alderman Jones'. But John Jones, Member of Parliament becomes 'John Jones, MP' on the envelope and 'Dear Mr Jones' in the letter.

Some ministers and ex-ministers are also privy counsellors, entitling them to 'Rt. Hon.' before their names, and 'PC' after them. Envelopes should be addressed to 'The Rt. Hon. Edward Heath, PC, MP' but letters should begin 'Dear Mr Heath'.

Doctors and Academics

Medical doctors who carry the initials 'MD' after their names should be addressed as 'Dear Dr —'. Surgeons, however, who carry the initials 'MS' are addressed as 'Dear Mr —', as are dentists.

A Ph.D. (doctor of philosophy) may also be addressed as 'Dear Dr —', particularly if he is working in a university or other academic institution. This form, however, is not normally used for those who have honorary degrees, such as Doctor of Letters.

Professors (including Emeritus and Regius Professors) are normally addressed as 'Dear Professor —'

Initials after the name

The extent to which you worry about including these on envelopes depends on the individual to whom you are writing, on the field in which he works, and on the extent to which your letter concerns his work. Honours awarded by the Crown — OBE, MBE, etc. — should always be added, at least in formal style: 'Stuart Fisher, Esq., MBE', for example. So should military decorations. Otherwise, the initials are strictly necessary only where the holder is working in a field relevant to his qualifications or awards, and where you are writing to him in that official or professional capacity.

To take the most common example, BA (Bachelor of Arts) is rarely used by, say, a chartered accountant. He or she would prefer FICA (Fellow of the Institute of Chartered Accountants). Those teaching or lecturing in schools, universities, or polytechnics, on the other hand, would use BA.

Invitations

Suppose that Susan, now married to John Bowden, is an old friend of yours whom you have not met for some time, and you would like to invite her to dinner. Here are two examples of how you might write.

Letter A

Dear Susie,

I saw Jane Sykes the other day and she made me think of you. Do you remember what a marvellous time we used to have together at college? Jane is married to a man called Brian now.

It would be lovely to see you again and nice if you could pop over for a bite two weeks on Wednesday evening. Isn't the weather awful?

Letter B

Dear Susie,

Peter and I would be very pleased if you and John could come to dinner on Wednesday 23rd July (7.30 p.m.).

It is so long since we've seen you and I thought of you the other day when I met our old college friend, Jane Sykes. I have invited Jane and her husband, Brian, on the same date and I am looking forward to recalling the marvellous times we used to have together. I am also hoping that Graham and Celia Harris—Graham teaches at the school where I work—will be able to come.

I do hope you can make it. Please let me know.

Letter B is, of course, greatly superior. It comes straight to the point and has an informative, business-like tone, without being over-formal or stilted. Letter A has a rambling opening, which disguises the main purpose of the letter.

It is not clear what Susie is being invited to (is 'a bite' a full meal or a few cheese sandwiches?). No precise date is given, nor any time. Susie is left without any indication as to whether her husband is invited too or, indeed, as to whether you are aware that she has a husband at all. Nor can she be certain that you are married. (In an age when marriages break up with alarming frequency, it is essential to give the full picture.)

Another weakness of letter A is that it does not indicate the size of the dinner party. The opening reference to 'Jane Sykes' suggests that she and Brian may be invited, too, but it is far from clear. Guests are entitled to some idea of what to expect, if only so that they can dress appropriately. The second letter gives just the right amount of detail. It is a small, fairly intimate dinner party, but not all those present will be old college friends. Susie is told just enough about Graham to understand his relationship to you; she does not need a life-history.

Finally, letter A ends with a complete irrelevance. Since the whole invitation is so vague, it is not absolutely clear that Susie is expected to reply. Letter B ends, as a letter should, by indicating what further action is expected.

So how should Susie, assuming that you send her letter B, reply? This time, the two examples are both adequate—one is a refusal, the other an acceptance.

Dear Pat,

Thank you so much for inviting us to dinner on the 23rd. Alas, we cannot make it. We had already accepted an invitation from John's boss for dinner that evening and, of course, we cannot possibly refuse now.

I hope you have a lovely evening. It is such a shame because I would have loved to have talked to you and Jane again, and was thinking of you both only yesterday. Perhaps we can arrange another date soon, at our house. Do give my love to Jane, and my best wishes to Peter.

Dear Pat,
It was lovely to hear from you again. Of course John and I will be delighted to come to dinner on Wednesday 23rd.
I am so looking forward to seeing you and Peter and it will be marvellous to see Jane again after all these years.

Both these letters are clear, polite and to the point. The date of the dinner is repeated lest there should be any fear of a mix-up; but not the time, which would make the response sound too formal. Susie expresses appropriate enthusiasm both for Pat and for Jane. In the first letter, she explains why she cannot accept the invitation. She also expresses genuine regret without saying 'we would much rather have dinner with you than with these boring people', which is both unnecessary and (because Pat or Peter may know John's boss) dangerous. Finally, she indicates a wish for future contact, without any definite commitment. Note that the first letter should be a little longer than the second; refusals, no matter how good the reasons, should not seem curt.

Thank-you Letters

The function of these is very simple. It is to express your appreciation of a present, dinner, or party and, possibly, to reassure the recipient on some point—that the present arrived safely, for example, or that you did not drive the car into a lamp-post on the way home.

So the formula is simple:-

Dear Frank and Susie,
Many thanks for a wonderful evening. Lively company and good food—what more could we want! You must let me have the recipe for that soufflé.
I am glad to report that Raymond's driving was above reproach after the black coffee. Hope to see you both again very soon.

Nothing more than that is necessary. It is wise to include a small detail (such as the soufflé) to show that something about the evening has stuck in your mind and was specially appreciated. But praising the merits of each dish in turn would be excessive, and might well seem insincere.

The rules are similar when thanking people for presents:

Dear Uncle George,
Thank you so much for the bed-linen you sent us as a

wedding present. Claire and I both think that it matches the bedroom curtains perfectly.

We were sorry that you couldn't make it to the wedding. We missed you very much, though we understand that the journey would have been too long. Let's hope we can see you at Christmas.

Again, the one simple comment about the present is perfectly adequate.

Bereavement

These are among the most difficult letters to write. Here is one example:

Dear Aunt Betty,

How terrible to hear that Uncle Freddie dropped down dead in the street. It must have been an awful shock to you to see him lying there. The same thing happened to Uncle Bill, and Aunt Sarah's nerves have been terrible ever since. Of course, it was worse for her because he was much younger.

I believe it was a heart attack and I suppose it was because he smoked so much. It should be a comfort to you that it was sudden and that he didn't go into a slow decline with that awful bronchitis of his. Anyway, you did your best for him. You musn't blame yourself for what happened; you just can't stop some people smoking.

I shall be arriving the day after tomorrow to help you sort out Uncle Freddie's things, which is always a pretty morbid job. I don't know how you will be able to manage on your own, now that he has gone, but we shall all do our best to rally round.

This letter could well be written with genuine sympathy but, of course, almost every word is hopelessly ill-chosen. The bereaved do not want you to dwell on the circumstances and causes of the death; they do not want to be reminded of others 'in the same boat' perhaps worse off; they are not comforted by suggestions that death is 'a blessing in disguise'.

It is doubtful that Aunt Betty would think of blaming herself unless you put the idea into her head. She may well be worried about the future, but does not need your apparent lack of confidence in her. Above all, the bereaved do not want people to descend on them, uninvited, to take over their affairs as if they had been rendered instantly helpless.

A good letter of condolence includes a restrained expression of genuine sympathy; a detail showing that you value the deceased's memory (in contrast to the above writer who conveys the image of a wheezy nicotine addict); and, if appropriate, an *offer* of practical help, which you must able to deliver gladly if it is taken up:

Dear Aunt Betty,

I was so sorry to hear of Uncle Freddie's death. It must have been a shock to you, particularly as it was so sudden. I remember him with great affection and especially for all the patient help he gave me in learning to play tennis.

Please don't hesitate to let me know of anything I can do to help. I can easily hop on a train and be with you in a couple of hours. In the meantime, try and keep your chin up—we are all thinking of you here.

The strength of this letter is in the third sentence. It recalls Uncle Freddie when he was very much alive, not the circumstances and causes of his death. Comments about the after-life are sometimes included in letters of condolence ('he is now in a better place where you can now look forward to joining him') but, even for the religious, these are unlikely to be of much help.

Replies to letters of condolence are much easier to write. Ideally, they should include some personal touch—perhaps a comment on the deceased's affection for the writer. They may also include some brief indication of how you have been affected by the death. But, in the circumstances, most people will understand if the note is short:

Dear Mr Grant,

Thank you very much for your kind thoughts and words on the death of my husband. It gives me great comfort to know that you and others thought so highly of Freddie. I know that he greatly admired your contribution to the tennis club over so many years.

It was a great shock to me, because, as you know, we were very close, but I am slowly beginning to adjust to life without him.

The first two sentences are perfectly acceptable on their own; but the addition of the last two makes it a far better letter.

Job Applications

These are among the most important letters you will ever write. Personnel officers, particularly of big companies, may receive thousands of letters a year. Since they cannot possibly interview all the applicants, they are going to use letters, c.v.s, references, and qualifications—the written material that you provide—to sift out the most promising cases.

The important factual information about yourself and your education should be in a curriculum vitae (c.v.) which you should type or have typed for you. Here is an example taken from the *Sunday Times Good Careers Guide* by Peter Wilby (Granada, 1985):

Name Sarah Wonderful (Miss)

Home Address 20 Any Road, Sometown, Hereshire HR2 3ZZ
Phone 007–12345
College Address Egghead Hall, Eggtown, Thereshire EG7 2DR
Phone 321–99199
Nationality British
Date of Birth 18/4/62

EDUCATION

Secondary Sometown High School 1973–1980
University Egghead Hall, Thereshire University 1980–1984
Academic qualifications:
O levels English Language, French, History, Maths, Physics
A levels French (B), Maths (E), Physics (A)
BA Hons Degree French (2:2)

EMPLOYMENT

Summer 1983	Hereshire Bookstore	Sales Assistant
Summer 1982	French Sunnytours	Tour Courier
Winter 1981	Hereshire Bakery	Sales Assistant

ADDITIONAL INFORMATION

Typing: 30 wpm   Current Driving Licence

OTHER INTERESTS

Acting, Netball (University 2nd team), President of Egghead Hall Young Liberals, Voluntary work at Hereshire Hospital.

Note that the information should be precise and detailed, with dates. The employer will want to know your degree subject, not just that you studied at Egghead Hall. He will want to know what you did during your vacation employment, not just the name of the employer. He will value not just your academic qualifications, but your ability to drive and type. You should keep several copies of a c.v., so that you can use it whenever you apply for a job.

The covering letter need not be typed; in fact, a neatly-written letter is better than a badly-typed one. The other rules are:

1. The letter should start by stating the position for which you are applying. If you are responding to an advertisement, say where it appeared.

2. It should repeat the most recent points from the c.v.

3. It should give some idea of why you want to work for that particular organization in that particular job and indicate any reasons why you think you are particularly suited to the work.

4. It should give some indication of when you are available for interview and when you could start work.

5. Give the names, addresses and positions of referees. (You may not want to include them in the c.v., lest you decide to nominate different referees for different jobs.) You should ask the referees' permission in advance.

6. Avoid excessive detail. At this stage, the personnel manager will not want to read all the details of what you did in your vacation jobs or how you played the tragic heroine in the annual university play. If you put too much in the letter, you will, in any case, have nothing left to talk about at the interview.

7. Avoid pomposity, the commonest fault in application letters. You did not 'obtain a post as sales assistant for Hereshire Bookstore'. You 'worked as a sales assistant'. You do not 'beg to submit my application for the position advertised in the Sunday Recorder'. You are replying to an advertisement.

Here is an appropriate example:

Dear Mr Thompson,

I am replying to your advertisement in the Sunday Recorder for management trainees.

I have just graduated from Egghead Hall, Thereshire University, with an honours degree in French and am keen to start a career in retail management. Vacation employment in the retail trade has stimulated my interest and given me some background knowledge of what is involved. I am anxious to join a company that offers a varied, broadly-based training and good promotion opportunities for graduates.

I enclose a copy of my c.v. Mr Tom Brain, my French tutor, at Egghead Hall, Eggtown, Thereshire EG7 2DR will provide one reference. Mrs Jane Good, Director, French Sunnytours, Brittany Road, Sometown, Hereshire SO6 3ES will provide another.

I can attend an interview at any time during the next month, and will be available to start work from 1st September.

The important paragraph is the second one. This suggests that you are interested specifically in retailing (not in any kind of management training scheme), directs the recruiter's attention to an important part of your c.v., and gives a positive reason for joining this particular company.

Complaints

Complaints should be precise, business-like, and restrained. Here is one example of a letter to a firm's head office:

Dear Sir,

I have just bought a haversack from one of your shops and it is absolutely useless. It is a typical example of shoddy British workmanship; no wonder foreigners won't buy our goods. I will certainly never buy anything from you again. I want my money back now.

This letter does make it clear that the writer is angry. Otherwise, it raises as many questions as it answers. What kind of haversack? Bought from which shop? When? What exactly has gone wrong? How much did the writer pay? And why, in any case, has he not returned it to the shop?

Here is an improved example:

Dear Sir,

I am writing to complain about a 'Happy Wanderer' haversack which I bought from your store in Ripon High Street while on holiday last week. I regret to tell you that the stitching has already come away on one of the straps. As you can imagine, this makes it impossible to use.

I would be grateful if you could advise me on what to do now with a view to a refund of the purchase price, which was £25·95, or an exchange of the faulty article. Living in Brighton, it is, of course, impossible for me to return the article to Ripon. However, perhaps you can advise me if you have a local branch, where I could exchange it. I do have a receipt.

This letter contains all the necessary details and is far more likely to get satisfaction, not because it is more polite, but because it shows that the writer has some idea of what he is about.

So the rules for making complaints are:

1. Start by saying it is a complaint. If you use the word 'complaint' in the first sentence, the letter should get immediately to the right person.

2. State exactly what article you are complaining about, where you bought it and when.

3. State exactly what is wrong with it, and the extent to which, in your view, this affects the use and value of the article.

4. State any previous action taken over the complaint. (Have you taken the article back to the shop?)

5. Explain what action you want the manufacturer/retailer to take. (A free repair? New goods? Full refund? Partial refund?)

6. State what proof of purchase you have, if any.

Conclusion

Above, we have looked at just a few examples of occasions when people write letters. There are, of course, many others. But the basic principles are the same in all cases. Think first of all of *why* you are writing the letter. Think of the recipient. What do you want him or her to feel or do as a result of the letter? What kind of impression do you want to give?

There is no reason why you shouldn't write a plan or rough draft of an important letter, just as you would of a long university essay or an important paper at work. You can put down three headings in a plan. First, the purpose of the letter. (The beginning.) Second, the essential information or feelings you want to convey to the recipient. (The middle.) Third, what you expect to happen next. (The end.)

What you put under these headings will depend largely on whether the letter is a business or social letter. A business letter may well start with a reference number; but a social letter, unless it is simply written between friends or lovers, to keep abreast of news or to express continuing affection, should state immediately what purpose, if any, it has. In a business letter, the middle will mainly comprise information (about why you want an overdraft, about the extent to which your financial circumstances will support a mortgage, about why you are resigning your job or your club membership). In a social letter, it will attempt to convey thanks, feelings, or sympathy which are best shown, not by generalities, but by the single *personal* detail (what you particularly remembered about a party, or a weekend, for which you are thanking the hostess) which distinguishes it from a business letter.

Finally, the end of a business letter should be specific (you want the overdraft quickly, you can see the building society manager any weekday lunchtime). The end of a social letter may be more vague—an expression of a wish to continue social contact, for example. But, if your letter does require a specific response, make sure you invite that response (like the traditional RSVP on invitations) right at the very end and do not bury it in the middle, where it could be forgotten.

When you have written a letter, read it again. And, as well as correcting the grammar and spelling, put yourself, for a moment, in the recipient's position. How would you feel if *you* got this letter, what would *you* think about the writer?

There are those who argue that it is impossible to set rules for letters, that letters and other forms of writing should be spontaneous. And it is true that nobody should be unnecessarily constrained by conventions. But many of the rules explained in this section are designed to assist efficient communication, which is the prime purpose of a letter, and to ensure good manners, without which a letter (and its writer) may be consigned to the dustbin for ever.

At the other extreme, there are those who have turned their backs on letter-writing entirely, using commercially-printed cards for everything from condolences to congratulations. This removes all spontaneity and individuality, leaving our personal and social sentiments as packaged as supermarket vegetables or television soap-operas.

Letters should be written with consideration for other people. To do that, you must keep the individual recipient in mind, as well as observing the normal social conventions. In that sense, writing letters is no different from any other form of social behaviour.

WORDS COMMONLY MISSPELT

THE list below contains words (i) which occasion difficulty in spelling; (ii) of which various spellings exist; or (iii) which need to be distinguished from other words spelt similarly. In each case the recommended form is given, and in some cases, for the sake of clarity, is followed by the rejected variant. Where the rejected variant is widely separated in alphabetical position from the recommended form, the former has been given an entry preceded by the mark • and followed by 'use' and the recommended form. The wording added to some entries constitutes a guide to the sense, not an exhaustive definition or description.

abetter
abettor (in law)
absorptive • not *absorbative*
accepter
acceptor (in law and science)
accessory
accommodation
adaptation • not *adaption*
adapter
adaptor (in electricity)
administer • not *administrate*
adviser
• *aerie*: use *eyrie*
affront
ageing
agriculturist
ait • not *eyot*
algorithm • not *algorism*
align, *alignment* • not *aline*, *alinement*
alleluia
almanac (*almanack* only in some titles)
aluminium • Amer. *aluminum*
ambiance (term in art)
ambidextrous
ambience surroundings
amok • not *amuck*
ampere
ancillary • not *ancilliary*
annex (verb)
annexe (noun)
any one (of a number)
anyone anybody
any time
any way any manner
anyway at all events
apophthegm • Amer. *apothegm*
apostasy
archaeology
arcing
artefact

assimilable • not *assimilatable*
aubrietia
aught anything
autarchy despotism
autarky self-sufficiency
auxiliary
ay yes (plural *the ayes have it*)
aye always
babu • not *baboo*
bachelor
bail out obtain release, relieve financially
bale out parachute from aircraft
balk (verb)
balmy like balm
barbecue
barmy (informal) mad
baulk timber
bayoneted, *-ing*
behove • Amer. *behoove*
biased, *biasing*
bivouac (noun and verb) *bivouacked*, *bivouacking*
blond (of man or his hair)
blonde (of woman or her hair)
bluish
bogey (golf)
bogie wheels
bogy apparition
born: *be born* (of child)
borne: *have borne* have carried or given birth to; *be borne* be carried; *be borne by* be carried by or given birth to by (a mother)
brand-new
brier • not *briar*
bur clinging seed
burr rough edge, drill, rock, accent, etc.
cabbala, *cabbalistic*
caftan
calendar almanac
calender press
caliph
calligraphy
calliper leg support; (plural) compasses • not *caliper*
callous (adjective)
callus (noun)
camellia shrub
canvas (noun) cloth
canvas (verb) cover with canvas (past *canvased*)
canvass (verb) (past *canvassed*)
caravanner, *caravanning*
carcass
caviare
censer vessel
censor official
centigram
centred, *centring*
chameleon
chancellor
chaperon
Charollais
cheque (bank)
chequer (noun) pattern, (verb) variegate; • Amer. *checker*
chilli pepper
choosy
chord combination of notes, line joining points on curve
chukka boot
chukker (polo)
clarinettist • Amer. *clarinetist*
coco palm

cocoa chocolate
coconut
colander strainer
commit(ment)
comparative
complement make complete, that which makes complete
compliment praise
computer
conjuror
connection
conqueror
conscientious
consensus
conterminous
contractual • not *contractural*
contribuent
convection
convector
convener
copier
cord string, flex, spinal *cord*, rib of cloth
cornelian • not *carnelian*
corslet armour, underwear
cosy • Amer. *cozy*
council assembly
councillor member of council
counsel advice, barrister
counsellor adviser
court martial (noun)
court-martial (verb)
crape black fabric
crêpe crape fabric other than black; rubber; pancake
crevasse large fissure in ice
crevice small fissure
crosier
crumby covered in crumbs
crummy (informal) dirty, inferior
curb restrain, restraint
curtsy
• *czar*: use *tsar*
dare say • not *daresay*
database
debonair
deflexion
dependant (noun)
dependent (adjective)
depositary (person)
depository (place)
descendant
desiccated
• *despatch*: use *dispatch*
deterrable
dextrously
devest (only Law: gen. use *divest*)
didicoi (tinker)
dike
dilatation (medical)
dilator
dinghy boat
dingy grimy
disc • Amer. *disk*
discomfited
discreet judicious
discrete separate
disk (sometimes in computing) • Amer. in all senses of *disc*
dispatch
dissect
dissociate • not *disassociate*
disyllable
divest
doily
douse quench
dowse use divining rod
draft (noun) military party, money order, rough sketch (verb) sketch • Amer. in all senses of *draught*

draftsman one who drafts documents
draught act of drawing, take of fish, act of drinking, vessel's depth, current of air • Amer. *draft*
draughtsman one who makes drawings, plans, etc.; piece in game of draughts
drier drying machine
duffel
duress
dyeing (cloth)
ecology
ecstasy
ecumenical
educationist • not *educationalist*
effrontery
• *eikon*: use *icon*
eirenicon • not *irenicon*
embarrassment
embed
employee (masculine and feminine; no accent)
enclose
enclosure (but *Inclosure Acts*)
encroach
encrust
encyclopaedia
endorse
enquire ask
enquiry question
enrol
ensure make sure
entomology study of insects
envelop (verb)
envelope (noun)
erector
erupt break out
etymology study of word origins
every one (of a number)
everyone everybody
exalt raise, praise
exult rejoice
• *eyot*: use *ait*
eyrie • not *aerie*
faecal
faeces
fee'd (*a fee'd lawyer*)
feldspar
feldspathic
felloe (of wheel) • not *felly*
ferrule cap on stick
ferule cane
fetid • not *foetid*
fillip
flotation
flu • not *'flu*
flyer
focused, *focusing*
foetal, *foetus* • Amer. and medical *fetal*, *fetus*
fogy
forbade (past tense of *forbid*)
forbear abstain
forebear ancestor
forego precede
foregone (conclusion)
forestall
for ever for always
forever continually
forgather
forgo go without
formatted, *formatting*
forty
fount (type) • Amer. *font*
Francophile
fulfil
fullness
fungous (adjective)
fungus (noun)
furore • Amer. *furor*

fusilier
fusillade
gaol (official use) • Amer. *jail* (both forms found in Brit. literary use)
gaoler (as for *gaol*)
gauge measure
gazump • not *gazoomph*, etc.
genuflexion
gibe jeer
gild make gold
• *gild* association: use *guild*
gluing
glycerine
gorilla
gormandize eat greedily
gormless
gourmand glutton
gram
grammar
gramophone
grandad
granddaughter
granter
grantor (in law)
grayling (fish, butterfly)
grey • Amer. *gray*
griffin fabulous creature • not *gryphon*
griffon vulture, dog
grill for cooking
grille grating
grisly terrible
grizzly grey-haired; bear
groin (anatomy; architecture)
grommet • not *grummet*
groyne breakwater
guerrilla
guild association
gybe (nautical) • Amer. *jibe*
gypsy
haema-, *haemo-* (prefix meaning 'blood')
haemorrhage
haemorrhoids
hair-dos • not *hair-do's*
hallelujah
hallo
harass
hark
harum-scarum
haulm stem
hearken
hectarage
hiccup
Hindu
homoeopathy
homogeneous having parts all the same
homogenize make homogeneous
homogenous having common descent
honorific
• *hooping cough*: use *whooping cough*
horsy
horticulturist
humous (adjective)
humus (noun)
hurrah, *hurray* • not *hoorah*, *hooray*
hussy • not *huzzy*
hypocrisy
hypocrite
icon
idiosyncrasy
idyll
ignoramus plural *ignoramuses*
• *imbed*: use *embed*
impinging
impostor
• *inclose*, *inclosure*: use *en-*

incommunicado
incrustation
independent
indispensable
inflexion
inputting
inquire investigate
inquiry official investigation
in so far
insomuch
install
instalment
instil
insure take insurance
inure
investor
irenic
• *irenicon*: use *eirenicon*
irrupt enter violently
its of it
it's it is
jail (see *gaol*)
jailer (see *gaol*)
jalopy
jam pack tightly; conserve
jamb door-post
• *jibe*: use *gibe*, *gybe* • Amer. also = accord with
joust combat • not *just*
judgement (in general use)
judgment (in legal works)
jugful
• *kabbala*: use *cabbala*
• *kaftan*: use *caftan*
kebab
kerb pavement • Amer. *curb*
ketchup
• *khalif*: use *caliph*
kilogram
kilometre
koala
Koran
kowtow
labyrinth
lachrymal of tears
lachrymose tearful
lackey
lacquer
lacrimal (in science)
lacrimate, -ation, -atory (in science)
largess
latish
ledger account book
leger line (in music)
licence (noun)
license (verb)
licensee
lich-gate
lickerish greedy
lightening making light
lightning (accompanying thunder)
limeade
linage number of lines
lineage ancestry
lineament feature
liniment embrocation
Linnaean (but *Linnean Society*)
liquefy
liqueur flavoured alcoholic liquor
liquor
liquorice
litchi Chinese fruit
literate
literature
littérateur
littoral
loadstone
loath(some) (adjectives)
loathe (verb)
lodestar

longevity
longitude • not *longtitude*
lour frown
Mac (prefix) spelling depends on the custom of the one bearing the name, and this must be followed; in alphabetical arrangement, treat as Mac however spelt, *Mac*, *Mc*, *M*^{c}, or *M*‘
mac (informal) mackintosh
mackintosh
maharaja
maharanee
• *Mahomet*: use *Muhammad*
mamma
mandolin
manikin dwarf, anatomical model
manila hemp, paper
manilla African bracelet
mannequin (live) model
manœuvrable • Amer. *maneuverable*
mantel(piece)
mantle cloak
marijuana
marquis
marriage guidance counsellor
marshal (noun and verb)
marten weasel
martial of war (*martial law*)
martin bird
marvellous • Amer. *marvelous*
matins
matt lustreless
medieval • not *mediaeval*
menagerie
mendacity lying
mendicity the state of being a beggar
metaphor
millenary of a thousand; thousandth anniversary
millennium thousand years
millepede
milli- (prefix meaning one-thousandth)
milometer • not *mileometer*
miniature
minuscule • not *miniscule*
mischievous • not *mischievious*
miscible (in science)
missel-thrush
missis (slang) • not *missus*
misspell
mistletoe
mixable
mizen (nautical)
mnemonic
moneyed
moneys
mongoose (plural *mongooses*)
mortgager (in general)
mortgagor (in law)
moustache • Amer. *mustache*
mouth (verb) • not *mouthe*
mucous (adjective)
mucus (noun)
Muhammad
murky
Muslim • not *Moslem*
naïve, *naïvety*
naught nothing
négligé
negligible
nerve-racking • not *-wracking*
net not subject to deduction
neurone
nonet

nonsuch unrivalled person or thing
no one nobody
nought the figure zero
noviciate
numskull
nurseling • Amer. *nursling*
O (interjection) used to form a vocative (*O Caesar*) and when not separated by punctuation from what follows (*O for the wings of a dove*)
occurrence
octet
• *of*: not to be written instead of *have* in such constructions as '*Did you go?*' '*I would* have, *if it hadn't rained.*'
olefin
omelette
on to • not *onto*
orangeade
Orangeism
orang-utan
outcast person cast out
outcaste (India) person with no caste
outputting
ouzel
oyez!
paediatric
palaeo- (prefix = ancient)
palate roof of mouth
palette artist's board
pallet mattress, part of machine, organ valve, platform for loads
pallor
panda animal
pander pimp; to gratify
panellist • Amer. *panelist*
paraffin
parakeet
parallel, *paralleled*, *paralleling*
partisan
pasha
pastel (crayon)
pastille
pavior
pawpaw (fruit) • not *papaw*
pedal (noun) foot lever, (verb) operate pedal
peddle follow occupation of pedlar; trifle
pederast
pedigreed
pedlar vendor of small wares • Amer. *peddler*
peen (verb) strike with pein
peewit
pein of hammer
Pekinese dog
Pekingese inhabitant of Peking
pendant (noun)
pendent (adjective)
peninsula (noun)
peninsular (adjective)
pennant (nautical) piece of rigging, flag
pennon (military) long narrow flag
peony
phone (informal) telephone • not *'phone*
phoney
pi pious
picnicker, *picnicking*
pidgin simplified language
pie jumbled type
piebald

pigeon bird; *not one's pigeon* not one's affair
piggy-back • not *pick-a-back*
pi-jaw
pilaff • not *pilau*, *pilaw*
pilule small pill
pimento • not *pimiento*
plane (informal) aeroplane • not *'plane*
plenitude • not *plentitude*
plimsoll (shoe) not *plimsole*
plough • Amer. *plow*
pommel knob, saddle-bow
poppadam
pore (*over* e.g. a map)
postilion
powwow
practice (noun)
practise (verb)
predacious • not *predaceous*
predominant(ly) • not *predominate(ly)*
premise (verb) to say as introduction
premises (plural noun) foregoing matters, building
premiss (in logic) proposition
primeval
principal chief
principle fundamental truth, moral basis
prise force open
Privy Council
Privy Counsellor
program (in computing) • Amer. in all senses
programme (general)
proletariat
promoter
propellant (noun)
propellent (adjective)
prophecy (noun)
prophesy (verb)
pukka
pummel pound with fists
pupillage
putrefy
putt (in golf)
pygmy
pyjamas • Amer. *pajamas*
quadraphony, *quadraphonic* • not *quadri-* or *quadro-*
quartet
quatercentenary • not *quarter-*
questionnaire
queuing
quintet
rabbet groove in woodwork (also *rebate*)
racket (for ball games) • not *racquet*
rackets game
racoon • not *raccoon*
radical (chemistry)
radicle (botany)
raja • not *rajah*
rarefaction
rarefy
rarity
rattan plant, cane (also *rotan*)
raze • not *rase*
razzmatazz
recce (slang) reconnaissance
recompense
reflection
Renaissance • not *Renascence*
renege • not *renegue*
repairable (of material) able to be repaired
reparable (of loss) able to be made good

reverend (deserving reverence; title of clergy)
reverent (showing reverence)
review survey, reconsideration, report
revue musical entertainment
rhyme • not *rime*
revue musical entertainment
rhyme • not *rime*
rickety
rigor (medical) shivering-fit
rigour severity
Riley (slang: *the life of Riley*)
rill stream
rille (on moon)
rogues' gallery
role (no accent)
roly-poly
Romania
routeing (from the verb *route*)
rule the roost • not *roast*
rumba • not *rhumba*
saccharin (noun)
saccharine (adjective)
salutary beneficial
salutatory welcoming
salvage (of ships)
sanatorium • Amer. *sanitarium*
Sanhedrin
satire literary work
satiric(al) of satire
satyr woodland deity
satyric of Greek drama with satyrs
savannah
scallop • not *scollop*
scallywag • Amer. *scalawag*
sceptic • Amer. *skeptic*
scrimmage tussle • also term in Amer. football
scrummage (Rugby)
sear to scorch, wither(ed)
secrecy
seigneur feudal lord
seigneurial of a seigneur
seigniory lordship
selvage (of cloth)
septet
sere catch of gun-lock; term in ecology
sergeant (military, police)
serjeant (law)
sestet (in a sonnet)
• *sett* (noun): use *set*
settler one who settles
settlor (in law)
sextet (in music, etc.)
Shakespearian
shanty hut, song
sheath (noun)
sheathe (verb)
sheikh
shemozzle rumpus
sherif Muslim leader
sheriff county officer
show • not *shew*
sibyl
sibylline
silvan
silviculture
singeing
Sinhalese
ski'd, skiing
slew turn • not *slue*
smart alec
smiley
smooth (adjective and verb) • not *smoothe*
sobriquet
somersault
some time (*come and see me some time*)

sometime former, formerly
speleology
spirituel (masculine and feminine) having refinement of mind
sprightly • not *spritely*
sprite
spurt
squirearchy
stanch (verb) stop a flow
starey
State (capital S for the political unit)
stationary (adjective) at rest
stationery (noun) paper, etc.
staunch loyal
steadfast
stoep (South Africa) veranda
storey division of building • Amer. *story*
storeyed having storeys
storied celebrated in story
stoup for holy water, etc.
straight without curve
strait narrow
strait-jacket
strait-laced
sty for pigs; swelling on eyelid • not *stye*
subsidiary
subtly • not *subtlely*
sulphur • Amer. *sulfur*
sumac
summons (noun) a command to appear (plural *summonses*)
summons (verb) issue a summons (inflected *summonsed*)
superintendent
supportive
swap • not *swop*
swat hit sharply
swingeing
swot study hard
sycamine, *sycomore* (Biblical trees)
sycamore (member of maple genus)
syllabication • not *syllabification*
synthesist, *synthesize* • not *synthet-*
targeted, *targeting*
tear-gassed, *tear-gassing*
teasel (plant)
teetotalism
teetotaller
tehee (laugh)
tell (archaeology)
template • not *templet*
tenant occupant
tenet principle
tetchy
thank you • not *thankyou*
thank-you letter
thievery
tic contraction of muscles
tick-tack semaphore
timpani drums
tingeing
tiro
titbit • Amer. *tidbit*
titillate excite
titivate smarten up
today
tomorrow
tonight
tonsillar, *tonsillitis*
t'other
toupee
Trades Union Congress
trade union
traipse trudge • not *trapes*

tranquil
tranquillity, *tranquillize*
transferable
tranship(*ment*)
transonic
transsexual
trolley
troop assembly of soldiers
trooper member of troop
troupe company of performers
trouper member of troupe
tsar
turbaned
Turco- (combining form of Turkish)
tympanum ear-drum
tyre • Amer. *tire*
'*un* (informal for *one*)
underlie, *underlying*
unequivocal, *-ally* • not *unequivocable*, *-ably*
unheard-of
valance curtain, drapery
valence (in chemistry)
Vandyke beard, *brown*
veld
vendor
veranda
vermilion
vice tool • Amer. *vise*
villain evil-doer
villein serf
visor • not *vizor*
wagon
waiver forgoing of legal right
warrior
wastable
waver be unsteady
way: *under way* • not *under weigh*
whiskey (Irish and US)
whisky (Scotch)
whitish
Whit Monday, *Sunday*
Whitsunday (Scottish; not a Sunday)
whiz
whooping cough
who's who is
whose of whom
wistaria • not *wisteria*
withhold
woeful • not *woful*
wooed, *woos*
wrath anger
wreath (noun)
wreathe (verb)
wroth angry
yoghurt

CLICHÉS AND MODISH AND INFLATED DICTION

A CLICHÉ is a phrase that has become worn out and emptied of meaning by over-frequent and careless use. Never to use clichés at all would be impossible: they are too common, and too well embedded in the fabric of the language. On many occasions they can be useful in communicating simple ideas economically, and are often a means of conveying general sociability. When writing serious prose, however, in which clear and precise communication is intended, one should guard against allowing clichés to do the work which the words of one's own choosing could do better. 'Modish and inflated diction' is a rough and ready way of referring to a body of words and phrases that is familiar, but hard to delineate and delimit. In origin some of these expressions are often scientific or technical and are, in their original context, assigned a real and useful meaning; others are the creation of popular writers and broadcasters. What they all have in common is their grip on the popular mind, so that they have come to be used in all kinds of general contexts where they are unnecessary, ousting ordinary words that are better but sound less impressive. As their popularity and frequency increase, so their real denotative value drains away, a process that closely resembles monetary inflation. As with clichés, it would be difficult, and not necessarily desirable, to ban these expressions from our usage completely, but, again, one should carefully guard against using them either because they sound more learned and up to date than the more commonplace words in one's vocabulary, or as a short cut in communicating ideas that would be better set out in simple, clear, basic vocabulary.

The list that follows does not claim to be an exhaustive collection of clichés or of modish diction, but presents some contemporary expressions which are most frequently censured and are avoided by good writers.

actual (tautologous or meaningless, e.g. *Is this an actual Roman coin?*)
actually (as a filler, e.g. *Actually it's time I was going*)
articulate (verb = express)
at the end of the day

at this moment (or *point*) *in time*
-awareness (e.g. *brand-awareness*)
ball game (*a different*, etc., ——)
basically (as a filler)
by and large (sometimes used with no meaning)
-centred (e.g. *discovery-centred*)
conspicuous by one's absence
constructive (used tautologously, e.g. *A constructive suggestion*)
definitely
-deprivation (e.g. *status-deprivation*)
dialogue
dimension (= feature, factor)
-directed (e.g. *task-directed*)
dispense (= give)
environment
escalate (= increase, intensify)
eventuate (= result)
framework (in the framework of)
fresh (= new, renewed, etc.)
grind to a halt (= end, stop)
identify (= find, discover)
if you like (explanatory tag)
integrate, integrated
in terms of
in the order of (= about)
in this day and age
-ize (suffix, forming vogue words, e.g. *normalize*, *permanentize*, *prioritize*, *respectabilize*)
leave severely alone
life-style
look closely at
loved ones (= relatives)
low profile (*keep, or maintain, a* ——)
massive (= huge)
matrix
meaningful (can often be omitted without any change in meaning)
methodology (= method)
-minded (e.g. *company-minded*)
name of the game, the
-oriented (e.g. *marketing-oriented*)
overkill
participate in

persona (= character)
proliferation (= a number)
proposition
quantum jump
real (especially in *very real*)
-related (e.g. *church-related*)
simplistic (= oversimplified)
sort of (as a filler)
spell (= mean, involve)
target (figuratively used)
terminate (= end)
totality of, the
track-record (= record)
until such time as
utilize (= use)
viability
vibrant
you know (as a filler)
you name it

See also the entries in 'Vocabulary' above for:

antithetical
author
aware
character
crucial
decimate
dichotomy
differential
dilemma
event (in the event that)
excess (in excess of)
exposure
feasible
following
hopefully
impact
industrial action
interface
ironic
literally
locate
maximize
nature
neighbourhood (in the neighbourhood of)
no way
obligate
ongoing
overly
overview
parameter
pivotal
predicate
pre-empt
pristine
proportion
region (in the region of)
scenario
situation
substantial

FOREIGN ALPHABETS

THE GREEK ALPHABET

Capital	*Lower-case*	*Name*	*English transliteration*
Α	α	alpha	a
Β	β	beta	b
Γ	γ	gamma	g
Δ	δ	delta	d
Ε	ε	epsilon	e
Ζ	ζ	zeta	z
Η	η	eta	ē
Θ	θ	theta	th
Ι	ι	iota	i
Κ	ϰ	kappa	k
Λ	λ	lambda	l
Μ	μ	mu	m
Ν	ν	nu	n
Ξ	ξ	xi	x
Ο	ο	omicron	o
Π	π	pi	p
Ρ	ϱ	rho	r
Σ	σ, (at end of word)ς	sigma	s
Τ	τ	tau	t
Υ	υ	upsilon	u
Φ	φ	phi	ph
Χ	χ	chi	kh
Ψ	ψ	psi	ps
Ω	ω	omega	ō

‘ (rough breathing) over vowel = prefixed h (ἁ = ha)
over rho = suffixed h (ῥ = rh)

’ (smooth breathing) over vowel or rho: not transliterated

(iota subscript) under vowel = suffixed i (ᾳ = āi)

THE RUSSIAN ALPHABET

Capital	*Lower-case*	*English transliteration*
А	а	a
Б	б	b
В	в	v
Г	г	g
Д	д	d
Е	е	e
Ё	ё	ë
Ж	ж	zh
З	з	z
И	и	i
Й	й	ĭ
К	к	k
Л	л	l
М	м	m
Н	н	n
О	о	o
П	п	p
Р	р	r
С	с	s
Т	т	t
У	у	u
Ф	ф	f
Х	х	kh
Ц	ц	ts
Ч	ч	ch
Ш	ш	sh
Щ	щ	shch
Ъ	ъ	″ (‘hard sign’)
Ы	ы	y
Ь	ь	′ (‘soft sign’)
Э	э	é
Ю	ю	yu
Я	я	ya

APPROXIMATE ENGLISH EQUIVALENTS OF FOREIGN LETTERS

This table shows (very approximately) the sound-values of single, double, combined, accented, and special characters in a number of European languages. It also includes some of the special values of letters used in the Pinyin transliteration of Chinese (this is the most recent transliteration system and the one preferred by the Chinese government; in it, the name of the capital of China is written Beijing).

The equivalents given in the third column should not be regarded as a complete guide to the pronunciation of these languages. They simply explain some of the most noteworthy divergences in the use of the Latin alphabet between these languages and English.

It is hoped that this table may enable some difficult foreign personal and place-names to be pronounced with greater accuracy.

Key to languages

Chin.	Chinese (in the Pinyin transliteration)
Cz.	Czech
Da.	Danish
Du.	Dutch
Fin.	Finnish
Ger.	German
Hun.	Hungarian
It.	Italian
N.	Norwegian
Pol.	Polish
Port.	Portuguese
Rom.	Romanian
Sp.	Spanish
Sw.	Swedish
Tk.	Turkish
Yug.	Yugoslav, i.e. Croatian mainly (Slovene in some cases)

Character	*Language*	*Meaning and rough value*
á	Cz.	
	Hun.	long *a* as in *ah*
ä	Ger.	
	Sw.	open *e*-sound like *e* in *there*
	Fin.	front *a*-sound; *a* in *cat*

å	Da.	
	N.	
	Sw.	*o*-sound roughly like *aw* in *law*
ã	Port.	nasal *a*; French *un*
ą	Pol.	nasal *a*; French *on*
ă	Rom.	central *a* like *a* in *above*
aa	Du.	
	Fin.	
	Ger.	long *a* as in *ah*
æ	Da.	
	N.	open *e*-sound like *ere* in *there*
ai	Chin.	
	Fin.	
	Ger.	*ai* diphthong as in *aisle*
ao	Chin.	as *ow* in *cow*
au	Du.	
	Fin.	
	Ger.	*au* diphthong; like *ow* in *cow*
äu	Ger.	similar to *oy* in *toy*
c	Chin.	
	Cz.	
	Hun.	
	Pol.	
	Yug.	*ts* in *cats*
	Tk.	*j* in *job*
c before e, i	Sp.	*th* in *thing*
	It.	*ch* in *church*
ć	Pol.	
	Yug.	palatal *t* like *t* in *tube*
ç	Port.	soft *c* like *s* in *sit*
	Tk.	*ch* in *church*
č	Cz.	
	Yug.	*ch* in *church*
ch	Cz.	
	Ger.	
	Du.	
	Pol.	*kh*; i.e. *ch* in *loch*
	It.	*k*; i.e. as *ch* in *chemist*
	Port.	*sh* in *ship*
cs	Hun.	*ch* in *church*
cz	Hun.	*ts* in *cats*
	Pol.	*ch* in *church*

d’	Cz.	palatal *d* like *d* in *due*, *verdure*
đ	Yug.	palatal *d* like *d* in *due*, *verdure*
é	Cz.	
	Hun.	long *e* like *eh*, but prolonged
ę	Pol.	nasal *e*; French *ei* in *plein*
ě	Cz.	*ye* in *yes*
ee	Du.	
	Fin.	
	Ger.	*e* as in *eh*, prolonged
ei	Chin.	
	Du.	
	N.	similar to *ei* in *vein*
	Ger.	like *ei* in *height*
en	Chin.	like *an* in *another*
eng	Chin.	like *ung* in *sung*
eu	Du.	like *eu* in *milieu*, prolonged
	Ger.	similar to *oy* in *toy*
g before e, i	Port.	*zh*; i.e. *s* in *vision*
	Sp.	*kh*; i.e. *ch* in *loch*
ğ	Tk.	*y* consonant as *y* in *yes*
gu before e, i	Sp.	hard *g* in *guest*
gy	Hun.	palatal *d*; as *d* in *verdure*
h	It.	
	Port.	
	Sp.	not pronounced
	Chin.	
	Yug.	*kh*; i.e. *ch* in *loch*
ı	Tk.	*y* vowel; between *ee* and *oo*
í	Cz.	
	Hun.	long *i* as *i* in *machine*
î	Rom.	*y* vowel; between *ee* and *oo*
ie	Du.	
	Ger.	as *ie* in *thief*
	Chin.	
	Fin.	as *ie* in *kyrie*, *Vietnam*
ii	Fin.	long *i* as *i* in *machine*
ij	Du.	similar to *ei* in vein
j	Cz.	
	Da.	
	Fin.	
	Ger.	
	Hun.	

j	Du.	
	N.	
	Pol.	
	Sw.	
	Yug.	*y* in *yes*
	Port.	
	Tk.	*zh*; i.e. *s* in *vision*
	Sp.	*kh*; i.e. *ch* in *loch*
ł	Pol.	*w* in *word*
lh	Port.	palatal *l*; i.e. *l* in *failure*
ll	Sp.	palatal *l*; i.e. *l* in *failure*
ly	Hun.	palatal *l*; i.e. *l* in *failure*
ń	Pol.	palatal *n*; i.e. *n* in *canyon*
ñ	Sp.	palatal *n*; i.e. *n* in *canyon*
ň	Cz.	palatal *n*; i.e. *n* in *canyon*
nh	Port.	palatal *n*; i.e. *n* in *canyon*
ny	Hun.	palatal *n*; i.e. *n* in *canyon*
ó	Cz.	
	Hun.	long *o* like *oh*, but prolonged
	Pol.	as *o* in *move*
ö	Ger.	
	Fin.	
	Hun.	
	Sw.	
	Tk.	rounded *e* as *eu* in *milieu*
õ	Port.	nasal *o*; French *on*
ő	Hun.	long *ö* (umlaut); similar to French *œu* in *cœur*
ø	Da.	
	N.	rounded *e* as *eu* in *milieu*
oe	Du.	as *oe* in *shoe*
ong	Chin.	like *oong*
oo	Du.	
	Fin.	
	Ger.	long *o* as in *oh*, prolonged
ou	Chin.	like *ow* in *know*
	Du.	similar to *ou* in *out*
q	Chin.	like *ch* in *cheese*
qu before e,i	Sp.	*k*
ř	Cz.	palatal *r* as *ri* in *deteriorate*
rz	Pol.	*zh*; i.e. *s* in *vision*
s	Hun.	*sh* in *ship*

ś	Pol.	palatal *s* as in *capsule*
ş	Rom.	
	Tk.	*sh* in *ship*
š	Cz.	
	Yug.	*sh* in *ship*
sc before e,i	It.	*sh* in *ship*
sch	Ger.	*sh* in *ship*
	Du.	*s-kh*; i.e. *s*, then *ch* in *loch*
sj	Da.	
	Du.	
	N.	
	Sw.	*sh* in *ship*
sz	Hun.	*s* in *sit*
	Pol.	*sh* in *ship*
ß	Ger.	*s* in *hiss*
ţ	Rom.	*ts* in *cats*
t'	Cz.	palatal *t* as *t* in *tube*
ú	Cz.	
	Hun.	long *u* as *u* in *blue*
ü	Chin.	
	Ger.	
	Hun.	
	Tk.	front *u*; French *u* in *tu*
ů	Cz.	long *u* as *u* in *blue*
ű	Hun.	long front *u*; French *u* in *mur*
ui	Chin.	like *way*
	Du.	similar to *uy* in *buy*
uu	Du.	long front *u*; French *u* in *mur*
	Fin.	long *u* as *u* in *blue*
w	Ger.	
	Pol.	*v* in *vine*
x	Chin.	*sh* in *ship*
	Port.	*sh* in *ship* (often)
y	Da.	
	Fin.	
	Ger.	
	N.	
	Sw.	front *u*; i.e. French *u* in *tu*
ý	Cz.	long *i* as *i* in *machine*
yy	Fin.	long front *u*; French *u* in *mur*
z	Chin.	*dz* as in *adze*
	Sp.	*th* in *thing*

z	It.	*ts* in *cats* or *dz* in *adze*
ź	Pol.	palatal *z* as *z* in *azure*
ž	Cz.	
	Yug.	*zh*; i.e. *s* in *vision*
ż	Pol.	*zh*; i.e. *s* in *vision*
zh	Chin.	*j* in *job*
zs	Hun.	*zh*; i.e. *s* in *vision*

PART TWO
THE SPOKEN WORD

PRONUNCIATION

> For one thing, you speak quite differently from Roy. Now mind you, I'm not saying that one kind of voice is better than another kind, although . . the B.B.C. seems to have very definite views on the subject.
>
> (Marghanita Laski, *The Village*)

THIS section aims at resolving the uncertainty felt by many speakers both about some of the general variations in the pronunciation of English, and about a large number of individual words whose pronunciation is variable. Accordingly, the section is in two parts: A, general points of pronunciation, and B, a list of preferred pronunciations.

The aim of recommending one type of pronunciation rather than another, or of giving a word a recommended spoken form, naturally implies the existence of a standard. There are of course many varieties of English, even within the limits of the British Isles, but it is not the business of this section to describe them. The treatment here is based upon Received Pronunciation (RP), namely 'the pronunciation of that variety of British English widely considered to be least regional, being originally that used by educated speakers in southern England'.* This is not to suggest that other varieties are inferior; rather, RP is here taken as a neutral national standard, just as it is in its use in broadcasting or in the teaching of English as a foreign language.

A. *General points of pronunciation*

This first part of the section is concerned with general variations and uncertainties in pronunciation. Even when RP alone is taken as the model, it is impossible to lay down a set of rules that will establish the correct pronunciation of every word and hold it constant, since pronunciation is continually changing. Some changes affect a particular sound in its every occurrence throughout the vocabulary,

* *A Supplement to the OED*, Volume 3.

while others occur only in the environment of a few other sounds. Some changes occur gradually and imperceptibly; some are limited to a section of the community. At any time there is bound to be considerable variation in pronunciation. One of the purposes of the entries that follow is to draw attention to such variation and to indicate the degree of acceptability of each variant in standard English. Uncertainty about pronunciation also arises from the irregularity of English spelling. It is all too often impossible to guess how a particular letter or group of letters in an unfamiliar word should be pronounced. Broadly speaking, there are particular letters and letter sequences which repeatedly cause such uncertainty (e.g. *g* (hard and soft); final *-ed*; final *-ade*). To settle these uncertainties is the other main purpose of the entries that follow.

The entries are arranged in alphabetical order of heading; the headings are not, of course, complete words, but are either individual letters of the alphabet or sequences of letters making up parts (usually the beginnings or endings) of words. Some entries cover sounds that are spelt in various ways: the heading given is the typical spelling. There are also three entries of a different sort: they deal with (*a*) the main distinguishing features of American pronunciation, (*b*) the reduction of common words in rapid speech, and (*c*) patterns of stress.

a

1. There is variation in the pronunciation of *a* between the sound heard in *calm*, *father* and that heard in *cat*, *fan*, in

(*a*) the suffix *-graph* (in *photograph*, *telegraph*, etc.) and

(*b*) the prefix *trans-* (as in *transfer*, *translate*, etc.).

(*a*) In *-graph*, *a* as in *calm* seems to be the more generally acceptable form in RP. Note that when the suffix *-ic* is added (e.g. in *photographic*), only *a* as in *cat* can be used.

(*b*) In *trans-*, either kind of *a* is acceptable.

2. The word endings *-ada*, *-ade*, and *-ado* occasion difficulty, since in some words the pronunciation of the *a* is as in *calm*, in others as in *made*.

(*a*) In *-ada* words, *a* is as in *calm*, e.g. *armada*, *cicada*.

(*b*) In most *-ade* words, *a* is as in *made*, e.g. *accolade*, *barricade*, *cavalcade*.
Exceptions: *a* as in *calm* in

aubade	*façade*	*roulade*
ballade	*pomade*	*saccade*
charade	*promenade*	

and in unassimilated loan-words from French, e.g. *dégringolade*, *œillade*.

(*c*) In most *-ado* words, *a* is as in *calm*, e.g.

aficionado	*avocado*	*desperado*
amontillado	*bravado*	*Mikado*

Exceptions: *a* as in *made* in *bastinado*, *gambado*, *tornado*.

3. *a* in the word-ending *-alia* is like *a* in *alien*, e.g. in *marginalia*, *pastoralia*, *penetralia*.

4. *a* before *ls* and *lt* in many words is pronounced either like *aw* in *bawl* or *o* in *doll*, e.g. in

alter	*halt*	*salt*
false	*palsy*	*waltz*

The same variation occurs with *au* in *fault*, *vault*.
Note: in several words *a* before *ls* and *lt* can only be pronounced like *a* in *sally*, e.g.

Alsatian	*altruism*	*salsify*
alter ego	*caltrop*	*saltation*

5. The word endings *-ata*, *-atum*, and *-atus* occasion difficulty. In most words the *a* is pronounced as in *mate*, e.g. in

apparatus	*flatus*
datum (plural *data*)	*hiatus*
desideratum (plural *desiderata*)	*meatus*
	ultimatum

Exceptions: *cantata*, *erratum*, *sonata*, *toccata* with *a* as in *calm*; *stratum*, *stratus* with *a* as in *mate* or as in *calm*.

-age

The standard pronunciation of the following words of French origin ending in *-age* is with stress on the first syllable, *a* as in *calm*, and *g* as in *régime*.

barrage	*fuselage*	*mirage*
camouflage	*garage*	*montage*
dressage	*massage*	*sabotage*

Note that *collage* is stressed on the second syllable.

● The pronunciation of *-age* as in *cabbage* in any of these words is non-standard. The placing of the stress on the final syllable in some of these words is a feature of Amer. pronunciation.

□ The substitution of the sound of *g* as in *large* for that in *régime* by some speakers in several of these words is acceptable.

American pronunciation

Where the Amer. pronunciation of individual forms and words significantly differs from the British, this is indicated as part of the individual entries in this Section. There remain certain constant features of 'General American'* pronunciation that, being generally distributed, are not worth noting for every word or form in which they occur. The principal features are these:

1. *r* is sounded wherever it is written, i.e. after vowels finally and before consonants, as well as before vowels, e.g. in *burn*, *car*, *form*.

2. The sound of *l* is 'dark' (as in British *bell*, *fill*) everywhere; the British sound of *l* as in *land*, *light* is not used.

3. (*t*)*t* between vowels sounds like *d* (and this *d* often sounds like a kind of *r*), e.g. in *latter*, *ladder*, *tomato*.

4. The vowel of *boat*, *dote*, *know*, *no*, etc. is a pure long vowel, not a diphthong as in British English.

5. Where British English has four vowels, (i) *a* as in *bat*, (ii) *ah* as in *dance*, *father*, (iii) *o* as in *hot*, *long*, and (iv) *aw* as in *law*, Amer. English has only three, differently distributed, viz.: (i) *a* as in *bat*, *dance*, (ii) *ah* as in *father*, *hot*, and (iii) *aw* as in *long*, *law*.

6. The sound of *you* (spelt *u*, *ew*, etc.) after *s*, *t*, *d*, *n*, is replaced by the sound of *oo*, e.g. in *resume*, *Tuesday*, *due*, *new*, etc.

7. The sound of *u* as in *up* (also spelt *o* in *come*, etc.) sounds like the obscure sound of *a* as in *aloft*, *china*.

8. *er* is pronounced as in *herd* in words where it is like *ar* in *hard* in British English, e.g. in *clerk*, *derby*.

9. The vowels in the first syllables of (*a*) *ferry*, *herald*, *merry*, etc., (*b*) *fairy*, *hairy*, *Mary*, etc., and (*c*) *carry*, *Harry*, *marry*, etc. (i.e. when

* 'A form of U.S. speech without marked dialectal or regional characteristics' (*A Supplement to the OED*, Volume 1).

r follows) are not distinguished from one another by most General American speakers.

10. In words of four syllables and over, in which the main stress falls on the first or second syllable, there is a strong secondary stress on the last syllable but one, the vowel of which is fully enunciated, not reduced as in British English, e.g. *cóntemplàtive*, *témporàry*, *térritòry*.

-arily

In a few adverbs that end in the sequence *-arily* there is a tendency to place the stress on the *a* rather than the first syllable of the word. The reason lies in the stress pattern of four- and five-syllable words.

Adjectives of four syllables ending in *-ary* which are stressed on the first syllable are generally pronounced with elision of one of the middle syllables, e.g. *military*, *necessary*, *temporary* pronounced milit'ry, necess'ry, temp'rary. This trisyllabic pattern is much easier to pronounce.

The addition of the adverbial suffix *-ly* converts the word back into an unwieldly tetrasyllable that cannot be further elided: *milit*(*a*)*rily*, *necess*(*a*)*rily*, *temp*(*o*)*rarily*. Hence the use of these adverbs is sometimes avoided by saying *in a military fashion*, *in a solitary way*, etc.

A number of these adverbs are, however, in common use, e.g.

arbitrarily	*necessarily*	*temporarily*
momentarily	*ordinarily*	*voluntarily*

Because of the awkwardness of placing the stress on the first syllable, colloquial speech has adopted a pronunciation with stress on the third syllable, with the *a* sounding like *e* in *verily*. This is probably a borrowing from Amer. English, in which this pronunciation problem does not arise. In adjectives like *necessary* the ending *-ary* quite regularly receives a secondary stress (see **American pronunciation** above), which can then be converted into a main stress when *-ly* is added.

This pronunciation is much easier and more natural in rapid, colloquial speech, in which it would be pedantic to censure it.

● In formal and careful speech, the standard pronunciation of *arbitrarily*, *momentarily*, *necessarily*, *ordinarily*, *temporarily*, and *voluntarily* is with stress on the first syllable.

The case of the word *primarily* is somewhat different. It contains only four syllables, which, with stress on the first, can be reduced by elision of the second syllable to the easily pronounced spoken form prim'rily.

● There is therefore no need to pronounce the word with stress on the second syllable, pri-*merr*-ily, or even worse, pri-*marr*-ily. These are widely unacceptable.

-ed

1. In the following adjectives the ending *-ed* is pronounced as a separate syllable:

accursed	*naked*	*wicked*
cragged	*rugged*	*wretched*
deuced	*sacred*	

Note: *deuced* can also be pronounced as one syllable.

2. The following words represent two different spoken forms each with meanings that differ according to whether *-ed* is pronounced as a separate syllable or not. In most cases the former pronunciation indicates an adjective (as with the list under 1 above), the latter the past tense and past participle of a verb, but some are more complicated.

	(*a*) *-ed* as separate syllable	(*b*) *-ed* pronounced '*d*
aged	= very old (*he is very aged, an aged man*)	= having the age of (one, etc.) (*he is aged three, a boy aged three*); past of *to age* (*he has aged greatly*)
beloved	used before noun (*beloved brethren*); = beloved person (*my beloved is mine*)	used as predicate (*he was beloved by all*)
blessed	= fortunate, holy, sacred (*blessed are the meek, the blessed saints*); = blessed person (*Isles of the blessed*)	part of *to bless*; sometimes also in senses listed in left-hand column
crabbed	= cross-grained, hard to follow, etc.	past of *to crab*

crooked	
= not straight, dishonest	= having a transverse handle (*crooked stick*); past of *to crook*
cursed	
before noun = damnable	past of *to curse*
dogged	
= tenacious	past of *to dog*
jagged	
= indented	past of *to jag*
learned	
= erudite	past of *to learn* (usually *learnt*)
ragged	
= rough, torn, etc.	past of *to rag*

-edly, -edness

When the further suffixes *-ly* (forming adverbs) and *-ness* (forming nouns) are added to adjectives ending in the suffix *-ed*, an uncertainty arises about whether to pronounce this *-ed-* as a separate syllable or not. The adjectives to which these suffixes are added can be divided into three kinds.

1. Those in which *-ed* is already a separate syllable (*a*) because it is preceded by *d* or *t* or (*b*) because the adjective is one of those discussed in the entry for ***-ed*** above; e.g. *belated, decided, excited, levelheaded, wicked.* When both *-ly* and *-ess* are added, *-ed-* remains a separate syllable, e.g. (i) *belatedly, decidedly, excitedly, wickedly*; (ii) *belatedness, levelheadedness, wickedness.*

2. Those in which the syllable preceding *-ed* is unstressed, i.e. if -(*e*)*d* is removed the word ends in an unstressed syllable; e.g. *bad-tempered, embarrassed, hurried, self-centred.* When both *-ly* and *-ness* are added, *-ed-* remains non-syllabic (i.e. it sounds like 'd), e.g.

(i)		
abandonedly	*frenziedly*	*old-fashionedly*
bad-temperedly	*good-humouredly*	*self-centredly*
biasedly	*hurriedly*	*shamefacedly*
dignifiedly	*ill-naturedly*	*worriedly*
embarrassedly		

(ii) *bad-temperedness* *self-centredness* (= -center'dness)
hurriedness *shamefacedness*

3. Those in which the syllable preceding *-ed* is stressed, i.e. if -(*e*)*d* is removed the word ends in a stressed syllable, or is a monosyllable, e.g. *assured, fixed.*

• (i) When *-ly* is added *-ed* becomes an extra syllable, e.g.

advisedly *declaredly* *professedly*
allegedly *deservedly* *resignedly*
amusedly *designedly* *surprisedly*
assuredly *displeasedly* *undisguisedly*
avowedly *fixedly* *unfeignedly*
constrainedly *markedly* *unreservedly*

Exceptions:

There are a few definite exceptions to this rule, e.g. *subduedly*, *tiredly* (*ed* is not a separate syllable). There are also several words in which variation is found, e.g. *confessedly*, *depravedly*, *depressedly* (three or four syllables according to *OED*); *inspiredly* (four syllables in *OED*, but now probably three).

• Note that some adverbs formed on adjectives in *-ed* sound awkward and ugly whether *-ed-* is pronounced as a separate syllable or not. Because of this, some authorities (e.g. *MEU*) discourage the formation of words like *boredly*, *charmedly*, *discouragedly*, *experiencedly*.

(ii) When *-ness* is added, there is greater variation. The older usage seems to have been to make *-ed-* an extra syllable. In *OED* the following are so marked:

absorbedness *estrangedness* *forcedness*
assuredness *exposedness* *markedness*
confirmedness *fixedness* *surprisedness*

The following have *ed* or *'d* as alternative pronunciation:

ashamedness *pleasedness*
detachedness *preparedness*

But *'d* is the only pronunciation in *blurredness*, *subduedness*. However, many other words are not specially marked, and it seems likely that it has become increasingly rare for *-ed-* to be separately sounded.

□ It is acceptable *not* to make *-ed-* a separate syllable in words of this type.

-ein(e)

The ending *-ein(e)* (originally disyllabic) is now usually pronounced like *-ene* in *polythene* in

caffeine *casein* *codeine* *protein*

-eity

The traditional pronunciation of *e* in this termination is as in *me*, e.g. in

contemporaneity *corporeity* *deity* *heterogeneity* *homogeneity* *simultaneity* *spontaneity* *velleity*

Among younger speakers there is a marked tendency to substitute the sound of *e* in *café*, *suede*. The reasons for this are probably:

1. The difficulty of making the sounds of *e* (as in *me*) and *i* distinct when they come together. Cf. the words *rabies*, *species*, *protein*, etc. in which *e* and *i* were originally separate syllables but have now fused. Because of this difficulty, many users of the traditional pronunciation of *e* actually make the first two syllables of *deity* sound like *deer*, and so with the other words.

2. The influence of the reformed pronunciation of Latin in which *e* has the sound of *e* in *café*.

The same variation is found in the sequence *-ei-* in the words *deism*, *deist*, *reify*, *reification* (but not *theism*, *theist*).

● The pronunciation of *e* as in *me* is the only generally acceptable one in all these words.

-eur

This termination, occurring in words originally taken from French, in which it is the agent suffix, normally carries the stress and sounds like *er* in *deter*, *refer*, e.g. in:

agent provocateur *coiffeur* *colporteur* *connoisseur* (con-a-*ser*) *entrepreneur* *litterateur* *masseur* *poseur* *raconteur* *restaurateur* *sabreur* *seigneur* *tirailleur* *voyeur*

Stress is on the first syllable usually in

amateur (and *amateurish*: *am*-a-ter-ish)
chauffeur *saboteur*

Stress can be either on the first or the third syllable in *secateurs*.

Feminine nouns can be formed from some of these by the substitution of *-se* for *-r*: the resulting termination is pronounced like *urze* in *furze*, e.g. *coiffeuse*, *masseuse*, *saboteuse*.

liqueur is pronounced li-*cure* (Amer. li-*cur*).

g

A. In certain less familiar words and words taken from foreign languages, especially Greek, there is often uncertainty as to whether *g* preceding *e*, *i*, and (especially) *y* is pronounced hard as in *get* or soft as in *gem*.

1. The prefix *gyn*(*o*)- meaning 'woman' now always has a hard *g*.

2. The element *-gyn-* with the same meaning, occurring inside the word, usually has a soft *g*, as in *androgynous*, *misogynist*.

3. The elements *gyr-* (from a root meaning 'ring') and *-gitis* (in names of diseases) always have a soft *g*, as in

gyrate
gyration
gyre (poetic, = gyrate, gyration)
gyro (*-scope*, *compass*, etc.)
laryngitis
meningitis

4. The following, among many other more familiar words, have a hard *g*:

gibbous
gig (all senses)
gill (fish's organ)
gingham

5. The following have a soft *g*:

gibber
gibe
gill (measure)
gillyflower
giro (payment system)
gybe
gypsophila
gypsum
gyrfalcon
gyve
panegyric

6. There is variation in:
demagogic, *-y*, *gibberish*, *hegemony*, *pedagogic*, *-y*.

● *g* should be hard in *analogous*.

B. See **-age**, pp. 229 f.

-gm

g is silent in the sequence *gm* at the end of the word:

apophthegm	*paradigm*
diaphragm	*phlegm*

But *g* is pronounced when this sequence comes between vowels:

apophthegmatic	*paradigmatic*
enigma	*phlegmatic*

h

1. Initial *h* is silent in *heir*, *honest*, *honour*, *hour*, and their derivatives; also in *honorarium*. It is sounded in *habitué*.

2. Initial *h* used commonly to be silent if the first syllable was unstressed, as in *habitual*, *hereditary*, *historic*, *hotel*. This pronunciation is now old-fashioned. (See also **a or an**, pp. 21f.)

-ies

The ending *-ies* is usually pronounced as one syllable (like *ies* in *diesel*) in:

caries	*rabies*	*series*
congeries	*scabies*	*species*
facies		

● The reduction of this ending to a sound like the ending of the plural words *armies*, *babies*, etc., is best avoided.

-ile

The ending *-ile* is normally pronounced like *isle*, e.g. in

docile	*fertile*	*sterile*
domicile	*missile*	*virile*

● The usual Amer. pronunciation in most words of this kind is with the sound of *il* in *daffodil* or *pencil*.

The pronunciation is like *eel* in:

automobile	*-mobile* (suffix)
imbecile	

-ile forms two syllables in *campanile* (rhyming with *Ely*), *cantabile* (pronounced can-*tah*-bi-ly), and *sal volatile* (rhyming with *philately*).

ng

There is a distinction in Standard English between *ng* representing a single sound (which is represented by *n* alone before *c*, *k*, *q*, and *x*, as in *zinc*, *ink*, *tranquil*, and *lynx*) and *ng* representing a compound consisting of this sound followed by the sound of hard *g*.

1. The single sound is the only one to occur at the end of a word, e.g. in

bring *furlong* *song* *writing*

2. The single sound also occurs in the middle of words, but usually in words that are a compound of a word ending in *-ng* (as in 1 above) + a suffix, e.g.

bringer *kingly* *stringy*
bringing *longish* *wrongful*
hanged *singable*

3. The compound sound, *ng* + *g*, is otherwise normal in the middle of words, e.g.

anger *hungry* *language* *singly*

And exceptionally, according to rule 2, in *diphthongize*, *longer*, *-est*, *prolongation*, *stronger*, *-est*, *younger*, *-est*.

● 4. It is non-standard:

(*a*) To use *-in* for *-ing* (suffix), i.e. to pronounce *bringing*, *writing* as bringin, writin.
(*b*) To use *n* for *ng* in *length*, *strength*. (The pronunciation lenkth, strenkth is acceptable.)
(*c*) To use *nk* for *ng* in *anything*, *everything*, *nothing*, *something*.
(*d*) To use the compound sound *ng* + *g* in all cases of *ng*, i.e. in words covered by rules 1 and 2 as well as 3. This pronunciation is, however, normal in certain regional forms of English.

o

1. In many words the sound normally represented in English by *u* as in *butter*, *sun* is written instead with *o*, e.g. *above*, *come*, *front*. There are a few words in which there is variation in pronunciation between the above sound (as in *come*, etc.) and the more usual sound of *o* (as in *body*, *lot*, etc.). The earlier pronunciation of most of these was with the *u*-sound; the *o*-sound was introduced under the influence of the spelling.

(*a*) More usually with the *u*-sound:

accomplice *frontier* *pommel*
accomplish *mongrel*

(*b*) More usually with the *o*-sound:

combat *hovel* *pomegranate*
conduit *hover* *sojourn*
dromedary

(*c*) Still variable (either is acceptable):

comrade *constable*

2. Before *ff*, *ft*, *ss*, *st*, and *th*, in certain words, there was formerly a variety of RP in which *o* was pronounced like *aw* in *law* or *oa* in *broad*, so that *off*, *often*, *cross*, *lost*, and *cloth* sounded like *orf*, *orphan*, etc.

● This pronunciation is now non-standard.

3. Before double *ll*, *o* has the long sound (as in *pole*) in some words, and the short sound (as in *Polly*) in others.

(*a*) With the long sound:

boll *roll* *toll*
droll *scroll* *troll*
knoll *stroll* *wholly*
poll *swollen*

(*b*) With the short sound:

doll, *loll*, and most words in which another syllable follows, e.g. *collar*, *holly*, etc.

4. Before *lt*, *o* is pronounced long, as in *pole*, e.g. *bolt*, *colt*, *molten*, *revolt*.

● The substitution of short *o*, as in *doll*, in these words is non-standard.

5. Before *lv*, *o* is pronounced short, as in *doll*, e.g.

absolve *evolve* *revolve*
devolve *involve* *revolver*
dissolve *resolve* *solve*

● The substitution of long *o*, as in *pole*, in these words is non-standard.

ough

Difficult though this spelling is for foreign learners, most words in which it occurs are familiar to the ordinary English speaker. Pronunciation difficulties may arise, however, with the following words:

brougham	(a kind of carriage) *broo*-am or broom
chough	(bird) chuff
clough	(ravine) cluff
hough	(animal's joint), same as, and sounds like, *hock*
slough	(bog) rhymes with *plough*
slough	(snake's skin) sluff
sough	(sound) suff (can also rhyme with *plough*)

phth

This sequence should sound like *fth* (in *fifth*, *twelfth*), e.g. in *diphtheria*, *diphthong*, *monophthong*, *naphtha*, *ophthalmic*.

● It is non-standard to pronounce these as if written *dip-theria*, etc.

Initially, as in the words *phthisical*, *phthisis*, the *ph* can be silent; it is also usually silent in *apophthegm*.

pn-, *ps-*, *pt-*

These sequences occur at the beginning of many words taken from Greek. In all of them it is normal not to pronounce the initial *p-*. The exception is *psi* representing the name of a Greek letter, used, e.g., as a symbol.

r

1. When *r* is the last letter of a word (always following a vowel, or another *r*) or precedes 'silent' final *e* (where it may follow a consonant, e.g. in *acre* which really = aker), it is normally silent in RP, e.g. in

aware	*four*	*pure*
err	*here*	*runner*
far	*kilometre*	

But when another word, beginning with a vowel sound, follows in the same sentence, it is normal to pronounce the final *r*, e.g. in

aware of it	*four hours*	*pure air*
to err is human	*here it is*	*runner-up*
far away	*a kilometre of track*	

This is called the 'linking *r*'.

- It is standard to use linking *r* and unnatural to try to avoid it.

2. A closely connected feature of the spoken language is what is called 'intrusive *r*'.

(*a*) The commonest occurrence of this is when a word ending with the obscure sound of *a*, as *china*, *comma*, *Jonah*, *loofah*, etc. is immediately followed by a word beginning with a vowel sound. An intrusive *r* is added to the end of the first word as if it were spelt with *-er* so as to ease the passage from one word to the next. Typical examples are:

the area-r *of the island*
the pasta-r *is cooked*
sonata-r *in E flat*
an umbrella-r *organization*
a villa-r *in Italy*

Here the sound spelt *-a* at the end of *area*, *pasta*, etc., which sounds the same as *-er*, *-re* at the end of *runner*, *kilometre*, is treated as if it were spelt with an *r* following.

(*b*) In the same way, some speakers unconsciously equate (i) the spelling *a* or *ah* in *grandma*, *Shah* with the identical-sounding *ar* in *far*, (ii) the spelling *aw* in *law*, *draw* with the similar *our* in *four* or *ore* in *bore*, *tore*, and (iii) the spelling *eu* in *milieu*, *cordon bleu* with the similar *er*(*r*) in *err*, *prefer*. Thus, just as linking *r* is used with *far*, *four*, *bore*, *tore*, *err*, and *prefer*, such speakers introduce an intrusive *r* in, e.g.

is grandma-r *at home?*
The Shah-r *of Iran*
draw-r *a picture*
law-r *and order*
a milieu-r *in which . .*
a cordon bleu-r *in the kitchen*

(*c*) Intrusive *r* is often introduced before inflexional endings, e.g.

The boys are keen on scubering (i.e. *scubaing*) (Berkely Mather)
oohing and ah-r-*ing*
draw-r-*ing room*

and even within the word *withdraw*-r-*al*.

(*d*) Intrusive *r* has been noted since the end of the eighteenth century. In the mid nineteenth century it was regarded as unpardonable in an educated person, but acknowledged to occur widely even among the cultivated. Its use after obscure *a* (as described under (*a*) above), where it greatly aids the flow of the sentence and is relatively unobtrusive, is acceptable in rapid, informal speech. The avoidance of intrusive *r* here by the insertion of a hiatus or a catch in the breath would sound affected and pedantic.

• The use of intrusive *r* after the sounds of *ah*, *aw*, and *eu* (described under (*b*)) is very widely unacceptable and should be avoided if possible. Its use before inflexional endings ((*c*) above) is illiterate or jocular.

• In formal speech, the use of intrusive *r* in any context conveys an impression of unsuitable carelessness and should not be used at all.

3. There is a tendency in certain words to drop *r* if it is closely followed (or in a few cases, preceded) by another *r* at the beginning of an unstressed syllable, e.g. in

deteriorate mispronounced deteriate
February mispronounced Febuary
honorary mispronounced honary (prefer hon'rary)
itinerary mispronounced itinery
library mispronounced lib'ry
secretary mispronounced seketry or seketerry
temporary mispronounced tempary (prefer temp'rary)

• This pronunciation should be avoided, especially in formal speech.

reduced forms

In rapid speech, many of the shorter words whose function is essentially grammatical rather than lexical, being lightly stressed, tend to be reduced either by the obscuring of their vowels or the loss of a consonant or both. They may even be attached to one another or to more prominent words. Similarly, some words such as pronouns and auxiliary verbs are in rapid speech omitted altogether, while longer words of frequent occurrence are shortened by the elision of unstressed syllables. Typical examples are:

gunna, *wanna* = going to, want to
kinda, *sorta* = kind of, sort of
gimme, *lemme* = give me, let me
'snot = it's not
innit, *wannit* = isn't it, wasn't it
doncha, *dunno* = don't you, I don't know
what's he say, *where d'you find it*, *we done it*, *what you want it for?*
'spect or *I'xpect* = I expect
(*I*) *spose* = I suppose
cos, *course*, *on'y*, *praps*, *probly* = because, of course, only, perhaps, probably

• Most of these reduced forms (with the possible exception of *innit*, *wannit*) are natural in informal RP, but severely mar the quality and clarity of careful and prepared discourse, where they should be avoided.

s, sh, z, and zh

In certain kinds of word, where the spelling is *ci*, *si*, or *ti*, or where it is *s* before long *u*, there is variation between two or more of the four sounds which may be phonetically represented as:

s	as in *sun*	*zh*	representing the
sh	as in *ship*		sound of *s* in *leisure*
z	as in *zone*		or *g* in *régime*

1. There is variation between *s* and *sh* in words such as:

appreciate	*association*	*negotiation*
appreciation	*negotiate*	*sociology*
associate		

This variation does not occur in all words with a similar structure: only *s* is used in *glaciation*, *pronunciation* (= -see-*ay*-shon), and only *sh* in *partiality* (par-shee-*al*-ity). Note that there can be a variant having the sound of *s* only with words in which the following *i* constitutes a separate syllable; hence only *sh* occurs in *initial*, *racial*, *sociable*, *spatial*, *special*, etc. It is possible that speakers avoid using *sh* in words that end in *-tion*, which also contains the *sh*-sound, so as to prevent the occurrence of this sound in adjacent syllables, e.g. in *appreciation* = appreshi-ashon.

2. There is variation between *s* and *sh* in *sensual*, *sexual*, *issue*, *tissue*, and between *z* and *zh* in *casual*, *casuist*, *visual*.

3. There is variation between *sh* and *zh* in *aversion*, *equation*, *immersion*, *transition*, *version*.

□ Either variant is acceptable in each of these kinds of word, although in all of them *sh* is the traditional pronunciation.

4. In the names of some countries and regions ending in *-sia*, and in the adjectives derived from them, there is variation between *sh* and *zh*, and in some cases *z* and *s* as well. So:

Asian	= *A*-shan or *A*-zhan
Asiatic	= A-shi-*at*-ic or A-zhi-*at*-ic or A-zi-*at*-ic or A-si-*at*-ic
Friesian	= *Free*-zi-an or *Free*-zhan
Indonesian	= Indo-*nee*-shan or -zhan or -zi-an or -si-an
Persian	= *Per*-shan or *Per*-zhan

Polynesian (varies like *Indonesian*)
Rhodesian = Ro-*dee*-shan or -zhan or -zi-an or -si-an

• In all except *Friesian* the pronunciation with *sh* is traditional in RP and therefore the most widely acceptable. The pronunciation with *zh* is also generally acceptable.

stress

1. The position of the stress accent is the key to the pronunciation of many English polysyllabic words. If it is known on which syllable the stress falls, it is very often possible to deduce the pronunciation of the vowels. This is largely because the vowels of unstressed syllables in English are subject to reduction in length, obscuration of quality, and, quite often, complete elision. Compare the sound of the vowel in the stressed syllable in the words on the left with that of the vowel in the same syllable, unstressed, in the related words on the right:

a:	humánity	húman
	monárchic	mónarch
	practicálity	práctically (-ic'ly)
	secretárial	sécretary (-t'ry)
e:	presént (verb)	présent (noun)
	protést	protestátion
	mystérious	mýstery (= myst'ry)
i:	satírical	sátirist
	combíne	combinátion
	anxíety	ánxious (= anksh'ous)
o:	ecónomy	económic
	oppóse	ópposite
	históric	hístory (= hist'ry)
u:	luxúrious	lúxury
	indústrial	índustry

Because the position of the stress has such an important effect on the phonetic shape of the word, it is not surprising that many of the most hotly disputed questions of pronunciation centre on the placing of the stress. For example, in *controversy*, stress on the first syllable causes the four vowels to sound like those of *collar turning*, while stress on the second causes them to sound like those of *an opposite*: two quite different sequences of vowels.

2. It is impossible to formulate rules accounting for the position of the stress in every English word, whether by reference to the spelling or on the basis of grammatical function. If it were, most of

the controversies about pronunciation could be cleared up overnight. Instead, three very general observations can be made.

(*a*) Within very broad limits, the stress can fall on any syllable. These limits are roughly defined by the statement that more than three unstressed syllables cannot easily be uttered in sequence. Hence, for example, five-syllable words with stress on the first or last syllable are rare. Very often in polysyllabic words at least one syllable besides the main stressed syllable bears a medium or secondary stress, e.g. *cáterpìllar*, *còntrovèrtibílity*.

(*b*) Although there is such fluidity in the occurrence of stress, some patterns of stress are clearly associated with some patterns of spelling or with grammatical function (or, especially, with variation of grammatical function in a single word). For example, almost all words ending in the suffixes *-ic* and *-ical* are stressed on the syllable immediately preceding the suffix. There is only a handful of exceptions: *Arabic*, *arithmetic* (noun), *arsenic*, *catholic*, *choleric*, *heretic*, *lunatic*, *politic*(*s*), *rhetoric*.

(*c*) If the recent and current changes and variations in stress in a large number of words are categorized, a small number of general tendencies can be discerned. Most of these can be ascribed to the influence exerted by the existing fixed stress patterns over other words (many of which may conform to other existing patterns of stress). It will be the purpose of the remaining part of this entry to describe some of these tendencies and to relate them to the existing canons of acceptibility.

3. *Two-syllable words*

While there is no general rule that says which syllable the stress will fall on, there is a fixed pattern to which quite a large number of words conform, by which nouns and adjectives are stressed on the first syllable, and verbs on the second.

A large number of words beginning with a (Latin) prefix have stress on the first syllable if they are nouns or adjectives, but on the second if they are verbs, e.g.

accent	*import*	*transfer*
compound	*present*	*transport*
conflict	*suspect*	

The same distinction is made in some words ending in *-ment*, e.g.

ferment	*segment*
fragment	*torment*

And words ending in *-ate* with stress on the first syllable are usually nouns, while those with stress on the second are mainly verbs, e.g.

nouns:	verbs:
climate	*create*
curate	*dictate*
dictate	*frustrate*
mandate	*vacate*

This pattern has recently exercised an influence over several other words not originally conforming to it. The words

ally *defect* *rampage*
combine *intern*

were all originally stressed on the second syllable; as verbs, they still are, but as nouns, they are all usually stressed on the first. Exactly the same tendency has affected

dispute *recess* *research* *romance*

but in these words, the pronunciation of the noun with stress on the first syllable is rejected in good usage. The following nouns and adjectives (not corresponding to identically spelt verbs) show the same transference of stress: *adept*, *adult*, *chagrin*, *supine*.

In the verbs *combat*, *contact*, *harass*, and *traverse*, originally stressed on the first syllable, a tendency towards stress on the second syllable is discernible, but the new stress has been accepted only in the word *traverse*.

4. *Three-syllable words*

Of the three possible stress patterns in three-syllable words, that with stress on the first syllable is the strongest and best-established, exercising an influence over words conforming to the other two patterns.

(*a*) Words with stress on the final syllable are relatively rare. A number of them have been attracted to the dominant pattern; in some this pattern (stress on the first syllable) is acceptable in RP, e.g. *artisan*, *commandant*, *confidant*, *partisan*, *promenade*; in others it is not, e.g. *cigarette*, *magazine*.

(*b*) Many words originally having stress on the second syllable now normally or commonly have stress on the first, e.g.

abdomen	*decorous*	*recondite*
acumen	*obdurate*	*remonstrate*
albumen	*precedence*	*secretive*
aspirant	*precedent* (noun)	*sonorous*
communal		*subsidence*
composite	*quandary*	*vagary*

Other words are also affected by this tendency, but the pronunciation with stress on the first syllable has not been accepted as standard, e.g. in

Byzantine	*contribute*
clandestine	*distribute*

Note: This tendency to move the stress back from the second to the first syllable of three-syllable words has been observed for at least a century. A case that typically illustrates it is the word *sonorous*. In 1884 W. W. Skeat, in his *Etymological Dictionary of the English Language* (edn. 2), wrote: 'Properly *sonórous*; it will probably, sooner or later, become *sónorous*.' The first dictionary to recognize the change was *Webster's New International* of 1909, which adds the newer pronunciation with the comment 'now often, esp. in British usage'. Fifty years after Skeat, G. B. Shaw wrote to *The Times* (2 Jan. 1934): 'An announcer who pronounced decadent and sonorous as dekkadent and sonnerus would provoke Providence to strike him dumb'—testifying both to the prevalence of the new pronunciation and to the opposition it aroused. In 1956 Compton Mackenzie, in an Oxford Union Debate, protested against the pronunciation of *quandary*, *sonorous*, and *decorous* with stress on the first syllable (B. Foster, *The Changing English Language*, 1968, p. 243). Foster (ibid.), however, records his surprise in about 1935 at hearing a schoolmaster use the older pronunciation of *sonorous*. The newer pronunciation was first mentioned in the *Concise Oxford Dictionary* in 1964; the two pronunciations are both heard, but the newer one probably now prevails.

(*c*) There is a tendency in a few words to move the stress from the first to the second syllable. It is generally resisted in standard usage, e.g. in

combatant	*exquisite*	*urinal*
deficit	*stigmata*	

all of which have stress on the first syllable. But it has prevailed in *aggrandize*, *chastisement*, *conversant*, *doctrinal*, *environs*, *pariah*.

5. *Four-syllable words*

In a very large group of four-syllable words there is a clash between two opposing tendencies. One is the impulse to place the stress on the first syllable; the other is the influence of antepenultimate stress which is so prevalent in three-syllable words. Broadly speaking, it has been traditional in RP to favour stress on the first syllable, so that the shift to the second syllable has been strongly resisted in:

applicable	*demonstrable*	*intricacy*
aristocrat	*formidable*	*kilometre*
capitalist	*hospitable*	*lamentable*
controversy	*illustrative*	*remediless*
contumacy		

In many words the two tendencies can be reconciled by the elision of one of the two middle unstressed syllables:

adversary	*necessary*	*promissory*
comparable	*participle*	*referable*
migratory	*preferable*	*voluntary*
momentary	*primarily*	

However, many words traditionally stressed on the first syllable have been, or are being, adapted to the antepenultimate stress pattern, e.g.

centenary	*hegemony*	*nomenclature*
despicable	*metallurgy*	*pejorative*
disputable	*miscellany*	*peremptory*
explicable		

Because antepenultimate stress has been accepted in most of these words, it is difficult to reject it in the words in the first list simply on the ground of tradition. Analogy is the obvious argument in some cases, i.e. the analogy of *capital*, *demonstrate*, *illustrate*, *intricate*, *kilocycle* (or *centimetre*), and *remedy* for the words related to them in the list, but this cannot be used with the remaining words.

6. *Five-syllable words*

Five-syllable words originally stressed on the first syllable have been affected by the difficulty of uttering more than three unstressed syllables in sequence (see 2(*a*) above). The stress has been shifted to the second syllable in *laboratory*, *obligatory*, whereas in *veterinary* the fourth syllable is elided, and usually the second as well. For *arbitrarily*, *momentarily*, etc., see **-arily,** pp. 231 f.

t

1. In rapid speech, *t* is often dropped from the sequence *cts*, so that *acts*, *ducts*, *pacts* sound like *axe*, *ducks*, *packs*.

• This should be avoided in careful speech.

2. The sounding of *t* in *often* is a spelling pronunciation: the traditional form in RP rhymes with *soften*.

th

1. Monosyllabic nouns ending in *-th* after a vowel sound (or vowel + *r*) form the plural by adding *-s* in the usual way, but the resulting sequence *ths* is pronounced in two different ways. In some words it is voiceless as in *myths*, in others voiced as in *mouths*.

(*a*) The following are like *myth*:

berth	*girth*	*sleuth*
birth	*growth*	*sloth* (animal)
breath	*hearth*	*smith*
death	*heath*	*wraith*
faith	*moth*	
fourth		

(*b*) The following are like *mouth*:

bath	*sheath*	*wreath*
oath	*swath*	*youth*
path	*truth*	

cloth, *lath* vary, but are now commonly like *myth*.

2. Note that final *th* is like *th* in *bathe*, *father* in:

bequeath	*booth*
betroth	*mouth* (verb)

u

The sound of long *u*, as in *cube*, *cubic*, *cue*, *use* is also spelt *eu*, *ew*, and *ui*, as in *feud*, *few*, *pursuit*. It is properly a compound of two sounds, the semivowel *y* followed by the long vowel elsewhere written *oo*. Hence the word *you* (= y + oo) sounds like the name of the letter *U*, *ewe*, and *yew*.

When this compound sound follows certain consonants the *y* is lost, leaving only the *oo*-sound.

1. Where it follows *ch*, *j*, *r*, and the sound of *sh*, the *y* element was lost in the mid eighteenth century.

So *brewed*, *chews*, *chute*, *Jules*, *rude*, sound like *brood*, *choose*, *shoot*, *joules*, *rood*.

The *y* element was also lost at about the same time or a little later where it follows an *l* preceded by another consonant; so *blew*, *clue*, *glue*, etc. sound as if they were spelt *bloo*, *cloo*, *gloo*, etc.

2. Where this compound sound follows an *l* not preceded by another

consonant, loss of the *y*-element is now very common in a syllable that bears the main or secondary stress. *COD*, for instance, gives only the *oo* pronunciation in many words, e.g. *Lewis*, *Lucifer*, *lucrative*, *lucre*, etc., and either pronunciation for many others, e.g. *lubricate*, *Lucan*, *lucid*, *ludicrous*, etc.

It is equally common in internal stressed syllables; in *COD* the words *allude*, *alluvial*, *collusion*, *voluminous*, etc. are given both pronunciations. So also in a syllable which bears a secondary stress: *absolute*, *interlude*.

□ In all syllables of these kinds, the *oo*-sound is probably the predominant type, but either is acceptable.

• In *unstressed* syllables, however, it is not usual for the *y*-element to be lost. The *yoo*-sound is the only one possible in, e.g.

curlew	*purlieu*	*value*
deluge	*soluble*	*volume*
prelude	*valuable*	

Contrast *solute* (= *sol*-yoot) with *salute* (= sa-*loot*).

3. After *s*, there is again variation between the compound sound and the *oo*-sound. The latter has now a very strong foothold. Very few people, if any, pronounce *Susan* and *Sue* with a *yoo*, and most people pronounce *super* (the word and the prefix) with *oo*. On the other hand, most people probably use *yoo* in *pseudo-* and in internal syllables, as in *assume*, *presume*, *pursue*. Common words such as *sewage*, *sewer*, *suet*, *suicide*, *sue*, and *suit* show wide variation: some people pronounce the first four (in which another vowel follows *ew* or *u*) with *oo*, but the last two with *yoo*.

In an unstressed syllable, the *y*-sound is kept, as with *l* in 2 above:

capsule	*consular*	*insulate*
chasuble	*hirsute*	*peninsula*

□ Apart from in *Susan*, *Sue*, and *super*, and the words in which the vowel occurs in an unstressed syllable, either pronunciation is acceptable, although *yoo* is the traditional one.

4. After *d*, *n*, *t*, and *th*, the loss of the *y*-sound is non-standard, e.g. in *due*, *new*, *tune*, *enthusiasm*.

Note: In Amer. English loss of the *y*-sound is normal after these consonants and *l* and *s*.

• The tendency to make *t* and *d* preceding this sound in stressed syllables sound like *ch* and *j*, e.g. *Tuesday*, *duel* as if *Choosday*, *jewel*, should be avoided in careful speech. In unstressed syllables (e.g. in *picture*, *procedure*) it is normal.

ul

After *b*, *f*, and *p*, the sequence *ul* sounds like *ool* in *wool* in some words, e.g. in *bull*, *full*, *pull*, and like *ull* in *hull* in others, e.g. in *bulk*, *fulminate*, *pulp*. In a few words there is uncertainty about the sound of *u*, or actual variation.

(*a*) Normally with *u* as in *hull*:

Bulgarian	*fulminate*	*pulmonary*
ebullient	*pullulate*	*pulverize*
effulgent		

(*b*) Normally with *u* as in *bull*:

bulwark *fulmar* *fulsome* *fulvous*

(*c*) With variation: *fulcrum*

urr

In Standard English the stressed vowel of *furry* and *occurring* is like that of *stirring*, not that of *hurry* and *occurrence*.

● The identity of the two sounds is normal in Amer. English.

wh

In some regions *wh* is distinguished from *w* by being preceded or accompanied by an *h*-sound.

□ This pronunciation is not standard in RP, but is acceptable to most RP-speakers.

B. *Preferred pronunciations*

The entries in this list are of three kinds. Some of the words in it have only one current pronunciation, which cannot, however, be deduced with certainty from the written form. These are mainly words that are encountered in writing and are not part of the average person's spoken vocabulary. Another class of words included here have a single, universally accepted pronunciation, which, in rapid or careless speech, undergoes a significant slurring or reduction. These reduced forms are noted, with a warning to use the fully enunciated form in careful speech so as to avoid giving an impression of sloppiness or casualness. Much the largest group are words for which two or more different pronunciations exist. Both (or all) are given, with notes giving a rough guide to the currency and acceptability of each.

The approach adopted here is fairly flexible, allowing for the inevitable subjectivity of judgements about pronunciation and the fact that there is variation and inconsistency even in the speech of an individual person.

Where the American pronunciation is significantly different from the British (disregarding the differences that are constant, such as the American pronunciation of *r* where it is silent in British speech), a note of it has been added, usually in brackets at the end of the entry. In a few cases the American pronunciation stands alone after the recommended one, implying that the use of the American form is incorrect in British speech. It will be found that in many cases the American pronunciation coincides with an older British one that is now being ousted. It is hoped that this will dispel the impression that all innovations are Americanisms, and give a clearer idea of the relationship between the two varieties of English pronunciation.

The symbol ● is used to warn against forms especially to be avoided; □ introduces most of the cases of peaceful coexistence of two variant pronunciations.

abdomen: stress on 1st syllable in general use; on 2nd in the speech of many members of the medical profession.

accomplice, accomplish: the older (and Amer.) pronunciation has 2nd syllable as in *comma*; but pronunciation as *come* is now predominant.

acoustic: 2nd syllable as *coo*, not *cow*.

acumen: stress on 1st syllable.

adept, adult (adjective and noun): stress on 1st syllable.

adversary: stress on 1st syllable.

aficionado: a-fiss-eon-*ah*-do.
aggrandize: stress on 2nd syllable.
ague: 2 syllables.
albumen: stress on 1st syllable.
ally (noun): stress on 1st syllable; (verb) on 2nd syllable; **allied** preceding a noun is stressed on 1st syllable.
analogous: *g* as in *log*; not a-*na*-lo-jus.
Antarctic: ● do not drop the first *c*.
anti- (prefix): rhymes with *shanty*, not, as often Amer., *ant eye*.
antiquary: stress on 1st syllable.
apache (Indian): rhymes with *patchy*; (street ruffian) rhymes with *cash*.
apartheid: 3rd syllable like *hate*. ● Not *apart-ite* or *apart-hide*.
apophthegm: *a*-po-them.
apparatus: 3rd syllable like *rate*; not appar-*ah*-tus.
applicable: stress on 1st syllable.
apposite: 3rd syllable like that of *opposite*.
arbitrarily: stress properly on 1st syllable, in informal speech on 3rd.
Arctic: ● do not drop the first *c*.
Argentine: 3rd syllable as in *turpentine*.
aristocrat: stress on 1st syllable. ● Not (except Amer.) a-*rist*-ocrat.
artisan: stress originally on 3rd syllable; pronunciation with stress on 1st syllable is Amer., and now common in Britain.
aspirant: stress on 1st syllable.
asthma: *ass*-ma is the familiar pronunciation; to sound the *th* is didactic (Amer. *az*-ma).
ate: rhymes with *bet* (Amer. with *bate*).
audacious: *au* as in *audience*, not as in *gaucho*.
auld lang syne: 3rd word like *sign*, not *zine*.
azure: the older pronunciation was with *-zure* like *-sure* in *pleasure*; now usually *az*-yoor.
banal: 2nd syllable like that of *canal* or *morale* (Amer. rhymes with *anal*).
basalt: 1st *a* as in *gas*, 2nd as in *salt*; stress on either.
bathos: *a* as in *paper*.
blackguard: *blagg*-ard.
bolero (dance): stress on 2nd syllable; (jacket) stress on 1st.
booth: rhymes with *smooth* (Amer. with *tooth*).
bouquet: first syllable as *book*, not as *beau*.
Bourbon (dynasty): 1st syllable as that of *bourgeois*; (US whisky) 1st syllable as *bur*.
breeches: rhymes with *pitches*.

brochure: stress on 1st syllable.
brusque: should be Anglicized: broosk or brusk.
bureau: stress on 1st syllable.
burgh (in Scotland): sounds like *borough*.
Byzantine: stress on 2nd syllable.
cadaver: 2nd syllable as in *waver*.
cadaverous: 2nd syllable like 1st of *average*.
cadre: rhymes with *harder*.
caliph: rhymes with *bailiff*.
camellia: rhymes with *Amelia*.
canine: □ 1st syllable may be as *can* or *cane* (the latter probably prevails).
canton (subdivision): 2nd syllable as 1st of *tonic*; (military, also in **cantonment**) 2nd syllable as that of *cartoon*.
capitalist: stress on 1st syllable.
carillon: rhymes with *trillion* (Amer. *carry*-lon).
caryatid: stress on 2nd *a*.
catacomb: 3rd syllable, in the older pronunciation, as *comb*; now frequently rhyming with *tomb*.
centenary: sen-*tee*-nary (Amer. *sen*-te-nary).
cento: *c* as in *cent*, not *cello*.
centrifugal, centripetal: stress originally on 2nd syllable; but pronunciation with stress on 3rd syllable seems to be usual among younger speakers.
certification: stress on 1st and 4th syllables, not 2nd and 4th.
cervical: □ stress either on 1st syllable (with last two syllables as in *vertical*) or on 2nd (rhyming with *cycle*): both pronunciations have been common for at least a century and a half (Amer. only the first pronunciation).
chaff: rhymes with *staff*.
chagrin: stress on 1st syllable; 2nd as *grin* (Amer. stress on 2nd syllable).
chamois (antelope): *sham*-wah; (leather) shammy.
chastisement: traditionally with stress on 1st syllable; now often on 2nd.
chimera: *ch* = k, not sh.
chiropodist: strictly *ch* = k, but pronunciation as sh is common.
choleric: 1st two syllables like *collar*.
cigarette: stress on 3rd syllable (Amer. on 1st).
clandestine: stress on 2nd syllable.
clangour: rhymes with *anger*.
clientele: kleeon-*tell*.

clique: rhymes with *leak*, not *lick*.
coccyx: *cc* = ks.
colander: 1st syllable as *cull*.
combat (verb), **combatant, -ive:** stress on 1st syllable (Amer. on 2nd).
combine (noun): stress on 1st syllable.
commandant: stress originally on 3rd syllable; now often on 1st.
communal: stress on 1st syllable.
commune (noun): stress on 1st syllable.
comparable: stress on 1st syllable, not on 2nd.
compensatory: the older (and Amer.) pronunciation has stress on 2nd syllable, but stress on 3rd is now common.
compilation: 2nd syllable as *pill*.
composite: stress on 1st syllable; 3rd as that of *opposite* (Amer. stress on 2nd syllable).
conch: originally = *conk*; now often with *ch* as in *lunch*.
conduit: last three letters like those of *circuit* (Amer. *con*-doo-it).
confidant(e): the older pronunciation has stress on last syllable, which rhymes with *ant*; stress on 1st syllable is now common.
congener: stress on 1st syllable; *o* as in *con*; *g* as in *gin*.
congeries: □ con-*jeer*-eez or con-*jeer*-y-eez.
congratulatory: stress on 2nd syllable; pronunciation with stress on 4th syllable is also common.
conjugal: stress on 1st syllable.
consuetude: stress on 1st syllable; *sue* like *swi* in *swift*.
consummate (adjective): stress on 2nd syllable; (verb) on 1st syllable, 3rd syllable as *mate*.
contact (noun and verb): stress on 1st syllable.
contemplative: stress on 2nd syllable.
contrarily (on the contrary): stress on 1st syllable; (perversely) stress on 2nd syllable.
contribute: stress on 2nd syllable. ● The former pronunciation with stress on 1st syllable has survived in dialect and is frequently heard, but is not standard.
controversy: stress on 1st syllable. ● The pronunciation with stress on 2nd syllable seems to be increasingly common, but is strongly disapproved by many users of RP.
contumacy: stress on 1st syllable (Amer. on 2nd).
contumely: 3 syllables with stress on the 1st.
conversant: now usually stressed on 2nd syllable; formerly on 1st.
courier: *ou* as in *could*.
courteous: 1st syllable like *curt*.
courtesan: 1st syllable like *court*.

courtesy: 1st syllable like *curt*.
covert: 1st syllable like that of *cover*. ● Does not rhyme with *overt*.
culinary: *cul-* now usually as in *culprit*; formerly as in *peculiar*.
dais: originally one syllable; now only with two.
data: 1st syllable as *date*. ● Does not rhyme with *sonata*.
decade: stress on 1st syllable.
defect (noun): stress on 1st syllable is now usual.
deficit: stress on 1st syllable.
deify, deity: *e* as in *me*. ● Pronunciation with *e* as in *suede*, *fête* is common among younger speakers, but is disapproved of by many users of RP.
delirious: 2nd syllable as 1st of *lyrical*, not *Leary*.
demesne: 2nd syllable sounds like *main*.
demonstrable: stress on 1st syllable.
deprivation: 1st two syllables like those of *deprecation*.
derisive, derisory: 2nd syllable like *rice*.
despicable: in formal speech, stress on 1st syllable; informally, especially for greater emphasis, on 2nd.
desuetude: as for **consuetude.**
desultory: stress on 1st syllable.
deteriorate: ● do not drop 4th syllable, i.e. not deteri-ate.
detour: *dee*-tour not *day*-tour (Amer. de-*tour*).
deus ex machina: *day*-us ex *mak*-ina, not ma-*shee*-na.
dilemma: 1st syllable like *dill*.
dinghy: ding-gy, not rhyming with *stringy*.
diphtheria, diphthong: *ph* = f not p.
disciplinary: the older (and Amer.) pronunciation has stress on 1st syllable, but it is now usually on the 3rd (with *i* as in *pin*).
disputable: stress on 2nd syllable.
dispute (noun): stress on 2nd syllable, not on 1st.
dissect: 1st syllable as *Diss*. ● Does not rhyme with *bisect*.
distribute: stress on 2nd syllable.
doctrinal: the older pronunciation has stress on 1st syllable, but it is now usually on the 2nd (with *i* as in *mine*).
dolorous, dolour: 1st syllable like *doll* (Amer. like *dole*).
dour: rhymes with *poor* not *power*.
dubiety: last 3 syllables like those of *anxiety*.
ducat: 1st syllable like *duck*.
dynast, dynastic, dynasty: 1st syllable like *din* (Amer. like *dine*).
ebullient: *u* as in *dull*, not as in *bull*.
economic: □ *e* as in *extra* or as in *equal*: both are current.
Edwardian: 2nd syllable as *ward*.

e'er (poetry, = *ever*): sounds like *air*.
efficacy: stress on 1st syllable, not 2nd.
ego: 1st syllable as that of *eager*.
egocentric, egoism, etc.: 1st syllable like *egg* (Amer. usually as **ego).**
either: *ei* as in *height* or *seize*: both are widely current (Amer. only the second pronunciation).
elixir: rhymes with *mixer*.
enclave: *en-* as in *end*, *a* as in *slave*.
entirety: now usually entire-ety; formerly entire-ty.
envelope: *en-* as in *end*, not *on*.
environs: rhymes with *sirens*.
epos: *e* as in *epic*.
epoxy: stress on 2nd syllable.
equerry: stress properly on 2nd syllable, but commonly on 1st.
espionage: now usually with *-age* as in *camouflage*.
et cetera: etsetera. • Not eksetera.
explicable: stress originally on 1st syllable, but now usually on 2nd.
exquisite: stress on 1st syllable.
extraordinary: 1st *a* is silent.
fakir: sounds like *fake*-ear.
falcon: *a* as in *talk*, not as in *alcove*.
fascia: rhymes with *Alsatia*.
fascism, fascist: 1st syllable like that of *fashion*.
February: • do not drop the 1st *r*: feb-roor-y, not *feb*-yoor-y or *feb*-wa-ry or *feb*-yoo-erry (Amer. *feb*-roo-erry).
fetid, fetish: *e* as in *fetter*.
fifth: in careful speech, do not drop the 2nd *f*.
finance: □ stress on 1st syllable (only with *i* as in *fine*) or on 2nd (with *i* as in *fin* or *fine*).
forbade: 2nd syllable like *bad*.
formidable: in careful speech, stress on 1st syllable; informally, on 2nd.
forte (one's strong point): originally (and Amer.) like *fort*, but now usually like the musical term *forte*.
foyer: *foy*-ay or *fwah*-yay (Amer. *foy*-er).
fracas (singular): *frack*-ah, (plural) *frack*-ahz (Amer. *frake*-us).
fulminate: *u* as in *dull*.
fulsome: *u* formerly as in *dull*, now always as in *full*.
furore: 3 syllables (Amer. **furor** with 2).
Gaelic: 1st syllable as *gale*.
gala: 1st *a* as in *calm*. • The former pronunciation with *a* as in *gale* is still used in the North and US.

gallant (brave, etc.): stress on 1st syllable; (polite and attentive to ladies) stress on 1st or 2nd syllable.

garage: stress on 1st syllable, *age* as in *camouflage* (or rhyming with *large*). • Pronunciation so as to rhyme with *carriage* is non-standard (Amer. ga-*rahge*).

garrulity: stress on 2nd syllable, which sounds like *rule*.

garrulous: stress on 1st syllable.

gaseous: 1st syllable like *gas*.

genuine: *ine* as in *engine*.

genus: *e* as in *genius*; **genera** (plural) has *e* as in *general*.

gibber, gibberish: now usually with *g* as in *gin*; *g* as in *give* was formerly frequent in the first word and normal in the second.

glacial: 1st *a* as in *glade*.

golf: *o* as in *got*. • The pronunciation goff is old-fashioned.

gone: *o* as in *on*. • The pronunciation gawn is non-standard.

government: • In careful speech, do not drop the 1st *n* (or the whole 2nd syllable).

gratis: *a* properly as in *grate*; but grahtis and grattis are commonly heard.

greasy: □ *s* may be as in *cease* or *easy*.

grievous: • does not rhyme with *previous*.

gunwale: gunn'l.

half-past: • In careful speech, avoid saying hah past or hoff posst.

harass(ment): stress on 1st syllable (Amer. often on 2nd).

have: in rapid speech, the weakly stressed infinitive *have* is reduced to '*ve* and sounds like the weakly stressed form of the preposition *of*. When stress is restored to it, it should become *have*, not *of*, as in '*You couldn't 've done it*', '*I could* have' (not '*I could* of').

hectare: 2nd syllable like *tar*, not *tare*.

hegemony: stress on 2nd syllable, *g* as in *get* or (as also Amer.) as in *gem*.

Hegira: stress on 1st syllable, which is like *hedge*.

heinous: *ei* as in *rein*.

homo- (prefix = same): *o* as in *from*.

homoeopath: 1st two syllables rhyme with *Romeo*.

homogeneous: last three syllables sound like *genius*.

honorarium: *h* silent, *a* as in *rare*.

hospitable: stress properly on 1st syllable.

hotel: *h* to be pronounced.

housewifery: stress on 1st syllable, *i* as in *whiff*.

hovel, hover: *o* as in *hot*. • The former pronunciation with *o* as in *love* is now only Amer.

idyll: *i* as in *idiot*; it may be like *i* in *idea* in **idyllic** (with stress on 2nd syllable) and usually is in **idyllist** (with stress on 1st syllable).
illustrative: stress on 1st syllable (Amer. on 2nd).
imbroglio: *g* is silent; rhymes with *folio.*
impious: stress on 1st syllable; on 2nd in **impiety**.
importune: stress on 3rd syllable or (with some speakers) on 2nd.
inchoate: stress on 1st syllable.
indict: *c* is silent; rhymes with *incite.*
indisputable: stress on 3rd syllable.
inexplicable: stress originally on 2nd syllable, but now usually on 3rd.
infamous: stress on 1st syllable.
inherent: 1st *e* as in *here.*
intaglio: *g* is silent, *a* as in *pal* or *pass.*
integral: stress on 1st syllable.
intern (verb): stress on 2nd syllable; (noun, Amer.) on 1st.
internecine: stress on 3rd syllable, last two syllables like *knee sign.*
interstice: stress on 2nd syllable.
intestinal: stress on 2nd syllable; 3rd syllable like *tin.*
intricacy: stress on 1st syllable.
invalid (sick person): stress on 1st syllable, 2nd *i* as in *lid* or *machine;* (verb) stress on 1st or 3rd syllable, 2nd *i* as in *machine*; (not valid) stress on 2nd syllable.
inveigle: originally rhyming with *beagle*, but now commonly with *Hegel.*
inventory: like *infantry* with *v* instead of *f.*
irrefragable: stress on 2nd syllable.
irrelevant: • not *irrevalent*, a blunder sometimes heard.
irreparable: stress on 2nd syllable.
irrevocable: stress on 2nd syllable.
issue: *ss* as in *mission*; but pronunciation to rhyme with *miss you* is very common.
isthmus: do not drop the *th.*
January: *jan*-yoor-y (Amer. *jan*-yoo-erry).
jejune: stress on 2nd syllable.
jewellery: jewel-ry. • Not jool-ery.
joule (unit): rhymes with *fool.*
jubilee: stress on 1st syllable • Not 3rd.
jugular: 1st syllable like *jug*: formerly as in *conjugal.*
junta: pronounce as written. • Hoonta, an attempt to reproduce the Spanish pronunciation, is chiefly Amer.
kilometre: stress on 1st syllable, as with *kilocycle*, *kilolitre.* • Not on

2nd syllable; the pattern is that of *millimetre*, *centimetre* (units), not that of *speedometer*, *milometer*, etc. (devices).

knoll: *o* as in *no*.

laboratory: stress on 2nd syllable. ● The former pronunciation, with stress on 1st syllable, is now chiefly used by Amer. speakers (with *o* as in *Tory*).

lamentable: stress on 1st syllable.

languor: as for **clangour**.

lasso: stress on 2nd syllable, *o* as in *do*.

lather: rhymes with *gather*, not *rather*.

launch: rhymes with *haunch*, not *branch*.

leeward (in general use): *lee*-ward; (nautical) like *lured*.

leisure: rhymes with *pleasure* (Amer. with *seizure*).

length: *ng* as in *long*. ● Not lenth.

levee (reception, assembly): like *levy*; (Amer., embankment) may be stressed on 2nd syllable.

library: in careful speech avoid dropping the 2nd syllable (li-bry).

lichen: sounds like *liken*.

lieutenant: 1st syllable like *left*; in Navy, like *let* (Amer. like *loot*).

liquorice: licker-iss.

longevity: *ng* as in *lunge*.

longitude: *ng* as in *lunge*. ● Not (*latitude and*) *longtitude*, an error sometimes heard.

long-lived: originally rhyming with *arrived*, but now usually like past tense *lived*.

lour: rhymes with *hour*.

lugubrious: loo-*goo*-brious.

machete: *ch* as in *attach*; rhymes with *Betty* (or with some speakers, *Katie*).

machination: *ch* as in *mechanical*, not as in *machine*.

machismo, macho: *ch* as in *attach*, not as in *mechanical*.

magazine: stress on 3rd syllable (Amer. and Northern pronunciation has stress on 1st).

maieutic: 1st syllable like *may*.

mandatory: stress on 1st syllable.

margarine: *g* as in *Margery*.

marital: stress on 1st syllable.

massage: stress on 1st syllable (Amer. on 2nd).

matrix: *a* as in *mate*; **matrices** (plural) the same, with stress on 1st syllable.

medicine: two syllables (med-sin). ● The pronunciation with three syllables is normal in Scotland and the US, but disapproved of by many users of RP.

mediocre: 1st syllable like *mead.*

metallurgy, -ist: stress on 2nd syllable. ● The older pronunciation with stress on 1st syllable, becoming rare in Britain, is chiefly Amer.

metamorphosis: stress on 3rd syllable.

metope: two syllables.

midwifery: stress on 1st syllable, *i* as in *whiff.*

mien: sounds like *mean.*

migraine: 1st syllable like *me* (Amer. like *my*).

migratory: stress on 1st syllable.

millenary: stress on 2nd syllable, which is like *Len* or *lean.*

miscellany: stress on 2nd syllable (Amer. on 1st).

mischievous: stress on 1st syllable. ● Not rhyming with *previous.*

misericord: stress on 2nd syllable.

mocha (coffee): originally (and Amer.) rhyming with *coca*, now often like *mocker.*

momentary, -ily: stress on 1st syllable.

municipal: stress on 2nd syllable.

nadir: *nay*-dear.

naïve: nah-*Eve* or nigh-*Eve.*

naïvety: has 3 syllables.

nascent: *a* as in *fascinate.*

necessarily: in formal speech, has stress on 1st syllable, with reduction or elision of *a*; informally, especially in emphatic use, stressed on 3rd syllable (e.g. *not necess*ar*ily!*).

neither: as for **either**.

nephew: *ph* sounds like *v* (Amer. like *f*).

nicety: has three syllables.

niche: nitch has been the pronunciation for two or three centuries; neesh, now common, is remodelled on the French form.

nomenclature: stress on 2nd syllable. The pronunciation with stress on 1st and 3rd syllables is now chiefly Amer.

nonchalant: stress on 1st syllable, *ch* as in *machine.*

nuclear: *newk*-lee-er. ● Not as if spelt *nucular.*

nucleic: stress on 2nd syllable, which has *e* as in *equal.*

obdurate: stress on 1st syllable.

obeisance: 2nd syllable like *base.*

obligatory: stress on 2nd syllable.

obscenity: *e* as in *scent.*

occurrence: 2nd syllable like the 1st in *current.*

o'er (poetry, = over): sounds like *ore*.
of: see **have**.
often: the *t* is silent, as in *soften*.
ominous: 1st syllable as that of *omelette*.
ophthalmic: *ph* = f not p.
opus: *o* as in *open*.
ormolu: *orm*-o-loo with weak 2nd *o* as in *Caroline*.
p (abbreviation for *penny*, *pence*): in formal context, say *penny* (after 1) or *pence*. ● 'Pee' is informal only.
pace (with all due respect to): like *pacey*.
paella: pah-*ell*-a.
panegyric: stress on 3rd syllable, *g* as in *gin*, *y* as in *lyric*.
paprika: stress on 1st syllable (Amer. on 2nd).
pariah: the older pronunciation has the stress on 1st syllable, rhyming with *carrier*; the pronunciation with stress on 2nd syllable, rhyming with *Isaiah*, is now common (and normal Amer.).
participle: stress on 1st syllable; 1st *i* may be dropped.
particularly: in careful speech, avoid dropping the 4th syllable (particuly).
partisan: as **artisan**.
pasty (pie): *a* now usually as in *lass*; the older sound, as in *past*, is sometimes used in *Cornish pasty*.
patent: 1st syllable like *pate*. ● Some who use this pronunciation for the general sense, have 1st syllable like *pat* in *Patent Office*, *letters patent*.
pathos: as for **bathos**.
patriarch: 1st *a* as in *paper*.
patriot(ic): *a* as in *pat* or *paper*.
patron, patroness: *a* as in *paper*.
patronage, patronize: *a* as in *pat*.
pejorative: stress on 2nd syllable.
peremptory: stress on 2nd syllable (Amer. on 1st).
perhaps: in careful speech, two syllables with *h*, not *r*, sounded; informally praps.
pharmacopoeia: stress on *oe*; *-poeia* rhymes with *idea*.
philharmonic: 2nd *h* is silent.
phthisis: *ph* is silent.
pianist: stress on 1st *i*, *ia* as in *Ian*.
piano (instrument): *a* as in *man*; (musical direction) *a* as in *calm*.
piazza: *zz* = ts.
pistachio: *a* as in *calm* or *man*, *ch* as in *machine*.
plaid, plait: rhyme with *lad*, *flat*.

plastic: rhymes with *fantastic*. • The pronunciation with *a* as in *calm* sounds affected to many people.

pogrom: originally with stress on the 2nd syllable (as in Russian); now usually on the 1st.

pomegranate: the older pronunciation was with 1st *e* silent, *o* as in *come* or *from*, and stress either on *o* or the 1st *a*; the pronunciation *pom*-gran-it is still used by some speakers, but *pommy*-gran-it is now usual.

porpoise: *oise* like *ose* in *purpose*.

posthumous: *h* is silent.

pot-pourri: stress on 2nd syllable (Amer. on 3rd), *pot-* like *Poe*.

precedence: originally with stress on 2nd syllable, now usually on 1st, which sounds like *press*.

precedent (adjective): stress on 2nd syllable; (noun) as for **precedence**.

precedented: as for **precedence**.

preferable: stress on 1st syllable.

premise (verb): stress on 2nd syllable, rhyming with *surmise*.

prestige: stress on 2nd syllable, *i* and *g* as in *régime*.

prestigious: rhymes with *religious*.

prima facie: *pry*-ma *fay*-shee.

primarily: stress on 1st syllable, with *a* reduced or elided. • The pronunciation with stress on the 2nd syllable, used by some (but not all) Americans, is disapproved of by many users of RP.

Primates: (order of mammals) originally with 3 syllables, but now often with 2.

primer (elementary school-book): *i* as in *prime*. • The older pronunciation with *i* as in *prim* survives in Australia and New Zealand.

privacy: □ *i* as in *privet* or *private*; the former is probably commoner; the latter is the older and Amer. pronunciation.

probably: in careful speech, 3 syllables; informally often probbly.

proboscis: pro-*boss*-iss.

process (noun): *o* as in *probe*. • An older pronunciation with *o* as in *profit* is now only Amer.

process (verb, to treat): like the noun; (to walk in procession) stress on 2nd syllable.

promissory: stress on 1st syllable.

pronunciation: 2nd syllable like *nun*. • Not pro-*noun*-ciation.

prosody: 1st syllable like that of *prospect*.

protean: stress on 1st syllable.

protégé: 1st syllable like that of *protestant* (Amer. like that of *protest*).

proven: *o* as in *prove*.

proviso: 2nd syllable as that of *revise*.
puissance (show-jumping): pronounced with approximation to French, *pui* = pwi, *a* nasalized; (in poetry) may be *pwiss*-ance or *pew*-iss-ance, depending on scansion.
pursuivant: *Percy*-vant.
pyramidal: stress on 2nd syllable.
quaff: rhymes with *scoff*.
quagmire: *a* originally as in *wag*, now usually as in *quad*.
qualm: rhymes with *calm*; the older pronunciation, rhyming with *shawm*, is now rare.
quandary: stress on 1st syllable; the older pronunciation, with stress on 2nd syllable, is rarely, if ever, heard.
quasi: the vowels are like those in *wayside*.
quatercentenary: *kwatt*-er-, not *quarter*-.
questionnaire: 1st two syllables like *question*.
rabid: 1st syllable like that of *rabbit*.
rabies: 2nd syllable like *bees*, not like the 2nd syllable of *babies*.
rampage (verb): stress on 2nd syllable; (noun) on 1st syllable.
rapport: stress on 2nd syllable, which sounds like *pore* (Amer. like *port*).
ratiocinate: 1st two syllables like *ratty*, stress on 3rd.
rationale: *ale* as in *morale*.
really: rhymes with *ideally*, *clearly*, not with *freely*.
recess (noun and verb): stress on 2nd syllable.
recognize: ● do not drop the *g*.
recondite: stress on 1st or 2nd syllable. The former is the commoner, the latter, the older, pronunciation.
recuperate: 2nd syllable like the 1st of *Cupid*.
referable: stress on 1st syllable.
remediable, -al: stress on 2nd syllable, *e* as in *medium*.
remonstrate: stress on 1st syllable; the older pronunciation, with stress on 2nd syllable, is rare.
Renaissance: stress on 2nd syllable, *ai* as in *plaice*.
renege: the traditional pronunciation rhymes with *league*. □ A pronunciation to rhyme with *plague*, for long dialectal, is now common. ● *g* is hard as in *get*, not as in *allege*.
reportage: *age* as in *camouflage*, but with stress.
research (noun): stress on 2nd syllable (Amer. on 1st).
respite: stress on 1st syllable, 2nd like *spite* (Amer. like *spit*).
restaurant: pronunciation with final *t* silent and second *a* nasalized is preferred by many, but that with *ant* = ont is widespread.
revanchism: *anch* as in *ranch*.

ribald: 1st syllable like *rib*.
risible: rhymes with *visible*.
risqué: □ *rees*-kay or *riss*-kay.
romance: stress on 2nd syllable. ● Pronunciation with stress on 1st syllable, usually in sense 'love affair, love story', is non-standard (except when used jocularly).
Romany: 1st syllable as that of *Romulus*.
rotatory: stress on 1st syllable.
rowan: *ow* often as in *low*, although in Scotland, whence the word comes, it is as in *cow*.
rowlock: rhymes with *Pollock*.
sacrilegious: now always rhymes with *religious*.
sahib: *sah*-ib.
salsify: *sal*-si-fee.
salve (noun, ointment; verb, soothe): properly rhymes with *halve*, but now usually with *valve* (Amer. with *have*).
salve (save ship): rhymes with *valve*.
satiety: as for **dubiety**.
Saudi: rhymes with *rowdy*, not *bawdy*.
scabies: as for **rabies**.
scabrous: 1st syllable like that of *scabious* (Amer. like *scab*).
scallop: rhymes with *wallop*.
scarify (make an incision): rhymes with *clarify*. ● Not to be confused with slang *scarify* (terrify) pronounced *scare*-ify.
scenario: *sc* as in *scene*, *ario* as in *impresario* (Amer. with *a* as in *Mary*).
schedule: *sch* as in *Schubert* (Amer. as in *school*).
schism: properly, *ch* is silent (siz'm); but skiz'm is often heard.
schist (rock): *sch* as in *Schubert*.
schizo-: skitso.
scilicet: 1st syllable like that of *silent*.
scone: rhymes with *on*.
second (to support): stress on 1st syllable; (to transfer) on 2nd.
secretary: *sek*-re-try. ● Not *sek*-e-try or *sek*-e-terry or (Amer.) *sek*-re-terry.
secretive: stress on 1st syllable.
seise, seisin: *ei* as in *seize*.
seismic: 1st syllable like *size*.
seraglio: *g* silent, *a* as in *ask*.
sheikh: sounds like *shake* (Amer. like *chic*).
simultaneous: *i* as in *simple* (Amer. as in *Simon*).
sinecure: properly, *i* as in *sign*, but *i* as in *sin* is common.
Sinhalese: sin-hal-*ese*.

Sioux: soo.
sisal: 1st syllable like the 2nd of *precise*.
sixth: in careful speech, avoid the pronunciation sikth.
slalom: *a* as in *spa*.
slaver (dribble): *a* as in *have*.
sleight: sounds like *slight*.
sloth: rhymes with *both*.
slough (bog): rhymes with *bough*; (to cast a skin) with *tough*.
sobriquet: 1st syllable like that of *sober*.
sojourn: 1st *o* as in *sob* (Amer. as in *sober*).
solder: *o* as in *sob* (Amer. pronunciation is sodder or sawder).
solecism: *o* as in *sob*.
solenoid: stress on 1st syllable, *o* as in *sober* or as in *sob*.
sonorous: stress on 1st syllable, 1st *o* as in *sob*.
soporific: 1st *o* now usually as in *sob* (formerly also as in *sober*).
sough (rushing sound): rhymes with *tough*.
sovereignty: *sov*'renty. ● Not sov-*rain*-ity.
Soviet: *o* as in *sober*. The pronunciation with *o* as in *sob* is also very common.
species: *ci* as in *precious*. ● Not *spee*-seez.
spinet: □ may be stressed on either syllable.
spontaneity: as for **deify, deity.**
stalwart: 1st syllable like *stall*.
status: 1st syllable like *stay*. ● Not *statt*-us.
stigmata: stress on 1st syllable. ● Not with *ata* as in *sonata*.
strafe: rhymes with *staff*.
stratosphere: *a* as in *Stratford*.
stratum, strata: *a* of first syllable like 1st *a* of *sonata*.
strength: *ng* as in *strong*. ● Not *strenth*.
suave, suavity: *a* as 1st *a* in *lava*.
subsidence: stress originally on 2nd syllable with *i* as in *side*; pronunciation with stress on 1st syllable and *i* as in *sit* is increasingly common.
substantial: 1st *a* as in *ant*, not *aunt*.
substantive (in grammar): stress on 1st syllable; (having separate existence, permanent) on 2nd syllable.
suffragan: *g* as in *get*.
supererogatory: stress on 4th syllable.
superficies: super-*fish*-(i-)eez.
supine (adjective): stress on 1st syllable (Amer. on 2nd).
suppose: ● in careful speech, avoid the elision of the *u*; informal *I s'pose so*, *s'posing it happens?*

surety: now usually three syllables (*sure*-et-y); originally two (*sure*-ty).
surveillance: ● do not drop the *l*; = sur-*vey*-lance, not sur-*vey*-ance.
suzerain: *u* as in *Susan*.
swath: *a* as in *water*; in plural, *th* as in *paths*.
syndrome: two syllables (formerly three).
taxidermist: □ stress on 1st or 3rd syllable.
temporarily: stress on 1st syllable (with weakening or dropping of *o*): *temp*-ra-rily. ● Not tempo-*rar*-ily.
Tibetan: 2nd syllable like *bet*, not *beat*.
tirade: tie-*raid*.
tissue: as for **issue**.
tonne: sounds like *ton*. ● To avoid misunderstanding, *metric* can be prefixed; but in most spoken contexts the slight difference between the imperial and metric weights will not matter.
tortoise: as for **porpoise**.
tourniquet: 3rd syllable like the 2nd of *croquet* (Amer. like *kit*).
towards: the form with two syllables is now the most common; some speakers use the pronunciation tords in all contexts, others only in some.
trachea: stress on *e* (Amer. on 1st *a*, pronounced as in *trade*).
trait: 2nd *t* is silent (in Amer. pronunciation, it is sounded).
trajectory: stress properly on 1st syllable; now often (and Amer.) on 2nd.
transferable: stress on 1st syllable is implied by the single *r* (see p. 25); but the form *transferrable* was formerly common, and accounts for the common pronunciation with stress on 2nd syllable.
transition: □ tran-*sizh*-on or tran-*zish*-on.
transparent: □ last two syllables either like those of *apparent* or like *parent*.
trauma, traumatic: *au* as in *cause* (Amer. as in *gaucho*).
traverse (noun): stress on 1st syllable; (verb) on 2nd syllable. (The original pronunciation of the verb exactly like the noun is still usual in Amer. English.)
trefoil: stress on 1st syllable, *e* as in *even* or as in *ever*.
triumvir: 1st two syllables like those of *triumphant*.
troth: rhymes with *both* (Amer. with *cloth*).
trow: rhymes with *know*.
truculent: 1st *u* as in *truck;* formerly as in *true*.
turquoise: □ *tur*-kwoyz or *tur*-kwahz.
ululate: *yool*-yoo-late. The alternative pronunciation *ull*-yoo-late seems now to be chiefly Amer.

umbilical: stress on 2nd syllable.
unprecedented: 2nd syllable like *press*.
untoward: the older pronunciation rhymed with *lowered*, but the pronunciation with stress on the 3rd syllable is now usual.
Uranus: stress on 1st syllable.
urinal: stress on 1st syllable.
usual: in careful speech, avoid complete loss of *u* (*yoo*-zh'l).
uvula: *yoo*-vyoo-la.
uxorious: 1st *u* as *Uxbridge*.
vagary: the original pronunciation was with stress on 2nd syllable, but this has been almost entirely superseded by that with stress on 1st syllable.
vagina, vaginal: stress on 2nd syllable, *i* as in *china*.
valance: rhymes with *balance*.
valence, -cy (chemistry): *a* as in *ale*.
valet: those who employ them sound the *t*.
Valkyrie: stress on 1st syllable.
vase: *a* as in *dance* (Amer. rhymes with *face* or *phase*).
veld: sounds like *felt*.
venison: the old pronunciation *ven*-z'n is now rare; *ven*-i-z'n or *ven*-i-s'n are usual.
veterinary: stress on 1st syllable, with reduction or elision of 2nd *e* and *a* (*vet*-rin-ry). ● Not *vet*-nary or (Amer.) *vet*-rin-ery.
vice (in the place of): rhymes with *spicy*.
vicegerent: three syllables, 2nd *e* as in *errant*.
victualler, victuals: sound like *vitt*-ell-er, vittles.
viola (instrument): stress on 2nd syllable, *i* as in *Fiona*; (flower) stress on 1st syllable, *i* as in *vie*.
vitamin: *i* as in *hit* (Amer. as in *vital*).
viz. (= videlicet): when reading aloud, it is customary to substitute *namely*; 'viz' is chiefly jocular.
voluntarily: stress on 1st syllable.
waistcoat: the older pronunciation was *wess*-kot (with 2nd syllable like that of *mascot*); but the pronunciation as spelt has replaced it, except among older speakers.
walnut, walrus: ● do not drop the *l*.
werewolf: 1st syllable like *weir*.
whoop (cry of excitement, *whoop it up*): = woop; (cough, *whooping cough*) = hoop; both rhyme with *loop*.
wrath: rhymes with *cloth* (Amer. with *hath*).
wroth: as for **troth**.
yoghurt: *yogg*-urt (Amer. *yoh*-gurt).

zoology: in careful speech, best pronounced with 1st *o* as in *zone*; there are a number of other compounds of *zoo-* in technical use, in which this is the normal pronunciation.

ENGLISH OVERSEAS

OUTSIDE the United Kingdom and the Republic of Ireland, English is an important language in many regions – especially the United States, Canada, Australia, New Zealand, South Africa, the Caribbean, and India. Despite the great distances separating these five English-speaking communities from each other and from the British Isles, and the great social and cultural differences between them, the forms of English which they use remain mutually intelligible to a remarkable degree. Partly this is because all English-speaking communities have held to a standard spelling system. There are a number of points of difference in spelling between the English of the United States and that of Britain (the other communities follow the British mode, except that many US spellings are usual, or acceptable, in Canada); but these are all relatively minor. The major differences are in pronunciation, vocabulary, and to a lesser degree, grammar.

The United States

The main differences between General American pronunciation and British Received Pronunciation are set out on pp. 230f. The General American accent is a supra-regional way of speaking acceptable throughout the country, but there are very marked differences of accent between different regions of the United States. Two varieties familiar in Great Britain are 'Brooklynese' (the New York City accent), in which *earl* and *oil* sound alike (the sound is somewhere between the two), and the southern 'drawl' (the accent of the states from Virginia southward) in which *I* and *time* sound like *ah* and *tahm*.

The difference in vocabulary between American and British English is too well known to need extensive illustration. Most British people are familiar with many American equivalents for British terms, e.g. *bathrobe* (dressing gown), *checkers* (draughts), *cookie* (biscuit), *elevator* (lift), *flyer* (handbill), *gas* (petrol), *vest* (waistcoat). It is not so often realized that many words and phrases now normal in Britain originated in North America, e.g. *to fall for*, *to fly off the handle*, *off-beat*, *punch line*, *quiz* (as a noun), *round trip*, *round-up*, *to snoop*. Nor is it fully realized how many words and phrases used every day in the United States are unknown, or nearly so, in Britain, and show no sign of being adopted here. Many, but not all, are colloquial, e.g. *realtor* (estate agent), *rotunda* (concourse), *running gear* (vehicle's wheels and axles), *sassy* (cheeky), *scam* (fraud), *scofflaw* (habitual law-breaker), *to second-guess* (be wise after the event), *tacky* (seedy, tatty). Many words have slightly different meanings in the United States, e.g. *jelly* (jam), *mean* (nasty, *not* stingy), *nervy* (impudent, *not* nervous). Some familiar words have a slightly different form, e.g. *behoove*, *crawfish*, *dollhouse*, *math*, *normalcy*, *rowboat*, *sanitarium* (British *sanatorium*), *tidbit*. There are some notable differences between American and British grammar and construction, e.g. *aside from* (apart from), *back of* (behind), *different than*, *in school*, *most* (almost), *protest* (protest against), *some* (to some extent), *through* (up to and including); *he ordered them arrested*, *I just ate* (I have just eaten), *to teach school*, *on the street*, *a quarter of ten*.

While, therefore, the formal and literary varieties of British and American English are mutually intelligible, the most colloquial spoken varieties of each are in some ways very different, and each can, in some contexts, be almost incomprehensible to a speaker of the other.

Canada

Canadian English is subject to the conflicting influences of British and American English. On the whole British English has a literary influence, while American has a spoken one. The Canadian accent is in most respects identical with General American. But where British English has four vowels in (i) *bat*, (ii) *dance*, *father*, (iii) *hot*, *long*, (iv) *law*, and General American three, Canadian has only two: *bat* and *dance* with a front *a*, and *father*, *hot*, *long*, and *law* with a back *ah*-sound. Peculiar to the Canadian accent is a distinction between two varieties of the *I*-sound and two of the *ow*-sound: *light* does not have the same vowel as *lied*, nor *lout* as *loud*. Canadians pronounce some words in the American way, e.g. *dance*, *half*, *clerk*, *tomato*, but others in the British way, e.g. *lever*, *ration*, *process*, *lieutenant*, and the name of the letter *Z*. Some American spellings have caught on, e.g. *honor*, *jail*, *plow*, *program*, *tire*, but many, such as *-er* in words like *center*, single *l* in *traveled*, *jeweler*, and the short *ax*, *catalog*, *check*, have not. In vocabulary there is much US influence: Canadians use *billboard*, *gas*, *truck*, *wrench* rather than *hoarding*, *petrol*, *lorry*, *spanner*; but on the other hand, they agree with the British in using *blinds*, *braces*, *porridge*, *tap*, rather than *shades*, *suspenders*, *oatmeal*, *faucet*. The

Canadian vocabulary, like the American, reflects the contact between English and various American Indian peoples, e.g. *pekan* (a kind of weasel), *sagamite* (broth or porridge), *saskatoon* (a kind of bush, or its berry). It also reflects close contact with the large French-speaking community of Canada and with Eskimo peoples, e.g. *aboiteau* (dike), *inconnu* (a kind of fish), *to mush* (travel by dog-sled); *chimo* (an Eskimo greeting), *kuletuk* (a garment resembling a parka). And as there have been different degrees of settlement by the various non-English-speaking European nationalities in Canada than in the United States, so the range of European loan-words in Canadian English is markedly different, many American colloquialisms being unknown. On the other hand, there are several regional dialects that differ markedly from the standard language, notably that of Newfoundland.

Australia and New Zealand

There are no important differences in written form between the English of Great Britain and that of Australia, New Zealand, or indeed South Africa. The literary language of the four communities is virtually identical. Grammatically, too, the English of all four is uniform, except that each has developed its own colloquial idioms. Thus it is in the everyday spoken language that the main differences lie. The Australian accent is marked by a number of divergences from the British. (i) The vowels of *fleece*, *face*, *price*, *goose*, *goat*, and *mouth* all begin with rather open, slack sounds not unlike those used in cockney speech. (ii) The vowels of *dress*, *strut*, *start*, *dance*, *nurse* have a much closer, tighter, more fronted sound than in RP. (iii) In unstressed syllables, typically *-es* or *-ed* (*boxes*, *studded*), where RP would have a sound like *i* in *pin*, Australian English has a sound like *e* in *open* or *a* in *comma*. (iv) In unstressed syllables, typically *-y*, or *-ie* + consonant (*study*, *studied*), where RP has the sound of *i* in *pin*, Australian English has a close *-ee* sound, as in *tree*. The result of (iii) and (iv) is that in Australia *boxes* and *boxers* sound the same, but *studded* and *studied*, which are the same in RP, sound different. (v) *-t-* between vowels, and *l*, are often sounded rather as they are in American English. A number of individual words are differently pronounced, e.g. *aquatic* and *auction* with an *o* sound as in *hot* in the stressed syllable; *Melbourne* with a totally obscured second syllable, but *Queensland* with a fully pronounced one (the reverse of the RP). Australian vocabulary reflects, of course, the very different nature of the landscape, climate, natural history, and way of life. Familiar English words like *brook*, *dale*, *field*, and *forest* are unusual, whereas *bush*, *creek*, *paddock*, and *scrub* are normal. There are of course a large number of terms (often compounded from English elements) for the plants and animals peculiar to the country, e.g. *blue gum*, *stringybark* (plants), *flathead*, *popeye mullet* (fish). The borrowings from Aboriginal languages hardly need extensive illustration; many are familiar in Britain, e.g. *billabong*, *boomerang*, *budgerigar*, *didgeridoo*, *wallaby*. Many of them have taken on transferred meanings and have lost their Aboriginal associations, e.g. *gibber* (boulder, stone), *mulga* (an inhospitable region), *warrigal* (wild, untamed person or animal). But above all it is in the colloquial language that Australian English differs from British. Not only are there terms relating to Australian life and society, e.g. *jackaroo*, *rouseabout*, *walkabout*, but ordinary terms, e.g. *to chiack* (tease), *crook* (bad, irritable, ill), *dinkum*, *furphy* (rumour), *to smoodge* (fawn, caress); formations and compounds like those ending in *-o* (e.g. *arvo* (afternoon), *Commo* (communist), *smoko* (teabreak)); *to overland*, *ratbag* (eccentric, troublemaker), *ropeable* (angry); and expressions like *come the raw prawn*, *she'll be right*, *have a shingle short*. While it is true that many Australianisms are known in Britain, and form the basis of various kinds of humorous entertainment, and while British English has borrowed some Australian vocabulary (e.g. the verb *to barrack* or the noun *walkabout*), there is yet a wide gap between the popular spoken forms of the two kinds of English.

The gap is less wide in the case of New Zealand English, where British influence has on the whole remained stronger. To a British ear, the New Zealand accent is hardly distinguishable from the Australian. Its main peculiarities are: (i) *i* as in *kit* is a very slack sound almost like *a* in *cadet*; (ii) *a* as in *trap* and *e* as in *dress* are almost like British *e* in *pep* and *i* in *this*; (iii) the vowels of *square* and *near* are very tense and close, and may even be sounded alike; (iv) the vowels of *smooth* and *nurse* are sounded forward in the mouth, and rather close. The chief differences between New Zealand and Australian English are lexical. The words of aboriginal origin are mostly unknown in New Zealand, while the New Zealand words drawn from Maori are unknown in Australia. Many of the latter, naturally, refer to natural history and landscape specific to the country, e.g. *bid-a-bid* (kind of plant), *cockabully*, *tarakihi* (kinds of fish), *pohutukawa* (kind of tree). There is a large everyday vocabulary, much of it, but by no means all, colloquial or slang, used neither in Britain nor in Australia, e.g. *booay* (remote rural district), *greenstone* (stone used for ornaments), *return to the mat* (resume Maori way of life), *shake* (earthquake), *tar-sealed* (surfaced with tar macadam), *Taranaki gate* (gate made of wire strands attached to upright battens). While a fair amount of colloquial vocabulary is shared by Australia and New Zealand (e.g. *sheila*, *Pommy*, *paddock* (field), *shout* (to treat to drinks)), there are important nuances. In both *to bach* is to live as a bachelor, but in New Zealand only is there a noun *bach*, a small beach or holiday house. Similar organizations are the *RSA* (Returned Servicemen's Association) in New Zealand, but the *RSL* (Returned Servicemen's League) in Australia; the initials of the one would be meaningless to a member of the other. *Mopoke* or *morepork* is the name for a kind of owl in New Zealand, but for either a nightjar, or a different kind of owl, in Australia.

South Africa

English is one of the two official languages of the Republic of South Africa, the other being Afrikaans (derived from Dutch, but now an entirely independent language). Afrikaans has had a fairly strong influence on the English of the Republic: the South African accent is distinctly 'clipped'; *r* is often rolled, and the consonants *p*, *t*, and *k* have a sharper articulation, usually lacking the aspiration (a faint *h* sound) found in other varieties of English. *I* is sometimes very lax (like *a* in *along*), e.g. in *bit*, *lip*, at other times very tense (like *ee*), e.g. in *kiss*, *big*; the vowels of *dress*, *trap*, *square*, *nurse* are very tense and close, while that of *part* is very far back, almost like *port*. As in the other forms of English of the Southern Hemisphere, the different landscape, flora and fauna, and way of life are reflected in the South African vocabulary, e.g. *dorp* (village), *go-away bird*, *kopje*, *nartjie* (tangerine), *rand*, *rhenosterbos* (a kind of plant), *roman*, *snoek* (both fish), *springbok*, *stoep* (veranda), *veld*. There are many loan-words from Afrikaans and African languages, e.g. (besides most of those above) *braai* (barbecue), *donga* (eroded watercourse), *erf* (building plot), *gogga* (insect), *impala* (kind of antelope), *indaba* (meeting for discussion), *lekker* (nice), *rondavel* (hut). There are also many general colloquial words and phrases, e.g. *the farm* (the country), *homeboy* (African from one's own area), *location* (Black township), *robot* (traffic light), *tackies* (plimsolls). Some of these reflect the influence of Afrikaans idiom, e.g. *to come there* (arrive), *just now* (in a little while), *land* (a field), *to wait on* (wait for). Only a few words have entered the main stream of English, but they are important ones, including *apartheid*, *commandeer*, *commando*, *laager*, *trek*, and the slang *scoff* (to eat; food).

The Caribbean

The standard English spoken in the Caribbean differs slightly from standard British English in some features of stress, intonation, pronunciation, and vocabulary. More different from standard English are the dialects of Caribbean English Creole (CEC). This language evolved through the contact between African and European populations during the slave trade and plantation periods of the 17th–18th centuries. CEC has derived most of its vocabulary from English, but a number of African languages, particularly the Niger–Congo family, including Yoruba, Twi, and Mandingo, and the Bantu languages, have contributed to its vocabulary, sound system, and grammar. In some areas, such as Trinidad and Guyana, proximity to areas where other languages are spoken, or the presence of speakers of other languages, have greatly influenced CEC, particularly in vocabulary. Spanish, French Creole, and Hindi–Bhojpuri are the most noticeable influences.

There is considerable social as well as geographical variation in English and English Creole usage in the Caribbean. Forms most different from English have been characterized as 'broken' or 'bad' English, but this attitude is changing considerably towards a more positive one. Most West Indians control a range of language varieties used within the overall speech community. Written language is usually English, although some newspapers show Creole influence. 'Dialect' writing in various forms of CEC is mostly confined to advertisements, dialogue in plays and novels, and humorous articles.

The verb systems of CEC are characterized by particles used to mark the verb. Once a time reference is established, the tense in focus is usually unmarked; this is particularly noticeable in the past, e.g., *yesterday he walk home*. Aspect, such as continuous or habitual action, is always marked, e.g., *me a go* 'I am going'. The particles can be combined, as in *me bin da go* 'I was going (a long time ago)'. In several CEC varieties, there is some direct translation whereby English words are used but have CEC grammatical meanings, e.g., *every day I does wait for bus*, where *does* marks the habitual. The verb is not marked for third person singular.

The verb *be* in sentences such as *Samwel* a *tiela* 'Samuel is a tailor', is almost always expressed in some form. *Be* is also expressed for place, as in *im* de *in di gyaaden* 'he/she is in the garden'. No *be* is necessary in the present tense before an adjective, as in *I tired*, *that nice*. Verbs and adjectives often behave differently than in

English, e.g., *he bury yesterday* 'he was buried yesterday', *it did cheap* 'it was cheap', *mi sick* 'I am sick', *mi go sick* 'I will be sick'.

Possession is usually indicated by juxtaposition, e.g. *mi brada haas* 'my brother's horse' or by the particle *fi* (primarily in Jamaica and Guyana), e.g., *dis wan a fi mi* 'this one is mine'. (*Fi* has a number of other functions, as in *a wan fi go* 'I want to go'.) Pronouns often do not change case endings as in English, e.g., Jamaican *im a go* 'he/she is going' and Trinidadian *I like she* 'I like her'. In most cases, a distinction is made between second person singular, e.g. *you*, *yuh*, and plural, e.g. *unu*, *allyuh*, *yinna*. Definite animate plurals are usually unmarked, but may be marked with a pronoun, as in *di dog-dem* 'the dogs'. Some words have an invariant form which appears plural, e.g., *a ants*, *one matches*. Comparatives often follow the form *John more big than him*. There are several widespread emphatic sentence patterns, e.g., *a big im big* or *is big he big* 'he's really big', and *a hau mi go see dat?* or *is how ah go see dat?* 'how will I see that?'.

The sound system of CEC differs considerably throughout the region, but there are some widespread features: (i) the use of the sounds *t* and *d* ('stops') where standard accents would have the voiceless and voiced *th* sounds ('fricatives') as in *thing* and *brother*; (ii) the reduction of final consonant clusters, as in *han* 'hand' and *neks* 'next'; (iii) a sound like French *ui* in *cuisine* as the sound of *w* in words like *wet* and *wheel*; and (iv) the use of 'clear' *l* (as in British *let*) in all positions.

Some areas, such as Jamaica, Tobago, and Guyana, share striking sound similarities despite their distances from each other and differences from their immediate neighbours. A good example is *r*. In Barbados, it is pronounced in all positions. In the Leewards and Trinidad, however, *r* is not present before consonants, e.g. in *start*, or at the end of a word, e.g. *beer*, although the vowel is lengthened. Jamaica and Guyana have also lost *r* before consonants, but retain it at the end of a word.

The vowels of words such as *face* and *goat* are pure vowels without glides in Barbados, Guyana, Trinidad, and some varieties elsewhere. However, in basilectal Jamaican and Leewards speech they have developed preceding glides so that they resemble *fyace* and *gwoat*. In Barbados, Guyana, and Trinidad, and in some isolated areas elsewhere, a sequence resembling *ong* replaces *own* in words like *town*. A decreasing number of areas have a *y* sound following *k* and *g* sounds before some vowels, e.g., *gyaaden* 'garden' and *kyan* 'can'.

There is some evidence that there are significant stress or tone patterns distinguishing word pairs such as *Taylor/tailor*. Several features of the intonation patterns are distinctive, but not well studied; one striking feature of the overall sound of CEC is the tendency to give each syllable equal weight, hence *Mi-chael*, rather than *Mi*-k'l.

The vocabulary of Caribbean English includes all of standard English plus local words. CEC includes a large part—potentially all—of English vocabulary, plus local words. Although there is considerable variation by country or local area, many CEC lexical items are found in many areas, e.g., *cut-eye* (a hostile glance), *study your head* 'to think hard', *hard-ears* 'stubborn, disobedient', *gravilicious/cravetious* 'greedy', *next* 'next, another, the other', *a dead* 'a corpse', *force-ripe* 'precocious in a bad way', *fufu* (a dish, usually of pounded root vegetables). The influence of many languages is quite evident in vocabulary, e.g., the Amerindian *agouti* (a rodent) and *carat* (a palm), the Indian *roti* (a flat bread folded over a filling), Chinese *whe-whe* (a gambling game), French Creole *jab-jab* (a devil masquerade), Spanish *rebucan* (secondary cocoa harvest), African *susu* (a revolving savings system) and *eye-water* (tears).

India

India, with about 23 million speakers of English, is the third largest English-speaking nation after the USA and UK—that is, if only three per cent of its 1985 population is considered bilingual in English. It was T. B. Macaulay's (1800–59) controversial Minute of 2 February 1835 that institutionalized bilingualism in English in Indian education and sociocultural settings. After 1947, independent India's constitution gave English the status of an 'associate' official language. Hindi is the 'official' language of the Republic. English is the state language of Meghalaya and Nagaland.

In India's intricate sociolinguistic context of an estimated 1652 languages and dialects, English is a vital pan-Indian link language. In typical Indian functions, English has developed several local varieties ranging from educated Indian English (IE) to restricted pidginized bazār varieties. Educated IE provides a standard for teaching, the media, and for interaction among the elite. Although spoken IE is distinctly Indian, in grammar and spelling, the educated British norm has a standardizing effect. The contact of English with Indian languages and cultures, and its specific Indian functions, manifest themselves in various processes of Indianization. The following generalizations are illustrative; however, some variation depends on the IE user's first language, region, and education.

In pronunciation, the alveolar series of consonants (e.g. *t*, *d*) is replaced by the retroflex series (pronounced with the tongue-tip curled up towards the hard palate); fricatives (e.g. *f*, and *th* in *thin* and *thus*) are pronounced as aspirated consonants *p+h*, *t+h*, *d+h* (or plain *d*); consonant clusters such as *sk-*, *st-*, and *sp-* do not occur in word-initial position; initial *p*, *t*, and *k* are not aspirated (as they are in British English); diphthongs (e.g. those in *lay*, *low*) generally change to monophthongs; the stress system is primarily used for emphasis and suffixes are stressed; unstressed vowels are pronounced as full vowels (e.g. in *photography* all the syllables are given full value unlike in British English), and no distinction is made between the strong and weak forms of vowels. All IE speakers share syllable-timed rhythm as opposed to the stress-timed rhythm of native varieties of English.

In syntax, interrogative structures do not always have subject–auxiliary inversion (*What you would like to eat?*); articles are used arbitrarily; certain selection constraints are violated, e.g., stative verbs (e.g. *have*, *know*) are used in progressive tenses (*John is having two books*, *I was knowing that you would come*); and reduplication is used for emphasis and for expressing a distributive meaning (*I want hot hot rice*, *Give them one one piece*).

The Indianness in IE vocabulary shows, for example, in borrowings from Indian languages to refer to typical Indian objects and concepts, e.g. *ahimsa* (non-violence), *bandh* (shutdown), *bhakti* (devotion), *chapati* (bread), *guru* (teacher), *panchayat* (village council)—only a few of such borrowings have been absorbed in British or American English (e.g. *pandit*, *pyjama*, *shampoo*); hybridization of local words and English, e.g. *lathi-charge* (to charge with baton), *swadeshi-cloth* (home-made cloth); translating contextually appropriate collocations from Indian languages, e.g. *twice-born* (a Brahmin), *dining leaf* (a leaf on which food is served); compounding based on Sanskrit patterns, e.g. *welcome address* (an address of welcome), *God-love* (love of God); and extending or restricting the semantic range of English words, e.g. kinship terms such as *brother*, *sister*, *mother* are additionally used as modes of reference and address, and *communal*, *interdine*, *intermarriage* have acquired specific meanings in Hindu–Muslim relationships, as have *holy-thread*, *pollute*, and *defile* in the context of caste system.

Indianized rhetorical strategies and styles are noticeable in stylistic and thematic experimentation in IE literature and in registers such as journalism and administration. One such strategy is 'mixing' words, phrases, clauses, and idioms from Indian languages in the stream of discourse in IE.

The localized model of IE has national currency and intelligibility. The international uses are restricted. In such uses, once the attitudinal barriers are crossed, and the IE innovations are understood in their proper sociolinguistic context, educated IE speakers are internationally intelligible. The functions of IE are, however, essentially Indian, and in its nativized form, IE has become, as it were, another Indian language.

HINTS ON SPEECH-MAKING AND TOASTS

'You have that in your countenance which I would fain call master.'
'What's that?'
'Authority.'

(William Shakespeare)

To the public speaker authority 'in countenance' is important; the voice and the eyes are equally faithful reflectors of both confidence and insecurity. The speaker needs confidence in himself, and the audience needs to *find* confidence in his ability.

As the voice is the chief communicator the aspiring speaker will work continually to improve it. An analysis of examination results in public speaking shows that poor voice production and quality is almost as frequent a cause of failure as inadequate speech construction.

The voice is flawed if:

(*a*) It is weakly supported by breath.

(*b*) It is husky and toneless.

(*c*) It has a pinched, strident quality.

(*d*) It is unresonant and difficult to hear at the furthest reaches of the audience.

It must be remembered that the voice is a musical instrument easily damaged by misuse.

Weaknesses such as these demand the attention of qualified and experienced teachers. It cannot be a do-it-yourself job.

Control of breath is the foundation on which voice is built. Tone should be balanced on a sufficient and steadily controlled supply of breath. Too *much* inhaled air fogs the tone; too *little* weakens supply *and* tone, and makes assured phrasing impossible. Simply, air breathed out sets the 'machine' in motion: air breathed in renews the fuel supply.

Most of us are sensitive to vocal quality; a harsh, shrill tone is offensive to our ears. Voices under stress are prone to distortion.

Teachers with weak class-control tend to have voices unnaturally pitched, squeezed, and forced in their vain attempts to quell a noisy class. Sadly, this is a 'Catch 22' situation; a noisy class makes a noisy teacher and a noisy teacher makes a noisy class.

Little can be achieved without relaxation. Anxiety tightens the muscles which control the free passage of air. When we yawn we (involuntarily) loosen the muscles of the throat, opening wide the arch at the back, so a series of wide, sustained yawns, each ending with a contented sigh, can do much to help. Try also to loosen the neck and shoulder muscles by shrugging and gentle head-rolling. Stand, feet comfortably apart. Place your hands, palms flat, against the lower ribs and breathe in slowly through an open mouth. You will feel the ribs expand to accommodate the inhaled air. Hold air in the lungs for three seconds, then breathe out *very slowly*, concentrating on an absolutely smooth exhalation. In this exercise the upper chest will rise a little when air is inhaled. There should be minimal shoulder movement. Repeat ten times, *with concentration*.

When long sentences or lines of verse are spoken this controlled legato is invaluable.

In its passage from lungs to mouth breath passes through the 'reeds' of the vocal cords causing them to vibrate and create sound waves. These are amplified by cavities in the head and the great cavity of the mouth, which is the chief resonator and amplifier.

To obtain good tone the voice must be focused well *forward*. Incorrect placing produces a muffled, unresonant tone. There are books which recommend useful exercises to achieve forward production, but there is no substitute for constant practice.

When the voice is strengthened and enriched by resonance it adds vitality and carrying-power. Humming is a simple, effective way of reinforcing the natural resonance created within the nasal cavities. It is important to avoid dropping the soft palate during vowel production; it causes unpleasant nasality. The rapid repetition of the word 'amo*ng*'—with emphasis on the final sound—will help to strengthen a lazy palate.

Diction is the process of cutting and shaping sound into articulate speech in its two main divisions—vowels, which gives it musical quality, and consonants, which give it clarity.

George Bernard Shaw maintained that it was impossible for one Englishman to open his mouth without making some other Englishman hate or despise him, and certainly pronunciation is closely related to class distinction. He also said: 'The English have no respect for their own language and will not teach their children to speak it', which is nearer the truth.

Lord Chesterfield's advice is more relevant to the public speaker's needs:

'Words are the dress of thought, which should be no more presented in rags and tatters than our persons should.'

The sensible public speaker—*irrespective of what regional pronunciation he may have*—should concentrate upon:

(*a*) A firm shaping of words so that they are cleanly begun and properly finished.

(*b*) An unforced delivery.

(*c*) An effective arrangement of the words into sense-groups.

(*d*) Sufficient variation of pace and inflexion to avoid monotony.

(*e*) Imaginative and emotional involvement so that meaning, colour and vitality are communicated.

(*f*) Competent projection of the voice over the whole speaking area.

The speaker must be aware that prose has a natural rhythm of its own (say aloud: 'Kippers for breakfast, herrings for tea') and that its free flow is important. The voice of the cuckoo is heard in our land whenever a public speaker 'promotes' the indefinite article 'a' into 'āy' instead of 'ŭ'. The following statement will, if read aloud, prove the póint:

'It is AY great disgrace that AY group of persons, in the name of democracy, should cause AY split in AY formerly united body.'

This absurd and unnecessary mangling of the neutral vowel sound (the little aah-ing noise we make when groping for a word) grossly impedes the free flow of rhythm and causes the phrase to sound stilted and unnatural. No good speaker would adopt it.

Writers and speakers know the frustration of 'waiting for the idea'. Charles Dickens, describing the odious Smallweed in *Bleak House*, writes:

Anything that he ever put away in his mind was a grub at first and a grub at last. In all his life he had never bred a single butterfly.

If ideas are to breed other and better ideas it is necessary to clear out stale thoughts that have lain inactive for a long time. There are moments in the day when the mind is in neutral gear—when some routine matter is in hand. It is then that an idea may be mulled over creatively. Chance favours the prepared mind.

Edward De Bono's *Practical Thinking* will be found helpful. Consider the preparation of a speech:

> In language clarity is everything.
>
> (Confucius)

The speaker should not confine this definition to mere excellence of diction. It embodies clearness of thought and the means of expression. If *Truth* married *Simplicity* and they bred *Interest*, *Brevity*, and *Communication* they would make an admirable public-speaking family. The arrangement of a speech should follow these guidelines.

The speaker may find it helpful to write down ideas in rough, then read them over slowly and thoughtfully, add or subtract, shuffle them around to improve their impact, then put the whole thing away for hours or days. A later reading will reveal weaknesses not realized earlier. Now the speaker should find a lively, striking beginning that will compel attention at once. (See 'The After-Dinner Speech'.) A similarly memorable ending should be prepared so that the audience is left interested and wishing for more. If the speech is well made and the points telling the speaker can begin with confidence in his material, at least.

Most of our little defeats are caused by negative thought. We cut the ground from under our own feet. The negative public speaker stumbles unhappily through alleys of potential failure peopled, it seems, with contemptuous critics. He longs for the conclusion before ever he has had a chance to redeem a weak, self-deprecating beginning. Communication is still-born.

The positive thinker leaves apprehension outside his venue and concentrates on the task in hand. He does not apologize in advance for a weakness he has no intention of displaying.

As you prepare your speech then, read it aloud. You are not preparing a reading. How the words sound *matters*. The nearer that sound to simple and *delighted* conversation the better. A small boy in Southern Ireland enchanted his examiner by saying spontaneously 'D'ye know what it is, sir; I *love* that pome.' His face glowed with sincerity. The poet would have been equally impressed. If *you* don't like your subject-matter it is unlikely to move anyone else. Choose simple, working, lively words. Churchill wrote: 'A vocabulary of truth and simplicity will be of service throughout life.' The deliberate use of involved language to impress displays a total contempt for a beautiful and flexible language. It is not impressive to speak of contumaciousness when you mean disobedience; an encumbrance is better described as a burden.

Avoid jargon and cliché and mindless phrases in common use around us. We can all make our own lists. A few examples may start you off:

Obscene for a proposal you don't agree with; *at the end of the day* for eventually; *to take on board* for to understand; *at this moment in time* for at present, or now. And many others.

The speaker should be aware always of the dominant words in phrases or sentences and not waste time placing stress on unimportant ones. If heavy stress is given indiscriminately in an attempt to make everything equally important meaning is confused and delivery made ridiculous.

A discriminating use of inflexion gives charm and variety to language, but beware of the 'soaring' inflexion, a sudden leap up for no discernible reason and without relevance to the sense. It is used in a self-conscious attempt to be musical.

Language should clarify meaning, never confuse it. Nothing should stand in the way of clear thought and communication. The pedlars of verbosity should study the magnificent simplicity of the Authorized Version of the Bible.

Executives in industry and commerce, Civil Servants, and others have to present reports to employers and committees. This is public speaking in which emotion plays little part. The speaker should present facts and figures at moderate speed and with great clarity. These should be arranged logically. If the speaker is expected to draw his own conclusion he should do so as briefly as possible. He should anticipate questions and have answers ready. If speaking to his own employers it is important for him to be poised, calm, and apparently confident.

The political speech: A classic example (excerpt)

I stand before you, sir, as an individual being tried for certain offences against the State. You are a symbol of that State. But I am something more than an individual also; I, too, am a symbol at the present moment, a symbol of Indian nationalism, resolved to break away from the British Empire and achieve the independence of India.

It is not me that you are seeking to judge and condemn, but rather the hundreds of millions of the people of India, and that is a large task even for a proud Empire.

Perhaps it may be that, although I am standing before you on my trial, it is the British Empire itself that is on its trial before the bar of the world. There are more powerful forces at work in the world today than courts of law; there are elemental urges for freedom and food and security which are moving vast masses of people, and history is being moulded by them. The future recorder of this history might well say that in the hour of supreme trial the Government of Britain and the people of Britain failed because they could not adapt themselves to a changing world. He may muse over the fate of empires which have always fallen because of this weakness and call it destiny. Certain causes inevitably produce certain results. We know the causes; the results are inexorably in their train.

It is a small matter to me what happens to me in this trial or subsequently. Individuals count for little; they come and go, as I shall go when my time is up. Seven times I have been tried and convicted by British authority in India, and many years of my life lie buried within prison walls. An eighth time or a ninth, and a few more years makes little difference.

But it is no small matter what happens to India and her millions of sons and daughters. That is the issue before me, and that ultimately is the issue before you, sir. If the British government imagines it can continue to exploit them and to play about with them against their will, as it has done for so long in the past, then it is grievously mistaken. It has misjudged their present temper and read history in vain.

(Jawaharlal Nehru: at his trial for sedition in 1940)

This excerpt from Nehru's defence has a literacy and dignity that seems an age removed from the crude outbursts we hear today when *playing to the media* is so important.

The political speech has two clear requirements: to refute the opposition's case and to advance your own. It is partisan (seldom objective), controversial, and unsparing. It may be derisive, persuasive, indignant, and many other things. It is often far too long and too vocally monotonous to retain interest for long.

Points to bear in mind:

(*a*) Read what the opposition have written and listen to what they have said on radio and television or in public. Unless you have studied their claims it is difficult to deal intelligently with them.

(*b*) Read and remember anything injudicious that may have been written or said in the past; it may be possible to 'hang them with their own garters'.

(*c*) Prepare your 'attack' with dramatic technique; leave the most telling points to the end and make that memorable. A good speech never fizzles out.

(*d*) Do not try to slay too many dragons at once. Better short and telling than long and diffused. Avoid common abuse but do not hesitate to use sardonic humour if it is appropriate. Churchill described Attlee as a 'sheep in sheep's clothing'.

(*e*) In putting your own case look to the past if you must but concentrate on the future. Most people are more concerned with what *may* happen to them than with what has. Have some hopeful thoughts to offer; have an alternative strategy which the electorate may be persuaded to consider. It is not enough to promise this and that. The political road is paved with broken promises: say *how* you think your strategy could be carried out to everyone's benefit and, if you have the courage, estimate the cost to the taxpayer! Anticipate objections; have answers ready; be direct: shun the shifty sidestepping so amusingly illustrated in 'Yes, Minister'.

(*f*) Keep vocabulary simple and sentences short. Avoid jargon, especially the economic new-speak of Common Marketeers. Education, too, is becoming infected with such horrors as: 'He makes the minimal contribution to his peer-group and is an emerging under-achiever.' Do not condescend or imply that those with whom you disagree are morons, and *never* use belligerent, hand-chopping gestures to armour-plate violent language. This belongs to the rabble-rouser, not the serious politician.

The politician is apt to develop irritating mannerisms—head-wagging, a throwing-up of the eyes at the end of a statement as one who says: 'God has spoken,' a sudden surge of volume on an upward inflexion for the sake of emphasis. For their own good, such speakers should be filmed occasionally and made to watch the result.

In a special category is the *After-Dinner Speech*.

This, being spoken on a social occasion, must be amiable, relaxed in presentation, and *brief*. It should be a welcome part of the evening's entertainment, not an ordeal for speaker and audience alike. The speaker should aim to achieve the kind of directness and spontaneity that characterize Alistair Cooke's 'Letters from America', but behind this seemingly impromptu delivery there should be very careful and thorough preparation.

Notes must not be READ

A speaker who is nose-deep in notes is wearing self-imposed

blinkers: he cannot communicate effectively. It is enough to have a few *headline* notes printed clearly on a postcard and placed unobtrusively on the table. A quick glance prompts the memory without distracting the audience.

Because the company have so many things to distract *them*—things to nibble, to drink, to fidget with—it is important that the speaker avoids fidgeting with his glasses, his handkerchief, the cutlery, money in his pocket, and the like. An audience fascinated or irritated by such antics is not attentive to the speech.

The speaker must remember two key words—*communicate* and *entertain*.

Speakers who begin with apologies for inadequacies they have not yet had time to prove have a kind of death-wish, yet this self-debasement is common.

The after-dinner speaker has even more need of a strong, compelling opening than most and this should be planned with some imagination. For example, a speech to a Gastronomic Society might begin:

> I mind my belly very studiously, and very carefully; for I look upon it that he who does not mind his belly, will hardly mind anything else.
>
> (Dr Samuel Johnson)

The opening might simply be an anecdote, but whatever its character it must be pithy.

At dinners the tables are often arranged to suit the waiters rather than the speaker, and some tables are on difficult sight-lines. This tempts the speaker to address himself exclusively to the better-placed tables. This should be avoided. No one likes to feel excluded.

It is a delusion to suppose that a speech cannot be entertaining unless it provokes frequent gales of laughter. Indeed, the 'comic' who mistakes crude joking for eloquence is a great trial. The best speeches are often those which elicit a *smiling* response from the audience. This demands wit rather than humour and a nice degree of timing.

The *Concise Oxford Dictionary* defines 'to entertain' as 'to amuse; to occupy agreeably'. This should not, in either definition, be beyond the reach of any speaker who likes his fellow men.

Toasts

Since the first troglodyte raised his stone mug and said the equivalent of 'Cheers!' men and women have toasted each other's health.

On important occasions a Toastmaster is engaged to organize the evening's events and call upon the speakers in a formal, established manner. He will have been given a list of the guests who are to speak and will have been told who is to propose the toasts and who will reply, and in what order.

The Toastmaster calls upon speakers in a formula which the speaker must note carefully since he is to imitate it exactly.

'My lords, ladies and gentlemen,' the Toastmaster may begin, or 'Mr President, distinguished guests' (etc.), '. . . pray silence for . . . who will propose the toast to . . .' The speaker will then repeat the Toastmaster's salutation and propose the toast. When this has been done the Toastmaster repeats the toast, the company stand, and all drink. The ritual salutation is repeated in turn by the person who will reply to the toast.

If the title of the toast is already printed on the menu the Toastmaster will not name it.

The toasts begin with the service of coffee, the loyal toast coming first in two simple words: 'The Queen!' No service is allowed until this toast has been drunk.

Guests who are to reply to the toast to themselves, or to the institutions they represent, are rightly aggrieved if the proposer rambles on about something quite irrelevant, turning to his proper subject only at the end. Care must be taken to keep everyone in good humour as a host should.

The person replying to the toast will be wise to note a few of the proposer's remarks and refer briefly to them, if only to prove that he was listening! He should thank his host courteously, say that he is honoured by the invitation (never that he doesn't know why he was asked) and he has enjoyed the hospitality, offer a brief anecdote (preferably humorous) about himself, and make agreeable comments upon the body which has invited him.

No toast, proposed or replied to, should occupy more than *three minutes*.

The Wedding Toast

It would be presumptuous to advise on the content of toasts at weddings or even to suggest time-limitations. The occasion is happy and personal. Provided the recognized order is observed the best thing to remember is:

> 'What comes from the heart goes to the heart.'

The *order* is as follows:

1. The toast to the bride and groom, usually proposed by a family friend, *not* by parents.
2. A reply by the groom on his wife's behalf and his own. This must express gratitude to those who have worked to make the day so memorable.
3. Before closing, the groom must thank the donors for their presents.
4. The groom then proposes a toast to the bridesmaids.
5. The best man replies on their behalf, with suitably flattering comments, and then proposes a toast to the parents, who by this time deserve one.

Impromptu Speaking by Vera Gough (Pergamon Press) is a valuable little book, giving specimen toasts on such occasions.

Making Presentations

Retirement, promotion, leaving the district, going to get married are among the reasons for presentations. They are small-group occasions, usually held at lunch-time or after office hours. They should not be dismissed lightly. A retirement presentation is particularly important to the person concerned. It marks a separation after many years from habit, custom, and colleagues. The speech on such an occasion must bear witness to the years of service and to friendships formed. It should have warmth and dignity and it should never be laboured.

All the speeches in this category should be friendly and *comfortable*. Notes should never be used. It is very bad form to rush off from such an occasion the moment the last word has been said.

Talking To The Young

Regrettably, many speakers talk to young people as if they belonged to a separate branch of humanity. Children of primary-school age can make a wonderful audience if a few simple facts are remembered.

The subject-matter should be appropriate to their age and present understanding. It should be practical rather than abstract and it should involve their imaginations. It will be enhanced by the use of good visual aids and models. The talk should be given at a moderate pace and with lively inflexions and an effective use of *pause*. Humour—if it is not sophisticated—is appreciated and the atmosphere should be friendly and relaxed.

However, in these less disciplined days, it is most unwise to allow shouted interruptions and questions, cat-calls, and the like. There may be a few unruly children and these must be treated firmly. It is fatal to try to be one of them in manner or idiom; they will regard you with contempt. Never buy peace at the expense of your own dignity.

Speaking to secondary-school children and young students allows a more sophisticated vocabulary, though simplicity should still be regarded as important. Visual and sound aids are valuable and notes may be used unobtrusively.

Discourage domination of question-time by one or two extrovert characters. It is foolish to assume that quiet listeners have nothing useful to say; draw them out when you can.

Be patient with the occasional crass remark or apparently silly question. These sometimes arise out of self-consciousness: it is not always easy to join in.

Advanced speakers may like to attempt the Public Speaking Examinations of the London Academy of Music and Dramatic Art, ranging from Bronze, Silver and Gold Medals to the Associate Public Speaking Diploma (ALAM) which demands an extremely high standard of performance before two examiners. This lasts an hour. The assessments are based upon voice, diction, and deportment, the quality of three prepared *contrasting* speeches and an impromptu speech, as well as a discussion on the technique involved. The pass mark is 150 out of 200 (honours 175). The candidate for the Diploma must already have gained the Gold Medal.

Full details may be obtained from the Administrator of Examinations, LAMDA, Tower House, 226 Cromwell Road, London SW5.

It seems appropriate to end with

A Speaker's Prayer

Lord, give me confidence, humility
and humour so that I may communicate
with ease; and when I sit down may
no one be moved to give thanks to you.

VERBAL FORMS OF ADDRESS

ONE of the frequent complaints made over the years by HRH Prince Charles, Prince of Wales, is that when he is enjoying the start of a good conversation, all too often the man or woman to whom he has been introduced suddenly becomes tongue-tied and lost for words. Other members of the royal family, equally adept at making people feel at ease, suffer the same experience.

The problem is that despite the great easing of protocol in modern times, people often remain nervous when they find themselves in the company of royalty because they do not know the rules of verbal address. 'Grey areas' still exist which only serve to complicate matters. For instance, although the days are over when it was rigidly observed, whilst in conversation with royalty, never to speak until spoken to, never to introduce topics of conversation, and not to ask questions, it is still *usual* for royalty to speak first.

For the uninitiated this new flexibility presents difficulties when talking not only to royalty, but to members of the peerage, the judiciary (especially women), the clergy, diplomats, academics, and civic leaders.

The spoken form of address to members of the royal family is relatively uncomplicated.

On meeting the Queen for the first time she is addressed as 'Your Majesty', and subsequently as 'Ma'am', to rhyme with 'Pam' and not 'palm'.

In conversation with the Queen 'Your Majesty' is substituted for 'you'. In such an exchange references to other members of the royal family are made to 'His Royal Highness' or 'Her Royal Highness' or to the individual title, viz., The Duke of Edinburgh or the Duchess of Kent.

The same rules apply to Queen Elizabeth the Queen Mother, who is addressed in the same way as the sovereign.

All other members of the royal family are addressed as 'Your Royal Highness' on introduction and subsequently as 'Sir' or 'Ma'am'.

However, at informal meeting I have found that after a formal introduction has taken place some of the younger members of the royal family are content to be addressed as 'you'.

In talking with members of the royal family it is a grave error to refer to an immediate relative as 'your husband', 'your sister', 'your wife', or 'your cousin'. Titles are *always* used.

Speeches: when the Queen or the Queen Mother is present the preamble begins 'May it please Your Majesty . . .'.

If a member of the royal family holds a specific office he or she is referred to as, for instance, 'Your Royal Highness and President . . .'.

To denote their rank as children of the sovereign, the Queen's three younger children are officially referred to in conversation as '*The* Princess Anne', '*The* Prince Andrew', and '*The* Prince Edward'.

Confusion can arise in another area for those not versed in royal protocol.

Whereas the wife of a royal prince takes on the style of her husband, viz., 'Her Royal Highness Princess Michael of Kent', this does *not* apply to the husband of a royal princess. Thus the Honourable Angus Ogilvy (the prefix denotes he is the younger son of an earl) has no claim, as the husband of Princess Alexandra, to any special form of address.

Men in his position 'should only be addressed as "Sir" if his seniority is such that he would be addressed as "Sir" in any case'.

The most difficult forms of verbal address concern the peerage, which is divided into five main groups: Duke, Marquess, Earl, Viscount, and Baron. To complicate matters there is often a formal, social, and employee form of address.

Only a duke is ever addressed by his actual rank. Formal address: 'Your Grace'. Social: 'Duke'. Employee: 'Your Grace'.

There is an easy pitfall if several dukes attend a gathering. If reference is made to only one duke he is called 'the Duke' but if a distinction is necessary or there is more than one duke present he should be called, for example, 'The Duke of Rutland'.

The formal address for a duchess is 'Your Grace'. Social: 'Duchess'. Employee: 'Your Grace'.

A dowager duchess, widow of a duke, is also addressed as 'Duchess'.

If a marriage to a duke has been dissolved, his former wife continues to use her former title but preceded by her Christian name, viz., Jane, Duchess of Somewhere—unless she remarries.

She is addressed formally as 'Madam'. Social: 'Duchess'. Employee: 'Madam'.

The eldest son of a duke, marquess, or earl takes as a courtesy title the second title of his father; e.g., the eldest son of the Duke of Norfolk is the Earl of Arundel and is addressed as 'Lord Arundel'.

Younger sons of dukes and marquesses are introduced as 'Lord Charles Merton' and addressed thereafter as 'Lord Charles'.

Daughters of dukes, marquesses, and earls are introduced as 'Lady Mary Merton' and addressed thereafter as 'Lady Mary'.

A marquess and narchioness, earl and countess, viscount and viscountess, and baron and baroness are *all* addressed as 'Lord and Lady So-and-So'.

A baronet and his wife are addressed as 'Sir John and Lady Surname'.

There are only two hereditary knights, the Knight of Kerry who is the Green Knight, and the Knight of Glin who is the Black Knight.

Both are addressed as 'Knight'.

If you were staying with either one of them it would be correct on retiring to say, 'Goodnight, Knight'!

A dame (the female equivalent of a knighthood) is introduced as 'Dame Mary Surname' and addressed as 'Dame Mary'.

A peeress in her own right (at present all are either countesses or baronesses) is addressed as 'Lady Surname'.

A life peer or peeress is 'Lord Surname' or 'Lady Surname'. Although some life peeresses prefer the style, for example, 'Baroness Phillips' they are verbally addressed with their title, *never* just 'Baroness'. If in doubt check with the peeress concerned.

Remember, however, that whereas the wife of a life peer is styled as her husband and addressed as 'Lady Surname', the husband of a life peeress takes no title.

Unless the husband has a title of his own such a couple are addressed as 'Lady Surname and Mr Surname'.

Also remember that it is customary to continue to address the heir of a peerage or a baronetcy, when a peer or baronet dies, by the style by which he was formerly known until *after* his predecessor's funeral.

The style of 'The Honourable' is never used in verbal address.

Rules are different in Scotland and Ireland with their chiefs, chieftains, and lairds.

The chief of a clan is addressed by clan or territorial designation and not by surname. Thus in Scotland you would say, 'Hello, Lochiel' or 'Goodbye, Mackintosh'.

Irish chieftains, however, are addressed by their titles: O'Conor Don is addressed as 'O'Conor', the O'Neill of Clanaboy as 'O'Neill' and the O'Kelly of Gallagh and Tycooly as 'O'Kelly'.

There are no simple guide-lines for the pronunciation of peerages. The right way to pronounce a person's surname is the way he or she likes it pronounced. This is a good reason for listening carefully when you are introduced to a member of the peerage.

Here is a short list of surnames (and there are many) which are not pronounced as written:

Beaulieu	Bewly
Cecil	Sissil
Cholmondeley	*Chum*ly
Derby	Darby
Gifford	Jifford
Buccleuch	Buc*loo*
Fiennes	Fynes
Rhondda	*Ron*-tha
Knollys	Noles
Drogheda	Droider

OTHER FORMS OF VERBAL ADDRESS

Political

The Prime Minister: 'Prime Minister' or by name.

Members of HM Government: by appointment or by name. Usual form: 'Minister'.

There is no special form of address for a Privy Counsellor (prefix 'The Rt. Hon.') or a Member of Parliament.

The Clergy

Church of England.

The Archbishops of Canterbury and York are addressed formally as 'Your Grace' and socially as 'Archbishop'.

Bishop: 'Bishop' or 'My Lord'. Until 1968 the style 'My Lord' was always used but today verbal address for a Bishop is a matter of personal preference.

Roman Catholic Church.

The Pope:	'Your Holiness'.
Cardinal:	Formal: 'Your Eminence'.
	Social: 'Cardinal So-and-So'.

Archbishop: Formal: 'Your Grace'.
Social: 'Archbishop'.
Bishop: 'My Lord' or 'My Lord Bishop'.

The Jewish Community.

Rabbi: 'Rabbi Surname' or 'Dr Surname' (if a doctor).

Diplomatic

An ambassador accredited to the Court of St James or a Commonwealth High Commissioner is addressed as 'Your Excellency' at least once in conversation and thereafter as 'Sir'.

The wife of an ambassador or High Commissioner is not entitled to the style of 'Your Excellency' but it is sometimes used by courtesy. Usual form of address: 'Madam'.

Armed Forces

If an officer in the Army, Navy, or Air Force has a title he is addressed as 'Lord So-and-So' unless he prefers to be addressed by his service rank.

Junior officers in any of the armed services address senior officers as 'sir' whether titled or not.

Judiciary

The Lord Chancellor (always a peer); 'Lord So-and-So'.

Master of the Rolls: according to his judicial rank.

Lord Justice of the Court of Appeal. Formal: 'My Lord' or 'Your Lordship'. Social: 'Lord Justice'.

Judge of the High Court. Formal: 'Sir'. Judicial matters and on the bench: 'My Lord' or 'Your Lordship'. Social: 'Sir John'.

Judge of the High Court (woman). Formal: 'Madam'. Judicial matters: 'My Lady' or 'Your Ladyship' Social: 'Dame Elizabeth'.

Medical

A Doctor of Medicine who practises *medicine* is called 'Doctor Surname'.

A surgeon (usually with a Fellowship in Surgery) is '*Mr* Surname'. Women surgeons, whether married or not, are called '*Miss* Surname'.

Civic Leaders

Lord Mayor: 'My Lord Mayor' or 'Lord Mayor'.

Lady Mayoress: 'My Lady Mayoress' or 'Lady Mayoress'.

Mayor: 'Mr Mayor' ('Your Worship' is archaic except when the Mayor is sitting as a magistrate, for which he must be a Justice of the Peace).

Mayoress: 'Mayoress'.

Aldermen: 'Alderman Surname'.

Academic

Chancellor of a University: 'Chancellor' or by name.

Vice-Chancellor: 'Vice-Chancellor' or by name.

The recipient of a doctorate conferred by a university or other such body is addressed as 'Doctor' unless he is a peer, baronet, or knight, and then by his appropriate rank.

Some doctorates:

Doctor of Civil Law (LL D).

Doctor of Letters (D.Lit. or Lit(t).D.).

Doctor of Literature (Lit.D.).

Doctor of Music (D.Mus. or Mus.D.).

Doctor of Philosophy (Ph.D. or D.Phil.).

Doctors of Divinity are usually but not always clergymen. The degree can, in some universities, be taken by or conferred on laymen and they are addressed as 'Doctor'.

Some holders of honorary doctorates use the title of 'Doctor' and their individual preference should be followed.

The comments of Mrs Massey Lyon on verbal address in her voluminous book, *Etiquette—a Guide to Public and Social Life* (Cassell, London), published in 1927, are still apt almost sixty years later.

She wrote, 'The use of titles is important but unlike many blunders both in etiquette and other matters, errors here are regular solecisms.

'That is why it is so important, first of all, to become familiar with the correct way to address people formally and colloquially in speech, and secondly to be careful to translate abstract knowledge into fact.

'To forget the right to the Christian name possessed by daughters of Peers above the rank of Viscount, and the sons of Marquesses and Dukes, after the prefix of Lord or Lady, is a sure sign of the social outsider.'

Mrs Massey Lyon went on to warn her readers, 'To say "there are three lords on the committee" savours at least of a solecism; it should be "three peers".'

One can do no better in summing up the problem of verbal address than to quote the late Sir Iain Moncreiffe of that Ilk, Bt., Ph.D., FSA, DL, Albany Herald of Arms.

In 1976 he observed, 'I was in Salt Lake City when I was interviewed by successive telephone calls on the American wireless. Questioner after questioner asked, "What does *Sir* Moncreiffe think about . . .?" until the studio bell rang and a voice said, "Mr Moncreiffe? I do call you *Mr* don't I?" I caught him out with the reply, "Well, you could call me *Mr* as I'm a Master of Arts but you can call me *Dr* if you prefer."

'The other side of the coin turned up at a press conference in Denmark. An intelligent journalist said, "I see you are a Doctor of Philosophy. Why do you prefer to be called *Sir* Iain?"

'The reply then was, "Because as a baronet I am a living memorial to a greater man than myself, while having earned a doctorate myself, I would only be swanking if I pretended it bettered his life work".'

Correct form of address for the late Sir Iain Moncreiffe of that Ilk (which simply means 'Moncreiffe of that same') was: 'Sir Iain' (pronounced 'Ian').

He delighted in his quaint name because, he said, 'it gives other people such fun'.

THE ORAL TRADITION

THERE is a tendency to regard literature as the prose fiction of named authors as printed in books, yet this is only a comparatively recent development of the last two or three centuries. The novel form itself, developed by professional writers, emerged from the eighteenth century. Poets have a more ancient history, but the concept of the professional poet or novelist, publishing works in book form, is still a relatively modern one.

Long before the invention of printing in the fifteenth century, popular literature and language was shaped by the oral tradition, since literacy and higher education were for the privileged few. Folklorists use the term 'oral tradition' to indicate the great body of imaginative poetry, stories, rhymes, and sayings communicated by word of mouth over the centuries, from mother or nurse to child, father to son, bard to audience, independently of manuscript or print.

The folklore of the oral tradition included stories, epic poems, heroic ballads and songs, riddles, jokes, and nursery rhymes. Although the ruling classes and aristocracy had always enjoyed their own poetry and prose, the greater body of folklore was the culture of poor people, of peasants, farmers, and artisans. It is convenient to classify the two traditions as high and low literature, the terms indicating social status rather than literary merit. Indeed, some of the most beautiful and inspiring imagery stems from the folk ballads of ordinary people.

At different times in history, the two cultures of high and low literature have interacted, usually resulting in mutual enrichment, although sometimes producing stilted and artificial imitations. Such interaction was particularly characteristic of the eighteenth and early nineteenth centuries, when sophisticated gentlemen became aware of the literary quality of traditional balladry, as sung by peasants, and began to print their verses. At the same time, peasant poets who were close to nature strove to imitate the sophisticated style of aristocratic verse.

But the literary and metrical structure of traditional materials is only one aspect of the oral tradition. It is the *way* in which these things are recited or sung that is the key to their astonishing vitality, adding an almost magical dimension to formal structure. The living performance of the oral tradition involves characteristic rhythms, inflexions, tones, and vocal ornamentations that are often of greater antiquity than the form in which they are currently manifest. It is this dynamic aspect of the oral tradition, independent of manuscript or print, that was often missed by early folklorists, intent on rescuing the words of old ballads and folk-songs for posterity, but in the process recovering only the skeleton of a living tradition.

Certain aspects of the oral tradition cut across class and regional boundaries. Nursery stories and rhymes have circulated at all levels of society independently of manuscript and print. Iona and Peter Opie, world authorities on children's lore, stated in the introduction to their book *The Oxford Dictionary of Nursery Rhymes* (Oxford, 1951):

An oft-doubted fact attested by the study of nursery rhymes is the vitality of oral tradition. This vitality is particularly noticeable where children are concerned for, as Jane Austen shows in *Emma*, and as V. Sackville-West has put it, children say 'tell it again, tell it just the same', and will tenaciously correct the teller who varies in the slightest particular from the original recital. It is this trait in children which makes their lore such a profitable subject for research.

The infrequency with which the rhymes were recorded before the nineteenth century establishes that the written word can have had little to do with their survival. The song 'The King of France', said in 1649 to be one which 'good fellowes often sing', was familiar to Victorian nurses, although it does not seem to have been once written down in 180 years. Similarly, 'If all the world were paper', found tucked away at the end of an adult anthology of 1641, next makes an appearance in a nursery anthology of 1810.

The characteristic chanting and singing of children's rhymes is often from an older oral tradition than the format of the verses themselves, which frequently change their wording while retaining their style and emotional impact. On the issue of origins, the Opies stated:

On the whole, fewer of the nursery rhymes come from antiquity than seems to be popularly supposed. Because there is said to have been a Prince Cole in the third century A.D., 'a gode man and welbeloved among the Brytonnes', it does not follow that the song 'Old (or Good) King Cole' dates back to that period, even in the unlikely event of it referring to this chieftain. A large number of our rhymes have not been found recorded before the nineteenth century, while some, as has been pointed out in the previous section, are actually of recent manufacture. It is, we feel, from the beginning of the seventeenth century onwards that the majority of the rhymes must be dated.

However, from the little sample of children's song quoted in the gospels (Matthew xi. 17; Luke vii. 32), from the Roman nurses' lullaby *Lalla, lalla, lalla, aut dormi, aut lacte*, in a scholium on Persius, and from Horace's *puerorum nenia* recited by children, possibly while playing 'King of the Castle', it is clear that nursery lore 2,000 years ago was not really different from that which obtains today. The earliest pieces still surviving are the unrhymed folk chants with their numerous equivalents throughout Europe, the counting-out formulas hardly even of onomatopoeic sense, the simpler infant amusements, and a number of riddles. Haphazard references in the Middle Ages confirm the existence of some of them.

The extraordinary tenacity of the oral tradition is shown by the persistence of such formulas as the 'Eeny, Meeny, Myna mo' type of counting-out rhyme. The Opies cited numerous regional variants and showed the connection with Celtic numerals surviving in the old words used by shepherds for counting sheep and fisherman for reckoning their catch. The Opies stated:

The theory is that, when the Romans and then the Saxons invaded and occupied Britain, it was in Scotland, in Wales, and in the west country that the Celts managed to retain their language and customs. The rest, in the course of years, came more and more completely under the influence of their conquerors. An exception was those whose work was lonely and who were left unmolested, particularly by the Romans, because of their value to the garrisons in supplying provisions: such were the stock-breeders. This is demonstrated by the snatches of language preserved through almost two milleniums by (i) people living in mountainous and outlandish parts, (ii) shepherds, (iii) children in their games. For children, as has been noted, are conservative and exact, and tend to be in touch with the non-working (oldest) members of the family, who themselves delight in recounting their earliest memories.

Many nursery rhymes have crossed international barriers, and the Opies listed analogues of British rhymes throughout Europe and Scandinavia. In a later work, *The Lore and Language of Schoolchildren* (Oxford, 1959), the authors drew attention to the speed with which even modern children's rhymes have travelled throughout Britain and even as far as the US. Such transmission appears to be largely independent of the printed word or other mass media.

Long before the spread of literacy, lullabies, riddles, proverbs, rhymes, stories, ballads, and songs were transmitted from nurse to child, father to son, and through peer-group culture. Sometimes verses from old ballads or songs were transformed into nursery rhymes, and the Opies have quoted examples.

Part of the fascination of the oral tradition is the fluctuation between tradition and topicality. The metrical and rhetorical structure of chanted lines is essentially conservative, but topical allusions are often introduced through new interpretations of assonantal values or conscious and unconscious punning. Sometimes the meaning of a word is lost through distortion in oral transmission, but gradually transmuted into new meanings through generations of singers. In *English Folk-Song: Some Conclusions* (London, 1907; reprinted 1936, 1965), Cecil J. Sharp noted various transmutations of the chorus line of the song 'The Lover's Tasks' from 'Parsley, sage, rosemary and thyme' to:

> Sing, ivy, leaf, sweet william and thyme.
> Every rose grows merry in thyme.
> Sober and grave grows merry in time.
> Whilst every grove rings with a merry antine.

In *The Lore and Language of Schoolchildren*, the Opies analysed similar changes in children's rhymes:

> Thus we find that variations, even apparently creative ones, occur more often by accident than by design. Usually they come about through mis-hearing or misunderstanding, as in the well-known hymnal misapprehension:
>
> > Can a woman's tender care
> > Cease towards the child she-bear?
>
> A line in the song 'I'm a knock-kneed sparrow' quickly becomes 'I'm a cockney sparrow'. 'Calico breeches', no longer familiar to youth today, become 'comical breeches'. 'Elecampane' becomes 'elegant pain'. 'Green gravel, green gravel' becomes by association 'Greengages, greengages'. And the unmeaning 'Alligoshee, alligoshee', in the marching game, is rationalized to 'Adam and Eve went out to tea'.

The richest and most significant area of the oral tradition is that concerned with the old ballads and folk-songs that circulated amongst poor people for centuries, and which provided their entertainment and cultural fulfilment. Like nursery rhymes, these were widely diffused, with analogous versions throughout Europe and Scandinavia. Traditional ballads are usually studied with reference to the canon of Professor Francis J. Child of Harvard, whose monumental work *The English and Scottish Popular Ballads* (5 vols., Boston, 1882–98; reprinted New York, 1957, 1965) discussed 305 main ballad types, of which variants are found in many countries. It is fascinating to see how certain themes and stories have spread internationally, taking on local characteristics.

One of the most valuable studies of ballad diffusion is found in the chapter 'How Ballads Spread' in W. J. Entwistle's *European Balladry* (Oxford, 1939), which charts the movement of ballad motifs and tunes, concluding:

> Wherever there is no difficult frontier of language or culture to surmount, traditional ballads are able to travel from mouth to mouth without impediment. The dialect used for their performance takes on slowly new characteristics as the song passes over the ground, until it may reach the limits of the linguistic area. It is not translation but substitution that occurs. The substitution may be left incomplete when the original is sufficiently understood. One may see this state of language in the Castilian-Catalan ballads, or in the Faeroese *Nykkurs visa*, several verses of which are in the original Danish. Borrowing, not spontaneous creation, in such cases is the rule.
>
> The words of ballads are, in fact, complexes of motifs just as their tunes are complexes of notes. The chances against fortuitous coincidence in the words are scarcely less heavy than against fortuitous coincidence in melody. These two aspects of the full performance have each their history of rise, expansion, and decline.

The universal problems of the human situation found in ballad themes also crossed social and class boundaries as well as international frontiers.

In my book *The Broadside Ballad: A Study in Origins and Meaning* (London, 1962; reprinted Hatboro, Pa./Wakefield, 1978), I showed how the basic theme of the Scottish love ballad 'The Two Magicians' (Child No. 44) was earlier expressed in an old Scandinavian folk-tale, and long before that in the ancient Hindu scripture *Brihadaranyaka Upanishad* (1st adhyaya, 4th brahmana).

Many other ballad themes may be traced to Hindu sources, part of the diffusion of culture from the great Indo-European migrations of ancient times. The old ballad 'Riddles Wisely Expounded' (Child No. 1) is surely a recasting of the seventy riddles of the rakshasi Karkati in the scripture *Yoga-Vasishtha Maharamayana*, where the life of the individual questioned hangs upon answers which contain metaphysical truths. In my book *The History of Street Literature* (Newton Abbot, 1973) I discussed other analogues, and cited the brilliant paper by Charles B. Lewis 'The Part of the Folk in the Making of Folklore' (*Folklore*, March 1935), in which the popular folk-songs 'Dabbling in the Dew' and 'Where are you going to, my pretty maid' are related to medieval French pastourelles and earlier to the cult of the Phrygian goddess Cybele. The great English and Scottish popular ballads, sung by the peasantry for centuries, descended in part from the same stories danced and sung by noble families in Scandinavia centuries earlier, while the troubadours and minstrels who were honoured by kings and princes became ancestors to the rogues and vagabonds of Shakespeare's England who hawked printed ballads on penny broadside sheets. Throughout such changes from high to low literature and back again, the oral tradition, in its variant forms, has retained some mysterious, almost magical quality.

Part of this mysterious appeal of the ballad and folk-song lies in vivid imagery and poetic techniques. There are colourful phrases which become commonplaces from one ballad to another—milk-white steeds, hair like molten gold, and blood-red wine. The compound 'true-love' for a sweetheart has added emphasis, so that the negative form of 'false true-love' has additional impact.

The characters of the ballads are high-born lords and ladies, loyal pages and faithful servants, living in castles, gallant outlaws like Robin Hood. The stories abound in chivalrous love, faithful unto death, treacherous plots, and heroic battles. Sometimes there are supernatural elements like the return of the dead from beyond the grave.

The ballad story unfolds in sharply incised scenes, often reinforced by what the ballad scholar Professor Francis B. Gummere called 'leaping and lingering'—the story varying between sudden leaps forward in scene and lingering over essential details. Such techniques recall the modern devices of montage and close-ups in cinema story-telling.

Sometime the stock phrases of ballad commonplaces exist side by side with astonishingly dramatic imagery, as in verses from 'Thomas Rymer and Queen of Elfland' (Child No. 37):

> She turned about her milk-white steed,
> And took True Thomas up behind
> And aye wheneer her bridle rang,
> The steed flew swifter than the wind.
>
> For forty days and forty nights
> He wade thro red blude to the knee,
> And he saw neither sun nor moon,
> But heard the roaring of the sea.

Another effective device, which Gummere designated 'incremental repetition', involves the repetition of certain formulas, which are brought to a sudden climax by a variation of wording, as in 'The Cruel Brother' (Child No. 11), where a dying bride makes her testament after being stabbed by her brother:

> 'O what will you leave to your father dear?'
>   With a hey ho and a lillie gay
> 'The silver-shode steed that brought me here.'
>   As the primrose spreads so sweetly.
>
> 'What will you leave to your mother dear?'
> 'My velvet pall and my silken gear.'
>
> 'What will you leave to your brother John?'
> 'The gallows-tree to hang him on.'

The refrains, probably from earlier danced versions of ballads, often heighten suspense by punctuating the narrative at dramatic points or occasionally adding ironic point, as in 'Fine Flowers in the Valley' (Child No. 20):

> She sat down below a thorn,
>   *Fine flowers in the valley*
> And there she has her sweet babe born.
>   *And the green leaves they grow rarely.*
>
> 'Smile na sae sweet, my bonie babe,
> And ye smile sae sweet, ye'll smile me dead.'
>
> She's taen out her little pen-knife,
> And twinnd the sweet babe o its life.

Ballads derive their maximum emotional impact from being sung, so that the swinging rhythms, haunting melodies, and recurring rhymes and refrains carry the singer and audience along. In modern times, however, ballads tend to be studied in printed versions. As James Kinsley reminded us in his Preface to the new edition of *The Oxford Book of Ballads* (Oxford, 1969), the ballads should be sung:

> 'When is a ballad not a ballad?' asks Professor Bronson; 'When it has no tune.' In gathering the extant tunes to the 'Child' ballads here and in America, Bronson has made the greatest single contribution to ballad scholarship in this century: for the interaction of words and music has been demonstrated on the grand scale, and the coherence of the ballad form restored. We are beginning to see how music controls rhetoric and phrasing, the shape of the dialogue, the measure of 'obliqueness' possible to the ballad poet.

With the innovation of printing in the fifteenth century, literature became the printed culture of sophisticated classes with access to education, while ballads and folk-songs remained the culture of uneducated peasants. From the sixteenth century onwards, there was a gradual expansion of literacy, but books remained beyond the means of poor people until the mass literacy of the nineteenth century.

However, poor and middle-class people began to have some limited access to reading through the penny broadside ballad sheets and chapbook pamphlets circulated by pedlars. The ballads printed on broadside sheets were usually illustrated by a crude woodcut, often only tenuously connected with the subject, and did not print music, referring instead to some well-known tune (often a folk-dance) or simply carrying the tag 'to a new tune'. As the ballads were usually sung by the pedlars who sold them in the streets, it was the new words for which one paid—a pennyworth of literature. Even if people never heard the piece sung they would usually have little difficulty in improvising some kind of tune.

The broadsides became a kind of musical journalism, the link between oral folklore and the popular press, forerunners of the cheap newspapers of the nineteenth century. The chapbooks, which were basically broadsides folded into small pamphlets, contained prose materials such as riddles, jokes, and stories, as well as songs.

The broadside verses were normally unsigned; they were written by poets, courtiers, and priests, as well as by the drunken alehouse poets and literary hacks of the day. On political topics it was prudent to conceal authorship. If you didn't get hung for treason, you might get your ears cut off. For the most part, broadside ballads carried a newer culture of topicality, of political and religious controversy and urban thought, that gradually supplanted country tradition. But many old ballads from the oral tradition were printed on broadsides, side by side with more topical songs on everyday news, politics, fashions, love songs (including bawdy ballads), the follies and humours of life. Because of this, many broadsides of old ballads or new songs in the old style actually became carriers of the oral tradition, refreshing fading memories or providing new words to old tunes.

With the development of literacy, broadside ballads and chapbooks became the literature of poor people who could not afford books and did not have opportunity or time to read them. Broadsides were pasted up on cottage walls or in inns, and passed eagerly from hand to hand. They played a considerable part in the development of literacy, although often at the expense of the simpler beauty of the oral tradition.

While poor people were discovering sophisticated literature, the cultured classes were becoming interested in the ballads of peasants. In 1711, Addison published his famous essay in the *Spectator* praising 'the darling songs of the common people', citing the old ballad 'Chevy Chase', which had moved the heart of Sir Philip Sidney 'more than a trumpet', and the pathetic broadside story of 'The Children in the Wood'. With the publication of Bishop Thomas Percy's *Reliques of Ancient English Poetry* in 1765, cultured interest in traditional balladry influenced high literature, and printed broadsides and chapbooks were also studied as artefacts of the oral tradition. Bishop Percy had visited broadside printers and taken away old ballad-sheets for study. James Boswell also visited the same ballad warehouse and started a collection of chapbooks.

Of course Percy's ballads were taken largely from an old folio manuscript, and it was some time before writers and scholars recognized that there was still a living oral tradition and that old ballads could be 'collected from the mouths of the people'. However, the emphasis on the words of ballads divorced from their melodies was based on a misunderstanding of the real nature of the oral tradition, and it was not until the nineteenth century that broadminded country parsons like the Revd John Broadwood and the Revd Sabine Baring-Gould began the movement to collect words and music of folk-songs.

The distinctive features of orality and printing are well described by W. J. Entwistle in *European Balladry*:

> Both the epic and the ballad, however, were directed to an unlettered public, not necessarily quite illiterate, but accustomed to get entertainment orally. They are addressed to those who have ears to hear; not to readers. When a ballad is written down and printed it may find a new circle of readers, but it becomes stereotyped and begins to shed the characteristics of traditional literature. A schism appears in the public; readers are different from listeners, and the former have more, the latter less and less prestige. Instead of addressing the people, the ballad-monger has before him the plebs, and ballads become vulgar and insignificant. It is to humanists that we owe the preservation of so many delightful ballad texts; far more than were contained in the repertoire of any traditional minstrel; but humanism, however pious, is a deadly opponent of the genre. It takes ballads out of the line of oral transmission, into the textual; they are the less heard or performed, the more they are read and discussed.

Meanwhile the powerful poetry of the folk ballads was not wholly extinguished by printed texts, and much of their technique and imagery had a stimulating effect on the artificialities of much of eighteenth-century high literature. By introducing popular balladry to polite society, Bishop Percy gave a new impulse to European literature, culminating in the romanticism of Herder, Bürger, and Sir Walter Scott.

Wordsworth was familiar with broadsides and chapbooks, and both he and Coleridge deliberately set out to use the techniques and style of the broadside ballad. In turn, Wordsworth's poem 'We Are Seven' was printed in chapbooks, and so too were the poems of Robert Burns, which had derived from folk tradition.

At the same time, high literature influenced peasant poets like Robert Bloomfield and John Clare, who were also familiar with the oral tradition of their own villages and attempted something of a fusion between high and low literature.

Many esteemed poets from the eighteenth century onwards were influenced by traditional balladry or broadsides; these include Keats, Tennyson, Kingsley, Dante Gabriel Rossetti, and Swinburne. For a valuable anthology of such poetry see *The Literary Ballad* by Anne Henry Ehrenpreis (London, 1966). In recent times, other poets who have experimented in the ballad idiom or adapted its commonplaces are Walter de la Mare, W. H. Auden, and W. B. Yeats. Even the music of folk-songs and ballads has inspired many composers, including Bartok and Vaughan Williams.

But with the development of a more uniform mass media society over the last two centuries, there has been no real place for a folk culture of old ballads and songs. Broadsides and chapbooks died out with the spread of cheap printing and higher standards of education. Farms became highly mechanized, and the whole pace of agricultural life worked against the old-fashioned peasant culture. Nowadays we are all exposed to a common culture through schools, radio, and television.

Some pockets of oral tradition lingered for a while. A few old men in country districts remembered the songs and ballads they had learnt in the oral tradition. Between 1916 and 1918, the folklorist Cecil Sharp collected some 500 British ballads and songs in a living oral tradition in isolated Southern Appalachian mountain communities in the US. These people, descendants of English and Scots-Irish settlers, used many antique English expressions such as 'light down' (alight from your horse), found in ballads, even in a period when travellers rode motor cars. There are still singers in the oral tradition in such communities today, but they are lingering survivors rather than a living tradition. Of course the style of singing, the tones, inflexions, and rhythms, were missing from the printed texts which Sharp published in *English Folk Songs from the Southern Appalachians* (2 vols., London, 1932). However, the recordings of Anglo-American ballads issued on discs by the Library of Congress Archive of Folk Song, established in 1928, give a good indication of the magical beauty of the oral tradition, in spite of primitive recording techniques of the time.

The mainstream of the oral tradition has ceased, but the folk-music revival of the 1950s generated a folk-club movement in Britain, drawing its strength from a revival of traditional singing, captured and propagated by recordings from old country singers. Here the tape recorder, like the broadside, has become a carrier of the oral tradition, but preserving essential characteristics which the printed word cannot record.

The oral tradition has certainly influenced high literature in its metrical and poetic structure, its imagery, and its colourful and succinct techniques of story-telling. These characteristics have been preserved and developed by printing, but the magic of the living performance has largely disappeared in the growing emphasis on printing and reading. Much of literature has come to be regarded as simply something studied from books, but we must not forget that the shapes of the written and printed words are only symbols of an oral tradition of considerable antiquity and power. This tradition is best studied in authentic recordings of singers who have preserved traditional style.

SLANG

THERE are two broad categories of language covered by the term 'slang'. Both derive principally from the spoken language (few authors sit down to invent slang language—or slanguage as it is sometimes called), and both represent categories of informal speech. The first is the specialized cant or jargon of particular subgroups within a community, and is identified as characteristic of that subculture. This slang consists of words, senses, and idioms peculiar to, for example, sections of the criminal fraternity (*screw*, prison warder; *snout*, tobacco), drug-users (*horse*, heroin; *uppers*, amphetamines), and on a more reputable level, servicemen (*kite*, aeroplane; *gong*, medal or decoration), computer buffs (*nibble*, half a byte; *hacker*, computer buff), and the theatrical world (*angel*, financial backer; *super*, supernumerary actor). It is a sort of secret language primarily comprehensible to its own in-group. The second category of slang is less restricted than this: it comprises highly colloquial words (and particular senses of words), along with complete phrases, which are commonly known and used in everyday speech by the general public, but which are felt to exist somehow below the level of the standard (or 'proper') language. The categories are by no means mutually exclusive, and many words chart a progression along the continuum from subculture jargon to general slang, sometimes eventually becoming adopted as part of the standard language.

The derivation of the word *slang* is as obscure as that of many of the words it describes. It first appears in print in English around 1750, both as an adjective and as a noun, and in contexts which suggest that it had already been current for several years. There are no similar contemporaneous words from which it might derive, and none of the various etymological proposals for its derivation are proven. An earlier term was *cant* (known since the sixteenth century, though from the seventeenth in this sense: it was based upon Latin *cantus*, singing, chant). *Cant* had rather contemptuous, dismissive overtones, and this—as well as the continual search for linguistic novelty—might partially account for its being ousted by *slang*. *Slang* is recorded in the sense 'language of a low and vulgar type' in the mid eighteenth century (and in the subsense 'specialized jargon of a trade or calling' by the early nineteenth century), and by the mid nineteenth century it was used quite commonly for both varieties of slang mentioned above, superseding the once-popular *flash*, and always commoner than the more technical *argot*.

It is not surprising that we know little about the origin of so many slang terms. In general, etymology (the science or study of word-derivation) works by observation and hypothesis, using as its materials the various layers of word-forms recorded throughout a language's history, and linking these with other forms in related languages. There are no rules for establishing word-derivation in oral language, which is just the place we look for the genesis of slang. This holds true for slang neologisms, words freshly coined in slang (*codswallop*—despite the stories about Mr Codd's weak beer; *spondulicks*, money; etc.). In the case of slang senses of existing words, the picture is different, as slang customarily introduces a new meaning to an old word: the connection is often self-evident (*brass*, money; *rap*, talk; etc.).

One of the features of much slang is its unusualness. Its terms strike us as strange on first hearing, but on further acquaintance they develop a familiarity and even an appropriateness. On the face of it (to take an example), *funk* 'fear, panic' has a rather barbaric, un-English appearance. It appears to come from the subclass of Oxford English known as Oxford University slang, at some time around 1750. The earliest commentators associated it with the Flemish word *fonck*, which is possible, but hard to substantiate. Others have thought it developed from an older slang term *funk* 'tobacco smoke' (ultimately related to Latin *fumus* 'smoke'). The impossibility of re-creating the precise linguistic environment into which the English word was born precludes further speculation, while increasing the word's mystique. Oral evidence is typically lost as soon as it is spoken. It is interesting to notice, in addition, that *funk* moved on from the small world of eighteenth-century university slang to the level of general slang by the nineteenth century, where it coalesced with an old use of *blue* (meaning 'dismayed, depressed, or low-spirited') to create the collocation *blue funk*, and that nowadays *funk* hovers uneasily somewhere between general slang and standard English—quite accepted and yet still standing slightly off-centre. It is not related to the other word *funk*, a variety of jazz music, which apparently derives from a dialect word meaning 'mouldy, earthy, foul-smelling', obsolescent in England but alive in the regions of North America when this form of music was created.

Similar processes are at work with the modern slang word *wally*, 'a fool or simpleton'. We cannot be certain how it arose, even though it is probably only twenty or twenty-five years old. The situation is the usual one. For the first ten years or so *wally* was used by only a tiny segment of the population (which of course had no reason to document its origin). By the time it was 'established' (i.e., it had reached the scripts of broadcast comedy programmes) no one remembered where it came from. It may be associated with the Sixties rock culture, as has often been maintained, but this hypothesis is tempered by a mass of conflicting evidence. It is just another example of respectability coming too late to rescue the facts.

Slang is probably endemic to language. Our knowledge of it in ancient languages is weakened by the type of documentary evidence which survives. Slang does not belong to the register of language used in formal records, epic poetry, religious prose, and other varieties of literature that illustrate the vocabulary of former societies. Even today it is sometimes regarded (subjectively) as substandard, or 'dustbin' language. In the pre-printing era, when books were expensive to prepare and as costly to duplicate, the language of the people is sparsely represented. Nevertheless, we can occasionally glimpse cracks in this formulaic armoury in the more playful areas of, for example, Greek drama. Eric Partridge, the past master of slang study in English, notes that 'in the Frogs (of Aristophanes), patient Xanthias tells pompous Dionysus that he's afraid the latter is *cracked*. Dionysus himself speaks of *grit*, and Heracles . . . admits (of some poetry) that it's *devilish tricky*.' Every schoolboy knows (or would have known a century ago) that the Latin word for 'tile', *testa*, was used metaphorically to mean 'head', from which we have the modern French word *tête*. But the full count of slang terms in these cultured and developed languages, as well as in early English, is small.

We are far better served linguistically in the years immediately following the Middle Ages, for not only are there printed records of a more general kind, but also the first glossaries and accounts of slang. They are evidence of a new interest in noting down the strange and colourful vocabulary which was emerging throughout Europe alongside the words and expressions which were known and understood. Sometimes the purpose was objective, but as often as not it was cautionary, for the first body of slang vocabularies documented the language of the sixteenth-century underworld, at a time when the underworld and the everyday world of 'polite' society often found themselves inescapably rubbing shoulders. Amongst others, there were Robert Copeland's *Hye Waye to the spyttel House* (?1536) and Thomas Harman's celebrated *Caveat for Commen Cursetors* (1567). Not only did these works evince a general interest in the exciting (perhaps rather frightening) idioms of the road, but they found their way to a wide audience by being pillaged by writers such as Robert Greene, in his cony-catching pamphlets, a guide to the unwary amongst card-sharps and other tricksters. Furthermore, they attest to quite notable observations, such as that slang vocabulary consists principally of nouns, and to a lesser extent, of verbs and adjectives, with the remaining parts of speech being sparsely represented.

The first dictionaries of English (from Robert Cawdrey's *Table Alphabeticall* of 1604) paid little or no heed to the vocabulary of slang. They were primarily dictionaries of 'hard' (often Latinate) words, reflecting the Renaissance interest in science and classical culture. So whereas slang was expanding daily in common speech, it was still held to one side by the self-professed authorities. The first dictionary to admit any sizeable body of canting vocabulary was Elisha Coles's *English Dictionary* of 1676. Coles was a schoolmaster, like many of his contemporary lexicographers, but he had an ear for the common language. It was from Richard Head's *Canting Academy* of 1643 that he took most of his slang terms, just as it was in John Ray's *Collection of English Words not generally used* that he found most of his regional vocabulary. The inclusion of slang in a mainstream English dictionary heralded a feeling that slang had reached a level, if not of acceptability, then at least of general noteworthiness. Samuel Johnson's attitude towards slang is well documented. In his great *Dictionary* of 1755 there is a marked antipathy towards the vulgar idioms of the street-corner, but he could hardly deny that they should somehow be recorded, though they were poorly represented in the authorities to whom he turned for most of his illustrative examples of vocabulary. Yet we know that he made use of one of his assistants, Francis Steward, for help with 'low cant phrases' and the terminology of gambling and of cards.

The Victorian age saw a two-sided perspective on slang. On the one hand, the simple and often rather crude language of the lower strata of society represented much that was inimical to the world-view of a civilized and expansionist people. Slang was evidence of the blacker under-side of life, a threat to the refined order of a successful economic power. But at the same time it remained an object of curiosity, and was observed by early sociologists and social reformers such as Henry Mayhew, in his monumental *London Labour and the London Poor* (1851–62). To Mayhew and his fellows, slang illustrated both a strong social tradition amongst the traders and street-performers who were the subjects of their studies, which was in danger of disappearing, and also concomitant evidence of the mental and physical poverty of the London poor, which could only be improved by sweeping social amelioration. It is from the Victorian period that we inherit most strongly the sense that slang is socially disturbing, and it is from this time that we most powerfully mark that distinction between the 'unacceptable' slang of the underworld, and the lighter-hearted 'acceptable' slang of the (Victorian) middle and upper classes. It is a distinction which still obtains in many quarters today, though we are typically less harsh in our judgements.

As in so many areas, we can pin-point the end of the Victorian era not in 1901, but in 1914. The effect of war upon slang is fundamental. Slang has always arisen out of cultural interchange; indeed cultural interchange has been the greatest single force behind most linguistic change. The fact that British, American, Australian, and other soldiers were forced so much together, away from their homes, heralded an enormous advance in the general count of slang terms. The catalyst of this development is enforced familiarity, the need to survive with others of one's own country or of another. In the ranks, there is little or no formality, correspondence is by word of mouth, by backchat, jokes, marching songs. The Australians brought their slang to the European theatre of war, as did the Americans and others, and it passed easily between the different nationalities. Sharing slang acts as a powerful bond. From the time of the First World War—before the era of the cinema or the television—a fusion of slang in English was created. As the servicemen returned to their homes, they took with them a wealth of new language which irreversibly permeated their country's speech. In comparison with this, the slang which arose from the technological advances of the twentieth century was for many years trifling. The tabloid newspapers and the international media of the cinema and television had a new vital base of receptive speakers on which to operate. By the time of the Lady Chatterley trial, the social tolerance of even the coarsest slang had been proved everywhere except in court.

The power of slang can be observed most closely by analysing its characteristics. The foregoing discussion has already assumed a certain degree of understanding of the term. We have seen that slang consists of words used in an informal context, in senses which they do not possess in formal language. Often slang provides new senses of existing words, less frequently it coins new words of its own. Typically slang is used throughout a small subculture of society, after which some of its terms seep through to a general audience. At first, it is used by the subculture to emphasize its differences from the dominant culture, and the terms may be discarded at the lower level when they are adopted by the parent society. The words are often colourful or exciting, either in their own right, or in the informal contexts in which they are employed. They may not last long in the main culture. In fact, they often seem to have a built-in obsolescence in the 'polite' world.

This can be seen by comparing the currency of a set of slang terms over a period of time. *A New Dictionary of the Canting Crew* was published about 1700. It declared itself 'useful for all sorts of People (especially foreigners) to secure their money and preserve their lives; besides very diverting and entertaining, being wholly new'. The blurb-writer's art is hardly new. A random selection of ten adjacent entries reads as follows:

> *bonny-clapper*, sower butter-milk
> *booby*, a dull heavy lob
> *booberkin*, the same
> *boon*, a gift, reward, or gratification
> *boon-companion*, a merry drinking fellow
> *boot*, a Scotch torture, or rack, for the leg
> *what boots it?* What avails it?
> *booty-play*, false cheating, also plunder
> *boracho*, a but, a drunkard, and a hogskin
> *borde*, a shilling

In general, the defining words are still known today (all except *lob* and *hogskin* occur in the *Concise Oxford Dictionary*), but the status of the slang vocabulary has changed radically. Only five of these terms are still recorded in the current edition of the *Concise Oxford Dictionary* (*booby*, *boon*, *boon companion*, *boot*, *What boots it?*), and none of these is labelled 'slang'— though perhaps *booby* might have been. *What boots it?* is archaic, and *boot* is historical. *Boon* and *boon companion* would not nowadays be regarded as slang. This suggests that these five words have moved into a new register over the centuries (or possibly that they were mislabelled by the dictionary's editor). The slang of one century is often the standard vocabulary of the next. Of the other five terms, *bonny-clapper* is (and always has been) regional—it is Anglo-Irish; *booberkin* is otherwise unrecorded, as is *booty-play* (though *to play booty* was certainly current in the seventeenth century); *boracho* is a variant spelling of *borachio*, an obsolete word for a 'wine-skin', and hence a 'drunkard'; and *borde* has likewise disappeared. In terms of derivation, the sample also shows the variability of slang origin: *bonny-clapper* is an Irish word commandeered into English; *boracho* and probably *booby* were borrowed from Italian/Spanish; *borde* probably represents a transferred use of an English word for a shield (presumably from the coin's design), whereas the other items come principally through more traditional routes into English (Anglo-Saxon, Middle English, Old French). Furthermore, several of the words were quite new in 1700. In general, the picture of slang then as now is of a seam of language picking words promiscuously from foreign languages or from the native tongue; of old slang terms mixing with newer ones; of a catalogue of nouns; of words which drift into slang and out again, some dropping entirely out of use, others remaining as archaic or historical fossils. The status of these terms in current American English, Australian English, and other Englishes, is much the same as it is in British English.

Throughout the world, slang revolves around the actions and objects of everyday life. Not only is it familiarity between fellows that engenders slang, but also our familiarity with the common world. Slang terms abound in the sphere of human relationships (*trouble and strife*, wife; *cobber*, friend (Australia); *broad*, woman (United States)—especially in derogatory expressions. Slang (often used euphemistically) is characteristically associated with sexuality (*fanny*, *to get one's oats*) and drunkenness (*paralytic*, *three sheets to the wind*). It expresses the strength of feeling, and often distrust, between English speakers from different countries (*pommy*, *limey*, *bog-hopper*). In the case of the North American *limey*, the word has a well-documented origin: *lime-juicer* or *limey* dates from the days when lime juice was served in the British navy for medicinal purposes, against scurvy. Slang permeates areas of human achievement, especially success and failure (carrying exhilarative or condemnatory overtones: *flop*, *dive-bomb*, *hit*, *to get the sack*). The best slang is often monosyllabic, or at least concise—frequently curtailing or clipping some longer word or expression. The lower depths of human experience are caught by the rigmarole of slang words for prison, death, and dying (*jug*, *clink*, *stir*, *porridge*; *to kick the bucket*, *push up daisies*, *croak*).

There is a marked reliance in slang upon using the unusual to express the commonplace. If the unusual is surprisingly appropriate, then so much the better. Nowhere is this more apparent than in rhyming slang, traditionally the hallmark of the cockney, but also rife in the States, and to an extensive degree in Australia. Appropriateness, humorous or real, stands out in *loaf* (*of bread*), head; *bird*(*-lime*), time (spent in prison); perhaps even in the Australian *Gregory* (*Peck*), neck. But the typical feeling of community and familiarity is apparent in other items such as *apples and pears*, stairs, and *rub-a-dub* (*-dub*), Australian rhyming slang for 'pub'. Rhyming slang is a slanguage which has to be mastered, and this is also a characteristic of all good subcultural slang. It survives outside the enclaves of London because it is fun, and relatively easy to understand and learn—if not so simple to use effectively. Less successful forms of slang include back slang (usually illustrated by the single word *yob*, though this type was commoner in the nineteenth and early twentieth centuries, if we trust the slang glossaries of the period). The difficulty with back slang is that it is slang refined to an almost academic degree. The target word can usually be guessed in rhyming slang. In back slang, the newcomer has to overcome sterner obstacles, which make it less likely to cross into the general arena. Much the same is true of pig Latin, in which the initial consonant or consonant cluster is moved to the end of each word, and another sound (usually *-ay*) tagged on at the end. Iona and Peter Opie state, in their *Lore and Language of Schoolchildren*, that 'Pig Latin . . . has been spoken by children since before the First World War'. As an example of this form they offer 'Unejay ithsmay isay igpay (June Smith is a pig)'. Though more comprehensible than back slang, the rhythms of pig Latin seem to preclude its being widely adopted. As a secret language it works excellently, but the secret is too hard for the general slang user to master.

In keeping with the slang of former times, today's slang contains a mixture of transitory and settled expressions. There is constant passage along the continuum from jargon to standard words and phrases. Slang arises, as we have seen, from a wide variety of sources. It is possible to isolate particular modes of linguistic formation responsible for much slang—remembering all the time that the words are for use rather than for analysis. This is bound to be the case, as slang is not introspective, however small its user-group. It stands out from regular speech-forms. The appropriateness of much slang stems from its use of metaphor: a *clot* (a variant of *clod*) is both a heavy mass of earth, and a dull, slow-witted person; a *sky-pilot*, slang for a clergyman, is someone who is charged with guiding souls to heaven; a *pineapple* is a bomb, especially a hand-grenade or a light trench mortar; a *bug* is an irritating fault or gremlin (a *glitch*) in a computer program; a *brick* is a 'solid fellow'; *to hit the deck* recalls servicemen dropping for cover in the face of attack; *to hit the sack* uses a comparable metaphor. Metaphor uses existing terminology in a new light, and as this is common to much slang, metaphor is a natural way to create new slang senses from terms already familiar in other contexts. As a matter of course, it is always easier to form new meanings from old than it is to introduce entirely new words—a factor that is instrumental in secondary linguistic formation at whatever level.

What holds for metaphor also holds for simile: *as sick as a parrot*, *like a bat out of hell*. The formulas were around for many years before they were employed with these slang twists. When slang borrows words from abroad, the origin may soon be forgotten, satisfying the 'simple' technique of creation from existing words, while soon giving the slang words the appearance of being new (*bosh* from a Turkish word for 'empty'; *bloke*, perhaps from Shelta, Irish tinkers' jargon). This is also clear in the tendency of slang to reduce common words to a new slang format, as with the offhand creativity of *clippie*, a clipper (of bus-tickets), a ticket-collector, or *dipso* (dipsomaniac), *acid* (lysergic acid diethylamide), *sus* (suspicion), *scouse* (from *lobscouse*, a sailor's meat stew). Further reduction takes place when the final element is omitted, helping to disguise the sense: *butcher's*, for *butcher's hook*, rhyming slang for 'look'. Distortion serves much the same function: *pix* for *pics* (= 'pictures'), or *san fairy ann*, 'ça ne fait rien (it does not matter)'—often thought of as private slang, but in fact widely recorded. *Bumf* is frequently thought perfectly polite (its origin as 'bum-fodder' unnoticed). Occasionally, slang consciously alters a word's meaning, as with *gay*, 'homosexual', an example of linguistic positive discrimination. Brevity attracts abbreviations to slang: *ac/dc*, bisexual; *aka*, also known as; and the ubiquitous *OK* (first recorded in 1839 as a shortening of 'orl korrect').

In all of these terms there is an element of misrepresentation (in sense, form, derivation), and knowledge or suspicion of this sets the slang user apart from others. The misrepresentation—or new representation—stems from the desire of a group to establish a form of speech different from the larger community. The knowledge of a shared language at odds with the normal is part of the essence of slang, a mystique which may produce short-lived terms with built-in obsolescence, but which also gives rise to words and expressions that filter through to a wider audience which uses them to boost its sense of familiarity with and awareness of the actions and processes of everyday life.

PART THREE
THE LANGUAGE OF LITERATURE

EVERYDAY QUOTATIONS

HOW TO USE THIS SECTION

THE arrangement is alphabetical by the names of authors; sections such as the Anonymous one, the Bible, etc., are included in the alphabetical order.

Under each author, quotations are arranged by the alphabetical order of the titles of the works from which they come: books, plays, poems. These are printed in bold italic type. Titles of pieces (e.g., articles, essays, short stories) that constitute part of a published volume are in bold roman (the volume title having been given in bold italic). Quotations from diaries, letters, speeches, etc., however, are given in chronological order, and normally follow the literary works quoted. Poetry quotations precede prose ones for poets; and vice versa for writers most of whose work was in prose. Quotations cited from biographies or other writers' works are kept to the end under each author; sources are then given conventionally with titles of books or plays in italic (not bold) type. Books of the Bible are presented in canonical order, not alphabetically.

Numerical source references are given for the first line of each quotation, by, e.g., act, scene, and, if appropriate line number; by chapter or by page or section of verse number. Each quotation without a full source given depends from its immediate predecessor. If no source reference is given at all, the quotation is from the same poem or chapter or whatever as the last preceding named or numbered one.

DEAN ACHESON 1893–1971

• Great Britain has lost an Empire and has not yet found a role

Speech at the Military Academy, West Point, 5 Dec. 1962

LORD ACTON 1834–1902

• Power tends to corrupt and absolute power corrupts absolutely.

Letter to Bishop Mandell Creighton, 3 Apr. 1887. See *Life and Letters of Mandell Creighton* (1904), i, 372.

MRS. ALEXANDER 1818–1895

• All things bright and beautiful,
All creatures great and small,
All things wise and wonderful,
The Lord God made them all.

All Things Bright and Beautiful **(1848)**

• The rich man in his castle,
The poor man at his gate,
God made them, high or lowly,
And order'd their estate.

ANONYMOUS

ENGLISH

• A Company for carrying on an undertaking of Great Advantage, but no one to know what is is.

The South Sea Company Prospectus, 1711, Cowles, *The Great Swindle* (1963), ch. 5

• Adam
Had 'em.

On the antiquity of Microbes. (Claimed as the shortest poem.)

• All human beings are born free and equal in dignity and rights.

Universal Declaration of Human Rights (1948), Article 1

- All present and correct.
  King's Regulations (*Army*). Report of the Orderly Sergeant to the Officer of the Day
- All this buttoning and unbuttoning.
  18th-century suicide note
- Along the electric wire the message came:
  He is not better—he is much the same.
  Said to be from a poem on the illness of the Prince of Wales, afterwards Edward VII, often attr. to Alfred Austin.
- Dear Sir, Your astonishment's odd:
  I am always about in the Quad.
  And that's why the tree
  Will continue to be,
  Since observed by Yours faithfully, God.
  Reply to Knox's limerick on idealism.
- From ghoulies and ghosties and long-leggety beasties
  And things that go bump in the night,
  Good Lord, deliver us!
  Cornish
- God be in my head,
  And in my understanding;
  God be in my eyes,
  And in my looking;
  God be in my mouth,
  And in my speaking;
  God be in my heart,
  And in my thinking;
  God be at my end,
  And at my departing.
  Sarum Missal
- Lizzie Borden took an axe
  And gave her mother forty whacks;
  When she saw what she had done
  She gave her father forty-one!
  Lizzie Borden was acquitted of murdering her father and stepmother on 4 Aug. 1892 in Fall River, Massachusetts
- Please to remember the Fifth of November,
  Gunpowder Treason and Plot.
  We know no reason why gunpowder treason
  Should ever be forgot.
  Traditional since 17th century
- That this house will in no circumstances fight for its King and country.
  Motion passed at the Oxford Union, 9 Feb. 1933
- The almighty dollar is the only object of worship.
  Philadelphia Public Ledger, 2 Dec. 1836
- The eternal triangle.
  Book Review in the *Daily Chronicle*, 5 Dec. 1907
- Thirty days hath September,
  April, June, and November;
  All the rest have thirty-one,
  Excepting February alone,
  And that has twenty-eight days clear
  And twenty-nine in each leap year.
  Stevins MS (*c.*1555)
- We hold these truths to be self-evident, that all men are created equal, that they are endowed by their Creator with certain unalienable rights, that among these are life, liberty and the pursuit of happiness.
  The American Declaration of Independence, 4 July 1776
- Would you like to sin
  With Elinor Glyn
  On a tiger-skin?
  Or would you prefer
  to err
  with her
  on some other fur?
  *c.*1907. A. Glyn, *Elinor Glyn* (1955), pt. II. 30
- You pays your money and you takes your choice.
  From a peepshow rhyme. See V. S. Lean, *Collectanea* (1902–4).

FRENCH

- *Cet animal est très méchant,*
  Quand on l'attaque il se défend.
  This animal is very bad; when attacked it defends itself.
  La Ménagerie, by Théodore P. K., 1828
- *Chevalier sans peur et sans reproche.*
  Knight without fear and without blemish.
  Description in contemporary chronicles of Pierre Bayard, 1476–1524
- *Honi soit qui mal y pense.*
  Evil be to him who evil thinks [of it].
  Motto of the Order of the Garter, originated by Edward III, probably on 23 Apr. of 1348 or 1349
- *Liberté! Égalité! Fraternité!*
  Freedom! Equality! Brotherhood!
  Motto of the French Revolution, but of earlier origin
- *Tout passe, toute casse, tout lasse.*
  Everything passes, everything perishes, everything palls.
  Cahier, *Quelques six mille proverbes*

GREEK

- Know thyself.
  Inscribed on the temple of Apollo at Delphi. Plato, *Protagoras*, 343 b, ascribes the saying to the Seven Wise Men.
- Nothing in excess.

LATIN

- *Ad majorem Dei gloriam.*
  To the greater glory of God.
  Motto of the Society of Jesus
- *Ave Caesar, morituri te salutant.*
  Hail Caesar; those who are about to die salute you.
  Gladiators saluting the Roman Emperor. See Suetonius, *Claudius*, 21.
- *Et in Arcadia ego.*
  And I too in Arcadia.
  Tomb inscription often depicted in classical paintings. The meaning is disputed.

ARCHIMEDES 287–212 BC

- Eureka! (I've got it!)
Vitruvius Pollio, *De Architectura*, ix. 215

NEIL A. ARMSTRONG 1930–

- That's one small step for a man, one giant leap for mankind.
On landing on the moon, 21 July 1969

W. H. AUDEN 1907–1973

- I'll love you till the ocean
    Is folded and hung up to dry
And the seven stars go squawking
    Like geese about the sky.
As I Walked Out One Evening
- O plunge your hands in water,
    Plunge them in up to the wrist;
Stare, stare in the basin
    And wonder what you've missed.
- Private faces in public places
Are wiser and nicer
Than public faces in private places.
Collected Poems, ii *1927–1932, Shorts*
- To the man-in-the-street, who, I'm sorry to say,
    Is a keen observer of life,
The word 'Intellectual' suggests straight away
    A man who's untrue to his wife.
iv *1939–47, Shorts*

JANE AUSTEN 1775–1817

- The sooner every party breaks up the better. [Mr. Woodhouse.]
Emma, ch. 25
- A woman especially, if she have the misfortune of knowing any thing, should conceal it as well as she can.
Northanger Abbey, ch. 14
- All the privilege I claim for my own sex ... is that of loving longest, when existence or when hope is gone. [Anne.]
Persuasion, ch. 23
- It is a truth universally acknowledged, that a single man in possession of a good fortune, must be in want of a wife.
Pride and Prejudice, ch. 1

FRANCIS BACON 1561–1626

- Silence is the virtue of fools.
De Dignitate et Augmentis Scientiarum, I, vi, 31. Antitheta, 6 (ed. 1640, tr. Gilbert Watts)
- If the hill will not come to Mahomet, Mahomet will go to the hill. (Proverbially, 'If the mountain will not ...')
12. **Boldness**

WALTER BAGEHOT 1826–1877

- The Sovereign has, under a constitutional monarchy such as ours, three rights—the right to be consulted, the right to encourage, the right to warn.
The English Constitution (1867), 3. **The Monarchy** (continued)

PHINEAS T. BARNUM 1810–1891

- There's a sucker born every minute.
Attr.

BERNARD M. BARUCH 1870–1965

- Let us not be deceived—we are today in the midst of a cold war.
Speech before South Carolina Legislature, 16 Apr. 1947. Mr. Baruch said the expression 'cold war' was suggested to him by H. B. Swope, former editor of the New York *World*.

SAMUEL BECKETT 1906–

- *Estragon:* Let's go.
Vladimir: We can't.
Estragon: Why not?
Vladimir: We're waiting for Godot.
Waiting for Godot (1954), I

STEPHEN VINCENT BENÉT 1898–1943

- Bury my heart at Wounded Knee.
American Names

JEREMY BENTHAM 1748–1832

- The greatest happiness of the greatest number is the foundation of morals and legislation.
The Commonplace Book

SIR JOHN BETJEMAN 1906–1984

- You ask me what it is I do. Well actually, you know,
I'm partly a liaison man and partly P.R.O.
Essentially I integrate the current export drive
And basically I'm viable from ten o'clock till five.
Executive
- Phone for the fish-knives, Norman,
    As Cook is a little unnerved;
You kiddies have crumpled the serviettes
    And I must have things daintily served.
How to Get On in Society
- Come, friendly bombs, and fall on Slough
It isn't fit for humans now.
Slough
- Miss Joan Hunter Dunn, Miss Joan Hunter Dunn,
How mad I am, sad I am, glad that you won.
A Subaltern's Love Song

ANEURIN BEVAN 1897–1960

- The Tory Party ... So far as I am concerned they are lower than vermin.
Speech at Manchester, 4 July 1948

- You will send a Foreign Minister, whoever he may be, naked into the conference chamber.
  M. Foot, *Aneurin Bevan*, vol. ii (1973), ch. 15. Speech at Labour Party Conference, 3 Oct. 1957, against unilateral nuclear disarmament.

ERNEST BEVIN 1881–1951

- My [foreign] policy is to be able to take a ticket at Victoria Station and go anywhere I damn well please.
  Spectator, 20 Apr. 1951

THE BIBLE

OLD TESTAMENT

- In the beginning God created the heaven and the earth.
  Genesis 1: 1
- And God said, Let there be light: and there was light.
  3
- And the evening and the morning were the first day.
  5
- And God saw that it was good.
  10
- Male and female created he them.
  27
- Be fruitful, and multiply, and replenish the earth, and subdue it.
  28
- And they sewed fig leaves together, and made themselves aprons [breeches in Genevan Bible, 1560].
  And they heard the voice of the Lord God walking in the garden in the cool of the day.
  3: 7
- In sorrow thou shalt bring forth children.
  16
- In the sweat of thy face shalt thou eat bread.
  19
- For dust thou art, and unto dust shalt thou return.
- Am I my brother's keeper?
  4: 9
- Esau selleth his birthright for a mess of potage.
  Heading to chapter 25 in Genevan Bible
- Behold, Esau my brother is a hairy man, and I am a smooth man.
  27: 11
- Ye shall eat the fat of the land.
  45: 18
- I have been a stranger in a strange land.
  Exodus 2: 22. See Exodus 18: 3.
- Behold, the bush burned with fire, and the bush was not consumed.
  3: 2
- A land flowing with milk and honey.
  8
- Let my people go.
  7: 16
- Life for life,
  Eye for eye, tooth for tooth, hand for hand, foot for foot.
  21: 23
- Thou shalt love thy neighbour as thyself.
  Leviticus 19: 18. See Matt. 19: 19.
- The Lord bless thee, and keep thee:
  The Lord make his face shine upon thee, and be gracious unto thee:
  The Lord lift up his countenance upon thee, and give thee peace.
  Numbers 6: 24
- Hear, O Israel: The Lord our God is one Lord.
  Deuteronomy 6: 4
- For the Lord thy God is a jealous God.
  15
- A dreamer of dreams.
  13: 1
- Be strong and of a good courage; be not afraid, neither be thou dismayed: for the Lord thy God is with thee, whithersoever thou goest.
  Joshua 1: 9
- Hewers of wood and drawers of water.
  9: 21
- Intreat me not to leave thee, or to return from following after thee: for whither thou goest, I will go; and where thou lodgest, I will lodge: thy people shall be my people, and thy God my God.
  Ruth 1: 16
- Speak, Lord; for thy servant heareth.
  1 Samuel 3: 9
- Quit yourselves like men, and fight.
  4: 9
- God save the king.
  10: 24
- A man after his own heart.
  13: 14
- Tell it not in Gath, publish it not in the streets of Askelon.
  2 Samuel 1: 19
- Saul and Jonathan were lovely and pleasant in their lives, and in their death they were not divided.
  23
- How are the mighty fallen in the midst of the battle!
  25
- Thy love to me was wonderful, passing the love of women.
  26
- Behold, the half was not told me.
  1 Kings 10: 7

- The navy of Tharshish, bringing gold, and silver, ivory, and apes, and peacocks.
22
- My father hath chastised you with whips, but I will chastise you with scorpions.
12: 11
- There ariseth a little cloud out of the sea, like a man's hand.
18: 44
- A still small voice.
19: 12
- The Lord gave, and the Lord hath taken away; blessed be the name of the Lord.
Job 1: 21
- Man is born unto trouble, as the sparks fly upward.
5: 7
- No doubt but ye are the people, and wisdom shall die with you.
12: 2
- I am escaped with the skin of my teeth.
19: 20
- I know that my redeemer liveth, and that he shall stand at the latter day upon the earth.
25
- The price of wisdom is above rubies.
28: 18
For psalms in the Book of Common Prayer see PRAYER BOOK.
- For whom the Lord loveth he correcteth.
Proverbs 3: 12
- Her ways are ways of pleasantness, and all her paths are peace.
17
- Get wisdom: and with all thy getting get understanding.
4: 7
- Hope deferred maketh the heart sick.
13: 12
- The way of transgressors is hard.
15
- He that spareth his rod hateth his son.
24
- A soft answer turneth away wrath.
15: 1
- A merry heart maketh a cheerful countenance.
13
- Pride goeth before destruction, and an haughty spirit before a fall.
16: 18
- Train up a child in the way he should go: and when he is old, he will not depart from it.
22: 6
- Look not thou upon the wine when it is red.
23: 31
- Heap coals of fire upon his head.
25: 21
- As cold waters to a thirsty soul, so is good news from a far country.
25
- Who can find a virtuous woman? for her price is far above rubies.
31: 10
- Vanity of vanities, saith the Preacher, vanity of vanities; all is vanity.
Ecclesiastes 1: 2
- There is no new thing under the sun.
9
- All is vanity and vexation of spirit.
14
- He that increaseth knowledge increaseth sorrow.
18
- To every thing there is a season, and a time to every purpose under the heaven:
A time to be born, and a time to die; a time to plant, and a time to pluck up that which is planted.
3: 1
- A time to love, and a time to hate; a time of war, and a time of peace.
8
- A living dog is better than a dead lion.
9: 4
- The race is not to the swift, nor the battle to the strong.
11
- Cast thy bread upon the waters: for thou shalt find it after many days.
11: 1
- Though your sins be as scarlet, they shall be as white as snow.
Isaiah 1: 18
- They shall beat their swords into plowshares, and their spears into pruninghooks: nation shall not lift up sword against nation, neither shall they learn war any more.
2: 4
- The people that walked in darkness have seen a great light.
9: 2
- For unto us a child is born, unto us a son is given: and the government shall be upon his shoulder: and his name shall be called Wonderful, Consellor, The mighty God, The everlasting Father, The Prince of Peace.
6
- And there shall come forth a rod out of the stem of Jesse.
11: 1
- The wolf also shall dwell with the lamb, and the leopard shall lie down with the kid; and

the calf and the young lion and the fatling together; and a little child shall lead them.
6

- Set thine house in order.
38: 1
- There is no peace, saith the Lord, unto the wicked.
48: 22
- How beautiful upon the mountains are the feet of him that bringeth good tidings, that publisheth peace.
52: 7
- Saying, Peace, peace; when there is no peace.
Jeremiah 6: 14
- Is there no balm in Gilead?
8: 22
- Can the Ethiopian change his skin, or the leopard his spots?
13: 23
- The heart is deceitful above all things, and desperately wicked.
17: 9
- Cast into the midst of a burning fiery furnace.
Daniel 3: 6
- And this is the writing that was written, MENE, MENE, TEKEL, UPHARSIN.
5: 25
- According to the law of the Medes and Persians, which altereth not.
6: 8
- They have sown the wind, and they shall reap the whirlwind.
Hosea 8: 7
- I will restore to you the years that the locust hath eaten, the cankerworm, and the caterpillar, and the palmerworm.
Joel 2: 25
- Beat your plowshares into swords, and your pruninghooks into spears.
3: 10

APOCRYPHA

- I shall light a candle of understanding in thine heart, which shall not be put out.
2 Esdras 14: 25
- We will fall into the hands of the Lord, and not into the hands of men.
Ecclesiasticus 2: 18
- Let us now praise famous men, and our fathers that begat us.
44: 1
- Their name liveth for evermore.
14

NEW TESTAMENT

- There came wise men from the east to Jerusalem,
Saying, Where is he that is born King of the Jews? for we have seen his star in the east, and are come to worship him.
St Matthew 2: 1
- Man shall not live by bread alone, but by every word that proceedeth out of the mouth of God.
4: 4. See Deut. 8: 3.
- Thou shalt not tempt the Lord thy God.
7 and Deut. 6: 16
- Follow me, and I will make you fishers of men.
19
- Blessed are the poor in spirit: for theirs is the kingdom of heaven.
Blessed are they that mourn: for they shall be comforted.
Blessed are the meek: for they shall inherit the earth.
Blessed are they which do hunger and thirst after righteousness: for they shall be filled.
Blessed are the merciful: for they shall obtain mercy.
Blessed are the pure in heart: for they shall see God.
Blessed are the peacemakers: for they shall be called the children of God.
5: 3
- Ye are the salt of the earth.
13
- Let your light so shine before men, that they may see your good works.
16
- After this manner therefore pray ye: Our Father which art in heaven, Hallowed be thy name.
Thy kingdom come. Thy will be done in earth, as it is in heaven.
Give us this day our daily bread.
And forgive us our debts, as we forgive our debtors.
And lead us not into temptation, but deliver us from evil:
For thine is the kingdom, and the power, and the glory, for ever. Amen.
6: 9 and Luke 11: 2
- Lay not up for yourselves treasures upon earth, where moth and rust doth corrupt, and where thieves break through and steal: But lay up for yourselves treasures in heaven.
19
- No man can serve two masters ... Ye cannot serve God and mammon.
24
- Consider the lilies of the field, how they grow; they toil not, neither do they spin.
28
- Solomon in all his glory was not arrayed like one of these.
29

- Take therefore no thought for the morrow: for the morrow shall take thought for the things of itself. Sufficient unto the day is the evil thereof.
  34
- Judge not, that ye be not judged.
  7: 1. See Luke 6: 37.
- Why beholdest thou the mote that is in thy brother's eye, but considerest not the beam that is in thine own eye?
  3
- Neither cast ye your pearls before swine.
  6
- Ask, and it shall be given you; seek, and ye shall find; knock, and it shall be opened unto you.
  7
- Strait is the gate, and narrow is the way, which leadeth unto life.
  14
- Beware of false prophets, which come to you in sheep's clothing, but inwardly they are ravening wolves.
  15
- Do men gather grapes of thorns, or figs of thistles?
  16
- By their fruits ye shall know them.
  20
- Let the dead bury their dead.
  8: 22
- Why eateth your Master with publicans and sinners?
  9: 11
- Neither do men put new wine into old bottles.
  17
- When he depart out of that house or city, shake off the dust of your feet.
  10: 14
- Be ye therefore wise as serpents, and harmless as doves.
  16
- He that is not with me is against me.
  12: 30 and Luke 11: 23
- He findeth it empty, swept, and garnished.
  44
- One pearl of great price.
  13: 46
- A prophet is not without honour, save in his own country, and in his own house.
  57
- If the blind lead the blind, both shall fall into the ditch.
  15: 14
- The signs of the times.
  16: 3
- Get thee behind me, Satan.
  23
- What is a man profited, if he shall gain the whole world, and lose his own soul?
  26 and Mark 8: 36
- Except ye be converted, and become as little children, ye shall not enter into the kingdom of heaven.
  18: 3
- Whoso shall offend one of these little ones which believe in me, it were better for him that a millstone were hanged about his neck, and that he were drowned in the depth of the sea.
  6. See Luke 17: 2.
- If thine eye offend thee, pluck it out, and cast it from thee.
  9
- For where two or three are gathered together in my name, there am I in the midst of them.
  20
- What therefore God hath joined together, let not man put asunder.
  19: 6
- It is easier for a camel to go through the eye of a needle, than for a rich man to enter into the kingdom of God.
  24. See Luke 10: 25.
- With men this is impossible; but with God all things are possible.
  26
- But many that are first shall be last; and the last shall be first.
  30
- For many are called, but few are chosen.
  22: 14
- Render therefore unto Caesar the things which are Caesar's; and unto God the things that are God's.
  21
- Well done, thou good and faithful servant.
  25: 21
- Unto every one that hath shall be given, and he shall have abundance: but from him that hath not shall be taken away even that which he hath.
  29
- They covenanted with him for thirty pieces of silver.
  26: 15
- Jesus took bread and blessed it, and brake it, and gave it to the disciples, and said, Take, eat; this is my body.
  26
- This night, before the cock crow, thou shalt deny me thrice.
  34
- Eli, Eli, lama sabachthani? ... My God, my God, why hast thou forsaken me?
  27: 46. See Psalms 22: 1.

- And, lo, I am with you alway, even unto the end of the world.
28: 20
- The sabbath was made for man, and not man for the sabbath.
St Mark 2: 27
- If a house be divided against itself, that house cannot stand.
3: 25
- She brought forth her firstborn son, and wrapped him in swaddling clothes, and laid him in a manger; because there was no room for them in the inn.
St Luke 2: 7
- Shepherds abiding in the field, keeping watch over their flock by night.
And, lo, the angel of the Lord came upon them, and the glory of the Lord shone round about them: and they were sore afraid.
8
- Behold, I bring you good tidings of great joy.
10
- Glory to God in the highest, and on earth peace, good will toward men.
14
- Lord, now lettest thou thy servant depart in peace, according to thy word.
29
- Wist ye not that I must be about my Father's business?
49
- Physician, heal thyself.
4: 23
- Love your enemies, do good to them which hate you.
6: 27
- Rejoice with me; for I have found my sheep which was lost.
15: 6
- Joy shall be in heaven over one sinner that repenteth, more than over ninety and nine just persons, which need no repentance.
7
- The crumbs which fell from the rich man's table.
16: 21. See Matthew 15: 27.
- The kingdom of God is within you.
17: 21
- Father, forgive them: for they know not what they do.
23: 34
- Father, into thy hands I commend my spirit.
46. See Psalms 31: 6.
- In the beginning was the Word, and the Word was with God, and the Word was God.
St John 1: 1
- The wind bloweth where it listeth.
3: 8
- God so loved the world, that he gave his only begotten Son, that whosoever believeth in him should not perish, but have everlasting life.
16
- Rise, take up thy bed, and walk.
5: 8
- He that is without sin among you, let him first cast a stone at her.
8: 7
- Neither do I condemn thee: go, and sin no more.
11
- The poor always ye have with you.
12: 8
- Let not your heart be troubled.
14: 1
- In my Father's house are many mansions.
2
- I am the way, the truth, and the life: no man cometh unto the Father, but by me.
6
- Greater love hath no man than this, that a man lay down his life for his friends.
15: 13
- And suddenly there came a sound from heaven as of a rushing mighty wind.
Acts of the Apostles 2: 2
- Silver and gold have I none; but such as I have give I thee.
3: 6
- Breathing out threatenings and slaughter.
9: 1
- Saul, Saul, why persecutest thou me?
4
- It is hard for thee to kick against the pricks.
5
- God is no respecter of persons.
10: 34. See Romans 2: 11.
- It is more blessed to give than to receive.
20: 35
- Who against hope believed in hope.
Romans 4: 18
- Shall we continue in sin, that grace may abound?
6: 1
- Death hath no more dominion.
9
- The wages of sin is death.
23
- Present your bodies a living sacrifice, holy, acceptable unto God.
12: 1
- Vengeance is mine; I will repay, saith the Lord.
19

- Overcome evil with good.
21
- Your body is the temple of the Holy Ghost.
1 Corinthians 6: 19
- It is better to marry than to burn.
7: 9
- Though I speak with the tongues of men and of angels, and have not charity, I am become as sounding brass, or a tinkling cymbal.
13: 1
- Though I have all faith, so that I could remove mountains, and have not charity, I am nothing.
2
- Charity suffereth long, and is kind, charity envieth not; charity vaunteth not itself, is not puffed up.
4
- Beareth all things, believeth all things, hopeth all things, endureth all things.
7
- For we know in part, and we prophesy in part.
9
- When I was a child, I spake as a child, I understood as a child, I thought as a child: but when I became a man, I put away childish things.
11
- For now we see through a glass, darkly.
12
- And now abideth faith, hope, charity, these three; but the greatest of these is charity.
13
- Be not deceived; God is not mocked: for whatsoever a man soweth, that shall he also reap.
Galatians 6: 7
- Rejoice in the Lord alway: and again I say, Rejoice.
Philippians 4: 4
- The peace of God, which passeth all understanding, shall keep your hearts and minds through Christ Jesus.
7
- Whatsoever things are true, whatsoever things are honest, whatsoever things are just, whatsoever things are pure, whatsoever things are lovely, whatsoever things are of good report; if there be any virtue and if there be any praise, think on these things.
8
- I have fought a good fight, I have finished my course, I have kept the faith.
2 Timothy 4: 7
- Unto the pure all things are pure.
Titus 1: 15

VULGATE

- *Dominus illuminatio mea.*
The Lord is the source of my light.
Psalm 26: 1 (AV Psalm 27: 1)
- *Vanitas vanitatum, dixit Ecclesiastes; vanitas vanitatum, et omnia vanitas.*
Vanity of vanities, said the preacher; vanity of vanities, and everything is vanity.
Ecclesiastes 1: 2
- *Magnificat anima mea Dominum.*
My soul doth magnify the Lord. [Tr. Book of Common Prayer]
Ev. S. Luc. 1: 46
- *Nunc dimittis servum tuum, Domine, secundum verbum tuum in pace.*
Lord, now lettest thou thy servant depart in peace: according to thy word. [Tr. Book of Common Prayer]
2: 29
- *Pax Vobis.*
Peace be unto you.
24: 36
- *Quo vadis?*
Where are you going?
Ev. S. Joann. 16: 5
- *Ecce homo.*
Behold the man.
19: 5
- *Consummatum est.*
It is achieved.
30
- *Noli me tangere.*
Do not touch me.
20: 17

PRINCE BISMARCK 1815–1898

- *Die Politik ist die Lehre von Möglichen.*
Politics is the art of the possible.
In conversation with Meyer von Waldeck, 11 Aug. 1867

WILLIAM BLAKE 1757–1827

- To see a World in a Grain of Sand,
  And a Heaven in a Wild Flower,
Hold Infinity in the palm of your hand,
  And Eternity in an hour.
Auguries of Innocence, 1
- And did those feet in ancient time
Walk upon England's mountains green?
Milton, preface
- And did the Countenance Divine
Shine forth upon our clouded hills?
And was Jerusalem builded here
Among these dark Satanic mills?

  Bring me my bow of burning gold!
  Bring me my arrows of desire!
  Bring me my spear! O clouds, unfold!
  Bring me my chariot of fire!

I will not cease from Mental Fight,
Nor shall my Sword sleep in my hand,
Till we have built Jerusalem,
In England's green & pleasant Land.

- Tyger! Tyger! burning bright
In the forests of the night,
What immortal hand or eye
Could frame thy fearful symmetry?
***Songs of Experience*, The Tyger**

- I was in a printing house in Hell, and saw the method in which knowledge is transmitted from generation to generation.
A Memorable Fancy, pl. 12–13

- If the doors of perception were cleansed everything would appear as it is, infinite.
pl. 14

LESLEY BLANCH 1907–

- She was an Amazon. Her whole life was spent riding at breakneck speed along the wilder shores of love.
The Wilder Shores of Love, 2. **Jane Digby El Mezrab**

HUMPHREY BOGART 1899–1957

- If she can stand it I can. Play it!
Casablanca (1942), script by Julius J. Epstein, Philip G. Epstein, Howard Koch. Often quoted as 'Play it again, Sam'.

LORD BOWEN 1835–1894

- The rain it raineth on the just
And also on the unjust fella:
But chiefly on the just, because
The unjust steals the just's umbrella.
Walter Sichel, *Sands of Time*

- On a metaphysician: A blind man in a dark room—looking for a black hat—which isn't there.
Attr. See *N. & Q.*, clxxxii. 153.

JOHN BRIGHT 1811–1889

- The angel of death has been abroad throughout the land; you may almost hear the beating of his wings.
House of Commons, 23 Feb. 1855

- England is the mother of Parliaments.
Birmingham, 18 Jan. 1865

CHARLOTTE BRONTË 1816–1855

- Reader, I married him.
***Jane Eyre*,** ch. 38

RUPERT BROOKE 1887–1915

- Blow out, you bugles, over the rich Dead!
The Dead

- These laid the world away; poured out the red
Sweet wine of youth.

- Stands the Church clock at ten to three?
And is there honey still for tea?
The Old Vicarage, Grantchester

- If I should die, think only this of me:
That there's some corner of a foreign field
That is for ever England.
The Soldier

- And laughter, learnt of friends; and gentleness,
In hearts at peace, under an English heaven.

ELIZABETH BARRETT BROWNING 1806–1861

- How do I love thee? Let me count the ways.
***Sonnets from the Portuguese*,** 43

ROBERT BROWNING 1812–1889

- I feel for the common chord again . . .
The C Major of this life.
***Abt Vogler*,** xii

- Ah, but a man's reach should exceed his grasp,
Or what's a heaven for?
***Andrea del Sarto*,** l. 97

- Oh, to be in England
Now that April's there.
Home-Thoughts, from Abroad

- That's the wise thrush; he sings each song twice over,
Lest you should think he never could recapture
The first fine careless rapture!

- I sprang to the stirrup, and Joris, and he;
I galloped, Dirck galloped, we galloped all three.
How they brought the Good News from Ghent to Aix

- Escape me?
Never—
Beloved!
Life in a Love

- Just for a handful of silver he left us,
Just for a riband to stick in his coat.
The Lost Leader

BEAU BRUMMELL 1778–1840

- I always like to have the morning well-aired before I get up.
Charles Macfarlane, *Reminiscences of a Literary Life*, 27

PROF. ARTHUR BULLER 1874–1944

- There was a young lady named Bright,
Whose speed was far faster than light;
She set out one day
In a relative way,
And returned home the previous night.
Punch, 19 Dec. 1923

JOHN BUNYAN 1628–1688

- As I walk'd through the wilderness of this world.
  The Pilgrim's Progress (1678), pt. i
- The name of the slough was Despond.
- The valley of Humiliation.
- It beareth the name of Vanity-Fair, because the town where 'tis kept, is lighter than vanity.
  See Psalms 62: 9
- Hanging is too good for him, said Mr Cruelty.
- A man that could look no way but downward, with a muckrake in his hand.
  pt. ii
- He that is down needs fear no fall,
  He that is low no pride.
  Shepherd Boy's Song

GELETT BURGESS 1866–1951

- I never saw a Purple Cow,
  I never hope to see one;
  But I can tell you, anyhow,
  I'd rather see than be one!
  Burgess Nonsense Book. **The Purple Cow**
- Ah, yes! I wrote the 'Purple Cow'—
  I'm sorry, now, I wrote it!
  But I can tell you anyhow,
  I'll kill you if you quote it!

DEAN BURGON 1813–1888

- Match me such marvel save in Eastern clime,
  A rose-red city 'half as old as Time'!
  Petra (1845)

ROBERT BURNS 1759–1796

- Should auld acquaintance be forgot,
  And never brought to mind?
  Auld Lang Syne
- We'll take a cup o' kindness yet,
  For auld lang syne.
- Gin a body meet a body
  Coming through the rye;
  Gin a body kiss a body,
  Need a body cry?
  Coming Through the Rye (taken from an old song, ***The Bob-tailed Lass***)
- Man's inhumanity to man
  Makes countless thousands mourn!
  Man was made to Mourn
- O, my Luve's like a red red rose
  That's newly sprung in June.
  My Love is like a Red Red Rose
- Wee, sleekit, cow'rin', tim'rous beastie,
  O what a panic's in thy breastie!
  To a Mouse

NICHOLAS MURRAY BUTLER 1862–1947

- An expert is one who knows more and more about less and less.
  attr. to a Commencement Address, Columbia University

LORD BYRON 1788–1824

- The Assyrian came down like the wolf on the fold,
  And his cohorts were gleaming in purple and gold.
  Destruction of Sennacherib

ROY CAMPBELL 1901–1957

- You praise the firm restraint with which they write—
  I'm with you there, of course:
  They use the snaffle and the curb all right,
  But where's the bloody horse?
  On Some South African Novelists

THOMAS CARLYLE 1795–1881

- A well-written Life is almost as rare as a well-spent one.
  Critical and Miscellaneous Essays, vol. i. **Richter**
- The three great elements of modern civilization, Gunpowder, Printing, and the Protestant Religion.
  State of German Literature. See Bacon, ***Novum Organum, bk. I***, *aphor. 129*

LEWIS CARROLL 1832–1898

- What I tell you three times is true.
  The Hunting of the Snark, Fit 1. **The Landing**
- They sought it with thimbles, they sought it with care;
  They pursued it with forks and hope;
  They threatened its life with a railway-share;
  They charmed it with smiles and soap.
  Fig 5. **The Beaver's Lesson**
- 'What is the use of a book', thought Alice, 'without pictures or conversations?'
  Alice's Adventures in Wonderland, ch. 1
- Curiouser and curiouser!' cried Alice.
  ch. 2
- How doth the little crocodile
  Improve his shining tail,
  And pour the waters of the Nile
  On every golden scale!
  See Watts.
- Oh my dear paws! Oh my fur and whiskers!
  ch. 4
- 'You are old, Father William,' the young man said,
  'And your hair has become very white;
  And yet you incessantly stand on your head—
  Do you think, at your age, it is right?'
  ch. 5

- 'Will you walk a little faster?' said a whiting to a snail,
'There's a porpoise close behind us, and he's treading on my tail.'
ch. 10

- 'Twas brillig, and the slithy toves
 Did gyre and gimble in the wabe;
All mimsy were the borogoves,
 And the mome raths outgrabe.
Through the Looking-Glass, ch. 1

- How, *here*, you see, it takes all the running *you* can do, to keep in the same place.
ch. 2

- 'Contrariwise,' continued Tweedledee, 'if it was so, it might be; and if it were so, it would be: but as it isn't, it ain't. That's logic.'
ch. 4

- 'If seven maids with seven mops
 Swept it for half a year,
Do you suppose,' the Walrus said,
 'That they could get it clear?'
'I doubt it,' said the Carpenter,
 And shed a bitter tear.

- The rule is, jam to-morrow and jam yesterday—but never jam to-day.
ch. 5

- 'When *I* use a word,' Humpty Dumpty said in a rather scornful tone, 'it means just what I choose it to mean—neither more nor less.'
ch. 6

- He's an Anglo-Saxon Messenger—and those are Anglo-Saxon attitudes.
ch. 7

EDITH CAVELL 1865–1915

- Standing, as I do, in the view of God and eternity I realize that patriotism is not enough. I must have no hatred or bitterness towards anyone.
Spoken to the chaplain who attended her before her execution by firing squad, 12 Oct. 1915. *The Times*, 23 Oct. 1915

NEVILLE CHAMBERLAIN 1869–1940

- I believe it is peace for our time . . . peace with honour.
After Munich Agreement, 30 Sept. 1938

KING CHARLES II 1630–1685

- Let not poor Nelly starve.
Burnet, *History of My Own Time*, vol. II, bk. iii, ch. 17

- He had been, he said, an unconscionable time dying; but he hoped that they would excuse it.
Macaulay, *Hist. England*, 1849, vol. i, ch. 4, p. 437

G. K. CHESTERTON 1874–1936

- I tell you naught for your comfort,
 Yea, naught for your desire,
Save that the sky grows darker yet
 And the sea rises higher.
Ballad of the White Horse, bk. i

- Before the Roman came to Rye or out to
  Severn strode,
The rolling English drunkard made the
  rolling English road.
The Rolling English Road

- The night we went to Birmingham by way
  of Beachy Head.

WINSTON CHURCHILL 1874–1965

- I cannot forecast to you the action of Russia. It is a riddle wrapped in a mystery inside an enigma.
Broadcast talk, 1 Oct. 1939

- I have nothing to offer but blood, toil, tears and sweat.
House of Commons, 13 May 1940

- We shall go on to the end, we shall fight in France, we shall fight on the seas and oceans, we shall fight with growing confidence and growing strength in the air, we shall defend our island, whatever the cost may be, we shall fight on the beaches, we shall fight on the landing grounds, we shall fight in the fields and in the streets, we shall fight in the hills; we shall never surrender.
4 June 1940

- Let us therefore brace ourselves to our duties and so bear ourselves that if the British Empire and its Commonwealth last for a thousand years men will still say, 'This was their finest hour'.
18 June 1940

- Never in the field of human conflict was so much owed by so many to so few.
20 Aug. 1940

- Give us the tools, and we will finish the job.
Radio Broadcast, 9 Feb. 1941

- When I warned them [the French Government] that Britain would fight on alone whatever they did, their Generals told their Prime Minister and his divided Cabinet: 'In three weeks England will have her neck wrung like a chicken.'
Some chicken! Some neck!
To the Canadian Parliament, 30 Dec. 1941

- This is not the end. It is not even the beginning of the end. But it is, perhaps, the end of the beginning.
Mansion House, 10 Nov. 1942. (Of the Battle of Egypt.)

- To jaw-jaw is better than to war-war.
Washington, 26 June 1954

SAMUEL TAYLOR COLERIDGE 1772–1834

- It is an ancient Mariner,
  And he stoppeth one of three.
  'By thy long grey beard and glittering eye,
  Now wherefore stopp'st thou me?'
  The Ancient Mariner, pt. i
- As idle as a painted ship
  Upon a painted ocean.
  pt. ii
- Water, water, every where,
  And all the boards did shrink;
  Water, water, every where.
  Not any drop to drink.
- At this moment he was unfortunately called out by a person on business from Porlock.
  Kubla Khan, Preliminary note
- In Xanadu did Kubla Khan
  A stately pleasure-dome decree:
  Where Alph, the sacred river, ran
  Through caverns measureless to man
  Down to a sunless sea.

NOËL COWARD 1899–1973

- Mad dogs and Englishmen go out in the mid-day sun.
  Mad Dogs and Englishmen
- Don't put your daughter on the stage, Missis Worthington.
  Mrs. Worthington

DESCARTES 1596–1650

- *Cogito, ergo sum.*
  I think, therefore I am.
  Le Discours de la Méthode

CHARLES DICKENS 1812–1870

- 'God bless us every one!' said Tiny Tim.
  A Christmas Carol, stave 3
- 'I am a lone lorn creetur', 'were Mrs Gummidge's words, ... 'and everythink goes contrairy with me.'
  David Copperfield, ch. 3
- Barkis is willin'.
  ch. 5
- Annual income twenty pounds, annual expenditure nineteen nineteen six, result happiness. Annual income twenty pounds, annual expenditure twenty pounds ought and six, result misery. [Mr. Micawber.]
  ch. 12
- With affection beaming in one eye, and calculation shining out of the other. [Mrs. Todgers.]
  Martin Chuzzlewit, ch. 8
- He'd make a lovely corpse. [Mrs. Gamp.]
  ch. 25

BENJAMIN DISRAELI 1804–1881

- Though I sit down now, the time will come when you will hear me.
  Maiden speech, 7 Dec. 1837. Meynell, *Disraeli*, i. 43
- The Continent will not suffer England to be the workshop of the world.
  House of Commons, 15 Mar. 1838
- Is man an ape or an angel? Now I am on the side of the angels.
  Meeting of Society for Increasing Endowments of Small Livings in the Diocese of Oxford, 25 Nov. 1864

LORD ALFRED DOUGLAS 1870–1945

- I am the Love that dare not speak its name.
  Two Loves

T. S. ELIOT 1888–1965

- Teach us to care and not to care
  Teach us to sit still.
  Ash Wednesday, 1
- Time present and time past
  Are both perhaps present in time future,
  And time future contained in time past.
  Four Quartets. **Burnt Norton**, 1
- Human kind
  Cannot bear very much reality.
- In my beginning is my end.
  East Coker, 1
- We are the hollow men
  We are the stuffed men
  Leaning together
  Headpiece filled with straw. Alas!
  The Hollow Men, 1
- *Here we go round the prickly pear*
  Prickly pear prickly pear.
  5
- This is the way the world ends
  Not with a bang but a whimper.
- Let us go then, you and I,
  When the evening is spread out against the sky
  Like a patient etherised upon a table.
  The Love Song of J. Alfred Prufrock
- In the room the women come and go
  Talking of Michelangelo.
  The yellow fog that rubs its back upon the windowpanes.
- I have measured out my life with coffee spoons.
- I should have been a pair of ragged claws
  Scuttling across the floors of silent seas.
- I grow old ... I grow old ...
  I shall wear the bottoms of my trousers rolled.
- I have heard the mermaids singing, each to each;
  I do not think that they will sing to me.

- Macavity, Macavity, there's no one like Macavity,
  There never was a Cat of such deceitfulness and suavity.
  Macavity: The Mystery Cat
- At whatever time the deed took place—
  MACAVITY WASN'T THERE!
- April is the cruellest month, breeding
  Lilacs out of the dead land.
  The Waste Land. 1. **The Burial of the Dead**
- And I will show you something different from either
  Your shadow at morning striding behind you,
  Or your shadow at evening rising to meet you
  I will show you fear in a handful of dust.

F. SCOTT FITZGERALD 1896–1940

- In the real dark night of the soul it is always three o'clock in the morning.
  The Crack-Up, ed. E. Wilson (1945), John Peale Bishop, *The Hours*. The phrase 'dark night of the soul' was used as the Spanish title of a work by St. John of the Cross known in English as *The Ascent of Mount Carmel* (1578–80)
- Let me tell you about the very rich. They are different from you and me.
  The Rich Boy. 'Notebooks E' in ***The Crack-Up*** records Ernest Hemingway's rejoinder: 'Yes, they have more money.'

HENRY FORD 1863–1947

- History is more or less bunk.
  Chicago Tribune, 25 May 1916

E. M. FORSTER 1879–1970

- All men are equal—all men, that is to say, who possess umbrellas.
  Howards End, ch. 6
- Only connect!
  ch. 22
- I hate the idea of causes, and if I had to choose between betraying my country and betraying my friend, I hope I should have the guts to betray my country.
  Two Cheers for Democracy, pt. 2. **What I Believe**

BENJAMIN FRANKLIN 1706–1790

- Remember, that time is money.
  Advice to Young Tradesman (1748)
- No nation was ever ruined by trade.
  ***Essays.* Thoughts on Commercial Subjects**

ROBERT FROST 1874–1963

- I have looked down the saddest city lane.
  I have passed by the watchman on his beat
  And dropped my eyes, unwilling to explain.
  Acquainted with the Night
- Forgive, O Lord, my little jokes on Thee
  And I'll forgive Thy great big one on me.
  ***In the clearing,* Cluster of Faith**
- Poetry is what gets lost in translation.
  Attr.

KING GEORGE II 1683–1760

- Mad, is he? Then I hope he will *bite* some of my other generals.
  Reply to the Duke of Newcastle who complained that General Wolfe was a madman. Wilson, *The life and letters of James Wolfe*, ch. 17

STELLA GIBBONS 1902–

- Something nasty in the woodshed.
  Cold Comfort Farm (1932), *passim*

HERMANN GOERING 1893–1946

- Guns will make us powerful; butter will only make us fat.
  Radio Broadcast, summer of 1936, often misquoted as 'Guns before butter'

SAMUEL GOLDWYN 1882–1974

- You can include me out.
  See Zierold, *The Hollywood Tycoons* (1969), ch. 3

KENNETH GRAHAME 1859–1932

- Believe me, my young friend, there is *nothing*—absolutely nothing—half so much worth doing as simply messing about in boats.
  The Wind in the Willows (1908), ch. 1

LORD GREY OF FALLODON 1863–1933

- The lamps are going out all over Europe; we shall not see them lit again in our lifetime.
  3 Aug. 1914. ***Twenty-Five Years, 1892–1916*** (1925), vol. ii, ch. 18

SIR JOHN HARINGTON 1561–1612

- Treason doth never prosper, what's the reason?
  For if it prosper, none dare call it treason.
  Epigrams (1618), bk. iv, No. 5. **Of Treason**

IAN HAY 1876–1952

- What do you mean, funny? Funny-peculiar or funny-ha-ha?
  The Housemaster (1936), Act III

J. MILTON HAYES 1884–1940

- There's a one-eyed yellow idol to the north of Khatmandu,
  There's a little marble cross below the town;
  There's a broken-hearted woman tends the grave of Mad Carew
  And the Yellow God forever gazes down.
  The Green Eye of the Yellow God (1911)

LILLIAN HELLMAN 1905–

- I cannot and will not cut my conscience to fit this year's fashions.
  Letter to the Honourable John S. Wood, Chairman of the House Committee on un-American Activities, 19 May 1952

A. P. HERBERT 1890–1971

- Let's find out what everyone is doing,
  And then stop everyone from doing it.
  Let's Stop Somebody

W. E. HICKSON 1803–1870

- If at first you don't succeed,
  Try, try again.
  Try and Try Again

THOMAS HOBBES 1588–1679

- The life of man, solitary, poor, nasty, brutish, and short.
  Leviathan (1651), pt. i, ch. 13

G. W. HUNT 1829–1904

- We don't want to fight, but, by jingo if we do,
  We've got the shops, we've got the men, we've got the money too.
  We Don't Want to Fight. Music hall song, 1878

CHRISTOPHER ISHERWOOD 1904–1986

- I am a camera with its shutter open, quite passive, recording, not thinking.
  ***Goodbye to Berlin*, A Berlin Diary**, Autumn 1930

PRESIDENT THOMAS JEFFERSON 1743–1826

- The tree of liberty must be refreshed from time to time with the blood of patriots and tyrants. It is its natural manure.
  Letter to W. S. Smith, 13 Nov. 1787
- When a man assumes a public trust, he should consider himself as public property.
  Remark to Baron von Humboldt, 1807. Rayner, *Life of Jefferson* (1834), p. 356

JEROME K. JEROME 1859–1927

- Love is like the measles; we all have to go through it.
  The Idle Thoughts of an Idle Fellow (1889). **On Being in Love**
- I like work: it fascinates me. I can sit and look at it for hours. I love to keep it by me: the idea of getting rid of it nearly breaks my heart.
  Three Men in a Boat (1889), ch. 15

HIRAM JOHNSON 1866–1945

- The first casualty when war comes is truth.
  Speech, US Senate, 1917

SAMUEL JOHNSON 1709–1784

- Sir, we are a nest of singing birds.
  Of Pembroke College, Oxford. Boswell, *Life of Johnson* (L.F. Powell's revision of G.B. Hill's edition), vol. i, p. 75. 1730
- They teach the morals of a whore, and the manners of a dancing master.
  Of Lord Chesterfield's *Letters*. p. 266. 1754
- Ignorance, madam, pure ignorance.
  When asked by a lady why he defined 'pastern' as the 'knee' of a horse, in his *Dictionary*. p. 293. 1755
- Lexicographer: a writer of dictionaries, a harmless drudge.
  p. 296. 1755
- A man, Sir, should keep his friendship in constant repair.
  p. 300. 1755
- Being in a ship is being in a jail, with the chance of being drowned.
  p. 348. 16 Mar. 1759
- The triumph of hope over experience.
  Of a man who remarried immediately after the death of a wife with whom he had been very unhappy. p. 128. 1770
- Read over your compositions, and where ever you meet with a passage which you think is particularly fine, strike it out.
  Quoting a college tutor. p. 237. 30 Apr. 1773
- It is wonderful, when a calculation is made, how little the mind is actually employed in the discharge of any profession.
  p. 344. 6 Apr. 1775
- Patriotism is the last refuge of a scoundrel.
  p. 348. 7 Apr. 1775
- No man but a blockhead ever wrote, except for money.
  vol. iii, p. 19. 5 Apr. 1776
- If I had no duties, and no reference to futurity, I would spend my life in driving briskly in a post-chaise with a pretty woman.
  p. 162. 19 Sept. 1777
- Depend upon it, Sir, when a man knows he is to be hanged in a fortnight, it concentrates his mind wonderfully.
  p. 167. 19 Sept. 1777
- When a man is tired of London, he is tired of life; for there is in London all that life can afford.
  p. 178. 20 Sept. 1777
- Claret is the liquor for boys; port for men; but he who aspires to be a hero must drink brandy.
  p. 381. 7 Apr. 1779
- Worth seeing? yes; but not worth going to see.
  Of the Giant's Causeway. p. 410. 12 Oct. 1779

- Sir, I look upon every day to be lost, in which I do not make a new acquaintance.
p. 374. Nov. 1784
- What is written without effort is in general read without pleasure.
Johnsonian Miscellanies (1897), vol. ii, p. 309
- Marriage has many pains, but celibacy has no pleasures.
Rasselas (1759), ch. 26

AL JOLSON 1886–1950

- You ain't heard nothin' yet, folks.
In the first talking film, *The Jazz Singer*, July 1927

BEN JONSON 1573?–1637

- Drink to me only with thine eyes,
  And I will pledge with mine;
Or leave a kiss but in the cup,
  And I'll not look for wine.
The Forest (1616), ix. **To Celia**

JUVENAL *c.*60–*c.*130

- *Sed quis custodiet ipsos Custodes?*
But who is to guard the guards themselves?
Satires, vi. 347

ALPHONSE KARR 1808–1890

- *Plus ça change, plus c'est la même chose.*
The more things change, the more they are the same.
Les Guêpes, Jan. 1849. vi

JOHN KEATS 1795–1821

- A thing of beauty is a joy for ever:
Its loveliness increases; it will never
Pass into nothingness.
Endymion (1818), bk. i, l. 1
- Oh, what can ail thee, Knight at arms
  Alone and palely loitering;
The sedge is wither'd from the lake,
  And no birds sing.
La Belle Dame Sans Merci
- Thou still unravish'd bride of quietness,
  Thou foster-child of silence and slow time.
Ode on a Grecian Urn
- Heard melodies are sweet, but those unheard
  Are sweeter.
- 'Beauty is truth, truth beauty,'—that is all
  Ye know on earth, and all ye need to know.
- O for a beaker full of the warm South,
  Full of the true, the blushful Hippocrene,
    With beaded bubbles winking at the brim.
Ode to a Nightingale
- Already with thee! tender is the night.

JOHN FITZGERALD KENNEDY 1917–1963

- And so, my fellow Americans: ask not what your country can do for you—ask what you can do for your country.
Inaugural address. 20 Jan. 1961. Not the first use of this form of words: a similar exhortation may be found in the funeral oration for John Greenleaf Whittier.
- All free men, wherever they may live, are citizens of Berlin. And therefore, as a free man, I take pride in the words *Ich bin ein Berliner*.
Speech at City Hall, West Berlin, 26 June 1963

REVD. MARTIN LUTHER KING 1929–1968

- I have a dream that one day this nation will rise up, live out the true meaning of its creed.
Washington, 27 Aug. 1963. The phrase 'I have a dream' was used by him in other speeches during the summer of that year.

RUDYARD KIPLING 1865–1936

- Oh, East is East, and West is West, and never the twain shall meet.
The Ballad of East and West
- Gentleman-rankers out on the spree,
Damned from here to Eternity,
God ha' mercy on such as we,
    Baa! Yah! Bah!
Gentleman-Rankers
- Though I've belted you an' flayed you,
By the livin' Gawd that made you,
You're a better man than I am, Gunga Din!
Gunga Din
- If you can keep your head when all about you
  Are losing theirs and blaming it on you.
If—
- If you can dream—and not make dreams your master.
- If you can meet with Triumph and Disaster
  And treat those two impostors just the same.
- If you can talk with crowds and keep your virtue,
  Or walk with Kings—nor lose the common touch.
- If you can fill the unforgiving minute
  With sixty seconds' worth of distance run,
Yours is the Earth and everything that's in it,
  And—which is more—you'll be a Man, my son!
- God of our fathers, known of old,
Lord of our far-flung battle-line.
Recessional (1897)

- The tumult and the shouting dies;
The Captains and the Kings depart.

LADY CAROLINE LAMB 1785–1828

- Mad, bad, and dangerous to know.
Of Byron, in her journal after their first meeting at a ball in March 1812. See Jenkins, *Lady Caroline Lamb* (1932), ch. 6.

PHILIP LARKIN 1922–1985

- Nothing, like something, happens anywhere.
I Remember, I Remember

EDWARD LEAR 1812–1888

- 'How pleasant to know Mr Lear!'
Who has written such volumes of stuff!
Some think him ill-tempered and queer,
But a few think him pleasant enough.
Nonsense Songs (1871), preface

- Far and few, far and few,
Are the lands where the Jumblies live;
Their heads are green, and their hands are blue,
And they went to sea in a Sieve.
The Jumblies

- The Owl and the Pussy-Cat went to sea
In a beautiful pea-green boat.
They took some honey, and plenty of money,
Wrapped up in a five-pound note.
The Owl and the Pussy-Cat

LE CORBUSIER 1887–1965

- *La maison est une machine à habiter.*
A house is a living-machine.
Vers une architecture (1923), p. ix

LIBERACE 1920–

- I cried all the way to the bank.
Liberace: An Autobiography, ch. 2. After hostile criticism.

ABRAHAM LINCOLN 1809–1865

- You can fool all the people some of the time, and some of the people all the time, but you can not fool all the people all of the time.
Attr. words in a speech at Clinton, 8 Sept. 1858. Attr. also to Phineas Barnum

- If I could save the Union without freeing any slave, I would do it; and if I could save it by freeing all the slaves, I would do it; and if I could save it by freeing some and leaving others alone, I would also do that.
Letter to Horace Greeley, 22 Aug. 1862

HENRY WADSWORTH LONGFELLOW 1807–1882

- I shot an arrow into the air,
It fell to earth, I knew not where.
The Arrow and the Song

- By the shore of Gitche Gumee,
By the shining Big-Sea-Water,
Stood the wigwam of Nokomis,
Daughter of the Moon, Nokomis.
The Song of Hiawatha (1855), iii. **Hiawatha's Childhood**

- From the waterfall he named her,
Minnehaha, Laughing Water.
iv. **Hiawatha and Mudjekeewis**

- Ships that pass in the night, and speak each other in passing.
Tales of a Wayside Inn, pt. III (1874), **The Theologian's Tale. Elizabeth**, iv

- Under the spreading chestnut tree
The village smithy stands;
The smith, a mighty man is he,
With large and sinewy hands.
The Village Blacksmith

- When she was good
She was very, very good,
But when she was bad she was horrid.
B. R. T. Machetta, *Home Life of Longfellow*

ANITA LOOS 1893–1981

- A girl like I.
Gentlemen Prefer Blondes (1925), *passim*

- Kissing your hand may make you feel very very good but a diamond and safire bracelet lasts forever.
ch. 4

- Fun is fun but no girl wants to laugh all of the time.

LOUIS XIV 1638–1715

- *L'État c'est moi.*
I am the State.
Attr. remark before the Parlement de Paris, 13 Apr. 1655. Dulaure, *Histoire de Paris* (1834), vol. 6, p. 298. Probably apocryphal.

LOUIS XVIII 1755–1824

- *Il n'est aucun de vous qui n'ait dans sa giberne le baton du duc de Reggio; c'est à vous à l'en faire sortir.*
There is not one of you who has not in his knapsack the field marshal's baton; it is up to you to bring it out.
Speech to the Saint-Cyr cadets, 9 Aug. 1819. *Moniteur*, 10 Aug. 1819

LORD MACAULAY 1800–1859

- And how can man die better
Than facing fearful odds,
For the ashes of his fathers,
And the temples of his Gods?
Lays of Ancient Rome (1842). **Horatius**, 27

- 'Now who will stand on either hand,
And keep the bridge with me?'
29

- But those behind cried 'Forward!'
And those before cried 'Back!'
50

- The gallery in which the reports sit has become a fourth estate of the realm.
***Historical Essays Contributed to the 'Edinburgh Review'*. Hallam's 'Constitutional History'** (Sept. 1828)

MARSHALL McLUHAN 1911–

- The medium is the message.
Understanding Media (1964), pt. i, ch. 1

HAROLD MACMILLAN (LORD STOCKTON) 1894–

- Let's be frank about it; most of our people have never had it so good.
20 July 1957. 'You Never Had It So Good' was the Democratic Party slogan in the US election campaign of 1952
- The wind of change is blowing through this continent.
Cape Town, 3 Feb. 1960. The speech was drafted by Sir David Hunt as described by him in *On the Spot: An Ambassador Remembers* (1975)

LOUIS MACNEICE 1907–1963

- All of London littered with remembered kisses.
***Autumn Journal*,** iv
- It's no go the merrygoround, it's no go the rickshaw,
All we want is a limousine and a ticket for the peepshow.
Bagpipe Music
- The glass is falling hour by hour, the glass will fall for ever,
But if you break the bloody glass, you won't hold up the weather.
- Time was away and somewhere else,
There were two glasses and two chairs
And two people with the one pulse
(Somebody stopped the moving stairs).
Meeting Point

JOSEPH DE MAISTRE 1753–1821

- *Toute nation a le gouvernement qu'elle mérite.*
Every country has the government it deserves.
***Lettres et Opuscules Inédits*,** i, p. 215, 15 Aug. 1811

GEORGE LEIGH MALLORY 1886–1924

- Because it is there.
Answer to the question 'Why do you want to climb Mt. Everest?' D. Robertson, *George Mallory* (1969), p. 215

MAO TSE-TUNG 1893–1976

- Every Communist must grasp the truth, 'Political power grows out of the barrel of a gun.'
Selected Works (Peking, 1961), vol. ii. **Problems of War and Strategy,** ii, 6 Nov. 1938
- All reactionaries are paper tigers.
vol. iv. **Talk with Anna Louise Strong,** Aug. 1946

QUEEN MARIE-ANTOINETTE 1755–1793

- *Qu'ils mangent de la brioche.*
Let them eat cake.
On being told that her people had no bread. Attributed to Marie-Antoinette, but much older. Rousseau refers in his *Confessions*, 1740, to a similar remark, as a well-known saying.

KARL MARX 1818–1883

- A spectre is haunting Europe—The spectre of Communism.
The Communist Manifesto (1848), opening words.
- The workers have nothing to lose in this [revolution] but their chains. They have a world to gain. Workers of the world, unite!
closing words
- From each according to his abilities, to each according to his needs.
Criticism of the Gothic Programme (1875). See Bakunin.
- Religion . . . is the opium of the people.
Critique of Hegel's Philosophy of Right (1843–4), Introduction

JOHN MASEFIELD 1878–1967

- Quinquireme of Nineveh from distant Ophir
Rowing home to haven in sunny Palestine,
With a cargo of ivory,
And apes and peacocks,
Sandalwood, cedarwood, and sweet white wine.
Cargoes. See 1 Kings 10
- Dirty British coaster with a salt-caked smoke stack,
Butting through the Channel in the mad March days,
With a cargo of Tyne coal,
Road-rail, pig-lead,
Firewood, iron-ware, and cheap tin trays.
- I must down to the seas again, to the lonely sea and the sky,
And all I ask is a tall ship and a star to steer her by.
Sea Fever
- I must down to the seas again, for the call of the running tide
Is a wild call and a clear call that may not be denied.
I must down to the seas again, to the vagrant gypsy life,
To the gull's way and the whale's way where the wind's like a whetted knife;
And all I ask is a merry yarn from a laughing fellow-rover,
And quiet sleep and a sweet dream when the long trick's over.

LORD MELBOURNE 1779–1848

- I like the Garter; there is no damned merit in it.
  On the Order of the Garter. H. Dunckley, *Lord Melbourne* (1890)
- Things have come to a pretty pass when religion is allowed to invade the sphere of private life.
  Remark on hearing an evangelical sermon. G. W. E. Russell, *Collections and Recollections*, ch. 6

JOHN STUART MILL 1806–1873

- Unearned increment.
  Dissertations and Discussions, vol. iv (1876), p. 299
- The liberty of the individual must be thus far limited; he must not make himself a nuisance to other people.
  On Liberty (1859), ch. 3

A. A. MILNE 1882–1956

- They're changing guard at Buckingham Palace—
  Christopher Robin went down with Alice.
  Alice is marrying one of the guard.
  'A soldier's life is terrible hard,'
  Says Alice.
  When We Were Very Young (1924), **Buckingham Palace**
- You must never go down to the end of the town if you don't go down with me.
  Disobedience
- I do like a little bit of butter to my bread!
  The King's Breakfast
- Little Boy kneels at the foot of the bed,
  Droops on the little hands, little gold head;
  Hush! Hush! Whisper who dares!
  Christopher Robin is saying his prayers.
  Vespers
- I am a Bear of Very Little Brain, and long words Bother me.
  Winnie-the-Pooh (1926), ch. 4
- Time for a little something.
  ch. 6

JOHN MILTON 1608–1674

- Come, knit hands, and beat the ground,
  In a light fantastic round.
  Comus (1634), l. 143
- That I incline to hope rather than fear,
  And gladly banish squint suspicion.
  l. 412
- To sport with Amaryllis in the shade.
  Lycidas (1637), l. 68
- Fame is the spur that the clear spirit doth raise
  (That last infirmity of noble mind).
  l. 70
- Their lean and flashy songs
  Grate on their scrannel pipes of wretched straw,
  The hungry sheep look up, and are not fed.
  l. 123
- Look homeward, Angel, now, and melt with ruth.
  l. 163
- Of Man's first disobedience, and the fruit
  Of that forbidden tree, whose mortal taste
  Brought death into the world, and all our woe,
  With loss of Eden.
  Paradise Lost (1667), 1668 edn. bk. i, l. 1
- Things unattempted yet in prose or rhyme.
  l. 16
- I may assert eternal Providence,
  And justify the ways of God to Men.
  l. 25
- Better to reign in hell, than serve in heav'n.
  l. 263
- And when night
  Darkens the streets, then wander forth the sons
  Of Belial, flown with insolence and wine.
  l. 500
- Who overcomes
  By force, hath overcome but half his foe.
  l. 648
- Let none admire
  That riches grow in hell, that soil may best
  Deserve the precious bane.
  l. 690
- From morn
  To noon he fell, from noon to dewy eve,
  A summer's day; and with the setting sun
  Dropt from the zenith like a falling star.
  l. 742
- A little onward lend thy guiding hand
  To these dark steps, a little further on.
  Samson Agonistes (1671), l. 1
- Eyeless in Gaza, at the mill with slaves.
  l. 41
- O dark, dark, dark, amid the blaze of noon,
  Irrecoverably dark, total eclipse
  Without all hope of day!
  l. 80
- How soon hath Time, the subtle thief of youth
  Stoln on its wing my three and twentieth year.
  Sonnet ii. **On his having arrived at the age of twenty-three**

- Thousands at his bidding speed
  And post o'er Land and Ocean without rest:
  They also serve who only stand and wait.
  xvi. **On His Blindness**
- For what can war but endless war still breed?
  On the Lord General Fairfax
- Peace hath her victories
  No less renowned than war.
  To the Lord General Cromwell, May 1652
- As good almost kill a man as kill a good book.
  Areopagitica (1644)

MARGARET MITCHELL 1900–1949

- After all, tomorrow is another day.
  Gone with the Wind (1936), closing words.

MOLIÈRE (J.-B. POQUELIN) 1622–1673

- *Il faut manger pour vivre et non pas vivre pour manger.*
  One should eat to live, and not live to eat.
  L'Avare (1668), III. v

HORATIO, LORD NELSON 1758–1805

- I have only one eye,—I have a right to be blind sometimes: . . . I really do not see the signal!
  At the battle of Copenhagen. Southey, *Life of Nelson*, ch. 7
- England expects that every man will do his duty.
  At the battle of Trafalgar
- Thank God, I have done my duty.
- Kiss me, Hardy.

SIR HENRY NEWBOLT 1862–1938

- There's a breathless hush in the Close to-night—
  Ten to make and the match to win.
  ***The Island Race*. Vitaï Lampada**
- Play up! play up! and play the game!'

EMPEROR NICHOLAS I OF RUSSIA 1796–1855

- *Nous avons sur les bras un homme malade—un homme gravement malade.*
  We have on our hands a sick man—a very sick man.
  [The sick man of Europe, the Turk.]
  Parliamentary Papers. Accounts and Papers, vol. lxxi, pt. 5. Eastern Papers, p. 2. Sir G. H. Seymour to Lord John Russell, 11 Jan. 1853

FRIEDRICH NIETZSCHE 1844–1900

- *Ich lehre euch den Übermenschen. Der Mensch ist Etwas, das überwunden werden soll.*
  I teach you the superman. Man is something to be surpassed.
  ***Also Sprach Zarathustra*.** Prologue (1883)
- *Gott ist tot.*
  God is dead.
  ***Die fröhliche Wissenschaft*,** III. 108

GENERAL R.-G. NIVELLE 1856–1924

- *Ils ne passeront pas.*
  They shall not pass.
  Used as a slogan throughout the defence of Verdun and often attributed to Marshal Pétain. Nivelle's Order of the Day dated 26 Feb. 1916 read '*Vous ne les laisserez pas passer.*' Taken up by the Republicans in the Spanish Civil War as '*No pasarán!*' !

WILLIAM OCCAM *c.*1280–1349

- *Entia non sunt multiplicanda praeter necessitatem.*
  No more things should be presumed to exist than are absolutely necessary.
  'Occam's Razor'. Ancient philosophical principle, often attributed to Occam, but used by many earlier thinkers. Not found in this form in his writings, though he frequently used similar expressions, e.g. *Pluralitas non est ponenda sine necessitate* (***Quodlibeta*,** *c.*1324, V, Q. i)

ADOLPH S. OCHS 1858–1935

- All the news that's fit to print.
  Motto of the *New York Times*

DANIEL O'CONNELL 1775–1847

- [Sir Robert] Peel's smile: like the silver plate on a coffin.
  Quoting J. P. Curran (1750–1817), Irish politician and lawyer. See *Hansard*, 26 Feb. 1835.

FRANK WARD O'MALLEY 1875–1932

- Life is just one damned thing after another.
  Attr. See *Literary Digest*, 5 Nov. 1932. Also attr. Elbert Hubbard

BARONESS ORCZY 1865–1947

- We seek him here, we seek him there,
  Those Frenchies seek him everywhere.
  Is he in heaven?—Is he in hell?
  That demmed, elusive Pimpernel?
  The Scarlet Pimpernel (1905), ch. 12

GEORGE ORWELL 1903–1950

- All animals are equal but some animals are more equal than others.
  Animal Farm (1945), ch. 10
- Big Brother is watching you.
  1984 (1949), p. 1

WILFRED OWEN 1893–1918

- Above all, this book is not concerned with Poetry.

The subject of it is War, and the Pity of War.
The Poetry is in the pity.
Poems (1920), Preface

- All the poet can do today is to warn.
- Red lips are not so red
  As the stained stones kissed by the English dead.
  Greater Love

LORD PALMERSTON 1784–1865

- Die, my dear Doctor, that's the last thing I shall do!
  Attr. last words

DOROTHY PARKER 1893–1967

- Men seldom make passes
  At girls who wear glasses.
  News Item
- She ran the whole gamut of the emotions from A to B.
  Of Katharine Hepburn in a Broadway play
- How could they tell?
  [On being told of the death of President Coolidge.]
  John Keats, *You might as well live* (1971), Foreword

C. NORTHCOTE PARKINSON 1909–

- Work expands so as to fill the time available for its completion.
  Parkinson's Law (1958), I, opening words

EDWARD JOHN PHELPS 1822–1900

- The man who makes no mistakes does not usually make anything.
  Speech at Mansion House, 24 Jan. 1899

WILLIAM PITT 1759–1806

- England has saved herself by her exertions, and will, as I trust, save Europe by her example.
  Guildhall, 1805
- Roll up that map; it will not be wanted these ten years.
  On a map of Europe, after hearing the news of the Battle of Austerlitz Dec. 1805. Lord Stanhope, *Life of the Rt. Hon. William Pitt* (1862), vol. iv, p. 369

EDGAR ALLAN POE 1809–1849

- Quoth the Raven, 'Nevermore'.
  The Raven (1845), xvii

MADAME DE POMPADOUR 1721–1764

- *Après nous le déluge.*
  After us the deluge.
  Madame de Hausset, *Mémoires*, p. 19

ALEXANDER POPE 1688–1744

- I am his Highness' dog at Kew;
  Pray, tell me sir, whose dog are you?
  Epigram Engraved on the Collar of a Dog which I gave to his Royal Highness
- Sir, I admit your gen'ral rule
  That every poet is a fool;
  But you yourself may serve to show it,
  That every fool is not a poet.
  Epigram from the French
- As yet a child, nor yet a fool to fame,
  I lisp'd in numbers, for the numbers came.
  Epistle to Dr. Arbuthnot, l. 127
- Damn with faint praise, assent with civil leer,
  And, without sneering, teach the rest to sneer.
  l. 201
- Nature, and Nature's laws lay hid in night:
  God said, *Let Newton be!* and all was light.
  Epitaphs. Intended for Isaac Newton
- Some have at first for wits, then poets pass'd,
  Turn'd critics next, and prov'd plain fools at last.
  An Essay on Criticism, l. 36
- A little learning is a dang'rous thing;
  Drink deep, or taste not the Pierian spring:
  There shallow draughts intoxicate the brain,
  And drinking largely sobers us again.
  l. 215
- To err is human, to forgive, divine.
  l. 525
- All seems infected that th'infected spy,
  As all looks yellow to the jaundic'd eye.
  l. 558
- The bookful blockhead, ignorantly read,
  With loads of learned lumber in his head.
  l. 612
- For fools rush in where angels fear to tread.
  l. 625
- Hope springs eternal in the human breast;
  Man never Is, but always To be blest.
  An Essay on Man. Epistle i, l. 95

PRAYER BOOK 1662

- We have erred, and strayed from thy ways like lost sheep. We have followed too much the devices and desires of our own hearts.
  General Confession
- We have left undone those things which we ought to have done; And we have done those things which we ought not to have done; And there is no health in us.

- Lighten our darkness, we beseech thee, O Lord.
  Evening Prayer. Third Collect
- Have mercy upon us miserable sinners.
  The Litany
- Hear them read, mark, learn, and inwardly digest them.
  Collects. 2nd Sunday in Advent
- An open and notorious evil liver.
  Holy Communion. Introductory rubric
- I should renounce the devil and all his works.
  Catechism
- To keep my hands from picking and stealing, and my tongue from evil-speaking, lying, and slandering.
- An outward and visible sign of an inward and spiritual grace.
- If any of you know cause, or just impediment, why these two persons should not be joined together in holy Matrimony, ye are to declare it.
  Solemnization of Matrimony. The Banns
- Forsaking all other, keep thee only unto her, so long as ye both shall live?
  Betrothal
- To have and to hold from this day forward, for better for worse, for richer for poorer, in sickness and in health, to love, cherish, and to obey, till death us do part.
- With this Ring I thee wed, with my body I thee worship, and with all my worldly goods I thee endow.
  Wedding
- Those whom God hath joined together let no man put asunder.
- In the midst of life we are in death.
  Burial of the Dead. First anthem
- Earth to earth, ashes to ashes, dust to dust.
  Interment
- Why do the heathen so furiously rage together?
  Psalms 2: 1
- Out of the mouth of very babes and sucklings hast thou ordained strength.
  8: 2
- The Lord is my shepherd: therefore can I lack nothing. He shall feed me in a green pasture: and lead me forth beside the waters of comfort.
  23: 1
- Yea, though I walk through the valley of the shadow of death, I will fear no evil: for thou art with me; thy rod and thy staff comfort me.
  Thou shalt prepare a table before me against them that trouble me: thou hast anointed my head with oil, and my cup shall be full.
  But thy loving-kindness and mercy shall follow me all the days of my life: and I will dwell in the house of the Lord for ever.
  4
- The earth is the Lord's, and all that therein is: the compass of the world, and they that dwell therein.
  24: 1
- O that I had wings like a dove: for then would I flee away, and be at rest.
  55: 6
- Which refuseth to hear the voice of the charmer: charm he never so wisely.
  58: 5
- Let them fall upon the edge of the sword: that they may be a portion for foxes.
  63: 11
- The zeal of thine house hath even eaten me.
  69: 9
- Thy rebuke hath broken my heart: I am full of heaviness.
  21
- The iron entered into his soul.
  105: 18
- They that go down to the sea in ships: and occupy their business in great waters;
  These men see the works of the Lord: and his wonders in the deep.
  107: 23
- I will lift up mine eyes unto the hills: from whence cometh my help.
  My help cometh even from the Lord: who hath made heaven and earth.
  He will not suffer thy foot to be moved: and he that keepeth thee will not sleep.
  Behold, he that keepeth Israel: shall neither slumber nor sleep.
  121: 1
- The Lord shall preserve thy going out, and thy coming in: from this time forth for evermore.
  8
- By the waters of Babylon we sat down and wept: when we remembered thee, O Sion.
  137: 1
- How shall we sing the Lord's song: in a strange land?
  If I forget thee, O Jerusalem: let my right hand forget her cunning.
  4
- Such knowledge is too wonderful and excellent for me: I cannot attain unto it.
  139: 5
- I will give thanks unto thee, for I am fearfully and wonderfully made.
  13
- O put not your trust in princes, nor in any child of man: for there is no help in them.
  146: 2

- To bind their kings in chains: and their nobles with links of iron.
  149: 8

PIERRE-JOSEPH PROUDHON 1809–1865

- *La propriété c'est le vol.*
  Property is theft.
  Qu'est-ce que la Propriété? (1840), ch. 1

MARCEL PROUST 1871–1922

- *Longtemps je me suis couché de bonne heure.*
  For a long time I used to go to bed early.
  A la Recherche du Temps Perdu, tr. C. K. Scott-Moncrieff and S. Hudson (1922–31), **Du côté de chez Swann,** opening sentence

PUNCH

- Advice to persons about to marry.—'Don't.'
  vol. viii, p. 1. 1845
- Never do to-day what you can put off till to-morrow.
  vol. xvii, p. 241. 1849
- Go directly—see what she's doing, and tell her she mustn't.
  vol. lxvii, p. 202. 1872
- It's worse than wicked, my dear, it's vulgar.
  Almanac. 1876

ISRAEL PUTNAM 1718–1790

- Men, you are all marksmen—don't one of you fire until you see the whites of their eyes.
  Bunker Hill, 1775. Frothingham, *History of the Siege of Boston* (1873), ch. 5, note. Also attributed to William Prescott (1726–95)

PYRRHUS 319/8–272 BC

- One more such victory and we are lost.
  Plutarch, *Pyrrhus*. After defeating the Romans at Asculum, 279 BC

SIR WALTER RALEIGH 1861–1922

- I wish I loved the Human Race;
  I wish I loved its silly face;
  I wish I liked the way it walks;
  I wish I liked the way it talks;
  And when I'm introduced to one
  I wish I thought *What Jolly Fun!*
  Laughter from a Cloud (1923), p. 228. **Wishes of an Elderly Man**

HENRY REED 1914–

- To-day we have naming of parts.
  Yesterday
  We had daily cleaning. And tomorrow
  morning,
  We shall have what to do after firing. But
  to-day,
  To-day we have naming of parts.
  Naming of Parts (1946)

GENERAL JOSEPH REED 1741–1785

- I am not worth purchasing, but such as I am, the King of Great Britain is not rich enough to do it.
  US Congress, 11 Aug. 1878. Reed understood himself to have been offered a bribe on behalf of the British Crown.

JULES RENARD 1864–1910

- *Les bourgeois, ce sont les autres.*
  The bourgeois are other people.
  Journal, 28 Jan. 1890

DR MONTAGUE JOHN RENDALL 1862–1950

- Nation shall speak peace unto nation.
  Written as the motto of the BBC in 1927 by Dr Rendall, one of the first Governors of the Corporation

GRANTLAND RICE 1880–1954

- For when the One Great Scorer comes
  To write against your name,
  He marks—not that you won or lost—
  But how you played the game.
  Alumnus Football

MANDY RICE-DAVIES 1944–

- He would, wouldn't he?
  When told that Lord Astor had denied her allegations. Trial of Stephen Ward, 29 June 1963

PRESIDENT FRANKLIN D. ROOSEVELT 1882–1945

- I pledge you—I pledge myself—to a new deal for the American people.
  Chicago Convention, 2 July 1932. (See also *N. & Q.*, cxciv, p. 529.)
- Let me assert my firm belief that the only thing we have to fear is fear itself.
  First Inaugural Address, 4 Mar. 1933

CHRISTINA ROSSETTI 1830–1894

- My heart is like a singing bird
  Whose nest is in a watered shoot;
  My heart is like an apple-tree
  Whose boughs are bent with thickset
  fruit;
  My heart is like a rainbow shell
  That paddles in a halcyon sea;
  My heart is gladder than all these
  Because my love is come to me.
  A Birthday

DANTE GABRIEL ROSSETTI 1828–1882

- I have been here before,
  But when or how I cannot tell:
  I know the grass beyond the door,
  The sweet keen smell,
  The sighing sound, the lights around the
  shore.
  Sudden Light, i

GIOACCHINO ROSSINI 1792–1868

- *Monsieur Wagner a de beaux moments, mais de mauvais quart d'heures.*
  Wagner has lovely moments but awful quarters of an hour.
  Said to Emile Naumann, April 1867. Naumann, *Italienische Tondichter* (1883), IV, 541

JEAN-JACQUES ROUSSEAU 1712–1778

- *L'homme est né libre, et partout il est dans les fers.*
  Man was born free, and everywhere he is in chains.
  Du Contrat Social, ch. 1

DAMON RUNYON 1884–1946

- More than somewhat.
  Phrase used frequently in Runyon's work, and adopted as book-title in 1937.

JOHN RUSKIN 1819–1900

- I have seen, and heard, much of Cockney impudence before now; but never expected to hear a coxcomb ask two hundred guineas for flinging a pot of paint in the public's face.
  [On Whistler's 'Nocturne in Black and Gold']
  Fors Clavigera letter lxxix, 18 June 1877
- All violent feelings ... produce in us a falseness in all our impressions of external things, which I would generally characterize as the 'Pathetic Fallacy'.
  Modern Painters (1888), vol. iii

BERTRAND RUSSELL 1872–1970

- Mathematics, rightly viewed, possesses not only truth, but supreme beauty—a beauty cold and austere, like that of sculpture.
  Mysticism and Logic (1918), ch. 4

SIR WILLIAM HOWARD RUSSELL 1820–1907

- They dashed on towards that *thin red line tipped with steel.*
  The British Expedition to the Crimea (1877), p. 156. Of the Russians charging the British.

'SAKI' (H. H. MUNRO) 1870–1916

- The cook was a good cook, as cooks go; and as cooks go she went.
  Reginald on Besetting Sins

LORD SALISBURY 1830–1903

- If you believe the doctors, nothing is wholesome: if you believe the theologians, nothing is innocent: if you believe the soldiers, nothing is safe.
  Letter to Lord Lytton, 15 June 1877. Lady Gwendolen Cecil, *Life of Robert, Marquis of Salisbury*, vol. II, ch. 4
- By office boys for office boys.
  Of the Daily Mail. See H. Hamilton Fyfe, *Northcliffe, an Intimate Biography*, ch. 4

JEAN-PAUL SARTRE 1905–1980

- *L'Enfer, c'est les Autres.*
  Hell is other people.
  Huis Clos, scene v
- *Trois heures, c'est toujours trop tard ou trop tôt pour tout ce qu'on veut faire.*
  Three o'clock is always too late or too early for anything you want to do.
  ***La Nausée,* Vendredi**

SIEGFRIED SASSOON 1886–1967

- Does it matter?—losing your legs? . . .
  For people will always be kind.
  Does it Matter?
- Does it matter?—losing your sight? . . .
  There's such splendid work for the blind.
- You are too young to fall asleep for ever;
  And when you sleep you remind me of
  the dead.
  The Dug-Out

CARL SCHURZ 1829–1906

- Our country, right or wrong! When right, to be kept right; when wrong, to be put right!
  Speech, US Senate, 1872

C. P. SCOTT 1846–1932

- Comment is free but facts are sacred.
  Manchester Guardian, 6 May 1926
- Television? The word is half Latin and half Greek. No good can come of it.
  Attr.

CAPTAIN ROBERT FALCON SCOTT 1868–1912

- For God's sake look after our people.
  Journal, 25 Mar. 1912
- Had we lived, I should have had a tale to tell of the hardihood, endurance, and courage of my companions which would have stirred the heart of every Englishman.
  Message to the Public

SIR WALTER SCOTT 1771–1832

- Hail to the Chief who in triumph
  advances!
  The Lady of the Lake (1810), II. xix
- O, young Lochinvar is come out of the
  west,
  Through all the wide Border his steed was
  the best.
  Marmion (1808), V. xii
- So faithful in love, and so dauntless in
  war,
  There never was knight like the young
  Lochinvar.
- O what a tangled web we weave,
  When first we practise to deceive!
  VI. xvii

- O Woman! in our hours of ease,
  Uncertain, coy, and hard to please.
  xxx

W. C. SELLAR 1898–1951
and R. J. YEATMAN 1898?–1968

- The Roman Conquest was, however, a *Good Thing*.
  1066, And All That (1930), ch. 1
- The Cavaliers (Wrong but Wromantic) and the Roundheads (Right but Repulsive).
  ch. 35

ROBERT W. SERVICE 1874–1958

- Ah! the clock is always slow;
  It is later than you think.
  ***Ballads of a Bohemian.* Spring,** ii

WILLIAM SHAKESPEARE 1564–1616

The line number is given without brackets where the scene is all verse up to the quotation and the line number is certain, and in square brackets where prose makes it variable. All references are to the Oxford Standard Authors Shakespeare in one volume.

- A young man married is a man that's marred.
  All's Well That Ends Well, II. iii. [315]
- My salad days,
  When I was green in judgment.
  Antony and Cleopatra, I. v. 73
- The barge she sat in, like a burnish'd throne,
  Burn'd on the water.
  II. ii. [199]
- Age cannot wither her, nor custom stale
  Her infinite variety.
  [243]
- Let's have one other gaudy night: call to me
  All my sad captains.
  III. xi. 182
- To business that we love we rise betime,
  And go to 't with delight.
  IV. iv. 20
- Finish, good lady; the bright day is done,
  And we are for the dark.
  V. ii. 192
- Sweet are the uses of adversity,
  Which like the toad, ugly and venomous,
  Wears yet a precious jewel in his head.
  As You Like It, II. i. 12
- All the world's a stage,
  And all the men and women merely players.
  vii. 139
- And then the whining schoolboy, with his satchel,
  And shining morning face, creeping like snail
  Unwillingly to school.
  145
- Seeking the bubble reputation
  Even in the cannon's mouth.
  152
- Second childishness, and mere oblivion,
  Sans teeth, sans eyes, sans taste, sans everything.
  165
- Blow, blow, thou winter wind,
  Thou art not so unkind
  As man's ingratitude.
  174
- My gracious silence, hail!
  Coriolanus, II. i. [194]
- Boldness be my friend!
  Arm me, audacity.
  Cymbeline, I. vi. 18
- For this relief much thanks; 'tis bitter cold
  And I am sick at heart.
  Hamlet, I. i. 8
- But, look, the morn, in russet mantle clad,
  Walks o'er the dew of yon high eastern hill.
  166
- A little more than kin, and less than kind.
  ii. 65
- Seems, madam! Nay, it is; I know not 'seems'.
  76
- O! that this too too solid flesh would melt,
  Thaw, and resolve itself into a dew.
  129
- How weary, stale, flat, and unprofitable
  Seem to me all the uses of this world.
  133
- Frailty, thy name is woman!
  146
- He was a man, take him for all in all,
  I shall not look upon his like again.
  187
- The friends thou hast, and their adoption tried,
  Grapple them to thy soul with hoops of steel.
  iii. 62
- Neither a borrower, nor a lender be.
  75
- This above all: to thine own self be true,
  And it must follow, as the night the day,
  Thou canst not then be false to any man.
  78
- It is a custom
  More honour'd in the breach than the observance.
  iv. 15
- Angels and ministers of grace defend us!
  39
- Something is rotten in the state of Denmark.
  90

- Leave her to heaven,
  And to those thorns that in her bosom lodge,
  To prick and sting her.
  v. 86
- My tables,—meet it is I set it down,
  That one may smile, and smile, and be a villain.
  105
- There are more things in heaven and earth, Horatio,
  Than are dreamt of in your philosophy.
  166
- The time is out of joint; O cursed spite,
  That ever I was born to set it right!
  188
- Brevity is the soul of wit.
  II. ii. 90
- Though this be madness, yet there is method in't.
  [211]
- There is nothing either good or bad, but thinking makes it so.
  [259]
- O God! I could be bounded in a nut-shell, and count myself a king of infinite space, were it not that I have bad dreams.
  [264]
- What a piece of work is a man!
  [323]
- I know a hawk from a handsaw.
  [406]
- The play, I remember, pleased not the million; 'twas caviare to the general.
  [465]
- What's Hecuba to him or he to Hecuba
  That he should weep for her?
  [593]
- The play's the thing
  Wherein I'll catch the conscience of the king.
  [641]
- To be, or not to be: that is the question:
  Whether 'tis nobler in the mind to suffer
  The slings and arrows of outrageous fortune,
  Or to take arms against a sea of troubles,
  And by opposing end them?
  III. i. 56
- To sleep: perchance to dream: ay, there's the rub;
  For in that sleep of death what dreams may come
  When we have shuffled off this mortal coil,
  Must give us pause.
  65
- Thus conscience doth make cowards of us all;
  And thus the native hue of resolution
  Is sicklied o'er with the pale cast of thought.
  83
- Get thee to a nunnery: why wouldst thou be a breeder of sinners?
  [124]
- The glass of fashion, and the mould of form.
  [162]
- Speak the speech, I pray you, as I pronounced it to you, trippingly on the tongue.
  ii. 1
- The lady doth protest too much, methinks.
  [242]
- My words fly up, my thoughts remain below:
  Words without thoughts never to heaven go.
  iii. 97
- Thou wretched, rash, intruding fool, farewell!
  iv. 31
- A king of shreds and patches.
  102
- I must be cruel only to be kind.
  178
- How all occasions do inform against me,
  And spur my dull revenge!
  IV. iv. 32
- There is a willow grows aslant a brook,
  That shows his hoar leaves in the glassy stream;
  There with fantastic garlands did she come.
  vii. 167
- Alas, poor Yorick. I knew him, Horatio; a fellow of infinite jest, of most excellent fancy.
  V. i. [201]
- There's a divinity that shapes our ends,
  Rough-hew them how we will.
  ii. 10
- If it be now, 'tis not to come; if it be not to come, it will be now; if it be not now, yet it will come: the readiness is all.
  [232]
- A hit, a very palpable hit.
  [295]
- The rest is silence.
  [372]
- Now cracks a noble heart. Good-night, sweet prince,
  And flights of angels sing thee to thy rest!
  [373]
- Rosencrantz and Guildenstern are dead.
  [385]

- If all the year were playing holidays,
  To sport would be as tedious as to work.
  Henry IV, Part 1, I. ii [226]
- I am not only witty in myself, but the cause that wit is in other men.
  Henry IV, Part 2, I. ii. [10]
- Thy wish was father, Harry, to that thought.
  IV. v. 91
- O! for a Muse of fire, that would ascend
  The brightest heaven of invention.
  Henry V, Chorus, 1
- Can this cockpit hold
  The vasty fields of France? or may we cram
  Within this wooden O the very casques
  That did affright the air at Agincourt?
  11
- Now all the youth of England are on fire,
  And silken dalliance in the wardrobe lies.
  II. Chorus, 1
- Once more unto the breach, dear friends, once more;
  Or close the wall up with our English dead!
  III. i. 1
- A little touch of Harry in the night.
  IV. Chorus, 47
- I think the king is but a man, as I am: the violet smells to him as it doth to me.
  i. [106]
- If we are mark'd to die, we are enow
  To do our country loss; and if to live,
  The fewer men, the greater share of honour.
  iii. 20
- Then will he strip his sleeve and show his scars,
  And say, 'These wounds I had on Crispin's day.'
  Old men forget: yet all shall be forgot,
  But he'll remember with advantages
  What feats he did that day.
  47
- We few, we happy few, we band of brothers.
  60
- Beware the ides of March.
  Julius Caesar, I. ii. 18
- The fault, dear Brutus, is not in our stars,
  But in ourselves, that we are underlings.
  139
- Let me have men about me that are fat;
  Sleek-headed men and such as sleep o' nights;
  Yond' Cassius has a lean and hungry look;
  He thinks too much: such men are dangerous.
  191
- Cowards die many times before their deaths;
  The valiant never taste of death but once.
  II. ii. 32
- I am constant as the northern star,
  Of whose true-fix'd and resting quality
  There is no fellow in the firmament.
  III. i. 60
- *Et tu, Brute?*
  77
- Cry, 'Havoc!' and let slip the dogs of war.
  273
- Not that I loved Caesar less, but that I loved Rome more.
  ii. [22]
- Friends, Romans, countrymen, lend me your ears;
  I come to bury Caesar, not to praise him.
  The evil that men do lives after them,
  The good is oft interred with their bones.
  [79]
- There is a tide in the affairs of men,
  Which, taken at the flood, leads on to fortune.
  IV. iii. 217
- Bell, book, and candle shall not drive me back,
  When gold and silver becks me to come on.
  King John, III. iii. 12
- Nothing will come of nothing: speak again.
  King Lear, I. i.]92]
- I grow, I prosper;
  Now, gods, stand up for bastards!
  ii. 21
- How sharper than a serpent's tooth it is
  To have a thankless child!
  iv. [312]
- O! let me not be mad, not mad, sweet heaven;
  Keep me in temper; I would not be mad!
  v. [51]
- Blow, winds, and crack your cheeks! rage! blow!
  III. ii. 1
- I am a man
  More sinned against than sinning.
  [59]
- The prince of darkness is a gentleman.
  iv. [148]
- Poor Tom's a-cold.
  [151]
- Study is like the heaven's glorious sun,
  That will not be deep-search'd with saucy looks.
  Love's Labour's Lost, I. i. 84

- A wightly wanton with a velvet brow,
With two pitch balls stuck in her face for eyes.
III. i. [206]

- When daisies pied and violets blue
And lady-smocks all silver-white
And cuckoo-buds of yellow hue
Do paint the meadows with delight,
The cuckoo then, on every tree,
Mocks married men; for thus sings he,
Cuckoo;
Cuckoo, cuckoo; O, word of fear,
Unpleasing to a married ear!
V. ii. [902]

- Fair is foul, and foul is fair:
Hover through the fog and filthy air.
Macbeth, I. i. 9

- Nothing in his life
Became him like the leaving it.
iv. 7

- Yet I do fear thy nature;
It is too full o' the milk of human kindness.
v. [16]

- If it were done when 'tis done, then 'twere well
It were done quickly.
vii. 1

- Is this a dagger which I see before me,
The handle toward my hand?
II. i. 33

- That which hath made them drunk hath made me bold.
ii. 1

- Methought I heard a voice cry, 'Sleep no more!
Macbeth does murder sleep,' the innocent sleep,
Sleep that knits up the ravell'd sleave of care.
36

- Double, double toil and trouble;
Fire burn and cauldron bubble.
IV. i. 10

- By the pricking of my thumbs,
Something wicked this way comes.
44

- Out, damned spot! out, I say!
V. i. [38]

- Yet who would have thought the old man to have had so much blood in him?
[41]

- What! will these hands ne'er be clean?
[47]

- Here's the smell of the blood still: all the perfumes of Arabia will not sweeten this little hand.
[55]

- She should have died hereafter;
There would have been a time for such a word,
To-morrow, and to-morrow, and to-morrow,
Creeps in this petty pace from day to day,
To the last syllable of recorded time;
And all our yesterdays have lighted fools
The way to dusty death. Out, out, brief candle!
Life's but a walking shadow, a poor player,
That struts and frets his hour upon the stage,
And then is heard no more; it is a tale
Told by an idiot, full of sound and fury,
Signifying nothing.
v. 16

- Lay on, Macduff;
And damn'd be him that first cries, 'Hold, enough!'
vii. 62

- Be absolute for death; either death or life
Shall thereby be the sweeter.
Measure for Measure, III. i. 5

- By my troth, Nerissa, my little body is aweary of this great world.
The Merchant of Venice, I. ii. 1

- Hath not a Jew eyes? hath not a Jew hands, organs, dimensions, senses, affections, passions?
III. i. [63]

- If you prick us, do we not bleed? if you tickle us, do we not laugh? if you poison us, do we not die? and if you wrong us, shall we not revenge?
[69]

- Tell me where is fancy bred.
Or in the heart or in the head?
ii. 63

- A harmless necessary cat.
IV. i. 55

- The quality of mercy is not strain'd,
It droppeth as the gentle rain from heaven
Upon the place beneath.
[184]

- And earthly power doth then show likest God's
When mercy seasons justice.
[196]

- Why, then the world's mine oyster.
The Merry Wives of Windsor, II. ii. 2

- To live a barren sister all your life,
Chanting faint hymns to the cold fruitless moon.
A Midsummer Night's Dream, I. i. 72

- The course of true love never did run smooth.
134

- Love looks not with the eyes, but with the mind,
  And therefore is wing'd Cupid painted blind.
  234
- I will roar you as gently as any sucking dove.
  ii. [85]
- The lunatic, the lover, and the poet,
  Are of imagination all compact.
  V. i. 7
- The poet's eye, in a fine frenzy rolling,
  Doth glance from heaven to earth, from earth to heaven;
  And, as imagination bodies forth
  The forms of things unknown, the poet's pen
  Turns them to shapes, and gives to airy nothing
  A local habitation and a name.
  12
- Speak low, if you speak love.
  Much Ado About Nothing, II. i. [104]
- Sigh no more, ladies, sigh no more,
  Men were deceivers ever.
  iii. [65]
- Your daughter and the Moor are now making the beast with two backs.
  Othello, I. i. [117]
- Keep up your bright swords, for the dew will rust them.
  ii. 59
- It is the cause, it is the cause, my soul.
  V. ii. 1
- Put out the light, and then put out the light.
  7
- Speak of me as I am; nothing extenuate,
  Nor set down aught in malice: then, must you speak
  Of one that lov'd not wisely but too well.
  341
- Teach thy necessity to reason thus;
  There is no virtue like necessity.
  Richard II, I. iii. 277
- The setting sun, and music at the close.
  II. i. 12
- Methinks I am a prophet new inspir'd.
  31
- This royal throne of kings, this scepter'd isle,
  This earth of majesty, this seat of Mars,
  This other Eden, demi-paradise.
  40
- This happy breed of men, this little world,
  This precious stone set in the silver sea.
  45
- This blessed plot, this earth, this realm, this England.
  50
- O! call back yesterday, bid time return.
  III. ii. 69
- For God's sake, let us sit upon the ground
  And tell sad stories of the death of kings.
  155
- Now is the winter of our discontent
  Made glorious summer by this sun of York.
  Richard III, I. i. 1
- A horse! a horse! my kingdom for a horse!
  V. iv. 7
- O! she doth teach the torches to burn bright.
  Romeo and Juliet, I. v. [48]
- He jests at scars, that never felt a wound.
  But, soft! what light through yonder window breaks?
  It is the east, and Juliet is the sun.
  II. ii. 1
- O Romeo, Romeo! wherefore art thou Romeo?
  33
- What's in a name? that which we call a rose
  By any other name would smell as sweet.
  43
- Good-night, good-night! parting is such sweet sorrow
  That I shall say good-night till it be morrow.
  185
- No, 'tis not so deep as a well, nor so wide as a church door; but 'tis enough, 'twill serve.
  III. i. [100]
- A plague o' both your houses!
  [112]
- Night's candles are burnt out, and jocund day
  Stands tiptoe on the misty mountain tops.
  v. 9
- What seest thou else
  In the dark backward and abysm of time?
  The Tempest, I. ii. 49
- Full fathom five thy father lies;
  Of his bones are coral made:
  Those are pearls that were his eyes:
  Nothing of him that doth fade,
  But doth suffer a sea-change
  Into something rich and strange.
  394
- If music be the food of love, play on;
  Give me excess of it, that, surfeiting,
  The appetite may sicken, and so die.
  Twelfth Night, I. i. 1
- Some men are born great, some achieve greatness, and some have greatness thrust upon them.
  II. v. [158]

- Crabbed age and youth cannot live together:
  Youth is full of pleasance, age is full of care.
  The Passionate Pilgrim, xii
- To the onlie begetter of these insuing sonnets, Mr. W.H.
  Sonnets, Dedication (also attr. Thomas Thorpe)
- Shall I compare thee to a summer's day?
  Thou are more lovely and more temperate:
  Rough winds do shake the darling buds of May,
  And summer's lease hath all too short a date.
  18
- Full many a glorious morning have I seen
  Flatter the mountain-tops with sovereign eye.
  33
- No longer mourn for me when I am dead
  Than you shall hear the surly sullen bell.
  71
- When in the chronicle of wasted time
  I see descriptions of the fairest wights,
  And beauty making beautiful old rime,
  In praise of ladies dead and lovely knights.
  106
- Love's not Time's fool, though rosy lips and cheeks
  Within his bending sickle's compass come;
  Love alters not with his brief hours and weeks,
  But bears it out even to the edge of doom.
  If this be error, and upon me prov'd,
  I never writ, nor no man ever lov'd.
  116
- Item, I give unto my wife my second best bed, with the furniture.
  Will, 1616

GEORGE BERNARD SHAW 1856–1950

- You can always tell an old soldier by the inside of his holsters and cartridge boxes. The young ones carry pistols and cartridges: the old ones, grub.
  Arms and the Man (1898), Act I
- I'm only a beer teetotaller, not a champagne teetotaller.
  Candida (1898), Act III
- All professions are conspiracies against the laity.
  The Doctor's Dilemma (1906), Act I
- The one point on which all women are in furious secret rebellion against the existing law is the saddling of the right to a child with the obligation to become the servant of a man.
  Getting Married (1908), Preface
- The greatest of evils and the worst of crimes is poverty.
  Major Barbara (1907), Preface
- You darent handle high explosives; but youre all ready to handle honesty and truth and justice and the whole duty of man, and kill one another at that game. What a country! What a world!
  Act III
- A lifetime of happiness! No man alive could bear it: it would be hell on earth.
  Man and Superman (1903), Act I
- Vitality in a woman is a blind fury of creation.
- The true artist will let his wife starve, his children go barefoot, his mother drudge for his living at seventy, sooner than work at anything but his art.
- The Golden Rule is that there are no golden rules.
  Maxims for Revolutionists (by 'John Tanner'): **'The Golden Rule'**
- He who can, does. He who cannot teaches.
  'Education'
- Marriage is popular because it combines the maximum of temptation with the maximum of opportunity.
  'Marriage'
- Every man over forty is a scoundrel.
  'Stray Sayings'
- It is impossible for an Englishman to open his mouth, without making some other Englishman despise him.
  Pygmalion (1912), Preface

PERCY BYSSHE SHELLEY 1792–1822

- I never was attached to that great sect,
  Whose doctrine is that each one should select
  Out of the crowd a mistress or a friend,
  And all the rest, though fair and wise, commend
  To cold oblivion.
  Epipsychidion (1821), l. 149
- I met Murder in the way—
  He had a mask like Castlereagh.
  The Mask of Anarchy (1819), II
- O wild West Wind, thou breath of Autumn's being,
  Thou, from whose unseen presence the leaves dead
  Are driven, like ghosts from an enchanter fleeing.
  Ode to the West Wind (1819), l. 1
- Be through my lips to unawakened earth
  The trumpet of a prophecy! O, Wind,
  If Winter comes, can Spring be far behind?
  l. 68
- I met a traveller from an antique land.
  Ozymandias

- Hail to thee, blithe Spirit!
  Bird thou never wert.
  To a Skylark (1819)

LOGAN PEARSALL SMITH 1865–1946

- To suppose, as we all suppose, that we could be rich and not behave as the rich behave, is like supposing that we could drink all day and keep absolutely sober.
  Afterthoughts (1931), ch. 4. **In the World**
- Thank heavens, the sun has gone in, and I don't have to go out and enjoy it.
  Last Words (1933)

STEVIE SMITH 1902–1971

- Nobody heard him, the dead man,
  But still he lay moaning:
  I was much further out than you thought
  And not waving but drowning.
  Not Waving But Drowning

JOHN L. B. SOULE 1815–1891

- Go West, young man, go West!
  Editorial, *Terre Haute* (Indiana) *Express* (1851)

STEPHEN SPENDER 1909–

- I think continually of those who were
  truly great—
  The names of those who in their lives
  fought for life,
  Who wore at their hearts the fire's centre.
  I Think Continually of Those
- What I had not foreseen
  Was the gradual day
  Weakening the will
  Leaking the brightness away.
  Preludes, 12

MME DE STAËL 1766–1817

- *Tout comprendre rend très indulgent.*
  To be totally understanding makes one very indulgent.
  Corinne (1807), lib. iv, ch. 2

JOSEPH STALIN 1879–1953

- The Pope! How many divisions has *he* got?
  When asked by Laval to encourage Catholicism in Russia to conciliate the Pope, 13 May 1935. Churchill, *The Second World War*, vol. i, 'The Gathering Storm', ch. 8

SIR HENRY MORTON STANLEY
1841–1904

- Dr Livingstone, I presume?
  How I found Livingstone (1872), ch. 11

GERTRUDE STEIN 1874–1946

- Rose is a rose is a rose is a rose.
  Sacred Emily
- What *is* the answer? ... In that case, what is the question?
  Last words. Donald Sutherland, *Gertrude Stein, A Biography of her Work* (1951), ch. 6

ROBERT LOUIS STEVENSON
1850–1894

- Fifteen men on the dead man's chest
  Yo-ho-ho, and a bottle of rum!
  Drink and the devil had done for the
  rest—
  Yo-ho-ho, and a bottle of rum!
  Treasure Island (1883), ch. 1
- To travel hopefully is a better thing than to arrive, and the true success is to labour.
  Virginibus Puerisque (1881), VI. **El Dorado**

HARRIET BEECHER STOWE
1811–1896

- 'Do you know who made you?' 'Nobody, as I knows on,' said the child, with a short laugh ... 'I 'spect I grow'd.'
  Uncle Tom's Cabin (1852), ch. 20

HANNEN SWAFFER 1879–1962

- Freedom of the press in Britain is freedom to print such of the proprietor's prejudices as the advertisers don't object to.
  In conversation with Tom Driberg, *c.*1928

JONATHAN SWIFT 1667–1745

- When a true genius appears in the world, you may know him by this sign, that the dunces are all in confederacy against him.
  Thoughts on Various Subjects (1706)
- So, naturalists observe, a flea
  Hath smaller fleas that on him prey;
  And these have smaller fleas to bite 'em,
  And so proceed *ad infinitum.*
  On Poetry (1733), l. 337
- In Church your grandsire cut his throat;
  To do the job too long he tarry'd,
  He should have had my hearty vote,
  To cut his throat before he marry'd.
  Verses on the Upright Judge

ALGERNON CHARLES SWINBURNE
1837–1909

- When the hounds of spring are on
  winter's traces,
  The mother of months in meadow or
  plain
  Fills the shadows and windy places
  With lisp of leaves and ripple of rain.
  Atalanta in Calydon (1865). Chorus

CHARLES-MAURICE DE TALLEYRAND 1754–1838

- *Ils n'ont rien appris, ni rien oublié.*
  They have learnt nothing, and forgotten nothing.
  Attributed to Talleyrand by the Chevalier de Panat in a letter to Mallet du Pan, Jan. 1796

NAHUM TATE 1652–1715
and NICHOLAS BRADY 1659–1726

- While shepherds watch'd their flocks by night,
All seated on the ground,
The Angel of the Lord came down,
And glory shone around.
Supplement to the New Version of the Psalms (1700). **While Shepherds Watched**

JANE TAYLOR 1783–1824

- Twinkle, twinkle, little star,
How I wonder what you are!
Up above the world so high,
Like a diamond in the sky!
The Star

ALFRED, LORD TENNYSON
1809–1892

- I come from haunts of coot and hern,
I make a sudden sally
And sparkle out among the fern,
To bicker down a valley.
The Brook, l. 23
- For men may come and men may go,
But I go on for ever.
l. 33
- Half a league, half a league,
Half a league onward.
The Charge of the Light Brigade
- 'Forward the Light Brigade!'
Was there a man dismay'd?
Not tho' the solder knew
Some one had blunder'd:
Theirs not to make reply,
Theirs not to reason why,
Theirs but to do and die:
Into the valley of Death
Rode the six hundred.
Cannon to right of them
Cannon to left of them,
Cannon in front of them
Volley'd and thunder'd.
- We needs must love the highest when we see it.
The Idylls of the King. **Guinevere,** l. 655
- God make thee good as thou art beautiful.
The Holy Grail, l. 136
- Never morning wore
To evening, but some heart did break.
In Memoriam A.H.H., vi
- Ring out, wild bells, to the wild sky,
The flying cloud, the frosty light:
The year is dying in the night;
Ring out, wild bells, and let him die.
cvi
- Kind hearts are more than coronets,
And simple faith than Norman blood.
Lady Clara Vere de Vere, vi
- Out flew the web and floated wide;
The mirror crack'd from side to side;
'The curse is come upon me,' cried
The Lady of Shalott.
The Lady of Shalott, pt. iii
- In the Spring a young man's fancy lightly turns to thoughts of love.
Locksley Hall, l. 20
- Faultily faultless, icily regular, splendidly null.
Maud, pt. I. ii
- Come into the garden, Maud,
For the black bat, night, has flown.
xxii. 1
- Sink me the ship, Master Gunner—sink her, split her in twain!
Fall into the hands of God, not into the hands of Spain.
The Revenge, xi
- And they praised him to his face with their courtly foreign grace.
xiii
- Far on the ringing plains of windy Troy.
Ulysses, l. 17
- It may be we shall touch the Happy Isles,
And see the great Achilles, whom we knew.
l. 63
- To strive, to seek, to find, and not to yield.
l. 70

BRANDON THOMAS 1856–1914

- I'm Charley's aunt from Brazil—where the nuts come from.
Charley's Aunt (1892), Act I

DYLAN THOMAS 1914–1953

- Do not go gentle into that good night,
Old age should burn and rave at close of day;
Rage, rage against the dying of the light.
Do not go gentle into that good night
- And before you let the sun in, mind it wipes its shoes.
Under Milk Wood
- Gomer Owen who kissed her once by the pig-sty when she wasn't looking and never kissed her again although she was looking all the time.
- Nothing grows in our garden, only washing. And babies.

JAMES THOMSON 1700–1748

- Rule, Britannia, rule the waves;
Britons never will be slaves.
Alfred: a Masque (1740), Act II, Scene the last

LORD THOMSON OF FLEET 1894–1977

- It's just like having a licence to print your own money.

(After the opening of Scottish commercial television.) Braddon, *Roy Thomson of Fleet Street*, p. 240

JAMES THURBER 1894–1961

- It's a Naïve Domestic Burgundy, Without Any Breeding., But I Think You'll be Amused by its Presumption.

Men, Women and Dogs. Cartoon caption

LEO TOLSTOY 1828–1910

- All happy families resemble one another, but each unhappy family is unhappy in its own way.

Anna Karenina (1875–7), pt. i, ch. 1. Tr. Maude

- It is amazing how complete is the delusion that beauty is goodness.

The Kreutzer Sonata, 5. Tr. Maude

HARRY S. TRUMAN 1884–1972

- The buck stops here.

Hand-lettered sign on President Truman's desk. Phillips, *The Truman Presidency*, ch. 12

MARK TWAIN 1835–1910

- There was things which he stretched, but mainly he told the truth.

The Adventures of Huckleberry Finn (1884), ch. 1

- When angry, count four; when very angry, swear.

Pudd'nhead Wilson's Calendar, March

- The report of my death was an exaggeration.

Cable from Europe to the Associated Press

- A verb has a hard time enough of it in this world when its all together. It's downright inhuman to split it up. But that's just what those Germans do. They take part of a verb and put it down here, like a stake, and they take the other part of it and put it away over yonder like another stake, and between these two limits they just shovel in German.

Address at dinner of the Nineteenth Century Club, New York, 20 Nov. 1900, to the toast, 'The Disappearance of Literature'

QUEEN VICTORIA 1819–1901

- This mad, wicked folly of 'Woman's Rights'.

Letter to Sir Theodore Martin, 29 May 1870

- We are not amused.

Attr. *Notebooks of a Spinster Lady*, 2 Jan. 1900

- We are not interested in the possibilities of defeat; they do not exist.

To A. J. Balfour, in 'Black Week', Dec. 1899

PHILIPPE-AUGUSTE VILLIERS DE L'ISLE-ADAM 1838–1889

- *Vivre? les serviteurs feront cela pour nous.* Living? The servants will do that for us.

Axël (1890), IV, sect. 2

HORACE WALPOLE, FOURTH EARL OF ORFORD 1717–1797

- This world is a comedy to those that think, a tragedy to those that feel.

To the Countess of Upper Ossory, 16 Aug. 1776

SIR ROBERT WALPOLE, FIRST EARL OF ORFORD 1676–1745

- They now *ring* the bells, but they will soon *wring* their hands.

On the declaration of war with Spain, 1739. W. Coxe, *Memoirs of Sir Robert Walpole* (1798), vol. i, p. 618

- The balance of power.

House of Commons, 13 Feb. 1741

BISHOP WILLIAM WARBURTON 1698–1779

- Orthodoxy is my doxy; heterodoxy is another man's doxy.

To Lord Sandwich. Priestley, *Memoirs* (1807), vol. i, p. 372

GEORGE WASHINGTON 1732–1799

- Father, I cannot tell a lie, I did it with my little hatchet.

Attr. Mark Twain, *Mark Twain as George Washington*

ISAAC WATTS 1674–1748

- How doth the little busy bee
  Improve each shining hour!

xx. **Against Idleness and Mischief**

- For Satan finds some mischief still
  For idle hands to do.

DUKE OF WELLINGTON 1769–1852

- The battle of Waterloo was won on the playing fields of Eton.

See Montalembert, *De l'Avenir Politique de l'Angleterre* (1856). The attribution was refuted by the 7th Duke.

- I always say that, next to a battle lost, the greatest misery is a battle gained.

Frances, Lady Shelley, *Diary*, p. 102

- Ours [our army] is composed of the scum of the earth—the mere scum of the earth.

Stanhope, *Notes of Conversations with the Duke of Wellington*, 4 Nov. 1831

- Up Guards and at them again!

Letter from Captain Batty, 22 June 1815. Booth, *Battle of Waterloo*. See also Croker, *Correspondence and Diaries* (1884), III, 280

- Publish and be damned.
Attr. According to legend, Wellington wrote these words across a blackmailing letter from Stockdale, publisher of Harriette Wilson's *Memoirs*, and posted it back to him. See Elizabeth Pakenham, *Wellington: The Years of the Sword* (1969), ch. 10

H. G. WELLS 1866–1946

- Human history becomes more and more a race between education and catastrophe.
The Outline of History, ch. 40 of the 1951 edn.

MAE WEST 1892?–1980

- 'Goodness, what beautiful diamonds.'
'Goodness had nothing to do with it, dearie.'
Night After Night (1932), script by Vincent Lawrence
- Why don't you come up sometime, see me?
She Done Him Wrong (1933). Commonly misquoted as 'Come up and see me sometime'.

JOHN FANE, LORD WESTMORLAND 1759–1841

- *Merit*, indeed! . . . We are come to a pretty pass if they talk of *merit* for a bishopric.
Noted in Lady Salisbury's diary, 9 Dec. 1835. C. Oman, *The Gascoyne Heiress* (1968), V

EDITH WHARTON 1862–1937

- Mrs Ballinger is one of the ladies who pursue Culture in bands, as though it were dangerous to meet it alone.
Xingu (1916), ch. 1

JAMES McNEILL WHISTLER 1834–1903

- [Answering Oscar Wilde's 'I wish I had said that']
You will, Oscar, you will.
L. C. Ingleby, *Oscar Wilde*, p. 67

WALT WHITMAN 1819–1892

- Silent and amazed even when a little boy.
A Child's Amaze
- I think I could turn and live with animals, they are so placid and self-contain'd.
Song of Myself, 32
- They do not sweat and whine about their
  condition,
They do not lie awake in the dark and
  weep for their sins,
They do not make me sick discussing their
  duty to God.

OSCAR WILDE 1854–1900

- Yet each man kills the thing he loves,
  By each let this be heard,
Some do it with a bitter look,
  Some with a flattering word.
The coward does it with a kiss,
  The brave man with a sword!
The Ballad of Reading Gaol (1898), I. vii
- For he who lives more lives than one
  More deaths than one must die.
III. xxxvii
- The truth is rarely pure, and never simple.
The Importance of Being Earnest (1895), Act I
- In married life three is company and two none.
- To lose one parent, Mr Worthing, may be regarded as a misfortune; to lose both looks like carelessness.
- All women become like their mothers. That is their tragedy. No man does. That's his.
- The good ended happily, and the bad unhappily. That is what Fiction means. [Miss Prism on her novel.]
Act II
- On an occasion of this kind it becomes more than a moral duty to speak one's mind. It becomes a pleasure.
- I couldn't help it. I can resist everything except temptation.
Lady Windermere's Fan (1891), Act I
- We are all in the gutter, but some of us are looking at the stars.
Act III
- A man who knows the price of everything and the value of nothing.
Definition of a cynic
- The English country gentleman galloping after a fox—the unspeakable in full pursuit of the uneatable.
A Woman of No Importance (1893), Act I
- *Lord Illingworth:* The Book of Life begins with a man and a woman in a garden.
Mrs Allonby: It ends with Revelations.
- Children begin by loving their parents; after a time they judge them; rarely, if ever, do they forgive them.
- I have put my genius into my life; all I've put into my works is my talent.
To André Gide. Gide, *Oscar Wilde: In Memoriam*
- [At the New York Custom House]
I have nothing to declare except my genius.
F. Harris, *Oscar Wilde* (1918), p. 75
- Work is the curse of the drinking classes.
H. Pearson, *Life of Oscar Wilde* (1946), ch. 12
- [A huge fee for an operation was mentioned]
'Ah, well, then, I suppose that I shall have to die beyond my means.'
R. H. Sherard, *Life of Oscar Wilde* (1906), p. 421

JOHN WILKES 1727–1797

- 'Wilkes,' said Lord Sandwich, 'you will die either on the gallows, or of the pox.'
'That,' replied Wilkes blandly, 'must depend on whether I embrace your lordship's principles or your mistress.'
Charles Chenevix-Trench, *Portrait of a Patriot*

(1962), ch. 3. But see H. Brougham, *Statesmen of George III*, third series (1843), p. 189. Also attr. Samuel Foote.

P. G. WODEHOUSE 1881–1975

- Jeeves shimmered out and came back with a telegram.
  Carry on Jeeves (1925). **Jeeves Takes Charge**
- He spoke with a certain what-is-it in his voice, and I could see that, if not actually disgruntled, he was far from being gruntled.
  The Code of the Woosters (1938)
- The Right Hon was a tubby little chap who looked as if he had been poured into his clothes and had forgotten to say 'When!'
  Very Good Jeeves (1930). **Jeeves and the Impending Doom**

CHARLES WOLFE 1791–1823

- Not a drum was heard, not a funeral note,
  As his corse to the rampart we hurried.
  The Burial of Sir John Moore at Corunna, i

WILLIAM WORDSWORTH 1770–1850

- Bliss was it in that dawn to be alive,
  But to be young was very heaven!
  French Revolution, as it Appeared to Enthusiasts (1809), and ***The Prelude***, bk. xi, l. 108
- I wandered lonely as a cloud
  That floats on high o'er vales and hills,
  When all at once I saw a crowd,
  A host, of golden daffodils.
  I Wandered Lonely as a Cloud (1807)
- For oft, when on my couch I lie
  In vacant or in pensive mood,
  They flash upon that inward eye
  Which is the bliss of solitude;
  And then my heart with pleasure fills,
  And dances with the daffodils.
- His little, nameless, unremembered, acts
  Of kindness and of love.
  Lines composed a few miles above Tintern Abbey (1798), l. 34
- The still, sad music of humanity.
  l. 91
- The rainbow comes and goes,
  And lovely is the rose.
  Ode. Intimations of Immortality (1807), ii
- But yet I know, where'er I go,
  That there hath passed away a glory from the earth.
- Whither is fled the visionary gleam?
  Where is it now, the glory and the dream?
  v
- Trailing clouds of glory do we come
  From God, who is our home:
  Heaven lies about us in our infancy!
  Shades of the prison-house begin to close
  Upon the growing boy.
- Earth has not anything to show more fair.
  ***Sonnets.* Composed upon Westminster Bridge**
- This City now doth, like a garment, wear
  The beauty of the morning.
- Dear God! the very houses seem asleep;
  And all that mighty heart is lying still!
- It is a beauteous evening, calm and free,
  The holy time is quiet as a nun,
  Breathless with adoration.
  It is a beauteous evening
- Milton! thou shouldst be living at this hour:
  England hath need of thee.
  Milton! thou shouldst
- Surprised by joy—impatient as the Wind
  I turned to share the transport—Oh! with whom
  But Thee, deep buried in the silent tomb.
  Surprised by joy
- The world is too much with us; late and soon,
  Getting and spending, we lay waste our powers.
  The world is too much with us

W. B. YEATS 1865–1939

- O body swayed to music, O brightening glance,
  How can we know the dancer from the dance?
  Among School Children, VIII
- That dolphin-torn, that gong-tormented sea.
  Byzantium
- All changed, changed utterly:
  A terrible beauty is born.
  Easter 1916
- Too long a sacrifice
  Can make a stone of the heart.
- Only God, my dear,
  Could love you for yourself alone
  And not your yellow hair.
  For Anne Gregory
- The years to come seemed waste of breath,
  A waste of breath the years behind
  In balance with this life, this death.
  An Irish Airman For-sees his Death
- I will arise and go now, and go to Innisfree,
  And a small cabin build there, of clay and wattles made:
  Nine bean-rows will I have there, a hive for the honey-bee,
  And live alone in the bee-loud glade.
  The Lake Isle of Innisfree
- Turning and turning in the widening gyre
  The falcon cannot hear the falconer;
  Things fall apart; the centre cannot hold.
  The Second Coming

- The best lack all conviction, while the worst
  Are full of passionate intensity.

EDWARD YOUNG 1683–1765

- Procrastination is the thief of time.

The Complaint: Night Thoughts, Night i, l. 393

ÉMILE ZOLA 1840–1902

- *J'accuse.*
  I accuse.

Title of an open letter to the President of the French Republic, in connection with the Dreyfus case, published in *L'Aurore*, 13 Jan. 1898

EVERYDAY PROVERBS AND PHRASES

ALL is gas and gaiters Everything is fine; the situation, or state of affairs, is ideal. The phrase comes from Dickens, *Nicholas Nickleby* (1838–9), 49.

It takes ALL sorts to make a world Originates from Shelton's translation of *Don Quixote*, 'in the world there must bee of all sorts', but in present form first found in D. W. Jerrold, *Story of a Feather* (1844), xviii.

ANY port in a storm Means any refuge will do when one is in trouble. First recorded in J. Cleland, *Memoirs of a Woman of Pleasure* (1749), ii.

If ANYTHING can go wrong, it will Commonly known as *Murphy's Law*, the saying has numerous variations. It is said to have been invented by George Nichols in 1949. Nichols was then a project manager working in California for the American firm of Northrop, and developed the maxim from a remark made by a colleague, Captain E. Murphy, of the Wright Field-Aircraft Laboratory. The contexts of the early quotations appear to support this explanation: 'Murphy's Law: If an aircraft part can be installed incorrectly, someone will install it that way' (*Aviation Mechanics Bulletin*, May–June 11, 1955). 'Dr Schaefer's observation confirms this department's sad experience that editors as well as laboratory workers are subject to Murphy's Laws, to wit: 1. If something can go wrong it will' (*Scientific American*, Apr. 1956).

An APPLE a day keeps the doctor away Earliest known version is Pembrokeshire proverb recorded in *Notes and Queries* (1866), 3rd Ser., ix: 'Eat an apple on going to bed, And you'll keep the doctor from earning his bread.'

ATTACK is the best form of defence A paradoxical statement based on military tactics, used also to describe methods of argument, or competitive manœuvres between people or groups in any sphere of activity. It is first recorded in 1775 as 'It is a maxim, that it is better to attack than to receive one' (W. H. Drayton in R. W. Gibbes, *Documentary Hist. American Revolution* (1855), i) and George Washington expressed it thus: 'Make them believe, that offensive operations, often times, is the surest, if not the only ... means of defence' (*Writings* (1940), xxxvii).

BAD money drives out good Commonly known as Gresham's Law, after Sir Thomas Gresham (*c.*1519–79), founder of the Royal Exchange. Gresham saw the economic need to restore the purity of the coinage, though there is no evidence that he actually used this expression. It was first recorded in 1858 as 'He [Gresham] was the first to perceive that a bad and debased currency is the cause of the disappearance of the good money' (H. D. Macleod, *Elements of Political Economy*, 477).

A BAD penny always turns up The proverb, also used allusively in simile and metaphor, usually refers to the predictable, and often unwanted, return of a disreputable or prodigal person to his place of origin after some absence. Recorded in L. H. Butterfield *et al.*, *Adams Family Correspondence* (1963), i, as being first used in 1766 by A. Adams: 'Like a bad penny it returnd, to me again'.

A BAD workman blames his tools From 13th-c. French, 'a bad workman will never find a good tool'. First recorded in English in R. Cotgrave, *Dict. French & English* (1613), s.v., as 'A bungler cannot find (or fit himselfe with) good tooles'.

Not with a BANG but a whimper A catch-phrase describing something not having a spectacular, magnificent or terrifying conclusion or downfall, but one that collapses or just fades away insignificantly. It is the last line of the poem, *The Hollow Men* (1928), by T. S. Eliot: 'This is the way the world ends / Not with a bang but a whimper.'

His BARK is worse than his bite Someone who is not as dangerous, bad tempered, aggressive, etc. as he gives the appearance of being. First recorded in Scott, *The Antiquary* (1816), II. vii, as 'Monkbarns's bark,' said Miss Griselda Oldbuck . . . 'is muckle waur than his bite.'

If you can't BEAT them, join them In US 'lick' not beat, and is first recorded in 1941 as 'if you can't lick 'em, jine 'em', in Q. Reynolds, *Wounded don't Cry*, i. Does not appear in above form until P. Gallico, *English Immortals* (1953), xvii.

BEAUTY is in the eye of the beholder Estimating beauty is a subjective judgement. First appears in present form in M. W. Hungerford, *Molly Bawn* (1878), I. xii.

We're only here for the BEER A catch-phrase that means a person or persons are only present for the drink, or for whatever is available, not to help or show goodwill. It comes from an advertisement for 'Double Diamond' beer.

Set a BEGGAR on horseback, and he'll ride to the Devil A proverb (now frequently used elliptically) with many variations, meaning that one unaccustomed to power or luxury will abuse or be corrupted by it. First recorded in G. Pettie, *Petit Palace* (1576), 76, as 'Set a Beggar on horsebacke, and he wyl neuer alight'.

BEGGARS can't be choosers 'Can't' has replaced 'must not' only recently. This first appears in a slightly different form in J. Heywood, *Dialogue of Proverbs* (1546), i.

To BELL the cat To do something which is dangerous to oneself in order to help or protect others. It comes from a fable about some mice who thought it would be a good idea to hang a bell round a cat's neck, but could not find a mouse willing to risk doing this. The earliest record of its use comes from the story, or legend, of when in 1482 certain of the Scottish barons formed a conspiracy to put down the obnoxious favourites of James III. A moment of grave suspense followed the enquiry as to who would undertake to enter the royal presence and seize the victims. It was terminated by the exclamation of Archibald Douglas, Earl of Angus, 'I will bell the cat', whence his historical appellation of 'Archibald Bell-the-cat'.

The BEST things in life are free From the 1927 song of that title by B. G. de Silva *et al.*

The BEST-laid schemes of mice and men, etc. From 'The best laid schemes o' Mice an' Men, / Gang aft agley' (go oft awry). See Burns, *Poems* (1876), 140. Nowadays often shortened to 'the best-laid schemes, etc.'

The BEST of all possible worlds A state in which all that one could desire could happen, though it usually implies that it would. It comes from Voltaire, *Candide* (1759), xxx, tr. W. Rider, where Dr Pangloss states: 'All is for the best in the best of all possible worlds.'

BETTER late than never Originated from the Greek 'It is better to start doing what one has to late than not at all' (Dionysius of Halicarnassus, *Roman Antiquities*, ix).

BETTER the devil you know than the devil you don't know It is better, easier, to tolerate, cope with, somebody/something evil, unpleasant or undesirable who/which is familiar and understood, than to risk having to cope with somebody/something unknown, who/which may prove to be worse. A version of this first recorded in Erasmus, *Adages* (1539), and well expressed in G. Pettie, *Petit Palace* (1576), 84: 'You had rather keepe those whom you knowe, though with some faultes, then take those whom you knowe not, perchaunce with moe faultes.'

'Tis BETTER to have loved and lost, than never to have loved at all In Tennyson's *In Memoriam* (1850), xxvii, though Congreve has a very similar phrase in *The Way of the World* (1700), II.

It is BETTER to travel hopefully than to arrive First found as, 'To travel hopefully is a better thing than to arrive', in R. L. Stevenson, *Virginibus Puerisque* (1881), iv, but first recorded reference in above form is in J. Duncan, *My Friend Muriel* (1959), ii.

The BIGGER they are, the harder they fall Though similar proverbs go back to the 15th c., the above is usually attributed to the boxer Robert Fitzsimmons, before a bout *c.*1900. 'Come' nowadays commonly replaces 'are'.

A BIRD in the hand is worth two in the bush Don't risk what you have by trying to get more. Originates from the Latin, 'one bird in the hands is worth more than two amongst the foliage', but the first reference as above is in Bunyan, *Pilgrim's Progress* (1678), i.

BIRDS of a feather flock together People of the same (usually unscrupulous) character associate together. Originates in the 16th c. and in present form is first found in J. Minsheu, *Spanish Grammar* (1599), 83.

You can't get BLOOD out of a stone Expression of resignation to signify it is useless trying to extract a statement, money, etc. from someone. This originated in the 15th c. and Dickens used a minor variation. Used as above in F. Thompson, *Lark Rise to Candleford* (1945), xix. Also frequently found in the form 'like getting blood out of a stone'.

BLOOD is thicker than water Normally used to indicate that a family relationship is more important than any other. Listed in J. Ray, *English Proverbs* (edn. 5) (1813), 281, but variations go back to the 12th c.

A BLOT on the escutcheon Someone, or something, that brings dishonour or discredit on a family or a group. An escutcheon is a shield or badge bearing a coat of arms.

BREVITY is the soul of wit From Shakespeare, *Hamlet* (1600–1), II, where its meaning was 'the essence of wisdom'.

To BUY a pig in a poke Purchasing or agreeing something without first judging its value properly. Hence, to enter into an engagement in ignorance of the responsibilities incurred. First recorded in 1562 as 'Ye loue not to bye the pyg in the poke' (J. Heywood, *Prov. & Epig.* (1867), 80).

Let the BUYER beware A warning that the buyer must satisfy himself of the nature and value of a purchase before proceeding with the transaction. The Latin tag *caveat emptor* is also frequently found. First recorded in J. Fitzherbert, *Husbandry* (1523), 36, as 'And [i.e. if] he [a horse] be tame and haue ben rydden vpon than caveat emptor be ware thou byer'.

CAESAR'S wife must be above suspicion According to Plutarch, this was Julius Caesar's reply when asked why he had divorced his wife, Pompeia. He considered his honour and position compromised, as she had been indirectly associated with Publius Clodius' trial for sacrilege.

A CALAMITY Jane A pessimistic person who is always expecting the worst to happen. It usually, but not always, refers to a woman. It was the nickname of Martha Jane Burke (*née* Canary) (?1852–1903), a famous American horse-rider and markswoman. The phrase was first used in the *Cheyenne* (Wyoming) *Daily Leader* in 1876.

If the CAP fits wear it Refers to the description of someone who demonstrably behaves, or is named, as he is described. Used in various forms since the 17th c.

CAST not a clout till May be out A warning that warm clothes may be needed until the end of May. It does not refer to May blossom as is sometimes assumed. First found in J. Stevens, *Spanish and English Dictionary* (1706), and in present form is first recorded in A. Henderson, *Scottish Proverbs* (1832).

A CAT may look at a king A version of this proverb is first recorded in J. Heywood, *Dialogue of Proverbs* (1546), ii, and is described in N. Bailey, *English Dictionary* (1721), as 'a saucy proverb, generally made use of by pragmatical persons'.

Don't CHANGE horses in mid-stream Sometimes quoted as 'to change horses in mid-stream'. A slightly different version of this was first recorded in 1864 and is quoted in Lincoln, *Collected Works* (1953), vii.

Monday's CHILD is fair of face Each line of the verse quoted below, which comes from A. E. Bray, *Traditions of Devon* (1838), II, may be used separately.

> Monday's child is fair of face,
> Tuesday's child is full of grace,
> Wednesday's child is full of woe,
> Thursday's child has far to go,
> Friday's child is loving and giving,
> Saturday's child works hard for its living,
> And a child that's born on Christmas (or Sabbath) day,
> Is fair and wise and good and gay.

The CHILD is father to the man An assertion of the unity of character from childhood to maturity. A similar idea occurs in Milton, *Paradise Regained* (1671), iv, and in above form in a poem called 'My Heart Leaps Up' (1807) by Wordsworth quoted in his *Poems* (1952), i. 226.

CHILDREN should be seen and not heard This proverb originally applied specifically to girls. J. Mirk, *Festial* (*c.*1400) (EETS), 1230, quotes 'an old Englysch sawe: "A mayde schuld be seen, but not herd."' Recorded as first applying to children in 1820 in J. Q. Adams, *Memoirs* (1875), v.

To have a CHIP on one's shoulder To bear a grudge or grievance about the world in general or about something specific. See *Long Isl. Tel.* (Hempstead, NY) dated 20 May 1830: 'When two churlish boys were *determined* to fight, a *chip* would be placed on the shoulder of one, and the other demanded to knock it off at his peril.'

CHIPS with everything A symbol of lower-class and unimaginative taste in food or anything else. It was popularized by Arnold Wesker's play, *Chips with Everything* (1962).

CLEANLINESS is next to godliness A version of this proverb appears in Bacon, *Advancement of Learning* (1605), ii, and above wording was used by Wesley in 1791, his meaning being that cleanliness is next in order, numerically, to godliness. See his *Works* (1872), vii. 16.

Every CLOUD has a silver lining A poetic sentiment that even the blackest outlook has some hopeful or consoling aspect. The existence of this seems to be evidenced in Milton, *Comus* (1634), i, but does not appear in its present form until P. T. Barnum, *Struggles and Triumphs* (1869), 460.

A man is known by the COMPANY he keeps This was originally used as a moral maxim or exhortation in the context of (preparation for) marriage and is first recorded in M. Coverdale's translation of H. Bullinger, *Christian State of Matrimony* (1541), F6. The modern use first appears in 1854 as quoted in H. Melville, *Complete Short Stories* (1951), 182.

COMPARISONS are odious A saying that means people or things should be judged on their own merits and not measured against someone or something else. It comes from early 14th-c. French: 'comparisons sont haineuses' and was being used in English by the middle of the 15th c.

The CORRIDORS of power The higher levels of government, administration, etc. where men, either for reasons of personal ambition, or to further a cause or their convictions, compete and intrigue for power and position. It was a phrase coined by C. P. Snow in the 1950s and later used by him as the title for one of his novels.

Don't COUNT your chickens before they are hatched Advice not to make, or act upon, an assumption (usually favourable) which might turn out to be incorrect. The metaphorical phrase, 'to count one's chickens', is also used. First recorded in T. Howell, *New Sonnets* (*c.*1570), C2, as 'Counte not thy Chickens that vnhatched be'.

In the COUNTRY of the blind, the one-eyed man is king Someone of limited intelligence will be considered a genius amongst foolish people. First recorded in Latin. See Erasmus, *Adages*, iii.

The COURSE of true love never did run smooth Any love affair will have its trouble, problems, difficulty. From Shakespeare, *Midsummer Night's Dream* (1595), I: 'Ah me! for aught that ever I could read, / Could ever hear by tale or history, / The course of true love never did run smooth.'

A CREAKING door hangs longest Usually said as a comfort to the infirm, though sometimes implying that the weak or faulty is a nuisance the longest. *Gate* sometimes replaces *door.* First recorded in T. Cogan, *John Buncle, Junior* (1776), i, as 'They say a creaking gate goes the longest upon its hinges; that's my comfort'.

When the CRUNCH comes The time of crisis or confrontation when it is necessary to come to a decision. The word 'crunch' in this context was first used by W. Churchill in *Daily Telegraph*, 23 Feb. 1939: 'Whether Spain will be allowed to find its way back to sanity and health . . . depends . . . upon the general adjustment or outcome of the European crunch.' The phrase 'When it comes to the crunch' is also commonly used and is first recorded in *The Times* (21 July 1960): 'Even the holders of Government bonds turn out to be chiefly philanthropic institutions and trade unions when it comes to the crunch.'

It is no use CRYING over spilt milk No point in regretting a misfortune when it is too late to correct it. First recorded as 'no weeping for shed milk', in J. Howell, *Proverbs* (British) (1659), 40, and in present form in J. Payn, *Canon's Ward I* (1884), xv.

CURIOSITY killed the cat Similar to another proverb 'care killed the cat', which comes from Shakespeare, *Much Ado About Nothing* (1598–9), v, the above is first recorded in E. O'Neill, *Diff'rent* (1921), II.

The CURSE of Cain The lot or fate of someone who has to live a vagabond life, who wanders or is forced to move from place to place in a profitless way. The phrase comes from the Old Testament, *Genesis* 4.

Don't CUT off your nose to spite your face A warning against spiteful revenge which results in one's own hurt or loss. The metaphorical phrase *to cut off one's nose to spite one's face* is very frequently found. It is first recorded in Latin—'he who cuts off his nose takes poor revenge for a shame inflicted on him'—and in English in *Deceit of Women* (*c.*1560), i: 'He that byteth hys nose of, shameth hys face'.

They that DANCE must pay the fiddler Similar to *He who PAYS the piper calls the tune*, where the emphasis is reversed. *To pay the piper* (*fiddler*, etc.) means 'to bear the cost (of an enterprise)'. The proverb is now predominantly found in US use. It is first recorded in J. Taylor, *Taylor's Feast* in *Works* (1876), 94, as 'One of the Fidlers said, Gentlemen, I pray you to remember the Musicke [i.e. company of musicians], you have given us nothing yet . . . Alwayes those that dance must pay the Musicke.' As above in A. Lincoln, *Speech*, 11 Jan. 1837 (*Works* (1953), i): 'I am decidedly opposed to the people's money being used to pay the fiddler. It is an old maxim and a very sound one, that he that dances should always pay the fiddler.'

DEAD men tell no tales A variant first recorded in T. Becon, *Works* (1560), ii, and in above form in G. Farquhar, *Inconstant* (1702), v.

DESPERATE diseases must have desperate remedies There are many variations on this proverb, the commonest being 'desperate situations require desperate remedies'. First recorded version is in Latin as 'extreme remedies for extreme ills'. The earliest version in English is in Erasmus, *Adages* (1539), 4, tr. R. Taverner.

DIAMOND cuts diamond Used of persons well matched in wit or cunning. Also often found as a descriptive phrase, 'diamond cut diamond'. Earliest recorded version is in Nashe, *Christ's Tears* (1593), ii.

DIAMONDS are a girl's best friend Diamonds, or gifts with a lasting cash value, especially from a lover, are an insurance for the future. The phrase comes from a song of that name in the musical comedy, *Gentlemen Prefer Blondes* (1949). Quote from Zsa Zsa Gabor: 'Diamonds are a girl's best friend and a dog is a man's best friend. Now you know which sex is smarter.'

The DIFFICULT is done at once; the impossible takes a little longer This is first recorded in 1873 in Trollope, *Phineas Redux*, ii, as 'What was it the French Minister said. If it is simply difficult it is done. If it is impossible, it shall be done.'

Throw DIRT enough, and some will stick Persistent slander will eventually pass for truth. First recorded in Latin as 'slander strongly and some will stick'. It first appears in English in 1656 in *Trepan*, 34: 'She will say before company, Have you never had the French Pox? speak as in the sight of God: let them Reply what they will, some dirt will stick.'

DISCRETION is the better part of valour A variation of this is recorded in Caxton, *Jason* (*c.*1477) (EETS), 23, and Shakespeare, *Henry IV, Pt. 1* (1597–8), v, has 'The better part of valour is discretion'. First appears as above in C. Lowe, *Prince Bismarck* (1885), i.

DIVIDE and rule A political axiom that government is more easily maintained if factions are set against each other, and not allowed to unite against the ruler. It comes from the Latin tag *divide et impera* and is first found in English in 1588 in a translation of *M. Hurault's Discourse upon the Present State of France*, 44: 'It hath been alwaies her [Catherine de Medici's] custome, to set in France, one against an other, that in the meane while shee might rule in these diuisions.'

The DOG days High summer. In the Roman calendar the six or eight weeks of greatest summer heat, when the influence of Sirius, the Dog-star, rising with the sun, was thought to increase its heat thus causing difficult conditions, pestilence, etc. It is now used more commonly to indicate a time of tedium or apathy. It was also said to be a time when dogs ran mad. Earliest example of use is Elyot, *Dict. Canicula* (1538): 'a sterre, whereof canicular or dogge days be named *Dies caniculares*'.

The EARLY bird catches the worm The person who seizes the earliest opportunity of doing something (e.g. getting up before others, reacting faster than others to a situation, etc.) will get what he wants, be successful at the expense of others. First found in W. Camden, *Remains concerning Britain* (edn. 5) (1636), 307.

EAST, west, home's best Also 'there's no place like home'. The above originates from Germany and is quoted in W. K. Kelly, *Proverbs of All Nations* (1859), 36, as 'east and west, at home the best'.

A curate's EGG Used to describe something that is good and bad in parts, of mixed quality. The phrase comes from an 1895 *Punch* cartoon which showed a nervous curate breakfasting on a boiled egg at his bishop's table. 'I'm afraid your egg is bad, Mr Jones.' 'Oh, no, my lord, I assure you! Parts of it are excellent.'

Don't put all your EGGS in one basket Don't chance everything on a single venture; spread your risk. 'To put all one's eggs in one basket' is commonly used as a metaphorical phrase. This is Italian in origin and is quoted in G. Torriano, *Italian Proverbs* (1662), 125, as 'To put all ones eggs in a paniard, viz. to hazard all in one bottom', where bottom means ship's hull or boat.

EMPTY vessels make the most sound Foolish or witless persons are the most talkative or noisy. Vessel means, in this case, a receptacle for liquid. First recorded in Lydgate, *Pilgrimage of Man* (1430), l. 15933, and Shakespeare used 'The empty vessel makes the greatest sound' in *Henry V* (1599), IV.

A fair EXCHANGE is no robbery First appears as above in J. Kelly, *Scottish Proverbs* (1721), 105, but a variant is recorded as early as 1546 in J. Heywood, *Dialogue of Proverbs*, ii.

What the EYE doesn't see, the heart doesn't grieve over From the Latin, 'what the eye sees not, the heart does not grieve at', and is first recorded in English in Erasmus, *Adages* (1545) (edn. 2), 13, tr. R. Taverner, as 'that the eye seeth not, the hart rueth not'.

FACT is stranger than fiction An alliterative version of 'truth is stranger than fiction'. First recorded in T. C. Haliburton, *Sam Slick's Wise Saws* (1853), 5, as 'Facts are stranger than fiction, for things happen sometimes that never entered into the mind of man to imagine or invent.'

FAINT heart never won fair lady First recorded as above in Richardson, *Grandison* (1754), i, though the earliest version can be traced to Gower, *Confessio Amantis* (*c.*1390), v. Earlier versions refer to a castle as well as a lady and the meaning of 'faint' was cowardly or timorous.

All's FAIR in love and war The gist of this proverb appears first in English in Lyly, *Euphues* (1578), i, as 'Anye impietie may lawfully be committed in loue, which is lawlesse', and Cervantes in *Don Quixote*, ii, tr. by T. Shelton (1620), says, 'love and warre are all one . . . It is lawfull to use sleights and stratagems to . . . attaine the wished end.'

FAMILIARITY breeds contempt Continued experience of, or association with, somebody/something leads to loss of appreciation, respect, attention, etc. formerly shown. This proverb is first recorded in Latin in Augustine, *Scala Paradisi*, 8. A different version was used by Chaucer in *Tale of Melibee*, 1, in 1390, and in its present form was first recorded in T. Fuller, *Comment on Ruth* (1654), 176.

The FAMILY that prays together stays together This saying was invented in the US by a professional commercial-writer, Al Scalpone, and used as a slogan of the Roman Catholic Family Rosary Crusade which began in 1942. A variant, 'the family that plays together stays together', was used by *Parents' Magazine* in 1954.

FEAR the Greeks bearing gifts From Virgil, *Aeneid*, ii, 'I fear the Greeks, even when bringing gifts' (said by Laocoön as a warning to the Trojans not to admit the wooden horse).

A FEATHER in one's cap Something achieved that constitutes a victory, triumph, or credit for oneself. The phrase has been said to come from a former custom of various peoples, among them the American Indians, of adding a feather to their headgear for every enemy killed. However, the phrase was used with the same meaning as early as 1581 as recorded in Pettie, *Guazzo's Civ. Conv.* Pref., (1586): 'Though a man shake the feather after the best fashion, and take upon him never so biglie, hee (etc.).'

To FEATHER one's (own) nest To look after one's own interests, especially by accumulating financial assets, the implication being that greed, selfishness, or dishonesty is involved.

FEED a cold and starve a fever Possibly meant as two separate pieces of advice. Starving a fever is first mentioned as early as 1574, but the linking of the two is not found until E. Fitzgerald, *Polonius* (1852), p. ix. An alternative interpretation is quoted in C. Morley, *Kitty Foyle* (1939), xxxi: 'I said I better go downstairs and eat a square meal, "feed a cold and starve a fever" . . . "You misunderstand that," he said. "It means if you feed a cold you'll have to starve a fever later".'

The FEMALE of the species is more deadly than the male 'The she-bear thus accosted rends the peasant tooth and nail, / For the female of the species is more deadly than the male', Kipling in *Morning Post*, 20 Oct., 1911.

To FIDDLE while Rome burns To behave frivolously, or uncaringly, in a serious situation. The phrase comes from Suetonius, *De Vita Caesarum*: *Nero*, bk. vi, who tells the story of how Nero set fire to Rome (to see what Troy looked like when it was in flames), and sang as he watched the blaze which raged for six days and seven nights. 'It is fiddling while Rome is burning to spend more pages over the sorrows of . . . Rose Salterne, while the destinies of Europe are hanging on the marriage between Elizabeth and Anjou' (C. Kingsley, *Westward Ho!* (1855), 10).

He who FIGHTS and runs away, may live to fight another day Of Greek origin, this proverb is first recorded in English before 1250 as 'wel fight that wel flight' and is recorded in *Owl and Nightingale* (1960). I. J. Ray, *Complete Hist. Rebellion* (1747), 61, expresses the meaning of it clearly in the rhyme, 'He that fights and runs away, / May turn and fight another day; / But he that is in battle slain, / Will never rise to fight again.'

FINDERS keepers losers weepers A colloquial variant of 'findings keepings'—first expressed in the Latin phrase, 'he may keep that finds', in Plautus, *Trinummus* I. Originally the proverb was 'finders keepers losers seekers', as recorded in J. Brockett, *Glossary of North Country Words* (1825), 89.

FIRST catch your hare Commonly thought to originate in the recipe for hare soup in Mrs Glasse's *Art of Cookery* (1747) or in Mrs Beeton's *Book of Household Management* (1851). But it is not in either, and first appears in its present form in Thackeray, *Rose & Ring* (1855), xiv, though its meaning, 'begin at the beginning', was first expressed around the start of the 14th c. in Bracton, *De Legibus Angliae*, iv.

There are as good FISH in the sea as ever came out of it Now often used as a consolation to rejected lovers, 'there are plenty more fish in the sea'. Recorded in G. Harvey, *Letter-Book* (1884), 126, as being first used *c.*1573: 'In the mayne sea theres good stoare of fishe, And in delicate gardens . . . Theres alwayes greate varietye of desirable flowers.'

There's no FOOL like an old fool From J. Heywood, *Dialogue of Proverbs* (1546), ii: 'But there is no foole to the olde foole, folke saie.'

FOOLS rush in where angels fear to tread From Pope, *Essay on Criticism* (1711), i: 'No place so sacred from such fops is barr'd, / Nor is Paul's Church more safe than Paul's Churchyard: / Nay, fly to Altars; there they'll talk you dead; / For fools rush in where Angels fear to tread.'

There's no such thing as a FREE lunch Originally a colloquial axiom in US economics, though now in general use, the implication of this proverb is that you cannot get something for nothing. 'I was taught . . . the first and only law of economics; there is no such thing as a free lunch', *Newsweek*, 52, 29 Dec. 1969.

A FRIEND in need is a friend indeed The origin of this proverb, 'a sure friend is known in unsure times', is found in Latin in Ennius, *Scaenica*, 210 (Vahlen). It first appears in English in about 1035 in the *Durham Proverbs*, 10, as a 'friend shall be known in time of need'.

GATHER ye rosebuds while ye may Seize what pleasures you can before the passage of time removes them or you. It comes from a poem by R. Herrick (1591–1674), 'To the Virgins. To make much of Time'.

Those who live in GLASS houses shouldn't throw stones Don't criticize others for a fault you yourself have, especially if you're vulnerable to retaliation. First appears in Chaucer, *Troilus & Criseyde* (*c.*1385), ii, as 'Who that hath an hed of verre [glass], / Fro cast of stones war hym in the werre!' By 1640 it is recorded in G. Herbert, *Outlandish Proverbs*, 196, as having become 'Whose house is of glasse, must not throw stones at another'.

All that GLITTERS is not gold Things are not always how they appear at first glance. This is first expressed in the Latin, 'not all that shines is gold', and is used variously by Chaucer (*Canon's Yeoman's Tale*, i. 962), Shakespeare (*Merchant of Venice*, II. vii. 65), and Charlotte Brontë (*Jane Eyre*, II. ix), but in exact wording as above it first appears in 1880 in *Dict. of English Proverbs* (Asprey Reference Library), 39.

If GOD did not exist, it would be necessary to invent him This comes from *Épîtres* by Voltaire. Nowadays it is often adapted and parodied.

If the GOING gets tough, the tough get going A favourite family saying of Joseph P. Kennedy, US politician, businessman, and father of the late President. It is recorded in J. H. Cutler, *'Honey Fitz'* (1962), xx: 'Joe [Kennedy] made his children stay on their toes . . . He would bear down on them and tell them, "When the going gets tough, the tough get going".'

If you can't be GOOD, be careful The advice behind this proverb has existed since the 14th c. and appears in R. Brunne, *Handling Synne* (1303), i. But in its modern form first appears in A. M. Binstead, *Pitcher in Paradise* (1903), viii.

The only GOOD Indian is a dead Indian Used as an expression of hatred for an enemy, especially of another nationality. Attributed to the US general, P. H. Sheridan (1831–88), but first recorded as 'I have never in my life seen a good Indian [i.e. North American Indian]—and I have seen thousands—except when I have seen a dead Indian', J. M. Cavanaugh, *Congressional Globe* (US), 2368, 28 May 1868.

There's many a GOOD tune played on an old fiddle From Butler, *The Way of All Flesh* (1903), lxi: 'Beyond a haricot vein in one of my legs I'm as young as ever I was. Old indeed! There's many a good tune played on an old fiddle.'

GREAT minds think alike Derived from 'Good wits doe iumpe [coincide]', which appears in D. Belcher, *Hans Beer-Pot* (1618), but as above is not recorded until 1922, in *Punch*, 27 Dec.

A HAIR of the dog An alcoholic drink which is taken, especially the morning after a heavy drinking session, to counter a hangover. First recorded in 1546 as 'I pray the leat me and my felow haue A heare of the dog that bote us last night' (J. Heywood, *Prov.* (1867), 37). Also used by Dickens in *Barnaby Rudge* (1840), lii: 'Drink again. Another hair of the dog that bit you, Captain.'

One HAND for oneself and one for the ship A nautical proverb, also used in variant forms in similar contexts. First recorded in 1799 as 'Did I not tell you never to fill both hands at once. Always keep one hand for the owners, and one for yourself' (*Port Folio* (Philadelphia, 1812), vii). Its meaning is best explained in B. Lubbock, *Round Horn* (1902), 58: 'The old rule on a yard is, "one hand for yourself and one for the ship", which means, hold on with one hand and work with the other'.

The HAND that rocks the cradles rules the world First recorded in 1865 in a verse by W. R. Wallace, 'A mightier power and stronger/Man from his throne has hurled,/For the hand that rocks the cradle/Is the hand that rules the world', which appears in J. K. Hoyt, *Cyclopaedia of Practical Quotations* (1896).

HANDSOME is as handsome does Handsome in this context originally meant chivalrous or genteel behaviour, not, as is popularly thought, good looks. At its second occurrence in the proverb the word is properly an adverb. In another form it is in A. Munday, *View of Sundry Examples* (*c.*1580), which is recorded in J. P. Collier, *John A Kent* (1851). But as above it is first recorded in *Spirit of the Times*, 297, 23 Aug. 1845.

HARD cases make bad law Difficult cases cause the clarity of the law to be obscured by exceptions and strained interpretations. According to G. Hayes in W. S. Holdsworth, *Hist. English Law* (1926), ix, it was first used in 1854.

A HARD day's night Comment after staying up all night, invariably in order to enjoy oneself. The phrase comes from a song by Paul McCartney: 'It's been a hard day's night, / And I've been working like a dog. / It's been a hard day's night, / I should have been sleeping like a log.'

More HASTE less speed The original meaning of the word 'speed' in this proverb is quickness in the performance of some action or operation. It dates back to around 1350 when it is found in *Douce* MS 52, no. 86, 'the more hast, the worse spede'.

You cannot HAVE your cake and eat it You cannot have it both ways in an argument or situation. The position of 'have' and 'eat' are sometimes reversed. First recorded as, 'Wolde ye bothe eate your cake, and haue your cake?' in J. Heywood, *Dialogue of Proverbs* (1546), ii.

If you don't like the HEAT, get out of the kitchen If you don't like the pressure under which you are working, living, etc. then it is up to you to change your circumstances. From *Time* magazine, 19, 28 Apr. 1952: 'President [Truman] gave a . . . down-to-earth reason for his retirement, quoting a favorite expression of his military jester, Major

General Harry Vaughan: "If you don't like the heat, get out of the kitchen".'

He who HESITATES is lost Originally, this proverb referred specifically to women. 'When love once pleads admission to our hearts . . . The woman that deliberates is lost', from Addison, *Cato* (1713), IV, but the first record of 'he' being used is not until 1878 in J. H. Beadle, *Western Wilds*, xxi: 'In Utah it is emphatically true, that he who hesitates is lost—to Mormonism.'

The HIDDEN persuaders Advertising and its techniques as they indirectly influence people to think, believe, or desire to have, things they might not otherwise have done. The phrase comes from the title of the seminal work on the power of advertising by Vance Packard (1957).

HOMER sometimes nods Even the best, or cleverest, people have lapses and make mistakes. The phrase comes from Horace (*Ars Poetica*, 359), who said 'I am aggrieved when good Homer sleeps.'

HOPE springs eternal Coined by Pope in *Essay on Man* (1732), i: 'Hope springs eternal in the human breast. / Man never Is, but always to be blest.'

You can take a HORSE to the water, but you can't make him drink 'The' is often omitted. First appears *c.*1175 in *Old English Homilies* (EETS), 1st Ser. 9, as 'who can give water to the horse that will not drink of its own accord?'

HORSES for courses Originally an expression in horse-racing meaning that different horses are suited to different race-courses, but is now commonly used in other contexts. First record of original use is in A. E. T. Watson, *Turf* (1891), vii, and its modern use is well expressed in *Punch*, 430, 18 Sept. 1963: 'People enjoy what they are capable of enjoying—horses for courses.'

Where IGNORANCE is bliss, 'tis folly to be wise Now frequently abbreviated to 'ignorance is bliss'. Coined by Gray in 1742 in his poem *Ode on a Distant Prospect of Eton College*: 'Yet ah! why should they know their fate? / Since sorrow never comes too late, / And happiness too swiftly flies. / Thought would destroy their paradise. / No more; where ignorance is bliss, / 'Tis folly to be wise.'

It's an ILL wind that blows nobody any good A nautical metaphor invoked to explain good luck deriving from the misfortunes of others. First recorded in J. Heywood, *Dialogue of Proverbs* (1546), ii, as 'An yll wynde that blowth no man to good, men saie.'

IMITATION is the sincerest form of flattery First recorded in C. C. Colton, *Lacon* (1820), i, as 'imitation is the sincerest of flattery'.

IN for a penny, in for a pound Said by someone who commits himself totally to an action. First recorded in E. Ravenscroft, *Canterbury Guests* (1695), v.

An IRON fist/hand in a velvet glove Firm control or severe treatment, but one which gives the appearance of being quite the opposite. T. Carlyle in *Latter-Day Pamphlets* (1850), ii, wrote: 'Soft of speech and manner, yet with an inflexible rigour of command ... "iron hand in a velvet glove", as Napoleon defined it'.

The IRON curtain The westernmost boundary of the group of eastern European states politically and economically dominated by the Soviet Union. The phrase was popularized by Winston Churchill, who first used it in a cable to President Truman on 4 June 1945. But its first recorded use was in Ethel Snowden, *Through Bolshevik Russia* (1920), and it was also used by Dr Goebbels in an article in *Das Reich*, dated 25 Feb. 1945, which was reported in both *The Times* and the *Manchester Guardian*.

The IVY League The group of older US universities, including Harvard, Yale, Princeton, and Columbia, which confers academic and social prestige on those who have taught or studied there. The phrase 'ivy colleges' was used in the *New York Herald Tribune* in 1933, but the above is not recorded until 1939 when it appeared in the *Princeton Alumni Weekly*: 'The "Ivy League" is something which does not exist and is simply a term which has been increasingly used in recent years by sports writers, applied rather loosely to a group of eastern colleges.'

JAM tomorrow and jam yesterday—but never jam today Often used when something is promised but never occurs. From L. Carroll, *Through the Looking-Glass* (1871), v: '"The rule is, jam to-morrow and jam yesterday—but never jam to-day." "It *must* come sometimes to 'jam to-day'," Alice objected. "No, it can't," said the Queen.'

Why KEEP a dog and bark yourself? There's little point in employing, keeping, someone/something for a job and then doing it yourself. This first appears in 1583 in B. Melbancke, *Philotimus*, 119, as, 'it is smal reason you should kepe a dog, and barke yourselfe.'

KNOW thyself Motto inscribed on the 6th c. BC temple of Apollo at Delphi and quoted by several ancient writers (some attributing it to Solon). See Pausanias, x, and Juvenal, *Satires*, xi.

A LAND fit for heroes to live in A catch-phrase for a nation that rewards those who have fought for their country with good conditions of life and work as civilians. It comes from a speech by the British Prime Minister, Lloyd George, in Nov. 1918, when he said 'What is our task? To make Britain a fit country for heroes to live in.'

It is the LAST straw that breaks the camel's back The metaphor is also used allusively, especially in the phrase 'the last straw'. This proverb is first expressed as, 'it is the last feather may be said to break an Horses back', in J. Bramhall, *Defence of True Liberty of Human Actions* (1655), 54. In 1793 it was written as 'the last feather will sink the camel' (*Publications of Colonial Society of Massachusetts*, xxxvi. 298, 1954), before becoming 'As the last straw breaks the laden camel's back' in Dickens, *Dombey & Son* (1848), ii.

LAUGH and the world laughs with you; weep and you weep alone An alteration of the sentiment expressed by Horace in *Ars Poetica*, 101: 'men's faces laugh on those who laugh, and correspondingly weep on those who weep.' It also appears in the New Testament, Romans xii: 15, in a slightly different version, but in its modern form it was coined in a verse by E. W. Wilcox published in the *New York Sun*, 3, 25 Feb. 1883: 'Laugh, and the world laughs with you; / Weep, and you weep alone. / For the sad old earth must borrow its mirth, / But has trouble enough of its own.'

The LAW of the jungle A phrase which now describes the morals and attitude of those who better themselves by using their wealth, strength, unscrupulousness, etc. at the expense of those weaker than themselves. It was used by Kipling in his *Jungle Book* (1894), 31: 'Baloo was teaching him the Law of the Jungle . . . Young wolves will only learn as much of the Law of the Jungle as applies to their own pack and tribe.'

LAY-OVERS for meddlers An answer to an impertinent or inquisitive child and others. The expression is found chiefly in the north of England, and in the US. *Lay-overs*, also contracted to *layers* or *layors*, are light blows or smacks given to the meddlesome, though A. E. Baker, *Glossary of Northamptonshire Words & Phrases* (1854), i, states 'lay-o'ers-for-meddlers' is a 'a contraction of *lay-overs*, i.e. things *laid over*, covered up, or protected from meddlers.' First recorded in 1699 as '*Lare-over*, said when the true Name of the thing must (in decency) be concealed' (B. E., *New Dict. Canting Crew*, s.v.).

LEAST said, soonest mended Lengthy recriminations, explanations, excuses, are often a mistake as they tend to exaggerate the importance of a (perhaps trivial) mistake, misunderstanding, or quarrel. First recorded *c.*1460 as 'Who sayth lytell he is wyse . . . And fewe wordes are soone amend' (W. C. Hazlitt, *Remains of Early Popular Poetry* (1864), iii. In above form first appears in T. Cogan, *John Buncle, Junior* (1776), i.

The LEOPARD does not change his spots It is impossible to change something that is as basic to someone's personality or character as the spots on a leopard. From Old Testament, Jeremiah 13: 'Can the Ethiopian change his skinne? or the leopard his spots?'

If you LIE down with dogs, you will get up with fleas An assertion that human failings, such as dishonesty and foolishness, are contagious. First recorded in Latin as 'they who lie with dogs will rise with fleas', and in English in 1573 as 'He that goeth to bedde wyth Dogges, aryseth with fleas' (J. Sanforde, *Garden of Pleasure*).

LIFE begins at forty People of 40 are mature but still fit, will generally have established their values, be freer from emotional, financial and career problems, responsibilities of child-rearing, etc. The phrase comes from W. B. Pitkin, *Life Begins at Forty* (1932), i: 'Life begins at forty. This is the revolutionary outcome of our New Era . . . Today it is half truth. Tomorrow it will be an axiom.'

LIFE isn't all beer and skittles Life can't all be fun and games. This adage is first recorded in T. C. Haliburton, *Nature & Human Nature* (1855), i:

'"This life ain't all beer and skittles." Many a time . . . when I am disappointed sadly I say that saw over.'

Where there's LIFE there's hope However adverse the circumstances, or however long someone is enduring bad luck, ill health, etc., they should not give up, as their fortunes could always change for the better. The phrase is first found in Latin in Cicero, *Ad Atticum*, ix. It first appeared in English in Erasmus, *Adages* (1539), tr. R. Taverner: 'The sycke person whyle he hath lyfe, hath hope.'

LIGHTNING never strikes the same place twice An unusual event, or something that happens by chance, is not likely to be repeated in exactly the same circumstances or to the same people. It was first used in P. H. Myers, *Prisoner of Border* (1857), xii: 'They did not hit me at all . . . Lightning never strikes twice in the same place, nor cannon balls either, I presume.'

LITTLE things please little minds This phrase was first recorded in Latin as 'small things enthral light minds' (Ovid, *Ars Amatoria*, i), and first appears in English as 'A litle thyng pleaseth a foole' (G. Pettie, *Petit Palace* (1576), 139). Its meaning is well explained in C. H. Spurgeon, *John Ploughman's Pictures* (1880), 81: 'Precious little is enough to make a man famous in certain companies . . . for . . . little things please little minds.'

He who LIVES by the sword dies by the sword Those who live either literally or metaphorically by using force are more likely to have their way of life, or their lives, terminated in a similar manner. The phrase comes from New Testament, Matthew 26: 'All they that take the sword shall perish with the sword.'

LOOK before you leap From *Douce* MS 52, no. 150, *c.*1350: 'First loke and aftirward lepe.' The meaning of this proverb is well expressed in W. Painter, *Palace of Pleasure* (1567), ii: 'He that looketh not before he leapeth, may chaunce to stumble before he sleapeth.'

LOVE is blind Being in love with somebody blinds one to shortcomings in the loved one. It comes from the Greek (Theocritus, 10. 19 f.) and is first recorded in English in Chaucer, *Merchant's Tale* (*c.*1390): 'For love is blynd alday, and may nat see.'

LUCKY at cards, unlucky in love First recorded in Swift, *Polite Conversation* (1738), iii, as: 'Well, Miss, you'll have a sad Husband, you have such good Luck at Cards.'

MAD as a hatter Along with the phrase 'mad as a March hare', first recorded in Skelton, *Replyacion* (1529), 35, and others, this is used to describe someone who is behaving abnormally. The above is often thought to derive from L. Carroll, *Alice in Wonderland*, which has a character in it called the Mad Hatter, but the phrase was first recorded in 1837–40 as 'Sister Sall . . . walked out of the room, as mad as a hatter' (Haliburton, *Clockmaker* (1862), 109).

MAKE hay while the sun shines To make the best use of one's opportunities while fortune favours one. First recorded in J. Heywood,

Dialogue of Proverbs (1546), i, as 'When the sunne shynth make hey'.

As you MAKE your bed, so you must lie upon it G. Harvey, *Marginalia* (1913), records a version of this, 'Lett them ... go to there bed, as themselues shall make it', as first appearing in about 1590. As above it first appears in S. Warren, *Diary of Late Physician* (1832), ii: 'As soon as his relatives ... heard ... they told him ... that as he had made his bed, so he must lie upon it.'

MAN cannot live by bread alone Man needs spiritual, intellectual, emotional nourishment as well as food to sustain him through life. The phrase originally came from Old Testament, Deuteronomy 8: 'Man doth not liue by bread alone, but by euery word that proceedeth out of the mouth of the Lord doth man liue' (Tyndale's version).

MAN bites dog A catch-phrase which defines what is newsworthy, especially that which is reported in the popular press. It comes from an article by C. A. Dana, *What is News?*, in the *New York Sun* in 1882.

MANY a mickle makes a muckle A corruption of 'Many a little makes a mickle' where 'little' is sometimes replaced by 'pickle', meaning a small quantity or amount (Scottish). 'Mickle' means a large quantity or amount. 'Muckle' is merely a variation of 'mickle', which shows that the corruption makes no sense. It was first used by George Washington in 1793 (*Writings* (1939), xxxii). The correct version first recorded in 1614 in *Remains concerning Britain* (edn. 2), 310, and the proverb's meaning goes back to before 1250, as recorded in *Ancrene Wisse* (1962 ed.), 32.

There's MANY a slip 'twixt cup and lip Mistakes happen even when it looks as if something has been all but accomplished. First recorded in Latin by Erasmus and in English in Erasmus, *Adages* (1539), 15, tr. R. Taverner, as 'Many thynges fall betwene the cuppe and the mouth ... Betwene the cuppe and the lyppes maye come many casualties.'

A MARE's nest A reported discovery, event, situation of a wonderful or startling nature which turns out to be a hoax or a misinterpretation of the facts. First recorded before 1619 in Fletcher, *Bonduca*, v, as 'Why dost thou laugh? What mares nest hast thou found?'

MARRY in haste and repent at leisure A marriage hastily entered into is liable to result in one's regretting it over a long period. First expressed in E. Tilney, *Duties in Marriage* (1568), B4, as 'Some haue loued in post hast, that afterwards haue repented them at leysure.' As above it is well used by Congreve in *The Old Bachelor* (1693): 'This grief still treads upon the heels of pleasure: / Marry'd in haste, repent in leisure.'

One man's MEAT is another man's poison What seems good or pleasing to one person may be bad or unsuitable for another. First recorded in Latin in Lucretius, *De Rerum Natura*, iv: 'What is food to one person may be bitter poison to others.' It first appears in English around 1576 as 'on bodies meat iz an otherz poison' (T. Whythorne, *Autobiography* (1961 ed.), 203).

A MISS is as good as a mile The syntax of this proverb has been distorted by abridgement. The original structure is apparent from how it was first recorded: 'An ynche in a misse is as good as an ell' from W. Camden, *Remains concerning Britain* (1614) (edn. 2), 303. An 'ell' is about 45 inches.

MORE means worse A catch-phrase for the dilemma that the more people have access to public facilities the more the standards in education, the arts, commodity distribution, etc. are lowered. It is an alteration of Kingsley Amis's remark in 1960 that 'more will mean worse'.

Out of the MOUTHS of babes— Young children may speak disconcertingly wisely at times. The proverb is used in a variety of abbreviated and allusive forms, often without a knowledge of the complete Biblical quotations. The best-known from the Bible is 'Jesus saith unto them [the Pharisees], Yea; have ye never read, Out of the mouth of babes and sucklings thou hast perfected praise' (Matthew 21).

Where there's MUCK there's brass Dirty work means profitable work: slag-heaps, mill-chimneys, etc. are signs of wealth for somebody. First recorded in J. Ray, *English Proverbs* (1678) (edn. 2), 179, as, 'Muck and money go together.' As above it appears in *Punch* (1967): '"Where there's muck there's brass" synopsised for many a North-country businessman the value of dirt in the profit-making process.'

MUTTON dressed as lamb A phrase often used to describe a person, usually a woman, who dresses and tries to look, often absurdly so, like someone of a much younger age. First recorded in Kipling, *Brushwood Boy*, in *Day's Work* (1898), 348: 'Look at young Davies makin' an ass of himself over mutton-dressed-as-lamb old enough to be his mother!'

NATURE abhors a vacuum From the Latin, 'natura abhorret vacuum', and is first recorded in English in 1551 as 'naturall reason abhorreth vacuum' in Cranmer, *Answer to Gardiner*, 299.

If you gently touch a NETTLE it'll sting you for your pains; grasp it like a lad of mettle, an' as soft as silk remains The metaphorical phrase *to grasp the nettle*, to tackle a difficulty boldly, is also found. It is first recorded in 1578 in Lyly, *Euphues*, i: 'True it is Philautus that he which toucheth ye nettle tenderly, is soonest stoung.'

It is NEVER too late to learn A later variation of 'it is never too late to mend' and 'never too old to learn', the above is first recorded in R. L'Estrange, *Seneca's Morals* (1678), iii: 'It is never too late to learn what is always necessary to know.'

NEW brooms sweep clean The phrase 'new broom'—someone new who makes changes in personnel or procedures—derives from this proverb. First recorded as 'som therto said, the grene new brome swepith cleene', in J. Heywood, *Dialogue of Proverbs* (1546), ii.

You can't put NEW wine in old bottles The quote from the New Testament, Matthew 9, where the proverb originated, is self-explanatory: 'Neither do men put new wine in old bottles: else the bottles break, and the wine runneth out, and the bottles perish: but they put new wine into new bottles, and both are preserved.'

NO man is a hero to his valet Attributed to Madame Cornuel (1605–94): 'il n'y a pas de heros pour son valet-de-chambre.' Its meaning is well expressed in S. Foote, *Patron* (1764), II: 'It has been said ... that no man is a hero to his valet de chambre; now I am afraid when you and I grow a little more intimate ... you will be horribly disappointed in your high expectations.'

NO names, no pack-drill If nobody is named as being responsible for something, then nobody can be blamed and punished. Also used more generally in favour of reticence on a subject. 'Pack-drill' is a military punishment in which the offender is compelled to march up and down in full marching order. First recorded in O. Onions, *Peace in our Time* (1923), i.

A NOD's as good as a wink to a blind horse A fanciful assertion that the slightest hint is enough to convey one's meaning to someone. First recorded in W. Godwin, *Caleb Williams* (1794), i, and is nowadays often shortened to 'a nod is as good as a wink'.

There is NOTHING new under the sun The world-weary, especially the elderly, have seen every combination of events and what may seem highly original to the young is to them only a dreary re-run. It comes from the Old Testament, Ecclesiastes 1: 'There is no new thing under the sun.'

There is NOTHING so good for the inside of a man as the outside of a horse A proverb asserting the benefit of horse-riding to health. 'The Squire will wind up ... with an apocryphal saying which he attributes to Lord Palmerston—"There's nothing so good for the inside of a man as the outside of a horse"' (G. W. E. Russell, *Social Silhouettes* (1906), xxxii).

NOTHING succeeds like success Success brings one the confidence in oneself and respect from others that lead to opportunities for further and greater successes. It comes from the French, 'rien ne réussit comme le succès', and is first recorded in English in A. D. Richardson, *Beyond Mississippi* (1867), xxxiv.

NOTHING venture, nothing gain A variation of 'nothing venture, nothing have' which first appears in Chaucer, *Troilus & Criseyde* (*c.*1385), ii, as 'he which that nothing undertaketh, Nothyng n'acheveth'. In 1624 it is recorded in T. Heywood, *Captives*, iv, as 'I see hee that nought venters, nothinge gaynes'.

There's NOWT so queer as folk Quoted in *English Dialect Dict.* (1905), iv, as an old saying.

Beware of an OAK, it draws the stroke; avoid an ash, it counts the flash; creep under the thorn, it can save you from harm Advice on where to shelter from lightning during a thunderstorm that is first recorded in *Folk-Lore Record* (1878), i. A variation is recorded in F. Thompson, *Lark Rise* (1945), xvii: 'Some one would ... warn him to keep away from trees during a thunderstorm . . . Others would quote: Under oak there comes a stroke, Under elm there comes a calm, And under ash there comes a crash.'

You cannot put an OLD head on young shoulders First recorded as 'It is not good grafting of an olde head vpon young shoulders, for they will neuer beare it willingly but grudgingly' in H. Smith, *Preparative to Marriage* (1591), 14.

OLD soldiers never die Comment on the dogged persistence, cheerfulness, etc. of long-serving, or retired, soldiers, etc. It is recorded in Brophy & Partridge, *Songs & Slang of the British Soldier 1914–18* (1930), ii, as an anonymous song sung during the First World War. It is also the title of a song by J. Foley, 1920.

You cannot make an OMELETTE without breaking eggs One cannot achieve a desired victory, reform, or other (important) aim without sacrificing something, causing loss or damage to somebody/something involved. From French, 'on ne fait pas d'omelette sans casser des œufs'; first recorded in English in T. P. Thompson, *Audi Alteram Partem* (1859), ii, as 'We are walking upon eggs and . . . the omelet will not be made without the breaking of some.'

ONCE bitten, twice shy Somebody who has suffered a particular kind of misfortune is extremely cautious about incurring it again. First expressed in R. S. Surtees, *Sponge's Sporting Tour* (1853), xxxvii, as 'Jawleyford had been bit once, and he was not going to give Mr Sponge a second chance.' Recorded as above in G. F. Northall, *Folk-Phrases* (1894), 20.

ONE for sorrow, two for mirth; three for a wedding, four for a birth A traditional country proverb current before 1846. It is found in a variety of forms and refers to the number of magpies seen on a particular occasion. First recorded in B. Haydon, *Autobiography* (1853), i.

To OPEN Pandora's box To bring about, especially in the hope of achieving something, a host of troubles either previously unknown or under control. The phrase comes from Greek mythology in which Pandora, the first woman, received from Jove the gift of a box—subsequently opened by her husband—in which all the troubles that could affect mankind had been safely sealed.

An OPEN sesame An easy means of access to a place, to a social, government, academic, or business circle, or to a particular commodity. The phrase comes from the magic words 'Open Sesame!' which caused the door of the robbers' cave to open in the story 'Ali Baba and the Forty Thieves', which is in *The Arabian Nights*.

The OPERA isn't over till the fat lady sings First recorded in the *Washington Post*, 13 June 1978: 'One day three years ago, Ralph Carpenter, who was then Texas Tech's sports information director, declared to the press box contingent in Austin, "The rodeo ain't over till the bull riders ride". Stirred to top that deep insight, San Antonio sports editor

Dan Cook countered with, "The opera ain't over till the fat lady sings".'

OPPORTUNITY never knocks twice at any man's door *Fortune* occurs instead of *opportunity* in earlier forms of the saying. The proverb is used in various forms. In some versions opportunity knocks once or more, in others once only. It is first recorded in 1567 in G. Fenton, *Bandello*, 216, as 'Fortune once in the course of our life, dothe put into our handes the offer of a good torne.'

OUT of sight, out of mind First recorded *c.*1250 as 'He that is ute bi-loken [shut] He is inne sone foryeten [forgotten]' (*Proverbs of Alfred* (1907), 46).

To be PAR for the course What one would expect to happen, or for somebody to be or to behave. Par in golf is the number of strokes that has been set as a standard for a good player to play each hole or the whole course. First recorded in *Partisan Review* (1947), xiv: 'Nancy had married and moved to San Francisco and had had three children immediately. "Par for the course," said Seymour to Jasper.'

If you PAY peanuts, you get monkeys Normally used with reference to pay negotiations. First recorded in L. Coulthard, *Director* (Aug. 1966), 228: 'Shareholders want the best available businessmen to lead the companies and recognise that you get what you pay for. If you pay in peanuts, you must expect to get monkeys.'

He who PAYS the piper calls the tune A similar proverb is 'they that dance must pay the fiddler' except that the emphasis is reversed. First recorded in *Daily News*, 9, 18 Dec. 1895, as 'Londoners had paid the piper, and should choose the tune.'

You PAYS your money and you takes your choice You choose whatever alternative course, explanation, etc. you like. It comes from a cockney stallholder's cry to prospective customers and is first recorded in *Punch* (1846), x.

Do not throw PEARLS to swine Don't waste something valuable on the valueless. Often used allusively, especially in the phrase 'to cast pearls before swine'. From New Testament, Matthew 7, where it is recorded as 'Give not that which is holy unto the dogs, neither cast ye your pearls before swine.'

The PEN is mightier than the sword The idea of this proverb is first expressed in Latin in Cicero, *De Officiis*, i, as 'arms give way to persuasion'. In English it is first recorded in G. Whetstone, *Heptameron of Civil Discourses* (1582), iii, as 'The dashe of a Pen, is more greeuous then the counter use of a Launce.'

The PERMISSIVE society A society, like Britain during the 1960s, that tolerates freedom of moral choice to its members in everything except criminal activity, and especially freedom in sexual relationships. First recorded in *Listener* (4 Jan. 1968): 'This dreadful dilemma of the puritan in a permissive society.'

PHYSICIAN, heal thyself From New Testament, Luke 4: 23. Its meaning is well explained in S. Smiles, *Thrift* (1875), ii: 'How can a man . . . teach sobriety or cleanliness, if he be himself drunken or foul? "Physician, heal thyself", is the answer of his neighbours.'

See a PIN and pick it up, all the day you'll have good luck; see a pin and let it lie, bad luck you'll have all the day This proverb is first alluded to in Pepys, *Diary* (1668), ix: 'I see your Majesty doth not remember the old English proverb, "He that will not stoop for a pin will never be worth a pound".'

POACHER turned gamekeeper Somebody who uses the knowledge and skills acquired in one trade or role to operate in another which is directly opposite in purpose.

POSSESSION is nine points of the law There is no specific legal ruling which supports this proverb—though the concept is widely acknowledged—but in early use the satisfaction of ten (sometimes twelve) points was commonly asserted to attest full entitlement or ownership. Possession, represented by nine (or eleven) points, is therefore the closest substitute for this. First recorded in above form in T. Draxe, *Adages* (1616), 163.

The POT calling the kettle black A saying that is used when somebody accuses another for a fault he himself has in an equal degree. The proverb existed before 1700 and is first recorded in B. E., *New Dict. Cant. Crew,* s.v.: 'The Pot calls the kettle black A–, when one accuses another of what he is as Deep in himself.'

PRACTICE makes perfect Repeated exercise in a skill, or craft, is the way to become a master of it. First recorded in T. Wilson, *Art of Rhetoric* (1553), 3.

PRACTISE what you preach Live and act in a way one believes in, or recommends others to do. First recorded in Langland, *Piers Plowman* (1377), B. xiii, as 'He perforneth yuel [performeth evil], That he precheth he preueth [demonstrates] nought.'

PRAISE the Lord and pass the ammunition A catch-phrase for those who are religious but who nevertheless fight their country's enemies. It comes from a comment attributed to a US naval lieutenant, Howell Forgy, during the attack on Pearl Harbor in December 1941.

PREVENTION is better than cure It is wiser, better, easier, etc. to prevent illness, or some other trouble, than to try and cure it afterwards. It is first recorded in Latin in Bracton, *De Legibus* (*c.*1240), v, as 'it is better and more useful to meet a problem in time than to seek a remedy after the damage is done.' It first appears in English in 1618 as 'Preuention is so much better then healing, because it saues the labour of being sicke' (T. Adams, *Happiness of Church*, 146).

PRIDE goes before a fall Recorded in Old Testament, Proverbs 16, as 'Pride goeth before destruction, and an haughty spirit before a fall.'

The PROOF of the pudding is in the eating The true value of somebody or something can be judged only from practical experience and not from appearance, theory, etc. In this context 'proof' means 'test' rather than the normal 'verification, proving to be true'. First appears in about 1300 in *King Alisaunder* (EETS), i, but as above is first recorded in W. Camden, *Remains concerning Britain* (1623) (edn. 3), 266.

A PROPHET is not without honour save in his own country Somebody is recognized as a great thinker, teacher, writer, artist, etc. except by his own family, associates, countrymen, etc. It comes from New Testament, Matthew 13: 'Is not this the carpenter's son? . . . And they were offended in him. But Jesus said unto them, "a prophet is not without honour, save in his own country and in his own house".'

PROVIDENCE is always on the side of the big battalions From a letter of Mme de Sévigné, 22 Dec. 1673: 'la fortune est toujours, comme disait le pauvre M. de Turenne, pour les gros bataillons.'

Any PUBLICITY is good publicity It's better to be talked, written, about adversely than not at all if you want publicity. First recorded in P. Cave, *Dirtiest Picture Postcard* (1974), xiv: 'Haven't you ever heard the old adman's adage . . . "any publicity is good publicity"?'

PUNCTUALITY is the politeness of princes Attributed to Louis XVIII (1755–1824), who said: 'l'exactitude est la politesse des rois', and first quoted as above in M. Edgeworth, *Helen* (1834), ii.

A PYRRHIC victory An unprofitable victory where losses are greater than is justified by anything gained. It comes from the fact that King Pyrrhus of Epirus defeated the Roman army at Asculum in 279 BC, but with so great a slaughter of his men that he said 'one such more victory and we are lost'.

You cannot get a QUART into a pint pot First recorded in *Daily News*, 23, 4 July 1896, as 'They had been too ambitious. They had attempted what he might describe in homely phrase as putting a quart into a pint pot.'

It never RAINS but it pours Incidents, troubles, visitors, business orders, etc. tend to come together in large numbers or in rapid succession. First recorded as the title of a work written by J. Arbuthnot in 1726, 'It cannot rain but it pours', where 'but' was used to introduce an inevitable accompanying circumstance.

He who RIDES a tiger is afraid to dismount Once a dangerous or troublesome venture is begun, the safest course is to carry it through to the end. First quoted in W. Scarborough, *Collection of Chinese Proverbs* (1875), no. 2082.

I'm all RIGHT, Jack I have been lucky, clever, or careful enough to make sure that I'm safe, comfortable, etc., and I don't care what happens to anyone else. First recorded in D. W. Bone, *Brassbounder* (1910), iii: 'It's "damn you Jack—I'm all right!" with you chaps.'

The ROAD to hell is paved with good inventions Blame, or punishment, is incurred by having good motives which either are not put into practice or have evil or harmful results. The proverb originates from French (St Francis de Sales, *Letter*, lxxiv) and first appears in English in 1574 in *Guevara's Epistles*, 205, tr. E. Hellowes, as 'Hell is full of good desires.' A later quote (1736) is 'hell is paved with good intentions', but the form above is not recorded until H. G. Bohn, *Hand-Book of Proverbs* (1855), 514.

All ROADS lead to Rome Whatever means or methods are chosen any one of them, or all of them, will eventually reach the same objective. This phrase comes from the fact that in ancient and medieval times Rome was considered the political, cultural, and religious centre of the European world. It originated from the Latin phrase 'a thousand roads lead man for ever towards Rome', and first appears in English in Chaucer, *Astrolabe* (*c.*1391), Prologue, i, as 'Right as diverse pathes leden diverse folk the righte way to Rome'.

A ROLLING stone gathers no moss A person who moves a lot from place to place, from job to job does not accumulate property, real friends, or social ties. First quoted in Erasmus, *Adages*, iii, as 'a rolling stone is not covered with moss.'

There is always ROOM at the top Used to encourage competition. First recorded use is in 1900 by William James (*Letter*, 2 Apr. (1920), 11. 121): 'Verily there is room at the top. S— seems to be the only Britisher worth thinking of.'

You cannot RUN with the hare and hunt with the hounds A person cannot try to keep on friendly terms with two opposing parties or have an interest in both of two opposing objectives. This was originally quoted in Lydgate, *Minor Poems* (*a.* 1449) (EETS) as 'He . . . holdeth bothe with hounde and hare', but does not appear as above until 1896 when it is recorded in M. A. S. Hume, *Courtships of Queen Elizabeth*, xii.

There is SAFETY in numbers One has better protection against ill luck or making a bad judgement or decision as a member of a group; finding a variety of activities, friends, and interests makes one less vulnerable. It is recorded in the Old Testament, Proverbs 11, as 'In the multitude of counsellors there is safety.'

One's SALAD days The time when one is young, innocent, inexperienced, etc. The phrase comes from Shakespeare, *Antony and Cleopatra*, I: 'My salad days / When I was green in judgement, cold in blood.'

What's SAUCE for the goose is sauce for the gander Originally this meant that what is suitable for a woman is also suitable for a man, but is now also used in a wider context. First recorded in J. Ray, *English Proverbs* (1670), 98.

SCRATCH a Russian and you find a Tartar This proverb is also used allusively, especially of other nationalities. It is attributed to Napoleon, and dates back to 1823 (J. Gallatin in *Diary* (1914)).

SEE no evil, hear no evil, speak no evil This proverb is conventionally represented by the three wise monkeys, one covering his eyes, the second his ears, and the third his mouth. First recorded in 1926 in the *Army & Navy Stores Catalogue*.

SEEK and ye shall find First recorded as above in the New Testament, Matthew vii. 7, but first expressed in Sophocles, *Oedipus Tyrannus*, i, as 'what is sought is found; what is neglected evades us.'

The SEVEN-year itch Boredom, restlessness, desire for sexual variety, that is supposed to set in after about seven years of married life.

Do not spoil the SHIP for a ha'porth of tar 'Ship' is a dialectal pronunciation of 'sheep', and the original literal sense of the proverb was, 'do not allow sheep to die for the lack of a trifling amount of tar', tar being used to protect sores and wounds on sheep from flies. It was first recorded in 1623 in W. Camden, *Remains concerning Britain* (edn. 3), 265, but is best illustrated in its original form in J. Smith, *Advertisements for Planters* (1631), xiii: 'Rather . . . lose ten sheepe, than be at the charge of halfe penny worth of Tarre.' Its modern form is first found in C. Reade, *Cloister & Hearth* (1861), i: 'Never tyne [lose] the ship for want of a bit of tar.'

SHIPSHAPE and Bristol fashion When something is in good order and tidy. The reference being to the time when Bristol was an important commercial port for sailing vessels. First recorded in *Nautical Magazine* (1839), 165: 'Neither shipshape nor Bristol fashion.' The word 'shipshape' alone was used in 1644 in Manwayring, *Seaman's Dict*.

From SHIRTSLEEVES to shirtsleeves in three generations Shirtsleeves denote the need to work hard for one's living. This saying has been attributed to A. Carnegie (1835–1919), manufacturer and philanthropist, but is not found in his published writings. 'No artificial class distinctions can long prevail in a society like ours (in the US) of which it is truly said to be often but three generations "from shirtsleeves to shirtsleeves"' (N. M. Butler, *True & False Democracy* (1907), ii).

SILENCE is golden A shorter version of 'speech is silver, but silence is golden'. It is desirable, and may be more effective, to remain silent.

You can't make a SILK purse out a sow's ear You can't make something out of nothing. First expressed in A. Barclay, *Eclogues* (1518) (EETS), v, but in present form in Gosson, *Ephemerides of Phialo* (1579), 62.

Let SLEEPING dogs lie Do not provoke, disturb, or interfere with somebody or something that is giving no trouble though he/it might, or could, do so. From early 14th-c. French, 'n'esveillez pas lou chien qui dort', and appears in Chaucer, *Troilus & Criseyde* (*c.*1385), 764, as 'it is nought good a slepying hound to wake.'

SMALL is beautiful From title of book by E.F. Schumacher, 1973. Schumacher's thesis is that mankind is being distorted by the worship of economic growth and needs to adjust its thinking if it is to survive. The phrase is now used in a wider context as an axiom that sheer size (of a corporation, building, etc.) is not in itself automatically a good thing.

SOFTLY, softly, catchee monkey Let 'gently, slowly and cautiously' be the maxim: easy/gently does it. Quoted in G. Benham, *Cassell's Book of Quotations* (1907), 849, as, '"Softly, softly," caught the monkey'.

If you're not part of the SOLUTION, you're part of the problem From M. Bradbury, *History Man* (1975), v.

Never SPEAK ill of the dead From the Greek 'speak no evil of the dead', attributed to the Spartan ephor or civil magistrate Chilon, 6th c. BC.

A SPRAT to catch a mackerel Something of relatively small importance, etc. that is sacrificed, risked, or offered in the hope of securing a much greater gain. There are a number of variants and it is first recorded in Reade, *Never Too Late* (1856), lix, as 'Did you never hear of the man that flung away a sprat to catch a whale?' The above first recorded in *Notes & Queries* (1864), 3rd Ser., vi.

It is too late to shut the STABLE-door after the horse has bolted When originally used this proverb referred to horse-stealing and 'has bolted' is a modern substitution for the traditional 'is stolen'. From Medieval French, 'the stable is shut too late, when the horse is lost'. First appears in English around 1350 in *Douce* MS 52, no. 22.

One man may STEAL a horse, while another may not look over a hedge People may take different degrees of liberty depending on our opinion of them. First recorded in J. Heywood, *Dialogue of Proverbs* (1546), ii, as 'This prouerbe . . . saith, that some man maie steale a hors better, Than some other maie stande and loke vpone.'

STICKS and stones may break my bones, but words will never hurt me Similar to the proverb 'hard words break no bones'. From G. F. Northall, *Folk-Phrases* (1894), 23.

STILL waters run deep Now commonly used to assert that a placid exterior hides a passionate nature. First recorded about 1400 as 'There the flode is deppist the water standis stillist' (*Cato's Morals* in *Cursor Mundi* (EETS), 1672).

A STITCH in time saves nine This proverb was originally a couplet. The number 'nine' was apparently introduced fancifully for the sake of assonance. First recorded as, 'A stitch in Time May save nine' in T. Fuller, *Gnomologia* (1732).

A STORM in a teacup A lot of fuss, disturbance, fear about something that is, or eventually proves to be, of very little importance. The idea was first expressed in 1590 and by 1678 had become 'a storm in a cream bowl' and by 1830 'a storm in a wash-hand basin'. But 'teacup' did not appear until 1872, when it was used in William Black, *The Strange Adventures of a Phaeton*, xvi: 'She has raised a storm in a tea-cup by her . . . unwarranted assault.'

A STRAW in the wind An incident, rumour, expression of opinion, etc. that indicates how a situation may be developing. First recorded in Lytton, *Rienzi* (*c.*1835), ii, as 'The Provençal, who well knew how to construe the wind by the direction of the straws'.

STRIKE while the iron is hot This proverb originally alluded to the blacksmith's art and is first recorded in French in the late 13th c. as 'one must strike the iron while it is hot'. Chaucer used it in *Melibee* (*c.*1390), 2226: 'Whil that iren is hoot, men sholden smyte.'

From the SUBLIME to the ridiculous is only one step Nowadays is often shortened to exclude the last four words. Comes from the French, 'du sublime au ridicule il n'y a qu'un pas', and is attributed to Napoleon. First recorded in 1879 in M. Pattison, *Milton*.

If at first you don't SUCCEED, try, try, try again The short poem 'Try (try) again' was often quoted in 19th-c. children's literature, especially in the United States. It is popularly attributed to W. E. Hickson, who quoted it (with three *try*s) in his *Moral Songs* (1857), but T. H. Palmer used it in 1840 in *Teacher's Manual*, 223: ''Tis a lesson you should heed, / Try, try again. / If at first you don't succeed, / Try, try, again.'

Never give a SUCKER an even break This proverb, which means you should never give a fool a fair chance, has been attributed to several people, including E. F. Albee and W. C. Fields. It was popularized by Fields, who is said to have used it in the musical comedy *Poppy* (1923), though it does not appear in the libretto. First appeared in print in *Collier's*, 28 Nov. 1925, when it is quoted by Fields.

He who SUPS with the Devil should have a long spoon A proverb advocating caution when dealing with dangerous persons. First appears in Chaucer, *Squire's Tale* (*c.*1390), i, as, 'Therfore bihoueth hire a ful long spoon that shal ete with a feend.'

One SWALLOW does not make a summer From the Greek, 'one swallow does not make a spring', and first appears in English in 1539 in Erasmus, *Adages*, 25, tr. R. Taverner.

It is idle to SWALLOW the cow and choke on the tail It is senseless to give up when a great task is almost completed. It is first recorded in J. Howell, *Proverbs* (English) (1659), 13, as 'To swallow an Ox, and be choaked with the tail.'

SWEET Fanny Adams Nothing at all. It comes from a girl so named murdered in the 19th c. and chopped to pieces. It is also sailor's slang for tinned mutton.

TALK of the Devil, and he is bound to appear Nowadays usually shortened to 'talk of the devil', and used when a person just talked about appears. 'The English say, Talk of the Devil, and he's presently at your elbow' (G. Torriano, *Italian Proverbs* (1666), 134.

You can't TEACH an old dog new tricks The older someone is the more difficult it is to correct their behaviour or way of doing things. First recorded in J. Fitzherbert, *Husbandry* (1530) (edn. 2), G1, as 'The dogge must lerne it when he is a whelpe, or els it wyl not be; for it is harde to make an olde dogge to stoupe.'

Don't TEACH your grandmother to suck eggs A caution against offering advice to someone who is wiser than you. First recorded in Quevedo's *Comical Works* (1707), iv, tr. J. Stevens, as 'You would have me teach my Grandame to suck Eggs.'

Don't THROW the baby out with the bathwater This proverb is of German origin and is first recorded in J. Kepler, *Tertius Interveniens* (1610), as 'this is a caution . . . lest you throw out the baby with the bath', but does not appear in English until 1853 in Carlyle, *Nigger Question* (edn. 2), 29, as 'You must empty out the bathing-tub, but not the baby along with it.'

TIME and tide wait for no man Originally expressed by Chaucer in *Clerk's Tale* (*c.*1390), 1, as 'for thogh we slepe or wake, or rome, or ryde, Ay fleeth the tyme; it nil no [will no] man abyde', and in above form in Scott, *Nigel* (1822), iii.

TIME is money From the Greek, 'the most costly outlay is time', attributed to Antiphon. First recorded as above in 1748, when it was probably coined by Benjamin Franklin (*Papers*, iii. 306 (1961)).

Other TIMES other manners A saying which asserts that in other, or different, times customs were different also. The phrase comes from the translation of the French expression 'autres temps, autres mœurs'.

TOO many cooks spoil the broth The date of this proverb's first appearance is uncertain but is probably 1575, as 'There is the proverb, the more cooks the worse pottage' (J. Hooker, *Life of Carew* (1857), 33). As above in B. Gerbier, *Principles of Building* (1662), 24.

TRAVEL broadens the mind First recorded in A. Powell, *Venusberg* (1933), as 'Seeing the world broadens the outlook. You can learn a lot abroad', but not till 1949 as above, in N. Streatfield, *Painted Garden* (1949), iii.

Many a TRUE word spoken in jest First recorded in Chaucer, *Monk's Prologue* (*c.*1390), 1, as 'Be nat wrooth, my lord, though that I pleye. Ful ofte in game a sooth [truth] I have herd seye!', and in above form about 1665 in *Roxburghe Ballads* (1890), vii.

TWO is company, but three is none This proverb is often used with the alternative ending 'three's a crowd', and is first recorded in J. Stevens, *Spanish & English Dict.* (1706), as 'A Company consisting of three is worth nothing. It is the Spanish Opinion, who say that to keep a Secret three are too many, and to be Merry they are too few.' First appears in above form in W. C. Hazlitt, *English Proverbs* (1869), 442.

It takes TWO to tango From song title by Hoffman & Manning, 1952, and its meaning is shown in *Listener*, 24 June 1965: 'As for negotiation . . . the President has a firm, and melancholy, conviction: it takes two to tango.'

TWO wrongs don't make a right This proverb was first recorded in 1783 as 'three wrongs will not make a right' (B. Rush, *Letter*, 2 Aug. 1951), but becomes two in J. Kerr, *Several Trials of David Barclay* (1814), 249.

UNITED we stand, divided we fall Coined in two American patriotic songs (the later one has the exact wording): 'Then join Hand in Hand brave Americans all, / By uniting we stand, by dividing we fall' ('Liberty Song' in *Boston Gazette*, 18 July 1768).

What goes UP must come down Commonly associated with bombing and anti-aircraft shrapnel in Second World War, but first recorded in 1939 in L. I. Wilder, *By Shore of Silver Lake*, xxviii.

VARIETY is the spice of life New, or different, things to do or experience, make life interesting, prevent one from becoming bored or dull. First recorded in W. Cowper, *Task* (1785), ii, as 'Variety's the very spice of life, That gives it all its flavour.'

One does not WASH one's dirty linen in public It is unwise to publicize private disputes or scandals. The saying is also used in the metaphorical phrase *to wash one's dirty linen in public*. It comes from the French, 'c'est en famille, ce n'est pas en publique, qu'on lave son linge sale', and is attributed to Napoleon. It is first recorded in 1809 in T. G. Fessenden, *Pills*.

WASTE not, want not 'Want' is variously used in the sense 'lack' and 'desire'. First recorded in 1772 as 'He will waste nothing, but he must want nothing' (J. Wesley, *Letter* (1931), v).

A WATCHED pot never boils Waiting attentively for something to happen, a stage to be reached, makes it seem to take longer. First recorded in 1848 in E. Gaskell, *Mary Barton*, ii: 'What's the use of watching? "A watched pot never boils".'

The WAY to a man's heart is through his stomach First recorded in 1814 as 'the shortest road to men's hearts is down their throats' (J. Adams, letter in *Works* (1851), vi).

The WEAKEST go to the wall Usually said to derive from the installation of seating (around the walls) in the churches of the late Middle Ages. 'To go to the wall' means figuratively 'to succumb in a conflict or struggle' and is first recorded in *Coventry Plays* (*a.* 1500) (EETS), 47.

Where there's a WILL, there's a way If one is sufficiently willing or determined, a way to do or obtain something can usually be found. First recorded in G. Herbert, *Outlandish Proverbs* (1640), no. 730, as 'To him that will, wais are not wanting', and in above form in Hazlitt, *New Monthly Magazine*, Feb. 1822.

WIN friends and influence people A catch-phrase which refers to business or political friendship and influence, and comes from the advertising slogan for Pelmanism, a commercial course for memory training and personality development. It was used by Dale Carnegie in the title of his book, *How to Win Friends and Influence People*, published in 1937.

You WIN a few, you lose a few An expression of consolation or resignation of American origin, also found in the form 'you win some; you lose some'. It is first expressed in Kipling, *Captains Courageous* (1897), x, as 'I lost some; and I gained some', but in above form does not appear until 1966 in P. O'Donnell, *Sabre-Tooth*, xiv. A proverb with a similar meaning is 'you can't win them all', and this first appears in R. Chandler, *The Long Good-Bye* (1953), xxiv.

The WIND(S) of change A catch-phrase that indicates signs of change, especially in political, or social, conditions. The phrase was first used by Harold Macmillan on 3 Feb. 1960 when Prime Minister with reference to the need for constitutional reforms in Africa and its gradual decolonization. He was speaking to the South African Houses of Parliament.

It is a WISE child that knows its own father First recorded in J. Withals, *Dict.* (rev. edn. 1584), L4, as 'Wise sonnes they be in very deede, / That knowe their Parentes who did them breede', and in above form in G. Wither, *Abuses* (1613), i.

If WISHES were horses, beggars would ride Everybody would be rich, talented, successful, popular, etc. if wishing was all that was required. First recorded in J. Carmichaell, *Proverbs in Scots* (*a.* 1628), no. 140, as 'And wishes were horse pure [i.e. poor] men wald ryde'.

A WOMAN's work is never done First recorded in T. Turner, *Husbandry* (rev. edn. 1570), 26, as 'Some respite to husbands the weather doth send, but huswiues affaires haue never none ende', and in above form in 1629 (*Roxburghe Ballads* (1880), iii).

Not to see the WOOD for the trees To be unable to understand, deal with, a main subject issue, problem, etc. because one is confused by, or too closely involved in, numerous or complex minor details. It was first recorded in 1546 as 'Plentie is no deintie, ye see not your own ease. I see, ye can not see the wood for trees' (J. Heywood, *Prov.* (1867) ii).

Many go out for WOOL and come home shorn Many seek to better themselves or make themselves rich, but end by losing what they already have. First recorded in J. Minsheu, *Dialogues in Spanish* (1599), 61: 'You will goe for wooll, and returne home shorne.'

All WORK and no play makes Jack a dull boy If there is too much concentration on working and not enough time for relaxation or other interests, the worker will become bored and the quality of his work will deteriorate. First recorded in J. Howell, *Proverbs* (1659) (English), 12.

Even a WORM will turn Even the humblest will strike back if harassed or borne upon too far. It is recorded first in J. Heywood, *Dialogue of Proverbs* (1546), ii, as 'Treade a worm on the tayle, & it must turne agayne.'

The ZERO option A proposal made by President Reagan's administration in Nov. 1981 that, in return for the removal of certain Soviet medium-range missiles aimed at European targets, the US and its allies would cancel their 1979 agreement to install new types of American missiles in various European countries. It is therefore a phrase which indicates a proposal which will, if successful, eventually result in both sides ending up with what they want by reducing what is being negotiated till none remain.

EVERYDAY CLASSICAL LITERATURE

* indicates a separate entry

Academy: 1. A park and gymnasium in the outskirts of Athens sacred to the hero Academus (or Hecademus). 2. The school or college established there by Plato, possibly as early as 385 BC.

Achilles: in mythology, son of Peleus and *Thetis. All the evidence goes to show that he was a man, real or imaginary, and not a 'faded' god, and that his widespread cult is almost solely because of *Homer's *Iliad.* During his infancy, Thetis plunged him in the *Styx, thus making his body invulnerable except in the heel, by which she held him. He went with the other Greek princes to recover *Helen from *Troy, and established a reputation as the bravest of the Greeks in the fighting. But when *Agamemnon deprived him of Briseis, Achilles retired to his tent, and refused to fight again, until his friend *Patroclus was killed. Bent on revenge, Achilles put on the armour made for him by *Hephaestus and slew *Hector who had killed Patroclus. Later, Achilles was wounded in the heel by *Paris and died.

Actium: a promontory in the south of Epirus, at the mouth of the Ambracian Gulf, off which Octavian defeated the fleets of Antony and Cleopatra in 31 BC. This battle marked the end of the Roman republic and introduced the Roman Empire.

Adonis: in mythology, the son of Cinyras, king of Cyprus, by an incestuous union with his daughter, according to the usual myth. The beautiful youth was beloved by *Aphrodite.

Adrastus: king of *Argos, leader of the expedition of the 'Seven against Thebes', and of the second expedition against Thebes, known as the war of the Epigoni.

Aeacus: in mythology, son of *Zeus and Aegina.

Aegeus: a mythical king of Athens and father of *Theseus.

Aeneas: son of Anchises and the goddess *Aphrodite, a famous Trojan leader in *Homer's *Iliad* and the hero of *Virgil's *Aeneid*.

Aeolus: the god of winds.

Aeschylus (525/4–456 BC): Attic tragedian, the son of Euphorion of Eleusis, who in his youth witnessed the end of tyranny at Athens and as an adult the growth of democracy. He fought at Marathon and probably at *Salamis, and has been described as the main father of Greek tragic drama.

Aesculapius: son of *Apollo and Coronis, who was taught the art of medicine by Cheiron, the *Centaur. At the prayer of *Artemis he restored her favourite, *Hippolytus, to life. *Zeus, angered at this interference, struck Aesculapius with lightning. After his death he was honoured as the god of medicine, and was represented holding in his hand a staff, round which is wreathed a serpent, a creature peculiarly sacred to him.

Aesop: famed as a teller of fables used metaphorically to illustrate a point, Aesop lived as a slave on the island of Samos in the early sixth century BC. Ancient chronological reckoning put his death in the year 564.

Agamemnon: in mythology, son of Atreus and brother of *Menelaus; king of Mycenae, or *Argos; probably a historical person. In *Homer's *Iliad* Agamemnon is the commander-in-chief of the Greek expedition against *Troy, who lacks resolution and is easily discouraged. On his return to Argos he was murdered by his wife, *Clytemnestra, and her lover Aegisthus.

Alcibiades (*c.*450–404 BC): son of Cleinias, Athenian general and statesman. He was brought up in the household of his guardian, *Pericles, and became the pupil and intimate friend of *Socrates.

Alexander III (356–323 BC): of Macedonia ('the Great'), son of Philip II and Olympias of Epirus. *Aristotle became his tutor, and he early showed his powers of intellect and command. He succeeded his father in 336 BC and set out to conquer the Persian Empire. In this he succeeded and even managed to penetrate parts of India before his troops refused to follow him further and he was forced to return. He was undoubtedly the greatest general of his race and probably of antiquity.

Amazons: in mythology, a people of female warriors, always situated on the borders of the known world.

Andromache: in mythology, daughter of Eetion king of Thebes and wife of *Hector.

Andromeda: in mythology, daughter of Cepheus king of the Ethiopians and his wife Cassiepeia or Cassiope. Cassiepeia boasted that Andromeda was more beautiful than the *Nereids; they complained to *Poseidon, who flooded the land and sent a sea-monster to ravage it. Cepheus learned that the only cure was to expose Andromeda to the monster, and she was accordingly fastened to a rock on the sea-shore, but was rescued by *Perseus, who fell in love with her and slaughtered the monster.

Antigone: a daughter of *Oedipus and Jocasta. When the strife between her brothers Eteocles and Polyneices had led to the death of the latter, she buried his body by night, against the order of King Creon, and was ordered by him to be buried alive. She took her own life before the sentence was executed, and Haemon, the king's son, who passionately loved her, killed himself on her grave.

Antisthenes: the founder of the Cynic school of philosophy.

Antoninus Pius (AD 86–161): Roman emperor from 138 to 161.

Aphrodite: the Greek goddess of love, identified by the Romans with *Venus. *Homer makes her the daughter of *Zeus and Dione.

According to *Hesiod she sprang from the foam (*aphros*) of the sea that gathered about the severed member of *Uranus when *Cronos mutilated him.

Apollo: also called Phoebus, often identified with the sun, he was the son of *Zeus and Latona. He was the god who brings back sunshine in spring, who sends plagues, and who founds states and colonies. He was the god of music and poetry and had the gift of knowing the future, so that his oracles were in high repute.

Arcadia: a mountainous district in the Peloponnese, the domain of Pan, the shepherd's god, taken as an ideal region of rustic contentment.

Archimedes (287–212 BC): a famous mathematician of Syracuse. He is said to have constructed a kind of orrery representing the movements of the heavenly bodies, to have invented the screw for raising water which bears his name, and to have set on fire with lenses the ships of the Roman consul Marcellus that were besieging Syracuse. It was he who exclaimed 'eureka' ('I have found it') when he discovered, by observing in his bath the water displaced by his body, the means of testing (by specific gravity) whether base metal had been introduced in Hiero's crown.

archon: the chief magistrate, or, after the time of Solon (*c.*638–558 BC), one of the nine magistrates, of Athens.

Ares: the god of war of the ancient Greeks, identified by the Romans with Mars. He was said to be the son of *Zeus and *Hera, and to have been detected by *Hephaestus in an amorous intrigue with *Aphrodite, caught in a net, and exposed to the ridicule of the assembled gods.

Argonauts: the name given to the heroes who accompanied *Jason on board the ship *Argo* to Colchis to recover the *Golden Fleece.

Argos: 1. A monster with a hundred eyes. 2. The dog of *Odysseus who recognized his master on his return from *Troy after an absence of twenty years. 3. A city in the southern part of the Argive plain. In *Homer's *Iliad* Argos was the kingdom of *Diomedes, who owned *Agamemnon's leadership. The great Argive goddess was *Hera.

Aristides: an Athenian general and statesman, surnamed 'The Just', who commanded his tribe at the battle of Marathon (490 BC) and was *archon in 489. He was ostracized (*see* ostracism) in 482, but fought at the battle of *Salamis, and commanded the Athenian contingent at the battle of Plataea. He died about 468 BC.

Aristophanes (*c.*448–*c.*380 BC): the great Athenian comic poet, whose comedies are of historical value for their caricatures of the leading personages of the time and their comments on current affairs.

Aristotle (384–322 BC): the great Greek philosopher, was born at Stageira in Chalcidice (Macedonia). He studied at Athens under *Plato, and stayed there for twenty years. He was subsequently appointed by Philip of Macedon to be tutor to his son Alexander. On the accession of the latter to the throne Aristotle returned to Athens, where he lectured many scholars while walking up and down, whence his school came to be known as the Peripatetic.

Artemis: *see* **Diana.**

Aspasia: the famous Greek courtesan, daughter of Axiochus of Miletus, came to Athens, where she acquired fame by her beauty, culture, and wit. She so captivated *Pericles that he made her his lifelong companion.

Athene: the goddess of wisdom, industry, and war, identified by the Romans with their goddess *Minerva. She was the daughter of *Zeus and Metis, and sprang fully grown and armed from the brain of her father, who had swallowed Metis when pregnant, fearing that her child would be mightier than he. It was she who gave Athens its name. She was also known as *Pallas*.

Atlas: one of the *Titans. As punishment for his part in the revolt of the Titans he was employed to support the heavens with his head and hands somewhere in the west of the earth. He was changed into a mountain by *Perseus, who, being refused hospitality by Atlas, turned the eyes of *Medusa upon him.

Attila (AD c.406–453): king of the Huns.

Augean stables: Augeas, king of Elis, had an immense herd of oxen, whose stables had never been cleansed. Their cleansing in one day was one of the labours imposed on *Hercules by Eurystheus.

Augustus (63 BC–AD 14): (Gaius Julius Caesar Octavianus), the nephew of Julius Caesar, and first Roman emperor, occupying the throne from 27 BC until his death. The title of Augustus was conferred on him by the Senate and people as a mark of their veneration, and was used by all subsequent Roman emperors.

Autolycus: in mythology, a son of *Hermes, celebrated for his craft as a thief, who stole the flocks of his neighbours and mingled them with his own.

bacchanalia: the mysteries or orgies celebrated in ancient Rome in honour of *Bacchus.

Bacchus: a name of the Greek god *Dionysus.

Belisarius: the great military commander during the reign of Justinian (AD 527–63).

Brutus, Lucius Junius: the legendary first consul of Rome.

Brutus, Marcus Junius (85–42 BC): joined *Pompey in the civil war, but after the battle of Pharsalia was pardoned by *Caesar. He nevertheless joined the conspirators who assassinated Caesar, in the hope of restoring republican government.

Bucephalus: the favourite horse of *Alexander the Great, which died after the battle on the Hydaspes. In its memory Alexander founded the town of Bucephala on the site.

Cadmus: son of Agenor, king of Phoenicia.

Caesar: the name of a patrician family of Rome, which *Gaius Julius Caesar* (*c.*102–44 BC), the conqueror of Gaul and dictator, raised to the highest eminence. He was not only a great general and statesman, but an orator and historian. The name Caesar was assumed by his adopted son, Octavianus, on whom the Senate conferred the title *'Augustus', and by *Tiberius as the adopted son of Augustus. Both names were used by successive emperors, whether of the family of Caesar or not. The word has survived as a title in *Kaiser* and *Tsar*.

Cassandra: daughter of *Priam, king of *Troy, received the gift of prophecy from *Apollo, who was enamoured of her. But as she slighted him, the god contrived that no trust should be placed in her predictions. After the fall of Troy she fell to the lot of *Agamemnon, who took her back to Greece and to whom she foretold the calamities that awaited him. She was murdered by *Clytemnestra.

Castor and Pollux: twin brothers, known as the *Dioscuri*, sons of *Zeus by *Leda. They took part in the expedition of the *Argonauts.

Cato the Censor (234–149 BC): was famous for his opposition in that office to the prevalent fashions of luxury.

Catullus (*c.*84–*c.*54 BC): (Gaius Valerius), a great Roman poet and epigrammatist, born in or near Verona.

censors: at Rome, two in number, were elected every five years to take the census of the people and carry out the solemn purification (*lustrum*) which accompanied it. Their period of office was eighteen months, but might be extended. They had a general supervision over the conduct of citizens, and in particular the duty of revising the roll of senators (*legere senatum*), removing those who were unworthy and replacing them by others. They also had the duty of making contracts for public works and for the farming of taxes, and of letting the State lands. The institution dated from about 440 BC.

Centaurs: a fabulous people of Thessaly, half horses. The legend of their existence perhaps arose from the ancient inhabitants of Thessaly having tamed horses and appearing to their neighbours mounted on horseback.

Ceres: *see* **Demeter.**

Charon: in Greek mythology, the ferryman of *Hades, who, for a small coin, ferried the souls of the dead over the rivers *Styx and Acheron to the infernal regions. It was usual among the ancients to place a piece of money under the tongue of the deceased for the purpose of this payment.

Charybdis: in Greek legend, a dangerous whirlpool in the straits of Messina which threatened the destruction of *Odysseus' fleet. It was said that Charybdis was an avaricious woman, who stole the oxen of Hercules, for which theft she was struck with a thunderbolt by *Zeus, and turned into a whirlpool.

Chimaera: in Greek mythology, a monster with the head of a lion, the body of a goat, and the tail of a dragon, the offspring of Typhon and Echidna.

Cicero, Marcus Tullius (106–43 BC): the great Roman orator was born near

Arpinum and after studying law and philosophy came forward as a pleader. His success in this capacity opened the way for him to the highest offices, and he became consul in 63 BC.

Circe: celebrated for her knowledge of magic and venomous herbs, inhabited an island called Aeaea. When *Odysseus visited the island his companions were changed by Circe's potions into swine. Odysseus, however, was fortified against her enchantment and, sword in hand, demanded the restoration of his companions. Circe complied, and Odysseus remained with her for a year, becoming by her the father of Telegonus, or, according to *Hesiod, of Agrius and Latinus.

Claudian: the last great poet of ancient Rome, who was a native of Alexandria.

Claudius: (Tiberius Claudius Drusus Nero Germanicus), Roman emperor AD 41–54, the nephew of Tiberius and younger brother of Germanicus. His learning, combined with a certain ungainliness and dullness of wit, has caused him to be compared to James I.

Cleisthenes: 1. The founder of Athenian democracy. After the fall of the tyrant Hippias (510 BC) there was an oligarchic movement in Athens headed by Isagoras and supported by Sparta. Cleisthenes put himself forward as the champion of democracy and overthrew the aristocrats. He completely reorganized the State on a democratic basis. 2. Of Sicyon, tyrant in the early 6th c. BC.

Clytemnestra: daughter of Tyndareus, king of Sparta, and *Leda, and wife of *Agamemnon, king of Argos. On the return of Agamemnon from the Trojan War (*see* Troy), she, with her paramour Aegisthus, murdered her husband, and was in turn slain by Orestes, Agamemnon's son.

consuls: at Rome, originally called *Praetors, were two in number and elected annually by the people. On the expulsion of the kings the consuls received the *imperium*, the military and judicial authority formerly wielded by the kings. This power was in course of time reduced by the creation of new magistracies, notably the censorship (*see* censors). The chief functions retained by the consuls were those of military command. Later they received as *proconsuls* an extension of their authority after the termination of their year of office, to enable them to carry on a military command or govern a province. Under the empire the consulate became more and more a mainly honorary office.

Coriolanus: (Gaius Marcius), according to tradition, a Roman patrician and a gallant general of the first half of the 5th c. BC, who earned the name Coriolanus for the capture of Corioli from the Volscians.

Corybantes: the companions of the goddess *Cybele, who followed her with wild dances and music.

Croesus: last king of Lydia (*c.*560–546 BC), who passed for the richest of mankind.

Cronos: or Kronos. In Greek mythology, one of the *Titans, a son of *Uranus and *Gaea, and father by *Rhea of *Hestia, *Demeter,

*Hera, *Poseidon, *Hades, and *Zeus. He succeeded Uranus as ruler of the universe, and was in turn dethroned by Zeus.

Cybele: an Asiatic goddess representing the fecundity of nature, worshipped especially in Phrygia. Thence her cult passed into Greece, where she was known as *Rhea.

Cyclopes: a race of giants having only one eye, in the middle of the forehead, who inhabited the island of Sicily.

Daedalus: an ingenious Athenian craftsman. He murdered his nephew Talus, his rival in ingenuity, and fled with his son Icarus to Crete, where he constructed the famous *labyrinth for King *Minos. Having incurred the king's displeasure, he was imprisoned, and escaped with Icarus by means of wings. But Icarus flew too high, and the heat of the sun melted the wax with which the wings were fastened, so that he fell into the sea west of Samos (hence called the Icarian Sea) and was drowned. Daedalus made his way to Sicily.

Danaë: the daughter of Acrisius, king of Argos.

Daphne: according to mythology, a daughter of the river Peneus, of whom *Apollo became enamoured. Daphne fleeing from his importunities entreated the assistance of the gods, who changed her into a laurel. Hence the laurel became the favourite tree of Apollo.

Demeter: known as *Ceres* to the Romans, Demeter was the Greek goddess of the corn-bearing earth and of agriculture. Mythology made her the daughter of *Cronos and sister of *Zeus, but she does not figure among *Homer's Olympian deities.

Democritus: a celebrated Greek philosopher, born at Abdera about 460 BC. He wrote on the natural sciences, mathematics, morals, and music. He advanced (with Leucippus) the theory that the world was formed by the concourse of atoms.

Demosthenes (*c.*383–322 BC): the Athenian orator, born in the Attic deme of Paeania.

Diana: a Roman goddess identified with the Greek Artemis. The latter was the daughter of *Zeus and Leto, and the twin sister of *Apollo. She lived in perpetual celibacy and was the goddess of the chase. She also presided over childbirth.

Diogenes the Cynic (*c.*400–*c.*325 BC): a Greek philosopher born at Sinope in Pontus who, after a dissolute youth, practised at Athens the greatest austerity, finally taking up his residence, it is said, in a large earthenware jar.

Diomedes: 1. Son of Tydeus and king of *Argos, he was one of the Greek princes who joined the expedition against *Troy, and, next to *Achilles, was the bravest. *Athene aided him in battle and enabled him to wound even *Ares and *Aphrodite. 2. King of the Bistones in Thrace. He owned famous mares, which he fed on human flesh. He was killed by *Hercules.

Dionysus: a Greek god, also known as *Bacchus*, the son of *Zeus and Semele, a god of fertility, a suffering god who dies and comes to life again. Also, and particularly, a god of wine, who loosens care and inspires man to music and poetry.

Dioscuri: *see* **Castor and Pollux.**

Electra: a daughter of *Agamemnon, who incited her brother Orestes to avenge their father's death by assassinating *Clytemnestra. She is the subject of plays by *Sophocles and *Euripides.

Elysium: a place or island in the western ocean, where, according to Greek mythology, the souls of the virtuous enjoy complete happiness and innocent pleasures.

Empedocles (c.493–c.433 BC): a learned and eloquent philosopher, of Agrigentum in Sicily. It is said that his curiosity to visit the crater of Etna proved fatal to him, for he threw himself into it.

ephors: magistrates in several Dorian states. At Sparta they were elected annually by the citizens, and the senior ephor gave his name to the year.

Epicurus (341–270 BC): the founder of the school of philosophy that bears his name. In ethics he regarded the absence of pain—peace of mind—as the greatest good.

Eros: god of love in Greek mythology.

Euclid: the celebrated geometrician who lived at Alexandria in the reign of the first Ptolemy (323–283 BC), but the place of his birth is not known.

Euripides (480–406 BC): the youngest and most 'modern-minded' of the three great Attic tragedians.

Eurydice: *see* **Orpheus.**

Fabius: (Quintus Fabius Maximus), nicknamed *Cunctator* or 'the delayer', was appointed dictator at Rome after the great victory won by *Hannibal over the Romans in 217 BC. He carried on a defensive campaign against Hannibal, avoiding direct engagements, and harassing the enemy. Hence the expressions, 'Fabian tactics', 'Fabian policy'.

Gaea: or Ge. In Greek mythology the personification of the Earth, a divine being, the wife of *Uranus and mother of the *Titans.

Galatea: a sea-nymph, loved by the Cyclops *Polyphemus, whom she treated with disdain, while Acis, a Sicilian shepherd, enjoyed her affection. The jealous Cyclops crushed his rival with a rock. Galatea could not bring him to life, so changed him into a river at the foot of Mt. Etna.

Gallic Wars: the name usually given to the campaigns by which *Caesar completed the Roman conquest of Gaul (58–51 BC).

Giants: according to Greek mythology, the Giants were the children of *Gaea, of great stature and strength, frequently confused with the *Titans. They are said to have conspired to dethrone *Zeus, and heaped Ossa on *Pelion in order to scale the walls of heaven. They were defeated and imprisoned in the earth.

Golden Fleece: Phrixus and Helle fled from the hatred of their stepmother on the back of a ram which had a golden fleece and wings. Helle became giddy and fell into a part of the sea which, as a consequence, is now called the Hellespont, but Phrixus arrived safely at the court of Aeetes, king of Colchis, and sacrificed the ram to *Zeus and dedicated the fleece. The king then murdered Phrixus to obtain the fleece and *Jason, in order to become king of Iolcus, set out with the bravest of the Greeks to avenge this murder in the *Argo*, hence the name *Argonauts. Aeetes promised to relinquish the golden fleece if Jason performed a series of tasks. With the help of the king's daughter, Medea, who had fallen in love with him, Jason performed the tasks and returned to Iolcus with the fleece and Medea.

Gorgons: the three sisters, Stheno, Euryale, and *Medusa. Of these the first two were immortal; Medusa was mortal and is the most celebrated. According to mythology, their hair was entwined with serpents, their hands were of brass, their bodies covered with impenetrable scales, their teeth like a wild boar's tusks, and they turned to stones all on whom they fixed their eyes.

Hades: or Pluto. In Greek mythology, the god of the nether world, the son of *Cronos and *Rhea, and brother of *Zeus and *Poseidon. He received, as his share of his father's empire, the kingdom of the infernal regions. The name 'Hades' was transferred to this kingdom, a gloomy sunless abode, where, according to *Homer, the ghosts of the dead flit about like bats. Its approach was barred by several rivers, including the *Styx. Tartarus was the region of Hades in which the most impious of men suffered retribution. The asphodel meadows were reserved for those who deserved neither bliss nor extreme punishment. The shades of the blessed were conveyed elsewhere (*see* Elysium), though *Virgil places Elysium in Hades.

Hadrian (AD 76–138): (Publius Aelius Hadrianus), a Roman emperor from 117 to 138. He was a patron of art and learning. He visited Britain and caused the wall to be built between the Solway and the mouth of the Tyne, known as *Hadrian's Wall*.

Hannibal (247–*c.*183 BC): the great Carthaginian general, who developed the Hellenistic system of combining infantry and cavalry till he could surround and annihilate the enemy. He was the great leader of the Carthaginians against Rome in the second *Punic War.

Hebe: the daughter of *Zeus and *Hera, and goddess of youth. She attended on Hera and filled the cups of the gods.

Hecate: a Greek goddess associated with the lower world and with night, a queen of ghosts and magic, the protectress of enchanters and witches.

Hector: a son of *Priam and *Hecuba, the most valiant of the Trojans who fought against the Greeks. He was slain by *Achilles.

Hecuba: the wife of *Priam, king of *Troy, and mother of *Hector, *Paris, and *Cassandra.

Helen: according to Greek legend, Helen was the most beautiful woman of her age. She was the daughter of *Zeus and *Leda. When still a child she was carried off by *Theseus, but was recovered by her brothers.

She selected *Menelaus, king of Sparta, for her husband, after her many suitors had bound themselves by an oath to defend her. She was subsequently seduced by *Paris and carried off to *Troy. To get her back, Menelaus assembled the Greek princes who had been her suitors, and these resolved to make war on Troy for her recovery. When Troy fell she was reconciled with Menelaus and lived with him at Sparta.

Helios: the Greek name of the sun-god, the son of (and sometimes identified with) Hyperion.

Hephaestus: the Greek god of fire, called by the Romans *Vulcan*

Hera: known as *Juno* by the Romans, Hera was the daughter of *Cronos and *Rhea and the sister and wife of *Zeus. She is represented in mythology as pursuing with inexorable jealousy the mistresses of Zeus and their children. She was mother of *Ares (Mars), *Hebe, and *Hephaestus (Vulcan). She was worshipped as queen of the heavens, the goddess representative of women, especially of wives, and protectress of marriage. The peacock among birds was specially sacred to her.

Heracles: *see* **Hercules.**

Hercules: in Greek *Heracles*. He was the son of *Zeus and Alcmena and was instructed in the various arts of war and music, and became the strongest and most valiant of men. After his death he obtained divine honours, having devoted the labours of his life to the benefit of mankind.

Hermes: called *Mercury* by the Romans, he was the son of *Zeus and Maia, the inventor of the lyre (he placed strings across the shell of a tortoise), and the messenger and herald of the gods.

Hermione: daughter of *Menelaus and *Helen, and the wife, first of Neoptolemus, then of Orestes.

Hero and Leander: a love-story, apparently of Alexandrian origin. Hero was priestess of *Aphrodite. Leander saw her at a festival and used nightly to swim the Hellespont to see her, until a storm put out the light by which she guided him across and he was drowned. She threw herself into the sea after him.

Herodotus (*c.*480–*c.*425 BC): a Greek historian who is known as the 'father of history', for he was the first to collect his materials systematically, test their accuracy so far as he was able, and arrange them agreeably. His work, in nine books, is the first masterpiece of Greek prose.

Hesiod (8th c. BC?): one of the earliest of Greek poets.

Hesperides: nymphs appointed to guard the golden apples that *Gaea gave to *Hera on the day of her nuptials with *Zeus.

Hestia: the Greek goddess of the hearth, daughter of *Cronos and *Rhea, akin to the Roman *Vesta.

hetairai: the Attic euphemism for those women, slave or free, who traded their sexual favours for long or short periods outside wedlock, whether they were streetwalkers, the inmates of civic or private brothels, or accomplished and expensive courtesans.

Hippocrates (*c*.460–357 BC): the most celebrated physician of antiquity. The so-called 'Hippocratic Oath', expressing the ethical doctrine of the medical profession, is attributed to him.

Hippolytus: a son of *Theseus and Hippolyta, he was famous for his virtue and misfortunes.

Homer: the great Greek epic poet, who was regarded by the ancients as the author of the *Iliad* and the *Odyssey*. Nothing is known about him for certain, not his birthplace, nor his date. It is now considered unlikely that the same man wrote both epics, or indeed that either, as now known, is the work of a single poet. The theory that a poet, 'Homer', living in the 8th c. BC, combined and remodelled earlier poems, and that his work was in its turn enlarged and remodelled by others, seems the most plausible account of their genesis.

Horace (65–8 BC): (Quintus Horatius Flaccus), the Roman poet, who was born at Venusia in Apulia. He was present on the losing side at the battle of Philippi, but obtained his pardon and returned to Rome.

Hygieia: the goddess of health, and daughter of *Aesculapius.

Hylas: a beautiful youth beloved by *Hercules, and his companion on board the ship *Argo*. When the *Argonauts landed for water he fell into the fountain and was drowned, or, according to the poets, was carried away by the nymphs for love of his beauty.

Icarus: *see* **Daedalus.**

Iris: according to mythology, the messenger of the gods, and particularly of *Zeus and *Hera. The rainbow was the path by which she travelled between the gods and men.

Isis: one of the great Egyptian deities.

Ithaca: the kingdom of *Odysseus, a small island in the Ionian Sea.

Janus: an ancient Italian deity, the god of the doorway.

Jason: a celebrated hero of antiquity, son of Aeson, king of Iolcus. When his father's kingdom was usurped by his uncle, Pelias, he undertook the expedition to Colchis to recover the *Golden Fleece. If he succeeded his uncle promised to surrender the kingdom to him.

Julian the Apostate: Roman emperor AD 361–3. He was brought up compulsorily as a Christian, and on attaining the throne proclaimed himself a pagan.

Juno: *see* **Hera.**

Jupiter: originally the elemental god of the Romans, he came to be identified with the Greek *Zeus, the myths concerning whom were transferred to Jupiter.

Juvenal (AD *c*.60–*c*.130): (Decimus Junius Juvenalis), the great Roman satirical poet.

labyrinth: a maze constructed by *Daedalus for *Minos, king of Crete. In it the *Minotaur was confined.

Laocoön: a legendary Trojan priest of *Apollo, who, when he was offering a sacrifice to *Poseidon, saw two serpents leave the sea and attack his sons. He rushed to their defence, but the serpents wreathed themselves about him and crushed him. This was said to be his punishment for temporarily dissuading the Trojans from admitting the wooden horse (*see* Trojan Horse) into *Troy.

Leda: a daughter of Thestius and wife of Tyndareus, king of Sparta. She was seen bathing in a river by *Zeus, who became enamoured of her and took the form of a swan in order to approach her. From their union were born *Castor and Pollux, and *Helen.

Lucretius (*c*.94–*c*.55 BC): (Titus Lucretius Carus), the Roman poet and philosopher.

Lycaon: an impious king of Arcadia, to punish whom *Zeus visited the earth. To test Zeus' divinity, Lycaon set before him a dish of human flesh. The god rejected the dish and slew Lycaon and his wicked sons, or turned them into wolves.

Lysander: a famous Spartan commander who captured the Athenian fleet in 405 BC. He fell at the battle of Haliartus in 395 BC.

Maenads: a name of the Bacchantes, or priestesses of *Bacchus.

Marathon: a crescent-shaped plain between the spurs of Pentelicus and Parnes and the sea, some 22 miles NE of Athens; the scene of the defeat of the invading Persians by Miltiades in 490 BC.

Marcus Aurelius Antoninus (AD 121–80): Roman emperor, AD 161–80. He left a collection of 'Meditations', in 12 books, private devotional memoranda written in Greek. Through many translations, they have influenced thousands who could not read the original.

Medusa: one of the three *Gorgons, and the only one who was mortal. According to *Ovid, by granting her favours to *Poseidon, she incurred the resentment of *Athene, who changed her locks which Poseidon admired into serpents.

Menander (*c*.342–292 BC): an Athenian dramatic poet.

Menelaus: king of Sparta, son of Atreus and brother of *Agamemnon. He was the successful suitor of *Helen and it was he who assembled the princes who had pledged themselves to protect her, so that she could be retrieved from *Paris who had taken her to *Troy.

Mercury: *see* **Hermes.**

Midas: a semi-legendary king of Phrygia, who, having hospitably entertained Silenus, the companion of *Dionysus, when he had lost his way, was given a wish, and wished that all he touched might become gold. But when he found that the very meat he attempted to eat became gold in his mouth, he asked to be relieved of the gift.

Minerva: the Roman goddess of wisdom and of arts and trades, subsequently identified with the Greek *Athene, which led to her being regarded also as the goddess of war. She was also held to have invented musical instruments.

Minos: a legendary king of Crete, son of *Zeus and Europa, who gave laws to his subjects and displayed so much justice and moderation that he was rewarded after death by being made supreme judge of the infernal regions. Attic legend, on the other hand, represented him as a cruel tyrant who imposed on Athens a yearly tribute of seven youths and seven maidens to be devoured by the *Minotaur.

Minotaur: a Cretan monster. *Minos refused to sacrifice to *Neptune a white bull which the god had given him for that purpose. The god to punish him caused his wife Pasiphaë to become enamoured of the bull, and she gave birth to the Minotaur. Minos confined it in the *labyrinth and it was later destroyed by *Theseus.

Momus: the god of fault-finding among the ancients, who criticized whatever the gods did.

Musaeus: 1. A legendary Greek poet, said to have been a pupil of *Orpheus. 2. A Greek poet, who perhaps lived about AD 500, the author of a poem on the story of *Hero and Leander.

Muses: the nine daughters of *Zeus and Mnemosyne, born in Pieria at the foot of Mt. Olympus, who presided over the various kinds of poetry, arts, and sciences.

Naiads: *see* **nymphs.**

Narcissus: a beautiful youth, son of the river-god Cephissus and the nymph Liriope. He saw his image reflected in a fountain and became enamoured of it, thinking it to be the nymph of the place. His fruitless attempts to approach this beautiful object drove him to despair and death. He was changed into the flower which bears his name.

Nemesis: according to *Hesiod a child of Night, she was in early Greek thought a personification of the gods' resentment at, and consequent punishment of, insolence (*hubris*) towards themselves.

Neptune: the Roman god of the sea, identified with the *Poseidon of the Greeks.

Nereids: *see* **nymphs.**

Nero: Roman emperor AD 54–68, the last of the Julio-Claudian dynasty, proverbial for his tyranny and brutality.

Nestor: king of Pylos in the Peloponnese, and a grandson of *Poseidon, led his subjects to the Trojan War (*see* Troy), where he distinguished himself among the Grecian chiefs.

Nike: the goddess of Victory in Greek religion.

Niobe: a daughter of *Tantalus and wife of Amphion. She was the mother of six sons and six daughters, and this so increased her pride that she boasted herself superior to Latona, the mother of *Apollo and *Artemis. For this arrogance her sons were slain by Apollo and all the daughters except one by Artemis. Niobe herself was changed into a stone, and still wept for her children in streams that trickled down the rock.

nymphs: in Greek mythology, female personifications of various natural objects, mountains, springs, rivers, and trees. The water-nymphs were the *Oceanides* (the daughters of Oceanus, nymphs of the Ocean), *Nereids* (nymphs of the Mediterranean Sea), and *Naiads* (nymphs of lakes, rivers, and fountains). The *Oreads* were nymphs of the mountains. The *Dryads* and *Hamadryads* were nymphs of trees. They possessed some divine gifts, such as that of prophecy, and were long-lived, but not immortal. They had no temples, but were honoured with gifts of milk, honey, fruit, etc.

Oceanus: in early Greek cosmology, the river supposed to encircle the plain of the Earth. Also personified as one of the *Titans, the progenitor (with his consort *Tethys) of the gods, and the father of the rivers and water-nymphs.

Odysseus: or, in Latin, *Ulysses*. He was son of Laertes and Anticles and king of the island of Ithaca. He became one of the suitors of *Helen, but despairing of success married *Penelope. It was he who advised Tyndareus, father of Helen, to bind her suitors by an oath to join together to protect her. When she was taken to *Troy Odysseus, after trying to evade his obligations by feigning madness, joined the other Greek princes in the expedition to recover her. After the war he embarked to return home but met on the way with a series of adventures which are recounted in *Homer's *Odyssey*. After twenty years away, he finally managed to reach Ithaca, and, with the help of his son, *Telemachus, destroyed the importunate suitors of Penelope. He lived on for another sixteen years before being killed by Telegonus, his son by *Circe, who did not know who he was.

Oedipus: son of Laius, king of *Thebes, and Jocasta. His father was informed by an oracle that he must perish at his son's hands. He consequently ordered the destruction of the child, but Oedipus was rescued by a shepherd. In ignorance of his parentage Oedipus later killed his father, and went on to Thebes where he solved the riddle of the Sphinx which was plaguing the city. He was given the kingdom and Jocasta's hand as a reward. They had two sons, Polyneices and Eteocles, and two daughters, Ismene and *Antigone. When he discovered the facts of his parentage, Oedipus put out his own eyes and Jocasta hanged herself.

Orpheus: a legendary pre-Homeric poet, said to be son of the muse Calliope. He was so skilled a player on the lyre that the wild beasts were spellbound by his music. He passionately loved his wife Eurydice and when she died he entered the infernal regions to recover her. He charmed *Pluto and *Persephone with his music and they consented to restore Eurydice to him provided he did not look behind him until he had emerged from *Hades. He forgot to obey and Eurydice immediately vanished.

Osiris: a great deity of the ancient Egyptians. As king of Egypt he civilized and educated his people. By the Greeks Osiris was identified with *Dionysus.

Ossa: *see* **Pelion.**

ostracism: an institution introduced at Athens by *Cleisthenes, designed to prevent any attempt against the established order. Each year the

Ecclesia considered the question 'whether it was expedient to apply ostracism'. In the event of an affirmative vote each citizen inscribed on potsherds (*ostraka*) the name of the person whose withdrawl from the State seemed to him necessary to the public safety. Any person so designated by a certain number of votes (6000 had to be cast in all) was to leave Athens for ten years, without loss of his property. Not more than ten citizens in all (among them *Aristides) ever suffered ostracism, and it was discontinued by the end of the 5th c. BC.

Ovid, Publius Ovidius Naso (43 BC–AD 18): the Roman poet. He was banished from Rome by *Augustus in AD 8 and died in exile. He wrote in elegiacs and was the favourite Latin poet of the Middle Ages.

paean: a song of thanksgiving for deliverance from evil or danger, addressed usually to *Apollo who, as god of healing, was given the name Paean. Later the word is used for a shout or song of triumph.

Palinurus: the helmsman of *Aeneas who was overcome by the god of Sleep, fell overboard, was washed up on the shore of Italy, and there murdered.

Pan: the god of shepherds and huntsmen, represented as a monster, with two small horns on his head, flat nose, ruddy complexion, and the legs and feet of a goat. He invented the flute with seven reeds, and his worship was widespread and particularly established in *Arcadia. Panic is the fear that seizes people without obvious cause; Pan was thought responsible for the alarms felt by people, especially travellers in remote and desolate places.

Paris: also known as *Alexander*. He was a son of *Priam, king of *Troy, and of *Hecuba. He was exposed as a child but was rescued and brought up by shepherds. He was appointed by the gods to judge the prize of beauty among the three goddesses, *Hera, *Aphrodite, and *Athene. He awarded the prize to Aphrodite after she had offered to make the fairest woman in the world his wife. He subsequently persuaded *Helen to elope with him, which brought about the expedition of the Greek princes to Troy. During the course of the war Paris was killed by an arrow shot by *Philoctetes.

patricians: members of certain distinguished families at Rome, a privileged class, as distinguished from the *plebeians.

Patroclus: one of the Grecian warriors during the Trojan War (*see* Troy), and the close friend of *Achilles. When the latter retired to his tent and refused to fight Patroclus followed his example, until *Nestor, in consequence of the many defeats of the Greeks, prevailed upon him to return. To this Achilles consented, and lent Patroclus his armour, but Patroclus was slain by Hector.

Pegasus: a winged horse sprung from the blood of *Medusa, when *Perseus cut off her head.

Pelion: a mountain in Thessaly, on which the Giants in their war with the gods heaped Mt. Ossa, in order to scale the heights of heaven.

Peloponnesian War: between Athens and Sparta and their respective allies,

431–404 BC. It ended in the surrender of Athens and the brief transfer of the leadership of Greece to Sparta.

Pelops: the son of *Tantalus and founder of the Pelopid dynasty from which the Peloponnese took its name.

Penelope: daughter of Icarius, wife of *Odysseus, and mother of *Telemachus.

Pericles: the great Athenian statesman and military commander, who controlled the affairs of the State from 460 BC until his death in 429 BC, including the earlier period of the *Peloponnesian War. During this administration Athens reached the summit of her power, and the Parthenon and Propylaea were built.

Peripatetics: *see* **Aristotle.**

Persephone: *see* **Proserpine.**

Persepolis: the capital of the Persian empire.

Perseus: the son of *Zeus and *Danaë. When King Polydectes became enamoured of Danaë he sent Perseus to fetch the head of *Medusa in order to be rid of him, for he thought he would be killed. But the gods favoured Perseus. *Pluto lent him a helmet that would make him invisible, *Athene a buckler resplendent as a mirror (so that he did not need to look directly at Medusa), and *Hermes wings for his feet. With the help of these aids Perseus took the head of Medusa and when *Atlas received him inhospitably he showed him the head and Atlas was changed into a mountain. He rescued *Andromeda and then slew Polydectes to protect his mother from the king's violence. While taking part in some funeral games he accidentally killed his grandfather with a quoit, thus fulfilling the prophecy concerning Danaë's son (*see* Danaë). He refused to ascend the throne of Argos, to which he now became the heir because of this calamity, but exchanged it for another and founded the new city of Mycenae. Another version has him withdrawing to Asia where his son Perseus became king of the Persians, supposed to be named after him.

Phaedra: a daughter of *Minos and Pasiphaë, and wife of *Theseus. She became enamoured of *Hippolytus, the son of Theseus, and when her advances were rejected she told Theseus his son had threatened her virtue and caused Hippolytus' death.

Philoctetes: one of the Greek heroes of the Trojan War (*see* Troy), who had inherited the bow and arrows of *Heracles. He was left on the island of Lemnos because of a bad wound in his foot, but in the tenth year of the war a seer revealed that only with his bow could Troy be beaten. So *Odysseus went to fetch him and after he had returned to Troy he slew *Paris.

Pindar (*c*.522–442 BC): the great Greek lyric poet, who was born at, or near, Thebes. He acquired fame at an early age and was employed by many winners at the Games to celebrate their victories.

Plato (*c*.429–347 BC): the great Greek philosopher, the son of an Athenian of ancient family. He became a pupil and devoted admirer of

*Socrates, and after his death in 399 retired to Megara, and subsequently paid three visits to the courts of Dionysius I and Dionysius II at Syracuse. After the first of these, about 386, he began teaching philosophy in the *Academy, an olive-grove near Athens, whence his school derives its name. He twice made some attempt to enter political life, but was repelled by the iniquities he encountered. The remainder of his life was mainly occupied with instruction and the composition of the Dialogues in which he embodied his views. One of Plato's principal contributions to philosophical thought is his 'Theory of Ideas'. The *idea* or *form* of a thing, in this theory, is somewhat of the nature of our abstract conception of that thing, but having a real existence outside the world of sense; it is the unchanging reality behind the changing appearance. The supreme *idea* is that of the Good. With Plato, as with Socrates, virtue is knowledge, knowledge of this supreme *idea*, which implies the effort to realize it. This perfect virtue is given to very few.

Plautus: Titus Maccius (*c.*254–184 BC), an early Roman dramatist.

plebeians: the Roman burgesses other than the patricians.

Pliny the Elder (AD 23–79): the author of the *Historia Naturalis*, and the intimate friend of *Vespasian. He perished while observing the eruption of Vesuvius.

Pliny the Younger (AD c.61–c.112): nephew of Pliny the Elder. He was an advocate who held many public offices, and an author.

Plotinus: born (AD *c.*205) probably at Lycopolis in Egypt, he was the chief exponent of Neoplatonism, which revived and developed the metaphysical side of the Platonic teaching. He was a man of an extremely spiritual and mystical character, the essence of whose philosophy was the desire to escape from the material world.

Plutarch: the biographer and moral philosopher, who was born before AD 50 and died after AD 120. He was the most popular of Greek authors at the time of the Renaissance.

Pluto: another name for the god *Hades.

Plutus: the son of *Demeter and the god of wealth.

Polyphemus: one of the *Cyclopes, a son of *Poseidon. He seized *Odysseus and twelve companions when they were driven on to the coast of Italy while returning from the Trojan War (*see* Troy). He confined them in a cave, blocked the entrance with a stone, and devoured two of them daily. Odysseus would have shared this fate had he not made the Cyclops drunk and put out his single eye with a firebrand. He then escaped by clinging to the wool under the belly of one of Polyphemus' rams when they were let out of the cave to feed.

Pompey (106–48 BC): surnamed 'The Great' (Gnaeus Pompeius), Pompey was a famous Roman general, who joined forces with Sulla and showed great military ability in the campaigns against the Marians. He later became the leader of the aristocracy and conservative party, and began the civil war with Caesar in 49. The following year he was defeated at Pharsalus, and sailed for Egypt. While landing from a boat, he was stabbed and killed by Septimus, formerly one of his centurions.

Poseidon: called *Neptune* by the Romans. He was, according to Greek mythology, a son of *Cronos and *Rhea, and brother of *Zeus and *Hades. He shared with these his father's empire, receiving as his portion the kingdom of the sea.

praetors: at Rome, originally the generic term for the holders of *imperium* or executive authority, and the name of the two magistrates who replaced the king, later called *consuls. Subsequently it was the title of the magistrate who administered justice between Roman citizens and the magistrate who did the same where foreigners were involved.

praetorians: under the Roman republic it was customary for a general to have a bodyguard of his friends and clients. These were replaced (towards the end of the republican period) by professional soldiers.

Praxiteles: Greek sculptor who worked in the 4th c. BC.

Priam: the last king of *Troy. He was the son of Laomedon, husband of *Hecuba, and father of many sons, 50 according to Homer, and daughters. He was slain by Neoptolemus when Troy was finally taken.

Priapus: a god of fertility. He was said to be the son of *Aphrodite and *Dionysus or some other god.

Procrustes: meaning 'the stretcher', or *Damastes*, a famous robber of Attica, who was killed by *Theseus. He tied travellers on a bed, and if their length exceeded it, he cut short their limbs; but if the bed proved longer, he stretched them to make them equal to it.

Prometheus: a son of the *Titan Iapetus and Themis or Clymene, and brother of Epimetheus. He made mankind out of clay, and when *Zeus oppressed them and deprived them of fire, he stole fire for them from heaven and taught them many arts. Zeus caused him to be chained to a rock, where, during the daytime, a vulture fed on his liver, which was restored each night. From this torture he was delivered by *Hercules.

Proserpine: according to her Greek name, *Persephone*, she was a daughter of *Zeus and *Demeter.

Proteus: an old man of the sea, who tended the flocks of *Poseidon.

Ptolemy, Claudius Ptolemaeus: 1. The celebrated mathematician, astronomer, and geographer who lived at Alexandria in the 2nd c. AD. 2. The name of all the Macedonian kings of Egypt.

Punic Wars: Rome, having by 270 BC made herself mistress of the Italian peninsula and become a Mediterranean power, found herself confronted across the Straits of Messina by the rival power of Carthage. To the political rivalry between the two states was added a trade rivalry. The first Punic War lasted from 264 to 241 BC and was won by the Romans, who, after a number of reverses, conquered Sicily by the naval victory off the Aegates Insulae (242). The second Punic War was launched when *Hannibal succeeded to the command of the Carthaginian army in Spain, and in spite of Roman protests captured Saguntum, a city in alliance with Rome. Hannibal reached Italy after an arduous passage over the Alps in 218, was joined by the Gauls of northern Italy, and defeated one great Roman army after another. The skilful policy adopted by Quintus *Fabius of following the invader and harassing him, while refusing a general engagement, proved successful; but it caused discontent at Rome, and was abandoned in 216, with the result that Hannibal overwhelmed the Roman army at Cannae. Nevertheless, the tide slowly turned in the favour of the Romans, and ended in victory for them in 202. The third and final Punic War started when Carthage was goaded into retaliating against an ally of Rome's in Africa, though Carthage had undertaken not to wage any wars there without Rome's consent. Carthage was captured and demolished in 146, and its dominions were for the greater part constituted a Roman province, thus ending the ancient commercial empire.

Pygmalion: a king of Cyprus and a sculptor. He became enamoured of a beautiful statue that he had made of a woman, and at his prayer *Aphrodite gave it life.

Pyrrho: a native of Elis in the Peloponnese, who lived in the time of Alexander the Great and joined his expedition. He was the founder of the Sceptical or Pyrrhonian school of philosophy, and maintained that certain knowledge on any matter was unattainable, and that suspension of judgement was true wisdom and the source of happiness.

Pyrrhus I (319/8–272 BC): king of Epirus from 307, he was second cousin of Alexander the Great. He was a skilful commander, a good organizer, and an ambitious military adventurer. The expression 'Pyrrhic victory', a victory won at too great a cost, alludes to an exclamation attributed to Pyrrhus after the battle of Asculum in 279, where he routed the Romans but lost the flower of his army: 'One more such victory and we are undone.'

Pythagoras: the Greek philosopher and mathematician, a native of Samos, who lived in the 6th c. BC. He settled in Cortona in Italy where he founded a brotherhood who combined ascetic practices and mystical beliefs with the study of mathematics. Pythagoras is credited with the discovery of the proof of the proposition that the square on the hypotenuse of a right-angled triangle is equal to the sum of the squares on the other two sides, which is called therefore the Pythagorean Theorem. He worked out a mathematical basis for music and supposed the heavenly bodies to be divided by intervals according to the laws of musical harmony, whence arose the idea of the harmony of the spheres. He discovered the rotation of the earth on its axis and found in this the causes of day and night.

Quintilian: (Marcus Fabius Quintilianus) (AD *c.*35–*c.*100), Roman rhetorician, educationist, and literary critic.

Rhea: an ancient Greek nature-goddess, commonly identified with the Asiatic *Cybele*, the wife of *Cronos.

rhetoric: in Greek, the art of speaking so as to persuade.

Romulus and Remus: these twin brothers were thrown into the Tiber, but were rescued and suckled by a she-wolf. When they undertook to build a city, the future Rome, the omens gave preference to Romulus, and he began to lay the foundations. Remus, in ridicule, leapt over them. This angered Romulus, who slew his brother. He then gathered fugitives and criminals in his city, and conquered the Sabines, who then came to live in Rome; and their king, Tatius, shared sovereignty with Romulus. The latter was deified and identified with Quirinus.

Rubicon: a small river rising in the Apennines and flowing into the Adriatic; it separated Italy from Cisalpine Gaul. By crossing it with an army and thus overstepping the boundaries of his province, Julius *Caesar committed himself to war against the Senate and *Pompey.

Sabines: an ancient people of Italy, whose lands were in the neighbourhood of Rome. They are celebrated in legend as having taken up arms against the Romans, to avenge the carrying off of their women by the latter at a spectacle to which they had been invited. Subsequently they are said to have made peace and migrated to Rome, where they settled with their new allies.

Salamis: an island separated by a narrow channel from the SW coast of Attica, near the Piraeus. It was for long a subject of contention between the Megarians and the Athenians, but was finally conquered by the latter as the result of a stirring appeal by *Solon. The adjoining sea was the scene of the great naval battle in 480 BC, in which the fleet of *Xerxes was defeated by the Greeks.

Sappho: a Greek lyric poetess, born in Lesbos probably about the middle of the 7th c. BC.

satrap: the title held by Persian provincial governors.

Saturn: an ancient Roman god of agriculture, subsequently identified with *Cronos.

satyr: in Greek mythology, one of a class of woodland spirits, in form partly human, partly bestial, supposed to be the companion of *Dionysus.

Sceptic: in philosophy, originally a follower of the school of *Pyrrho. He inferred from the contradictions presented by the evidence of the senses and the operations of the mind that knowledge of the nature of things is unattainable. Hence the proper attitude is one of suspension of judgement, mental quietude, and indifference to outward things.

Scipio (*c.*236–*c.*183 BC): (Africanus Major, Publius Cornelius), the conqueror of Spain, and of *Hannibal at the battle of Zama, and one of the greatest of the Romans.

Scylla: a nymph loved by *Poseidon, or according to *Ovid by Glaucus, one of the deities of the sea.

Senate: at Rome, may have originated in Roma Quadrata, before there was a king of Rome. Later it was the king's council. During republican times, it was at first a purely *patrician body, but *plebeians were constantly admitted to it during the 4th c. BC, and it became in practice an assembly of ex-magistrates. Nominations to it, at first made by the *consuls, were made from the latter part of the 4th c. by the *censors.

Seneca, Lucius Annaeus: the philosopher who was born at Corduba in Spain a few years before the Christian era and who died in AD 65. He was tutor to the young Nero and became one of Nero's chief advisers when Nero was emperor. He was accused of participating in a conspiracy and was ordered to take his own life, which he did.

sibyls: certain inspired women said to have lived in various parts of the ancient world, at Cumae, Delphi, Erythrae in Ionia, etc. The best known is the Cumaean (sometimes identified with the Erythraean) sibyl, Herophile by name, who was beloved by *Apollo.

sirens: fabulous creatures, two or three in number, who had the power of luring men to destruction by their song. Their names, according to one story, were Parthenope, Ligeia, and Leucosia, and they lived on an island off the SW coast of Italy. *Odysseus, informed of the power of their voices by *Circe, when passing by this point stopped the ears of his companions with wax and caused himself to be tied to the mast of the ship, and so passed them in safety. They also attempted to beguile the *Argonauts, but *Orpheus surpassed them in song.

Sisyphus: a legendary king of Corinth, famous for his cunning, who outwitted *Autolycus. When the latter stole his neighbours' cattle, Sisyphus, who mistrusted him, was able to pick out his own, having marked them under the feet. After his death, Sisyphus, on account of his misdeeds, was condemned in hell to roll to the top of a hill a large stone, which, when it reached the summit, rolled back to the plain, so that his punishment was eternal.

Socrates (469–399 BC): the great Greek philosopher, born near Athens. He served with credit in the army, saving the life of *Alcibiades at Potidaea (432 BC). Later in life he held public office and showed great moral courage in resisting illegalities. He was married to Xanthippe, who had a reputation as a scold. He occupied his life with oral instruction, frequenting public places and conversing with all and sundry, seeking the truth, and the exposure of pride and error. In consequence he incurred the malevolence of those who pretended to wisdom, was attacked by *Aristophanes, and finally accused of impiety, condemned by a narrow majority of the judges, and sentenced to death (by drinking hemlock). Socrates wrote nothing, but the general method and tendency of his teaching are preserved in the Dialogues of *Plato. The following appear to have been prominent features in his teaching: 1. the view that it is the duty of philosophy to investigate not physical phenomena, but ethical questions, how men should live and act; 2. the view that virtue is knowledge; no one is willingly wicked, for happiness lies in virtue; if a man is wicked, it is from ignorance. Socrates' concern was therefore to discover what the good is. The question of moral intentions was with him secondary. The

Socratic method of instruction was by questions aptly proposed so as to arrive at the conclusion he wished to convey.

Solon (*c*.638–558 BC): the great Athenian legislator, celebrated for his wisdom.

sophist: originally meaning one learned in some art or craft, then a wise man generally. Later, from the middle of the 5th c., the term was applied especially to persons who gave lessons for money in rhetoric, politics, and mathematics. They were useful in popularizing knowledge; but as time went on, they gave increasing importance to rhetoric, to the form of expression, rather than to the substance of knowledge. For this they were condemned by *Socrates and *Plato, and the term came to mean a quibbler.

Sophocles (496–406 BC): one of the three great Attic tragedians, who was born at Colonus near Athens. His first victory as a tragic poet was in 468 BC, when he won the prize against *Aeschylus. After this he was the favourite poet of the Athenians. He was the first to increase the number of actors from two to three.

Spartacus: Thracian gladiator who led a revolt against the Romans, starting in 73 BC.

Stoics: a school of Greek philosophers, founded by *Zeno of Citium about 310 BC, which derives its name from the fact that Zeno taught under the *Stoa Poikile* or 'Painted Portico' of Athens. Though the Stoic doctrine embraced a complete philosophical system, its chief importance lies on the moral side. It held that happiness consists in liberation from the bondage of the passions and appetites, and in approximation to God by obeying his will; that virtue is thus the highest good, and suffering a matter of indifference.

Styx: a gloomy river, a river of *Hades or the lower world, over which the shades of the departed were ferried by *Charon, and by which the gods swore their most solemn oaths.

Suetonius (*c*.70–*c*.160 AD): (Gaius Suetonius Tranquillus), Roman historian, friend of the younger *Pliny, and author of *Lives of the Caesars*.

Syrinx: in Greek mythology, an Arcadian damsel, who, being pursued by *Pan, threw herself into the river Ladon, where she was changed into a reed. Of this Pan made his pipe.

Tacitus Gaius(?) Cornelius (*c*.55–*c*.117 AD): the Roman historian.

Tantalus: in Greek mythology, the father of *Pelops and *Niobe. He is represented as punished in hell with an intense thirst and placed up to the chin in a pool of water which recedes when he attempts to drink it, while a bough laden with fruit hangs above his head but withdraws from his hand.

Tarquins: Tarquinius Priscus and Tarquinius Superbus (6th c. BC), the fifth and seventh legendary kings of Rome, of Etruscan origin. The former reigned with moderation and popularity, but the second, his son, was noted for his tyranny and arrogance. The Romans, provoked by his oppression, rose in rebellion and expelled the family from Rome.

Tartarus: *see* **Hades.**

Telemachus: a son of *Odysseus and *Penelope, who was still a child when his father went to the Trojan War (*see* Troy). When Odysseus did not return Telemachus went to seek him accompanied by *Athene in the guise of Mentor, and visited *Nestor and *Menelaus to obtain information.

Terpander: the father of Greek music, who probably flourished in the first half of the 7th c. BC. He is said to have made the lyre from a four-stringed into a seven-stringed instrument, and to have founded at Sparta the first Greek school of music.

Terpsichore: the *Muse who presided over dancing.

Tethys: in Greek mythology, one of the deities of the sea, daughter of *Uranus and *Gaea, the wife of *Oceanus. She was regarded as the mother of the chief rivers of the earth, and her daughters were known as the Oceanides (*see* nymphs).

Thebes: the capital of Boeotia in Greece, supposed to have been founded by *Cadmus, and the scene of the legend of *Oedipus.

Themis: in Greek mythology, a *Titaness and the mother of *Prometheus; later the personification of justice.

Theocritus: a great Greek pastoral poet, a native of Syracuse, who lived in the 3rd c. BC.

Thermopylae: a narrow pass between mountain and sea leading from Thessaly into Locris and Phocis, celebrated for the battle fought there in 480 BC, when 6000 Greeks including 300 Spartans under Leonidas, for three successive days, resisted the vast army of the Persians under *Xerxes.

Theseus: a son of *Poseidon, or, according to a later legend, of *Aegeus, king of Athens, by Aethra. He achieved many great feats including the destruction of the *Minotaur. He later ascended the throne of Athens, overcame the *Amazons, and carried off their queen, Hippolyta. He also descended to the infernal regions to carry away *Persephone, but *Pluto defeated him, and Theseus suffered a long imprisonment in *Hades until released by *Hercules.

Thespis: a Greek poet of Attica, who lived in the 6th c. BC. He is important in the history of tragedy, for he gave it a dramatic character by introducing an actor, who replied to the leader of the chorus. *Horace records a tradition that Thespis was a strolling player who travelled about with a wagon as temporary stage.

Thetis: one of the sea deities, who became the wife of Peleus.

Thucydides: the great Athenian historian, who was born about 460 BC and died about the end of the 5th c. BC.

Tiberius: born 42 BC, Roman emperor AD 14–37.

Timon: of Athens. A semi-legendary character, a famous misanthrope. He seems to have lived in the time of *Pericles.

Tiresias: a Theban soothsayer, who was struck with blindness in his youth for reasons variously given, one that he had seen *Athene bathing. As some compensation, he was given the power of prophecy, and a staff which guided his footsteps.

Titans: the sons and daughters of *Uranus and *Gaea. They included *Cronos (Saturn), *Rhea, *Oceanus, *Tethys, and Hyperion. The legend says that Uranus had thrown his elder sons into *Tartarus, and that Gaea incited the Titans to rise against him. This they did, deposed Uranus, and raised Cronos to the throne.

Trajan: (Marcus Ulpius Trajanus), Roman emperor AD 98–117, of Spanish birth, a great soldier, simple and unassuming, conqueror of the Dacians, whose territory he constituted a Roman province.

Triton: a sea deity, son of *Poseidon (Neptune) and Amphitrite.

Troilus: son of *Priam.

Trojan horse: the artifice by which the Greeks got possession of *Troy. They constructed a large wooden horse and filled it with armed men, and then withdrew their forces from the neighbourhood as if returning home. Sinon, son of *Sisyphus, allowed himself to be taken prisoner by the Trojans, pretending to have been maltreated by the Greeks, and persuaded *Priam to have the horse drawn into the city, on the ground that it was an offering to *Athene and would render Troy impregnable. When the horse was within the walls, Sinon, at dead of night, released the armed men, who made themselves masters of the city.

Troy: or *Ilium*, a city that stood near the Hellespont and the river Scamander in the NW of Asia Minor. According to legend, as related by *Homer in his *Iliad*, Troy was the capital of King *Priam, which was for ten years besieged by the Greeks in their endeavour to recover *Helen.

Uranus: in Greek mythology, the personification of the sky, the most ancient of the Greek gods and the first ruler of the universe. He married *Gaea, the earth, and was father of the *Titans.

Venus: identified with the *Aphrodite of the Greeks and the Astarte of the Syrians, Venus was the Roman name for the goddess of beauty and love.

Vespasian: (Titus Flavius Sabinus Vespasianus), Roman emperor AD 70–9. He was remarkable for the simplicity of his mode of life and the economy and efficiency of his administration. Among his public works at Rome were the Colosseum (completed by Titus or Domitian).

Vesta: akin to the Greek goddess *Hestia. She was worshipped by the Romans in every household as the goddess of the hearth.

vestals: in Roman religion, were virgins who represented the king's daughters of the regal period, and were charged with the preservation of the fire in the Temple of Vesta, the State hearth.

via Appia: the first of the great Roman roads, built by Appius Claudius

Caecus in his censorship (*see* censors) of 312 BC. It ran from Rome to Capua. It was by the Appian Way that St Paul entered Rome.

Virgil (70–19 BC): (Publius Vergilius Maro), the Roman poet, born at Andes, a village near Mantua. His chief works were the *Aeneid*, the epic poem of the Roman people; the *Georgics*; and the *Eclogues* or *Bucolics*.

Vulcan: or *Mulciber*. Vulcan was the Roman equivalent of the Greek god *Hephaestus.

Vulgate: Latin version of the Bible.

Xanthippe: the wife of *Socrates.

Xanthippus: father of *Pericles. He commanded the Athenian fleet after *Salamis and at Mycale.

Xenophon (c.430–c.355 BC): an Athenian writer, who was, when young, a pupil of *Socrates. He joined the Greek contingent raised by the younger Cyrus in 401 for his war with Artaxerxes, and was later elected one of the generals of the Greek force. Among his principal writings is *Anabasis*, or history of the expedition of the younger Cyrus and the retreat of the Greeks. It is in this that the Ten Thousand cry *Thalassa! Thalassa!* ('The sea! The sea!'), when from the summit of Mt. Theches they first see the Euxine after their wanderings in Asia Minor.

Xerxes: king of Persia between 485 and 465 BC. He bridged the Hellespont with boats and invaded Greece, but was defeated at *Salamis in 480 BC.

Zeno: of Citium in Cyprus. He was the founder of the *Stoic school of philosophy.

Zeus: the greatest of the Greek gods, in whom the myths of many different parts of the Greek world centred. The Roman god *Jupiter was identified with him, and the Greek myths were transferred to Jupiter. According to *Hesiod, Zeus was the son of *Cronos and *Rhea. He was regarded as the king and father of gods and men.

FAMOUS WRITERS AND THEIR WORKS

* indicates a separate entry

ADDISON, Joseph (1672–1719): educated at Charterhouse and Oxford, Addison was a distinguished classical scholar whose time as an MP from 1708 until his death included several government posts. He is best known for his contributions to the *Tatler*, founded in 1709 by his lifelong friend Richard Steele, *The Guardian*, and *The Spectator*, which he and Steele ran between 1711 and 1712. Addison's prose was acclaimed by Dr *Johnson as 'the model of the middle style; on grave subjects not formal, on light occasions not groveling . . .'. He was described as 'The First Victorian', and one of his most original and influential contributions to the history of literary taste was his reassessment of the popular ballad.

ALBEE, Edward (1928–): American playwright whose explorations of sexual fantasy, frustration, and domestic anguish recall the plays of T. *Williams. His plays include *Who's Afraid of Virginia Woolf?* (1962), *Tiny Alice* (1965), and *A Delicate Balance* (1966).

ALCOTT, Louisa M(ay) (1832–88): born in Pennsylvania, USA, Louisa Alcott was a friend of *Emerson and *Thoreau. From an early age she published sketches, stories, etc., to help support her father and family. She achieved fame and financial security with *Little Women* (1868–9), one of the most popular juvenile novels ever written, which was followed by several other similar works. She also wrote sensational novels and straight adult novels.

AMIS, Kingsley (1922–): educated at the City of London School and Oxford, Amis lectured first in Swansea, then at Cambridge (1949–63). He published volumes of poetry and achieved popular success with his first novel, *Lucky Jim* (1954). Its hero, lower-middle-class radical lecturer Jim Dixon, was full of subversive attitudes, which resulted in Amis being hailed as one of the 'angry young men', a journalistic catch-phrase of the time which was loosely applied to a number of playwrights and novelists of the mid 1950s. Its setting in a provincial university was also indicative of a new development in fiction (see Cooper, W., Larkin, and Braine), a movement that Amis confirmed in *That Uncertain Feeling* (1955) and *Take a Girl Like You* (1960). His other novels include *I Like it Here* (1958), *One Fat Englishman* (1963), *Ending Up* (1974), and *Jake's Thing* (1978). His enthusiasm for Ian *Fleming's works expressed itself in two novels, *The James Bond*

Dossier (1965) and *Colonel Sun* (1968), published under the pseudonym of Robert Markham.

ANDERSEN, Hans Christian (1805–75): Danish writer, born in Odense, Andersen's earliest ambitions were theatrical. His fairy stories were published in Danish from 1835 onwards and first appeared in English in 1846. Deeply rooted in Danish folklore, these stories were also shaped by Andersen's own psychological experiences and his at times morbidly acute sensitivity. Among his admirers were *Dickens and Elizabeth Barrett *Browning.

ANDERSON, Sherwood (1876–1941): born in Ohio, USA, Anderson first made his name as a leading naturalistic writer with his third book, *Winesburg, Ohio* (1919), a collection of short stories illustrating life in a small town. He published several other collections and a number of novels including the semi-autobiographical *Tar: A Midwest Childhood*.

ANOUILH, Jean (1910–): French dramatist, whose works include *Antigone* (1944; English tr., 1946), *L'Invitation au château* (1947; *Ring Round the Moon*, 1950), *La Valse des toréadors* (1952; *The Waltz of the Toreadors*, 1956), and a number of plays dealing with historical figures like Joan of Arc and Robespierre.

ARNOLD, Matthew (1822–88): eldest son of Thomas Arnold, the headmaster of Rugby (1828–42) who had such a profound and lasting influence on the public school system, Matthew Arnold was educated at Rugby, Winchester, and Oxford. He became a fellow of Oriel College and later the professor of poetry at Oxford, and for 35 years served as an inspector of schools (1851–86). His first volume of poems was published in 1849 and was followed by several others. But in his maturity he turned increasingly to prose, writing essays on literary, educational, and social topics that established him as the leading critic of the day and which greatly influenced writers as diverse as T. S. *Eliot, F. R. Leavis, and Raymond Williams.

AUDEN, W(ystan) H(ugh) (1907–73): educated at Gresham's School, Holt and Oxford, Auden began early on to explore the means of preserving 'private spheres' (through poetry) in 'public chaos'. Among his contemporaries, who were to share some of his left-wing near-Marxist response to the public chaos of the 1930s, were *MacNeice, *Day-Lewis, and *Spender, and they, as a group, became nicknamed the Pylon Poets, an allusion to some of the rather self-conscious use of industrial imagery in their work. His first volume, *Poems*, appeared in 1930; it was well received and established him as the most talented voice of his generation. During the 1930s he wrote a number of plays, some of them, including *The Ascent of F6* (1936), in collaboration with *Isherwood; and Benjamin Britten set many of his poems to music and later used his text for the opera *Paul Bunyan*. Auden also collaborated with MacNeice on *Letters from Iceland* (1937) and with Isherwood on *Journey to a War* (1939). In January 1939 he and Isherwood left

Europe for America (he became a US citizen in 1946) where he published *Another Time* (1940), which contained many of his most famous poems. Later, his work became increasingly Christian in tone, perhaps not unconnected with the death of his devout Anglo-Catholic mother in 1941.

Auden's absence during the war led to a poor reception of his works in England at that period, but the high quality of his later work reinstated him as an unquestionably major poet, and in 1956 he was elected professor of poetry at Oxford. His major later collections include *Nones* (1951, NY; 1952, London); *The Shield of Achilles* (1955), which is considered by many his best single volume; and *Homage to Clio* (1960). He also edited many anthologies and collections, wrote several books of prose criticism, and a number of librettos, notably for Stravinsky's *The Rake's Progress*. His influence on a succeeding generation of poets was incalculable, comparable only with that, a generation earlier, of *Yeats.

AUSTEN, Jane (1775–1817): born in the rectory at Steventon, Hampshire, she was the sixth child in a family of seven. Her father, the Revd George Austen, encouraged her both in her reading and her writing and as a child and a young woman she read widely. Her life was uneventful, but lived in the midst of a lively and affectionate family. She never married.

The Juvenilia, written in her early and mid teens, are already incisive and elegantly expressed. The youthful sketch *Elinor and Marianne* (1795–6) was rewritten in 1797–8 as *Sense and Sensibility*, revised again in 1809 and finally published in 1811. *First Impressions*, written in 1797, was refused without being read by the publisher Cadell. In 1809 it was re-created, renamed *Pride and Prejudice*, and published in 1813. *Northanger Abbey*, written in 1798–9, was sold for £10 in 1803 to a firm who never issued it, and it was finally published posthumously in 1818. Her last three completed novels, *Mansfield Park* (1814), *Emma* (1816), and *Persuasion* (1818), are known to have been written in the busy parlour at Chawton, where the family had moved to in 1809. When she died of Addison's disease she was working on *Sanditon*. *The Watsons*, which she had started in 1804 but abandoned the following year when her father died, also remained unfinished. The novels were generally well received from publication onwards, though both C. *Brontë and E. B. *Browning found her limited, and it was not until the publication of J. E. Austen's *Memoir* in 1870 that a Jane Austen cult began to develop. Since then her reputation has remained consistently high, though with significant shifts of emphasis.

BACON, Francis, first Baron Verulam and Viscount St Albans (1561–1626): Bacon was born in London and educated at Cambridge. He became a barrister in 1582 and was elected to Parliament in 1584. He subsequently held several important appointments, but in 1621 he admitted his guilt when charged with taking bribes as a judge, and retired from public life.

Bacon's writings are of many different kinds, the largest and most influential being philosophical in a broad sense of the term. He saw this as all forming part of a massive system, never to be completed, called *The Great Instauration*. His other works include *New Atlantis* (1627), which describes a Utopian community; various editions of *Essays*; *Maxims of the Law* (1597), in which he sketches his fundamental legal principles; and his *History of Henry VII* (1622). This last is not original so far as its raw material is concerned, but inaugurates a new era in being a genuinely explanatory account of its subject and not a mere chronicle.

BALDWIN, James (1924–   ): a Black American writer, Baldwin's first novel, *Go Tell it on the Mountain* (1953), set in Harlem where he was born, was followed by several on a more international scale, dealing with both homosexuality and the situation of American Blacks. He has also written short stories, political and autobiographical essays, and plays.

BALLANTYNE, R(obert) M(ichael) (1825–94): after working in the Hudson's Bay Company, Ballantyne returned to London and worked for Constable's printing firm. In 1856 he published his first adventure story, *Snowflakes and Sunbeams; or the Young Fair Traders*. After the success of *The Coral Island* in 1857 he became an extremely successful professional writer of stories for boys, writing over 80 novels. Among his best-known works are *The Gorilla Hunters* (1862) and *Black Ivory* (1873).

BALZAC, Honoré de (1799–1850): French novelist, author of the great series of co-ordinated and interconnected novels and stories known collectively as the *Comédie humaine*. The 91 separate completed works—137 were planned—that make up the whole were written between 1827 and 1847. His grand design was to give an authentic and comprehensive fictional representation of French society in the latter years of the 18th c. and the first half of the 19th c. The novels were classified under three main heads: 1. *Études de mœurs* (by far the largest category, subdivided into those dealing with private, provincial, and country life, Paris, military matters, and politics); 2. *Études philosophiques*; 3. *Études analytiques*. The cast of the *Comédie humaine* comprises more than 2000 characters, and the vitality of Balzac's creations and the breadth of his vision have led some (H. *James among them) to regard him as the greatest of novelists. His influence on later fiction has been immense, and his work is an essential reference-point in the history of the European novel.

BARNES, Djuna (1892–1982): a novelist, illustrator, short-story writer, and playwright, Djuna Barnes was an American born in Cornwall-on-Hudson. She is best remembered for *Nightwood* (1936), a novel which T. S. *Eliot described in his preface as one possessing 'a quality of horror and doom very nearly related to that of Elizabethan tragedy'.

BARRIE, Sir J(ames) M(atthew) (1860–1937): born in Kirriemuir, Scotland, Barrie began work with the *Nottinghamshire Journal*, an experience described in *When a Man's Single* (1888). There followed a number of stories and novels, and his first play, *Richard Savage*, was performed in London in 1891. This was followed in 1901 by his sentimental comedy, *Quality Street*, and in 1902 by the enduring successful play, *The Admirable Crichton. Peter Pan*, his internationally and abidingly famous children's play, grew from stories he had made up for the five sons of some friends, and was first performed in 1904. A book of the play was published in 1911. His other successful plays included *What Every Woman Knows* (1906) and *Dear Brutus* (1917).

BAUDELAIRE, Charles (1821–67): the French poet, whose *Les Fleurs du mal* (1857), a series of 101 exquisitely crafted lyrics in a variety of metres, including many sonnets, is one of the great collections of French verse. On its publication in 1857 Baudelaire was fined and six of the poems were banned from subsequent editions as offensive to public morals. He also wrote a number of prose works and his reputation as a critic, which has increased steadily since his death, is now firmly established.

BEAUMONT, Sir Francis (1584–1616): educated at Oxford, though he took no degree, Beaumont collaborated with *Fletcher in dramatic works from about 1606 to 1613. His earliest known play, *The Woman Hater*, was probably performed in 1605, published 1607: recent linguistic analysis assigns some scenes in this to Fletcher, whereas *The Knight of the Burning Pestle* (?1607) is now generally considered to be Beaumont's alone. Beaumont retired *c.*1613, when he married profitably and moved to Kent.

BECKETT, Samuel (1906–): born at Foxrock, near Dublin, Beckett was educated at Portora Royal School, Enniskillen, and at Trinity College, Dublin. He went to Paris, where he met and formed a lasting relationship with *Joyce, and after some years of wandering finally settled in France. His first published work was an essay on Joyce (1929), which was followed by a study of *Proust, short stories, and several novels, which included *Murphy* (1938) and *Watt* (1953). Both these last were written in English but his trilogy, *Molloy* (1951), *Malone Meurt* (1951; Beckett's own English version, *Malone Dies*, 1958), and *L'Innommable* (1953; *The Unnameable*, 1960), was originally written in French. Beckett's highly distinctive, despairing, yet curiously exhilarating voice reached a wide audience and public acclaim with the Paris performance in 1953 of *En attendant Godot* (pub. 1952). The English version, *Waiting for Godot* (1955), also made a great impact, and was followed by several other plays, including *Fin de parti* (English version, *Endgame*, pub. 1958); *Krapp's Last Tape* (1958, pub. 1959); and *Happy Days* (1961, pub. 1961).

From the time of *Waiting for Godot* Beckett became widely known as a playwright associated with The Theatre of the Absurd, the term used to characterize the work of a number of dramatists during the 1950s and early 1960s. As the term suggests, the function of such theatre is to give dramatic expression to the philosophical notion of the 'absurd', a notion that had received widespread diffusion following the publication of *Camus's essay *Le Mythe de Sisyphe* in 1942. To define the world as absurd is to recognize its fundamentally mysterious and indecipherable nature, and this recognition is frequently associated with feelings of loss, purposelessness, and bewilderment. To such feelings, the Theatre of the Absurd gives ample expression, and its use of the stage and of dramatic narrative and symbolism revolutionized drama in England and deeply influenced later playwrights like *Pinter and *Stoppard.

BEHAN, Brendan (1923–64): born in Dublin, the son of a house-painter, Behan wrote a number of plays, the best known being *Borstal Boy* (1958), *The Hostage* (1958), and *The Quare Fellow* (1959).

BELLOC, Hilaire (1870–1953): born in France, of part-French Catholic ancestry, and educated at the Oratory School and Oxford, Belloc was Liberal MP for Salford from 1906 to 1909 and again in 1910. He became a prolific and versatile writer of poetry and verse, essays, biography, travel, literary criticism, and novels. His books attacking and satirizing Edwardian society (some with G. K. *Chesterton) include *Pongo and the Bull* (1910) and *The Servile State* (1912). His many biographies include *Danton* (1899), *Cromwell* (1927) and *Charles II* (1940), and he also wrote a substantial *History of England* (1915). *The Cruise of the Nona* (1925), the most intimate of his books, contains many of his personal reflections. His verse collections include *Cautionary Tales* (1907) and *Sonnets and Verses* (1923), and amongst his novels *Mr Clutterbuck's Election* (1908), *The Girondin* (1911), *The Green Overcoat* (1912), and *Belinda* (1928) are amongst the best regarded.

BELLOW, Saul (1915–): born in Canada of Russian-Jewish parents, and educated from the age of 9 in Chicago, Bellow has written a number of highly acclaimed novels which include *Dangling Man* (1944), *The Victim* (1947), *The Adventures of Augie March* (1953), *Seize the Day* (1956), *Henderson the Rain King* (1959), *Herzog* (1964), *Dr Sammler's Planet* (1969), and *Humbolt's Gift* (1974). He has also written short stories and a play (*The Last Analysis*, 1964), and was awarded the Nobel Prize for Literature in 1976.

BENTLEY, Edmund Clerihew (1875–1956): educated at St Paul's, where he became a lifelong friend of *Chesterton, and Oxford, Bentley was called to the Bar, but then became a journalist. In *Biography for Beginners* (1905) he invented the wittily absurd verse-form called after his second name, and in *Trent's Last Case* (1913) he produced the prototype of the modern detective novel.

BETJEMAN, Sir John (1906–1984): born in Highgate and educated at Marlborough and Oxford, where he became friendly with *Auden and *MacNeice but left without a degree, Betjeman began writing, for the *Architectural Review*, in 1931. His first collection of verse, *Mount Zion*, appeared the same year, and was followed by a number of others, with his highly successful *Collected Poems* being published in 1958 and expanded in 1962. In 1960 he published his blank-verse autobiography, *Summoned by Bells*, which covers his boyhood and life at Oxford, and this was followed by two more volumes of verse. Betjeman writes of his 'topographical predilection' for 'suburbs and gaslights and Pont Street and Gothic Revival Churches and mineral railways, provincial towns and garden cities', a predilection also displayed in his editing and writing of Shell Guides and various works on architecture. His poetry, which has reached an unusually wide public (while numbering *Auden and *Larkin among its advocates), is predominantly witty, urbane, satiric, and light of touch, a comedy of manners, place-names, and contemporary allusions, but many have commented on the underlying melancholy, the chill of fear, the religion which dwells more on hope than faith. He was appointed Poet Laureate in 1972.

BINYON, Laurence (1869–1935): educated at St Paul's and Oxford, Binyon published many works on art, *Painting in the Far East* (1908) being the best known. He wrote several plays and his war poems include his much anthologized 'For the Fallen' ('... They shall grow not old, as we that are left grow old ...'). His other works included two long odes, *The Sirens* (1924) and *The Idols* (1928), *Collected Poems* (1931), and *Landscape in English Art and Poetry* (1931).

BLACKMORE, R(ichard) D(odderidge) (1825–1900): educated at Blundell's and at Oxford, Blackmore published several volumes of poems, translations, and 14 novels, his fame resting almost entirely on one of them, *Lorna Doone* (1869).

BLAKE, William (1757–1827): the third son of a London hosier, Blake did not go to school but was apprenticed to an engraver and then became a student at the Royal Academy, and from 1779 he was employed as an engraver. He engraved and published his *Songs of Innocence* in 1789, and also *The Book of Thel*, both works which manifest the early phases of his highly distinctive mystic vision, and in which he embarks on the evolution of his personal mythology. *The Book of Thel* heralds the increasing complexity of his writings, which include his principal prose work, *The Marriage of Heaven and Hell* (engraved *c.*1790–3), and several revolutionary volumes in which he develops his attitude of revolt against authority, combining political fervour and visionary ecstasy. By this time Blake had already established his poetic range, and he was once more to demonstrate his command of the lyric in *Songs of Experience* (1794), which includes 'Tyger! Tyger! burning bright', 'O Rose thou art sick', and others of his more accessible pieces.

In 1800 Blake moved to Felpham, Sussex, where he worked for his friend and patron William Hayley. After three years he returned to London to work on *Milton*, one of his longest and most complex mythological works, which is prefaced by his well-known lines 'And did those feet in ancient time', commonly known as 'Jerusalem'; and on *Jerusalem: the Emanation of the Giant Albion* (written and etched between 1804 and 1820). His last years were passed in obscurity, although he continued to attract the interest and admiration of younger artists, and a commission in 1821 produced his well-known illustrations for the Book of Job, published in 1826. At his death, general opinion held that he had been, if gifted, insane, but his later admirers included *Swinburne and *Yeats, and the 20th c. has seen an enormous increase in interest.

BLIXEN, Karen, *née* Dinesen (1885–1962): a Danish writer who wrote mainly in English, under the name of 'Isak Dinesen', Karen Blixen is best known for her first major publication *Seven Gothic Tales* (1934), a collection of stories, and for *Out of Africa* (1937), which recounts her life on a Kenyan coffee plantation.

BLUNDEN, Edmund (1896–1974): educated at Christ's Hospital and Oxford, Blunden was born in London but his family moved soon after to Kent, the countryside of which was to become one of the chief subjects of his poetry. He served in the trenches during the 1914–18 war and later wrote poems, such as 'Third Ypres' and 'Report on Experience', which have come to be regarded as among the best of their kind. In 1920 he published a small edition of MS poems of *Clare, whose work he rescued from obscurity, and his own volumes, largely on rural life, included *The Waggoner* (1920), *The Shepherd* (1922), and *English Poems* (1925), while his first *Collected Poems* appeared in 1930. His best-known work is *Undertones of War* (1928), in which he describes the double destruction of man and nature in Flanders. He also wrote a number of biographies. He was appointed professor of poetry at Oxford in 1966. Although heralded as a leader of the Georgians (see R. Brooke), Blunden belonged to no group. After many years in the making, his reputation stands high.

BLUNT, Wilfrid Scawen (1840–1922): poet, diplomat, traveller, anti-imperialist, and Arabist, Blunt's first volume of poetry, *Sonnets and Songs by Proteus* (1875, subsequently revised) passionately addresses various women. It was followed by several other volumes of verse, and he also wrote and agitated in support of Egyptian, Indian, and Irish independence.

BÖLL, Heinrich (1917–): German author of novels and short stories, mostly on the subject of wartime and post-war Germany. He is highly acclaimed for his realistic portrayal of the social problems of a country recovering from guilt and defeat, and in 1972 received the Nobel Prize for Literature.

BOND, Edward (1934–): a playwright whose dramas, which include *The*

Pope's Wedding (1962), *Saved* (1965), *The Fool* (1975, pub. 1976), and *Summer* (1982), are an outspoken indictment of capitalist society. His belief, that violence occurs in 'situations of injustice' and that it therefore flourishes as 'a cheap consumer commodity' under capitalism, continues to arouse extreme responses from critics and audiences.

BORGES, Jorge Luis (1899–1986): Argentine writer, born in Buenos Aires and educated (1914–18) in Geneva, Borges read English literature from an early age (notably the works of *Wilde, *De Quincey, R. L. *Stevenson, and *Chesterton). After some time in Spain he returned in 1921 to Argentina. His first volume of poetry, *Fervor de Buenos Aires* (1923), was followed by many other volumes of verse and essays, but he is best known for his short stories, of which the first volume, *Historia universal de la infamia* (1935; *A Universal History of Infamy*), has been acclaimed as a landmark in Latin American literature.

BOSWELL, James (1740–95): the eldest son of a Scottish judge, Boswell reluctantly studied law, his ambition being directed towards literature and politics, as was manifested by numerous pamphlets and verses which he published anonymously from 1760 onwards. He was in London in 1762–3, where he met Dr *Johnson on 16 May 1763. They made their celebrated tour of Scotland and the Hebrides in 1773 and Boswell's *Journal of a Tour of the Hebrides* was published in 1785. His last meeting with Johnson was in 1784, and his *Life of Samuel Johnson*, the most celebrated biography in the English language, appeared in 1791. His portrait is vivid and intimate, in his own words a 'Flemish picture' made up of trifling incidents as well as significant events.

BOWDLER, Thomas (1754–1825): an MD of Edinburgh, Bowdler published in 1818 his *Family Shakespeare*. As is shown by his Prefaces, his love and admiration of Shakespeare were profound; nevertheless, he believed that nothing 'can afford an excuse for profaneness or obscenity; and if these could be obliterated, the transcendent genius of the poet would undoubtedly shine with more unclouded lustre'. His method was to cut, not to substitute, and the cutting was severe. Bowdler's work was extremely successful and went through many editions. With the verb 'to bowdlerize', or expurgate, he joins the small band of those who have given their names to the language.

BOWEN, Elizabeth (1899–1973): Anglo-Irish novelist and short-story writer who was born in Dublin, Elizabeth Bowen spent much of her childhood in Co. Cork. Probably her best-known novels are *The Death of the Heart* (1938) and *The Heat of the Day* (1949). The war inspired many of her best short stories and her *Collected Stories* were published in 1980.

BRAINE, John (1922–): novelist, born and educated in Bradford, Braine's first novel, *Room at the Top* (1957), was an instant success. Its hero, Joe Lampton, was hailed as another of the provincial 'angry young men' (see Kingsley Amis) of the 1950s, and *Life at the Top* (1962) continues the story of his success and disillusion. Braine's later novels express his increasing hostility to the radical views with which he was once identified.

BRECHT, Bertolt (1898–1956): German dramatist and poet, Brecht emigrated to the United States and then settled in 1949 in East Berlin. *Die Dreigroschenoper* (*The Threepenny Opera*, 1928), his version of *The Beggar's Opera*, was one of the theatrical successes of Weimar Germany. His other plays include *Mutter Courage* (*Mother Courage*, 1941) and *Der kaukasiche Kreidekreis* (*The Caucasian Chalk Circle*, 1948), and these illustrate that he regarded a play as a series of loosely connected scenes, where dramatic climaxes were dispensed with, and songs were used to comment on the action. They call for highly stylized acting and also illustrate his theory of drama, which discards the notion that drama should seek to create the illusion of reality. Some of Brecht's plays have a particularly direct anti-capitalist theme, and others, like *Der aufhaltsame Aufstieg des Arturo Ui* (*The Resistible Rise of Arturo Ui*, 1941), combine this with the theme of Hitlerism. His didactic plays of the period around 1930 are closely connected with the interests of the Communist Party, but he was never a member and his relations with it, even in his last years in East Berlin, became rather uncertain. British playwrights of the 1960s, particularly *Bond and Arden, are clearly influenced by Brecht's radical approach, in theme and treatment, to drama. Brecht was also an outstanding lyric poet.

BRIDGES, Robert (1844–1930): educated at Eton and Oxford, Bridges afterwards studied medicine and he continued to practise until 1881. At Oxford he met G. M. *Hopkins, who became a close and influential friend, and whose complete poems Bridges eventually published in 1918. Bridges' first book, *Poems*, was published in 1873. Further volumes followed over many years, and his lyric verse has been much anthologized. Some of it (including 'London', 'A Passer-by', 'Asian Birds', and 'A Dead Child') has become widely known. He was much interested in the musical setting of words, and wrote the words for four works by the British composer Sir Hubert Parry. His collected prose works, mostly on poets and various literary topics, were published between 1927 and 1936. Though still respected, Bridges' general reputation does not stand as high as it once did.

BRONTË, Anne (1820–49): the youngest of the motherless family, Anne was the sister of Branwell, Charlotte, and Emily *Brontë. Her first novel, *Agnes Gray* (1847), appeared under the pseudonym Acton Bell, as did a selection of her poems, together with those of her sisters, in 1846. Her second novel, *The Tenant of Wildfell Hall*, appeared in 1848.

BRONTË, Charlotte (1816–55): daughter of Patrick Brontë, an Irishman, perpetual curate of Haworth, Yorkshire, from 1820 to his death in 1861; Charlotte Brontë's mother died in 1821, leaving five daughters and a son to the care of their aunt, Elizabeth Branwell. A period at a Clergy Daughters' School probably hastened the death of Charlotte's two elder sisters in 1825 and seriously impaired her own health, and the surviving children pursued their education at home. They read widely, and became involved in a rich fantasy life that owes much to their admiration of the *Arabian Nights*, of *Byron, and of Sir Walter *Scott. After a spell as a teacher and then a governess, Charlotte studied languages in Brussels with her sister Emily. A volume of verse entitled *Poems, by Currer, Ellis and Acton Bell* (the pseudonyms of Charlotte, Emily, and Anne) appeared in 1846, but did not sell and received little attention. By this time each had finished a novel. Charlotte's first, *The Professor*, never found a publisher in her lifetime, but her second, *Jane Eyre*, was published in 1847 and achieved immediate success. Through the tragic period when Branwell, Emily, and Anne all died within a year of each other she persevered with the composition of *Shirley*, which appeared in 1849, and this was followed by *Villette* (1853), both under the name of Currer Bell. In 1854 she married her father's curate but died a few months later. 'Emma', a fragment, was published in 1860 in the *Cornhill Magazine* with an introduction by *Thackeray, and many of her juvenile works have subsequently been published, adding to our knowledge of the intense creativity of her early years. She was the most admired of the Brontë sisters in her lifetime and her works continue to hold high popular and critical esteem.

BRONTË, Emily (1818–48): sister of Branwell, Charlotte, and Anne, Emily Brontë was educated largely at home, where she was particularly close to Anne, with whom she created the imaginary world of Gondal, the setting for many of her finest dramatic poems. She was for a time a governess and in 1847 went to Brussels with Charlotte to study languages, but returned when her aunt died and remained at Haworth for the rest of her brief life. In 1845 her poems were 'discovered' by Charlotte (or so Charlotte alleged), who projected a joint publication, *Poems, by Currer, Ellis and Acton Bell*, their three pseudonyms, published in 1846. *Wuthering Heights* was written between Oct. 1845 and June 1846, and published after some delay in 1847. It was met with more incomprehension than recognition, and it was only after Emily's death that it became widely acknowledged as a masterpiece. She is now established as much the most considerable poet of the three sisters, and one of the most original poets of the century, remembered for her lyrics (e.g. 'The night is darkening round me'), her passionate invocations from the world of Gondal ('Remembrance', 'The Prisoner'), and her apparently more personal visionary moments ('No coward soul is mine').

BROOKE, Rupert (1887–1915): educated at Rugby, where his father was a master, and at Cambridge, Brooke began to publish poems in journals in 1909, the year in which he settled at Grantchester (about which he later wrote his celebrated poem). *Poems 1911* was well received, but the following year he suffered a serious breakdown, and in 1913 he travelled widely. While in Tahiti he wrote 'Tiara Tahiti' and other poems, often thought to be among his best. His five 'War Sonnets', which included 'The Soldier' ('If I should die'), appeared early in 1915, and were ecstatically received and made him the nation's poet of war, a reputation further enhanced by the publication of *1914 and Other Poems* in 1915, after he had died of blood poisoning while serving in the RNVR.

Brooke's work in the first and second volumes of *Georgian Poetry*, edited by his friend Edward Marsh, was well received when they first appeared. This series, five in total, was planned by Brooke, H. Monro, and Marsh, and was published by Monro at the Poetry Bookshop between 1912 and 1922. The early volumes were widely influential and successful bringing a fresh vision and manner into the tired poetry of the time. Later volumes contained the work of *Blunden, *Sassoon, *Graves, and *Rosenberg. However, the poems of quality were few in the volumes of 1919 and 1922, several poets objected to being identified as 'Georgian', and the term began to acquire its present strong pejorative sense.

BROWNING, Elizabeth Barrett (1806–61): eldest of the twelve children of Edward Moulton Barrett, Elizabeth Barrett Browning spent her childhood at Hope End in Hertfordshire and was largely self-educated at home. In 1838 she became seriously ill and was sent to Torquay to live but returned to London, still an invalid, in 1841. In 1845 Robert *Browning began a correspondence with her which led to their meeting and eventually to their marriage, in Sept. 1846, after which they went to live in Italy. Their only child, a boy, was born in 1849. *The Seraphim, and Other Poems* (1838) was her first work to gain critical and public attention. Her next, *Poems* (1844), was so highly regarded that when *Wordsworth died in 1850 her name was widely canvassed as his most appropriate successor as Poet Laureate. It was followed by a number of other volumes, including her magnum opus, *Aurora Leigh* (1857), and *Last Poems*, issued posthumously in 1862, which contained some of her best-known lyrics. Throughout her married life her poetic reputation stood higher than Browning's in general contemporary opinion.

BROWNING, Robert (1812–89): the son of a clerk in the Bank of England, Browning received his education mainly in his father's large and eclectic library. His first published poem appeared anonymously in 1833 and attracted little notice. After his play, *Strafford*, was produced in 1837 he next published *Sordello* (1840), a narrative poem which had taken him over seven years to complete but whose hostile reception eclipsed his reputation for over 20 years. After his marriage to Elizabeth Barrett (see Browning, E. B.) in 1846 the couple eloped to Italy. In 1855 Browning published the masterpiece of his middle period, *Men and Women*, which, together with *Dramatis Personae* (1864), began to revive his reputation, a revival that was completed by the triumph of *The Ring and the Book* (1868–9). After the death of his wife in 1861 he returned to London where he continued to write. Fifteen volumes of his work were published between 1871 and 1889, and collections were issued in 1849, 1863, 1868, and 1888–9.

BUCHAN, John (1875–1940): first Baron Tweedsmuir, born in Perth and educated at Glasgow and Oxford, Buchan published his first novel, *Sir Quixote of the Moors* (1895), while still at University. He wrote many works of non-fiction, but is remembered for his adventure stories, the most popular of which include *The Thirty-nine Steps* (1915), *Greenmantle* (1916), *Mr Standfast* (1918), and *John Macnab* (1925).

BUNTING, Basil (1900–85): born in Northumberland, Bunting worked abroad for many years. Although he had a considerable reputation among younger American poets, he was virtually unknown in his own country until the appearance of his long, semi-autobiographical and deeply Northumbrian poem, *Briggflatts* (1966), which firmly established his presence. His *Collected Poems* were published in 1968.

BUNYAN, John (1628–88): born at Elstow, near Bedford, Bunyan learnt to read and write at the village school. After serving in the Parliamentary army he joined a Nonconformist church. In Nov. 1660 he was arrested for preaching without a licence and spent most of the next 12 years in gaol. During the first half of this period he wrote nine books and during the second half probably composed sections of *The Pilgrim's Progress*. The first part, written while again serving a short prison sentence in 1676, was published in 1678, and the second, together with the whole work, in 1684. His other principal works are *The Life and Death of Mr Badman* (1680) and *The Holy War* (1682).

BURGESS, Anthony (1917–): born in Manchester and educated at the university there, Burgess had a varied early career which included some years (1954–60) as an education officer in the colonial service in Malaya and Borneo. During this period he wrote his first three novels, set in the Far East, which were later published together as *The Malayan Trilogy* (1972). His many other works include *A Clockwork Orange* (1962), *Earthly Powers* (1980), and the comic trilogy about the gross and fitfully inspired poet Enderby (*Inside Mr Enderby*, 1963, under the pseudonym 'Joseph Kell'; *Enderby Outside*, 1968; *Clockwork Testament*, 1974). Burgess has also written critical works, screenplays, and television scripts, as well as many orchestral works.

BURNETT, Frances Hodgson (1849–1924): a prolific author, who wrote many novels and other books for adults, Frances Hodgson Burnett is now remembered for her work for children; in particular for the immensely successful (but much derided) *Little Lord Fauntleroy* (1886) and for *The Secret Garden* (1911).

BURNEY, Fanny (1752–1840): after publishing her first novel, *Evelina* (1778), anonymously, Fanny Burney achieved immediate fame when she was revealed as its author. It enjoyed huge success, numbering Dr *Johnson among its admirers, who preferred it to the work of *Fielding. She published *Cecilia* in 1782, and in 1786 was appointed second keeper of the robes to Queen Charlotte. In 1796 she published *Camilla.* These three major novels take as their theme the entry into the world of a young girl of beauty and understanding but no experience.

BURNS, Robert (1759–96): one of seven children born to a cottar near Alloway in Ayrshire, Burns was given a thorough education at the various schools he attended. He read voraciously and began to write occasional verses while still at school, though his spare time was fully employed on his father's ailing farm as labourer and ploughman. After his father's death in 1784 he and his brother continued to farm. To this period belong a number of well-known poems, including 'To a Mouse'. When they were published under the title *Poems, chiefly in the Scottish Dialect* (1786) they were an immediate success. After a second edition appeared the same year Burns started to collect old Scottish songs. He collected, amended, and wrote some 200, which include many of his best-known lyrics, such as 'Auld Lang Syne', 'O my luve's like a red, red rose', 'Ye Banks and Braes', and 'Scots wha hae'. In 1788 he married and settled on a poor farm, but then secured a post as an excise officer. In 1791, the year he published his last major poem, 'Tam o' Shanter', he relinquished his farming life with relief and moved to Dumfries. His work was much admired by his contemporaries, and his popularity with his fellow countrymen is still reflected by the celebrations held all over the world on 'Burns Night', 25 Jan., his birthday.

BURTON, Sir Richard (1821–90): explorer, swordsman, anthropologist, and linguist, Burton left Oxford without graduating and after a spell in the Indian army travelled widely. He published over forty volumes of travel, but is best remembered for his unexpurgated versions of the *Arabian Nights* (1885–8), *The Kama Sutra* (1883), and *The Perfumed Garden* (1886, from the French).

BUTLER, Samuel (1835–1902): educated at Shrewsbury and Cambridge, Butler went to New Zealand in 1859 where he achieved success as a sheep-farmer. *A First Year in Canterbury Settlement* (1863), compiled by his father from Samuel's letters, was published in a New Zealand journal. It became the core of Butler's satirical novel, *Erewhon* ('Erewhon' is an anagram of 'nowhere'), which he published anonymously in 1872 after he had returned to England. A sequel, *Erewhon Revisited*, appeared in 1901, and his best-known work, the semi-autobiographical novel *The Way of All Flesh*, was published posthumously in 1903. He also wrote poetry, and a number of books on science, travel, and art.

BYRON, George Gordon (1788–1824): sixth baron, educated at Harrow and Cambridge, Byron had his first collection of poems, *Hours of Idleness*, published in 1807 when they were bitterly attacked in the *Edinburgh Review*. In 1809 he began the poem that was to become *Childe Harold* and completed two cantos; he wrote one of his most famous lyrics, 'Maid of Athens'; he swam the Hellespont; and he became fired with the wish, which was to lead to his return and death, that Greece should be freed from the Turks. His first great literary triumph came with the publication of the first two cantos of *Childe Harold's Pilgrimage* in March 1812. He was lionized by aristocratic and literary London, and several more volumes of poetry were published, but in 1816 he left England for good when rumours of his incest with his half-sister Augusta, whose child was almost certainly his, became widely known and widely condemned. Then started a peripatetic life in Europe, which took him to Geneva, Venice, and Rome. The first two cantos of *Don Juan* were published in 1819 and were denounced in *Blackwood's* as 'a filthy and impious poem'. However, it was much admired by *Goethe, a fact Byron found greatly encouraging. In 1820 he finished Cantos III and IV of *Don Juan*, which he continued to work on in the following years as well as writing several plays and more poetry which included *Werner* (1822), a poetic drama, *The Age of Bronze* (1823), and *The Island* (1823). In Jan. 1824 he arrived at Missolonghi, formed the 'Byron Brigade', but died of fever before he saw any serious fighting. Byron's poetry, although widely condemned on moral grounds, was enormously popular in England and even more so abroad. His legacy of inspiration in European poetry, music, the novel, opera, and painting, has been immense.

CAMUS, Albert (1913–60): French novelist and essayist, Camus was born in Algeria, which provides the setting for many of his works. Through *L'Étranger* (1942; English tr. *The Outsider*, 1946), *La Peste* (1947; *The Plague*, 1948), both novels; and *Le Mythe de Sisyphus* (1942; *The Myth of Sisyphus*, 1955) and *L'Homme Révolté* (1951; *The Rebel*, 1953), he explored the implications of the 'absurd' nature of the human condition. His novel *La Chute* appeared in 1956 (*The Fall*, 1957), and he also wrote short stories and a number of plays, and his work influenced those writing the type of drama which came to be known as the Theatre of the Absurd (see S. Beckett). He was awarded the Nobel Prize for Literature in 1957.

CANETTI, Elias (1905–): born in Bulgaria, Canetti was educated largely in Zurich and Frankfurt, and gained a doctorate in chemistry at the University of Vienna. His best-known work was published as *Blendung* (1935), and in an English translation by C. V. Wedgwood as *Auto da Fé* (1946). He has also published plays, essays, and two volumes of autobiography. In 1981 he was awarded the Nobel Prize for Literature.

CARLYLE, Thomas (1795–1881): born at Ecclefechan, Dumfriesshire, Carlyle was educated at Annan Academy and at the University of Edinburgh. He established his reputation with his *History of the French Revolution* (1837), which was followed by *Chartism* (1839) and *Past and Present* (1843) in which he applied himself to what he called 'the Condition-of-England question', attacking both *laissez-faire* and the dangers of revolution it encouraged. However, unlike some of his followers, Carlyle turned increasingly away from democracy towards a kind of feudalism. His admiration for both Cromwell and Frederick the Great was expressed in books, the former in a collection of letters and speeches, the latter in a lengthy biography published in 6 volumes between 1858 and 1865. His wife died in 1866 and he thereafter wrote little of importance, but his influence as social prophet and critic, and his prestige as a historian, were enormous during his lifetime. His reputation in the 20th c. waned, but many of his coinages have become accepted as part of the language, and his work continues to attract scholars and biographers.

CARROLL, Lewis: see **Dodgson, C. L.**

CATHER, Willa (1876–1946): born in Virginia, USA, Willa Cather was brought up in Nebraska and educated at the university there. After a period of teaching and journalism, during which she published her first book of poems and a book of short stories, she worked on the staff, then as editor, of a New York magazine. Her first novel, *Alexander's Bridge* (1912), was followed by a number of others, most notably *One of Ours* (1922), *The Professor's House* (1925), and *Death Comes for the Archbishop* (1927). She was a pioneer not only in her treatment of the frontiers of the West, but also in her development of the American novel.

CERVANTES SAAVEDRA, Miguel de (1547–1616): the great Spanish novelist and dramatist, Cervantes was born in Alcalá of an ancient but impoverished family. In 1571 he lost for life the use of his left hand at the battle of Lepanto and for five years was a prisoner of pirates in Algiers. His first attempt at fiction was a pastoral novel, *La Galatea* (1585), which was followed by his masterpiece, *Don Quixote*, the first part of which appeared in 1605, the second in 1615. He also wrote a number of plays and short stories.

CHAUCER, Geoffrey (c.1343–1400): the son of a London vintner, Chaucer's date of birth has been much argued, all views now placing it between 1339 and 1346. He married the sister of John of Gaunt's third wife and enjoyed Gaunt's patronage throughout his life. He held a number of positions at Court and in the King's service and travelled to France and Italy. His writings develop through his career from a period of French influence in the late 1360s (of which the culmination was *The Book of the Duchess* in about 1370), through his 'middle period' of both French and Italian influences (including *The House of Fame* in the 1370s and the mature Italian-influenced works of which the most important is *Troilus and Criseyde*, *c.*1385), to the last period of most of *The Canterbury Tales*, Chaucer's most celebrated work which was probably designed about 1387 and extends to 17 000 lines in prose and verse of various metres.

CHEKHOV, Anton (1860–1904): Russian dramatist and short-story writer.

He studied medicine in Moscow, where he began writing humorous stories for journals. Among the greatest of his mature stories are 'A Dreary Story' (1889), 'Ward No. Six' (1892), 'My Life' (1896), 'Ionych' and the trilogy 'The Man in a Case', 'Gooseberries', and 'About Love' (all 1898), and 'The Lady with the Little Dog' (1899). His first successful play was *Ivanov* (1895), and he then wrote several light one-act comedies. His status as a dramatist, however, rests on his four late plays: *The Seagull* (1895), *Uncle Vanya* (1900), *Three Sisters* (1901), and *The Cherry Orchard* (1904). Chekhov's success and influence has been immense. The stories of Katherine *Mansfield, an early admirer, are held to be the main channel through which his work influenced the English, and *Shaw declared that reading Chekhov's plays made him want to tear up his own.

CHESTERTON, G(ilbert) K(eith) (1874–1936): born in London and educated at St Paul's School, Chesterton made his name in journalism, writing, with his great friend *Belloc, for *The Speaker*, in which both took a controversial, anti-Imperial, pro-Boer line on the Boer war. His first novel, *The Napoleon of Notting Hill*, appeared in 1904. His many volumes of short stories include those which feature Father Brown, an unassuming priest highly successful in the detection of crime by intuitive methods, who first appears in *The Innocence of Father Brown* (1911). Chesterton also published verse—'The Rolling English Road' (1914) being perhaps his best known—literary criticism, and many volumes of political, social, and religious essays.

CLARE, John (1793–1864): born in Helpstone, Northamptonshire, a neighbourhood to which he remained deeply attached and where he worked as hedge-setter and day-labourer; Clare's successful first volume of poetry, *Poems Descriptive of Rural Life and Scenery* (1820), was followed by *The Village Minstrel* (1821), *The Shepherd's Calendar* (1827), and *The Rural Muse* (1835). In 1837 he was admitted as insane to an asylum. He escaped but was recertified as insane, and though he continued to write he spent the rest of his life in Northampton General Asylum. His sales declined and he remained little read until this century, but he is now recognized as a poet of great truth and power.

CLARKE, Marcus (1846–81): after emigrating to Australia in 1863, Clarke spent four years on a sheep station in Victoria before settling as a journalist in Melbourne. He is remembered for his novel *For the Term of his Natural Life* (1874), a powerful and sympathetic portrayal of an Australian penal settlement.

COBBETT, William (1763–1835): the son of a farmer near Farnham, Cobbett was a self-educated man who enlisted as a soldier and served in New Brunswick between 1784 and 1791. He published two books while living in America, returned to England in 1800, became an anti-Radical journalist, and founded and wrote *Cobbett's Political Register* (started 1802). His views soon began to change and he was imprisoned for his attack on flogging in the army. He published *Parliamentary*

Debates, afterwards taken over by Hansard, and a number of other books, but is best remembered for *Rural Rides* (1830), which first began to appear in the *Political Register* in 1821. In 1832 he became MP for Oldham.

COCTEAU, Jean (1889–1963): French poet, novelist, dramatist, film director, and critic, who worked with many of Europe's leading artists like Diaghilev, Picasso, and Stravinsky. His works included numerous volumes of poetry; several novels including *Les Enfants terribles* (1929; English tr., 1930, and, as *Children of the Game*, 1955); sketches for ballets, including *Parade* (1917); films, such as *La Belle et la bête* (1945); and a number of plays.

COLERIDGE, Samuel Taylor (1772–1834): the youngest son of the vicar of Ottery St Mary, Devon, Coleridge was educated at Christ's Hospital school, London, and Cambridge, where a brilliant career was diverted by French revolutionary politics, heavy drinking, and an unhappy love affair. He did not take a degree. He became friends with *Southey but they later quarrelled and Coleridge, now married, retired to a cottage at Clevedon where he edited a radical Christian journal and published his second volume of poems, which included the 'Monody on the Death of Chatterton' and 'The Eolian Harp'. In 1795 he met *Wordsworth and his sister Dorothy, and the intense friendship that sprang up between the three shaped their lives for the next 14 years. It proved to be one of the most creative partnerships in English Romanticism, the literary movement (politically inspired by the revolutions in America and France and by the wars of independence elsewhere) that created the profound shift in sensibility in Britain and the rest of Europe between 1770 and 1848. The Romantic movement emotionally expressed an extreme assertion of the self and the value of individual experience, together with the sense of the infinite and the transcendental. Socially it championed progressive causes and its stylistic keynote is intensity, its watchword 'imagination'.

Between July 1797 and Sept. 1798 Coleridge and the Wordsworths lived and worked intimately together, and it was during this time that Coleridge composed his celebrated opium-vision, 'Kubla Khan' (1816), and 'The Rime of the Ancient Mariner' which was published in *Lyrical Ballads* (1798), a selection of poetry by Coleridge and Wordsworth intended as an 'experiment' in English poetry. It received a poor critical reception, but then achieved a revolution in literary taste and sensibility. After a time in Germany, he moved, in 1880, to the Lake District with the Wordsworths, but his marriage was increasingly unhappy and his use of opium now became a crippling addiction. It was during these years that he began to compile his *Notebooks*, daily meditations on his life, writing, and dreams, which have proved among his most enduring and moving works. Although ill, Coleridge, in 1808, began his series of Lectures on Poetry and Drama, which he continued sporadically over the next decade to audiences including *Keats and

*Byron, and which, like his *Shakespearian Criticism*, introduced new concepts of 'organic' form and dramatic psychology. Though he tried to regain his health by travelling abroad, he became estranged from Sara Hutchinson, for whom he had left his wife, and from his old circle of intimates. In 1811 he moved to London, where he was sustained by various friends, and with the publication in 1816 of *Christabel and Other Poems*, which included 'Kubla Khan', his by now almost legendary reputation among the younger Romantics was assured. *Sibylline Leaves*, the first edition of his collected poems, was published in 1817 and expanded in 1828 and 1834. His remaining prose works had a more openly social and religious slant, and he wrote some haunting late poems. He foreshadows much of the spiritual 'anxiety' of European Existentialism (see Sartre), and his position (with Wordsworth) as one of the two great progenitors of the English Romantic spirit is assured. There is a religious and metaphysical dimension to all his best work, both poetry and prose, which has the inescapable glow of the authentic visionary.

COLETTE, Sidonie-Gabrielle (1873–1954): having achieved success in the music hall, Colette established her reputation as a writer with *Chéri* (1920) and *La Fin de Chéri* (1926), narratives evoking the tragic passion of a young man for an older woman. Her other works include *La Maison de Claudine* (1922) and *Gigi* (1943).

COLLINS, Wilkie (1824–89): named after his godfather, the painter David Wilkie, it was Collins who wrote the first full-length detective stories in English, and set a mould for the genre which has lasted for a century. He wrote numerous articles and short stories for periodicals edited by *Dickens, a collaborator and close friend of Collins, and for other journals, but his reputation rests on his novels, in which he displayed his expertise in mystery, suspense, and crime. They include *The Woman in White* (1860) and *The Moonstone* (1868).

COMPTON-BURNETT, Dame Ivy (1884–1969): a novelist, who embarked on a serious career as a writer only with *Pastors and Masters* (1925); Dame Ivy's highly condensed and abstracted novels, composed almost entirely in dialogue, were so unlike anyone else's that their impact was often compared to that of Post-Impressionism in painting. She held that 'nothing is so corrupting as power', and her inward-looking, self-contained, and heavily monitored high Victorian households provided her with an ideal environment in which to examine its misuse. Her chief formative influences were G. *Eliot, the Greek tragic dramatists, and *Butler. After 1925 she wrote a further 18 novels, perhaps the most outstanding being *A House and Its Head* (1935), *A Family and a Fortune* (1939), and *Manservant and Maidservant* (1947).

CONGREVE, William (1670–1729): born at Bardsey, near Leeds, Congreve was a fellow student of *Swift at Kilkenny school and Trinity College, Dublin. He gave up law for literature, published a novel, and in 1693 suddenly achieved fame with his comedy, *The Old Bachelor*.

Of his other comedies *The Double Dealer* was published in 1694 (first performed 1693), *Love for Love* in 1695, and *The Way of the World* in 1700. In these Congreve shows himself the master of Restoration comedy, the genre established after the restoration of the monarchy and the re-opening of the theatres, predominantly marked by a tone that was witty, bawdy, cynical, and amoral. The plays were mainly in prose, with passages of verse for the more romantic moments; the plots complex; and the principal theme was sexual intrigue, either for its own sake or for money. Its main writers, besides Congreve, were Etherege, Farquhar, Vanbrugh, and Wycherley.

CONNOLLY, Cyril (1903–74): educated at Eton and Oxford, Connolly founded *Horizon* in 1939 with *Spender, and edited it until it closed in 1950. His works include *Enemies of Promise* (1938), *The Unquiet Grave* (1944), and his only novel, *The Rock Pool* (Paris, 1936; London, 1947).

CONRAD, Joseph (1857–1924): born of Polish parents in the Russian-dominated Ukraine, Conrad longed to go to sea from an early age and in 1874 he began the career as a sailor which was to supply so much material for his writing. In 1886 he became a British subject and a master mariner and in 1894, after 20 years at sea, settled in England and devoted himself to writing. He married in 1895 and published his first novel, writing in English, his third language. Nevertheless, by his third novel, *The Nigger of the Narcissus* (1897), and his fourth, *Lord Jim* (1900), he showed himself a master of his craft. His narrative technique is characterized by a skilful use of breaks in time-sequence and uses a narrator, Marlow, who provides a commentary on the action not unlike that of a Greek chorus. His other novels include *Typhoon* (1902), *Nostromo* (1904), *The Secret Agent* (1907), *Under Western Eyes* (1911), *Chance* (1913), which brought him his first popular and financial success, and *The Rover* (1923). He also wrote short stories and in one of his best known, 'Heart of Darkness' (1902), he carries one of his chief preoccupations—man's vulnerability and corruptibility—to a terrifying conclusion. By the time of his death, Conrad was well established in the literary world, though his work was generally ill-received by both critics and the public alike, and he was plagued by money problems. A decline in interest in the 1930s was followed by a revival and in 1941 F. R. Leavis wrote in *Scrutiny* (later reprinted in *The Great Tradition*) that Conrad is placed 'among the very great novelists in the language'.

COOPER, James Fenimore (1789–1851): born in New Jersey, USA, Cooper spent part of his youth at sea but then settled down to write novels. His second book, *The Spy* (1821), brought him to prominence, and *The Pioneers* (1823) was the first of his best-known group of novels, *Leather-Stocking Tales*, called after the deerskin leggings of their pioneer scout hero, Natty Bumppo. Among the sequels were *The Last of the Mohicans* (1826), *The Pathfinder* (1840), and *The*

Deerslayer (1841). Cooper travelled widely in Europe between 1826 and 1833 and on his return wrote several highly critical accounts of European society, and he later wrote critically of American democracy and expressed his conservative opinions in a number of works.

COOPER, William (1910–): William Cooper is the pseudonym of Harry Summerfield Hoff. His most influential novel, *Scenes from Provincial Life* (1950, reissued 1969), was hailed as seminal by *Braine and other writers of the 1950s. It was followed by *Scenes from Married Life* (1961) and *Scenes from Metropolitan Life* (1982), originally written as the middle volume of the trilogy. A sequel, *Scenes from Later Life*, appeared in 1983.

CORNFORD, John (1915–36): the first Englishman to enlist against Franco in the Spanish Civil War, Cornford was killed in action the same year. His poems had been published in various periodicals and were collected with various prose pieces, mainly political, in *John Cornford: A Memoir*, ed. Pat Sloan, 1938.

CORVO, Baron: see **Rolfe, Frederick.**

COWPER, William (1731–1800): educated at Westminster, Cowper was called to the Bar in 1754 but suffered a nervous breakdown. From this time he was subject to periods of acute melancholia which took a religious form. He was befriended by the Revd Morley Unwin and lived with his widow after Unwin died. He also came under the influence of the evangelical curate, J. Newton, and with him wrote *Olney Hymns* (1779). His satires were written at the suggestion of Mrs Unwin and were published in 1782 with several shorter poems. In the same year he wrote *John Gilpin* which was followed by his best-known long poem *The Task* (1785). In 1786 he moved to Weston Underwood with Mrs Unwin, where he wrote various poems published after his death, including the verses 'On the Loss of the Royal George', 'To Mary', 'The Poplar-Field', and 'The Castaway'. His sympathetic feelings for nature presage Romanticism (see Coleridge); and his poems and much-admired letters (published posthumously) have been highly valued for their intimate portrait of tranquillity and for their playful and delicate wit.

CRABBE, George (1754–1832): born in Aldeburgh, Suffolk, Crabbe practised as the parish doctor before determining, in 1770, on a writing career. He went to London, where he became almost destitute before being befriended by Edmund Burke, who encouraged him to take orders. In 1783 he published *The Village*, a poem which painted a grim picture of rural poverty and established his reputation. After 1785 nothing of importance appeared until 1810 when he published *The Borough*, a poem in which he illustrates the life of a country town and which includes the tales of 'Peter Grimes' and 'Ellen Orford'. This was followed in 1812 by *Tales in Verse* and in 1819 by a series of varied stories called *Tales of the Hall*. Throughout the upheaval represented by the Romantic movement (see Coleridge) Crabbe persisted in his precise, closely observed, realistic portraits of rural life and landscape, writing mainly in heroic couplets.

CUMMINGS, E(dward) E(stlin) (1894–1962): born in Cambridge, Massachusetts, USA, and educated at Harvard, Cummings established an immediate international reputation with the publication of his first book, *The Enormous Room* (1922), an account of his stay in a French detention camp in 1917. In 1923 appeared the first of 12 volumes of poetry. The early poems attracted attention more for their experimental typography and technical skill than for their considerable lyric power. His other works include essays, plays, and a satirical ballet. Cummings opened new perspectives for an entire generation of American and British poets including *Auden and *Spender.

D'ANNUNZIO, Gabriele (1863–1938): after urging the entry of Italy in the First World War on the side of the Allies, D'Annunzio, with a small volunteer force, occupied Fiume in 1919 and remained as dictator until 1921. One of his novels, *Il piacere* (*The Child of Pleasure*, 1896), is one of the significant texts of European Decadence. Some of his plays were set to music, including that of Debussy and Mascagni. D'Annunzio is at his best in his lyrics in *Alcyone* and in *Maia*, part of a four-volume collection entitled *Laudi* (*Praises*, 1904).

DANTE ALIGHIERI (1265–1321): born at Florence of a Guelf family, Dante's early life is obscure, but we know that in 1277 he was formally betrothed to his future wife and that in 1289 he took part in military operations against Arezzo and Pisa. The precise dating of Dante's works presents problems as yet unsolved. The first in order of composition (apart from his earliest lyric poems) was the *Vita nuova*, written in the period 1290–4, in which Dante brings together 31 poems. The *Convivio* or *Banquet* is an unfinished philosophical work and the Latin treatise *De vulgari eloquentia* is also unfinished. The *Monarchia*, written in the period 1309–12, is a Latin treatise on the universal empire and the relations between emperor and pope. It is very uncertain when Dante began his masterpiece, *Divina Commedia*, which comprises the *Inferno*, the *Purgatorio*, and the *Paradiso*, in *terza rima.* It may have been begun as early as 1307, or possibly not until 1314 or later, and was finished just before his death.

DAVIES, W(illiam) H(enry) (1871–1940): born in Newport, Davies went as a young man to America where he spent several years on the road. On a second visit, to seek his fortune in the Klondike, he lost a leg in an accident, an experience recounted in his *Autobiography of a Super-Tramp*, published in 1908. This had a preface by *Shaw, who did much to encourage the young poet and who interested himself in Davies's first volume, *The Soul's Destroyer and other poems* (1905), which was followed by several others. Davies's *Complete Poems* appeared in 1963.

DAY-LEWIS, Cecil (1904–72): born in Ireland, Day-Lewis, who wrote as C. Day Lewis, was educated at Sherborne and Oxford, where he became associated with a group of young left-wing poets of which *Auden was the acknowledged leader, and with whom he edited *Oxford Poetry* (1927). He published a number of volumes of poetry, including *Transitional Poems* (1929) and *The Magnetic Mountain* (1933), and during the 1930s embarked, under the pseudonym of 'Nicholas Blake', on a successful career as a writer of detective fiction. After the war he consolidated his literary reputation with translations of Valéry and Virgil, and with collections of original verse. He was professor of poetry at Oxford from 1951 to 1956, the first poet of distinction to hold the post since M. *Arnold, and in 1968 was appointed Poet Laureate.

DEFOE, Daniel (1660–1731): born in London the son of James Foe, a butcher, Defoe changed his name from *c.*1695. He took part in Monmouth's rebellion, and in 1688 joined the advancing forces of William III. His immensely popular satirical poem, *The True-Born Englishman*, appeared in 1701. Between 1703 and 1714 he was employed as a secret agent and travelled about England in this capacity. He was an extremely versatile and prolific writer, and produced some 560 books, pamphlets, and journals, but his best-known works belong to his later years. *Robinson Crusoe* was published in 1719, with *Further Adventures* appearing a few months later. The next five years saw the appearance of his most important works of fiction, which included *Moll Flanders* (1722) and *Roxana* (1724). Defoe's influence on the evolution of the English novel was enormous. Many regard him as the first true novelist, and his peculiar gifts made him one of the greatest reporters of his time.

DE LA MARE, Walter (1873–1956): educated at St Paul's Choir school, de la Mare began work for an oil company aged 16 and stayed for 20 years. In 1902 he published his first volume of poetry, which attracted little notice. He subsequently published many more volumes, both for adults and children, *The Listeners* (1912), being his first successful one. He also wrote several novels, and his many volumes of short stories, for adults and children, were often arresting or bizarre. He also published anthologies as well as essays and some critical work. Remembered chiefly as a poet, for both adults and children, de la Mare was fluent, highly inventive, technically skilled, and unaffected by fashion.

DE QUINCEY, Thomas (1785–1859): educated at several schools and then at Manchester Grammar School, from which he ran away, De Quincey later went to Oxford, and—having made the acquaintance of *Coleridge and *Wordsworth—settled at Grasmere. While at Oxford he had begun to take opium and, from 1812, was an addict. *Confessions of an Opium Eater*, by which he made his name, was published in 1822, and for the next 30 years he earned a precarious living writing tales, articles, and reviews.

DICKENS, Charles (1812–70): born in Portsmouth, the son of a clerk in the navy pay office, Dickens spent the happiest period of his boyhood in Chatham; this was followed by a period of intense misery which deeply affected him, during which his father was imprisoned for debt and he himself, aged 12, worked in a blacking warehouse. Memories of this painful time inspired much of his fiction, notably the early chapters of *David Copperfield* (1849–50), which is, in some of its details, Dickens's veiled autobiography. 'Of all my books,' he wrote of it, 'I like this the best.'

Dickens later worked as an office boy, studied shorthand, and became a reporter of debates in the Commons for the *Morning Chronicle*. He contributed to several magazines, writing the articles which were subsequently republished as *Sketches by 'Boz', Illustrative of Every-Day Life and Every-Day People* (1836–7). These attracted much attention and led to an approach by publishers which resulted in the creation of Mr Pickwick, and the publication in monthly parts of *The Posthumous Papers of the Pickwick Club*, which was subsequently published in volume form in 1837. After a slow start the series achieved immense popularity and sealed Dickens's success as a writer. The same year *Oliver Twist* (1837–8) began to appear monthly in a new periodical of which Dickens was the first editor, and it was followed by *Nicholas Nickleby* (1838–9), *The Old Curiosity Shop* (1840–1), and *Barnaby Rudge* (1841). In 1842 he and his wife visited America, and the disillusionment he felt with the country was reflected in *American Notes* (1842). Both this and his portrayal of American stereotypes in *Martin Chuzzlewit* (1843–4) caused offence in America. The sales of the latter were disappointing but it was soon followed by other successes, including *A Christmas Carol* (1843), *Dombey and Son* (1848), *Bleak House* (1852–3), *Hard Times* (1854), *Little Dorrit* (1855–7), *A Tale of Two Cities* (1859), *Great Expectations* (1860–1), and *Our Mutual Friend* (1864–5). He died with his last novel, *The Mystery of Edwin Drood* (1870), unfinished.

Dickens captured the popular imagination as no other novelist had done and, despite some murmurs against his sensationalism and sentimentality and his inability to portray women other than as innocents or grotesques, he was also held in high critical esteem, admired by contemporaries as varied as Queen Victoria and *Dostoevsky. But it was not until this century that he began to attract serious academic attention.

See also article on 'Dickens and the English Language' by Dr Andrew Sanders on p. 544.

DICKINSON, Emily (1830–86): born in Amherst, Massachusetts, USA, Emily Dickinson was educated at the Academy there and at Mount Holyoke. Although witty and sociable during her early years, she gradually withdrew into an inner world, eventually, in her 40s, refusing to leave her home. She wrote poetry from girlhood onwards, but only seven poems out of nearly 2000 are known to have been published during her lifetime. At first regarded as an eccentric minor poet, she is now considered a major writer of startling originality. Her work presents recurrent themes—a mystic apprehension of the natural world, a preoccupation with poetic vocation, fame, death, and immortality—and is expressed in a rhetoric and language of her own, cryptic, elliptical, and at times self-dramatizing and hyperbolic.

DINESEN, Isak: see **Blixen, Karen.**

DISRAELI, Benjamin (1804–81): first Earl of Beaconsfield, politician and prime minister, Disraeli started writing at 15, and his first story was published in the *Indicator* in 1820. After an attempt to start a newspaper failed, Disraeli wrote his first novel, *Vivian Grey* (1826), probably to pay off his debts. There followed a number of other works, including the novels *Contarini Fleming* (1832) and *Alroy* (1833), which, with *Vivian Grey*, formed his first trilogy. But he is most renowned for the trilogy, *Coningsby* (1844), *Sybil* (1845), and *Tancred* (1847), written, he declared, because it was through novels that he felt he could best influence public opinion, and they may be regarded as the first truly political novels in English.

DODGSON, Charles Lutwidge (1832–98): educated at Rugby and Oxford, where he became a lecturer in mathematics in 1855, Dodgson wrote under the pseudonym Lewis Carroll. His most famous work, *Alice's Adventures in Wonderland* (1865), originated in a boat trip with the young daughters of H. G. Liddell, Lorina, Alice, and Edith; it was for Alice that he expanded an impromptu story into book form. *Through the Looking-Glass and What Alice Found There* followed in 1871. Both volumes were illustrated by Tenniel. His other works include *The Hunting of the Snark* (1876) and a light-hearted defence of Euclid, *Euclid and His Modern Rivals* (1879).

DONNE, John (1572–1631): born into a devout Catholic family, Donne went at the age of 11 to Hart Hall, Oxford (now Hertford College). Little is known of his adolescence before his admission as a law student in May 1592, but it was around this time that he apparently renounced his Catholic faith. He went on two naval expeditions, one to sack Cadiz (1596), the other to hunt Spanish treasure ships off the Azores (1597), and his poems 'The Storm' and 'The Calm' commemorate these voyages. After 14 years of trying to find responsible employment, he took orders in 1615 and in 1621 procured the deanery of St Paul's. One of the most celebrated preachers of his age, as well as its greatest non-dramatic poet, Donne was the founder of the 'school' of metaphysical poets—it included poets like *Marvell, Traherne, Cowley, and Cleveland—a label that was first used (disparagingly) by Dr *Johnson who identifies them as a 'race of writers' who display their learning, use far-fetched comparisons, and lack feeling. The label, however, is misleading, as these writers had little in common and no serious interest in metaphysics. Their reputation dwindled after the Restoration and was not revived until after the First World War. When it came, however, it was dramatic: indeed, the revaluation of metaphysical poetry, by T. S. *Eliot among others, was the major feature of the rewriting of English literary history in the first half of the 20th c. The metaphysical poets' virtues of difficulty and tough newness were felt to relate them closely to the modernists like *Pound, *Yeats, and T. S. Eliot, though more recent critics have questioned this.

DOS PASSOS, John (1896–1970): born in Chicago, USA, Dos Passos was educated at Harvard. His first important novel, *Three Soldiers* (1921), was followed by many others, as well as poetry, essays, travel writings, memoirs, and plays. He is chiefly remembered for his novels *Manhattan Transfer* (1925) and *U.S.A.* (1938) and a trilogy composed of *The 42nd Parallel* (1930), *1919* (1932), and *The Big Money* (1936).

DOSTOEVSKY, Fyodor (1821–81): born in Moscow, Dostoevsky studied at the St Petersburg Engineering Academy (1838–43). His first original work appeared in 1846, but in 1849 he was arrested as a member of the socialist Petrashevsky circle and sent to a Siberian penal settlement for four years, which was followed by four years as a private soldier. His *Notes from the House of the Dead* (1860–1) were based on his period of imprisonment. Throughout the 1860s he travelled widely abroad and the series of brilliant works which followed, *Notes from Underground* (1864), *Crime and Punishment* (1866), *The Idiot* (1868), *The Devils* (1872), and *The Brothers Karamazov* (1880), are those on which his reputation is based. He admired a number of English writers, particularly *Dickens, and many of his novels appeared in English in the 1880s. R. L. *Stevenson was an early admirer and the influence of *Crime and Punishment* on *Dr Jekyll and Mr Hyde* (1886) is apparent. In general, though, contemporary response to Dostoevsky in England was cool. However, he has now become the Russian writer most widely read and influential in England.

DOUGLAS, Keith (1920–44): educated at Christ's Hospital and Oxford; Douglas's verses began to appear in periodicals in the 1930s, but the only volume published in his lifetime was *Selected Poems* (1943). He was killed in Normandy, and inevitably is remembered largely as a war poet. His vivid experimental narrative of desert warfare, *Alamein to Zem Zem*, was published posthumously in 1946; his *Collected Poems* appeared in 1951 and the *Complete Poems* in 1979.

DOYLE, Arthur Conan (1859–1930): educated at Stonyhurst and Edinburgh, Doyle became a doctor and practised at Southsea (1882–90). He is chiefly remembered for the detective Sherlock Holmes, whose adventures began in *A Study in Scarlet* (1887), and continued through stories, chiefly in the *Strand Magazine*, which were collected in *The Adventures of Sherlock Holmes* (1892), *The Memoirs of Sherlock Holmes* (1894), *The Hound of the Baskervilles* (1902), and other works. He also wrote historical and other romances, notably *The Exploits of Brigadier Gerard* (1896), the first of many 'Gerard' tales, and *The Lost World* (1912), the first of a series of stories dominated by

Professor Challenger. He also wrote pamphlets, histories, and a one-act play.

DREISER, Theodore (1871–1945): born in Indiana, USA, Dreiser became a journalist in Chicago. His first novel, *Sister Carrie* (1900), was withheld from circulation by its publishers, who were apprehensive about Dreiser's frank and amoral treatment of Carrie's sexuality and ambition, and he was forced to continue as a hack journalist until the greater success of *Jennie Gerhardt* (1911). His other novels include *The Genius* (1915) and *An American Tragedy* (1925), and he also wrote several volumes of non-fiction. The power, originality, first-hand observations, and moral independence of his work have ensured him a lasting readership and a serious reputation as an artist.

DRYDEN, John (1631–1700): educated at Westminster School and Cambridge; Dryden's early writing was mostly for the theatre and included several rhymed heroic plays and a number of comedies. He was most original, however, with his tragi-comedies like *Marriage à-la-Mode* (1672). All these plays, together with several adaptations, reveal Dryden's considerable interest in philosophical and political questions. He became Poet Laureate in 1668, and Historiographer Royal in 1670.

Dryden constantly defended his own literary practice, and he wrote a number of critical works and essays. He also developed his critical principles in poems such as *MacFlecknoe*, in which he attacks his arch-opponent Shadwell, and in others about, or addressed to, fellow writers and artists like *Congreve and Kneller. The constitutional crisis of the late 1670s troubled him greatly and is reflected in his plays and other writings, and in the early 1680s he produced his most celebrated satires, which include *Absalom and Achitophel* (1681) and *The Medall* (1682). In 1688 he lost both his court offices and returned to the theatre. Two of his late plays, *Don Sebastian* (1689) and *Amphitryon* (1690), are excellent, and *Cleomenes* (1692) is intellectually impressive, but he then tired of the theatre and turned to criticism again, and to translating. His immense and splendid achievements in translating include pieces of Homer, Juvenal, Ovid, Boccaccio, and the whole of Virgil. His culminating and most impressive achievement both as a critic and a translator was *Fables Ancient and Modern*.

DUMAS, Alexandre (1802–70): known as 'Dumas *père*' to differentiate him from his writer-son of the same name; Dumas's reputation now chiefly rests on his historical novels. These began to appear serially at prodigious speed around 1840. *Les Trois Mousquetaires* (1844–5) and his masterpiece of mystery and suspense, *Le Comte de Monte Cristo* (1844–5), are the best known. He also wrote numerous books of travel, 22 volumes of *Mémoires* (1852–5), several children's stories, and a *Grand dictionnaire de cuisine* (1872, posthumous).

DURRELL, Lawrence (1912–): born in India, Durrell returned to England in his late teens, and thereafter travelled widely. Although he began to write and publish both verse and prose when very young his work made little impact for some years. He was first recognized as a poet, and his collections include *A Private Country* (1941), *On Seeming to Presume* (1948), and *The Tree of Idleness* (1955). His *Collected Poems* appeared in 1960. His first novel of interest, *The Black Book: an Agon*, heavily influenced by Henry *Miller, published in Paris in 1938, did not appear in Britain until 1973. It was with the publication of *Justine* (1957), the first volume of his *Alexandria Quartet*, that Durrell achieved fame: *Balthazar* and *Mountolive* followed in 1958, and *Clea* in 1960. His others novels include *Tunc* (1968), *Nunquam* (1970), *Monsieur* (1974), and *Constance* (1982). He has also written a number of travel books.

DÜRRENMATT, Friedrich (1921–): Swiss dramatist, a writer of grotesque black comedy, because he thinks that since the Second World War tragedy is a form no longer applicable to our modern 'upside-down world'. His best-known plays are *Der Besuch der alten Dame* (*The Visit*, 1956) and *Die Physiker* (*The Physicists*, 1962).

EDGEWORTH, Maria (1768–1849): after spending her infancy in Ireland, Maria Edgeworth received some schooling in England, and when she was 15 returned to live the rest of her life with her family in Ireland. Her first publication was *Letters to Literary Ladies* (1795), a plea for women's education. From then on she wrote prolifically for some 40 years and established a high reputation. Although not generally regarded as a novelist of the first rank, she appears to have initiated, in *Castle Rackrent* (1800), both the first fully developed regional novel and the first true historical novel in English. Her writings fall into three groups: those like *Castle Rackrent* and *The Absentee* (first published in *Tales of Fashionable Life* in 1812) based on Irish life (considered her finest); those depicting English society, such as *Belinda* (1801) and *Leonora* (1806); and her many popular lessons and stories for and about children.

ELIOT, George (1819–80): the youngest surviving child of an agent for a Warwickshire estate, George Eliot, whose real name was Mary Ann (later Marian) Evans, became converted to Evangelicalism at school, and although she was later freed from this she remained strongly influenced by religious concepts of love and duty. She pursued her education rigorously and devoted herself to completing a translation of Strauss's *Life of Jesus*, which appeared without her name in 1846. In 1850 she became a contributor to the *Westminster Review*, and in 1851 became its assistant editor. In 1854 she published a translation of Feuerbach's *Essence of Christianity* and at about the same time she started living with the writer G. H. Lewes, a union that lasted until his death. 'The Sad Fortunes of the Rev. Amos Barton', the first of the *Scenes of Clerical Life*, appeared in *Blackwood's Magazine* in 1857, and, with two other stories, at once attracted praise for their domestic realism, pathos, and humour, and speculation about the identity of

'George Eliot'. *Adam Bede* appeared in 1859 and at once established her as a leading novelist. This was followed by *The Mill on the Floss* (1860), *Silas Marner* (1861), *Romola*, published in the *Cornhill* in 1862–3, *Felix Holt, The Radical* (1866), *Middlemarch*, published in instalments in 1871–2, and *Daniel Deronda*, her last great novel, also published in instalments in 1874–6. Lewes died in 1878 and in 1880 she married the 40-year-old John Walter Cross, whom she had met in Rome in 1869 and who had become her financial adviser. After her death her reputation as the greatest novelist of her time declined somewhat, but in the late 1940s a new generation of critics, led by F. R. Leavis (*The Great Tradition*, 1948), introduced a new respect for and understanding of her mature works.

ELIOT, T(homas) S(tearns) (1888–1965): born at St Louis, Missouri, USA, and educated at Harvard, the Sorbonne, and Oxford, Eliot has been a major figure in English literature since the 1920s. In 1914 he met *Pound, who encouraged him to settle in England; in June 1915 he married, and in the same month his poem 'The Love Song of J. Alfred Prufrock' appeared (also with Pound's encouragement) in *Poetry*. Eliot taught briefly during the war, and then, in 1917, joined Lloyds Bank. His first volume of verse, *Prufrock and other Observations*, appeared the same year and was followed by *Poems* (1919), hand-printed by L. and V. *Woolf at the Hogarth Press. These struck a new note in modern poetry, satiric, allusive, cosmopolitan, at times lyric and elegiac. In 1922 Eliot founded a new quarterly, *The Criterion*; in the first issue appeared, with much éclat, *The Waste Land*, which established him decisively as the voice of a disillusioned generation. In 1925 he left Lloyds and became a director of the publishers, Faber & Faber, where he built up a list of poets (*Auden, Pound, *Spender, etc.) which represented the mainstream of the modern movement in poetry in England: from this time he was regarded as a figure of great cultural authority, whose influence was more or less inescapable.

In 1927 Eliot became a British subject and a member of the Anglican Church; his pilgrimage towards his own particular brand of High Anglicanism may be charted in his poetry through 'The Hollow Men' (1925), 'The Journey of the Magi' (1927) and 'Ash-Wednesday' (1930), to its culminating vision in *Four Quartets* (1935–42) In the 1930s he began his attempt to revive poetic drama with *Sweeney Agonistes* (1932), which was followed by *The Rock* (1934), *Murder in the Cathedral* (1935), *The Family Reunion* (1939), and three 'comedies': *The Cocktail Party* (1950), *The Confidential Clerk* (1954), and *The Elder Statesman* (1959). His book of verse for children, *Old Possum's Book of Practical Cats* (1939), reveals the aspect of his character that claimed the influence of *Lear.

Eliot also produced a number of critical works, including *The Sacred Wood: Essays on Poetry and Criticism* (1920) and *Notes Towards a Definition of Culture* (1948), and he was equally influential as critic and poet. In his combination of literary and social criticism he may be called the M. *Arnold of the 20th c. He was formally separated from his first wife in 1932–3; she died in 1947. The following year he was awarded the Nobel Prize for Literature and the Order of Merit. He married his second wife in 1957.

EMERSON, Ralph Waldo (1803–82): born in Boston, USA, Emerson was educated at Harvard, studied theology, was ordained and became a pastor in Boston, but resigned his charge because he felt unable to believe in the sacrament of the Lord's Supper. He visited England in 1833 where he met *Coleridge, *Wordsworth, and notably *Carlyle, who became a lifelong friend and correspondent. On his return to America Emerson became a lecturer, evolving the new quasi-religious concept of Transcendentalism. This form of mystic idealism and Wordsworthian reverence for nature was immensely influential in American life and thought, and Emerson, like his friend Carlyle, was revered as a sage and counted such writers as *Whitman and *Thoreau among his disciples. Many of his gnomic, rough-hewn, but frequently striking poems were published in *The Dial*, which was edited by Emerson between 1842 and 1844. His first volume of essays was published in 1841 and the second in 1844. In 1845 he delivered the lectures later published in 1850 as *Representative Man*. In 1847 he revisited England, where he was greatly admired, and his *English Traits* (1865) won him more readers. On his return to America he was actively engaged in the anti-slavery campaign, and continued to lecture and write (including poems and prose for *The Atlantic Monthly*) until, in his last decade, he lost his mental powers.

EMPSON, Sir William (1906–84): educated at Winchester and Cambridge, where he studied mathematics, then English, Empson taught in universities in China and Japan before becoming professor of English at Sheffield. He published two volumes of verse and his *Collected Poems* (revised) appeared in 1955. His poetry is extremely difficult, making use of analytical argument and imagery, drawn from modern physics and mathematics; a technical virtuoso, he offered (in his own words) 'a sort of puzzle interest', and employed metaphysical conceits and linguistic, metrical, and syntactical complexities. He published several works of criticism which include *Seven Types of Ambiguity* (1930), *Some Versions of Pastoral* (1935), and *Milton's God* (1961).

ERASMUS, Desiderius (c.1467–1536): the great Dutch humanist, born at Rotterdam, Erasmus under pressure from his guardians became an Augustan monk, but thanks to the protection of the Bishop of Cambrai was allowed to leave the cloister and travel extensively in Europe. Among his principal works were a new edition of the Greek New Testament (1516), *Encomium Moriae* (*The Praise of Folly*, 1511) and *Enchiridion Militis Christiani* (1503). His *Adagia* (1500), a collection of Latin and Greek proverbs traced to their source, one of the first works of the new learning, was much drawn upon by *Rabelais and by many English writers. His many editions and translations of the Bible, early Christian authors, and the classics revolutionized European literary culture. Erasmus prepared the way for the Reformation by his writings, and was at first sympathetic to the movement, but later refused to take sides.

FAULKNER, William (1897–1962): born in Mississippi, USA, where his family had long been settled, Faulkner used the history and legends of the South, and his own family, as material for his greater books. He met S. *Anderson while working as a journalist in New Orleans, who encouraged him to write his first novel, *Soldier's Pay* (1926). Then came *Sartoris* (1929), *The Sound and the Fury* (1929), and *As I Lay Dying* (1930). He made his name, however, not with these but with *Sanctuary* (1931), a more sensational work written to attract sales. This was followed by *Light in August* (1932), and *Absalom, Absalom!* (1936) which confirmed his reputation as one of the finest of modern novelists. Other important works include *The Hamlet* (1940) and *Intruder in the Dust* (1948), and several volumes of short stories, collected in 1950. He was awarded the Nobel Prize for Literature in 1949.

FIELDING, Henry (1707–54): educated at Eton, the son of an army officer, Fielding at 19 attempted to elope with a beautiful heiress, but failing in this settled in London, determined to earn his living as a dramatist. A distant cousin, Lady Mary Wortley Montagu, encouraged him, and in 1728 his play *Love in Several Masques* was successfully performed at Drury Lane. After studying at Leiden, he returned to London and between 1729 and 1737 wrote some 25 assorted dramas, largely in the form of farce and satire, and including two adaptations of *Molière and his most successful production *Tom Thumb*. In 1736 Fielding took over the management of the New Theatre, but the introduction of censorship by the Lord Chamberlain brought this career to an end and he entered the Middle Temple and began to read for the Bar. However, he became ill with gout and returned to earning a living as a dramatist and journalist. He probably began *The History of Tom Jones, a Foundling* in 1746 and it was enthusiastically received by the public, if not by *Richardson, *Smollett, Dr *Johnson, and other literary figures, when it was published in 1749. In 1748 he had been appointed a JP and from his court in Bow Street he struggled against corruption and lawlessness and strove to establish new standards of honesty and competence on the bench. In 1751 he published *Amelia*, which sold the best of all his novels. Fielding is generally agreed to be an innovating master of the highest originality. His three acknowledged masters were Lucian, *Swift, and *Cervantes. In breaking away from the epistolary method of his contemporary Richardson, and others, he devised what he described as 'comic epics in prose', which are in effect the first modern novels in English, leading straight to the works of *Dickens and *Thackeray.

FITZGERALD, Edward (1809–83): educated at the King Edward VI Grammar School, Bury St Edmunds, and Cambridge; FitzGerald's only celebrated work is his free translation of *The Rubáiyát of Omar Khayyám* (1859), but he also translated other works from Persian and a number of plays by Calderón, Aeschylus, and Sophocles.

FITZGERALD, F(rancis) Scott (1896–1940): born in Minnesota, USA, and educated at Princeton; Fitzgerald's first novel, *This Side of Paradise* (1920), made him instantly famous. Shortly after its publication he married the glamorous Zelda Sayre, and together they embarked on a life of high living, big spending, and party-going. He published stories in fashionable periodicals and these were collected as *Flappers and Philosophers* (1920) and *Tales of the Jazz Age* (1922), the latter including 'The Diamond as Big as the Ritz'. *The Beautiful and the Damned* (1922), a novel about a wealthy, doomed, and dissipated marriage, was followed by *The Great Gatsby* (1925), widely considered his finest work. More short stories followed as well as *Tender is the Night* (1934, but later in various revised versions) and *The Last Tycoon* (1941), which remained unfinished when he died of a heart attack in Hollywood while working there as a script-writer.

FLAUBERT, Gustave (1821–80): born in Rouen, Flaubert was one of the masters of 19th-c. fiction. His first published novel, *Madame Bovary* (1857), the story of the adulteries and suicide of a doctor's wife in provincial Normandy, was judged to be offensive to public morals, and Flaubert, his publishers, and his printers, were tried but acquitted. His other works include the novel *Salammbô* (1862), and his *Correspondence*, which contains searching reflections on the art of fiction and the life of the novelist, has earned him the reputation of the exemplary artist.

FLECKER, James Elroy (1884–1915): educated at Uppingham and Oxford, Flecker produced several volumes of lyrical romantic verse, some of which was included in *Georgian Poetry* (see R. Brooke). He also published an experimental, highly individual novel, *The King of Alsander* (1914), but the work for which he is best remembered is the poetic Eastern play, *Hassan*, published posthumously in 1922, and his other play, *Don Juan* (1925).

FLETCHER, John (1579–1625): born at Rye in Sussex, Fletcher was educated at Cambridge. Little is known of his early life; about 1605 he began to write plays in collaboration with Sir F. *Beaumont, and, before his death of the plague, he produced some 15 plays with him and some 16 of which he was the sole author, and collaborated with a number of writers, including *Jonson, in the writing of many other works. He also collaborated with *Shakespeare in *The Two Noble Kinsmen* and *Henry VIII*.

FORESTER, C(ecil) S(cott) (1899–1966): best remembered for his seafaring novels set during the Napoleonic wars, featuring Horatio Hornblower;

Forester's other works include *Brown on Resolution* (1929) and *The African Queen* (1955).

FORSTER, E(dward) M(organ) (1879–1970): educated at Tonbridge School, where he was deeply unhappy and developed a lasting dislike of public school values, and at Cambridge, Forster published his first story in 1904 and in 1905 he completed *Where Angels Fear to Tread* which appeared the same year. *The Longest Journey* appeared in 1907, *A Room with a View* in 1908, and *Howards End*, which established Forster's reputation as a writer of importance, in 1910. In 1912–13 he visited India and in 1913 wrote *Maurice*, a novel with a homosexual theme which he circulated privately; it was published posthumously in 1971. During the First World War he worked in the Red Cross in Alexandria, where he met Cavafy, whose works, on his return to England in 1919, he helped to introduce. In 1921–2 he revisited India. When *A Passage to India*, which he had begun before the war, was published in 1924 it was highly acclaimed. But it was to be his last novel and he devoted the remainder of his life to a wide range of literary activities. His other works include essays, short stories, and two biographies.

FOWLES, John (1926–): educated at Bedford School and Oxford; Fowles's first novel, *The Collector*, was published in 1963. This was followed by *The Aristos* (1965), an idiosyncratic collection of notes and aphorisms aimed at a 'personal philosophy'; four more novels, *The Magus* (1966, revised version 1977), which, with its narrative complexity and mythological dimension, is faintly suggestive of Magic Realism (see García Márquez), *The French Lieutenant's Woman* (1969), *Daniel Martin* (1977), and *A Maggot* (1985); and a collection of novellas, *The Ebony Tower* (1974).

FROST, Robert (1874–1963): born in San Francisco, USA, of New England stock, Frost was educated at both Dartmouth College and Harvard. In 1912 he came to England where he published his first volume of poems, *A Boy's Will* (1913), and *North of Boston* (1914), which contains 'Mending Wall' and 'Death of the Hired Man'. He met the Georgian poets (see R. Brooke) and formed a particularly close and fruitful friendship with E. *Thomas. Upon his return to America he settled in New Hampshire and continued to write poetry, supporting himself by successive teaching appointments in several colleges. His volumes include *Mountain Interval* (1916), which contains 'Birches' and 'The Road Not Taken'; *New Hampshire* (1923); *Collected Poems* (1930); *A Witness Tree* (1942); and *In the Clearing* (1962). He established himself as one of the most popular of 20th-c. American poets, admired for the blend of colloquial and traditional in his verse, and hailed as a fitting heir, in his response to the natural world, of *Wordsworth and *Emerson. But beneath the country lore and wisdom lay a more troubled spirit, expressed in such poems as 'Fire and Ice' (1923) and 'Bereft' (1928).

FRY, Christopher (1907–): born in Bristol of Quaker stock, Fry worked as schoolmaster, actor, and theatre director before making his name as a playwright with works that were hailed in the late 1940s as a sign of a new renaissance in poetic drama. His mystical and religious plays were frequently compared with those of T. S. *Eliot, though his comedies like *The Lady's not for Burning* (1949) and *Venus Observed* (1950) were more popular. The vogue for poetic drama proved short-lived and when *Curtmantle* appeared in 1962 it struck critics as dated. Fry also wrote several screenplays, and successful translations and adaptations of *Anouilh and Giraudoux.

FULLER, Roy (1912–): educated at Blackpool High School before becoming a solicitor, Fuller worked for many years for a building society. His first volume of verse, *Poems* (1939), shows the influence of *Auden and *Spender. *Collected Poems 1936–1961* (1962) forms a link between the poets of the 1930s and poets of the Movement (see Larkin), in its lucid, ironic, detached tone, and its formal accomplishment. His later volumes, while displaying an equal interest in technique, frequently strike a more personal note. He has published several novels, including, notably, *Image of a Society* (1956), and three volumes of memoirs.

GALSWORTHY, John (1867–1933): educated at Harrow and Oxford, Galsworthy, influenced by *Conrad, whom he met by chance, turned from the law to writing. His first volume of stories, *From the Four Winds*, appeared in 1897, and in 1898 his first novel, *Jocelyn*, which he never republished. The first appearance of the Forsyte family was in one of the stories in *Man of Devon* (1901) and the first of the Forsyte novels, *A Man of Property*, was published in 1906. It was followed by *In Chancery* (1920) and *To Let* (1921), which, together with two interludes, appeared collectively as *The Forsyte Saga* in 1922. The second part of the Forsyte chronicles, containing *The White Monkey* (1924), *The Silver Spoon* (1926), *Swan Song* (1928), and the two interludes 'A Silent Wooing' and 'Passers By', was published as *A Modern Comedy* in 1929. In 1931 Galsworthy followed the immense success of the Forsyte books with a further collection of stories, *On Forsyte Change*.

Galsworthy began his playwriting career in 1906 with *The Silver Box* and his reputation as a dramatist became firmly established with *Strife* (1909), and this was followed by a number of other plays. Posthumous publications included *Collected Poems* (1934) and *The End of the Chapter* (1935), a trilogy relating the family history of the Charwells, cousins of the younger Forsytes. Galsworthy received the Nobel Prize for Literature in 1932, by which time he had already been awarded the OM. Yet (although the Forsyte stories have had a history of continuing popularity) his work has never received high critical acclaim. His detached stance has tended to provoke the suspicion that some part of him respected the qualities he professed to satirize and that his satire lacked gall.

GARCÍA LORCA, Federico (1898–1936): born in Andalusia, and educated at the universities of Granada and Madrid, Lorca published his first volume of poems in 1921, which was followed by others including his extremely popular collection of gypsy ballads, *Romancero gitano* (1928). He also wrote several plays which include the lyrical, intense, poetic tragedies *Bodas de sangre* (*Blood Wedding*, perf. 1934); *Yerma* (perf. 1934); and *La casa de Bernarda Alba* (*The House of Bernarda Alba*, perf. and pub. posthumously, 1945). He also wrote several comedies and tragi-comedies, but is best known in England for his evocation of the profound and primitive passions of Spanish peasant life. He was murdered by Nationalist partisans in July 1936, shortly after the outbreak of the Civil War. His body was never found.

GARCÍA MÁRQUEZ, Gabriel (1928–): born in Aracataca, Colombia, and educated at a Jesuit college in Bogotá, García Márquez became a journalist at 18. In 1955 he was sent to Europe for the Liberal *El Espectador* and during this period began to write novels. His works include *La hojarasca* (1955; English tr. as *Leaf Storm*, 1972), a novella which introduces the village of Macondo, the setting for his most famous novel *Cien años de soledad* (1967; *One Hundred Years of Solitude*, 1970), *La mala hora* (1966; *In Evil Hour*, 1970), *El otoño del patriarca* (1975; *The Autumn of the Patriarch*, 1977), and various collections of short stories. He was awarded the Nobel Prize for Literature in 1982.

One Hundred Years of Solitude is a classic work of Magic Realism, the term coined in the 1920s to describe tendencies in the work of certain German artists, which has subsequently been used to describe the works of Latin American writers like García Márquez, *Borges, and Alejo Carpentier. Elements of it have also been noted in *Grass, Calvino, *Fowles, and other European writers. In the 1970s and 1980s it was adopted in Britain by several of the most original of younger fiction writers, including, notably, Emma Tennant and Angela Carter. Magic Realist novels and stories have, typically, a strong narrative drive, in which the recognizably realistic mingles with the unexpected and the inexplicable, and in which elements of dream, fairy story, or mythology combine with the everyday.

GASKELL, Mrs Elizabeth (1810–65): the daughter of a Unitarian minister, William Stevenson, Mrs Gaskell married William Gaskell in 1832 and they had four daughters, and a son who died in infancy. As a distraction from her sorrow at his death she wrote her first novel, *Mary Barton* (1848). It won the attention of *Dickens, at whose invitation most of her work was first published in his periodicals. Her other full-length novels include *Cranford* (1853), *North and South* (1855), and *Sylvia's Lovers* (1863). She also wrote the first and most celebrated biography of C. *Brontë, and many vivid and warm-hearted short stories and novellas, of which the finest was *Cousin Phyllis* (1864). Her contemporaries classed her as a novelist with the *Brontës and G.

*Eliot, but although *Cranford* has always remained a favourite with the general reader her other novels were underrated in critical esteem for a full century after her death.

GENET, Jean (1910–86): the French novelist and dramatist, who spent much of the earlier part of his life in reformatories or in prison. His literary work is clearly marked by those experiences. He has published the autobiographical *Journal du voleur* (1949; English tr., *The Thief's Journal*, 1954), and novels such as *Notre Dame des fleurs* (1944; *Our Lady of the Flowers*, 1949), and *Miracle de la rose* (1946; *Miracle of the Rose*, 1965). His plays include *Les Bonnes* (1948; *The Maids*, 1954) and *Le Balcon* (1956; *The Balcony*, 1957).

GERHARDIE (originally GERHARDI), William (1895–1977): born of English parents in St Petersburg, Gerhardie served during the First World War in the British embassy at Petrograd, then with the British military mission in Siberia. He then attended Worcester College, Oxford, where he wrote the first English book on *Chekhov and his first novel *Futility: a Novel on Russian Themes* (1922). During the next 15 years he produced many other novels admired by, among others, H. G. *Wells and E. *Waugh. They include *The Polyglots* (1925), perhaps his best-known work, *Pending Heaven* (1930), and *Of Mortal Love* (1936). His autobiography, *Memoirs of a Polyglot*, appeared in 1931.

GIDE, André (1869–1951): French novelist, essayist, critic, and dramatist, whose works included a number of short novels, including *L'Immoraliste* (1902; *The Immoralist*, 1930) and *La Symphonie pastorale* (1919; *The Pastoral Symphony*, 1931), and two longer ones, *Les Caves du Vatican* (1914; translated under various titles: *The Vatican Swindle*, 1925; *Lafcadio's Adventures*, 1928; *The Vatican Cellars*, 1952) and *Les Faux-monnayeurs* (1925; *The Counterfeiters*, 1927). He also wrote a number of autobiographical works, including *Si le grain ne meurt*... (1926; *If It Die*..., 1935), which describes his revolt against his Protestant upbringing, and his *Journal* for the years 1889 to 1949 (*The Journals of André Gide*, 1947–51). He was awarded the Nobel Prize for literature in 1947.

GOETHE, Johann Wolfgang von (1749–1832): born at Frankfurt am Main. Goethe, against his inclination, was trained for the law. In 1775 he was invited by the Duke of Weimar to his Court, and thereafter spent most of his life in Weimar, occupying positions of increasing importance in the government. In 1791 he was appointed director of the Weimar Court theatre, a post he held for many years. He was a man of wide-ranging interests who besides his literary accomplishments evolved a new theory of the character of light and made important discoveries in connection with plant and animal life.

In the field of literature Goethe's most famous work was the poetic drama *Faust*, the story of a wandering conjuror who lived in Germany about 1488–1541. It was published in two parts, the first in 1809, the second in 1832. His first important work, a drama called *Götz von Berlichingen mit der eisernen Hand* (1773), excited Sir W. *Scott, who translated it (inaccurately) in 1799. It was followed by a number of other plays; by novels, which include *Die Leiden des jungen Werthers* (*The Sorrows of Young Werther*, 1774), *Die Wahlverwandtschaften* (*Elective Affinities*, 1809), and the famous 'Wilhelm Meister' novels written at intervals between 1777 and 1829; and by several volumes of poetry. Though Goethe is most celebrated, particularly outside Germany, for *Faust* and the novels, he was also a lyric poet of great genius. Many of his poems, as well as the songs from 'Wilhelm Meister', were set to music by German Romantic composers.

Goethe's achievement in literature covers an astonishing range of forms, though all his works stand in a close relation to the social and emotional events of his life. The most decisive influences of his life were Herder, who introduced him to *Shakespeare, and *Schiller, with whom he began a close friendship in 1794. In Britain, Goethe exercised an enormous influence on *Carlyle, who translated him. Through Carlyle a whole generation of Victorians turned their attention to Goethe, and eminent authors like G. *Eliot and M. *Arnold paid tribute to his genius.

GOGOL, Nikolai (1809–52): born in the Ukraine, which he used as a setting for his early writings, Gogol left for St Petersburg in 1828. His first collection of stories, *Evenings on a Farm near Dikanka*, appeared in 1831–2, and was followed by two others, *Mirgorod* and *Arabesques* (1835), and by his brilliant St Petersburg stories which are set in a mad city where nothing is what it seems. His play, *The Government Inspector* (or *Inspector-General*), a savagely satirical picture of life in a provincial Russian town, appeared in 1836. From that year to 1848 Gogol lived mainly abroad and worked on his masterpiece, the comic epic *Dead Souls*; the first part was published in 1842, but he burnt both drafts of the second part. Gogol's prose is characterized by extraordinary imaginative power and linguistic originality, and his fictional world is unique and fantastic. He was much admired by the young *Dostoevsky.

GOLDING, William (1911–): educated at Marlborough Grammar School and Oxford, Golding published a volume of verse, *Poems*, in 1935, but his first novel, *Lord of the Flies*, did not appear until 1954 when it was an immediate success. It was followed by *The Inheritors* (1955), *Pincher Martin* (1956), *Brass Butterfly* (a play, 1958), *Free Fall* (1959), *The Spire* (1964), and a collection of essays, *The Hot Gates* (1965). His later novels include *Rites of Passage* which won the 1980 Booker Prize, and he was awarded the Nobel Prize for Literature in 1983. Golding often presents isolated individuals or small groups in extreme situations dealing with man in his basic condition stripped of trappings, creating a quality of a fable.

GOLDSMITH, Oliver (?1730–74): educated at Trinity College, Dublin, and then in Leiden after studying medicine in Edinburgh, Goldsmith embarked on a literary career in London as reviewer and hack-writer for a number of periodicals. In 1761 he met Dr *Johnson, who admired his work. They became friends and the following year Johnson sold for him the (possibly unfinished) manuscript of *The Vicar of Wakefield*, thereby saving Goldsmith from arrest for debt. It was published in 1766 and subsequently became one of the most popular works of fiction in the language. He also wrote a number of biographies, abridgements, and translations as hack-work which in all totalled more than 40 volumes. But he first achieved literary distinction with his poem *The Traveller*, which appeared in 1764, and after the publication of his most famous poem *The Deserted Village* (1770) published several volumes of lighter verse.

Goldsmith's first comedy, *The Good-Natur'd Man*, was rejected by Garrick but produced at Covent Garden in 1768 with moderate success; *She Stoops to Conquer* followed in 1773 with immense success.

GOWER, John (?1330–1408): from a family of gentry who owned land in Kent and Yorkshire, Gower probably lived in Kent throughout the first half of his life. He may have been trained in the law, but from 1377 to his death he lived at a priory in Southwark, devoted to his writing. His considerable learning is attested by his writing with accomplishment in three languages. In French he wrote his *Cinkante Balades*, written in Anglo-Norman before 1374, and presented to Henry IV in 1400, and his first large-scale work the *Mirour de l'Omme (Speculum Meditantis)*, an allegory written *c.*1376–8 in about 32 000 lines of octosyllabics in 12-line stanzas. His second major work was the much more considerable Latin *Vox Clamantis* (*c.*1379–81), an apocalyptic poem of seven books in 10 265 lines of elegiac couplets. In English he wrote the late poem 'In Praise of Peace' in 55 stanzas of rhyme royal, as well as his principal work, the *Confessio Amantis*. This is over 33 000 lines long, and contains 141 stories which draw widely on classical story (most prominently Ovid) and medieval romance. They are in octosyllabic couplets, which are handled with a metrical sophistication and skill unsurpassed in English. Several are paralleled by stories in *The Canterbury Tales* and other works by *Chaucer. The pairs of narratives are usually compared to Gower's disadvantage, because his stories lack the development and dramatic scope of Chaucer's; but the lucidity and pointedness, as well as the stylistic accomplishment, of Gower are admirable too. Perhaps his significance as an English writer is to have brought into the mainstream of the canon of the literature the disparate narratives of the classics and the popular romances.

GRAHAME, Kenneth (1859–1932): born in Edinburgh, Grahame went to school in Oxford and then entered the Bank of England, where he became Secretary in 1898. Though he gained success both in England and the US with earlier books (*The Golden Age*, 1895, and *Dream Days*, 1898), he is now best remembered for *The Wind in the Willows*, based largely on bedtime stories and letters to his son and never intended for publication. Its reception was muted when it was published in 1908 and it was some years before it became established as a children's classic.

GRAVES, Robert (1895–1985): educated at Charterhouse; Graves's first poetry appeared while he was serving during the First World War. In 1919 he went to St John's College, Oxford. He left without a degree but later successfully submitted a critical work as a thesis for a B.Litt.

Graves's output was prodigious; he wrote many volumes of poetry, essays, fiction, biography, and works for children, and published many free translations from various languages. Among his best-known works are his powerful autobiography, *Goodbye to All That* (1929), his two novels, *I, Claudius* and *Claudius the God* (both 1934), and *The White Goddess: a historical grammar of poetic myth* (1948). His volumes of verse appeared regularly over the years, and his *Collected Poems* of 1955 confirmed a world-wide reputation.

GRAY, Thomas (1716–71): educated at Eton and Cambridge, Gray published *Ode on a Distant Prospect of Eton College*, the first of his works to appear in print, in 1747. In 1750 he completed *Elegy Written in a Country Church-Yard*, which was published the following year, and in 1754 finished his Pindaric ode on *The Progress of Poesy*, and in 1757 a second Pindaric ode, *The Bard*. Both these last were published by Horace Walpole, a friend from his school-days, the first works printed by the Strawberry Hill Press. They were his last major poems, but by this time, owing largely to the *Elegy*, his poetry was extremely popular. His remaining years were devoted largely to antiquarian and botanical studies, and to travels to Scotland and the Lake District.

GREENE, Graham (1904–): educated at Berkhamsted School, where his father was headmaster, then at Oxford, Greene joined the Roman Catholic Church in 1926, married in 1927, and was from 1926 to 1930 on the staff of *The Times*. His first three novels (1929–31), which he later disclaimed, made little impression, but *Stamboul Train* (1932) sold well and was followed by many increasingly successful novels, short stories, books of reportage and travel, plays, children's books, etc. His novels include *England Made Me* (1935), *The Power and the Glory* (1940), *The Heart of the Matter* (1948), *The End of the Affair* (1951), *The Quiet American* (1955), *A Burnt-Out Case* (1961), *The Honorary Consul* (1973), and *The Human Factor* (1978). Other works of fiction he classed as 'entertainments': these include *Brighton Rock* (1938), *The Confidential Agent* (1939), *Loser Takes All* (1955), and *Our Man in Havana* (1958). *The Third Man* (1950), also described as an entertainment, was originally written as a screenplay and filmed (1949) by Carol Reed. Greene's plays include *The Living Room* (1953), *The Potting Shed* (1957), and *The Complaisant Lover* (1959). His range as a writer is wide, both geographically and in variations of tone, while his skilful variations of popular forms (the thriller, the detective story) have brought him a rare combination of critical and popular admiration. He was awarded the Order of Merit in 1986.

GRIMM, Jacob (1785–1863) and Wilhelm (1786–1859): the German brothers who pioneered the study of German philology, law, mythology, and folklore. They are chiefly known in England for their collection of fairy-tales, *Kinder- und Hausmärchen* (1812–15), of which an English translation, illustrated by Cruikshank, was published in 1823 under the title *German Popular Stories*.

HARDY, Thomas (1840–1928): born at Upper Bockhampton, near Dorchester in Dorset, Hardy was the son of a stonemason. His first published novel, *Desperate Remedies*, appeared in 1871, and the success of *Far from the Madding Crowd* (1874) enabled him to give up architectural work for writing, and to marry. The marriage produced intolerable strains, but it also produced, after his wife's death in 1912, some of Hardy's most moving poems. The underlying theme of many of his novels, the short poems, and the epic drama *The Dynasts* (a vast work in blank verse and prose published in three volumes in 1904, 1906, and 1908) is, in *Binyon's words, 'the implanted crookedness of things'; the struggle of man against the indifferent force that rules the world and inflicts on him the sufferings and ironies of life and love.

Hardy's novels and short stories, according to his own classification, fall into three groups: the Novels of Character and Environment like *Far from the Madding Crowd*, *The Return of the Native* (1878), *The Mayor of Casterbridge* (1886), *Tess of the D'Urbervilles* (1891), and *Jude the Obscure* (1896); Romances and Fantasies like *A Pair of Blue Eyes* (1873) and *A Group of Noble Dames* (1891); and Novels of Ingenuity like *Desperate Remedies* and *The Hand of Ethelberta* (1876). *A Changed Man, The Waiting Supper, and other Tales* (1913) is a reprint of 'a dozen minor novels' belonging to the various groups. He also published eight volumes of poetry, including *Wessex Poems* (1898) and his *Collected Poems* (1930), and over 40 short stories, most of which were collected in *Wessex Tales* (1888) and three other volumes.

HARTLEY, L(eslie) P(oles) (1895–1972): educated at Harrow and Oxford, Hartley began his literary career as a writer of short stories and as a fiction reviewer. His first full-length novel, *The Shrimp and the Anemone* (1944), was followed by *The Sixth Heaven* (1946) and *Eustace and Hilda* (1947), the last being the title by which the trilogy is known. But his best-known novel is *The Go-Between* (1953), which was followed by several others.

HAWTHORNE, Nathaniel (1804–64): born at Salem, Massachusetts, USA, Hawthorne published his first novel, *Fanshawe* (1828), at his own expense. His stories began to appear in journals and were collected in *Twice-Told Tales* (1837) and other volumes. In 1850 he met *Melville, who admired Hawthorne's work enormously, and indeed wrote an enthusiastic review comparing him to the Shakespeare of the tragedies. His other works include essays, some lasting books for children, and four novels, *The Scarlet Letter* (1850), *The House of the Seven Gables* (1851), *The Blithedale Romance* (1852), and *The Marble Faun* (1860). Hawthorne has long been recognized as one of the greatest of American writers, a moralist and allegorist much preoccupied with the mystery of sin, the paradox of its occasionally regenerative power, and the compensation for unmerited suffering and crime.

HAZLITT, William (1778–1830): born at Maidstone, Hazlitt was trained for the ministry but gave it up in the hope of becoming a painter. However, under the powerful influence of *Coleridge he decided on writing as a career. In London he became the friend of C. *Lamb, who introduced him to other literary men, and he began a long career as a prolific journalist, parliamentary reporter, dramatic and literary critic, essayist, and lecturer. Hazlitt was the first English writer to make a large part of his livelihood from descriptive criticism. His merits as a critic are not always agreed, yet even his detractors concede the great range of his reading and his achievement as a critical historian at a time when no history of English literature existed.

HELLER, Joseph (1923–): born in New York, USA, Heller served as a bombardier during the Second World War, an experience which resurfaced in his first novel, *Catch-22* (1961), which took him eight years to write and brought him instant fame. His other novels are *Something Happened* (1974) and *Good as Gold* (1979).

HEMINGWAY, Ernest (1899–1961): born in Illinois, USA, Hemingway worked as a Kansas City reporter before serving as a volunteer with an ambulance unit on the Italian front during the First World War, where he was wounded. He then worked as a reporter for the *Toronto Star* before settling in Paris, where he met *Pound, *Stein, and others described in his posthumously published *A Moveable Feast* (1964). His novels include *The Sun Also Rises* (1926; in England, as *Fiesta*, 1927), with which he made his name, *A Farewell to Arms* (1929), *For Whom the Bell Tolls* (1940), and *The Old Man and the Sea* (1952). He has been considered a finer writer of short stories than of novels, and his collections *Men Without Women* (1927) and *Winner Take Nothing* (1933) are especially notable. He was awarded the Nobel Prize for Literature in 1954 and wrote little thereafter.

HENRY, O. (1862–1910): pseudonym of William Sydney Porter. O. Henry had a chequered early career, which included a term in prison for embezzlement. He began to write short stories in prison and published the first of his many collections, *Cabbages and Kings*, in 1904. He was prolific, humorous, and highly ingenious, especially in his use of coincidence, and became the most famous writer of his kind of the day.

HERRICK, Robert (1591–1674): born in London, Herrick was apprenticed in 1607 to his uncle, a wealthy goldsmith. His earliest datable poem was written about 1610 to his brother Thomas. In 1613, having obtained release from his apprenticeship, he entered St John's College, Cambridge, but later moved to Trinity Hall. In 1623, after obtaining an MA, he was ordained priest. He evidently mixed with literary circles in London, particularly the group around *Jonson, and was well known as a poet by 1625. In 1630 he took up the living of a Devonshire village, Dean Prior, but as an ardent loyalist he was ejected from it by Parliament in 1647 and returned to London, where the following year his poems *Hesperides*, together with his religious poems *Nobel Numbers*, were published. In 1660 he was reinstated in his living and he remained there for the rest of his life but, apparently, wrote no more poems. As late as 1810 villagers there could repeat some of his verses. He is one of the finest English lyric poets, and has a faultless ear. *Swinburne, with little exaggeration, called him 'the greatest song-writer ever born of English race'.

HESSE, Hermann (1877–1962): the German author of several novels of a more or less mysterious nature which attracted a revival of interest in Germany and Britain in the 1960s, Hesse was awarded the Nobel Prize for Literature in 1946. They include *Siddhartha* (1922), *Der Steppenwolf* (1927), and *Das Glasperlenspiel* (*The Glass Bead Game*, 1943).

HOPKINS, Gerard Manley (1844–89): educated at Highgate School and Oxford, where he went in 1863, Hopkins published in the same year 'Winter with the Gulf Stream'. At Oxford he made many friends, including *Bridges, wrote much poetry, including 'Heaven-Haven' and 'The Habit of Perfection', and obtained a First Class degree. In 1868 he was received into the Roman Catholic Church and the following year resolved to become a Jesuit. For the next few years he wrote little, devoting himself to the life of a novice. In 1876 a new phase of creativity began with the writing of 'The Wreck of the Deutschland'. After his ordination he wrote 'Henry Purcell' and while working in various industrial parishes in Liverpool, 'Felix Randal' and 'Spring and Fall'. In 1884 he was appointed to the chair of Greek and Latin at University College, Dublin, where he wrote a number of 'Dark Sonnets', including 'Carrion Comfort' and 'No worst, there is none'. He wrote to Bridges describing his weakness and desolation, but managed to produce in these last years less desperate poems, including 'Harry Ploughman' and 'That Nature is a Heraclitean Fire'.

Apart from work in anthologies nothing was published of Hopkins's until 1918, when Bridges produced his *Poems*; Bridges, to whom many of Hopkins's poems and papers went after his death, had judged the public not ready to receive Hopkins's 'oddity', but initial bewilderment was followed by steadily rising admiration, and Hopkins is now recognized as a major poet. His poems, letters, and journals reflect his whole-hearted involvement in all aspects of his life—his sense of vocation (sometimes conflicting) as priest and poet, his love of beauty in nature and man, his technical interest in prosody, and his search for a unifying sacramental view of creation.

HOUSMAN, A(lfred) E(dward) (1859–1936): educated at Bromsgrove and Oxford, Housman, who was brilliant, failed his Finals and spent ten years as a clerk in the Patent Office in London, during which time he worked on Propertius, Ovid, Juvenal, and other classical authors, publishing articles when he could. In 1892 he was appointed a professor of Latin in London University, where he began to produce his definitive edition of Manilius, which appeared in five volumes, 1902–30. In 1896 he published at his own expense *A Shropshire Lad*, a series of 63 spare and nostalgic verses, based largely on ballad-forms, and mainly set in a half-imaginary Shropshire. Housman met with little encouragement, but initial public indifference to the poem slowly gave way to interest, and sales mounted steadily, and during the years of the First World War it became hugely popular. *Last Poems*, whose 41 poems met with great acclaim, was published in 1922, *More Poems* appeared in 1936, and his *Collected Poems* posthumously in 1939.

HUGHES, Richard (1900–76): educated at Charterhouse and Oxford, Hughes began writing at an early age and while at Oxford published a volume of poems, *Gipsy Night* (1922). His first ambition was to be a dramatist and he was commissioned by the BBC to write the first original radio play, *Danger*, produced in 1924. He gained fame with his first novel, *A High Wind in Jamaica* (1929), which paved the way for such works as *Golding's *Lord of the Flies*. It was followed by *In Hazard* (1938) and *Fox in the Attic* (1961), the first volume of an ambitious new project, 'The Human Predicament'. The second volume, *The Wooden Shepherdess*, was published in 1973. He also wrote three volumes of short stories and two plays, and his collected poems, *Confessio Juvenis*, appeared in 1926.

HUGHES, Ted (1930–): born in West Yorkshire, and educated at Mexborough Grammar School and Cambridge, Hughes as a boy spent much time on shooting and fishing expeditions, and his obsession with animals and his sense of the beauty and violence of the natural world appear in his first volume of verse, *The Hawk in the Rain* (1957). This was followed by *Lupercal* (1960), *Wodwo* (1967, prose and verse), and several books of children's verse. *Crow* (1970) is a sequence of poems introducing the central symbol of the crow, which recurs frequently in subsequent volumes. Later volumes include *Cave Birds* (1975), *Season Songs* (1976), and *Moortown* (1979). He has also published plays for children and a version of Seneca's *Oedipus* (1968), and edited various anthologies. He was appointed Poet Laureate in 1984.

HUGHES, Tom (1822–96): educated at Rugby School and Oxford, Hughes was a barrister and Liberal MP who devoted much energy to working men's education, the Co-operative movement, etc. He is remembered as the author of *Tom Brown's Schooldays* (1857, by 'An Old Boy'), which evokes the Rugby of his youth and his veneration for its headmaster, Dr T. Arnold. The sequel, *Tom Brown at Oxford* (1861), is less interesting. Hughes also wrote several biographies and memoirs, and one other novel.

HUGO, Victor (1802–85): the central figure of the Romantic movement in France, Hugo is regarded as one of the masters of French poetry, to which he brought a new freedom of subject, diction, and versification. His many collections include: *Odes* (1822), *Odes et Ballades* (1826), *Les Orientales* (1829), *Les Feuilles d'automne* (1831), *Les Chants du crépuscule* (1835), *Les Rayons et les ombres* (1840), and *Les Châtiments* (1853). The poems of *La Légende des siècles* (1859, 1877, 1883) compose an epic and prophetic treatment of history, of which the posthumously-published *La Fin de Satan* (1886) and *Dieu* (1891) were intended to form the final parts. Of Hugo's plays, *Cromwell* (1827), *Hernani* (1830), and *Ruy Blas* (1838) are variously important; the first because of its preface, which became a manifesto of the French Romantic movement. The first two performances of *Hernani* mark an epoch in the French theatre and have entered its mythology. *Ruy Blas* continued his success in verse drama. He also wrote a number of novels, among them the well-known *Notre Dame de Paris* (1831) and *Les Misérables* (1862).

HUXLEY, Aldous (1894–1963): educated at Eton and Oxford, Huxley at 16 developed serious eye trouble which made him nearly blind, though he recovered sufficiently to read English at Balliol College. By 1919 he had already published three volumes of verse, and a volume of short stories, *Limbo* (1920), was followed by *Chrome Yellow* (1921), a country-house satire which earned him a reputation for precocious brilliance and cynicism. While living in Europe during the 1920s and 1930s he wrote much fiction, including *Antic Hay* (1923), *Those Barren Leaves* (1925), *Point Counter Point* (1928), *Brave New World* (1932), *Eyeless in Gaza* (1936), *After Many A Summer* (1939), and *Island* (1962). He also wrote essays, historical studies, and travel books; *The Doors of Perception* (1954) and *Heaven and Hell* (1956) describe his experiments with mescalin and LSD. Although *Brave New World* has an assured place as a popular classic, Huxley's other novels have proved difficult to 'place' as literature. Their mixture of satire and earnestness, of apparent brutality and humanity, have led some to dismiss them as smart and superficial; others have seen them as brilliant and provocative 'novels of ideas'.

IBSEN, Henrik (1828–1906): Norwegian dramatist who is generally acknowledged as the founder of modern prose drama. His first successes, *Brand* (1866) and *Peer Gynt* (1867), created his name in Scandinavia, but it was over 20 years before he was established as a major dramatist in England. In 1889 a long review of Ibsen's work by Gosse was followed by a highly successful production of *A Doll's House* (1879). In 1891 a single performance of *Ghosts* (1881) and a commercial production of *Hedda Gabler* (1890) both caused a storm of outrage. Ibsen's earlier plays (such as *Ghosts* and *An Enemy of* *the People*, 1882) were concerned largely with social and political themes, but the last six (which include *Rosmersholm*, 1886; *The Master Builder*, 1892; and *Little Eyolf*, 1896) are more deeply concerned with the forces of the unconscious, and were greatly admired by Freud.

ISHERWOOD, Christopher (1904–86): educated at Repton School and Cambridge; Isherwood's first novels, *All the Conspirators* (1928) and *The Memorial* (1932), show the influence (as he acknowledged) of E. M. *Forster and V. *Woolf; his own voice appears distinctly in *Mr Norris Changes Trains* (1935) and *Goodbye to Berlin* (1939), works which reflect his experiences of living in Berlin between 1929 and 1933. They were planned as part of a long novel, to be entitled *The Lost*, which was never written. Isherwood travelled widely in Europe after leaving Berlin, went to China with *Auden in 1938, and in 1939 went with him to America; he became an American citizen in 1946. During the 1930s he collaborated with Auden in the writing of *The Ascent of F6* and several other works, and his later novels include *Down There on a Visit* (1962) and *A Single Man* (1964).

JAMES, Henry (1843–1916): after a desultory education in New York, London, Paris, and Geneva, James entered the law school at Harvard in 1862. He settled in Europe in 1875. He at first chiefly concerned himself with the impact of the older civilization of Europe upon American life, and to this period belong his novels *Roderick Hudson* (1876), his first important novel, *The American* (1877), *Daisy Miller* (1879), and *Portrait of a Lady* (1881). He next turned to a more exclusively English stage in *The Tragic Muse* (1890), *The Spoils of Poynton* (1897), and *The Awkward Age* (1899), in which he analysed English character with extreme subtlety, verging at times on obscurity. *What Maisie Knew* appeared in 1897. In his last three great novels, *The Wings of the Dove* (1902), *The Ambassadors* (1903), and *The Golden Bowl* (1904), he returned to the 'international' theme of the contrast of American and European character.

Besides more than 100 short stories (including the well-known ghost story *The Turn of the Screw*, 1898), James wrote several volumes of sketches of travel and a number of plays. His other works include the novels *Washington Square* (1881), *The Bostonians* (1886), and *The Aspern Papers* (1888). In 1915 he became a British subject and was awarded the OM the following year.

JEROME, Jerome K(lapka) (1859–1927): brought up in east London, Jerome became an actor and published a volume of humorous pieces about the theatre and another collection of light essays, *Idle Thoughts of an Idle Fellow* (1886). He achieved lasting fame with *Three Men in a Boat* (1889), which was followed by *Three Men on the Bummel* (1900) and an autobiographical novel, *Paul Klever* (1902). He also wrote many plays, in the manner of his friend *Barrie, including the most memorable, *The Passing of the Third Floor Back* (1907).

JOHNSON, Samuel (1709–84): educated at Lichfield Grammar School and Oxford—which he left after 14 months without taking a degree—Johnson worked briefly and unhappily as an under-master before starting a private school at Edial, near Lichfield. It was not a success, and in 1737 he set off with one of his few pupils, Garrick, to try his fortune in London. He had already contributed essays to the *Birmingham Journal* (none of which survive) and he now started contributing to *The Gentleman's Magazine* as well as writing prefaces and other editorial work. In 1738 he published his poem *London*, which may record his friendship with the poet Savage, whose nocturnal wanderings he often shared during this period of poverty and hack-work; his *Life of Mr Richard Savage* (1744) is a vivid evocation of Grub Street and a notable stage in the evolution of the art of biography. In 1746 he entered into an agreement with a publisher and others to write a dictionary, the first of its kind in English, and started work with six humble assistants in newly rented premises in Gough Square. It was published in 1755. He said his object was to produce 'a dictionary by which the pronunciation of our language may be fixed and its attainment facilitated; by which its purity may be preserved, its use ascertained, and its duration lengthened'. He wrote the definitions of over 40 000 words, illustrating them with about 114 000 quotations drawn from every field of learning and literature from the time of *Sidney onwards; his derivations suffer from the scantiness of etymological knowledge in his day, but the work as a whole remained without rival until the creation of the *Oxford English Dictionary*. His well-known definitions (e.g. *lexicographer*, 'a writer of dictionaries, a harmless drudge') represent a mere handful in the body of this enormous achievement.

In 1749 Johnson published *The Vanity of Human Wishes*, the first work to bear his own name, and in the same year Garrick produced his tragedy *Irene*, written in 1736 at Edial; it brought him almost £300. In 1750 he started *The Rambler*, a periodical written almost entirely by himself partly for money and partly for 'relief' from the *Dictionary*. When the *Dictionary* was published it firmly established his reputation and brought him the Oxford degree he had failed to achieve earlier. He continued to write essays, reviews, and political articles for various periodicals, and in 1765 appeared his edition of *Shakespeare, on which he had been at work for some years. Although superseded by later scholarship, it contained valuable notes and emendations, and its Preface is regarded as one of his finest works of critical prose. His later publications include *A Journey to the Western Islands of Scotland* (1775) and the crowning work of his old age, *The Lives of the English Poets* (1779–81).

In 1763 Johnson met his biographer, Boswell, and his reputation rests not only on his works but also on Boswell's evocation of his brilliant conversation, his eccentricities and opinionated outbursts, his interest in the supernatural, his generosity and humanity, and many other aspects of his large personality.

See also article on 'Dr Johnson and the English Language' by Professor Pat Rogers on p. 535.

JONSON, Ben(jamin) (1572/3–1637): dramatist, poet, scholar, and writer of Court masques, Jonson was educated at Westminster School. His first important play, *Every Man in his Humour*, with Shakespeare in the cast, was performed in 1598, and *Every Man out of his Humour* the following year. His first extant tragedy, *Sejanus*, was given at the Globe by Shakespeare's company in 1603, followed by *Volpone* (1605–6), *Epicene, or The Silent Woman* (1609–10), *The Alchemist* (1610), and *Bartholomew Fair* (1614).

Though he was not formally appointed the first Poet Laureate, the essentials of the position were conferred on Jonson in 1616, when a pension was granted to him by James I. In the same year he published a folio edition of his *Works*, which raised the drama to a new level of literary respectability. After *The Devil is an Ass* (1616), he abandoned the public stage for ten years, and his later plays show a relatively unsuccessful reliance on allegory and symbolism; *Dryden called them his 'dotages'. From 1605 onwards Jonson was constantly producing masques for the Court, and this form of entertainment reached its highest elaboration in his hands. His non-dramatic verse includes *Epigrams* and *The Forest*, printed in the folio of 1616, and *The Underwood* and a translation of Horace's *Ars Poetica*, printed in 1640. His chief prose works are *The English Grammar* and *Timber, or Discoveries*, printed in 1640.

During the reign of James I Jonson's literary prestige and influence were unrivalled. His reputation declined sharply from about 1700, as Shakespeare's, with whom he was inevitably compared, increased, but in this century it has revived.

JOYCE, James (1882–1941): a good linguist, Joyce from an early age read and studied widely, and in 1901 wrote a letter of profound admiration in Dano-Norwegian to *Ibsen. Other early influences were *Dante and *Yeats. After living in Trieste for some years, Joyce moved first to Zurich before finally settling in Paris after the First World War. His first published work was a volume of verse, *Chamber Music* (1907), followed by *Dubliners* (1914), a volume of short stories. When it appeared it was greeted with enthusiasm by *Pound, whose support greatly encouraged Joyce's career and reputation. *A Portrait of the Artist as a Young Man*, a largely autobiographical work, was published serially in 1914–15. His famous novel *Ulysses* was first published in Paris in 1922 and was received as a work of genius by writers as varied as T. S. *Eliot and *Hemingway, though others were less admiring. Another small volume of verse, *Pomes Penyeach*, appeared in 1927, and his second great work, *Finnegans Wake*, extracts of which had already appeared as 'Work in Progress', was published in its complete form in 1939. He also wrote a play, *Exiles*, which was performed unsuccessfully in Munich in 1918. *Ulysses* and *Finnegans Wake* revolutionized the form and structure of the novel, decisively influenced the development of the 'stream of consciousness' or 'interior monologue', and pushed language and linguistic experiment (particularly in the latter work) to the extreme limits of communication.

KAFKA, Franz (1883–1924): born in Prague, Kafka was the author of three novels, *Der Prozess* (*The Trial*, 1925), *Das Schloss* (*The Castle*, 1926), and the unfinished *Amerika* (1927), and also a large number of short stories, of which 'Das Urteil' ('The Judgement', 1913) and 'Die Verwandlung' ('The Metamorphosis', 1915) are among the best known. His novels were first published after his death by his friend Max Brod, and were translated into English, beginning with *The Trial* in 1930. Characteristic of Kafka's work is the portrayal of an enigmatic reality, in which the individual is seen as lonely, perplexed, and threatened, and guilt is one of his major themes.

KEATS, John (1795–1821): after attending Clarke's School, Enfield, Keats in 1816 was licensed to practise as an apothecary, but abandoned this to write poetry. In 1816 his poem 'O Solitude' and the sonnet 'On First Looking into Chapman's Homer' were published. He met *Shelley and Haydon and began to plan *Endymion*, which appeared in 1818. His first volume of poems was published in 1817 and though there were some pleasing reviews public interest was not aroused. During the winter of 1817–18 he saw something of *Wordsworth and *Hazlitt, both of whom much influenced his thought and practice. September 1818 marked the beginning of what is sometimes referred to as the Great Year; he wrote, amongst other poems, 'The Eve of St Agnes', 'The Eve of St Mark', the 'Ode to Psyche', 'La Belle Dame sans Merci', 'Ode to a Nightingale', and probably at about the same time the 'Ode on a Grecian Urn', 'Ode on Melancholy', and 'Ode on Indolence'. In the winter of 1819 he became increasingly ill and his great creative work was now over. His second volume of poems, *Lamia, Isabella, The Eve of St Agnes, and other Poems*, was published in 1820, and it was generally well received. He died the following February in Rome.

Keats has always been regarded as one of the principal figures in the Romantic movement (see Coleridge), and his stature as a poet has grown steadily through all changes of fashion.

KEROUAC, Jack (1922–69): born in Massachusetts, USA, of French-Canadian parents, Kerouac was educated at Columbia University. He is best known in Britain for his semi-autobiographical novel *On the Road* (1957). His other works include *The Dharma Bums* (1958) and *The Subterraneans* (1958).

Kerouac became a spokesman for the Beat generation, a phrase used to describe a group of American writers who emerged in the 1950s, and generally agreed to have been coined in this sense (with connotations of beatitude, disengagement, down-and-out 'street' language and experience, spontaneity, etc.) by him. The beat emphasis was on escape from conventional, puritanical, middle-class (termed 'square') mores, towards visionary enlightenment and artistic improvisation, approached via (Zen) Buddhism and other echoes of religious confessional, such as American Indian and Mexican peyote cults. Influential texts include Ginsberg's long poems and the laconic documentary collage novels of William Burroughs (*Junkie*, 1953; and *The Naked Lunch*, 1959). The experimental forms, metaphysical content, and provocative anti-intellectual, anti-hierarchical spirit of the movement were taken up by second- and third-generation writers (Yevtushenko, Bob Dylan, the Beatles), evolving a 'counter-culture' which had a widespread and in many ways lasting impact.

KINGSLEY, Charles (1819–75): educated at Helston Grammar School, King's College, London, and Cambridge, Kingsley became a curate and, in 1844, rector of Eversley in Hampshire. His first two novels *Yeast* (1850) and *Alton Locke* (1850) show his concern with the sufferings of the working classes. His other novels include *Westward Ho!* (1855), and *Hereward the Wake* (1866). He also wrote for the young, especially *The Water-Babies* (1863), and tracts on many topics. Though most of his poetry is forgotten, many of his songs and ballads, including 'Airly Beacon' and 'The Sands of Dee', remain popular, and some of his lines, like 'For men must work and women must weep', have become proverbial. Kingsley in his lifetime was a celebrated and revered figure, and although his works are now read largely for their social interest his complex personality continues to interest biographers.

KIPLING, Rudyard (1865–1936): born in Bombay, Kipling was brought to England in 1871 and his education there was later depicted in his schoolboy tales *Stalky & Co.* (1899). From 1882 to 1889 he worked as a journalist in India; many of his early poems and stories published there were later collected under various titles, including *Plain Tales from the Hills* (1888) and *Wee Willie Winkie* (1890). In 1889 he came to London, where he achieved instant literary celebrity, aided by the publication of many of the poems ('Danny Deever', 'Mandalay', etc.) later collected as *Barrack-Room Ballads* (1892).

Kipling's output was vast and varied, and has been variously judged. His early tales of the Raj, praised for their cynical realism, were compared to those of *Maupassant, but he was increasingly accused of vulgarity and jingoism in aesthetic and anti-imperialist circles. His most uncontroversial and durable achievements are perhaps his tales for children (principally *The Jungle Book*, 1894; *Just So Stories*, 1902; and *Puck of Pook's Hill*, 1906) and his picaresque novel of India, *Kim* (1901), generally considered his masterpiece.

KOESTLER, Arthur (1905–83): born in Budapest and educated at the University of Vienna, Koestler worked as foreign correspondent in the

Middle East, Paris, and Berlin. In 1932 he joined the Communist Party but broke from it in 1938. After being imprisoned under Franco during the Spanish Civil War, he came, in 1940, to England. His publications manifest a wide range of political, scientific and literary interests, and include his novel *Darkness at Noon* (1940) and several works of non-fiction.

LA FONTAINE, Jean de (1621–95): French poet, author of the *Fables,* a collection of some 240 poems, published in twelve books between 1668 and 1694 (English tr., 1734). The material for the fables is drawn from Eastern, classical, and modern sources, and a number of them have long enjoyed widespread popularity in France.

LAMB, Charles (1775–1834): educated at Christ's Hospital, where he became a lifelong friend of *Coleridge, Lamb was for a short time deranged and the threat of madness became a shadow on his life. He wrote several plays as well as essays, collections of stories, and criticism for a number of periodicals, including the *London Magazine*, in which appeared the first series of essays known as *Essays of Elia*, published in a collected volume in 1823. The second series appeared in 1833. Of his poems the best known are 'The Old Familiar Faces', the lyrical ballad 'Hester' (1803), and an elegy 'On an Infant dying as soon as born' (1827), probably his finest poem. *Album Verses* (1830) includes many other lyrics and sonnets. A. C. Bradley regarded Lamb as the greatest critic of his century, but few would follow Bradley quite so far.

LANGLAND, William (perhaps c.1330–c.1386): the author of the poem *Piers Plowman*, of whose identity and life very little is known for certain.

LARKIN, Philip (1922–85): educated at King Henry VIII School, Coventry, and at Oxford; Larkin's early poems appeared in an anthology, *Poetry from Oxford in Wartime* (1944), and a collection, *The North Ship* (1945). He then published a novel, *Jill* (1946), set in wartime Oxford, and a second novel, *A Girl in Winter*, appeared in 1947. His other works include three volumes of poetry, *The Less Deceived* (1955), *The Whitsun Weddings* (1964), and *High Windows* (1974), and a volume of essays, *Required Writing* (1983).

During the 1950s Larkin's name was associated with the Movement, a term coined in 1954 to describe a group of writers including *Amis, D. J. Enright, *Wain, and Robert Conquest. Two anthologies, Enright's *Poets of the 1950s* (1955) and Conquest's *New Lines* (1956) which included poems by Larkin, illustrate the Movement's predominately anti-romantic, witty, rational, sardonic tone.

LAWRENCE, D(avid) H(erbert) (1885–1930): born at Eastwood, Nottinghamshire, Lawrence won a scholarship to Nottingham High School but was forced to leave at 15. After working as a clerk, he became a pupil-teacher and in 1906 took up a scholarship at Nottingham University College to study for a teacher's certificate. He was already writing poetry and short stories and he now began his first novel, *The White Peacock* (1911), which was followed by *The Trespasser* (1912) and *Sons and Lovers* (1913). In 1912 he met Frieda Weekley, wife of his old professor at Nottingham, and together they eloped to Germany, though during the war years they lived in England where Lawrence formed friendships in literary and intellectual circles. His next novel, *The Rainbow* (1915), was seized by the police and declared obscene; his frankness about sex, and his use of four-letter words, was to keep him in constant trouble with the law. In 1916 he finished *Women in Love* but was unable to find a publisher until 1920 in New York, where an action against it failed, and 1921 in London. In 1917 he and Frieda left for Italy and the following years were spent travelling, to Ceylon and Australia and then to America and Mexico. His other novels include *Aaron's Rod* (1922), *Kangaroo* (1923), *The Plumed Serpent* (1926), and *Lady Chatterley's Lover*, which Lawrence had privately printed in Florence in 1928; an expurgated version appeared in London in 1932, but the full text was not published until 1960.

Lawrence's reputation as a short-story writer has always been high, many stories appearing first in small collections like *England, My England* (1922); there is a complete edition in three volumes (1955). At times uneven, his poetry always has the immediate and personal quality of his prose. He published several volumes, including *Love Poems* (1935), *Birds, Beasts and Flowers* (1923), and *Pansies* (1929). He also wrote several travel books and a number of other non-fiction works.

LEAR, Edward (1812–88): born in Holloway, the 20th child of a stockbroker, Lear worked as a zoological draughtsman until he came under the patronage of the Earl of Derby, for whose grandchildren he wrote *A Book of Nonsense* (1845), with his own limericks and illustrations. Later nonsense volumes included *Nonsense Songs, Stories, Botany and Alphabets* (1871), which contains 'The Owl and the Pussy-Cat' and 'The Jumblies', and *Laughable Lyrics* (1877).

LEHMANN, Rosamond (1901–   ): educated privately and at Cambridge, Rosamond Lehmann achieved a *succès de scandale* with her first novel, *Dusty Answer* (1927), which describes the awakening into womanhood of 18-year-old Judith Earle. Her second novel, *A Note in Music* (1930) also created a stir with its frank treatment of homosexuality. Her other novels include *Invitation to the Waltz* (1932), *The Ballad and the Source* (1944), and *The Echoing Grove* (1953).

LESSING, Doris (1919–   ): born in Persia of British parents who moved when she was 5 to a farm in Southern Rhodesia, Doris Lessing left school at 15 and in 1949 went to England, where her first novel, *The Grass is Singing*, appeared in 1950. Her quintet, *Children of Violence*, traces the history of Martha Quest from her childhood in Rhodesia, through post-war Britain, to an apocalyptic ending in AD 2000 (*Martha*

Quest, 1952; *A Proper Marriage*, 1954; *A Ripple From the Storm*, 1958; *Landlocked*, 1965; and *The Four-Gated City*, 1969). Perhaps her best-known book, *The Golden Notebook* (1962), is a lengthy and ambitious novel which was hailed as a landmark by the Women's Movement. Later novels enter the realm of 'inner space fiction', exploring mental breakdown and the breakdown of society; and the sequence collectively entitled *Canopus in Argus Archives*, published between 1979 and 1983, marks a complete break with traditional realism, describing the epic and mythic events of a fictional universe with a remarkable freedom of invention. Her *Collected Stories* (2 vols.) were published in 1978.

LEWIS, Alun (1915–44): born in a Welsh mining village, Lewis went to university at Aberystwyth and trained as a teacher before joining the army in 1940. His first volume of poems, *Raiders' Dawn*, appeared in 1942, and in 1943 a volume of stories, *The Last Inspection*, most of which deal with army life in England, as does his most anthologized poem, 'All Day it has Rained...', first published in 1941. He was killed in Burma.

LEWIS, Cecil Day: see **Day-Lewis.**

LEWIS, C(live) S(taples) (1898–1963): literary scholar and critic, Lewis is more widely known for his popular religious and moral writings such as *The Screwtape Letters* (1940). He also wrote three science fiction novels and with *The Lion, The Witch, and The Wardrobe* (1950) began a series of seven 'Narnia' stories for children.

LONDON, Jack (1876–1916): born in San Francisco, USA, London grew up in poverty and scratched a living in various legal and illegal ways, including taking part in the Klondike gold rush of 1897. These experiences provided the material for his works and made him a socialist. *The Son of the Wolf* (1900), the first of his many collections of tales, is based upon life in the far North, as is the book that brought him recognition, *The Call of the Wild* (1903). *The People of the Abyss*, an emotive documentary based on some weeks spent in the slums of London's East End, appeared the same year, and was followed by many other tales of struggle, travel, and adventure, including *The Sea-Wolf* (1904), *White Fang* (1906), and *Martin Eden* (1909). He was remembered by his friend the novelist Upton Sinclair as 'one of the great revolutionary figures' of America's history.

LONGFELLOW, Henry (1807–82): born in Maine, USA, and educated at Bowdoin, Longfellow later taught at Bowdoin and at Harvard. His prose romance, *Hyperion* (1839), was followed in 1841 by *Ballads and other Poems*, with such well-known pieces as 'The Wreck of the Hesperus' and 'The Village Blacksmith'. By 1843 he was already one of the most widely read poets in America, and subsequent volumes confirmed his reputation in the English-speaking world as second only to that of *Tennyson in popularity; these include *The Belfry of Bruges and other Poems* (1847), *The Song of Hiawatha* (1858), and *Tales of a*

Wayside Inn (1863), which follows the form of the *Canterbury Tales* and the *Decameron*. Other 'Tales of a Wayside Inn' followed in 1872 and his last volumes, *The Masque of Pandora* (1875), *Ultima Thule* (1880), and *In the Harbor* (1882), contain some poignant autumnal reflections on old age.

LORCA, Federico: see **García Lorca.**

LOWELL, Robert (1917–77): born in Boston, USA, of ancient New England families, Lowell was educated at Kenyon College. He became a fanatical convert to Roman Catholicism and his first volume of verse, *Land of Unlikeness* (1944), betrays the conflict of Catholicism and his Boston ancestry. His second volume, *Lord Weary's Castle* (1946), which contains 'The Quaker Graveyard in Nantucket' and 'Mr Edwards and the Spider', was hailed in extravagant terms and was followed by *The Mills of the Kavanaughs* (1951) and by several other volumes, including *Life Studies* (1959) and *Near the Ocean* (1967), and by translations, plays, etc. A legendary figure in his lifetime, both *poète maudit* and aristocrat, both classic and romantic, he suffered from the claims made on his behalf as the greatest American poet of his time, a heroic myth-maker whose work was compared favourably with that of *Yeats.

LOWRY, Malcolm (1909–57): under the influence of *Melville, *O'Neill, *Conrad, and Jack *London, Lowry went to sea on leaving school and travelled to the Far East before returning to take a degree at Cambridge. In 1933 he published *Ultramarine*, which shows a considerable debt to *Blue Voyage* by his friend Conrad Aiken. He travelled widely in Europe and the US, settling in Mexico from 1936 to 1938, where he worked on his novel *Under the Volcano* which was published in 1947. After living in Canada he later returned to England where he died. He was a chronic alcoholic, as are many of his characters. His posthumous publications include *Hear Us O Lord from Heaven Thy Dwelling Place* (1963) and *October Ferry to Gabriola* (1970).

MACAULAY, Thomas Babington (1800–59): after graduating at Trinity College, Cambridge, Macaulay was called to the Bar, but his essay on *Milton for the *Edinburgh Review* in 1825 brought him instant fame, and he became one of the acknowledged intellectual pundits of the age. After a spell as an MP, he accepted a place on the Supreme Council of India, and on his return in 1838 began to write a detailed history of England from the revolution of 1688. By now his literary fame was such that everything he published was a dazzling success, beginning in 1842 with *Lays of Ancient Rome*, a collection of poems which deal with episodes from traditional Roman history, such as the defence of the bridge leading to Rome against the Tuscans ('Horatius'). The first two volumes of his *History of England* appeared in 1849 and the next two volumes in 1855. It was one of the best-sellers of the century, and has never since gone out of print. It brought him great wealth and a peerage. He at first intended to take it up to 1830, then lowered his sights to 1714, but when he died he had only reached 1697.

MACKENZIE, Sir Compton (1883–1972): educated at St Paul's School and Oxford, Mackenzie became a prolific writer, who is best remembered for his novels, which include *Carnival* (1912), *Sinister Street* (2 vols., 1913 and 1914), and his most ambitious work, *The Four Winds of Love*, which appeared between 1937 and 1945 in six volumes. He published two volumes of war memoirs, *Gallipoli Memories* (1929) and *Greek Memories* (1932), and in 1947 *Whisky Galore*, a fictional account of an actual wreck of a ship loaded with whisky. The ten 'Octaves' of his autobiography, *My Life and Times*, were published between 1963 and 1971 and met with much popular and critical success. He is often thought to have written too much, too indiscriminately; but after a long period of neglect the best of his work is receiving increasing attention.

MacNEICE, Louis (1907–63): born in Belfast, MacNeice was educated at Marlborough and Oxford, where he met *Auden and *Spender. He lectured in Classics, made several unsuccessful attempts at writing for the theatre, and in 1941 joined the BBC as writer-producer. *Letters from Iceland* (1937) was written in collaboration with Auden. He published several volumes of poetry, including *Blind Fireworks* (1929), *Poems* (1935), *Autumn Journal* (1938), *Springboard* (1944), and *The Burning Perch* (1963). He used most of the classic verse-forms, but his distinctive contribution was his deployment of assonance, internal rhymes, and half-rhymes, and ballad-like repetitions that he had absorbed from the Irishry of his childhood. Although overshadowed in the 1930s and 1940s by Auden, and later by critical fashion, his reputation was revived by the publication in 1966 of his *Collected Poems*.

MAILER, Norman (1923–): American novelist and essayist, Mailer was educated at Harvard. His naturalistic first novel *The Naked and the Dead* (1948) was based on his experiences with the army in the Pacific. It was followed by other novels, including *Barbary Shore* (1951), *The Deer Park* (1955), and *An American Dream* (1965), but most of his work is of a more unorthodox genre, mixing journalism, autobiography, political commentary, and fictional passages in a wide range of styles.

MANDELSTAM, Osip (1891–?1938): brought up in St Petersburg and educated at the university there; Mandelstam's first poems appeared in 1910 and his first collection, *Stone*, was published in 1913. It was followed by two more collections, *Tristia* (1922) and *Poems* (1928), and by a major prose piece, *The Journey to Armenia* (tr. 1980). His first arrest, in 1934, resulted from his recitation of his famous poem denouncing Stalin. In exile he wrote his important late poetry the 'Voronezh Notebooks'. He was re-arrested and died of a heart attack on the way to a hard-labour camp. Two volumes of memoirs by his wife

Nadezhda Mandelstam, *Hope against Hope* (1971) and *Hope Abandoned* (1974), are the main source of information on the poet. Mandelstam's reputation continues to grow, and he is now regarded as one of the major poets of the 20th c. He has been widely translated into English, notably his *Selected Poems* (1973).

MANN, Thomas (1875–1955): born in Lübeck, Mann emigrated in the Nazi period. *Buddenbrooks* appeared in 1901 and quickly made him famous. *Tonio Kroger* (1903), one of his most celebrated novellas, is, like so many of his works, about the nature of the artist. *Der Tod in Venedig* (*Death in Venice*, 1912), influenced particularly by the thought of Schopenhauer and Nietzsche, was followed by other novels, which include *Der Zauberberg* (*The Magic Mountain*, 1924), the 'Joseph' novels (in four parts, 1933–43), *Dr Faustus* (1947), and *Felix Krull* (1954). He was awarded the Nobel Prize for literature in 1929.

MANSFIELD, Katherine (1888–1923): pseudonym of Kathleen Mansfield Beauchamp, who was born in Wellington, New Zealand, and educated at Queen's College, London. She returned to New Zealand to study music, then, in 1908, returned to London. Her first collection of stories, *In a German Pension*, appeared in 1911. This was followed by *Bliss and other stories* (1920), by which time she was increasingly recognized as an original and experimental writer, whose stories were the first in English to show the influence of *Chekhov, whom she greatly admired. *The Garden Party, and other stories* (1922) was the third collection to be published in her lifetime, but two others, *The Dove's Nest* (1923) and *Something Childish* (1924), were published posthumously, as well as various collections of letters, extracts from her journal, etc.

MARLOWE, Christopher (1564–93): educated at King's School, Canterbury, and Cambridge, Marlowe seems to have been of a violent and at times criminal temperament, and he came to a violent end after a tavern quarrel. *The Tragedie of Dido, Queene of Carthage*, published in 1594, may have been written while Marlowe was still at Cambridge, and in collaboration with Nashe. Part I of the drama in blank verse, *Tamburlaine*, was written not later than 1587, and Part II the following year; it was published in 1590. The next plays may have been *The Jew of Malta*, not published until 1633, and *Edward II*, published in 1594. *Massacre at Paris*, which survives only in a fragmentary and undated text, and *Dr Faustus*, published 1604, may both belong to the last year of Marlowe's life. He also published several translations and two books of an erotic poem *Hero and Leander* (1598). In spite of his violent life Marlowe was an admired and highly influential figure. Shakespeare's early histories are strongly influenced by Marlowe, and he paid tribute to him in *As You Like It* as the 'dead shepherd'.

MARRYAT, Captain Frederick (1792–1848): author, naval captain, and FRS, Marryat resigned his commission in 1830 after the success of his first novel, *The Naval Officer: or Scenes and Adventures in the Life of Frank Mildmay* (1829). He wrote another 15 novels, which include *Mr Midshipman Easy* (1836). With *Masterman Ready* (1841) he turned his attention to children's books, and it is chiefly for these he is remembered, with the popularity of *Children of the New Forest* (1847) lasting well into this century.

MARVELL, Andrew (1621–78): educated at Hull Grammar School and Cambridge, Marvell spent the years between 1643 and 1647 travelling in Europe. On his return he apparently moved in London literary circles, and in 1650 wrote 'An Horatian Ode upon Cromwell's Return from Ireland', perhaps the greatest political poem in English. From 1650 to 1652 Marvell tutored the daughter of a Parliamentarian general and in this period, it is usually assumed, he wrote 'Upon Appleton House' and lyrics such as 'The Garden' and the Mower poems. In 1654 with 'The First Anniversary' (pub. 1655) he began his career as unofficial laureate to Cromwell, and after Cromwell's death in 1658 mourned him in 'Upon the Death of His late Highness the Lord Protector'. In 1659 he was elected MP for Hull, and remained one of the Hull members until his death. At the Restoration his influence secured *Milton's release from prison. In 1667 he composed his finest satire, attacking financial and sexual corruption at Court and in Parliament, and in his prose works he continued to wage war against arbitrary royal power. His *Miscellaneous Poems* appeared in 1681 and *Poems on Affairs of State* between 1689 and 1697.

The history of Marvell's reputation is extraordinary. Famed in his day as patriot, satirist, and foe to tyranny, he was virtually unknown as a lyric poet. Even when his poems were published in 1681, they were greeted by two centuries of neglect. C. *Lamb started a gradual revival, but Marvell's poems were more appreciated in 19th-c. America than in England. It was not until after the First World War that the modern high estimation of his poetry began to prevail.

MASEFIELD, John (1878–1967): after training for the merchant navy, Masefield sailed for Chile in 1894, but suffered acutely from seasickness and endured some kind of breakdown, and was returned home. He sailed again but deserted ship and became a vagrant in America. When he returned to England he began a prolific writing career, which included some 50 volumes of verse, over 20 novels, and eight plays. His first published book, *Salt Water Ballads*, which included 'I must go down to the sea again', appeared in 1902, and *Ballads and Poems*, which contained 'Cargoes', in 1910. His *Collected Poems* (1923) sold in great numbers, as did several of his novels. He became Poet Laureate in 1930 and received the OM in 1935. Masefield's reputation sank rapidly in the 1930s, but his major narrative verse, many of his lyrics, and some of his prose are once again highly regarded.

MAUGHAM, W(illiam) Somerset (1874–1965): educated at King's School,

Canterbury and Heidelberg University, Maugham later trained as a doctor. His first novel, *Liza of Lambeth* (1897), was the beginning of a long and prolific career. Success was not instant, but he achieved fame in 1907 with the production of *Lady Frederick*, and in 1908 he had four plays running simultaneously in London. His other plays include *The Circle* (1921), *East of Suez* (1922), *The Constant Wife* (1926), and *For Services Rendered* (1932). His best-known novel, *Of Human Bondage*, appeared in 1915 and was followed by others like *The Moon and Sixpence* (1919), *Cakes and Ale* (1930), and *The Razor's Edge* (1944). Of his short stories particular mention should be made of 'Rain' (in *The Trembling of a Leaf*, 1921) and 'The Alien Corn' (in *Six Stories in the First Person Singular*, 1931). Despite his worldly success and great popularity as a writer, Maugham's view that he stood 'in the very first row of the second-raters' has been largely endorsed by literary critics.

MAUPASSANT, Guy de (1850–93): a literary disciple of *Flaubert, de Maupassant was one of the group of young Naturalistic writers (see Zola) that formed around Zola. To their collection of tales *Les Soirées de Médan*, he contributed 'Boule de suif', a story of the Franco-Prussian war that many regard as his finest. Besides the hundreds of stories that he published in a brief creative life, he wrote six novels, of which the best known are *Une vie* (1883), *Bel-Ami* (1885), and *Pierre et Jean* (1888).

MELVILLE, Herman (1819–91): born in New York, Melville sailed as a 'boy' on a packet to Liverpool, then in 1841 shipped on a whaler for the South Seas, where he jumped ship, joined the US Navy, and finally returned to begin writing. The fictionalized travel narrative of *Typee or a Peep at Polynesian Life* (1846), was Melville's most popular book during his lifetime. He then wrote a sequel and three other books before publishing *Moby-Dick, or, The Whale* (1851), which was inspired by the achievement of *Hawthorne. Its brilliance was noted by some critics and by very few readers, and was followed by other novels, poetry, and a collection of short stories.

Despite some revival of interest in Britain, Melville died virtually forgotten, with his novella *Billy Budd, Foretopman* still in manuscript: contemporary misunderstanding, censorship, and neglect, and the subsequent revision of Melville's reputation since the 1920s, have made him a classic case of the artist as reviled Titan. *Moby-Dick* is the closest approach the United States has had to a national prose epic.

MEREDITH, George (1828–1909): educated intermittently at Portsmouth and Southsea, and then at the unusual school of the Moravians at Neuwied in Germany, Meredith began his long literary career with 'Chillianwallah', a poem published in 1849. His first major novel, *The Ordeal of Richard Feverel* (1859), was followed by several others, though the only one to meet with general popularity was *Diana of the Crossways*. He then published several volumes of verse, more novels, and a collection of short stories. By the time he died Meredith had written steadily for 50 years and had become a greatly revered man of letters. He himself felt he was a poet first and a novelist after, but that has not been the verdict of his readers. His reputation stood very high well into this century, but the deliberate intricacy of much of his prose defeats many modern readers, and for the last 50 years his writings have not received any great popular or critical acclaim.

MILLER, Arthur (1915–): born in New York and educated at the University of Michigan, where he began to write plays, Miller made his name with *All My Sons* (1947) and established himself as a leading dramatist with *Death of a Salesman* (1949). This was followed by *The Crucible* (1952) and *A View from the Bridge* (1955). *The Misfits* (1961) is a screenplay written for his then wife, Marilyn Monroe, and was followed by *After the Fall* (1964) and *The Price* (1968). Miller has also published short stories and essays, and adapted *Ibsen's *An Enemy of the People* (1951).

MILLER, Henry (1891–1980): born in New York, Miller left America for Europe in 1930, and his autobiographical novel, *Tropic of Cancer*, was published in Paris in 1934; it was banned for decades (as were many of his works) in Britain and the US. This was followed by many other works which mingled metaphysical speculation with sexually explicit scenes, surreal passages, and scenes of grotesque comedy; they include *Tropic of Capricorn* (France, 1939; US, 1962), *The Colossus of Maroussi* (1941), *The Air-Conditioned Nightmare* (1945), and a sequence of three works, *Sexus* (1949), *Plexus* (1953), and *Nexus* (1960), known together as *The Rosy Crucifixion*. In 1944 he settled in California and gradually became accepted as a spiritual sage who greatly influenced the Beat generation (see Kerouac) in its search for salvation through extremes of experience.

MILNE, A(lan) A(lexander) (1882–1956): educated at Westminster School and Cambridge, Milne became a prolific author of plays, novels, poetry, short stories, biography, and essays, all of which have been overshadowed by his children's books. In 1924 his book of verses for children, *When We Were Very Young*, was immediately successful, outdone only by the phenomenal and abiding success of *Winnie-the-Pooh* (1926). Further popular verses, *Now We Are Six* (1927), were followed by *The House at Pooh Corner* (1928), no less successful than its predecessor.

MILTON, John (1608–74): educated at St Paul's School and Cambridge, where he began to write poetry, Milton's first distinctly Miltonic work, 'On the Morning of Christ's Nativity', was written at Christmas 1629. His 'masque' *Comus*, published anonymously in 1637, was written and performed at Ludlow in 1634. In 1637 he wrote *Lycidas*, an elegy; during the 20 years that elapsed between this and his composition of *Paradise Lost* Milton wrote little poetry. He travelled abroad and then his attentions were diverted by historical events to many years of pamphleteering and political activity, and to a tireless defence of religious, civil, and domestic liberties. By 1651 he was totally blind. At the Restoration he went into hiding briefly, then was arrested, fined, and released. He now returned to poetry and set about the composition of *Paradise Lost*, which is said to have been finished in 1663, but the agreement for his copyright was not signed until 1667. *Paradise Regained* was published in 1671 with *Samson Agonistes*. In 1673 appeared a second edition of his *Poems*, originally published in 1645, including most of his minor verse.

Milton's personality continues to arouse as much discussion as his works. As a writer, his towering stature was recognized early. Although appreciated as a master of polemical prose as well as of subtle lyric harmony, his reputation rests largely on *Paradise Lost*. Poets and critics in the 18th c. were profoundly influenced by Milton's use of blank verse (previously confined largely to drama) and he inspired many serious and burlesque imitations and adaptations. But even at this period there were murmurs of dissent, and in 1936 T. S. *Eliot described Milton as one whose sensuousness had been 'withered by book learning' and further impaired by blindness, who wrote English 'like a dead language'. He modified these views later, but they were endorsed by F. R. Leavis. The debate continues.

MITFORD, Nancy (1904–73): daughter of the second Lord Redesdale, who appears in many of her novels as the eccentric 'Uncle Matthew', Nancy Mitford published three novels before her first popular success, *The Pursuit of Love* (1945). Subsequent novels include *Love in a Cold Climate* (1949), *The Blessing* (1951), and *Don't Tell Alfred* (1960), and she also wrote several historical biographies and edited two volumes of family correspondence.

MOLIÈRE (1622–73): pseudonym of the French comic playwright and actor Jean-Baptiste Poquelin. Educated at the Jesuit Collège de Clermont, Molière at 21 abandoned his commercial prospects to found a professional theatre. Equally gifted as actor, director, and playwright, he was the creator of French classical comedy, who had a profound understanding of the incongruities of human life. His plays include *L'École des maris* (1661), *L'École des femmes* (1662), *Le Tartuffe* (1664), *Le Misanthrope* and *Le Médecin malgré lui* (1666), *Le Bourgeois Gentilhomme* (1670), and *Le Malade imaginaire* (1673). His major plays show that he was saturated in *Montaigne. His influence on English Restoration comedy (see Congreve) exceeded that of *Jonson: dramatists like *Dryden, Wycherley, Vanbrugh, and Shadwell quarried his plays for characters and situations.

MONTAIGNE, Michel de (1533–92): generally regarded as the inventor of the modern 'essay', a genre he fashioned out of the late medieval 'compilation', transforming it into a personal test of ideas and experience; Montaigne's first two books of *Essais* appeared in 1580. The fifth edition, containing the third book, appeared in 1588, and a posthumous edition in 1595, each successive version containing extensive additions to the existing material.

MURDOCH, Iris (1919–): educated at Badminton School and Oxford, Iris Murdoch worked for some time in the Civil Service, then lectured in philosophy in Oxford and London; her works on philosophy include *Sartre, Romantic Rationalist* (1953) and *The Sovereignty of Good* (1970). Her first novel, *Under the Net* (1954), was followed by many other successful works, including *The Bell* (1958), *A Severed Head* (1961), *The Red and the Green* (1965), *Bruno's Dream* (1969), and *The Sea, The Sea* (1978), which won the Booker Prize. She has also written three plays.

NABOKOV, Vladimir (1899–1977): the son of a leading member of the Kerensky Government, Nabokov had published only a small volume of poetry when his family left Russia for Germany in 1919. After studying French and Russian literature at Cambridge, he lived in Europe, writing mainly in Russian, under the pseudonym 'Sirin'. In 1940 he moved to the US. From then on all his novels were written in English. Nabokov's reputation as one of the major, most original prose writers of the 20th c., a stylist with extraordinary narrative and descriptive skill and a wonderful linguistic inventiveness in two languages, is based on his achievement in his novels, which, besides his outstanding success, *Lolita* (1955), include *The Defence* (1930), *Glory* (1932), *Laughter in the Dark* (1932), *Despair* (1936), *Invitation to a Beheading* (1938), *The Gift* (1938), *The Real Life of Sebastian Knight* (1941), *Bend Sinister* (1947), *Pnin* (1957), *Pale Fire* (1962), and *Look at the Harlequins!* (1974), and on several volumes of short stories.

NAIPAUL, V(idiadhar) S(urajprasad) (1932–): born in Trinidad of a Brahmin family, Naipaul was educated at Queen's Royal College, Port of Spain, and Oxford. He settled in England and embarked on a career of literary journalism. His first four books, *The Mystic Masseur* (1957), *The Suffrage of Elvira* (1958), *Miguel Street* (short stories, 1959), and *A House for Mr Biswas* (1961), were all set in Trinidad and were followed by his only novel set in London, *Mr Stone and the Knights Companion* (1963), and by *The Mimic Men* (1967), set on a fictitious Caribbean island. His other works include *In a Free State* (1971), which won the Booker Prize, and *A Bend in the River* (1979). Naipaul's recurrent themes of political violence, innate homelessness, and alienation inevitably give rise to comparisons with *Conrad.

OATES, Joyce Carol (1938–): American novelist and short-story writer, Joyce Carol Oates was educated at the universities of Syracuse and Wisconsin. Her novels, many of which portray extremes of human passions and violence, include *A Garden of Earthly Delights* (1967), *them* (1969), and *A Bloodsmoor Romance* (1982). She has also published many collections of short stories.

O'BRIEN, Edna (1932–): born in the west of Ireland; Edna O'Brien's first novel, *The Country Girls* (1960), was followed by *The Lonely Girl*

(1962), and *Girls in their Married Bliss* (1963), all of which follow the experiences of two girls who escape their country homes and convent education for first Dublin and then London. Her subsequent novels include *August is a Wicked Month* (1964), *A Pagan Place* (1971), and *Night* (1972). Her lyrical descriptive powers and lack of inhibition have led to comparisons with *Colette.

O'BRIEN, Flann (1911–66): the pseudonym of Brian O'Nolan or Ó Nualláin, who was born at Strabane, Co. Tyrone, and educated at University College, Dublin. His first novel, *At Swim-Two-Birds* (1939), is an exuberant work much influenced by *Joyce. His second, *An Béal Bocht* (1941), was written in Gaelic and translated into English in 1973 as *The Poor Mouth*. The best known of his other works is *The Third Policeman* (written 1940, pub. 1967).

O'CASEY, Sean (1880–1964): born in Dublin of Protestant parents, O'Casey, according to his own autobiographies, was educated in the streets there. He worked from the age of 14 at a variety of jobs, spending nine years from 1903 as a railway labourer. He began to publish articles, songs, and broadsheets under the name of Seán Ó Cathasaigh; his first plays were rejected by the Abbey Theatre, but *The Shadow of a Gunman* was performed in 1923, followed by *Juno and the Paycock* in 1924; they were published together as *Two Plays* (1925). *The Plough and the Stars* provoked nationalist riots at the Abbey in 1926. All three plays are tragi-comedies that deal realistically with the rhetoric and dangers of Irish patriotism, with tenement life, self-deception, and survival. His later works include *Within the Gates* (1933), *Red Roses for Me* (1942), *Cock-a-Doodle Dandy* (1949), and *The Bishop's Bonfire* (1955). He also published, in six volumes, a much-praised series of autobiographies.

O'HARA, John (1905–70): born in Pennsylvania, USA, O'Hara wrote more than 200 of his sharp, satiric short stories for the *New Yorker*. These were later collected under many different titles, from *The Doctor's Son* (1935) onwards. His novels, which gained wide popularity with their toughness, frankness, and sophistication, include *Appointment in Samarra* (1934), *Butterfield 8* (1935), *Pal Joey* (1940), and *A Rage to Live* (1949).

O'NEILL, Eugene (1888–1953): born in New York, O'Neill was the son of a well-known romantic actor. He had a varied career (as seaman, gold prospector, journalist, and actor) before associating himself (1916) with an experimental theatre group which staged several of his early one-act plays. His first big success was the full-length naturalistic drama, *Beyond the Horizon* (1920), which was followed by *The Emperor Jones* (1920) and *Anna Christie* (1921), and several others. His criticism of contemporary materialistic values was powerfully and poetically expressed in plays like *The Fountain* (1925) and *Marco Millions* (1927). *Mourning Becomes Electra* appeared in 1931, but after *Days Without End* (1934), there was a long absence from the stage, during which he was awarded the Nobel Prize for Literature (1936) and worked on several plays, including *The Iceman Cometh* (1946). His masterpiece, *Long Day's Journey into Night*, was written in 1940–1, and posthumously produced and published in 1956. His last play, *A Moon for the Misbegotten*, was written in 1943 and produced in 1947. Despite occasional lapses into melodrama and rhetoric, O'Neill's plays remain powerfully theatrical and original; he transcends his debt to *Ibsen and *Strindberg, producing an *œuvre* in which the struggle between self-destruction, self-deception, and redemption is presented as essentially dramatic in nature.

ORCZY, Baroness (Mrs Montague Barstow) (1865–1947): born in Hungary, Baroness Orczy lived from the age of 15 in London. She achieved fame with her romantic novel, *The Scarlet Pimpernel* (1905). The success of the novel followed its success in a dramatized version, written in collaboration with her husband. She wrote many other historical and romantic novels, including several sequels to *The Scarlet Pimpernel*.

ORTON, Joe (1933–67): born in Leicester, Orton left school at 16 to train as an actor. His comedies, which include *Entertaining Mr Sloane* (1964), *Loot* (1965), and the posthumously performed *What the Butler Saw* (1969), are black, stylish, and violent, and their emphasis on corruption and sexual perversion made them a *succès de scandale*.

ORWELL, George (1903–50): the pen-name of Eric Arthur Blair, who was born in Bengal, brought to England at an early age, and educated at Eton. He served with the Indian Imperial Police in Burma, 1922–7, and his experiences are reflected in his first novel, *Burmese Days* (1934). He returned to Europe and worked in Paris and London in a series of ill-paid jobs (see *Down and Out in Paris and London*, 1933). His second novel, *A Clergyman's Daughter* (1935), was followed by *Keep the Aspidistra Flying* (1936), and, after a journey north, by his vivid and impassioned documentary of unemployment and proletarian life *The Road to Wigan Pier* (1937). The Spanish Civil War (in which he fought for the Republicans and was wounded) intensified his political preoccupations and produced *Homage to Catalonia* (1939), and the threat of the coming war hung over his next novel, *Coming up for Air* (1939). By this stage Orwell saw himself primarily as a political writer, a democratic socialist who avoided party labels, hated totalitarianism, and was to become more and more disillusioned with the methods of Communism; his plain, colloquial style made him highly effective as pamphleteer and journalist. He also published several collections of essays, but his most popular works were undoubtedly his political satires *Animal Farm* (1945) and *Nineteen Eighty-Four* (1949), which brought inevitable comparisons with *Swift.

OSBORNE, John (1929–   ): born in Fulham, London, Osborne began to write plays while an actor in provincial repertory, the first of which was performed in 1950. He made his name with *Look Back in Anger* (1956, pub. 1957), which was followed by *Epitaph for George Dillon* (1957, pub. 1958; written in the mid 1950s in collaboration with Anthony Creighton), *The Entertainer* (1957), *Luther* (1961), *Inadmissible Evidence* (1964), and *A Patriot for Me* (1965). Iconoclastic, energetic, and impassioned, Osborne's works at their most positive praise the qualities of loyalty, tolerance, and friendship, but his later works (which include *West of Suez*, 1971; *A Sense of Detachment*, 1972; *Watch it Come Down*, 1976) have become increasingly vituperative in tone, and the objects of his invective have become apparently more arbitrary.

OWEN, Wilfred (1893–1918): born in Shropshire and educated in Liverpool and at Shrewsbury Technical College, Owen began to experiment with verse from an early age. He joined the army in 1915 and was soon commissioned. After concussion and trench-fever on the Somme he was invalided to hospital in Edinburgh, where he was greatly encouraged in his writing by *Sassoon. He returned to France in 1918, won the MC, and was killed a week before the Armistice. Only five of his poems were published in his lifetime, and they made little mark on a public revering Rupert *Brooke. However, his reputation slowly grew, greatly assisted by *Blunden's edition of his poems, and he is now generally regarded as a war poet of the first rank. The poems were chosen by Benjamin Britten for his *War Requiem* and were collected again in 1963, edited by *Day-Lewis.

PASTERNAK, Boris (1890–1960): born in Moscow, Pasternak studied philosophy at Marburg University and on his return to Russia published his first verse collection *A Twin in the Clouds* (1914). A second volume, *Above the Barriers*, appeared in 1917, but it was his third collection, *My Sister Life* (the poems of 1917, published 1922), which established his reputation. In the 1930s, when he began what he called his 'long silent duel' with Stalin, Pasternak's position became increasingly difficult and after 1933 no original work by him could be published for ten years. During this time he earned his living by translating, among other authors, *Goethe, *Keats, and *Shakespeare. His main literary concern in the final decades of his life, however, was the work he intended to be his testament, a witness to the experience of the Russian intelligentsia before, during and after the Revolution, the novel *Doctor Zhivago*. Despairing of publication in the USSR, he gave permission for publication in Italy, where the novel appeared in 1957. In 1958 he wrote a second 'Autobiographical Sketch', and was awarded the Nobel Prize for Literature, but, after a vehement and shameful campaign against him, he declined it. *Dr Zhivago*, on which his world-wide fame is based, has never been published in the USSR, where his reputation depends on the poetic achievement of *My Sister Life* and another major collection, *Second Birth* (1932).

PATMORE, Coventry (1823–96): after publishing his first volume of *Poems* in 1844, Patmore, in 1846, became assistant in the printed book department of the British Museum. His work was much admired by the Pre-Raphaelites (see D. G. Rossetti), with whom he became acquainted, and he contributed to *The Germ*. In 1847 he married his first wife, Emily, who inspired his long and popular sequence of poems in praise of married love, *The Angel in the House* (1854–63). Emily died in 1862 and two years later he married again, to a Catholic, and was himself converted to Catholicism, factors which may have contributed to the decline in his popularity as a poet.

PEAKE, Mervyn (1922–68): educated at Eltham College, Kent, Peake spent three years from 1934 with a group of artists on the island of Sark, then returned to London, where he taught art, exhibited his own work and illustrated books, published verse and stories for children, etc. He was invalided out of the army in 1943 but was later commissioned as a war artist. He published his first novel, *Titus Groan*, in 1946; it was followed by *Gormenghast* (1950) and *Titus Alone* (1959), which as a trilogy form the work for which Peake is best remembered, a creation of grotesque yet precise Gothic fantasy. He also published poetry, including *The Glassblowers* (1950) and *The Rhyme of the Flying Bomb* (1962), a ballad of the blitz.

PEPYS, Samuel (1633–1703): educated at St Paul's and Cambridge, Pepys entered the household of Sir Edward Montagu (afterwards first Earl of Sandwich), his father's first cousin, in 1656; and his subsequent successful career was largely due to Montagu's patronage. His famous *Diary* opens on 1 Jan. 1660, when Pepys was living in Axe Yard, Westminster, and was very poor. Soon after this he was appointed 'clerk of the King's ships' and clerk of the Privy Seal, and in 1672 made Secretary to the Admiralty. Owing to an unfounded fear of failing eyesight, he closed his diary on 31 May 1669. His diary remained in cipher (a system of shorthand) at Magdalene College, Cambridge, until 1825, when it was deciphered. An enlarged edition appeared in 1875–9, and an edition in ten volumes (1893–9) remained the standard text until the appearance of a new and unbowdlerized transcription (11 vols., 1970–83).

PETRARCH (Francesco Petrarca) (1304–74): Italian poet and humanist, and the most popular Italian poet of the English Renaissance. He was born at Arezzo, the son of a notary who was expelled from Florence and migrated to Avignon in 1312. Here in 1327 Petrarch first saw the woman, Laura, who inspired his love poetry; her true identity is unknown. Today Petrarch is best known for his 'Rime Sparse', the collection of Italian lyrics which includes the long series of poems in praise of Laura; but of his contemporaries and the generations that immediately succeeded him he was best known as a devoted student of classical antiquity. He is justly regarded as the father of Italian humanism and the initiator of the revived study of Greek and Latin literature, but for English writers his chief inspiration was to the early sonneteers.

PINERO, Sir Arthur (1855–1934): after leaving school at 10 to work in his father's solicitor's practice, Pinero was stage-struck from youth, and became an actor. He was noticed by Henry Irving, who later produced some of his plays. His first one-act play, *Two Hundred a Year*, performed in 1877, heralded a successful and prolific career. The first of his farces, *The Magistrate* (perf. 1885), brought him both fame and wealth. Later ones, *The Schoolmistress* (1887) and *Sweet Lavender* (1888), did nearly as well. His first serious play, on what was to be the recurrent theme of double standards for men and women, was *The Profligate* (1889), and was followed by a number of others, including *The Second Mrs Tanqueray* (1893), and a sentimental comedy *Trelawny of the 'Wells'* (1898).

PINTER, Harold (1930–): born in east London, and educated at Hackney Downs Grammar School, Pinter began to publish poetry in periodicals before he was 20, then became a professional actor, working mainly in repertory. His first play, *The Room*, was performed in Bristol in 1957, followed in 1958 by a London production of *The Birthday Party*. Pinter's distinctive voice was soon recognized, and many critical and commercial successes followed, including *The Caretaker* (1960), *The Homecoming* (1965), *Old Times* (1971), and *Betrayal* (1978). Pinter's gift for portraying, by means of dialogue which realistically produces the nuances of colloquial speech, the difficulties of communication, and the many layers of meaning in language, pause, and silence, have created a style labelled by the popular imagination as 'Pinteresque'.

PIRANDELLO, Luigi (1867–1935): Italian dramatist, short-story writer, and novelist, Pirandello was awarded the Nobel Prize for Literature in 1934. He exercised a pervasive influence on European drama by challenging the conventions of Naturalism (see Zola). Among his plays, ten of which he published as *Maschere nude* (*Naked Masks*, 1918–22), the best known are: *Così è (se vi pare)* (*Right You Are, If You Think You Are*, 1917), *Sei personaggi in cerca di autore* (*Six Characters in Search of an Author*, 1921), and *Enrico IV* (*Henry IV*, 1922). In these plays he anticipated the anti-illusionist theatre of *Brecht, *Wilder, and Peter Weiss; his exploration of the disintegration of personality foreshadowed *Beckett; his probing of the conflict between reality and appearance has echoes in the work of *O'Neill; and his examination of the relationship between self and persona, actor and character, face and mask, is a precursor of the work of *Anouilh, Giraudoux, and *Genet. Yet much of Pirandello's best work is to be found in his very short stories (28 of which were dramatized), where themes in common with his plays are more deeply explored.

PLATH, SYLVIA (1932–63): born in Boston, Massachusetts, USA, Sylvia Plath was educated at Smith College, Massachusetts, and Cambridge. She married Ted *Hughes in 1956. Her first volume of poetry, *The*

Colossus, appeared in 1960, and in 1963 her only novel *The Bell Jar*. Less than a month after its publication she committed suicide. In 1965 appeared her best-known collection, *Ariel*, which established her reputation with its courageous and controlled treatment of extreme and painful states of mind. Other posthumous volumes include *Crossing the Water* and *Winter Trees* (both 1971), and *Johnny Panic and the Bible of Dreams* (1977, collected prose pieces). Her *Collected Poems* appeared in 1981.

POE, Edgar Allan (1809–49): born in Boston, Massachusetts, USA, Poe published his first volume of verse anonymously and at his own expense; then enlisted in the US army, from which he was eventually dishonourably discharged. He now turned to journalism, worked as editor on several papers, and began to publish his stories in magazines. His first collection, *Tales of the Grotesque and Arabesque* (1839, for 1840), contains one of his most famous works, 'The Fall of the House of Usher'. In 1845 his poem 'The Raven', published in a New York paper and then as the title poem of *The Raven and other Poems* (1845), brought him fame, but not security. His posthumous reputation has been great; he was much admired by *Baudelaire, who translated many of his works, and in Britain by *Swinburne, *Wilde, *Rossetti, and *Yeats.

POPE, Alexander (1688–1744): his health ruined and his growth stunted by a severe illness at the age of 12, Pope was largely self-educated. He showed his precocious metrical skill in his 'Pastorals' written, according to himself, when he was 16. Wycherley introduced him to London life and his *Essay on Criticism* (1711) made him known to *Addison's circle, while his *Windsor Forest* (1713) won him the friendship of *Swift. *The Rape of the Lock* appeared in 1712 and was republished, enlarged, in 1714. His translations of Homer's *Iliad* and the *Odyssey* brought him financial independence and in 1718 he moved to Twickenham, where he spent the rest of his life. The first volume of his *Dunciad*, a satire on Dullness in three books, appeared anonymously in 1728 and an enlarged version in 1729. An additional book, *The New Dunciad*, appeared in 1742, and the complete *Dunciad*, in four books, was published in 1743.

With the growth of Romanticism (see Coleridge) Pope's poetry was increasingly seen as artificial and it was not until F. R. Leavis and *Empson that a serious attempt was made to rediscover his richness, variety, and complexity.

POUND, Ezra (1885–1972): born in Idaho, USA, Pound studied at Hamilton College, Pennsylvania and in 1908 came to Europe where he published several volumes of poems. He helped found the Imagist school of poets, advocating the use of free rhythms, concreteness, and concision of language and imagery. He also championed avant-garde writers and artists like *Joyce, Gaudier-Brzeska, and T. S. *Eliot, who described him as 'more responsible for the XXth Century revolution in poetry than any other individual'. Pound later turned away from Imagism, and moved towards the rich, grandly allusive, multi-cultural world of the *Cantos*, his most ambitious achievement; the first three Cantos appeared in 1917. In 1920 he moved from London to Paris and later settled in Rapallo where he continued to work on the Cantos, which appeared intermittently over the next decades until the appearance of the final *Drafts and Fragments of Cantos CX to CXVII* (1970). During the Second World War he broadcast over the Italian radio, and after the war was tried in Washington but was found unfit to plead. He was confined to a mental institution until 1958 when he returned to Italy where he died.

Inevitably, Pound's literary reputation was obscured by the tragedy of his last decades, and also by the difficulty of the work itself, which resides principally in its astonishingly wide range of reference and assimilation of cultures. Nevertheless, he is widely accepted both as a great master of traditional verse forms and as the man who regenerated the poetic idiom of his day.

POWELL, Anthony (1905–): Powell's initial reputation as a satirist and light comedian rests on five pre-war books, beginning with *Afternoon Men* (1931) which maps a characteristically seedy section of pleasure-loving, party-going London. After the war he embarked on a more ambitious sequence of 12 novels, *A Dance to the Music of Time*, which started with *A Question of Upbringing* (1951) and ended with *Hearing Secret Harmonies* (1975). The narrative is part humorous, part melancholy, and at times so funny that readers have tended if anything to underrate its sombre, even tragic, sweep and range.

POWYS, John Cowper (1872–1963): educated at Sherborne School and Cambridge, Powys became a prolific writer, who included poetry and many essays among his publications, as well as a remarkable *Autobiography* (1934). It is, however, for his highly individual novels that he is chiefly remembered. His first, *Wood and Stone* (1915, NY; 1917, London), was followed by a number of others, including *Rodmoor* (1916), *Ducdame* (1925), and his first major success, *Wolf Solent* (1929). *A Glastonbury Romance* (1932, NY; 1933, London), probably the best known of Powys's novels, is a work on a huge scale. He also wrote historical novels, the most successful being *Owen Glendower* (1940, NY; 1941, London). Much controversy centres on Powys's stature as a writer. Some regard him as unjustly neglected, an arresting and major novelist, while others find his talent spurious and verbose.

PRIESTLEY, J(ohn) B(oynton) (1894–1984): born in Bradford, Priestley served in the infantry during the First World War and afterwards took a degree at Cambridge. He then settled in London where he quickly made a name as journalist and critic. His first major popular success as a novelist was with the high-spirited, rambling *The Good Companions* (1929), which was followed by the grimmer novel of London life, *Angel Pavement* (1930). His many other novels include *Bright Day*

(1946), *Lost Empires* (1965), and *The Image Men* (1968). Priestley also wrote some 50 plays and dramatic adaptations, and published dozens of miscellaneous works, including a number of travel books and several volumes of autobiography.

PROUST, Marcel (1871–1922): in 1896 Proust published a collection of essays, poems, and short stories, *Les Plaisirs et les jours* (*Pleasures and Regrets*, 1948), but is now remembered as the author of *A la recherche du temps perdu* (1913–27; English tr., *Remembrance of Things Past*, 1922–31), a novel in seven sections. He also published a collection of literary parodies, *Pastiches et mélanges* (1919), and explored his own literary aesthetic in *Contre Sainte-Beuve* (1954; *By Way of Sainte-Beuve*, 1958).

PUSHKIN, Alexander (1799–1837): born in Moscow, Pushkin is Russia's greatest poet. He attended the Lyceum at Tsarskoe Selo, outside St Petersburg, where he began to write poetry. He worked in government service, but was expelled from St Petersburg in 1820 for writing revolutionary epigrams. He was fatally wounded in a duel with a French nobleman.

Pushkin wrote prolifically in a variety of genres: lyric poems, among the most important of which are 'Winter Evening' (1825), 'The Prophet' (1826), 'The Poet' (1827), and 'I loved you' (1829); narrative poems in various styles, including *Ruslan and Ludmilla* (1820), *The Gypsies* (1824), and *Poltava* (1829); the novel in verse *Eugene Onegin* (1823–31), his greatest and most sophisticated work; plays, including the blank-verse historical drama *Boris Godunov* (1825); and prose, on which he concentrated after 1830. No Russian writer of note since his time escaped his influence.

RABELAIS, François (c.1494–c.1553): the son of a Touraine lawyer, Rabelais became successively a Franciscan monk, the secretary of the Bishop of Maillezais, and a Bachelor of Medicine from Montpellier. He published various works on archaeology and medicine in Latin, and in French the satirical entertainments with the popular giants Gargantua and Pantagruel for which he is remembered. He travelled widely in France and Italy, and acquired a widespread reputation for his erudition and medical skill. His intellectual curiosity is insatiable, his knowledge of contemporary life and society without rival. His command of the vernacular, sustained by an encyclopaedic vocabulary and a virtuoso's rhetorical repertoire, and extending beyond French and its dialects to a dozen contemporary languages, remains unique in French literature.

RACINE, Jean (1639–99): informally educated by the Jansenists of Port-Royal, Racine wrote the majority of his plays while estranged from them between 1666 and 1677. His tragedies derive from various sources: from Greek and Roman literature, *Andromaque* (1667), *Iphigénie* (1674), and *Phèdre* (1677); from Roman history, *Britannicus* (1669), *Bérénice* (1670), and *Mithridate* (1673); from contemporary

Turkish history, *Bajazet* (1672); and from the Bible, *Esther* (1689) and *Athalie* (1691). He also wrote one comedy, *Les Plaideurs* (1668), drawn from Aristophanes. The plays were extensively translated into English from the 1670s, but differences in national tastes and dramatic conventions have rendered most English versions wildly unfaithful to their originals.

RATTIGAN, Sir Terence (1911–77): educated at Harrow and Oxford, Rattigan early embarked on a career as a playwright. His first West End success was a comedy, *French Without Tears* (1936, pub. 1937). This was followed by many other works, including *The Winslow Boy* (1946), *The Browning Version* (1948), *The Deep Blue Sea* (1952), *Separate Tables* (1954, pub. 1955), *Ross* (1960), and *Cause Célèbre* (1977, pub. 1978). When Rattigan's *Collected Works* were published in 1953, he wrote a preface to the second volume in which he created the character of 'Aunt Edna', the average middle-brow matinée attender whom playwrights must take into account. Critics were later to use this light-hearted invention as a focus for their complaints about the middle-class, middle-brow nature of his own plays, but his works are still much performed.

REMARQUE, Erich Maria (1898–1970): German novelist, author of *Im Westen nichts Neues* (*All Quiet on the Western Front*, 1929) and *Der Weg zurück* (*The Road Back*, 1931), a sequel.

RICHARDSON, Samuel (1689–1761): the son of a joiner, Richardson appears to have received, in his own words, 'only common School-learning'. As a boy he read widely, told stories to his friends, and by the age of 13 was employed writing letters for young lovers. He set up in business as a printer on his own in 1721, and all his working life he was extremely industrious, and his business prospered and expanded steadily. In 1739 he began the first of his three novels, *Pamela*, which started as a series of 'familiar letters' which fellow printers had encouraged him to write on the problems and concerns of everyday life. While these eventually grew into *Pamela*, they were also published separately as *Letters . . . to and for Particular Friends* (1741). *Pamela* was written in two months and was published, to very considerable acclaim, in 1740, with volumes 3 and 4 (*Pamela II*) appearing in 1741. This was followed by the first two volumes of *Clarissa*, which were published in 1747, and by a further five volumes in 1748. *Clarissa* was an undoubted success but there were complaints about both its length and its indecency, and it was not reprinted as often as *Pamela*. He had by now become friendly with Dr *Johnson, to whose *Rambler* he contributed, and in 1752 Johnson (together with many of Richardson's other friends) read the draft of *Sir Charles Grandison*, which was published in seven volumes in 1753–4. The novel sold well and rapidly became fashionable, but was assailed in various critical pamphlets for length, tedium, and doubtful morality.

Richardson is generally agreed to be one of the chief founders of the modern novel. All his novels were epistolary, a form he took from earlier works in English and French, which he appreciated for its immediacy, and which he raised to a level not attained by any of his predecessors.

RILKE, Rainer Maria (1875–1926): German poet; Rilke's early collections were not particularly interesting or distinguished. Of decisive importance were his two visits to Russia which, deepening his religious experience, led to *Das Stundenbuch* (*The Book of Hours*, 1905), in which death is the central theme. The subjective emotionalism of the early work began to give way to poetry of a more objective type, the transition to which is seen in *Das Buch der Bilder* (*The Book of Pictures*, 1902) and which finds its mature expression in the *Neue Gedichte* (*New Poems*, 1907–8). His other works included a full-scale prose work, *Die Aufzeichnungen des Malte Laurids Brigge* (*Sketches of Malte Laurids Brigge*, 1910) and *Die Sonette an Orpheus* (*Sonnets to Orpheus*, 1923). He is the most important lyric poet of 20-c. Germany, and his poetry has been translated into many languages.

RIMBAUD, Arthur (1854–91): one of the most revolutionary figures in 19th-c. literature, Rimbaud was, by the age of 16, in full revolt against every form of authority. By the age of 17 he had written his most famous poem, 'Le Bateau ivre', a hymn to the quest for unknown realities, which became a sacred text for the next two generations of writers. By the time he was 19 his poetic career was over. Between 1871 and 1873—the period of his association with *Verlaine and his sojourns in England—he undertook a programme of 'disorientation of the senses' in order to try to turn himself into a *voyant* or seer. This resulted in his most original work, two collections of prose poems, *Les Illuminations*, which explored the visionary possibilities of this experiment, and *Une Saison en enfer*, recording its moral and psychological failure. The remainder of his life has been described as a prolonged act of passive resistance.

ROLFE, Frederick (1860–1913): Rolfe, who liked to call himself 'Baron Corvo', or, equally misleadingly, Fr Rolfe, was by turns schoolmaster, painter, and writer. His most outstanding novel, *Hadrian the Seventh* (1904), appears to be a dramatized autobiography. His other writings include *Stories Toto Told Me* (1898), *Chronicles of the House of Borgia* (1901), *Don Tarquinio: A Kataleptic Phantasmatic Romance* (1905), and *The Desire and Pursuit of the Whole: a romance of modern Venice* (1934). Two other novels and several fragments were published posthumously. Rolfe's style is highly ornate and idiosyncratic; his vocabulary is arcane, his allusions erudite, and although he had admirers during his lifetime, he alienated most of them by his persistent paranoia and requests for financial support.

ROSENBERG, Isaac (1890–1918): the son of émigrés from western Russia, Rosenberg during his irregular East End schooling learned to paint and began to experiment with poetry. In 1911 another Jewish family paid for him to attend the Slade School of Art; in 1912 he published at his own expense a collection of poems, *Night and Day*, and was encouraged by *Pound and others. In 1915 he published another volume of verse, *Youth*, then joined the army, and was eventually killed in action. His poetry is forceful, rich in its vocabulary, and starkly realistic in its attitudes to war; Rosenberg greatly disliked *Brooke's 'begloried sonnets'. His reputation was slow to grow; a selection of his poems and letters appeared in 1922, but it was not until his *Collected Works* was published in 1937 that his importance became generally accepted.

ROSSETTI, Christina (1830–1894): the sister of D. G. *Rossetti and W. M. Rossetti, Christina Rossetti was educated at home and shared her brothers' intellectual interests. She contributed to the Pre-Raphaelite periodical, *The Germ*, where five of her poems appeared under the pseudonym 'Ellen Alleyn'. In 1861 *Macmillan's Magazine* published 'Uphill' and 'A Birthday', two of her best-known poems, which were followed by *Goblin Market and other poems* (1862) and several other volumes, and she also published many prose devotional works. Her work has often been compared with that of E. *Brontë, but, while both share a sense of mystical yearning, Rossetti's is more subdued, more hopeless, less fulfilled. Her technical virtuosity was considerable, and her use of short, irregularly rhymed lines is distinctive.

ROSSETTI, Dante Gabriel (1828–82): educated at King's College School, London, Rossetti studied painting with Millais and Holman Hunt, and in 1848, with them and four others, founded the Pre-Raphaelite Brotherhood. For many years he was known only as a painter, though he began to write poetry early. Several were published in *The Germ*, and others were later published in *The Fortnightly Review*. *Poems* (1870) contained 'Sister Helen', 'Jenny', and the first part of his sonnet sequence 'The House of Life' which was completed in *Ballads and Sonnets* (1881). Rossetti's poetry is marred for many readers by its vast and cloudy generalities about Life, Love, and Death, though some of his work shows in contrast a Pre-Raphaelite sharpness of detail, and much of it has an undeniable emotional and erotic power.

ROUSSEAU, Jean-Jacques (1712–78): born into a Protestant artisan family at Geneva, Rousseau later lived not only in Switzerland but France, Italy, and England. His lifelong interest in music and excursions into opera and drama, a voluminous correspondence, and important and influential contributions to social and political philosophy, the novel, autobiography, moral theology, and educational theory mark him out as one of the dominant writers and thinkers of the age. His essay *Discours sur les sciences et les arts*, on a subject proposed by the Academy of Dijon, won first prize and was published in 1750, and was followed by a variety of other essays, including *Du contrat social* (1762); by the novel *Julie, ou la Nouvelle Héloïse* (1761), his greatest popular success; and posthumously by his autobiographical works *Les*

Confessions (1781–8) and *Les Rêveries du promeneur solitaire* (1782), which remain landmarks of the literature of personal revelation and reminiscence.

RUSKIN, John (1819–1900): much of Ruskin's schooling was given at home and from 1836 to 1842 he was at Christ Church, Oxford, where he won the Newdigate Prize. Amongst his earliest publications were essays in the *Magazine of Natural History* and the *Architectural Magazine*, and the first of the five volumes of *Modern Painters* appeared in 1834, the last being published in 1860. Between them he published many pamphlets, books, and volumes of essays on architecture and art, including *The Seven Lamps of Architecture* (1849), *The Stones of Venice* (1851–3), and *The Political Economy of Art* (1857). In attacking the 'pseudo-science' of J. S. Mill and Ricardo in books published from 1860 Ruskin entered new territory and declared open warfare against the spirit and science of his times. This fight, against competition and self-interest, and for the recovery of heroic, feudal, and Christian social ideals, was to occupy him for the rest of his life.

SAINT-EXUPÉRY, Antoine de (1900–44): Saint-Exupéry, a Frenchman, was actively involved in the early years of commercial aviation, and his novels, which include *Vol de nuit* (1931; *Night Flight*, 1932), *Terre des hommes* (1939; *Wind, Sand and Stars*, 1939), and *Pilot de guerre* (1942; *Flight to Arras*, 1942), are intimately linked with his flying experiences. He also wrote a book for children, *Le Petit Prince* (1943; *The Little Prince*, 1944).

SAKI (1870–1916): the pseudonym of Hector Hugh Munro. Saki was known principally for his short stories. Born in Burma, but brought up in England, he joined the military police in Burma in 1893 but was invalided home and went to London to earn his living as a writer. His first characteristic volume of short stories, *Reginald*, was published under the pseudonym Saki in 1904, and was followed by several others. He also published two novels, *The Unbearable Bassington* (1912) and *When William Came* (1913). In 1914 he enlisted as a trooper and was killed in action in France.

SALINGER, J(erome) D(avid) (1919–): born in New York, Salinger is best known for his novel *The Catcher in the Rye* (1951), the story of adolescent Holden Caulfield who runs away from boarding-school. His other works include *Franny and Zooey* (1961) and *Raise High the Roof-Beam, Carpenters and Seymour: an Introduction* (1963), both containing two long short stories.

SAND, George (1804–76): pseudonym of the French novelist, Amandine-Aurore Lucille Dupin, Baronne Dudevant. Her fame now largely derives from two groups of novels, of the many that she wrote in a long career. The first, a series of romantic tales, portrayed the struggles of the individual woman against social constraints, especially those of marriage. The simple, artfully told idylls of rustic life that compose the second group are set in the region of Berry, where she had a country property. Her other works include *Elle et lui* (1859), which fictionalizes her liaison with Alfred de Musset; *Un hiver à Majorque* (1841), which describes an episode in her long relationship with Chopin; and her autobiography *Histoire de ma vie* (4 vols., 1854–5).

SANDBURG, Carl (1878–1967): born in Chicago, USA, of Swedish Lutheran immigrant stock, Sandburg challenged contemporary taste by his use of colloquialism and free verse, and became the principal among the authors writing in Chicago during and after the First World War. His first volume of verse, *Chicago Poems* (1916), was followed by several others, including *Good Morning America* (1928) and *Complete Poems* (1950). His major prose work is his monumental life of Abraham Lincoln (6 vols., 1926–39) and he also wrote a novel, *Remembrance Rock* (1948), and a volume of autobiography, *Always the Young Strangers* (1953).

SANSOM, William (1926–76): educated at Uppingham, Sansom was a short-story writer, travel writer, and novelist. His first volume, *Fireman Flower and other stories* (1944), reflects his experiences with the National Fire Service in wartime London, and was followed by many other collections. His most successful novel, *The Body*, appeared in 1949.

SARTRE, Jean-Paul (1905–80): educated at the École Normale Supérieure and at the French Institute in Berlin, Sartre was the principal exponent of Existentialism in France, and exercised a considerable influence on French intellectual life in the decades following the Second World War. Through the great range of his creative and critical energies, his personal involvement in many of the important issues of his time, and his unceasing concern with problems of freedom, commitment, and moral responsibility, he won a wide audience for his ideas. He made important contributions in many areas, which included Marxist and existentialist philosophy; the novel, including *La Nausée* (1938; *Nausea*, 1949) and three volumes of a projected tetralogy *Les Chemins de la liberté* (1945–7; *The Roads to Freedom*, 1947–50), comprising *L'Âge de raison*, *Le Sursis*, and *La Mort dans l'âme* (*The Age of Reason*, *The Reprieve*, and *Iron in the Soul*); drama, including *Les Mouches* (1943; *The Flies*, 1947) and *Huis Clos* (1945; *In Camera*, 1946; *No Exit*, 1947); biography, including studies of *Baudelaire and *Genet; and literary criticism. His autobiography, *Les Mots* (*Words*) appeared in 1964 and he was awarded the Nobel Prize for Literature the same year.

SASSOON, Siegfried (1886–1967): educated at Marlborough and Cambridge, Sassoon first published verse in private pamphlets, but it was in the trenches during the First World War that he began to write the poetry for which he is remembered; his bleak realism, his contempt for war leaders and patriotic cant, and his compassion for his comrades found expression in a body of verse which was not acceptable to a public revering R. *Brooke. During this first spell in the front line he was awarded the MC, which he later threw away. Dispatched as 'shell-shocked' to hospital, he encountered and encouraged W. *Owen, and organized a public protest against the war. In 1917 he published his war poems in *The Old Huntsman* and in 1918 further poems in *Counter-Attack*, both with scant success. Further volumes of poetry published in the 1920s finally established a high reputation, and collections were published in 1947 and 1961. From the late 1920s Sassoon began to think of himself as a religious poet and in 1957 he became a Catholic.

Meanwhile he was also achieving success as a prose writer. His semi-autobiographical trilogy (*Memoirs of a Fox-Hunting Man*, 1928; *Memoirs of an Infantry Officer*, 1930; and *Sherston's Progress*, 1936) were published together as *The Complete Memoirs of George Sherston* in 1937; and he also published three volumes of autobiography, *The Old Century and Seven More Years* (1938), *The Weald of Youth* (1942), and *Siegfried's Journey* (1945), and an important biography of G. *Meredith.

SCHILLER, Johann (1759–1805): German dramatist and lyric poet; Schiller's first play was *Die Räuber* (*The Robbers*, 1781), and its theme of authoritarianism and liberty gave it great popularity. His next important play was *Kabale und Liebe* (*Intrigue and Love*, 1784, the play on which Verdi based his opera *Luisa Miller*), but he achieved his greatest dramatic success with the historical tragedy of *Wallenstein* (1799), composed of three parts, the second and third of which were translated into English verse by Coleridge in 1800. *Maria Stuart* (1800) also dramatizes history, as does *Die Jungfrau von Orleans* (*The Maid of Orleans*, 1801). He then wrote a 'classical' drama with chorus, *Die Braut von Messina* (*The Bride of Messina*, 1803), and his last finished play was *Wilhelm Tell* (1804).

Schiller was also a fine poet. Some of his best-known poems are 'Die Kunstler' ('The Artists'), 'Das Ideal und das Leben' ('The Ideal and Life'), 'Die Glocke' ('The Bell'), and 'An die Freude' ('Ode to Joy'), which Beethoven set to music in his Ninth Symphony.

SCOTT, Sir Walter (1771–1832): educated at Edinburgh High School and University; Scott's interest in the old Border tales and ballads had early been awakened. His *Minstrelsy of the Scottish Border* appeared in three volumes in 1802–3; and in 1805 his first considerable original work, the romantic poem *The Lay of the Last Minstrel.* This was followed by several other long poems, including *The Lady of the Lake* (1810), *Rokeby* (1813), *The Lord of the Isles* (1815), and *Harold the Dauntless* (1817). Eclipsed in a measure by *Byron as a poet, in spite of the great popularity of his verse romances, Scott turned to the novel. They appeared anonymously and included, among many, *Waverley* (1814), *Rob Roy* (1817), *The Heart of Midlothian* (1818), *The Bride of Lammermoor* (1819), *Ivanhoe* (1819), *Redgauntlet* (1824), and *Castle Dangerous* (1831). Scott was created a baronet in 1820, and avowed the authorship of the novels in 1827. His other works include dramas, in which he did not excel, essays, and several historical works.

Scott's influence as a novelist was incalculable; he established the form of the Historical novel, and, according to V. S. Pritchett, the form of the short story (with 'The Two Drovers' and 'The Highland Widow'). He was avidly read and imitated throughout the 19th c., not only by historical novelists, but also by writers like Mrs *Gaskell, G. *Eliot, and the *Brontës. His reputation gradually declined but since the publication of three essays on him in 1951 there has been a considerable upsurge of scholarly activity and reappraisal, most of which concurs in regarding the Scottish 'Waverley' novels as his masterpieces.

SHAFFER, Peter (1926–): born in Liverpool and educated at Cambridge, Shaffer's first play, *Five Finger Exercise* (1958), was followed by many other successes, including *Royal Hunt of the Sun* (1964, pub. 1965), *Black Comedy* (1965, pub. 1967), *Equus* (1973), and *Amadeus* (1979, pub. 1980).

SHAKESPEARE, William (1564–1616): dramatist, man of the theatre, and poet, Shakespeare was baptized at his birthplace, Stratford-upon-Avon, on 26 April 1564. His birth is traditionally celebrated on 23 April, which is also known to have been the date of his death. He was the eldest son of John Shakespeare, a glover and dealer in other commodities who played a prominent part in local affairs, but whose fortunes later declined. Of the eight children his wife Mary Arden bore, four sons and one daughter survived childhood.

The standard and kind of education indicated by William's writings are such as he might have received at the local grammar school. We do not know how he was employed in early manhood; the best-authenticated tradition is Aubrey's: 'he had been in his younger yeares a Schoolmaster in the Countrey.' Nothing is known either of his beginnings as a writer, nor when or in what capacity he entered the theatre. He married Anne Hathaway in 1582 and they had three children, a daughter Susanna and twins, Hamnet—who died in 1596—and Judith.

The first printed allusion to Shakespeare's acting career appeared in 1592 and he was a leading member of the Lord Chamberlain's Men soon after their foundation in 1594. With them he worked and grew prosperous for the rest of his career as they developed into London's leading company, occupying the Globe Theatre from 1599, becoming the King's Men on James I's accession in 1603, and taking over the Blackfriars as a winter house in 1608. He is the only prominent playwright of his time to have had so stable a relationship with a single company.

Shakespeare's only writings for the press are the narrative poems *Venus and Adonis* (1593) and *The Rape of Lucrece* (1594), and the short poem 'The Phoenix and the Turtle' (1601). His sonnets, numbering 154 in total and dating probably from the mid 1590s, appeared in 1609, apparently not by his agency; they bear a dedication to the mysterious 'Mr W.H.' over the initials of the publisher. The volume also includes the poem 'A Lover's Complaint'.

Shakespeare's plays were published by being performed. Scripts of only half of them appeared in print in his lifetime, some in reported texts now known as 'bad quartos', for their texts are extremely corrupt as a result of their reconstruction from memory by a member, or members, of their cast. Records of performances are scanty and haphazard: as a result dates and order of composition, especially of the earlier plays, are often difficult to establish. The list that follows gives dates of first printing of all the plays other than those that first appeared in the 1623 Folio, of which 1200 were printed. In this First Folio 36 plays, 18 printed for the first time, were arranged by Heming and Condell into sections of comedies, histories, and tragedies. It was dedicated to William Herbert, Earl of Pembroke, and Philip Herbert, Earl of Montgomery, and contains the Droeshout portrait and a list of 'the Principall Actors in all these Playes', together with commendatory verses by contemporaries including *Jonson.

Probably Shakespeare began to write for the stage in the late 1580s. The ambitious trilogy on the reign of Henry VI, now known as *Henry VI* Parts One, Two, and Three, and its sequel *Richard III*, are among his early works. Parts Two and Three were printed in reported texts as *The First Part of the Contentions betwixt the Two Famous Houses of York and Lancaster* (1594) and *The True Tragedy of Richard, Duke of York* (1595). A bad quarto of *Richard III* appeared in 1597. Shakespeare's first Roman tragedy is *Titus Andronicus*, printed 1594, and his earliest comedies are *The Two Gentlemen of Verona*, *The Taming of the Shrew* (a derivative play, *The Taming of a Shrew*, was printed 1594), *The Comedy of Errors* (acted 1594), and *Love's Labour's Lost* (printed 1598). All these plays are thought to have been written by 1595.

Particularly difficult to date is *King John*: scholars still dispute whether a two-part play, *The Troublesome Reign of John, King of England*, printed 1591, is its source or a derivative. *Richard II*, printed 1597, is usually dated 1595. For some years after this, Shakespeare concentrated on comedy, in *A Midsummer Night's Dream* and *The Merchant of Venice* (both printed 1600), *The Merry Wives of Windsor* (related to the later history plays, and printed in a reported text 1602), *Much Ado About Nothing* (printed 1600), *As You Like It* (mentioned in 1600), and *Twelfth Night*, probably written in 1600 or soon afterwards. *Romeo and Juliet* (ascribed to the mid 1590s) is a tragedy with strongly comic elements, and the tetralogy begun by *Richard II* is completed by three comical histories: *Henry IV* Parts One and Two, each printed a year or two after composition (Part One 1598, Part Two 1600), and *Henry V*, almost certainly written 1599, printed, in a reported text, 1600. In 1598 a minor writer mentioned 12 of the plays so far listed (assuming that by *Henry the 4* he meant both Parts) along with another, *Love's Labours Won*, apparently either a lost play or an alternative title for an extant one.

Late in the century Shakespeare turned again to tragedy. A Swiss traveller saw *Julius Caesar* in London in September 1599. *Hamlet* apparently dates from a year or two later; it was entered in the register of the Stationers' Company in July 1602; a bad—very bad—quarto appeared in 1603, and a good text in late 1604 (some copies bear the date 1605). A play that defies easy classification is *Troilus and Cressida*, probably written 1602, printed 1609. The comedy *All's Well that Ends Well*, too, is probably of this period, as is *Measure for Measure*, played at Court in December 1604. The tragedy *Othello*, played at Court the previous month, reached print abnormally late in 1622. *King Lear* probably dates, in its first version, from 1605; the quarto printed in 1608, which some regard as a reported text, is gaining acceptance as an authoritative version. The text printed in the Folio appears to represent a revision dating from a few years later. Much uncertainty surrounds *Timon of Athens*, printed in the Folio from uncompleted papers, and probably written in collaboration with Thomas Middleton. *Macbeth* is generally dated 1606, *Antony and Cleopatra* 1606–7, and *Coriolanus* 1607–9.

Towards the end of his career, though while still in his early 40s, Shakespeare turned to romantic tragi-comedy. *Pericles*, printed in a debased text 1609, certainly existed in the previous year; it is the only play generally believed to be mostly, if not entirely, by Shakespeare that was not included in the 1623 Folio. Forman, the astrologer, records seeing both *Cymbeline* and *The Winter's Tale* in 1611. *The Tempest* was given at Court in November 1611.

The last three plays associated with Shakespeare appear to have been written in collaboration with J. *Fletcher. They are *Henry VIII*, which 'had been acted not passing 2 or 3 times' before the performance at the Globe during which the theatre burnt down on 29 June 1613; a lost play, *Cardenio*, acted by the King's Men in 1613 and attributed to the two dramatists in a Stationers' Register entry of 1653; and *The Two Noble Kinsmen*, which appears to derive in part from a 1613 masque by F. *Beaumont, and was first printed in 1634. No Shakespeare play survives in authorial manuscript, though three pages of revisions to a manuscript play, *Sir Thomas More*, variously dated about 1593 or 1601, are often thought to be by Shakespeare and in his hand.

Over 200 years after Shakespeare died, doubts were raised about the authenticity of his works. The product largely of snobbery—reluctance to believe that a man of humble origins wrote many of the world's greatest dramatic masterpieces—and of the desire for self-advertisement, they are best answered by the facts that the monument to William Shakespeare of Stratford-upon-Avon compares him with

Socrates and Virgil, and that Jonson's verse tributes to Shakespeare in the 1623 Folio identify its author as the 'Sweet Swan of Avon'.

See also article 'Shakespeare and the English Language' by Professor Stanley Hussey on p. 527.

SHAW, George Bernard (1856–1950): born in Dublin, Shaw moved to London in 1876 and began his literary career by ghosting music criticism and writing five unsuccessful novels. He wrote music, art, and book criticism for several periodicals and was already well known as a journalist and public speaker when his first play, *Widowers' Houses* (pub. 1893), was produced in 1892. There followed several others, but his first popular success did not come until *John Bull's Other Island* (1904, pub. NY 1907). Altogether he wrote over 50 plays, including *The Devil's Disciple* (perf. NY 1897, pub. 1901), *Mrs Warren's Profession* (pub. 1898, perf. 1902), *Man and Superman* (pub. 1903, perf. 1905), *Major Barbara* (1905, pub. 1907), *Pygmalion* (perf. Vienna 1913, pub. Berlin 1913), and *Heartbreak House* (pub. 1919, perf. 1920, both NY). The plays continued to be performed regularly both during and after his lifetime and his unorthodox views, his humour, and his love of paradox have become an institution. Amongst his other works should be mentioned *The Quintessence of Ibsenism* (1891, revised and expanded 1913), which reveals his debt to Ibsen as a playwright; and *The Intelligent Woman's Guide to Socialism and Capitalism* (1928). He was awarded the Nobel Prize for Literature in 1925.

SHELLEY, Percy Bysshe (1792–1822): educated at Eton and Oxford; Shelley's upbringing made him deeply unhappy and rebellious. At Oxford he read radical authors and in 1811 was summarily expelled for circulating a pamphlet, *The Necessity of Atheism.* Much of his early philosophy, both in poetry and politics, is expressed in *Queen Mab* (1813), with its remarkable notes; they show Shelley as the direct heir to the French and British revolutionary intellectuals of the 1790s. In 1814 his marriage collapsed and he eloped abroad with Mary Godwin and her 15-year-old stepsister. When they returned he wrote *Alastor* (1816), a non-political poem of haunting beauty, which first brought him general notice and reviews. The summer of 1816 was spent on Lake Geneva with *Byron. Mary began *Frankenstein*, and Shelley composed two philosophic poems much influenced by *Wordsworth. The same year his wife drowned herself, and Shelley married Mary and settled at Great Marlow where he wrote his polemical 'Hermit of Marlow' pamphlets and composed 'Laon and Cythna' which was published as *The Revolt of Islam* in 1818.

Harried by creditors, ill health, and 'social hatred', Shelley took his household to Italy in 1818. There he composed 'Julian and Maddalo' and started work on *Prometheus Unbound.* His domestic situation was increasingly strained, yet the 12 months from the summer of 1819 saw his most extraordinary and varied burst of major poetry. Much of this was inspired by news of political events, which also produced a number of short, angry propaganda poems. At the same time he dashed off several pure lyric pieces and completed a verse melodrama, *The Cenci* (1819). Yet he could get very little accepted for publication in England.

The quieter period at Pisa which followed saw him at work on a number of prose pieces, including his famous *Defence of Poetry* (1821). In the spring of 1821 news of the death of Keats produced *Adonais* (1821) and a platonic love-affair *Epipsychidion* (1821). In the winter of 1821 Byron also moved to Pisa, and a raffish circle formed round the two poets. Then in April 1822 Shelley moved his household to an isolated beach house. Here he began his last major poem, *The Triumph of Life* (1824), and composed a number of short lyrics of striking melodic grace. He was drowned in August 1822 when his schooner was sunk in a storm.

His lyric powers and romantic biography have until recently obscured Shelley's most enduring qualities as a writer. But among the English Romantics, he has now recovered his position as an undoubted major figure.

SHERIDAN, Richard (1751–1816): educated at Harrow, where he was regarded as a dunce, Sheridan's first play, *The Rivals* (1775) was highly successful and established Sheridan in the fashionable society he sought. It was followed by the farce, *St Patrick's Day*, again a success, and by an operatic play, *The Duenna*, which delighted its audiences. In 1776 Sheridan, with partners, bought Garrick's half-share in the Drury Lane Theatre and became its manager. *A Trip to Scarborough* appeared early in 1777 followed in the May by the universally acclaimed *The School for Scandal.* In 1779 he became the sole proprietor of Drury Lane, and began to live far beyond his means. In 1779 he produced his new play *The Critic*, which again was a huge success, and the world regarded him as the true heir of Garrick. But it was not what he wanted and in 1780 he became an MP and in 1783 became Secretary to the Treasury and established his reputation as a brilliant orator. But later his fortunes went into decline. In 1811 he lost his seat and in 1813 was arrested for debt. He wished to be remembered as a man of politics and to be buried next to Fox, but when he died he was laid near Garrick instead.

SHERRIFF, R(obert) C(edric) (1896–1975): born in Kingston upon Thames, Sherriff began to write plays to raise money for his rowing club. His best-known play was *Journey's End* (1928, pub. 1929), based on his experiences in the trenches during the First World War, but he wrote several others, including *Badger's Green* (1930) and *Home at Seven* (1950). He also wrote several novels.

SHOLOKHOV, Mikhail (1905–84): of mixed Cossack, peasant, and lower-middle-class background, Sholokhov became well known in the West for his novel *And Quietly Flows the Don* (4 vols., 1928–40), which has been much admired. His other works include a novel, *Virgin Soil Upturned* (1931), which chronicles life under a Five-Year Plan in south Russia. He was awarded the Nobel Prize for literature in 1965.

SIDNEY, Sir Philip (1554–86): educated at Shrewsbury School and Oxford, Sidney was the eldest son of Sir Henry Sidney who was thrice lord deputy governor of Ireland. He travelled widely in Europe in his youth, but did not achieve any official post until his appointment as governor of Flushing in 1585. His knighthood was awarded for reasons of Court protocol in 1582.

Years of comparative idleness enabled him to write and revise *Arcadia* (1590, and again in 1593 with the last three books of the earlier version appended), a prose romance that included poems and pastoral eclogues in a wide variety of verse forms, and to complete his essay, *Defence of Poetry* (1595), *The Lady of May*, a short pastoral entertainment first performed in 1578 or 1579, and *Astrophel and Stella*, a sequence of 108 sonnets and 11 songs, whose publication in 1591 began a craze for sonnet sequences.

During these years Sidney became a notable literary patron, receiving dedications from a variety of authors, the best known being that of *Spenser's *The Shepheardes Calendar* in 1579. He was interested in experimenting with classical metres in English, but it is unlikely that his discussion of this and other matters with Greville, Dyer, and Spenser amounted to anything so formal as an academy or learned society. The last year of his life was spent in the Netherlands, where he received a mortal wound while leading an attack on a Spanish convoy. None of Sidney's works were published during his lifetime and his posthumous reputation, as the perfect Renaissance patron, soldier, lover, and courtier, far outstripped his documented achievements, and can be seen as having a life independent of them which has become proverbial.

SILLITOE, Alan (1928–   ): after service in the RAF in Malaya, Sillitoe spent some years in Majorca where Robert *Graves encouraged him to write. His first volume of verse, *Without Beer or Bread* (1957), was followed by his much-praised first novel, *Saturday Night and Sunday Morning* (1958), and by several other works, including a collection of short stories, *The Loneliness of the Long Distance Runner* (1959).

SILONE, Ignazio (1900–78): founder member of the Italian Communist Party in 1921, Silone escaped Fascist persecution by going into exile in Switzerland in 1930 where he remained until 1945. His best-known novels are *Fontamara* (1930) and *Pane e vino* (pub. first in English, *Bread and Wine*, 1936; in Italian 1937, rev. 1955 as *Vino e pane*).

SIMENON, Georges (1903–   ): the Belgian-French popular novelist, Simenon is one of the most prolific of modern writers. He launched his celebrated detective, Maigret, in 1931, and his abilities have earned him a respect rarely accorded to writers in the genre of detective fiction.

SINGER, Isaac Bashevis (1904–): educated at the Warsaw Rabbinical Seminary, Singer emigrated to New York in 1935 and became a journalist. He wrote in Yiddish for the *Jewish Daily Forward*, which published most of his short stories. The first of his works to be translated into English was *The Family Moscat* (1950), which was followed by many other works, including *The Magician of Lublin* (1960), *The Slave* (1962), *The Manor* (1967) and its sequel *The Estate* (1969), and several volumes of short stories. Singer's writings have been increasingly admired internationally, and he was awarded the Nobel Prize for Literature in 1978.

SITWELL, Dame Edith (1887–1964): after publishing her first volume of verse in 1915, Dame Edith quickly acquired a reputation as an eccentric and controversial figure, which was quickly confirmed by the first public performance, in 1923, of *Façade*, a highly original entertainment (with music by William Walton) with verses in syncopated rhythms. Her prose works include *English Eccentrics* (1933) and *Victoria of England* (1936). Her only novel, *I Live under a Black Sun* (1937), was poorly received, but it was followed by a period of great acclaim, aroused by her poems of the blitz and the atom bomb. F. R. Leavis had claimed in 1932 that 'the Sitwells belong to the history of publicity, rather than that of poetry', but her status as a poet survived this dismissal, although it remains a matter of controversy.

SITWELL, Sir Osbert (1892–1969): educated at Eton, Sir Osbert served in the First World War and his early poetry is sharply satirical and pacifist in tone. He produced many volumes of verse, and his prose works include the novel *Before the Bombardment* (1926) and two travel books, *Winters of Content* (1932) and *Escape with me!* (1939). His most sustained achievement was his autobiography, in five volumes (*Left Hand! Right Hand!*, 1945; *The Scarlet Tree*, 1946; *Great Morning!*, 1948; *Laughter in the Next Room*, 1949; *Noble Essences*, 1950; with a later addition, *Tales my Father Taught Me*, 1962).

SITWELL, Sacheverell (1897–): brother of Osbert and Edith; Sacheverell's first volume of verse, which appeared in 1918, was followed by several others; his *Collected Poems* appeared in 1936, and a selection, *A Retrospect of Poems*, in 1979. Many of his prose works combine an interest in art and travel, and he also wrote biographies of Mozart and Liszt.

SKELTON, John (?1460–1529): created 'poet laureate' by the universities of Oxford, Louvain, and Cambridge, an academical distinction, Skelton became tutor to Prince Henry (Henry VIII) and enjoyed Court favours despite his outspokenness. His principal works include: *The Bowge of Courte*, a satire on the Court of Henry VII; *The Garlande of Laurell*, a self-laudatory allegorical poem; and *Phyllyp Sparowe*, a lamentation. Two of his satires contained attacks on Cardinal Wolsey. However, he seems to have repented of these, for

The Garlande of Laurell and his poem on the Duke of Albany, both of 1523, are dedicated to Wolsey. His most vigorous poem was *The Tunnyng of Elynour Rummyng* and his *Ballade of the Scottysshe Kynge* is a spirited celebration of the victory of Flodden.

SMOLLETT, Tobias (1721–71): after attending Glasgow University, Smollett was apprenticed to a surgeon and later served as one in the navy. In 1744 he set himself up as a surgeon in Downing Street and in 1746 his much-admired poem, 'The Tears of Scotland', was published. Further poems followed and in 1747 he wrote *The Adventures of Roderick Random* which appeared the following year and was a lasting success, though it was not until his *Complete History of England* was published in 1757–8 that he could feel financially secure. His other works include *The Adventures of Peregrine Pickle* (1751), *The Adventures of Ferdinand Count Fathom* (1953), *The Life and Adventures of Sir Launcelot Greaves* (1760), and his crowning achievement *The Expedition of Humphry Clinker* (1771).

Smollett's passion for controversy did not always endear him to the literary or fashionable world, but his major novels were admired and successful; his reputation sank considerably in the 19th and early 20th c., but now stands high.

SOLZHENITSYN, Alexander (1918–): born in the Caucasus, the son of a Russian army officer, Solzhenitsyn was arrested in 1945 for remarks critical of Stalin. He was sent to a labour camp and in 1956 returned to central Russia to work as a teacher. His first published story, *One Day in the Life of Ivan Denisovich* (1962), caused a sensation through its honest and pioneering description of camp life. His major novels, *Cancer Ward* (1968) and *The First Circle* (1969), could only be published abroad, and in late 1969 he was expelled from the Union of Soviet Writers. In 1970 he was awarded the Nobel Prize for Literature. The appearance abroad of the first volume of *The Gulag Archipelago* (1973–5) caused him to be deported from Russia. He settled in the United States, and continued a series of novels begun with *August 1914* (1971), offering an alternative picture of Soviet history.

SOUTHEY, Robert (1774–1843): after being expelled from Westminster, Southey went up to Oxford with 'a heart full of poetry and feeling, a head full of Rousseau and Werther, and my religious principles shaken by Gibbon'. He became friendly with *Coleridge and with him wrote *The Fall of Robespierre* (1794). From this time his literary output was prodigious. In 1795 he wrote *Joan of Arc* (1796) and between 1796 and 1798 wrote many ballads, including 'The Inchcape Rock' and 'The Battle of Blenheim', which had an influence in loosening the constrictions of 18th-c. verse; he also produced one of his best-known poems, 'The Holly Tree'. In 1800 he went to Spain and on his return settled in the Lake District, where he remained for the rest of his life as one of the 'Lake Poets'. His other works include *Thalaba* (1801), *Madoc* (1805), and *Roderick: the Last of the Goths* (1814), all narrative poems; his *History of the Peninsular War* (1823–32); and *Essays Moral and Political* (1832).

His longer poems, now little read, were admired by men as diverse as Fox and *Macaulay. The scope of his reading and of his writing was vast, and his clear, firm prose style has been much esteemed; but in no sphere was his work of the highest distinction.

SPARK, Muriel (1918–): after spending some years in Central Africa, which was to form the setting for several of her short stories, Muriel Spark returned to Britain where she worked for the Foreign Office during the Second World War. Her first novel, *The Comforters* (1957), was followed by many others, including *Memento Mori* (1959), *The Ballad of Peckham Rye* (1960), *The Prime of Miss Jean Brodie* (1961), *The Girls of Slender Means* (1963), *The Mandelbaum Gate* (1965), and *The Abbess of Crewe* (1974). She has also written plays and poems; her *Collected Poems* and *Collected Plays* were both published in 1967.

SPENDER, Sir Stephen (1909–): educated at University College School and Oxford, where he became friendly with *Auden and *MacNeice, Spender published his first collection of verse, *Twenty Poems*, in 1930. His *Poems* (1933) contained both personal and political poems, including 'The Pylons', which gave the nickname of Pylon Poets to himself and his friends. His interest in the public and social role and duty of the writer has tended to obscure the essentially personal and private nature of much of his own poetry, including his elegies for his sister-in-law, in *Poems of Dedication* (1947), and many of the poems in such later volumes as *Collected Poems 1928–1953* (1955). His other works include criticism, translations, and his autobiography *World Within World* (1951).

SPENSER, Edmund (c.1552–99): educated at Merchant Taylors' School and Cambridge, Spenser obtained a place in the household of the Earl of Leicester where he became acquainted with Sir Philip Sidney, to whom he dedicated his *Shepheardes Calendar* (1579). In the same year he began to write his greatest work, *The Faerie Queene*, of which the first three books were published in 1590, and the second three in 1596. In 1580 he was appointed secretary to Lord Grey of Wilton, then going to Ireland as lord deputy and settling there. His other works include *Amoretti* and *Epithalamion*, printed together in 1595, and *Prothalamion* (1596). His monument in Westminster Abbey describes him as 'THE PRINCE OF POETS IN HIS TYME'; there have been few later periods in which he has not been admired, and the poetry of both *Milton and *Keats had its origins in the reading of Spenser.

STEAD, Christina (1902–83): educated at the University Teachers' College in Sydney, where she was born, Christina Stead went to Europe in 1928. She lived there and in America until returning to Australia in 1968. Her wandering life and her left-wing views may have contributed to the neglect of her work, which towards the end of her life received renewed attention and admiration. Her first collection of stories, *The*

Salzburg Tales (1934), was followed by several full-length novels, which include her best-known work, *The Man who loved Children* (1940); *For Love Alone* (1945); and *Cotter's England* (1967; US as *Dark Places of the Heart*, 1966). Many of the novels manifest the author's admiration for *Zola, and her feminism and politics are deeply interwoven, independent, and personal.

STEELE, Sir Richard (1672–1729): educated at Charterhouse and Oxford; Steele's first play was the comedy, *The Funeral* (1701). In 1709 he started *The Tatler*, which he carried on with the help of *Addison till January 1711. He then started *The Spectator* and, with Addison, carried it on till 1712. In 1713 he became an MP, but was expelled the following year after publishing a pamphlet in favour of the Hanoverian succession. The tide turned in his favour on the accession of George I and he was appointed supervisor of Drury Lane Theatre, among other posts, and was knighted in 1715. His last comedy, *The Conscious Lovers*, was produced in 1722. Less highly regarded as an essayist than Addison, his influence was nevertheless great, and his reformed and sentimental dramas did much to create an image of polite behaviour for the new century.

STEIN, Gertrude (1874–1946): educated at Ratcliffe College and Johns Hopkins University, Gertrude Stein settled in Paris in 1902. Her friend, secretary, and companion from 1907 was a fellow American, Alice B. Toklas, whom she made the ostensible author of her own memoir, *The Autobiography of Alice B. Toklas* (1933). *Tender Buttons* (1914) is an example of her highly idiosyncratic poetry, and her other works include novels like *Three Lives* (1909) and *A Long Gay Book* (1932), literary theory, short stories, portraits of her friends, a lyric drama, and *Wars I Have Seen* (1945), a personal account of occupied Paris. Her characteristic repetitions and reprises, her flowing, unpunctuated prose, and her attempts to capture the 'living moment' represent a highly personal but nevertheless influential version of the stream-of-consciousness technique.

STEINBECK, John (1902–68): born in California, Steinbeck took his native state as the background for his early short stories and novels. *Tortilla Flat* (1935) was his first success, and he confirmed his growing reputation with two other novels, *In Dubious Battle* (1936) and *Of Mice and Men* (1937). His best-known work is *The Grapes of Wrath* (1939). His later novels are often marred by sentimentality and uncertainty of purpose, and by the time he was awarded the Nobel Prize for literature in 1962 his reputation had already declined in his own country.

STENDHAL (1783–1842): the pseudonym of the French novelist Henri Beyle. Stendhal spent his early years in his native Grenoble and later lived for long periods in Italy. His two recognized masterpieces, *Le Rouge et le noir* (1830) and *La Chartreuse de Parme* (1839), are remarkable for their political dimension, for the detail and variety of the experience portrayed, for the energy and passion of the principal characters, and for penetrating psychological analysis. Besides a number of other novels, Stendhal also wrote studies of music and musicians, several volumes of autobiography, and much occasional journalism.

STERNE, Laurence (1713–68): educated at Cambridge, where he encountered and embraced the philosophy of Locke, Sterne took holy orders and in 1741 became a prebendary of York cathedral. In 1759, in the course of an ecclesiastical quarrel, he wrote *A Political Romance* (later entitled *The History of a Good Warm Watch Coat*), a satire on local ecclesiastical courts so barbed that the authorities had it burned. In the same year he started his unique work *Tristram Shandy*, now generally regarded as the progenitor of the 20th-c. stream-of-consciousness novel. The first version of Vols. I and II was rejected by a London printer and the next version was published in York in 1759. Early in 1760 Sterne found himself famous. He went to London and (although his book was not liked by Dr *Johnson, *Goldsmith, *Richardson, and others) was fêted by society. In 1761 four more volumes appeared and in 1765 Vols. VII and VIII. The same year he undertook an eight-month tour of France and Italy, which clearly provided him with much of the material for *A Sentimental Journey* (1768). The ninth and last volume of *Tristram Shandy* appeared in 1767, but after his death a spate of forgeries appeared which included another volume of it.

Sterne is generally acknowledged as an innovator of the highest originality, and has been seen as the chief begetter of a long line of writers interested in the stream of consciousness. He acknowledges in *Tristram Shandy* his own debt in this respect to Locke.

STEVENSON, Robert Louis (originally Lewis) (1850–94): although admitted as an advocate in 1875, Stevenson had already determined to be a writer. In that year he was introduced to W. E. Henley, who became a close friend, and with whom he was to collaborate on four undistinguished plays. After travelling extensively to try and regain his health he returned to England where he consolidated a friendship with Henry *James. By this time he had published widely in periodicals, and many of his short stories, essays, and travel pieces were collected in volume form. His first full-length work of fiction, *Treasure Island*, published in book form in 1883, brought him fame, which increased with the publication of *The Strange Case of Dr Jekyll and Mr Hyde* (1886). This was followed by his popular Scottish romances, *Kidnapped* (1886), its sequel *Catriona* (1893), and *The Master of Ballantrae* (1889). He also published many other works, including travel books, poetry, and historical romances. In 1888 he set out with his family for the South Seas, becoming a legend in his lifetime. He finally settled in Samoa, and died there while working on his unfinished masterpiece, *Weir of Hermiston* (1896).

Although his more popular books have remained constantly in print, and have been frequently filmed, his critical reputation has been obscured by attention to his vivid personality and adventurous life. His delight in story-telling, swashbuckling romances, and historical 'tushery', as he called it, gave him an audience of readers rather than critics.

STOKER, Bram (1847–1912): born in Dublin, Stoker gave up his career as a Civil Servant there in 1878 to become Sir Henry Irving's secretary and touring manager for the next 27 years. He wrote a number of novels and short stories, and is chiefly remembered for *Dracula* (1897), a tale of vampirism influenced by 'Carmilla', one of the stories in Le Fanu's *In a Glass Darkly* (1872).

STOPPARD, Tom (1937–): Stoppard, who was born in Czechoslovakia, had his first play, *A Walk on the Water*, televised in 1963 (staged in London in 1968 as *Enter a Free Man*). He published a novel, *Lord Malquist and the Moon*, in 1965, and in 1966 his play *Rosencrantz and Guildenstern are Dead* attracted much attention. This was followed by many witty and inventive plays, including *The Real Inspector Hound* (1968), *Jumpers* (1972), *Dirty Linen* (1976), *Night and Day* (1978), and *The Real Thing* (1982).

STOWE, Mrs Harriet Elizabeth Beecher (1811–96): born in Connecticut, USA, Harriet Beecher was a schoolteacher before marrying C. E. Stowe, a professor at her father's theological seminary. Her anti-slavery novel, *Uncle Tom's Cabin*, which was serialized in 1851–2 and published in book form in 1852, had a sensational success and stirred up great public feeling. The novel's success brought Mrs Stowe to England three times where she was rapturously received, although she later alienated British opinion by her *Lady Byron Vindicated* (1870), in which she charged *Byron with incestuous relations with his half-sister. Her other works include *The Minister's Wooing* (1859), *Old Town Folks* (1869), and *Poganuc People* (1878).

STRINDBERG, August (1849–1912): born in Stockholm, Strindberg achieved theatrical success only after much difficulty and attempts at other careers, and his works, dramatic and non-dramatic, are marked by a deeply neurotic response to religion, social class, and sexuality. His first important play, *Master Olof* (written 1872–7, perf. 1881), was followed by others, including *The Father* (1887), *Miss Julie* (1888), and *Creditors* (1889). His later works are tense, symbolic, psychic dramas; they include *The Dance of Death* (1901), *A Dream Play* (1902), and *The Ghost Sonata* (1907), all distinctive and innovative works which influenced the psychological and symbolic dramas of *O'Neill. Strindberg's non-dramatic works include a novel, *The Red Room* (1879), short stories, and *Inferno* (written and published in French, 1898), an extraordinary account of his life in Paris after the collapse of his second marriage.

SURTEES, Robert (1805–64): educated at Durham Grammar School,

Surtees practised as a lawyer, but from 1830 built up a reputation as a sporting journalist. He contributed to the *Sporting Magazine*, and in 1831 helped found the *New Sporting Magazine* to which he contributed his comic sketches of Mr Jorrocks, the sporting cockney grocer, later collected as *Jorrocks's Jaunts and Jollities* (1838). Jorrocks reappears in *Handley Cross* (1843), one of Surtees's most successful novels, and in the less popular *Hillingdon Hall* (1845). His second great character, Mr Soapy Sponge, appears in *Mr Sponge's Sporting Tour* (1853), which is probably his best work. Another celebrated character was Mr Facey Romford, who appears in his last novel, *Mr Facey Romford's Hounds* (1865).

SVEVO, Italo (1861–1928): born in Trieste from a Jewish Italo-German background; Svevo's work as a novelist was unknown until *Joyce met him in Trieste and helped him to publish his masterpiece, *La coscienza di Zeno* (*Confessions of Zeno*, 1923). His other novels are *Una vita* (*A Life*, 1893), *Senilità* (a title translated by Joyce as *As a Man Grows Older*, 1898), and *La novella del buon vecchio e della bella fanciulla* (*The Tale of the Good Old Man and the Lovely Young Girl*, 1929). He was at work on a fifth, *Il vecchione* (*The Grand Old Man*, 1967), when he died in a car crash.

SWIFT, Jonathan (1667–1745): educated, with *Congreve, at Kilkenny Grammar School, and then at Trinity College, Dublin, Swift was ordained in 1694, received a small prebend, and became dean of St Patrick's in 1713. In 1697 he wrote *The Battle of the Books*, which was published in 1704 together with *A Tale of a Tub*, his celebrated satire on 'corruptions in religion and learning'. In the course of numerous visits to London he became acquainted with *Addison, *Steele, Congreve, and Halifax, and contributed to periodicals like *The Tatler* and *The Examiner*. He also wrote various political pamphlets and in 1726 published his satire *Gulliver's Travels*. During his last years in Ireland he wrote some of his most famous tracts and characteristic poems, which include *The Grand Question Debated* (1729), *Verses on the Death of Dr Swift* (1731, pub. 1739), *A Complete Collection of Polite and Ingenious Conversation* (1738); and the ironical *Directions to Servants* (written about 1731 and published after his death). His output was vast and included political writings, pamphlets on Ireland and on the Church, and poetry. His *Prose Works* were published in 16 volumes between 1939 and 1974.

Nearly all Swift's works were published anonymously, and for only one, *Gulliver's Travels*, did he receive any payment (£200). Many writers were alienated by his ferocity and coarseness, and his works tended to be undervalued in the late 18th and 19th c. The 20th c. has seen a revival of biographical and critical interest, stressing on the whole Swift's sanity, vigour, and satirical inventiveness rather than his alleged misanthropy.

SWINBURNE, Algernon (1837–1909): educated at Eton and Oxford,

Swinburne's first published volume, *The Queen-Mother; Rosamund* (1860), shows the influence of Elizabethan dramatists. It attracted little attention, but *Atalanta in Calydon* (1865), a drama in classical Greek form, with choruses (e.g. 'When the hounds of spring are on winter's traces') that revealed his great metrical skills, brought him celebrity. *Chastelard* (1865), the first of three dramas on the subject of Mary Queen of Scots, raised some doubts about the morality of Swinburne's verse, doubts reinforced by the first series of *Poems and Ballads* (1866), which brought down a torrent of abuse. The volume contains many of his best as well as his most notorious poems which clearly demonstrate the preoccupation with de Sade, masochism, and *femmes fatales*. *Bothwell* (1874) and a second Greek drama, *Erechtheus* (1876), were followed by the more subdued *Poems and Ballads: second series* (1878). He published many more volumes, but they lack the force of his earlier work, and often fall into a kind of self-parody. His published prose works include two novels and several works of perceptive criticism. His influence on fellow aesthetes like Pater and a later generation of poets was considerable, and was deplored by T. S. *Eliot and F. R. Leavis.

TENNYSON, Alfred, first Baron Tennyson (1809–92): educated privately and then at Cambridge, Tennyson's early career was dogged by poverty. In 1842 appeared a selection from *Poems, Chiefly Lyrical* (1830) and *Poems* (1833), many of the poems much revised, with new poems, including 'Morte d'Arthur', 'Locksley Hall', 'Ulysses', and 'St Simeon Stylites'. In 1847 he published *The Princess* and in 1850 *In Memoriam*, which he had been working on since 1833. He was appointed Poet Laureate in 1850 and wrote his 'Ode' on the death of Wellington in 1852 and 'The Charge of the Light Brigade' in 1854.

Tennyson's fame was by now firmly established, and *Maud, and other Poems* (1855) and the first four *Idylls of the King* (1859) sold extremely well. His other works include *The Holy Grail and Other Poems* (1869), *Ballads and Other Poems* (1880), and *Tiresias, and Other Poems* (1885), and a number of dramas. He was made a peer in 1884. In his later years there were already signs that the admiration he had long enjoyed was beginning to wane. Critical opinion has tended to endorse *Auden's view that 'his genius was lyrical', and that he had little talent for the narrative, epic, and dramatic forms to which he devoted such labour. T. S. *Eliot called him 'the great master of metric as well as of melancholia'. More recently there has been a revival of interest in some of the longer poems.

THACKERAY, William Makepeace (1811–63): educated at Charterhouse and Cambridge, which he left without taking a degree, Thackeray began his career in journalism by becoming the proprietor of a struggling weekly paper. It ceased publication a year later but the experience had given Thackeray an entrée to the London literary world. After a period living in Paris he began to contribute regularly to a number of periodicals and newspapers in London, including a long association with *Punch*, and during the 1840s began to make his name as a writer. He first came to the attention of the public with *The Yellowplush Papers*, which appeared in *Fraser's Magazine* in 1837–8. His first full-length volume, *The Paris Sketch-Book*, appeared in 1840, and *The Great Hoggarty Diamond* in 1841, both under his most familiar pseudonym, Michael Angelo Titmarsh. He also wrote as 'George Savage FitzBoodle'. *The Irish Sketch-book* of 1843 has a preface signed, for the first time, with Thackeray's own name. In 1847 his first major novel, *Vanity Fair*, began to appear in monthly numbers, and was followed by a number of others, including *Pendennis* (1848–50), *The History of Henry Esmond* (1852), *The Newcomes* (1853–5), and *The Virginians* (1857–9).

THOMAS, Dylan (1914–53): born in Swansea, the son of the English master at Swansea Grammar School, where he himself was educated, Thomas knew no Welsh. He began to write poetry while still at school, and worked in Swansea as a journalist before moving to London in 1934; his first volume of verse, *18 Poems*, appeared the same year. In 1937 he married Caitlin Macnamara; they settled for a while at Laugharne in Wales, returning there permanently after many wanderings in 1949. Despite some allegations of deliberate obscurity, Thomas's romantic, affirmative, rhetorical style gradually won a large following; it was both new and influential, and the publication of *Deaths and Entrances* (1946), which contains some of his best-known work (including 'Fern Hill' and 'A Refusal to Mourn the Death by Fire of a Child in London') established him with a wide public: his *Collected Poems 1934–52* (1952) sold extremely well. Thomas also wrote a considerable amount of prose, including two collections of short stories, *Portrait of the Artist as a Young Dog* (1955) and *Adventures in the Skin Trade* (1955). Shortly before his death he took part in a reading in New York of what was to be his most famous single work, the radio drama *Under Milk Wood*, which was first broadcast in 1954 and subsequently adapted for the stage.

THOMAS, Edward (1878–1917): educated at St Paul's and Oxford, Thomas married young and moved to Kent, supporting his family by producing many volumes of prose, much of it topographical and biographical. In 1913 he was introduced to *Frost, with whose encouragement he turned to poetry. In 1915 Frost returned to America and Thomas enlisted in the army and was killed at Arras. Most of his poetry was published posthumously, though a few pieces appeared under the pseudonym 'Edward Eastaway' between 1915 and 1917. Various collections followed; the fullest, *Collected Poems*, was published in 1978.

THOREAU, Henry (1817–62): born in Concord, Massachusetts, USA, Thoreau was educated at Harvard and became a follower and friend of *Emerson. He supported himself by a variety of occupations and made no money from literature. He published only two books in his lifetime. *A Week on the Concord and Merrimack River* (1849) describes a journey undertaken in 1839 with his brother. *Walden, or Life in the Woods* (1854) describes his two-year experiment in self-sufficiency. It attracted little attention, but has since been recognized as a literary masterpiece and as one of the seminal books of the century. His *Journals* (14 vols.) were published in 1906 and his collected *Writings* (20 vols.) the same year.

TOLKIEN, J(ohn) R(onald) R(euel) (1892–1973): Merton professor of English language and literature at Oxford between 1945 and 1959, Tolkien became internationally known for two books based on a mythology of his own: *The Hobbit* (1937) and its sequel *The Lord of the Rings* (3 vols., 1954–5). *The Silmarillion*, which has an earlier place in this sequence of stories, was published in 1977.

TOLSTOY, Count Leo Nikolaevich (1828–1910): born in central Russia; Tolstoy's first published work was *Childhood* (1852), the first part of a remarkably perceptive trilogy on his early years. This was followed by a number of other works, but in the decade following *Cossacks* (1863) he was mainly engaged in the creation of *War and Peace* (1863–9), which was followed by *Anna Karenina* (1873–7). From about 1880 Tolstoy's constant concern with moral questions developed into a spiritual crisis which led to the writing of such works as *A Confession* (1879–82), *What Men Live By* (1882), and *What I Believe* (1883). The major fictional works of this late period, bearing the imprint of changes in his thinking, include *The Kreutzer Sonata* (1889), *Master and Man* (1895), *Resurrection* (1899), and *Hadji Murad* (1904). Tolstoy's moral positions led to the banning of many of his works by the censorship, and to his excommunication by the Orthodox Church. But they also brought him a unique authority and influence, and his home became a place of pilgrimage.

TRAVEN, Ben (?1882–1969): the novelist and short-story writer, whose first stories appeared in German in Berlin in 1925 as *Die Baumwollpflücker* (*The Cottonpickers*) followed by his highly successful novel *The Death Ship* (1925). Traven, whose identity remained for many years shrouded in mystery, went to Mexico in the 1920s, whence appeared some 12 novels and collections of short stories, including *The Treasure of Sierra Madre* (1934). *The Man who was B. Traven* (1980) by W. Wyatt established that he was Albert Otto Max Feige, later known as Rex Marut, born in Świebodzin, a Polish town then in Germany.

TROLLOPE, Anthony (1815–82): educated at both Harrow and Winchester, where the family's poverty made him miserable, Trollope became a junior clerk in the General Post Office in London in 1834 and eventually became an important if also highly individual Civil Servant. Among his achievements is the introduction in Great Britain of the pillar-box for letters. His literary career began with the appearance of *The Macdermots of Ballycloran* in 1847, but not until his fourth novel,

The Warden (1855), did he establish the manner and material by which he is best known. This, the first of the 'Barsetshire' series, was followed by five others including *Barchester Towers* (1857) and *The Last Chronicle of Barset* (1867). His second series of novels is known as the 'Political' novels or—perhaps more appropriately—as the 'Palliser' novels, after Plantagenet Palliser, who appears in all of them. This series of six novels begins with *Can You Forgive Her?* (1864) and ends with *The Duke's Children* (1880).

Trollope established the novel-sequence in English fiction. His use of reappearing characters had been anticipated by *Balzac, but there is no evidence that Trollope was in any way indebted to the French author. He attributed his remarkable output, which included 47 novels, several travel books, biographies, as well as collections of short stories and sketches, to a disciplined regularity of composition, and he trained himself to produce a given number of words an hour.

TURGENEV, Ivan (1818–83): born in central Russia, Turgenev studied at Moscow and St Petersburg Universities. He fell in love with a singer and partly for this reason was to live much of his life abroad. His first important prose work was *A Hunter's Notes* (1847–51). It was followed by a series of novels, including *Rudin* (1856), *Fathers and Sons* (1862), and *Smoke* (1867). His greatest short stories are 'Asya' (1858), 'First Love' (1860), and 'Torrents of Spring' (1870). His best play is *A Month in the Country* (1850). Turgenev was the first major Russian writer to find success in the rest of Europe.

TWAIN, Mark (1835–1910): pseudonym of Samuel Langhorne Clemens. Twain was born in Florida, USA. From 1862 he worked as a newspaper correspondent for various magazines, adopting the pseudonym 'Mark Twain', familiar to him as the leadsman's call on the Mississippi, on which he had worked as a pilot between 1857 and 1861. Under this name he published his first successful story, 'Jim Smiley and his Jumping Frog'. This comic version of an old folk-tale became the title story of *The Celebrated Jumping Frog of Calaveras County, and other Sketches* (1867), which established him as a leading humorist, a reputation consolidated by *The Innocents Abroad* (1869). In 1876 and 1885 respectively appeared his most famous works, both deeply rooted in his own childhood, *The Adventures of Tom Sawyer* and its sequel *The Adventures of Huckleberry Finn*, which paint an unforgettable picture of Mississippi frontier life. His other works include *The Prince and the Pauper* (1882), *Life on the Mississippi* (1883), and *A Connecticut Yankee in King Arthur's Court* (1889).

UPDIKE, John (1932–): born in Pennsylvania, USA, and educated at Harvard; Updike's novels include the trilogy *Rabbit, Run* (1960), *Rabbit Redux* (1971), and *Rabbit is Rich* (1981), a small-town domestic tragi-comedy which traces the career of ex-basketball champion Harry Angstrom. His other novels include *Couples* (1968) and *The Coup* (1979), and he has also published several volumes of short stories.

VERLAINE, Paul (1844–96): French poet. Some of his poems appeared in *Le Parnasse contemporain* of 1866; his *Poèmes saturniens* were published in the same year; and his *Fêtes galantes* in 1869. From the end of 1871 he came under the influence of *Rimbaud and their problematical relationship culminated in Verlaine's arrest and imprisonment, in 1873, for wounding Rimbaud with a revolver. His most interesting work, characterized by an intense musicality and metrical inventiveness, appeared in *Romances sans paroles* in 1874.

VERNE, Jules (1828–1905): French novelist, who achieved great popularity with a long series of books combining adventure and popular science. Amongst his most successful stories are *Voyage au centre de la terre* (1864), *Vingt mille lieues sous les mers* (1869), and *Le Tour du monde en quatre-vingts jours* (1873).

WAIN, John (1925–): born in Stoke-on-Trent and educated at Oxford; Wain's first novel, *Hurry On Down* (1953), has been linked with those of W. *Cooper, K. *Amis, and J. *Braine as a manifestation of the spirit of the 'angry young men' (see K. Amis) of the 1950s. His other novels include *The Contenders* (1958), *A Travelling Woman* (1959), and *Strike the Father Dead* (1962). He has also published several volumes of verse, collected in *Poems 1949–79* (1981), and was professor of poetry at Oxford 1973–8.

WALTON, Izaak (1593–1683): born at Stafford, Walton wrote a number of biographies but is now known chiefly for *The Compleat Angler*. This was first published in 1653, and was largely rewritten for the second edition (1655), which is half as long again. Often reprinted, this work combines practical information about angling with folklore, quotations from a variety of writers, pastoral interludes of songs and ballads, and glimpses of an idyllic rural life of well-kept inns and tuneful milkmaids.

WAUGH, Evelyn (1903–66): educated at Lancing and Oxford, Waugh worked for some years (unhappily) as a schoolmaster which provided material for *Decline and Fall* (1928), his first and immensely successful novel. It was followed by a number of others, including *Vile Bodies* (1930), *Black Mischief* (1932), *A Handful of Dust* (1934), and *Scoop* (1938), all works of high comedy and social satire. He also established himself as journalist and travel writer with accounts of journeys through Africa and South America, and of Mussolini's invasion of Abyssinia. His later novels include *Put Out More Flags* (1942), *Brideshead Revisited* (1945), *The Loved One* (1948), *The Ordeal of Gilbert Pinfold* (1957), and the trilogy *Sword of Honour* (1965) which was originally published as *Men at Arms* (1952), *Officers and Gentlemen* (1955), and *Unconditional Surrender* (1961). He also wrote a number of biographies and a volume of autobiography, *A Little Learning* (1960).

WELLS, H(erbert) G(eorge) (1866–1946): born in Bromley, Kent, Wells became a teacher, studying at night and winning a scholarship in 1884 to the Normal School of Science in South Kensington, where he came under the lasting influence of T. H. Huxley. His literary output was vast and extremely varied. As a novelist he is perhaps best remembered for his scientific romances, among the earliest products of the new genre of science fiction. The first, *The Time Machine* (1895), was followed by a number of others, including *The Island of Doctor Moreau* (1896), *The Invisible Man* (1897), and *The War of the Worlds* (1898). Another group of novels evokes in comic and realistic style the lower-middle-class world of his youth and includes *Love and Mr Lewisham* (1900) and *Kipps* (1905). Among his other novels should be mentioned *Ann Veronica* (1909) and one of his most successful works, *Tono-Bungay* (1909). He also produced a number of volumes of short stories, his massive *The Outline of History* (1920), and many works of scientific and political speculation (including *The Shape of Things to Come*, 1933) which confirmed his position as one of the great popularizers and one of the most influential voices of his age.

WESKER, Arnold (1932–): born in Stepney and educated in Hackney, Wesker left school at 16 and worked at various jobs before making his name as a playwright. His first play, *Chicken Soup with Barley* (1958), was followed by many other successful productions, including *Roots* (1959), *I'm Talking about Jerusalem* (1960), *Chips with Everything* (1962), *The Four Seasons* (1965), *The Merchant* (1977), and *Caritas* (1981). He has also published essays, screenplays, and volumes of short stories.

WEST, Nathanael (1903–40): the pseudonym of Nathan Wallenstein Weinstein. West was born in New York and is known principally for two macabre and tragic novels, *Miss Lonelyhearts* (1933) and *The Day of the Locust* (1939). He was killed in a car crash.

WEST, Dame Rebecca (1892–1983): the adopted name of Cecily Isabel Fairfield, Rebecca West was educated in Edinburgh and trained briefly for the stage in London before becoming a feminist and a journalist, much influenced at this stage by the Pankhursts. Many of her shrewd, witty, and combative pieces have been collected and reprinted as *The Young Rebecca* (1982). Her first novel, *The Return of the Soldier* (1918), was followed by a number of others, including *The Judge* (1922), *The Thinking Reed* (1936), *The Fountain Overflows* (1956), and *The Birds Fall Down* (1966). Her other works include *Black Lamb and Grey Falcon* (1941) and *The Meaning of Treason* (1940).

WHITE, Patrick (1912–): born in England, White was taken to Australia (where his father owned a sheep farm) when he was six months old, but was educated in England, at Cheltenham College and Cambridge. He settled in London where he wrote several unpublished novels. After the war, in which he served in the RAF, he returned to Australia. His first published novel, *Happy Valley* (1939), was followed by several others, including *The Tree of Man* (1955) and *Voss* (1957). These two novels gave White an international reputation, which he strengthened with several subsequent works, including *Riders in the Chariot* (1961), *The Solid Mandala* (1966), *The Eye of the Storm* (1973), and *The Twyborn Affair* (1979). He has also published *Four Plays* (1965), volumes of short stories, and a frank self-portrait, *Flaws in the Glass* (1981). He was awarded the Nobel Prize for literature in 1973.

WHITE, T(erence) H(anbury) (1906–64): the author of several adult novels, White is best known for his novels on the Arthurian legend, published under the title *The Once and Future King* (1958). The first book in this sequence, *The Sword in the Stone*, originally published separately in 1937, is a classic children's novel, as is *Mistress Masham's Repose* (1947). He also wrote *The Goshawk* (1951), an account of how he trained a hawk.

WHITMAN, Walt (1819–92): born on Long Island, New York, and brought up partly in Brooklyn, Whitman had little formal education. He worked at various occupations, including that of a journalist, and after a journey to St Louis and Chicago his experience of the frontier merged with his admiration for *Emerson to produce the first edition of *Leaves of Grass*. When Emerson was sent a copy of the 12 poems he replied hailing the work, with good reason, as 'the most extraordinary piece of wit and wisdom that America has yet contributed'. The second edition (1856) added 21 poems, and the third edition (1860) 122. The six further editions that appeared in Whitman's lifetime were revised or added to, the work enlarging as the poet developed. His contact with the wounded during the Civil War affected him deeply, as can be seen in his prose *Memoranda during the War* (1875) and in the poems published under the title of *Drum-Taps* in 1865. In the *Sequel* to these poems (1865–6) appeared the great elegy on Lincoln, 'When Lilacs Last in the Dooryard Bloom'd'. In spite of his achievement, Whitman was disregarded by the public; though his reputation began to rise after recognition in England by, among others, D. G. *Rossetti and *Swinburne (who compared him to *Blake). The free, vigorous sweep of his verse conveys subjects at once national ('Pioneers! O Pioneers!', 1865), mystically sexual ('I sing the body electric', 1855) and deeply personal ('Out of the Cradle Endlessly Rocking', 1860), and his work proved a liberating force for many of his successors, including H. *Miller and D. H. *Lawrence.

WILDE, Oscar (1854–1900): born in Dublin, Wilde, a brilliant classical scholar, studied at Trinity College, Dublin, and then at Oxford, where his flamboyant aestheticism attracted attention, much of it hostile. In 1883 he attended the first night of his play *Vera* in New York but it was not a success. In 1884 he married, and in 1888 published a volume of fairy stories, *The Happy Prince and other tales*, written for his sons. In 1891 followed *Lord Arthur Savile's Crime, and other stories* and his only novel, *The Picture of Dorian Gray*. In 1891 he published more fairy stories, *A House of Pomegranates*. His second play, *The Duchess* *of Padua* (1891), brought theatrical success, and was followed by *Lady Windermere's Fan* (1892), *A Woman of No Importance* (1893), and *An Ideal Husband* (1895). His masterpiece, *The Importance of Being Earnest*, was produced in 1895, the same year as he was imprisoned for homosexual offences. He was released in 1897 and went to France where he wrote *The Ballad of Reading Gaol* (1898). He died in Paris.

WILDER, Thornton (1897–1975): born in Wisconsin, USA; Wilder's best-known novel is *The Bridge of San Luis Rey* (1927), but *The Ides of March* (1948), among others, is also notable. He scored considerable success in the theatre with *Our Town* (1938), *The Skin of Our Teeth* (1942), and *The Merchant of Yonkers* (1938), a comedy which was revised as *The Matchmaker* (1954) and adapted as the musical comedy *Hello Dolly!* (1963).

WILLIAMS, Tennessee (1911–83): born in Mississippi, USA, Williams studied at the Universities of Washington and Iowa, and in New York, while embarking on a career as playwright with *American Blues* (1939, pub. 1945, revised 1957 as *Orpheus Descending*). He achieved success with the semi-autobiographical *The Glass Menagerie* (1944, pub. 1945), a poignant and painful family drama set in St Louis. His next big success was *A Streetcar Named Desire* (1947), which was followed by many others, including *The Rose Tattoo* (1950), *Cat on a Hot Tin Roof* (1935), *Suddenly Last Summer* (1958), and *The Night of the Iguana* (1962). He also wrote a novella, *The Roman Spring of Mrs Stone* (1950), collections of poems, and his *Memoirs*, which appeared in 1975.

WILLIAMS, William Carlos (1883–1963): for many years a paediatrician in his home town in New Jersey, USA; Williams's profession as a doctor deeply affected his literary life. His poems range from the minimal, eight-line, sixteen-word 'The Red Wheelbarrow' (1923) to his most ambitious production, *Paterson* (1946–58), a long five-part, free-verse, collage-mixed evocation of a characteristic industrial city. He also wrote short stories, collected as *The Farmers' Daughters* (1961), and his other prose works include a series of essays, *In the American Grain* (1925). Williams's work was more or less disregarded in Britain until the 1950s, but recently interest has increased considerably.

WILLIAMSON, Henry (1895–1977): educated at Colfe's Grammar School, Lewisham, Williamson joined the army in the First World War. Afterwards he worked briefly in Fleet Street while writing his first novel, *The Beautiful Years* (1921: Vol. 1 of the *Flax of Dream* quartet). In 1921 he moved to North Devon, and embarked on a modest country life which produced his most widely known work, *Tarka the Otter* (1927), which was much admired and remains a popular classic. This was followed by other tales of wildlife and the countryside, including *Salar the Salmon* (1935). His most ambitious work was a series of 15 novels known under the collective title *A Chronicle of Ancient Sunlight*, a panoramic survey which opens in the mid 1890s with *The*

Dark Lantern (1951) and closes with *The Gate of the World* (1969). He also wrote a short, devastating account of trench warfare, *A Patriot's Progress* (1930), and about his friendship with T. E. Lawrence in *Genius of Friendship* (1941).

WILSON, Sir Angus (1913–): born in England, Wilson spent some of his childhood in South Africa, but was educated at Westminster and Oxford. His first two volumes, *The Wrong Set* (1949) and *Such Darling Dodos* (1950), were of short stories, and were followed by a number of novels, including *Hemlock and After* (1952), *Anglo-Saxon Attitudes* (1956), *The Middle Age of Mrs Eliot* (1958), *The Old Men at the Zoo* (1961), *No Laughing Matter* (1967), and *Setting the World on Fire* (1980). He has also written on *Zola, *Dickens, and *Kipling, and an interesting account of his own sources and creative processes, *The Wild Garden* (1963). His works display a brilliant satiric wit, acute social observation, and a love of the macabre and the farcical, combined with humanity, compassion, and a lively interest in human affairs.

WODEHOUSE, Sir P(elham) G(renville) (1881–1975): born in Guildford, Wodehouse was educated at Dulwich College. He soon abandoned a career in banking in Hong Kong for literature; he began by writing short stories for boys' magazines, and later published extensively in various periodicals, establishing himself as one of the most widely read humorists of his day. His first novel was published in 1902, and his prolific output, of over 120 volumes, included *The Man with Two Left Feet* (1917), the collection of stories which first introduced Jeeves and Bertie Wooster; a series of Jeeves volumes (*My Man Jeeves*, 1919; *The Inimitable Jeeves*, 1923; *Carry On, Jeeves*, 1925, etc.); and other works featuring such favourite characters as Lord Emsworth (and his prize sow, the Empress of Blandings), Mr Mulliner, Psmith, several redoubtable aunts, and many patrons of the Drones Club.

WOLFE, Thomas (1900–38): born in North Carolina, USA, and educated at university there and at Harvard, Wolfe made his name with his autobiographical novel *Look Homeward, Angel* (1929). This was followed by a sequel, *Of Time and the River* (1935), and various posthumous works, which include *The Web and the Rock* (1939) and its sequel *You Can't Go Home Again* (1930). He died of an infection following pneumonia.

WOOLF, Virginia (1882–1941): daughter of Leslie Stephen and Julia Duckworth, Virginia Woolf was born at Hyde Park Gate, but moved to Bloomsbury after the death of her father in 1904. There, she and the other Stephen children formed the nucleus of the Bloomsbury Group, which also included, among others, Lytton Strachey, David Garnett, E. M. *Forster, and Roger Fry. In 1905 she began writing for the *Times Literary Supplement* and in 1912 married Leonard Woolf. Her first novel, *The Voyage Out*, was published in 1915, and was followed by *Night and Day* (1919) and by *Jacob's Room* (1922) which was recognized as a new development in the art of fiction, in its indirect narration and poetic impressionism. Her subsequent major novels, *Mrs Dalloway* (1925), *To the Lighthouse* (1927), and *The Waves* (1931), established her reputation securely. The intensity of her creative work was accompanied by mental suffering and ill health, but she was able to intersperse her more serious works with more playful productions, such as *Orlando* (1928), a fantastic biography inspired by her friend V. Sackville-West. She was also a literary critic and journalist of distinction. *A Room of One's Own* (1929) is a classic of the feminist movement and her critical essays were published in several collections, including *The Common Reader* (1925; Second Series, 1932). *A Haunted House* (1943) collects earlier stories and some not previously published.

Virginia Woolf is now acclaimed as one of the great innovative novelists of the 20th c., many of whose experimental techniques (such as the use of the stream of consciousness, or interior monologue) have been absorbed into the mainstream of fiction; her novels have been particularly highly regarded from the 1970s onwards by the new school of feminist criticism.

WORDSWORTH, William (1770–1850): born at Cockermouth, Cumbria, Wordsworth was educated at Hawkshead Grammar School and Cambridge. In 1790 he went on a walking tour in Europe and then lived in France for a year; during this period he was fired by a passionate belief in the French Revolution and republican ideals, and also fell in love. After his return to England he published in 1793 two poems in heroic couplets, *An Evening Walk* and *Descriptive Sketches*. In 1795 he received a legacy intended to enable him to pursue his vocation as a poet, and in 1797 he met *Coleridge. There followed a period of intense creativity for both poets, which produced the *Lyrical Ballads* (1798), a landmark in the history of English Romanticism (see Coleridge). The winter of 1798–9 was spent in Germany, where Wordsworth wrote sections of what was to be *The Prelude* (pub. posthumously in 1850) and the enigmatic 'Lucy' poems. In 1799 he and his sister Dorothy moved to Grasmere; to the next year belong 'The Recluse', Book I (later *The Excursion*), 'The Brothers', 'Michael', and many of the poems included in the 1800 edition of the *Lyrical Ballads*. In 1802 he married Mary Hutchinson. The same year he composed 'Resolution and Independence', and began his ode on 'Intimations of Immortality from Recollections of Early Childhood', both of which appeared in *Poems in Two Volumes* (1807), along with many of his most celebrated lyrics. His productivity continued, and his popularity gradually increased. In 1813 he was appointed Stamp Distributor for Westmorland, a post which brought him some £400 a year, and in the same year he moved to Rydal Mount, Grasmere, where he lived the rest of his life. The great work of his early and middle years was now over, and Wordsworth slowly settled into the role of patriotic, conservative public man, abandoning the radical politics and idealism of his youth. In 1843 he succeeded *Southey as Poet Laureate. He died at Rydal Mount, after the publication of a finally revised text of his works (6 vols., 1849–50).

*De Quincey wrote of Wordsworth in 1835, 'Up to 1820 the name of Wordsworth was trampled underfoot; from 1820 to 1830 it was militant; from 1830 to 1835 it has been triumphant.' A great innovator, he permanently enlarged the range of English poetry, both in subject-matter and in treatment (a distinction he would not himself have accepted).

YEATS, William Butler (1865–1939): eldest son of J. B. Yeats and brother of Jack Yeats, both celebrated painters, Yeats at 21 abandoned art as a profession in favour of literature. Irish traditional and nationalist themes, and unrequited love, provided much of the subject-matter for *The Wanderings of Oisin and other Poems* (1889), *The Land of Heart's Desire* (1894), *The Wind among the Reeds* (1899), *The Shadowy Waters* (1900), and such of his later plays as *On Baile's Strand* (1904) and *Deirdre* (1907). With each succeeding collection of poems Yeats moved further from the elaborate Pre-Raphaelite style of the 1890s. *In the Seven Woods* (1903) was followed by *The Green Hamlet and Other Poems* (1910), *Poems Written in Discouragement* (1913), *Responsibilities: Poems and a Play* (1914), and *The Wild Swans at Coole* (1917). In 1917 he married Georgie Hyde-Lees, who on their honeymoon attempted automatic writing, an event that exercised a profound effect on his life and work. His wife's 'communicators' ultimately provided him with the system of symbolism described in *A Vision* (1925) and underlying many of his later poems. In the poems and plays written after his marriage he achieved a spare, colloquial lyricism wholly unlike his earlier manner, although many themes of his early manhood reach their full flowering in the later period. He also published several volumes of essays. In 1923 he received the Nobel Prize for literature.

ZOLA, Émile (1840–1902): the first volume (*La Fortune des Rougon*) of Zola's principal work, *Les Rougon-Macquart*, appeared in 1871. Nineteen more volumes followed, including *Germinal* (1885), the last, *Le Docteur Pascal*, appearing in 1893. In this series of novels, which was influenced by contemporary theories of heredity and experimental science, Zola chronicles the activities of the two branches (the Rougons and the Macquarts) of a family, whose conduct is seen as conditioned through several generations by environment and inherited characteristics, chiefly drunkenness and mental instability. The result is a panorama of mid-19th-c. French life. He also published a trilogy *Les Trois Villes* (*Lourdes*, 1894; *Rome*, 1896; *Paris*, 1898) and an unfinished work, *Les Quatre Évangiles* (*Fécondité*, 1899; *Travail*, 1901; *Vérité*, 1903). The last of these refers to the Dreyfus case in which Zola intervened with trenchant vigour, notably in his letter to the newspaper *L'Aurore*, 'J'Accuse'.

Zola was the dominant practitioner of Naturalism in prose fiction and the chief exponent of its doctrines. His novel *Thérèse Raquin* (1867), together with the Goncourts' *Germinie Lacerteux* (1865), are considered as marking the beginnings of the movement. Broadly speaking, Naturalism is characterized by a refusal to idealize experience and by the persuasion that human life is strictly subject to natural laws. The Naturalists shared with the earlier Realists the conviction that the everyday life of the middle and lower classes of their own day provided subjects worthy of serious literary treatment. These were to be rendered so far as possible without artificiality of plot and with scrupulous care for *documentation*, i.e. for the authenticity and accuracy of detail, thus investing the novel with the value of social history.

LITERARY AND POETIC TERMS

alexandrine: an iambic line of six feet, which is the French heroic verse, and in English is used, e.g., as the last line of the Spenserian stanza or as a variant in a poem of heroic couplets, rarely in a whole work. The name is derived from the fact that certain 12th- and 13th-c. French poems on Alexander the Great were written in this metre.

allegory: a figurative narrative or description, conveying a veiled moral meaning; an extended metaphor.

alliteration: the commencement of two or more words in close connection with the same sound, as in e.g. G. M. Hopkins's 'The Windhover':

> I caught this morning morning's minion, king-
> dom of daylight's dauphin, dapple-dawn-drawn Falcon . . .

It was used to excess by many late 19th-c. poets, notably Swinburne, whose 'lilies and languors of virtue' and 'raptures and roses of vice' are characteristic examples from 'Dolores'.

alliterative prose: a tradition of Old and Middle English prose elevated in style by the employment of some of the techniques of alliterative verse.

alliterative verse: the native Germanic tradition of English poetry and the standard form in Old English up to the 11th c., recurring in Middle English as a formal alternative to the syllable-counting rhymed verse borrowed from French. The Old English line was (normally) unrhymed, and made up of two distinct half-lines each of which contained two stressed syllables. The alliteration was always on the first stress of the second half-line, which alliterated with either, or both, of the stresses in the first half-line. In Middle English the alliterative rules were much less strict, although the alliteration was often very dense:

> 'I have lyved in Londe', quod I, 'My name is Longe Wille'
> (*Piers Plowman* B, xv. 152, by Langland)

Nothing after Middle English could categorically be said to be 'alliterative verse', despite its recurrent use as a device throughout English poetry, except perhaps for the rather self-conscious revival of the form in this century by such poets as Auden and Day-Lewis.

amphibrach: a foot consisting of a long between two short syllables.

anacoluthon: (Greek, 'wanting sequence'), a sentence in which a fresh construction is adopted before the former is complete.

anacrusis: 'striking up', an additional syllable at the beginning of a line before the normal rhythm, e.g. the 'and' in the second of the following lines:

> Till danger's troubled night depart
> And the star of peace return.
>
> (T. Campbell, 'Ye Mariners of England')

anapaest: (Greek, 'reversed'), a reversed dactyl, a metrical foot composed of two short followed by a long syllable.

anaphora: 'carrying back', the repetition of the same word or phrase in several successive clauses; for instance, 'Awake up, my glory; awake, lute and harp; I myself will awake right early' (Ps. 57: 9).

antistrophe: 'turning about', in a Greek chorus, the response to the strophe, recited as the chorus proceeded in the opposite direction to that followed in the strophe. The metre of strophe and antistrophe was the same.

aphorism: a term transferred from the 'Aphorisms of Hippocrates' to other sententious statements of the principles of physical science, and later to statements of principles generally. Thence it has come to mean any short pithy statement into which much thought or observation is compressed.

apologue: a fable conveying a moral lesson.

apophthegm: a terse, pointed saying, embodying an important truth in few words; a pity or sententious maxim.

apostrophe: (from Greek, 'to turn away'), a figure of speech in which the writer rhetorically addressed a dead or absent person or abstraction, e.g. 'Milton! thou shouldst be living at this hour' (Wordsworth, 'London, 1802').

assonance: the correspondence or rhyming of one word with another in the accented and following vowels, but not in the consonants, as e.g. in Old French versification. The term is now more broadly used to cover a wide range of vowel correspondences, from the deliberate reverberation of the last line of Yeats's 'Byzantium'—'That dolphin-torn, that gong-tormented sea'—to the subtle echoes and repetitions of Keats in 'To Autumn': 'Then in a wailful choir the small gnats mourn / Among the river sallows, borne aloft / Or sinking as the light wind lives or dies.'

ballad: originally a song intended as an accompaniment to a dance; hence a light, simple song of any kind, or a popular song, often one attacking persons or institutions. Broadside ballads were printed on one side of a single sheet and sold in the streets or at fairs. In the relatively recent sense, now most widely used, a ballad is taken to be a single, spirited poem in short stanzas, in which some popular story is graphically narrated, and in this sense the oral tradition is an essential element, though there has been much discussion as to the origin and composition of old English ballads. The form has continued to inspire poets, from Keats ('La Belle Dame Sans Merci') to W. Morris, Hardy, Yeats, and Causley, and flourishes in a popular folk form as well as in a more literary guise. The ingredients of ballads, both ancient and modern, vary, but frequently include the use of a refrain (sometimes altered slightly at the end of each stanza, to advance the story), stock descriptive phrases, and simple, terse dialogue.

ballade: strictly a poem consisting of one or more triplets of seven- or (afterwards) eight-lined stanzas, each ending with the same line as refrain, and usually an envoy addressed to a prince or his substitute. It was a dominant form in 14th- and 15th-c. French poetry, and one of its great masters was Villon. The form enjoyed a minor English revival in the late 19th c. in the work of Swinburne and others.

blank verse: verse without rhyme, especially the iambic pentameter of unrhymed heroic, the regular measure of English and dramatic and epic poetry, first used by the poet Henry Surrey, *c.*1540, in his translation of Books II and IV of the *Aeneid*.

bob and wheel: a metrical pattern used at the end of the strophes of the main narrative. The 'bob' is a short tag with one stress and the following 'wheel' is a quatrain of short lines rhyming abab.

caesura: in Greek and Latin prosody, the division of a metrical foot between two words, especially in certain recognized places near the middle of the line; in English prosody, a pause about the middle of a metrical line, generally indicated by a pause in the sense.

canto: a subdivision of a long narrative or epic poem, employed in the works of Dante and others; Spenser was the first to employ the term in English.

chiasmus: a figure of speech by which the order of the words in the first of two parallel clauses is reversed in the second, e.g. 'He saved others; himself he cannot save.'

choriamb: a metrical foot of four syllables, the first and last long, the two others short. A choree is a trochee.

classicism, classic: terms used in several different and at times overlapping senses. A 'literary classic' is a work considered first-rate or excellent of its kind, and therefore standard, fit to be used as a model or imitated; a series such as the World's Classics includes work from many different genres, including poetry, fiction, autobiography, biography, letters, and history. More narrowly, 'classicism' may be taken to denote the deliberate imitation of the works of antiquity, and in this sense is often qualified as 'neo-classicism', which flourished in England in the late 17th and 18th c. An elaboration of this concept leads to a distinction between Classicism and Romanticism; the Romantic movement, which dominated the early 19th c., and which saw itself in part as a revolt against Classicism, led in turn to a reaction at the beginning of the 20th c. from writers such as T. S. Eliot and T. E. Hulme, whose concern was to stress man's limitations rather than his perfectibility and illimitable aspirations, and who emphasized the virtues of formal restraint in literature rather than the virtues of inspiration and exuberance.

The shades of meaning which the terms have acquired lead at times to apparent confusion: when one speaks of the drama of Racine and Corneille as 'classical', and the drama of Shakespeare or Hugo as 'romantic', one is not depriving Shakespeare or Hugo of classic status, nor suggesting that Shakespeare himself had any sense of such a contrast; whereas Hugo wrote as a conscious rebel against classicism. Auden and Dylan Thomas, near-contemporaries, are frequently described as exemplars of, respectively, the classical and the romantic in modern poetry, and both are widely considered classics of their own period and aesthetic approach. The use of the phrase 'a minor classic' raises yet more problems of definition, indicating the adaptability rather than the precision of the term.

clerihew: an epigrammatic verse-form invented by Edmund Clerihew Bentley, consisting of two rhymed couplets, usually dealing with the character or career of a well-known person, e.g.

> Sir James Jeans
> Always says what he means;
> He is really perfectly serious
> About the Universe being Mysterious.

cliché: French, 'a stereotype block', a stock expression which by constant use has become hackneyed and lost its edge.

concrete poetry: a term used to describe a kind of experimental poetry developed in the 1950s and flourishing in the 1960s, which dwells primarily on the visual aspects of the poem (although two other forms of concrete poetry, the kinetic and the phonetic, have also been distinguished). Concrete poets experiment with typography, graphics, the 'ideogram concept', computer poems, collage, etc., and in varying degrees acknowledge influence from Dada, Hans Arp, Schwitters, and other visual artists. Ian Hamilton Finlay (1925–), one of the leading Scottish exponents, expresses his own affinity with 17th-c. emblems and poems which use the shape as well as the sense of a poem to convey meaning.

couplet: a pair of successive lines of verse, especially when rhyming with each other.

crambo poem: one designed to exhaust the possible rhymes with someone's name.

dactyl: a metrical foot consisting of one long followed by two short syllables, or of one accented followed by two unaccented.

dithyramb: a lyric poem in a lofty style with a flute accompaniment in the Phrygian mode. Supposedly invented by Arion (7th c. BC), it was originally antistrophic and sung in honour of Bacchus. Later dithyrambs were monostrophic and could be addressed to other gods.

doggerel: comic or burlesque, or trivial, mean, or irregular verse. The derivation is unknown, but cf. *dog-latin* (*OED*).

eclogue: the term for a short pastoral poem, which comes from the Greek 'a choice', the title given in Greek to collections of elegant extracts. The Latinized form *ecloga* was used, however, for any short poem and attached itself particularly to Virgil's pastorals which their author had called *bucolica*, a name commonly applied to the *Idylls* of Theocritus that Virgil had imitated. The terms eclogue, bucolic, and idyll have been widely used as synonyms, except that grammarians have made an effort to confine 'eclogue' to poems in dialogue form.

elegiac: 1. In prosody, the metre consisting of a dactylic hexameter and pentameter, as being the metre appropriate to elegies. 2. Generally, of the nature of an elegy.

elegy: from the Greek, the word has been variously used with reference to different periods of English. In Old English a group of short poems in the Exeter Book whose subject is the transience of the world, sometimes relieved by Christian consolations, are called elegies. From the 16th c. onwards the term was used for a reflective poem by poets such as Donne; later it was applied particularly to poems of mourning (from Milton's *Lycidas*), and the general reflective poem, as written by Coleridge and Yeats, is sometimes called 'reverie'. T. Gray's *Elegy Written in a Country Church-Yard* is a general poem of mourning, combined with the reflective mode.

elision: the suppression of a vowel or syllable in pronouncing.

ellipsis: the leaving out from a sentence of words necessary to express the sense completely.

enjambment: a technical term in verse, signifying the carrying on the sense of a line or couplet into the next.

envoy: the final stanza of a poem containing an address to the reader or the person to whom it is dedicated.

epic: a poem that celebrates in the form of a continuous narrative the achievements of one or more heroic personages of history or tradition.

epic simile: an extended simile which compares one composite action with another, often with a digressive effect; it originates in Homer, and was imitated by Virgil, Dante, and, in English, notably by Milton. It is frequently parodied by Fielding.

epigram: originally an inscription, usually in verse, e.g. on a tomb; hence a short poem ending in a witty turn of thought; hence a pointed or antithetical saying.

epistolary novel: a story written in the form of letters, or letters with journals, and usually presented by an anonymous author masquerading as 'editor'. The first notable example in English, written entirely in epistolary form, was a translation from the French in 1678, *Letters of a Portuguese Nun*. A. Behn published *Love-letters between a Nobleman and his Sister*, and many similar tales of illicit love and love-manuals followed. Thus when Richardson, the first and perhaps greatest master of the form, came to write *Pamela* (1741), he felt a duty to rescue the novel from its tainted reputation.

euphuism: taken from *Euphues*, a prose romance by Lyly, of which the first part was published in 1578 and the second in 1580. *Euphues* is famous for its peculiar style. Its principal characteristics are the excessive use of antithesis, which is pursued regardless of sense, and emphasized by alliteration and other devices; and of allusions to historical and mythological personages and to natural history drawn from such writers as Plutarch, Pliny, and Erasmus.

fable: a term most commonly used in the sense of a short story devised to convey some useful moral lesson, but often carrying with it associations of the marvellous or the mythical, and frequently employing animals as characters. Aesop's fables were well known and imitated in Britain by Chaucer and others, and La Fontaine, the greatest of modern fable writers, was also imitated. The form enjoyed something of a vogue in the 1920s and 1930s, and has always been popular in children's literature.

fabliau: a short tale in verse, almost invariably in octosyllabic couplets, dealing for the most part from a comic point of view with incidents of ordinary life. The fabliau was an important element in French poetry from the 12th to the 13th c., and was imitated by Chaucer.

faction: a term coined *c.* 1970 to describe fiction based on and mingled with fact, applied particularly to American works of fiction such as *In Cold Blood* (1966) by Truman Capote.

foot: a division of a verse, consisting of a number of syllables one of which has the principal stress.

Galliambic: the metre of the *Attis* of Catullus, so called because it was the metre used by the Galli, or priests of Cybele, in their songs. It was imitated by Tennyson in his 'Boadicea':

> So the Queen Boadicea, standing loftily charioted,
> Brandishing in her hand a dart and rolling glances lioness-like,
> Yell'd and shriek'd between her daughters in her fierce volubility.

Georgian: a term applied in a literary sense to the writers of the reign of George V (1910–36), and usually indicating poetry of a pastoral or, as later critics asserted, an escapist nature.

Gongorism: an affected type of diction and style introduced into Spanish literature in the 16th c. by the poet Luis de Góngora y Argote (1561–1627), a style akin to euphuism in England.

gothic novel: tales of the macabre, fantastic, and supernatural, usually set amid haunted castles, graveyards, ruins, and wild picturesque landscapes. They reached the height of their considerable fashion in the 1790s and the early years of the 19th c. The word 'gothic' originally implied 'medieval' but in the later 18th c. its meaning altered until its emphasis lay on the macabre, and the original medieval element was sometimes wholly disregarded. The first of the true gothic novels is generally accepted to be *The Castle of Otranto* (1764) by Horace Walpole.

haiku: a Japanese lyric form of 17 syllables in lines of 5, 7, 5 syllables. It emerged in the 16th c., flourished from the 17th to the 19th c., and dealt traditionally with images of the natural world; in this century it has been much imitated in Western literature.

hendecasyllabic: a verse line of 11 syllables, used by Catullus and by Tennyson:

O you chorus of indolent reviewers.

hendiadys: from the Greek words meaning 'one by means of two', a figure of speech by which a single complex idea is expressed by two words joined by a conjunction, e.g. 'Such as sit in darkness and in the shadow of death, being fast bound in misery and iron' (Ps. 107: 10).

heroic couplet: a pair of rhymed lines of iambic pentameter. The form was introduced into English by Chaucer, and widely used subsequently, reaching a height of popularity and sophistication in the works of Dryden and Pope.

heroic poetry: the same as epic.

heroic verse: that used in epic poetry: in Greek and Latin poetry, the hexameter; in English, the iambic of five feet or ten syllables; in French, the alexandrine of 12 syllables.

hexameter: a verse of six metrical feet, which in the typical form consists of five dactyls and a trochee or spondee; for any of the dactyls a spondee may be substituted, except in the fifth foot, where a spondee is rare. It is not frequently used in English, but has sometimes been employed to considerable effect.

hudibrastic: in the style of Butler's *Hudibras*; in octosyllabic couplets and with comic rhymes.

hypallage: from a Greek word meaning 'exchange', a transference of epithet, as 'Sansfoy's dead dowry' for 'dead Sansfoy's dowry' (Spenser).

hyperbole: the use of exaggerated terms not in order to deceive but to emphasize the importance or extent of something.

hysteron proteron: in grammar and rhetoric, a figure of speech in which the word or phrase that should properly come last is put first; in general, 'putting the cart before the horse'.

iamb, iambic trimeter, iambic pentameter: see **metre.**

idylls: see **eclogue.**

lampoon: the original meaning of this was a drinking song. It now means a virulent or scurrilous satire upon an individual.

lay: a short lyric or narrative poem intended to be sung; originally applied specifically to the poems, usually dealing with matters of history or romantic adventure, which were sung by minstrels.

Leonine verse: a kind of Latin verse much used in the Middle Ages, consisting of hexameters, or alternate hexameters and pentameters, in which the last word rhymes with that preceding the caesura; for instance:

His replicans clare tres causes explico quare
More Leonino dicere metra sino.

The term is applied to English verse of which the middle and last syllables rhyme. It is derived, according to Du Cange, from the name of a certain poet Leo, who lived about the time of Louis VII of France (1137–80) or his successor Philippe-Auguste (1180–1223).

limerick: a form of facetious jingle, of which the first instances occur in *The History of Sixteen Wonderful Old Women* (1820) and *Anecdotes and Adventures of Fifteen Gentlemen* (*c.*1821), subsequently popularized by Lear in his *Book of Nonsense.* The name is said to be derived from a custom at convivial parties, according to which each member sang an extemporized 'nonsense-verse', which was followed by a chorus containing the words 'Will you come up to Limerick?' (*OED*). Limericks have been composed on a great variety of subjects from philosophic doctrines to jokes of extreme obscenity.

In the older form of limerick, as written by Lear, D. G. Rossetti, and others, the first and last lines usually ended with the same word, but in more recent examples, such as the following comment on Berkeley's philosophy by Ronald Knox, a third rhyming word is supplied:

There once was a man who said: 'God
Must think it exceedingly odd
If he finds that this tree
Continues to be
When there's no one about in the Quad.'

A great number of the best-known limericks are, for obvious reasons, anonymous.

litotes: a figure of speech in which an affirmative is expressed by the negative of the contrary, e.g. 'a citizen of no mean city'; an ironical understatement.

lyric, lyric poetry: derived from the Greek adjective 'lurikos' ('for the lyre'), it was the name given in ancient Greece to verses sung to a lyre, whether as a solo performance (Sappho) or by a choir (Pindar). The Greek lyrists were then imitated in Latin at an artistic level by Catullus and Horace, but what appears to have been more important for the development of the genre was the tradition of popular song which existed both in Rome and among the German tribes. This continued to flourish in spite of the Church's disapproval and produced in all the medieval literatures of western Europe a lyric harvest that ranged from hymns to bawdy drinking songs and drew its authors from every social category. In England lyric poems flourished in the Middle English period, and in the 16th-c. heyday of humanism this already quite sophisticated lyric tradition was enriched by the direct imitation of ancient models and reached perfection in the song-books and plays of the Elizabethan age. During the next 200 years the link between poetry and music was gradually broken, and the term 'lyric' came to be applied to short poems expressive of a poet's thoughts or feelings, and which could not be classed under another heading. The convention that a poem communicates its author's feelings to a reader reached the high point of its popularity in the Romantic period, but soon afterwards Baudelaire introduced the modern form of lyric poetry in which the poet seems to struggle to express for his own satisfaction psychic experiences whose nature he at times only half understands.

macaronic verse: a term 'used to designate a burlesque form of verse in which vernacular words are introduced into a Latin context with Latin terminations and in Latin constructions . . . and loosely to any form of verse in which two or more languages are mingled together' (*OED*).

mandarin: used as an adjective to describe esoteric, highly decorative, or highbrow prose.

meiosis: an understatement, sometimes ironical or humorous, and intended to emphasize the size, importance, etc., of what is belittled. Except in litotes, which is a form of meiosis, the use of meiosis is chiefly colloquial; e.g. 'He's doing all right out of it'; 'That must be worth a few bob'.

metaphor: the transfer of a name or descriptive term to an object different from, but analogous to, that to which it is properly applicable, e.g. 'abysmal ignorance'. Mixed metaphor is the application of two inconsistent metaphors to one object.

metathesis: the transposition of letters or sounds in a word. When the transposition is between the letters or sounds of two words, it is popularly known as a 'Spoonerism', of which a well-known specimen, attributed to the Revd W. A. Spooner (1844–1930), warden of New College, Oxford, is 'Kinquering congs their titles take'.

metre: the sound patterns on whose recurrence rhythm depends were formed in antiquity by arrangements of long and short syllables. Lines of verse consisted of 'feet', the commonest being the iambus (⏑ -), trochee (- ⏑), anapaest (⏑ ⏑ -), dactyl (- ⏑ ⏑), and spondee (- -). The pyrrhic (⏑ ⏑), tribrach (⏑ ⏑ ⏑), amphibrach (⏑ - ⏑), cretic (- ⏑ -), paeon (- ⏑ ⏑ ⏑, etc.), bacchius (⏑ - -), ionic a minore (⏑ ⏑ - -), and choriambic (- ⏑ ⏑ -) featured mainly in lyric poems. The most popular ancient measure was the hexameter. Made up of four dactyls (replaceable by spondees) and then an invariable dactyl and a spondee or trochee, it was divided by a caesura (a break where a word ends before a foot is finished) usually in the third foot. Elegiac couplets linked the hexameter with a pentameter which, never found alone, consisted of two feet (dactyls or spondees) and a single long syllable before the caesura followed by two dactyls and a single syllable, always end-stopped. Dramatists used the iambic trimeter because of its closeness to common speech. This comprised six feet arranged in pairs (hence 'trimeter') where the iamb could be replaced by other feet according to strict rules. There were also numerous lyric metres. Alcaics, Sapphics, and Asclepiads organized trochees, dactyls, and spondees in various patterns, and trochaic hendecasyllabics flourished in satire.

The 5th c. AD brought, however, the beginnings of a radical change. The shape of the classical feet was retained, but stress became their determining feature, so that a trochee was an accented followed by an unaccented syllable. The trochaic tetrameter catalectic, which was divided by a caesura after the fourth trochee, the second half consisting of three trochees and a single syllable, provided the basis for most medieval hymns.

English prosody is similarly based on stress. The earliest measures to develop were trochaic, but soon iambic couplets of four or five feet linked by rhyme became more popular. In the four-foot couplet we find extensive modulation: often the first foot has only one syllable, and the final syllable in the fifth foot is dropped. The five-foot couplet had a strict form, end-stopped with a marked middle break, but also a form that allowed overflow from one line to the next and substitution of different two- or even three-syllable feet for the iamb. But it is not in the couplet that the five-foot iambic line (iambic pentameter) attained greatest importance. Introduced into poetic drama in 1562, it had a distinguished history as 'blank verse', with more modulations than in the couplet and the final foot often replaced by an amphibrach. When blank verse was used later in epic by Milton, the modulations, if more controlled, were also more frequent and the use of overflow developed into paragraph construction. Five-foot lines were also built into stanzas with a variety of rhyme schemes; rhyme royal (or rime royal; seven lines rhymed ababbcc), used for narrative from Chaucer to William Morris; the nine-line Spenserian stanza, ababbcbcc; and, principally, the sonnet, introduced by Wyatt and used since by every major English poet. (Wyatt copied Petrarch, dividing the sonnet into an octave rhymed abba, abba, and a sestet ccd, ccd or cde, cde; but Shakespeare preferred three quatrains ending with a couplet.) Other popular iambic metres include in Tudor times the awkward Poulter's Measure, a rhymed couplet where the first line had 12, the second 14 syllables. Broken by pause and internal rhyme, this makes a stanza 3343 which has been widely used by hymn writers. Fourteeners appear unresolved in Chapman's *Homer*, but provide, when divided 4343 and rhymed, the buoyant and well-known ballad stanza. Trochaic, anapaestic, and dactylic metres, though they figure in many poems, have not been as popular as the iambic.

Verse in the 20th c. has largely escaped the strait-jacket of traditional metrics.

neo-classicism: the habit of imitating the great authors of antiquity (notably its poets and dramatists) as a matter of aesthetic principle; and the acceptance of the critical precepts which emerged to guide that imitation.

nouveau roman: ('new novel'), a term applied to the work of a wide range of modern French novelists, including Nathalie Sarraute (1902–),

Marguerite Duras (1914–), and Alain Robbe-Grillet (1922–). What distinguishes these novelists is primarily a shared conviction as to the inadequacies of the traditional novel. Thus Robbe-Grillet argues that the traditional novel, with its dependence on an omniscient narrator, creates an illusion of order and significance which is denied by the reality of experience. The task of the new novel is therefore to foster change by dispensing with any technique which imposes a particular interpretation on events, or which organizes events in such a way as to endow them with a collective significance.

octave: see **metre.**

octosyllabics: consisting of eight syllables, usually applied to the eight-syllabled rhyming iambic metre of e.g. Milton's 'Il Penseroso'.

ode: in ancient literature, a poem intended or adapted to be sung; in modern use, a rhymed (rarely unrhymed) lyric, often in the form of an address, generally dignified or exalted in subject, feeling, and style, but sometimes (in earlier use) simple and familiar (though less so than a song) (*OED*).

onomatopoeia: the formation of a word by an imitation of the sound associated with the object or action designated: as 'hurlyburly', 'buzz', 'creak'. The term is also applied to the use of a combination of words to evoke by sound a certain image or mood, the most frequently quoted example being Tennyson's 'murmuring of innumerable bees'.

ottava rima: an Italian stanza of eight 11-syllabled lines, rhyming abababcc, employed by Tasso, Ariosto, etc. It was introduced into England by Wyatt, and used to great effect by Byron in *Don Juan*, with a 10-syllable iambic line.

oxymoron: from two Greek words meaning 'sharp', 'dull', a rhetorical figure by which two incongruous or contradictory terms are united in an expression so as to give it point; e.g. 'Faith unfaithful kept him falsely true' (Tennyson, *Idylls of the King*).

palindrome: from the Greek 'running back again', a word, verse, or sentence that reads the same forward or backwards, e.g.:

> Lewd did I live & evil I did dwel
>
> (Philips, 1706)

and the Latin line descriptive of moths:

> In girum imus noctes et consumimur igni.

parody: a composition in which the characteristic turns of thought and phrase of an author are mimicked and made to appear ridiculous, especially by applying them to ludicrously inappropriate subjects.

paronomasia: a play on words, a kind of pun, in which the repeated words are similar but not identical, e.g. Lady Macbeth: 'I'll gild the faces of the grooms withal, / For it must seem their guilt.'

pastiche: a literary composition made up from various authors or sources, or in imitation of the style of another author.

pastoral: a form of escape literature concerned with country pleasures, which is found in poetry, drama, and prose fiction. Its earliest examples appear in the *Idylls* of Theocritus. Neglected during the Middle Ages, the pastoral reappeared during the Renaissance. In the 17th c., however, the Theocritean vision which had so far satisfied men's desire to escape from the pressures of urban life gave place to a more realistic dream of enjoying a rural retreat. In its traditional form it died with the rise of Romanticism.

picaresque: from the Spanish *picaro*, a wily trickster; the form of novel accurately described as 'picaresque' first appeared in 16th-c. Spain with the anonymous *Lazarillo de Tormes* (1533) and Alemán's *Guzmán de Alfarache* (1599–1604), which relate the histories of ingenious rogues, the servants of several masters, who eventually repent the error of their ways. The term was first used in England in the 19th c. Nowadays the term is commonly, and loosely, applied to episodic novels, especially those of Fielding, Smollett, and others of the 18th c. which described the adventures of a lively and resourceful hero on a journey. *The Golden Ass* by Apuleius is regarded as a forerunner of the picaresque novel.

Pindaric: from the Greek lyric poet, Pindar (*c.*522–433 BC), the majority of whose surviving works are odes celebrating victories in the games at Olympia and elsewhere. Antiquity's most notable exponent of the Greater Ode, he served as an inspiration to all subsequent poets attempting this difficult genre. His compositions were elevated and formal, distinguished by the boldness of their metaphors and a marked reliance on myth and gnomic utterance. He used a framework of strophe, antistrophe, and epode which his imitators sought to copy, but in Pindar this rested on an elaborate prosodic structure that remained unknown until it was worked out by August Boeckh in his edition of the Odes (1811). The 17th- and 18th-c. writers of Pindarics—Cowley, Dryden, Pope, Gray—employed a much looser prosodic system, so that their odes, although elevated and rich in metaphor, lack Pindar's architectural quality.

quatrain: a stanza of four lines, usually with alternative rhymes; four lines of verse.

***roman-à-clef*:** i.e. a 'novel with a key', in which the reader (or some readers) are intended to identify real characters under fictitious names. The key is sometimes literal, sometimes figurative, and sometimes provided by the author, as in the case of Mrs Manley's *The New Atalantis*, sometimes published separately by others, as in the case of Disraeli's *Coningsby*.

romance: derived from the medieval Latin word *romanice*, 'in the Roman language'. The word *roman* in Old French was applied to the popular courtly stories in verse which dealt with three traditional subjects: the legends about Arthur, Charlemagne and his knights, and stories of classical heroes, especially Alexander. Defining them by theme is very difficult; they usually involved the suspension of the circumstances normally attendant on human actions (often through magic) in order to illustrate a moral point. From the 15th c. onwards English romances are mostly in prose, and some 16th-c. examples were the inspiration for Spenser and Shakespeare. A new interest in the medieval romance (in writers such as Scott and Keats) contributed to the naming of 19th-c. Romanticism, though the term was also used to embrace some sentimental novels from the 18th c. onwards, and is now a popular genre for paperback publishers.

***roman-fleuve*:** the French term for a novel-sequence. The practice of pursuing a family story through a number of related novels in order to render a comprehensive account of a social period ultimately derives from Balzac and Zola, but it reached its culmination between 1900 and 1940 by such writers as Romain Rolland (1866–1944), Roger Martin du Gard (1881–1958), Georges Duhamel (1884–1966), and Jules Romains (1885–1972). Translations of these authors have been popular in England, but the English version of the phenomenon, descending from Trollope and including such novelists as Galsworthy and C. P. Snow, did not have the same conviction and consistency.

rondeau: a French verse-form consisting of ten (or, in stricter sense, 13) lines, having only two rhymes throughout, and with the opening words used twice as a refrain. It became popular in England in the late 19th c. and was much used by Dobson, Swinburne, and others. The rondel is a form of rondeau, again using two rhymes and a refrain, usually of three stanzas.

saga: an Old Norse word meaning 'story', applied to narrative compositions from Iceland and Norway in the Middle Ages. There are three main types of saga: family sagas, dealing with the first settlers of Iceland and their descendants; kings' sagas, historical works about the kings of Norway; and legendary or heroic sagas, fantastic adventure stories about legendary heroes.

satire: a poem, now often a prose composition, in which prevailing vices or follies are held up to ridicule.

sestet: see **metre.**

sestina: a poem of six six-line stanzas (with an envoy) in which the line-endings of the first stanza are repeated, but in different order, in the other five (*OED*).

simile: an object, scene, or action, introduced by way of comparison for explanatory, illustrative, or merely ornamental purpose, e.g. 'as strong as an ox', or more poetically, 'The moon, like a flower / In heaven's high bower / With silent delight / Sits and smiles on the night' (Blake, 'Night', *Songs of Innocence*); or, in more modernist vein, 'the evening is spread out against the sky / Like a patient etherised upon a table' (T. S. Eliot, 'The Love Song of J. Alfred Prufrock'). *See also* epic simile.

sirvente: a form of poem or lay, usually satirical, employed by the troubadours.

skaldic verse: (also 'scaldic'), a form of Old Norse poetry distinguished by its elaborate metre, alliteration, consonance, and riddling diction. The most usual skaldic metre is 'dróttkvætt', a strophe which consists of eight six-syllable lines, each ending in a trochee. In regular 'dróttkvætt' each odd line contains two alliterating syllables in stressed positions, and the alliteration is continued on one stressed syllable in each following even line. Odd lines also contain two internal half-rhymes; even lines two full rhymes. The first known skald was Bragi Boddason who probably wrote in the late 9th c. Skaldic verse flourished in the 10th c. and on into the 11th, and much of it was composed to commemorate the deeds of chieftains who ruled Norway at this time. Such verses are preserved mainly in the kings' sagas; many 'lausavísur' or occasional verses, and some love poetry, are included in the narratives of family sagas (*see* **saga**).

Skeltonic verse: a verse whose name is derived from the favourite metre of the poet John Skelton (?1460–1529), 'a headlong voluble breathless doggerel, which rattling and clashing on through quick-recurring rhymes . . . has taken from the name of its author the title of Skeltonical verse' (J. C. Collins). As he himself said (*Collyn Cloute*, 53–8):

> For though my ryme be ragged,
> Tattered and jagged,
> Rudely rayne-beaten,
> Rusty and mothe-eaten,
> Yf ye take well therwith,
> It hath in it some pyth.

sonnet: a poem consisting of 14 lines (of 11 syllables in Italian, generally 12 in French and 10 in English), with rhymes arranged according to one or other of certain definite schemes, of which the Petrarchan and the Elizabethan are the principal, viz: (1) abbaabba, followed by two, or three, other rhymes in the remaining six lines, with a pause in the thought after the octave (not always observed by English imitators, of whom Milton and Wordsworth are prominent examples); (2) ababcdcdefefgg. The sonnets of Shakespeare are in the latter form.

The sonnet was introduced to England by Wyatt and developed by Surrey (*see also* metre) and was thereafter widely used, notably in the sonnet sequences of Shakespeare, Spenser, and others, most of which are amatory in nature, and contain a certain narrative development: later sonnet sequences on the theme of love include those of D. G. Rossetti and E. B. Browning. Milton, Donne, Keats, and Yeats have all used the form to great and varied effect, and it continues to flourish in the 20th c.

Spenserian stanza: the stanza invented by E. Spenser, in which he wrote *The Faerie Queene.* It consists of eight five-foot iambic lines, followed by an iambic line of six feet, rhyming ababbcbcc.

Spoonerism: see **metathesis.**

stanza: a group of lines of verse (usually not less than four), arranged according to a definite scheme which regulates the number of lines, the metre, and (in rhymed poetry) the sequence of rhymes; normally forming a division of a poem consisting of a series of such groups constructed according to the same scheme.

syllepsis: a figure of speech by which a word, or a particular form or inflection of a word, is made to refer to two or more words in the same sentence, while properly applying to them in different senses: e.g. 'Miss Bolo ... went home in a flood of tears and a sedan chair' (Dickens, *Pickwick Papers*, ch. 35). Cf. **zeugma.**

synecdoche: (pron. 'sinekdoki'), a figure of speech by which a more comprehensive term is used for a less comprehensive or vice versa, as whole for part or part for whole, e.g. 'There were six guns out on the moor' where 'guns' stands for shooters; and 'Oxford won the match', where 'Oxford' stands for 'the Oxford eleven'.

tail-rhyme: translated from the Latin *rhythmus caudatus*, the measure associated in particular with a group of Middle English romances in which a pair of rhyming lines is followed by a single line of different length and the three-line pattern is repeated to make up a six-line stanza. Chaucer's 'Sir Thopas' (*Canterbury Tales*, 17) is an example.

terza rima: the measure adopted by Dante in the *Divina Commedia*, consisting of lines of five iambic feet with an extra syllable, in sets of three lines, the middle line of each rhyming with the first and third lines of the next set (aba, bcb, cdc, etc.).

tribrach: see **metre.**

trimeter: see **metre.**

triolet: a poem of eight lines, with two rhymes, in which the first line is repeated as the fourth and seventh, and the second as the eighth.

triplet: three successive lines of verse rhyming together, occasionally introduced among heroic couplets, e.g. by Dryden.

trochee: see **metre.**

***vers de société*:** a term applied to a form of light verse dealing with events in polite society, usually in a satiric or playful tone, sometimes conversational, sometimes employing intricate forms such as the villanelle or the rondeau. English writers noted for their *vers de société* include Goldsmith and Dobson.

***vers libre*:** a term used to describe many forms of irregular, syllabic, or unrhymed verse, in which the ordinary rules of prosody are disregarded: Whitman pioneered a form of *vers libre* in America, and its independent evolution in France and Belgium had a great influence on the early Modernists such as T. S. Eliot and Pound.

vignette: an ornamental design on a blank space in a book, especially at the beginning or end of a chapter, of small size, and unenclosed in a border. The word is a diminutive of the French *vigne*, a vine; originally meaning an ornament of leaves and tendrils. It is now, by extension, used for any miniature work, visual, verbal, or musical.

villanelle: 'a poem, usually of a pastoral or lyrical nature, consisting normally of five three-lined stanzas and a final quatrain, with only two rhymes throughout. The first and third lines of the first stanza are repeated alternately in the succeeding stanzas as a refrain, and form a final couplet in the quatrain' (*OED*). The form has been much employed in light verse and *vers de société* by Lang, Dobson, and others, and in the 20th c. was used to more serious purpose by Auden, Empson ('slowly the poison the whole blood stream fills'), Dylan Thomas ('Do not go gentle into that good night'), and others.

virelay: 'a song or short lyric piece, of a type originating in France in the 14th c., usually consisting of short lines arranged in stanzas with only two rhymes, the end-rhyme of one stanza being the chief one of the next' (*OED*).

weak ending: the occurrence of an unstressed or proclitic monosyllable (such as a preposition, conjunction, or auxiliary verb) in the normally stressed place at the end of an iambic line.

zeugma: a figure of speech by which a single word is made to refer to two or more words in a sentence, when properly applying in sense to only one of them; e.g. 'See Pan with flocks, with fruits Pomona crowned'. Cf. **syllepsis**.

SHAKESPEARE AND THE ENGLISH LANGUAGE

How do we know what Shakespeare actually wrote? We have no copies of his plays as written down by Shakespeare himself, no collected works which he proof-read. The nearest we have is the First Folio of 1623, compiled seven years after his death by two members of his company and containing 36 of his plays. Some plays also exist in the smaller quartos whose value for establishing the text varies considerably. The book-keeper (or prompter) might make changes in the course of production, as conceivably could the author. Some scholars now believe that the two versions of *King Lear* (quarto and folio) represent an earlier and a later draft by Shakespeare himself. Further minor changes could be made by the printer, who might wish to produce a 'clean' page or alternatively might simply be in a hurry. And how reliable, anyway, was the written text from which the printer worked? Despite all these opportunities for change, we tend to assume that the language of our modern editions reflects Shakespeare's own words. In most cases this will be so, but the better editions often cite variant readings, and we need to be especially careful of their stage directions and their punctuation, which need not be his. Stage directions may be anybody's: Shakespeare's, prompter's, or later editor's. Elizabethan punctuation was both less than ours and meant for reading aloud, although italics are used not for emphasis but for proper names or quotations. Our punctuation reflects the grammatical construction of the sentence and is designed principally for silent reading. So where there are disputed readings in the text the modern editor's punctuation may serve as a form of interpretation.

Of the various aspects of language, spelling and pronunciation are likely to trouble the general reader least, if only because the productions he sees and the editions he uses will almost always modernize Shakespearean forms. The pronunciation of English long vowels had changed considerably between Chaucer and Shakespeare, but spelling had not kept up with the change, and the introduction of printing in the late fifteenth century helped to perpetuate the old spellings. For Shakespeare *clean* rhymes with *lane*, where we rhyme it with *lean*. For different reasons, *war* and *jar*, *watch* and *match*, *blood* and *good*, *swine* and *groin* may also rhyme. Yet he distinguishes, as we would not, between *see* and *sea* and perhaps *due* and *dew*. We should beware of accusing him of bad rhymes, even whilst recognizing that not all rhymes are exact.

As with rhymes, puns may depend on assonance rather than on exact correspondence. Several of Shakespeare's puns are, however, immediately intelligible to us. For instance, when Claudius is bidding for Hamlet's support, he addresses him (quotations throughout are from the New Penguin edition):

> But now, my cousin Hamlet, and my son.

Hamlet's comment, an aside, is

> A little more than kin, and less than kind!

Claudius continues

> How is it that the clouds still hang on you?

which provokes Hamlet's reply

> Not so, my lord. I am too much in the sun.

The *son/sun* pun is obvious, and in any case it is reinforced by the preference of the melancholic for the shade and, in Hamlet's case, for his 'customary suits of solemn black'. But what about *kin* and *kind*? These are Hamlet's very first words in the play and are characteristically sardonic in their tone. He is more than a *cousin*: indeed he is Claudius's stepson. But he is no natural relation, no *son*, and 'nature' was the earlier meaning of the noun *kind*. Other puns may be even more multifaceted, as with the concluding couplet of Sonnet 5:

> But flowers distilled, though they with winter meet,
> Lose but their show: their substance still lives sweet.

particularly the *still* in the last line. Does it mean 'unmoving' (the flowers are *distilled*) or 'everlasting' or 'nevertheless'? And there is the additional 'philosophical' pun on *show* ('outward form') and *substance* ('essential quality'). Nor should we assume that all Shakespearian puns are light-hearted, confined to comedy. 'I'll *gild* the faces of the grooms withal / For it must seem their *guilt*' says Lady Macbeth. John of Gaunt puns on his own name whilst on his death-bed. Professor Mahood (*Shakespeare's Wordplay*) believes that puns are often creative. Take Portia's well-known lines

> The quality of mercy is not strained,
> It droppeth as the gentle rain from heaven
> Upon the place beneath.

Strained clearly means 'constrained', but did it also suggest to Shakespeare 'filtered', 'squeezed', and so lead to *droppeth* in the following line? His scansion, too, may be different from ours. Words ending in *-sion* or *-tion* may need an extra syllable, especially at the end of a line. 'His eye begets occasion for his wit' (*Love's Labour's Lost*, II. i. 69) sounds perfectly natural to us, but 'Withhold thy speed, dreadful occasion!' (*King John*, IV. ii. 125) needs the extra syllable which forces us to linger on the last word. Sometimes the Shakespearian pronunciation of a word may even provide a clue to characterization. The name of Armado's page, Moth (*Love's

Labour's Lost) might suggest an airy, fairy-like figure, but in Elizabethan pronunciation *moth* and *mote* may have sounded alike and he *is* diminutive. If, as the New Penguin edition suggests, the pronunciation resembled *mott*, there may be a further pun in French *mot* ('word'—the final *t* was sounded then) and Mote (or Moth or Mott) does frequently answer his master back.

Some features of Shakespeare's grammar, illustrated at length in histories of the language, probably offer little difficulty in practice to the reader or theatre-goer. Such are the double comparatives ('As a wall'd town is *more worthier* than a village') or double superlatives ('This was the *most unkindest* cut of all'), where it might often be better to regard the *more* and *most* as simple intensifiers with the force of 'much' or 'very'. Or, again, the use of the relative pronouns *which* or *that* to refer to people ('I have known *those which* have walked in their sleep'; '*He that* hath kill'd my king and whor'd my mother'). Or even the fact that *its* was not common in English until well on into the seventeenth century (some ten instances only in the First Folio and none at all in the Authorized Version of 1611) and that therefore Shakespeare frequently uses *his* ('How far that little candle throws *his* beams') or even *it* (of the Ghost in *Hamlet*: 'It lifted up *it* head and did address / Itself to motion like as it would speak'). In such cases many modern editors normalize to *its* so that the reader is not even aware of the difference.

We need to be rather more careful, however, about the present tense forms in *-s* and *-eth*. These can exist in free variation:

> The quality of mercy is not strained,
> It *droppeth* as the gentle rain from heaven
> Upon the place beneath. It is twice blest,
> It *blesseth* him that *gives* and him that *takes*.

At first in sixteenth-century London, *-s* may have been regarded as informal, but it soon came into common use, and perhaps already by Shakespeare's later years *-eth* was beginning to suggest a conservative or formal tone simply because it was being used less often. If other features of the Shakespearian context suggest such conservatism, *-eth* may provide corroborative evidence: no more than that. Of course, the decision which to use may sometimes have been influenced by metre: *fights* is one syllable, *fighteth* two. But *hath* and *doth* always remain more common than *has* and *does*, and there may have been little difference in pronunciation between the two forms.

The little verb *do* can mislead as well. As for us, it can be a full verb with the meaning 'perform' ('The maid that milks and *does* the meanest chores') or a substitute verb ('It goes not forward, *doth* it?'). We use *do* to ask questions. Frequently Shakespeare does too, but he need not; there remained to him the older method of simply inverting subject and verb so that in questions the verb came first ('Did you call, sir?' but 'Know you where you are, sir?'). The choice of the one method or the other can occasionally contribute to the tone of a scene. When Hamlet interrogates his companions about the appearance of the Ghost to them (I. ii), the dominance of the shorter, inversion, form of the questions contributes to the build-up of tension. Similarly, about half of Shakespeare's negative sentences read exactly like present-day English:

I know your lady does not love her husband.
(*King Lear*, IV. v. 23)

but *do* is not necessary for a negative:

Indeed I think the young King loves you not.
(*2 Henry IV*, V. ii. 9)

And there was a further use of *do* which we have since lost. This *do* was semantically empty, adding nothing to the meaning:

No more of this; it *does offend* ('offends') my heart.
(*Coriolanus*, II. i. 161)

If ever I *did dream* ('dreamt') of such a matter.
(*Othello*, I. i. 5)

Some of these might suggest extra emphasis to us: it is unlikely that they did to Shakespeare's audience. Once again, the choice may have been dictated by the need for an extra syllable, and there is some (inconclusive) evidence that the use of this 'dummy' *do* became another method of indicating an old-fashioned style.

Shakespeare's characters, like us, address the Deity (or, in pagan plays, a deity) as *Thou*. But we also find both *thou* and *you* used to a single person in ordinary discourse. It is sometimes said that in such cases *you* is the polite form, used to superiors, and that *thou* signifies either inferiority or familiarity. This will have been so for Chaucer, but it seems more likely that, by Shakespeare's time, *you* had become the expected (what linguists term the 'unmarked') form and that, more and more, *thou* was becoming the unexpected ('marked') form, so that we need to watch for *thou* where the social situation would seem naturally to call for a *you*. In the opening scene of *King Lear*, Kent is so furious at Lear's banishment of Cordelia that he drops the respectful *you* and addresses his king as *thou*. Hamlet calls Horatio *thou* (is Horatio his only friend in Denmark?) but Horatio, as we would expect, uses *you* to his prince. In the struggle in Ophelia's grave, Hamlet and Laertes insult each other by using *thou*, whereas *you* might have been their usual pronoun in normal conversation. Claudius always calls Hamlet *you*, except when he is dispatching him to England when he relaxes with an expansive *thou*. The plural form of address is, of course, always *you*, although *ye* is frequently used for the nominative case.

One of the creative features of Renaissance English was the increased possibility of using one part of speech as if it were another, a practice sometimes called *conversion*. We ourselves do it a good deal: a *key* man in an organization; to *down* tools; that's a *must*. It is far less common in earlier periods of English because of the greater number of endings which signal grammatical functions (e.g. *-eth* is third person singular, present tense, indicative). Shakespeare seems to have exploited this change—the result of the disappearance of several earlier endings—more than his contemporaries and used it as a means of directing attention to a word he wished to emphasize. We pause for a second when we find a word we are accustomed to as a noun used as an adjective or a verb. Frequently such usages in Shakespeare are not just grammatically innovative but also metaphorical, and the audience needs to be able to savour the metaphor. Lear refers to Goneril and Regan as 'those *pelican* daughters', where *pelican* is adjectival. He is also reversing the significance of the old story where the pelican allows its starving young to peck at the parent's breast: in contrast, Lear's daughters are deliberately tearing him to pieces. Coriolanus, pressurized into flattering the plebs, says disgustedly 'I'll *mountebank* their loves'. But Shakespeare's grammatical daring goes beyond this: he will even use a converted form as part of a new compound. Hamlet hopes to use the play to trap Claudius:

> If his occulted guilt
> Do not itself *unkennel* in one speech,
> It is a damned ghost that we have seen.

Hotspur reminds his fellow-rebels of a previous period when Bolingbroke was anxious for whatever support he could get:

> Why, what a *candy* deal of courtesy
> This fawning greyhound then did proffer me.

By *Antony and Cleopatra*, however, Shakespeare has gone further with the same conversion-metaphor:

> The hearts
> That spanieled me at heels, to whom I gave
> Their wishes, do *discandy*, melt their sweets
> On blossoming Caesar; and this pine is barked
> That overtopped them all.

There are two other conversions here, *spanieled* and *barked* ('stripped of its bark') and the key word *discandy* is glossed by *melt their sweets*: not even Shakespeare can be too allusive.

Syntax, the ordering of words into longer units such as sentences, is more difficult to discuss briefly. All that can be said here is that we should watch for syntax that is clearly more complex or more simple than the norm of the scene and then try to gauge its effect. Much of Claudius's suavity, when he suggests he is in perfect control of events in Denmark (I. ii) or when, much later, he calms Laertes who bursts into the royal palace at the head of an angry mob (IV. v), is achieved by his use of long but perfectly controlled sentences. Macbeth, in his soliloquies, tries to weigh up the consequences of killing—or not killing—Duncan. Here the complex, balanced, almost see-saw syntax conveys the turmoil in his mind:

> If it were done when 'tis done, then 'twere well
> It were done quickly.

On the other hand, the simplicity of Romeo's 'Well, Juliet, I will lie with thee tonight', as he resolves on suicide, is, although we notice the pun on *lie*, essentially at odds with the extravagant language characteristic of earlier parts of the play. The same principle of contrast operates in a marked disturbance of the usual style level. The opening soliloquy of *Richard III* is wrong—deliberately wrong—when 'Grim-visaged war ... now ... *capers* nimbly in a lady's chamber'. Throughout this play Richard punctures the bubble of polite feudal conventions with his own brand of cynical colloquialism:

> Amen. And make me die a good old man.
> That is the *butt-end* of a mother's blessing;
> I marvel that her grace did leave it out.

Most readers of Shakespeare will be most interested in his use of words. When he began to write, probably *c.*1590, the earlier stigmatization of English as 'rough', 'inelegant', 'unpolished' was largely past. Latin was still regarded as being fixed, clearly defined, authoritative in a way English was not, and it gave access to a European audience rather than a merely English one, but there was already some eloquent English literature (Spenser, Lyly, Sidney) and in the 1590s some experimentation in styles other than the purely literary (Nashe, Greene, Dekker) had begun. There was, too, a standard written English. Dialects certainly reflected local pronunciation, but although we can recognize in Shakespeare a very few Warwickshire dialect words, it is likely that the language of, say, Edgar disguised as Poor Tom or the rustics in *A Midsummer Night's Dream* is meant to be stage, 'country' dialect rather than local. Some of the growing confidence in English as a language fit for all purposes reflects the increasing patriotism of the age. Puttenham's *Art of English Poesie* (1585) heads its second chapter 'That there may be an Art of our English Poesie as well as there is of the Latine and Greeke'. The earlier attempts of the purists to keep English 'unmixt and unmangled' with foreign words had largely been discarded in the face of the realization that Renaissance English (like the English of earlier periods) was dependent on borrowings from other languages, especially Latin and to a less extent Greek, to extend its vocabulary. A standard book such as A. C. Baugh and T. Cable, *A History of the English Language* will demonstrate the huge number of these loan-words. Many of the Latin borrowings were slightly changed, especially in their endings, to make them correspond more to the form of native words: Latin *-us* became *-ous* (*conspicuous*); the Latin past participle *-atus*/*-atum* appears as *-ate* (*literate*); *-alis* was changed to *-al* (*oral*). Those words borrowed into English directly from Greek (e.g. *catastrophe*, *criterion*, *heterodox*) seem to us less 'English'. Almost every great classical writer was translated into English; some of these translations, such as North's *Plutarch* or Golding's *Ovid*, we know that Shakespeare used. But if Shakespeare was uncertain about a word he could not simply look it up in the dictionary, for the first English dictionary, Robert Cawdrey's *A Table Alphabeticall*, did not appear until 1604 and it concentrates on 'hard' words, chiefly those introduced into the language in the previous generation or two. Most new words must have been passed on by reading, and sometimes by word of mouth—which is why Shakespeare can make good stage business of characters like Dogberry and Verges, Mistress Quickly, Costard, or Elbow who misunderstand such 'hard' words. Shakespeare himself may have introduced some 600 new words into English, words like *addiction*, *consign*, *contemplate*, *exposure*, *generous*, *hostile*, *majestic*, *negotiate*, *obscene*, *operate*, *pious*, *radiance*, *stricture*, *traditional*, *tranquil*. Many have remained; others, such as *combustious*, *disroot*, *illume*, *neglection*, have disappeared. Some are compounds: *over-credulous*, *sharp-toothed*, or the more poetical *wide-skirted*. He seems especially fond of compound adjectives whose second element is a past participle; perhaps these appealed to him because they preserve something of the concentration of action in the verb, whereas the alternative might have been a more lengthy simile. Others of his coinages are examples of affixation, where a prefix or suffix is added to an already existing word (amaze*ment*, *de*note, disgrace*ful*, employ*er*, fashion*able*, *in*auspicious, use*ful* and use*less*, *un*changing, *un*real, and several more in *un-*). He formed several new verbs from nouns ending in *-ion*: *arbitrate*, *contemplate*, *educate*, *operate*.

How can we know, though, which words seemed novel to the audience of 1600? The *Oxford English Dictionary* cites the first recorded use of a word in English and will provide some evidence of its frequency. A concordance, such as the *Harvard Concordance* compiled by Marvin Spevack, will show how often Shakespeare uses a particular word. Above all, the Shakespearian context will often suggest if a word is unfamiliar: does he gloss it by a more common synonym or even partly define it? The results of such investigation can prove illuminating. *Assassination* is found only with reference to Duncan; *equivocator*, too, is rare (three times in *Macbeth*, with *equivocate* twice and *equivocation* once; elsewhere *equivocation* occurs once—in *Hamlet*—and *equivocal* twice). If *Macbeth* is obviously a play about *assassination*, it is demonstrably even more about *equivocation*. Shakespeare may also use some of these newer words as members of groups of synonyms or near-synonyms:

> How weary, stale, flat, and unprofitable
> Seem to me all the uses of this world.
> (*Hamlet*, I. ii. 133)

> The bonds of heaven are slipped, dissolved and loosed,
> And with another knot, five-finger-tied,
> The fractions of her faith, orts of her love,

> The fragments, scraps, the bits and greasy relics
> Of her o'er-eaten faith, are given to Diomed.
> (*Troilus and Cressida*, v. ii. 153)

This is what the Elizabethans called *copious* language. It is meant to sound impressive, either because the subject is weighty (for example, affairs of state) or because a particular character is self-important. At the other extreme of vocabulary lies the word whose sense is very familiar to us but which seems not to fit the particular context. Here the meaning may have changed between Shakespeare's time and ours. *Ecstasy*, *humour*, *shrewd*, *suggestion*, *unvalued*, and several others may not mean in Shakespeare what they mean now.

Finally we should remember that, for the most part, Shakespeare was writing *drama*. Drama selects from the spoken language of its time, but the necessity to hold the audience's attention requires a greater concentration of sense than in ordinary speech. Yet it also has to seem spontaneous, to be spoken as if it had not been written first. Dialogue, in particular, is a complex business: it is full of assumptions, references back, implications. Questions are not always answered (or not immediately) nor commands obeyed. To investigate how Shakespeare used these features of normal language, whilst bearing in mind what was or was not possible in Renaissance English, may be one of the most profitable ways forward in the study of his language.

DR JOHNSON AND THE ENGLISH LANGUAGE

'THAT damned dictionary-making. He is all definitions.' This view of Samuel Johnson was expressed to Boswell by their common friend General Paoli, the Corsican patriot, in 1778. It expresses well a popular sense of Johnson which survives until today. In his own time he was celebrated as 'Dictionary' Johnson, but also mocked as 'the English Lexiphanes' (phrase-monger, speechifier), who promoted the 'Babylonish Dialect which learned Pedants much affect'. This sense of Johnson, either favourable or unfavourable, has to do not just with the great *Dictionary*, but also with the sort of English which Johnson is thought to have written as a result of his labours in lexicography. To understand his contribution to the way English has been used in the past two centuries, we must try to discover the full truth about Johnson and words, and not remain content with his definitions and damned dictionary-making.

I

Johnson is not a great creative writer in the same manner as Shakespeare or Dickens. These two are figures of transcendent imaginative power, who mediate an intense personal vision through sharply idiosyncratic dealings with language. Both of them (as, more recently, Joyce) bend, batter, and sculpt words to their purposes. They operate with a sublime innocence of the limitations which are supposed to confine and define 'normal' usage. Johnson stands at the very opposite extreme. His hold on English possesses a deeply impersonal, rather than personal, quality: it has to do with obeying, and not transgressing, the normal and normative forms we customarily obey. His whole approach to words could hardly be less innocent. It is knowledgeable, even knowing, and it does not start from poetic perception (though it may end up there), rather from such attributes as common sense, observation, sensitivity to the habitual phrases and rhythms of English, in short from an acceptance of the everyday communicative needs which language serves. For the great creative feat to be brought off—*King Lear*, *Bleak House*, *Ulysses*, *The Waste Land*—it is often necessary to take words where they have never been before. What Johnson is especially good at is tracing where words *have* been, and in what company; and (more tentatively) where they might be likely to go in future.

There is no single location where we can find all Johnson's linguistic views assembled in a neat bundle. But there is a group of sources which reveal most about his ideas on the subject. First, of course, the *Dictionary* of 1755—and here one must add the *Plan* published eight years earlier, as a trial kite flown to whet the interest of public and patrons. As regards the *Dictionary*, there is the splendidly eloquent Preface quite apart from the entries themselves. Second, Johnson's periodical essays, particularly *The Rambler* (1750–2), devote a fair amount of space to linguistic issues. The evidence here is scattered, and sometimes a little technical. Third, Johnson's works of formal literary criticism, above all the *Lives of the Poets* (1779–81), show him at work on English used at the highest level, under the pressure of the toughest creative exigencies in works by Milton, Dryden, and Pope. But even more important is Johnson's lifelong concern with Shakespeare, culminating (but not actually concluding) in his edition of the plays in 1765. Last, there is external evidence supplied by the comments of contemporaries, descriptions of Johnson's spoken and written style, satires, parodies, and much else. This last category obviously has to be handled with care, because not all the witnesses are disinterested or reliable. But they do record a very important part of the Johnsonian legacy, in that they show how people thought the Great Cham had influenced the English language. Their observations are interesting even when they happen to be wrong, though more interesting when they are right.

II

The *Dictionary* was published in two huge folio volumes, containing between them well over 2000 pages, in April 1755. Johnson was forty-five, a university drop-out, failed schoolmaster, frustrated scholar, and reluctant journalist who had been a non-graduate until recently. Then, two months before publication, Oxford was persuaded to award him the degree of Master of Arts 'by diploma', in recognition of *The Rambler* ('writings that have shaped the manners of his countrymen') and in anticipation of the *Dictionary*'s projected role of 'adorning and fixing our native tongue'. The original citation is in Latin, which is significant: for though lawcourts by this date used English, and public business would have ground to a halt if a deep acquaintance with the ancient tongues had been required, all matters ceremonial, academic, or obscene were still veiled in their decent obscurity. For Johnson, the main advantage was that he could put 'by Samuel Johnson, A.M.' on the title-page. This was a valuable point-of-sale recourse in the days before dust-jackets were used.

By the time of Johnson's death, almost thirty years later, five major editions had appeared of the full *Dictionary*, and another was on the way. Among these the most interesting, after the first, are the second edition (1755–6), in 165 weekly parts at sixpence a number; and the fourth (1773), one of the rare occasions when Johnson actually submitted to the discipline of revising his own work. This fourth edition contains a number of interesting changes, but in general when students of Johnson speak of the

Dictionary they mean the original version—so we can reasonably confine ourselves to the 1755 text.

It contains about 40 000 entries. This was much larger than the earliest English dictionaries, starting with Robert Cawdrey's *Table Alphabeticall* (1604), with a bare 3000 words. Seventeenth-century lexicography confines itself to 'hard words', that is to say obscure or learned expressions. It took generations for this highly selective approach to die out, and indeed no one before Johnson is remotely as good at discriminating between the shades of difference in the myriad extensions in meaning exhibited by the simplest word—Johnson has sixty-six subheadings for the transitive verb *put.* Each usage ('put up', 'put to it', and so on) has its own little illustrative passage, and these run the full gamut, as David Nokes has pointed out, from the sublime to the ridiculous.

Slowly English lexicography developed in the century before Johnson, although curiously there were good Italian, Welsh, or polyglot dictionaries long before there was an adequate monoglot English volume. There were contributions of limited value by Milton's nephew, Edward Philips, with his *New World of Words* (1658), and John Kersey, with a new venture (1702) 'chiefly designed for the benefit of young scholars, tradesmen, artificers and the female sex, who would learn to spell truely'. However, Johnson's most important predecessor was the schoolmaster Nathan Bailey, whose *Dictionarium Britannicum* (1730) Johnson had specially interleaved with blank pages and employed as the basis for his own compilation. Second in importance for Johnson was a different kind of enterprise, that is Ephraim Chambers's *Cyclopedia* (1728), which was the forerunner of the first edition of the *Encyclopaedia Britannica* in 1768. It may be added that other compilers of dictionaries in Johnson's lifetime were Daniel Defoe's unsatisfactory son Benjamin; John Wesley; and the elocution-master Thomas Sheridan, father of Richard Brinsley, the playwright.

Bailey achieves a respectable standard, even if he blurs the function of glossary and reference-book in a way that puzzles us today, so that a word like 'dulness' is liable to be followed by 'Dunmow, a town in Essex famous for its flitch'. Nevertheless, it was Johnson who raised the standard by a class or two, as indeed he raised the national consciousness of language by the renown of his volumes. In what, then, does he excel? Certainly not in his history of the English language, which is mostly routine, and not in his grammar of the English tongue, wonky and unreliable even in the unexacting philological context of the age. (John Cleland, author of *Fanny Hill*, was so far liberated by the primitive ideas of comparative linguistics which then held sway that he could produce a work in 1766, maintaining that Celtic (Welsh) was the aboriginal language of Europe. The same volume contained an essay on Freemasonry, a topic on which Cleland was scarcely better informed.) Nor, when we turn to the main entries, does Johnson shine in every respect. He gives no pronunciations, just marks of stress; whilst his etymologies are notoriously haywire on many occasions. Finally, he is dependent in many entries on previous compilers, such as Chambers and the writers of technical glossaries on such subjects as agriculture or naval affairs. There is always a danger that such interdependence of reference-books will produce accretions of error, like a coral reef of mis-statement, and Johnson does not quite avoid this.

But the positive side is much more important, and more striking. There is a Preface of surpassing majesty and intelligence, which remains one of the most culturally aware statements on the nature of language, though sociolinguistics was not yet even a cloud on the horizon. These days we hear a lot about 'reflexive' literature, that is writing which subjects itself to a critique of its own workings. Yet no one ever understood his or her own purposes in writing better than Johnson: the peroration to this essay is plangent and touching:

> In this work, when it shall be found that much is omitted, let it not be forgotten that much likewise is performed; and though no book was ever spared out of tenderness to the author, and the world is little solicitous to know whence proceeded the faults of that which it condemns; yet it may gratify curiosity to inform it, that the *English Dictionary* was written with little assistance of the learned, and without any patronage of the great; not in the soft obscurities of retirement, or under the shelter of academick bowers, but amidst inconvenience and distraction, in sickness and in sorrow.

Then, after referring to the partial success of the great continental dictionaries produced by teams from corporate bodies (the French Académie, the Accademia della Crusca in Florence), Johnson concludes:

> I have protracted my work till most of those whom I wished to please have sunk into the grave, and success and miscarriage are empty sounds. I therefore dismiss it with frigid tranquillity, having little to fear or hope from censure or praise.

This typically balanced cadence makes a noble sound in the reader's head (one has to read Johnson, as it were, with the mind's ear). But it is based on a profound truth: here was this disadvantaged and solitary hack, doing with the inconsiderable aid of a few rather feckless amanuenses what the great institutions of the land had failed to achieve in centuries of cloistered privilege. And, one might add, what it now takes committees, boards of advisers, and several hectares of software to set in motion.

It is the same with the wry self-mocking definitions. Take Grub Street: 'Originally the name of a street in Moorfields in London, much inhabited by writers of small histories, dictionaries, and temporary poems; whence any mean production is called *grubstreet*.' Or, even more famous, *Lexicographer*: 'A writer of dictionaries; a harmless drudge, that busies himself in tracing the original, and detailing the signification of words.' The ironies are delicious ('temporary', 'harmless', 'detailing'), and somehow not curdled by the pain that just shows through. And so with the joky or prejudiced definitions which everybody knows: the point is not that

Johnson is forgetting himself, but rather that he is able to express a serious and inward feeling for the experience embodied in language even when he appears to be fooling.

The definitions are in general outstandingly clear, accurate, and informative. When other lexicographers started to pillage from Johnson in order to produce their own compilations (as they soon began to do), it was convenient that they believed they had a perfect right to borrow his phrasing, word for word. It is in fact very hard to find a shorter or more pointed form of words than those Johnson habitually finds. But Johnson also discriminates neatly between competing senses, and shows an unsurpassed power to sort out literal and metaphorical meanings. Here it is vital that he was a practising creative writer, a student of great literature (above all Shakespeare), and a trained critic. One might notice, to take a single case at random, how he unlocks the various 'significations' of the complex and fast-changing term *sensible.* Unlike the *Oxford English Dictionary*, Johnson's *Dictionary* is organized on semantic rather than historical principles: that is, he starts from the nodal, root sense as it now appears, and follows the branching of various extended applications. This does not provide a chronological picture of the word's evolution, as does the method of the *OED*; but in some respects it performs a task of greater literary interest.

Finally, the huge advance of the *Dictionary* lies in the provision of illustrative passages from classical English writers. In fact, it was the work which more than any other defined the idea of a classical corpus of English texts, a canon of the most respected writers. There was then no great tradition for writers to join or reject. Nobody studied English literature at school or at university; there were no handy Oxford paperbacks, no Penguin anthologies, no classic serials on television, no A level texts—scarcely anything corresponding to that entire range of cultural markers we have stuck on books of the past, and which tell us as soon as we ever hear of the work that *Silas Marner* is a 'classic' in a way that the latest Barbara Cartland is not. Johnson chose his extracts with both care and judgement: he took trouble to ensure that heretical or immoral writers were not represented, and by his dense citation of Shakespeare, Bacon, Sir Thomas Browne, Milton, Locke, Dryden, and others helped to confirm their centrality. It took, then, a flash of intuition for Johnson to perceive what may nowadays seem obvious: that the illustrative quotations could be more than mere linguistic documentation, but could also become a sort of 'intellectual history'.

Johnson knew that no work, whatever eminence it may achieve, can stem linguistic change: his own Preface dilates most intelligently upon the effects to which language is subject as a result of social, political, and commercial developments ('They that have frequent intercourse with strangers . . . must in time learn a mingled dialect, like the jargon which serves the traffickers on the *Mediterranean* and *Indian* coasts'—a precognition of Pidgin English.) He stated that he had laboured '[to settle] the orthography . . . [regulate] the structures, and [ascertain] the structures of English words', but he knew that he was building sand-castles to be obliterated by an incoming tide of material and cultural change. He may have helped to standardize spelling a little, though on the whole this has more to do with printing conventions than any great literary impulse. He had no effect on pronunciation, since he did not record it. But his was certainly the first word, if not the last, when serious questions of meaning were involved: and until Noah Webster made a unilateral declaration of American independence in 1828, his writ also ran throughout the English-speaking world. It should not be forgotten that Franklin and Jefferson must have spoken pretty well impeccable 'native' English.

It did not take long for the work to achieve an immense renown. Boswell as a young man recorded the view that Johnson deserved the pension he had just been awarded, since 'his Dictionary was a kind of national Work so he has a kind of claim to the Patronage of the state'. It must be remembered that early study of the language had a quasi-patriotic function, amongst many other purposes. General Paoli told Boswell in 1769 that a great language was one 'in which great men have written; for it is by being moulded and animated by superior souls that a language becomes superior'. It was therefore the task of writers to dignify their national tongue by producing important works, but equally it was the job of a dictionary to enshrine this national self-tribute. Of course, some unenlightened persons were sceptical. There is a story that when Johnson was in the Scottish Highlands in 1773, he was introduced to a Gaelic-speaking crowd as (in English terms) 'the man who made the English language'. An old man on the edge of the crowd retorted in Gaelic, 'Well, he hadn't much to do!'

That may be apocryphal, but we know for certain of other encounters which testify to Johnson's repute. Boswell, on his Grand Tour came across a Herr Rogler MA, in Leipzig, who had made a voluminous German–English dictionary in which he 'amassed all the rubbish which Mr Johnson has with so much judicious care kept out of his book'. Generally Johnson bore his curious celebrity with good humour. Once Boswell, to while away a wet day (one of many) in Skye, showed Johnson some verses composed of uncommon words found in his *Dictionary*: to which the lexicographer retorted drily that he was 'not responsible' for all the words there. On another occasion, someone daringly gave Johnson a list of the work's imperfections. 'Are those all?' he asked cheerfully, 'I had thought there had been a thousand more.' His willingness to admit to error, as with the mistaken definition of a horse's pastern, is among his most winning qualities. It goes with a total lack of vanity on a personal level: Johnson takes his subject with great seriousness, but has none of the professional airs later linguistic studies have acquired.

III

'General philology' was Johnson's object of ambition as a young man, according to his biographer Arthur Murphy. By this expression is meant not very much more than 'polite learning', but it does suggest the way in which education of earlier centuries was rooted in the study of good letters. And although this had traditionally meant ancient literature, there were rapid changes in Johnson's lifetime which placed greater emphasis on Norse, medieval, 'Gothic' and Celtic antiquities, and which pointed the way towards the Romantic revival by stressing primitive and folk elements in culture. Many of Johnson's friends were deeply interested in the study of language. Boswell was always planning, and never actually writing, a Scottish dictionary. Mrs Thrale became increasingly obsessed with fanciful etymologies, learnt Hebrew for non-devotional reasons, and produced a *British Synonymy* (1794), incorporating some of her theories. It is true that Dr Burney discouraged his daughter Fanny from giving prolonged attention to grammar, on the grounds that it was too masculine a study; but at least girls were permitted to learn foreign languages, at a time when most intellectual activities of any utility were denied to them.

Johnson's own style as a writer was thrust into prominence by the *Dictionary*, although works such as *The Rambler* had earlier displayed its characteristic features. Nor was the ponderous use of long Latinate words its only distinguishing mark, for there are favourite devices of syntax and rhythm (parallelism and antithesis, inversion, and so on) which are just as important in obtaining the effect Johnson seeks. None the less, most of his critics fixed on the supposed abstract, general, 'Latin'—anyway un-English—and pompous character of his diction. For Charles Churchill, indeed, a considerable satiric poet, Johnson became Pomposo, 'Who, to increase his native strength / Draws words, six syllables in length.' As we have seen earlier, another critic dubbed Johnson 'Lexiphanes' and parodied his 'hard words and affected style'. The most amusing and elegant of Johnson's detractors is the letter-writer Horace Walpole, who wrote to a friend in 1775 of his 'teeth-breaking diction', and a few years later committed these thoughts to paper:

> He prefers learned Words to the simple and common—and on every occasion. He is never simple, elegant, or light. He destroys more Enemies with the Weight of his Shield than with his spear, and had rather make three mortal wounds in the same part than one.

Macaulay was to say almost the same thing when reviewing an edition of Boswell's *Life* in 1831. 'All his books', declares Macaulay, 'are written in a learned language, in a language which nobody hears from his mother or his nurse, a language in which nobody ever quarrels, or drives bargains, or makes love, in a language in which nobody ever thinks . . . He felt a vicious partiality for terms which, long after our own speech had been fixed, were borrowed from the Greek and Latin, and which, therefore . . . must be considered as born aliens, not entitled to rank with the King's English.' Interestingly, Macaulay made a distinction between Johnson's written style, which he viewed as 'systematically vicious', and the more 'natural' manner of his conversation as reported by Boswell. Victorian ideas of Johnson, in every respect, were strongly coloured by Macaulay, and writers such as Matthew Arnold echoed these fulminations against the 'pompous and long' words favoured by Johnson.

In this century a reaction has set in, and a general admiration for Johnson has brought with it a re-examination of his style. The scholar W. K. Wimsatt produced two important books, *The Prose Style of Samuel Johnson* (1941) and *Philosophic Words* (1948). These helped to dislodge Macaulay's crude estimate of the way Johnson uses words. We now recognize, for example, that he can employ generalized constructions with a quasi-concrete force and particularity; that his 'philosophic' diction is in fact an excitingly poetic use of scientific words just losing their strict literal sense and becoming metaphoric (see the important passage in the Preface to the *Dictionary*, beginning 'As by the cultivation of various sciences, a language is amplified, it will be more furnished with words deflected from their original sense . . .') . We appreciate the fact that Johnson's desire to clear the language from colloquial familiarities is not just a routine habit born of pomposity, but a process in tune with a whole ideal of decorum which saw each level of style as appropriate to a particular task in communication. We know from Mrs Thrale that the *Rambler* essays, *pace* Macaulay, expressed his true self 'in a style so natural to him, and so much like his common mode of conversing'.

It is the contemporary tributes, rather than the modern scholarly defences, which leave the strongest impression. There is the painter Ozias Humphrey observing that everything Johnson said was 'as correct as a second edition'. Or Thomas Tyers remarking that he said 'the most common things in the newest manner'. The biographer Sir John Hawkins agreed that Johnson spoke in a manner one would have expected to encounter from someone reading aloud. As well as these learned testimonies, there is the direct and simple response of a lady otherwise unknown to history, called Miss Beresford, who once travelled in a stage-coach to Oxford—aptly—with Johnson and Boswell. 'How he does talk,' whispered the 'agreeable' young American lady to Boswell, 'every sentence is an essay.'

Finally, there are Boswell's own splendid tributes to his mentor. As early as 1763, just after meeting the older man, Boswell was advising a friend, 'Read the work of Mr Johnson. There, indeed is style; there indeed is the full dignity of an English period.' In Venice in 1765, he told an acquaintance that David Hume was but a child in comparison to Johnson. 'When you see him, you will go down on your knees . . . His *Dictionary* is great philosophy: all the axiomatical knowledge of the language: clear ideas.' (A 'hot dispute' ensued.) Throughout the great *Life*, there are passages where Boswell confides his sense of Johnson's pre-eminence in thought, and the contribution which his unrivalled mastery of words played in that. A single brief example must suffice, from 12 April 1776: 'My record upon this occasion does great injustice to Johnson's expression, which was so forcible and brilliant, that Mr Cradock whispered me, "O that his words were written in a book!"'

There will probably always be some people who feel with Hippolyte Taine that Johnson's truths are too true, and that his words—by extension—are too wordy. But for very many of us his rich and varied personality serves as a perpetual support, and we come as close as anywhere to the heart of the man in his feeling for words. He said so many wise things on the subject: 'in lexicography . . . naked science is too delicate for the purposes of life.' Or this, from the same work, the 'Plan' of the *Dictionary*:

> [Words], like their author, when they are not gaining strength, . . . are generally losing it. Though art may sometimes prolong their duration, it will rarely give them perpetuity; and their changes will be almost always informing us, that language is the work of man, of a being from whom permanence and stability cannot be derived.

There is in this passage a sense of the dynamism of language, and a very modern-looking awareness of the social context of meaning. But there is also a characteristic recognition of what has been called 'the durable pastness of words'. From his long work on the *Dictionary*, from his hours grappling with the text of Shakespeare, from his own aspiring efforts as poet and dramatist, from his constant immersion in professional literary life, above all from his own wonderfully clear-headed approach to living—from all these Johnson derived his remarkable powers as a user and an analyst of the English language.

DICKENS AND THE ENGLISH LANGUAGE

LATE in the nineteenth century one of Dickens's most perceptive critics, Walter Bagehot, noted the importance of the novelist's relationship with the greatest city of his time, London. 'London is like a newspaper,' Bagehot wrote, 'everything is there, and everything is disconnected. There is every kind of person in some houses, but there is no more connection between the houses than between the neighbours in the lists of "births, marriages and deaths".' This sense of 'disconnection' is true too of Dickens's narratives. It is also a valid observation to make about his language. Victorian London epitomized the cosmopolitan, industrialized culture of Victorian Britain; it intermixed social classes and blurred gradations between classes; in its streets citizens rubbed shoulders with people born in the remotest villages of the realm and in the farthest outposts of empire; it attracted visitors from more elegant capitals and refugees from less liberal political climates. Much of Dickens's true originality as a writer, and much of his continuing impact on our culture derives from his understanding of the nature of the urban phenomenon and the use he makes of it in his fiction. The city was multifarious and its disconnections were inherent and inevitable. London proved the essential stimulus to Dickens's distinctive genius.

Very early in his career as a writer of fiction, Dickens recognized the extent to which the 'magic lantern' of London was necessary to him. He needed 'streets and crowds of people' both to feed his imagination and to help him find a proper focus in the process of writing. What fascinated and energized him seems to have had the opposite effect on many other writers of his time; finding the city too big, or too stressful, or too distressing, they withdrew to solitude or to contemplation of the century's shortcomings amid landscape. Dickens's mind, by contrast, seems to have worked more clearly in a street than on a mountain top and what others read as confusion he saw as evidence of the vigour and energy of life. It was the very sound of the streets which informs the linguistic intricacy of his fiction. His ear was best attuned not to still small voices, or to calmly ordered discourses, or to the recherché exchanges of cultured drawing-rooms, but to the variety of the patterns of speech which crossed and recrossed as he walked the length of High Holborn or Oxford Street. Dickens, it has often been remarked, saw details which seemed inconsequential to less acute observers; he also seems to have heard voices more distinctly and he echoed their disconnected rhythms in his novels.

Dickens is an outstanding user of language and of locution to individualize his characters. Anyone who has read his work will remember at least one distinct voice either because it stimulated laughter or because its oddity proved disconcerting or disturbing. The variety is itself phenomenal, from the grandiloquence of a Vincent Crummles or a Wilkins Micawber to the inarticulacy of the illiterate Jo or the traumatized Dr Manette. He can capture the effete unpleasantness of an eighteenth-century aristocrat like Sir John Chester and the stiff awkwardness of a déclassé nineteenth-century teacher like Bradley Headstone. He can delight in the quick wit and verbal inventiveness of Sam Weller and suggest a languorous jadedness in Eugene Wrayburn. He can move from the wonderful distortions of Mrs Gamp to the barely logical streams of ideas which issue from Flora Finching. In his most experimental novel, *Bleak House*, Dickens teases his readers not simply with his immensely complex double plot and his diverse range of characters but also with his employment of two distinct narrative voices. One part of the story is told by an impressionable, confused, but observant woman narrator in the first person singular and in the past tense; the other by a more meditative, knowing, and censorious sexless narrator who uses the third person singular and the present tense. The many voices of the characters are filtered through the already distinct narrative styles of the two story-tellers; often these voices cross between the narratives. One narrator appears detached from the story; the other has to learn secrets and discover identities through the process of the very story she purports to have lived and through the events she attempts to record.

That Dickens was particularly alert to the vernacular idioms of Victorian Londoners was evident to readers of his earliest works, the stories collected as *Sketches by Boz* and the vastly successful *Pickwick Papers*. The *Sketches* are expressive of a fascination with the ways in which characters can be both observed and heard. Tradesmen, cabmen, hucksters and washerwomen briefly articulate their professions and their view of themselves and their surroundings; they are glimpsed as if overheard, or as if readers share their company for the space of a short journey. This 'sketchy' device was one which Dickens would use effectively throughout his career, especially so in the later journalism collected as *Reprinted Pieces* and *The Uncommercial Traveller*. The encapsulation of character substantially through verbal traits, or through idiolect, rather than through an analysis of the workings of the mind, is an aspect of his art which disappointed some contemporary critics. George Eliot, who so carefully tried to represent an English Midlands artisan in *Adam Bede*, found Dickens's rendering of 'external traits' akin to a verbal 'sun picture' (as the new art of photography was called). Like many subsequent commentators she seems to have missed the density of Dickens's overall achievement in his novels by concentrating her critical comments on the 'humorous and external' devices in his early fiction. If we take a larger view and look at the totality of a mature Dickens novel it is evident that the details form themselves into more complex and various structures than are often dreamt of in the philosophy of those who espouse strict verisimilitude as a fictional device. Like a 'sun picture' Dickens gives us an intensity of detailing which can be startling; unlike the finest Victorian photographs he also exhibits an equally startling animation, a sense of movement built up through the energy and variety of his language. A Dickens novel is established from a series of changing impressions, sounds, moods, and evocations of place. Given the extraordinary intensity of Dickens's ways of representing character, and the large number of characters concerned in his fiction, the representation of inner lives, and the supposed voices of consciousness, begin to seem less essential than they do in the work of novelists with a radically different view of the art of the novel.

In his later work, Dickens increasingly experimented with settings and with ways of speaking that moved beyond the London and the Londoners of his first novels. Dickens had, however, always been aware of the diversity of London's population; he remembered seeing Spanish refugees in their cloaks in the shabby suburbs of his boyhood, and he was familiar with the magnetic pull London had always exerted on new generations of refugees and provincial seekers after fame or fortune or anonymity. His ear seems, though, to have gradually become more attuned to accents and idioms beyond those of the metropolis and the south-east of England. In *Oliver Twist* Mr Bumble sounds splendid enough, but his London inflexions disguise the fact that he is meant to be an official of a small provincial town somewhere to the north of the capital, and John Browdie the Yorkshire farmer in *Nicholas Nickleby* betrays more of Mummerset than the North Riding in his speech. The self-confident Americans of *Martin Chuzzlewit* have, however, a true enough ring (though interestingly enough the 'good' American, Mr Bevan, speaks standard English) and in *David Copperfield* Dickens researched the dialect of Norfolk and Suffolk in order to give the Peggottys a distinct accent. In *Hard Times*, a novel in which the juxtaposition of voices is so often of structural significance, he reveals a far keener grasp of Northern English than he had done in *Nickleby*, a result of his travels in Yorkshire and Lancashire and perhaps of his close acquaintance with the social fiction of Elizabeth Gaskell. Dickens's users of English as a second language form a category of their own. His own command of French was good, and during his extended visit to Italy in 1844 he seems to have acquired some fluency in a second Romance tongue. His affection for France and for the French is certainly tempered by the fact that most of his Francophone characters are either extravagant or villainous or both. Throughout *A Tale of Two Cities* he plays with a somewhat awkward representation of spoken French literally translated into English, but it is a device which works well in the climactic scene of the confrontation of the monoglot Miss Pross and Mme Defarge in which feelings take over from spoken language. Bilingual characters, like Manette and Darnay, are given a rather precise and stiff English which has all too often been interpreted as an indication of Dickens's own overformulization of the story. Elsewhere he shows some occasional dexterity in representing a French mind working in English while still forming French sentences. Lady Dedlock's French maid, Hortense, speculating on her rival provides an entertaining example:

> Ha, ha, ha! She Hortense, been in my Lady's service since five years, and always kept at the distance, and this doll, this puppet, caressed—absolutely caressed—by my Lady on the moment of her arriving at the house! Ha, ha, ha! 'And do you know how pretty you are, child?'—'No, my Lady.'—You are right there! 'And how old are you, child? And take care they do not spoil you by flattery, child!' Oh how droll! It is the *best* thing altogether.
>
> (*Bleak House*, ch. 12)

Dickens interpolates Hortense's reflection into the third-person narrator's own commentary, thus yet again alerting readers to the novel's shifting perspectives through stylistic devices. A further example, that of the virtuous Mr Riah in *Our Mutual Friend*, suggests something of Dickens's care in finding the right expression and some readers' dismay at the result. Riah, though clearly a native English speaker, still retains certain echoes of his Jewish culture which render his English deliberate and rhetorical rather than idiomatic:

> 'Thus I reflected, I say, sitting that evening in my garden on the housetop. And passing the painful scene of that day in review before me many times, I always say that the poor gentleman believed the story readily, because I was one of the Jews—that you believed the story readily, my child, because I was one of the Jews—that the story itself first came into the invention of the originator thereof, because I was one of the Jews.'
>
> (Book the Fourth, ch. 9)

Riah is having to explain himself, after much thought, to his peculiar interlocutor Jenny Wren. He has, like so many characters in *Our Mutual Friend*, been misunderstood. Such careful, balanced language as he chooses may sound as stiff as the Anglo-French dialogues of *A Tale of Two Cities*, but for Dickens the slight oddity of such ways of speaking contributes to a constantly shifting but accumulating series of impressions.

Like a dramatist Dickens establishes action and character through discourse rather than through monologue or through a translation of the processes of thought into words. He uses first-person narrators three times (in *David Copperfield*, *Bleak House*, and *Great Expectations*) but all three tend to be disinclined to careful self-analysis or introspection, and all three record dialogue in a verbatim manner rather than through the use of reported speech which a genuine 'autobiographer' might have found more succinct and accurate. Given Dickens's dramatic propensities, and the delight both he and his readers have often found (and find) in reading his works aloud, it is odd that he should have shown comparatively little talent as a playwright. He experimented in the theatre as a young writer, and he was, by all accounts, a highly gifted actor who remained fond of amateur dramatics, but otherwise his histrionic talents were concentrated on a highly successful series of public readings from his novels. It is, however, important that Dickens can be so easily *performed*. As some recent theatrical adaptations have demonstrated, his fiction can be successfully translated into fluid dramatic forms, his dialogue proving particularly effective on stage; even the crucial role of the narrator has been variously included in a series of roles. Dickens's works were performed even in his own time and it is likely that some of the most popularly cited quotations from his work derive their currency from versions performed in the theatre, or made later for the cinema and television (one thinks here of Scrooge's 'Humbug' or Sydney Carton's last words).

Despite the prominence of inventive dialogue in Dickens's novels it should not be forgotten that he is also a supreme master of descriptive prose. His language has a richness and a resourcefulness which derives in part from the literary tradition in which he wrote, one which had recently assimilated the new vocabulary of Romanticism and which was adjusting itself to the markets opened up by greater literacy and increased prosperity. Dickens's works are full of echoes of the King James Bible, the Anglican Prayer Book, and Shakespeare's plays. These we might take for granted in talking about any major writer of his generation. Dickens adds to these familiar, and intensely formative, norms a feel for poetry, both the largely ephemeral popular poetry he had heard quoted or sung as a young man and the works of his great contemporaries, most notably Tennyson, to whose work he responded as a means of articulating certain modes of feeling. He had also learnt much from earlier generations of novelists and dramatists. It was perhaps from Scott's extensive use of the vernacular that Dickens grasped the importance of a fiction which conveyed a forceful sense of place or, more pointedly, a sense of locality both in terms of geography and class. This specification derived from local inflexions of speech and from dialect also owes something to the city comedies of Ben Jonson (Dickens himself had directed an important revival of *Every Man in his Humour*) and to the novels of Fielding and Smollett. From these novelists he seems to have also learnt much in terms of his use of varied narrative tones and especially of irony (used with particular effect in *Oliver Twist*). Dickens found in the eighteenth-century novel the kind of fictional shape and the comic characterization with which he most relaxed as a reader; as a writer he remade an inherited form as the central artistic expression of the new century.

Dickens was the most popular writer of his day both in the English-speaking world and beyond it. He relished what he sensed was an intimate relationship with his readers and fostered it by accepting an inexpensive form of serial publication in monthly and weekly parts and by his later public appearances as a reader and lecturer. The language of his novels, firmly grounded in the spoken English of his day, suggests a further aspect of this relationship, that of a writer seeking immediacy and one who both reinforces some values while undermining others. Dickens remains reassuring in his celebration of human community; he remains challenging in his response to threats to that same community. This is perhaps why the language of his fiction is both playful and serious and why his jokes still sting. His delight in words began early. He later recalled being fascinated as a boy in the blacking-factory by the effect of seeing the words 'COFFEE ROOM' reflected backwards as 'MOOR EEFFOC'; the shifting quality of words and meanings remained important from Bill Stumps's mark in *Pickwick* to Durdles's epitaphs in *Edwin Drood.* It is not idly that he names his characters in the way that he does, nor that he should allow some of them to distort sounds and meanings (one thinks here of Mr Chadband's 'Terewth' or Jo's twisting of 'Consecrated Ground' into 'Consequential Ground'). His rhythms at moments of heightened emotion may drift towards the easy metre of blank verse but his finest passages of 'poetry' show a far more complex interest in patterning words. The celebrated opening to *Bleak House* avoids finite verbs and presents us with some sentences which are entirely verbless, while the first page of *Edwin Drood* poses a series of fragmentary questions which serve to throw us out of an assured sense of place and time. Dickens's prose can be purely mimetic, as in the use of accelerating rhythms to suggest the movement of a railway train in Chapter 20 of *Dombey and Son*, and he can tellingly employ extended metaphors (like the feline imagery associated with Carker in the same novel) and synecdoche (like the references to Mrs Merdle in *Little Dorrit* as 'the Bosom'). In all of these cases he plays with style in order to disconcert pleasingly and to accentuate the reader's sense of disconnections. Dickens has often been seen as a social reformer and a campaigner for progressive change; he was most impressively so in the manner in which he alerted his readers to the shifting nature of reality beyond the world of his novels. His popularity lay in the extraordinary versatility of his fictional expression and in his choice of a language of comic playfulness. In this he was, as an early nickname indicates, 'The Inimitable'.

PART FOUR

THE LANGUAGE OF SCIENCE, TECHNOLOGY, AND COMMERCE

SCIENTIFIC WRITING

SCIENTIFIC research is not complete until its results have been published, for science is very much a public affair: the observation-statements out of which science grows record what is for all to see, and the interpretations put upon such statements become public property. A scientific publication does not often take the form of a book but characteristically of a 'paper' to a learned journal, which may or may not have been the subject of a verbal communication before the society of which the journal represents the transactions. Because a paper in a learned journal is a rather dressy affair and scientific papers may sometimes be quite slight, publication may take a much shorter form, as a letter to *Nature* or a three- or four-page paper in a journal that makes space for shorter communications.

The author of a scientific paper writes under some constraint, for 'the spirit of John Stuart Mill', it has been said, 'glares out of the eyes of every editor of a learned journal'. Almost without exception editors take the view that the scientific process is what John Stuart Mill represented it to be—that is, an act of reasoning that begins with *facts*, or rather with simple observation-records that embody factual information. These are then compounded into more general statements, perhaps into natural laws, by the application of a number of 'rules on discovery', the entire process being as it were empirically fuelled by the accumulation of observations. It is well known that William Whewell and more recently Karl Popper rejected Mill's scheme in its entirety, substituting for it a conception in which the initiative comes not from facts but from hypotheses, which provide the incentive for making some observations rather than others and conducting experiments that help to discriminate between one hypothesis and another.

The editors of scientific journals, however, virtually insist upon a format that embodies the methodology of John Stuart Mill. The paper begins with an introduction, which may or may not adequately explain the nature of its subject-matter but which will normally contain acknowledgements of the work of other scientists who have groped their way towards solutions of the same problem. Then comes the meat of the paper, 'Observations and results'. This is a great orgy of factual information, usually containing no clue about why the facts were collected and why one observation was made rather than another. Then follows the 'Discussion' in which the author asks himself what it all means, just as if he had no glimmering about what the possible outcomes of his experiments might be. This is the format, then; what about the style? Joseph Glanvill, one of the early Fellows of the Royal Society, said it all more than three hundred years ago in his *Plus Ultra* (1668). The scientific style was to be 'manly and yet plain . . . It is not broken by ends of Latin, nor impertinent quotations, . . . not rendered intricate by long parentheses, nor gaudy by flaunting metaphors; not tedious by wide fetches and circumferences of speech', but 'as polite and as fast as marble'. ('Polite' means, of course, *polished*, not dainty or ingratiating.)

Glanvill's recommendations are pretty generally worded. It is clear, anyway, that scientists were to put away for ever what Abraham Cowley in his 'Ode to the Royal Society' (1663) referred to as 'the painted scenes and pageants of the brain'. Nothing in the Apollonian mode here, to be sure: the scientist was not seen as Shelley was to see him, as something akin to a poet, but rather as an accountant of natural affairs. Brevity, cogency, and clarity are the principal virtues and the greatest of these is clarity—something that will almost certainly entail the use of a specialized terminology, partly for brevity's sake and partly also to avoid all possible uncertainties and equivocations.

Almost always a scientific paper is written for an *in*-group comprising the limited number of people who can understand it. The ambition to make a technical scientific paper generally intelligible—that is, intelligible to scientists as a whole—is impossible to achieve. A paper on theoretical physics written in such a manner as to inform and interest biologists would almost certainly bore other theoretical physicists to extinction.

Henry Oldenburg, who was Secretary of the Royal Society in Joseph Glanvill's day, was inclined to think Glanvill's own style was somewhat florid, not a charge which could be drawn against any scientific writing of the present day; but scientific writing can be graceful and elegant and may even be decorated by literary elegances. Such was the writing of Sir D'Arcy Wentworth Thompson in his *Essay on Growth and Form* (1917). D'Arcy was Professor of Natural History in the University of Dundee and then of St

Andrews and sometime President of the Classical Associations of England and Wales and of Scotland. We can delight in all his melismata and fioriture because D'Arcy Thompson was a perfectly accomplished singer from whom such graces could reasonably be looked for and applauded. But a work such as this could not be written a second time: the wonder is that it was written once.

Thomas Sprat, author of the great *History of the Royal Society of London for the Improving of Natural Knowledge* (1668), thought much as Glanvill did. Scientific discourse was to be marked by 'a close, naked, natural way of speaking; positive expressions; clear senses; a native easiness bringing all things as near the mathematical plainness as they can, and preferring the language of artizans, countrymen and merchants before that of wits or scholars'. There was one matter, Sprat added, on which the Royal Society had been most solicitous: to be on its guard against the 'luxury and redundance of speech', for superfluity of talking had already 'overwhelmed most arts and professions insomuch that he could not forbear from concluding that eloquence ought to be banished in all civil societies as fatal to peace and Good Manners'; specious tropes and figures of speech 'gave the mind a motion too changeable and bewitching to consist with *right practice*'.

An outrageous old chauvinist but strangely prescient all the same, Thomas Sprat believed that English excelled all other languages in fitness to be the vehicle of scientific discourse.

Because of the quantitative preponderance of American research and scientific publications, broken English became the international language of science soon after the war, and English is now the preferred language at international conferences and even of scientific journals, especially in Scandinavia, Denmark, and the Low Countries. This hegemony of the English tongue is not readily assented to by the French, who for some time withheld travel grants from any French scientist who did not undertake to deliver his lecture in his native tongue. The ingenious subterfuges used by the French to annul this ruling soon brought it into total disrepute, and English-speaking people have been rewarded by the fact that some French writers—notably Jacques Monod and François Jacob—write English at least as well as, and sometimes better than, most Englishmen. Our native tongue could have no higher compliment than that.

The Restoration and *a fortiori* the eighteenth century would have been altogether too polished to accept Sprat's recommendations of the style of countrymen, artisans, and merchants, but today the wheel has turned so far as to reinstate rather aggressively the claims of straightforward demotic English and to depreciate the usages of educated speech and the smooth southern English accents that give them voice.

But living languages change, of course, and we may expect changes of address in the future at least as great as those which occurred between Sprat's day and the Enlightenment.

EVERYDAY COMMERCIAL AND LEGAL TERMS

* indicates a separate entry

Also see under 'General Abbreviations and Acronyms' and 'Foreign Words and Phrases'.

'A' ordinary shares: when *shares have the prefix of 'A' or 'B' it usually means that they have restrictions on them. 'A' shares are invariably non-voting shares. They are mostly issued when company shareholders (*see* share) want to raise more capital without diluting their control in the company and without having to guarantee a fixed annual dividend.

abandonment: 1. The act of giving up a legal right, particularly a right of ownership of property. Property that has been abandoned is *res nullius* (a thing belonging to no one), and a person taking possession of it therefore acquires a lawful title. In *marine insurance, abandonment is the surrender of all rights to a ship or cargo in a case of *constructive total loss. The insured person must do this by giving the insurer a *notice of abandonment.* 2. In civil litigation, the relinquishing of the whole or part of a claim made in an action or of an appeal. 3. The offence of a parent or guardian leaving a child under the age of 16 to its fate.

above par: a term used on the *Stock Exchange describing *shares which are priced above their face—or nominal—value.

abstract of title: written details of the *title deeds and documents that prove an owner's right to dispose of his land. An owner usually supplies an abstract of title to an intending purchaser or mortgagee, who compares it with the original title deed when these are produced or handed over on completion of the transaction.

accessory: one who is a party to a crime that is actually committed by someone else (the *perpetrator*).

account days: a term used on the *Stock Exchange for the days during which accounts—*bargains between members—are settled. Except for *gilt-edged securities which are accounted for on a daily basis, accounts are settled every week on a Tuesday, the purchaser of *shares having received a statement the previous Thursday. A purchaser can, if he so wishes, carry his account forward, but he is charged for this (*see* contango rate). A seller may also delay delivering the shares to the buyer (*see* backwardation).

account executive: an employee of an advertising agency who looks after one or more of that agency's clients, and is responsible that the contract with the client is implemented.

accounts: a statement of a company's financial position. All *registered companies must present accounts annually to company members at a *general meeting. Accounts consist of a *balance sheet and a *profit-and-loss account, with group accounts attached if appropriate. They are accompanied by a *directors' report and an *auditor's report. All *limited companies must deliver copies of their accounts to the *Companies Registry, where they are open to public inspection.

act of God: an event due to natural causes like storms, earthquakes, and floods, so exceptionally severe that no one could reasonably be expected to anticipate or guard against it.

actual total loss: (in marine insurance) a loss of a ship or cargo in which the subject-matter is destroyed or damaged to such an extent that it can no longer be used for its purpose.

actuary: a person employed by *insurance and *life assurance companies who estimates rates of premium calculated on life expectancy tables and other statistical evidence.

affidavit: a sworn statement used mainly to support certain applications and, in some circumstances, as evidence in court proceedings.

affiliation order: an order of a magistrates' court against a man alleged to be the father of an illegitimate child, obliging him to make payments towards the upkeep of the child.

affreightment: a contract for the carriage of goods by sea.

age of consent: the age, now 16, at which a girl can legally consent to sexual intercourse, or to an act that would otherwise constitute an indecent assault.

aggravated damages: *damages awarded when the conduct of the defendant or the surrounding circumstances increase the injury to the plaintiff by subjecting him to humiliation, distress, or embarrassment, particularly in such *torts as assault, false imprisonment, and *defamation.

airspace: in English and international law, the ownership of land includes ownership of the airspace above it, though outer space is not considered to be subject to ownership.

alibi: from the Latin: elsewhere. A defence to a criminal charge alleging that the defendant was not at the place at which the crime was committed and so could not have been responsible for it.

amortization: 1. Paying off a debt over a number of years by putting aside money each year, usually into a sinking fund. 2. Paying off a debt by making regular payments which include interest on the amount owed and part of that amount.

ancient lights: an *easement acquired by lapse of time resulting from 20 years' continuous enjoyment of the access of light to the claimant's land without any written consent from the owner of the land over which the easement is claimed.

anti-trust laws: laws passed in the United States from 1890 onwards which prohibit the creation of *monopolies by new or existing commercial and industrial organizations.

arbitrage: the name given to the purchasing of currency, commodities, or stock, and then immediately selling it in another market, making a profit either from the difference in price or because of the rate of exchange.

arrestable offence: an offence for which there is a fixed mandatory penalty (at the moment this applies only to murder and treason) or for which a sentence of imprisonment for a first offender is declared by statute to be at least five years (e.g. theft).

articles of association: regulations for the management of *registered companies. Under the Companies Act 1948 they constitute, together with the provisions of the *memorandum of association, a contract between company members and the company.

asset stripping: the name given to the business of buying up companies and then selling off their assets for a greater sum than the original purchase price before closing them down.

assurance: see **insurance**.

attorney: 1. A person authorized to act for another in legal matters. 2. In the United States an attorney-at-law is someone who acts on a person's behalf in a court of law.

Attorney-General: the principal law officer of the Crown. The Attorney-General is usually a Member of Parliament of the ruling party and holds ministerial office, although he is not normally a member of the Cabinet.

auction: a method of sale in which parties are invited to make competing offers (*bids*) to purchase an item. The auctioneer, who acts as the agent of the seller, announces completion of the sale in favour of the highest bidder by striking his desk with a hammer (or in any other customary manner). Until then any bidder may retract his bid and the auctioneer may withdraw the goods. The seller may not bid unless the sale is stated to be subject to the seller's right to bid.

auditor: a person appointed to examine the *books of account and the *accounts of a registered company, and to report upon them to company members. An *auditor's report* must state whether or not, in the auditor's opinion, the accounts have been properly prepared and give a true and fair view of the company's financial position.

authorized capital (nominal capital): the total value of the shares that a registered company is authorized to issue in order to raise capital.

average: 1 (in marine insurance). A loss or damage arising from an event at sea. 2. A reduction in the amount payable under an insurance policy in respect of a partial loss of property. All marine insurance policies are subject to average, and other policies may be subject to it if they contain express provision to that effect.

average adjuster: someone skilled in the law of marine insurance who is able to assess claims and decide who will bear the loss involved.

'B' shares: see **'A' shares**.

back freight: the sum payable by the owner of freight to get it back when he either does not, or cannot, take delivery of it at the specified time and the ship's master either takes it back to the port of loading or transfers it to another port.

backwardation: the percentage paid by a seller of *shares for the privilege of postponing delivery of them till the next account or to any other future date.

bailiff: an officer of a court (usually a county court) concerned with the serving of the court's processes and the enforcement of its orders.

bailiwick: the area within which a *bailiff or *sheriff exercises jurisdiction.

bailment: the transfer of the possession of goods by the owner (the *bailor*) to another (the *bailee*) for a particular purpose.

balance sheet: a document presenting in summary form a true and fair view of a company's financial position at a particular time.

Baltic Exchange: The proper name for this, one of the largest freight markets in the world, is the *Baltic Mercantile and Shipping Exchange*. It is situated in the City of London and deals with the chartering of ships and aircraft and the conveyancing of freight by them. The Exchange also includes a commodity market and a *futures market that deals in barley.

Bank of England: the country's central bank. It manages the service of the public debt, receives and accounts for the revenue when collected, and issues legal tender notes to an amount automatically regulated. It also acts as a normal bank for the Government, the commercial banks (*see* clearing banks), central banks in other countries, and a number of international organizations.

bankruptcy: the state of a person who has been adjudged by a court to be insolvent (*compare* winding-up). The court orders the compulsory administration of a bankrupt's affairs so that his assets can be fairly distributed among his creditors. To declare a debtor to be bankrupt a creditor or the debtor himself must make an application, known as a *bankruptcy petition*, either to the High Court or to a county court.

banns: the public announcement in church of an intended marriage. Banns must be published for three successive Sundays if a marriage is to take place in the Church of England other than by religious licence or a superintendent registrar's certificate.

Bar: see **barrister**.

bareboat charter: the term that covers the charter of a ship in which the charterer pays all the expenses during the time the ship is on hire to him. The shipowner provides the ship only; the charterer employs the crew, and pays all the running costs including fuel and insurance.

bargain: the term used on the *Stock Exchange when *shares are bought or sold.

barratry: 1. Any act committed wilfully by the master or crew of a ship to the detriment of its owner or charterer. 2. The former common-law offence, now abolished, of habitually raising or inciting disputes in the courts.

barrister: a legal practitioner admitted to plead at the *Bar. A barrister must be a member of one of the four *Inns of Court, by whom he is *called to the Bar* when admitted to the profession. The primary function of barristers is to act as advocates for parties in courts or tribunals, but they also undertake the writing of opinions and some of the work preparatory to a trial. With rare exceptions a barrister may only act upon the instructions of a *solicitor, who is also responsible for the payment of the barrister's fee.

bear: the term used on the *Stock Exchange for a dealer on the stock market who sells *shares he does not possess for delivery at a future date, anticipating that the price of the share will have fallen by the date he is obliged to buy and deliver them.

beneficial owner: an owner who is entitled to the use of land or its income for his own benefit.

bill of lading: a document acknowledging the shipment of a consignor's goods for carriage by sea.

blight notice: a statutory notice by which an owner-occupier can require a public authority to purchase land that is potentially liable to compulsory acquisition by them and therefore cannot be sold at full value on the open market.

bond: 1 (legal). A deed by which one person commits himself to another to do something or refrain from doing something. If it secures the payment of money, it is called a *common money bond*; a bond giving security for the carrying out of a contract is called a *performance bond.* 2. The term used in Britain to describe government or local authority fixed-interest securities. In the United States it is sometimes used for company loans.

bonded goods: goods from overseas which have been placed in a bonded warehouse pending payment of duties owed on them, or their re-exportation.

bonus issue (capitalization issue): a method of increasing a company's issued capital (*see* authorized capital) by issuing further shares to existing company members. These shares are paid for not by the shareholders but out of undistributed profits of the company or the *share premium account. The bonus issue is made to shareholders in proportion to their existing shareholding.

books of account: records that disclose and explain a company's financial position at any time and enable its directors to prepare its *accounts. The books, which registered companies are required to keep by the Companies Act, should reveal, on a day-to-day basis, sums received and expended, together with details of the transaction, assets and liabilities, and, where appropriate, goods sold and purchased.

bourse: the French equivalent of the Stock Exchange.

breach of contract: an actual failure by a party to a contract to perform his obligations under that contract or an indication of his intention not to do so. An indication that a contract will be breached in the future is called *repudiation* or an *anticipatory breach*, and may be either expressed in words or implied from conduct. Such an implication arises when the only reasonable inference from a person's acts is that he does not intend to fulfil his part of the bargain.

breach of the peace: a riot, affray, assault, battery, or any other act in which people's safety is put at risk. It is an offence to use threatening, abusive, or insulting words or behaviour in a public place that are intended or likely to provoke a breach of the peace.

breakdown of marriage: the deterioration of a marriage to such an extent that the court will grant a decree of *divorce. The breakdown must be *irretrievable*, which can be shown only by proof of one of the following facts: (1) that the other spouse has committed adultery *and* that the petitioner finds it intolerable (either because of the adultery or for some other reason) to live with him (or her); (2) that the other spouse has behaved in such a way that the petitioner (taking into account his (or her) particular characteristics and circumstances) cannot reasonably be expected to live with her (or him) (*see* unreasonable conduct); (3) that the other spouse has deserted the petitioner for at least two years (*see* desertion); (4) that the spouses have lived apart for at least two years (if the other spouse agrees to the divorce petition) or for five years (even if the other spouse does not agree to the petition). The spouses may live together for up to six months during the period of separation without breaking the period of living apart, but the time spent together cannot itself count towards the period of living apart.

bull: the term used on the *Stock Exchange for a dealer on the stock market who buys *shares at a fixed price which he must pay at an agreed future date, anticipating that by the time he has to pay for them they will have risen in price. A *bull market* is therefore one where it is anticipated that the price of shares will rise.

call: a demand by a company under the terms of the articles of association or an ordinary resolution requiring company members to pay up fully or in part the nominal value of their shares.

capital-intensive: the term used for those industries where the ratio of capital used for production to the workforce employed is high.

care order: a court order committing the care of a child to a local authority. It entitles a local authority to keep the child in its care despite any claims by a parent or guardian, and it has the same powers and duties as a parent or guardian, although it cannot alter the child's religion or give consent to his adoption.

cartel: 1. An agreement between belligerent states for certain types of non-hostile transactions, especially the exchange of prisoners. 2. A national or international association of independent enterprises formed to create a *monopoly in a given industry.

case law: the body of law set out in judicial decisions, as distinct from *statute law. *See also* precedent.

***casus belli*:** (Latin: occasion for war) an event giving rise to war or used to justify war. The only legitimate *casus belli* now is an unprovoked attack necessitating self-defence on the part of the victim.

caveat: (from Latin: let him beware) a notice, usually in the form of an entry in a register, to the effect that no action of a certain kind may be taken without first informing the person who gave the notice (the *caveator*).

change of name: a person may change his surname simply by using a different name with sufficient consistency to become generally known by that name. A change is normally given formal publicity (e.g. by means of a statutory declaration, deed poll, or newspaper advertisement), but this is not legally necessary. A young child, however, has no power to change his surname, nor does one parent have such a power without the consent of the other, even if that parent has sole custody of the child. (An injunction may be sought to prevent a parent from attempting to change a child's name unilaterally.) When a mother has remarried after divorce or is living with another person, and wishes to change the name of the child to that of her new partner, a court order may be obtained and the welfare of the child will be the first and paramount consideration.

chartered accountant: an accountant who is a member of the Institute of Chartered Accountants, which governs the profession.

chartered company: a company which has been created by royal charter.

charter-party: a written contract by which a person (the *charterer*) hires from a shipowner, in return for the payment of freight, the use of his ship or part of it for the carriage of goods by sea. The hiring may be either for a specified period (a *time charter*) or for a specified voyage or voyages (a *voyage charter*), and the charterer may hire the ship for carrying either his own goods alone or the goods of a number of shippers, who may or may not include himself.

chattel: any property other than freehold land.

chief executive: the term describing someone who has the overall responsibility for an organization on a day-to-day basis. The chief executive of a *limited company is normally the *managing director.

Chiltern Hundreds, stewardship of the: an appointment that, as a nominal office of profit under the

Crown, disqualifies its holder from membership of the House of Commons. Although the appointment has been a sinecure since the 18th century, it has been retained as a disqualifying office to enable members to give up their seats during the lifetime of a parliament (a member cannot by law resign his seat). After obtaining the stewardship—an application for which is never refused—the member resigns the office so as to make it available for re-use. A second office used for the same purpose is the stewardship of the *Manor of Northstead*.

c.i.f. (cost, insurance, freight) contract: a type of contract for the international scale of goods by which the seller agrees not only to supply the goods but also to make a contract of carriage with a sea carrier, under which the goods will be delivered at the contract port of destination, and a contract of insurance with an insurer, to cover them while they are in transit.

circumstantial evidence (indirect evidence): evidence from which the judge or jury may infer the existence of a fact in issue but which does not prove the existence of the fact directly.

citizen's arrest (private arrest): an arrest by a private person. This is permitted (1) if someone either is or is suspected of being in the process of committing an *arrestable offence; (2) if someone is suspected of having committed an arrestable offence; (3) to prevent a *breach of the peace; (4) if an *indictable offence is being committed in the night; and (5) when statute expressly gives a private person the power to arrest. A person who makes a citizen's arrest must take the arrested person to the police or a magistrate as soon as is practicable.

civil law: 1. The law of any particular state, now usually called municipal law. 2. Roman law. 3. A legal system based on Roman law, as distinct from the English system of *common law. 4. Private law, as opposed to criminal, administrative, military, and ecclesiastical law.

clearing banks: the term used for the six commercial banks which are members of the Bankers' Clearing House, which is an organization to deal with what one bank owes another as a consequence of its customers issuing cheques. Settlement is made by way of accounts which are held by the commercial banks at the *Bank of England. The names of the commercial banks are: Lloyds, Midland, Barclays, National Westminster, Coutts & Co., and Royal Bank of Scotland.

codicil: a document supplementary to a will, which is executed with the same formalities under the Wills Act 1837 (*see* execution of will) and adds to, varies, or revokes provisions in the will. A codicil normally republishes a will (*see* republication of will) and may revive a will that has been revoked if that is the testator's clear intention.

collateral: 1. Adjective describing the relationship between people who share a common ancestor but are descended from him through different lines of descent. 2. Ancillary: subordinate but connected to the main subject, etc. 3. Security that is additional to the main security for a debt.

collective bargaining: a mode of fixing the terms of employment by means of bargaining power between an organized body of employees, usually a trade union, and an employer, or association of employers.

collusion: an improper agreement or bargain between parties that one of them should bring proceedings against the other.

common law: the part of English law based on rules developed by the royal courts during the first three centuries after the Norman Conquest in 1066 as a system applicable to the whole country, as opposed to local customs. The Normans did not attempt to make new law for the country or to impose French law on it; they were mainly concerned with establishing a strong central administration and safeguarding the royal revenues, and it was through machinery devised for these purposes that the common law developed. Royal representatives were sent on tours of the shires to check on the conduct of local affairs generally, and this involved their participating in the work of local courts. At the same time there split off from the body of advisers surrounding the king (the *curia regis*) the first permanent royal court—the Court of Exchequer, sitting at Westminster to hear disputes concerning the revenues. Under Henry II, who reigned between 1154 and 1189 and who was principally responsible for the development of the common law, the royal representatives were sent out on a regular basis. Their tours were known as *circuits* and their functions began to be exclusively judicial whereby they took over the work of the local courts. In the same period there appeared at Westminster a second permanent royal court, the Court of Common Pleas. These two steps mark the real origins of the common law, for the judges of the Court of Common Pleas superimposed a single system on the multiplicity of local customs so successfully that, as early as the end of the 12th century, reference is found in court records to the custom of the kingdom. In this process they were joined by the judges of the Court of Exchequer, which began to exercise jurisdiction in many cases involving disputes between subjects rather than the royal revenues, and by those of a third royal court that gradually emerged—the Court of the King's Bench. The common law was subsequently supplemented by *equity, but it remained separately administered by the three courts of common law until they and the Court of Chancery were replaced by the *High Court in the 1870s.

common-law marriage: 1. A marriage recognized as valid at common law although not complying with the usual requirements for marriage. Such marriages are only recognized today if (1) they are celebrated outside England and there is no local form of marriage reasonably available to the parties or (2) they are celebrated by military chaplains in a foreign territory, or in a ship in foreign waters, and one of the parties to the marriage is serving in the Forces in that territory. 2. Loosely, the situation of two unmarried people living together as husband and wife.

Companies Registry: the office of the Registrar of Companies (*see* registration of a company).

completion: (in land law) the point at which ownership of lands that is the subject of a contract for its sale changes hands. The purchaser hands over any unpaid balance of the price in exchange for the title deeds and a valid conveyance of the land to him.

compound interest: this is the interest earned on a sum of money which, unlike simple interest, has previous interest payments added to it. Simple interest over two years on £100 at 10% per year accumulates the sum of £110 after the first year and £120 after the second. With compound interest the amount accumulated after the first year is again £110, but after the second it is £121, i.e. 10% of £110, not 10% of £100 as in simple interest.

comprehensive insurance: the term used in motor *insurance where the insured is covered not only for *third-party insurance but for every possible loss or damage from an accident while he, or a person with his permission, is driving the car that is insured. Some insurance companies stipulate that the insured names the people who will be driving the vehicle to be insured, and an additional premium may be charged if these names extend beyond the insured and his or her spouse.

compulsory winding-up by the court: a procedure for *winding up a company that is initiated when a *petition for winding-up* is presented to the court, usually by a creditor or a qualified *contributory. The usual ground for the petition is that the company is unable to pay its debts.

conjugal rights: the rights of either spouse of a marriage, which include the right to the other's consortium (company), cohabitation (sexual intercourse), and maintenance during the marriage. There is, however, no longer any legal procedure for enforcing these rights.

Consols: government consolidated stock that is issued at no fixed times at differing rates of interest. They have no *maturity (repayment) date.

constructive desertion: behaviour by one spouse causing the other to leave the matrimonial home. If the behaviour is so bad that the party who leaves is forced to do so, it is the spouse who stays behind who is considered, in law, to have deserted, and not the spouse who actually left.

constructive dismissal: termination of a contract of employment by an employee because his employer has shown that he does not intend to be bound by some essential term of the contract. Although the employee has resigned, he has the same right to apply to an industrial tribunal as one who has been unfairly dismissed by his employer. *See also* unfair dismissal.

constructive total loss: a loss of a ship or cargo that is only partial but is treated for the purposes of a *marine insurance policy as if it were an actual total loss.

contango rate: the percentage which the buyer of *shares pays to the seller to postpone transfer to the next settling day.

contempt of court: 1 (civil contempt). Disobedience to a court judgement or process, e.g. breach of an injunction or improper use of discovered documents. 2 (criminal contempt). Conduct that obstructs or tends to obstruct the proper administration of justice.

contract note: a note issued by *stockbrokers as proof that *shares have been bought or sold.

contributory: any of the past or present members of a company, who are potentially liable to contribute to the company's assets in the event of a *winding-up.

convertible loan stock: this is stock that companies sometimes issue which on a given date can be converted to ordinary or preference *shares.

conveyancing: the procedures involved in validly creating, extinguishing, and transferring ownership of interests in land.

copyright: the exclusive right to reproduce or authorize others to reproduce artistic, dramatic, literary, or musical works. Copyright lasts for the holder's lifetime plus 50 years from the end of the year in which he died; it can be assigned or transmitted on death.

coroner: an officer of the Crown whose principal function is to investigate deaths either by ordering a post-mortem examination or conducting an *inquest.

cost-benefit analysis: a systematic way of evaluating and analysing a planned course of action where social and economic factors, as much as profit and loss, are usually involved. Cost-benefit analysis, therefore, is normally undertaken on large projects affecting the local population, traffic flow, accident rate, and other environmental considerations.

covenant: see **deed**.

cover note: a temporary document which an insurance company issues to someone with whom it has a contract until the policy has been drawn up and delivered.

credit transfer: a method of paying an amount of money from one bank account to another through the banking system without issuing a cheque.

critical path analysis: a type of planning used to analyse highly complex undertakings. The project is broken down into a step-by-step operation so that each part can be carefully examined to make sure that it is not only efficient and economically viable in itself but relates logically and systematically to the next step.

'cum' dividend and 'ex' dividend: the price of a *share is quoted 'cum div' or 'ex div' and this shows that it either does, or does not, have the right to receive the next dividend.

damages: a sum of money awarded by a court as compensation for a *tort or a breach of contract. Damages are awarded as a lump sum. *Substantial damages* are given when actual damage has been caused, but *nominal damages* may be given for breach of contract and for some *torts in which no damage has been caused.

debenture: a document that states the terms of a loan, usually to a company. A debenture may be issued to an individual creditor (a *debenture holder*) or a debenture trust deed may be drawn up in favour of trustees for a large group of creditors (*debenture stock holders*).

decree absolute: a decree of *divorce, nullity, or presumption of death that brings a marriage to a legal end, enabling the parties to remarry. It is usually issued six weeks after the *decree nisi, unless there are exceptional reasons why it should be given sooner.

decree nisi: a conditional decree of *divorce, nullity, or presumption of death. For most purposes the parties to the marriage are still married until the decree is made absolute.

deed: a written document that is signed, sealed, and delivered. If it is a contractual document, it is referred to as a *contract under seal* (or *specialty*). A promise contained in a deed is called a *covenant* and is binding. Covenants may be either express or implied.

deed poll: a deed to which there is only one party; for example, one declaring a change of name.

***de facto*:** (Latin: in fact) existing as a matter of fact rather than of right.

defamation: the *publication of a statement about a person that tends to lower his reputation in the opinion of right-thinking members of the community or to make them shun or avoid him.

demurrage: liquidated damages payable under a charter-party at a specified daily rate for any days required for completing the loading or discharging of cargo after the *lay days have expired. Liquidated damages are the sum fixed in advance by the parties to a contract as the amount to be paid in the event of a breach of that contract.

desertion: the failure by a husband or wife to cohabit with his or her spouse. Desertion usually takes the form of physically leaving the home, but this is not essential: there may be desertion although both parties live under the same roof, if all elements of a shared life (e.g. sexual intercourse, eating of meals together) have ceased. Desertion must be a unilateral act carried out against the wishes of the other spouse, with the intention of bringing married life to an end. If it continues for more than two years, it may be evidence of *breakdown of marriage and entitle the deserted spouse to a decree of *divorce (*see also* constructive desertion).

dilapidations: at the end of a long-term lease the landlord can demand from the leaseholder that he return the land or building he has been leasing to the same condition they were in at the start of the tenancy. This obligation is known as liability for dilapidations.

direct debiting: this is the same as a standing order except that when signing a direct debit form the debtor is authorizing that the amount being debited from his account can fluctuate according to the amount the creditor requires.

director: an officer of a company appointed by or under the provision of the *articles of association. Directors may have a contract of employment with the company (*service directors* and *managing directors) or merely attend board meetings (*non-executive directors*).

dividend: the payment made by a company to its shareholders out of its distributable profits. It is calculated as a percentage of nominal value of their *shares, which is fixed for holders of preference shares and fluctuating for holders of ordinary shares.

divorce: the legal termination of a marriage and the obligations created by marriage, other than by a decree of nullity or presumption of death. Proceedings are initiated by either spouse filing a *petition for divorce*, stating the facts that have led to the breakdown of the marriage. Normally a divorce will not be given within the first three years after celebration of the marriage (except in cases of exceptional hardship or depravity). A divorce may only be given upon proof that the marriage has broken down completely (*irretrievable breakdown*), which may evidenced by a number of facts (*see* breakdown of marriage).

double-entry book-keeping: this is the basic method of modern book-keeping. There is a debit side and a credit side for each account, with the receiver being credited and the giver debited. These are recorded in the *ledger* and they should always balance. Cash account is often accounted for separately, in a *cash book*.

Dutch auction: unlike an ordinary *auction, where the auctioneer begins with a low price for the object being auctioned, the auctioneer in a Dutch auction starts at a very high price and then reduces it until he finds a bidder.

E. & O.E. (errors and omissions excepted): these initials are sometimes added to the bottom of an invoice to indicate to the receiver that any errors or omissions that are in it will be corrected at a later date.

easement: a right enjoyed by the owner of land (the *dominant tenement*) to a benefit from other land (the *servient tenement*). An easement benefits and binds the land itself and therefore continues despite any change of ownership of either dominant or servient tenement, although it will be extinguished if the two tenements come into common ownership.

embezzlement: the dishonest appropriation by an employee of any money or property given to him on behalf of his employer. Before 1968 there was a special offence of embezzlement; it is now, however, classified as a form of theft.

endowment assurance: see **life assurance**.

engagement to marry: an agreement, verbal or in writing, to marry at a future date. Such agreements are no longer treated as enforceable legal contracts, and no action can be brought for breach of such an agreement or to recover expenses incurred as a result of the agreement. Engagement rings are deemed to be absolute gifts and cannot be recovered when an engagement is broken. There is a special statutory provision that property rights between engaged parties (for example, in respect of a house purchased with a view to marriage) are to be decided in accordance with the rules governing property rights of married couples.

equity: 1. That part of English law originally administered by the Lord Chancellor and later by the Court of Chancery, as distinct from that administered by the courts of *common law. 2. An equitable right or claim. 3. A share in a limited company.

escalation clause: the term for a clause which is sometimes added to a contract where its completion is going to take some years and where prices could therefore be affected by inflation or market forces. The clause lays out by what percentage the costs in the contract are allowed to rise if they are affected by these factors.

escrow: the name given to a written document held by a third party which involves two other parties, the writer and the recipient. The recipient is not entitled to receive the document, which may be a contract, deed, or bond, until he has carried out satisfactorily what is required of him, e.g. performed some task or paid over a sum of money. While the document is in the possession of the third party it is known as being *in escrow*. The document can also be delivered to the recipient, but it does not become operative until a condition in it is complied with.

estoppel: a rule of evidence or a rule of law that prevents a person from denying the truth of a statement he has made or from denying facts that he has alleged to exist.

exchange of contracts: the point at which a purchaser of land exchanges a copy of the sale contract signed by him for an identical copy signed by the vendor. At that point the contract becomes legally binding on both parties.

'ex' dividend: see **'cum' dividend**.

execution of will: the process by which a testator's will is made legally valid. Under the Wills Act 1837 the will must be signed at the end by the testator or by someone authorized by him, and the signature must be made by the testator in the presence of at least two witnesses, present at the same time, who must themselves sign the will in the testator's presence. A will witnessed by a beneficiary is not void, but the gift to that beneficiary is void.

executor: a person appointed by a

will to administer the testator's estate.

factoring: the term given to a producer of goods who, for various reasons, chooses to have his invoice paid by a *factor*, usually a finance company, instead of waiting for his customer to pay. In this way the producer is paid promptly and is relieved of such matters as debt collection as this becomes the factor's responsibility. Naturally, the factor charges a commission for this service.

fair comment: the defence to an action for *defamation that the statement made was fair comment on a matter of public interest.

flags of convenience: the term given to the flags of those countries, principally Costa Rica, Honduras, Panama, and Liberia, which allow merchant ships of other nationalities to be registered there instead of in their country of origin, or in the country where their owners carry on their businesses. This is done to avoid taxes, and trade union regulations and wages, which are not, for the most part, in force in the countries named above. A merchant ship always flies the flag of the country in which it is registered.

flotation: a process by which a *public company can, by an issue of securities (shares or debentures), raise capital from the public. It may involve a *prospectus issue*, in which the company itself issues a prospectus inviting the public to acquire securities; an *offer for sale*, in which the company sells the securities on offer to an *issuing house*, which then issues a prospectus inviting the public to purchase the securities from it; or a *placing*, whereby an issuing house arranges for the securities to be taken up by its clients in the expectation that they will ultimately become available to the public on the open market.

flow chart: a diagram showing the movement of goods, materials, or personnel in any complex system of activities (as an industrial plant) and the sequence of operations they perform or processes they undergo. It can also be a diagram in which conventional symbols show the sequence of actual or possible operations and decisions in a data-processing system or computer program.

f.o.b. (free on board) contract: a type of contract for the international sale of goods in which the seller's duty is fulfilled by placing the goods on board a ship.

foreclosure: a remedy available to a mortgagee when the mortgagor has failed to pay off a *mortgage by the contractual date for redemption.

franchise: 1. A percentage below which the marine *underwriter incurs no responsibility. 2. The authorization granted to an individual or group by a company to sell its products or services in a particular area.

free from particular average: a term used in the *marine insurance market for a policy which excludes responsibility for all losses except a total loss and *general average loss.

free of all average: a term used in the *marine insurance market for a policy which will pay only in the case of a total loss.

fringe benefits: the term used to describe benefits a company can give an employee without the employee being taxed for them, or where the tax is minuscule in relation to the benefit's worth to the employee. A company car is an obvious example, private health care and cheap mortgages two others.

futures: the term used to describe a deal in the commodity market where a dealer contracts to buy or sell a commodity at a fixed price at a fixed future date.

garnishee: a person who has been warned by a court to pay a debt to a third party rather than to his creditor.

garnishee proceedings: a procedure by which a judgement creditor may obtain a court order against a third party who owes money to, or holds money on behalf of, the judgement debtor. The order requires the third party to pay the money, or part of it, to the judgement creditor.

gazumping: the withdrawal by a vendor from a proposed sale of land in the expectation of receiving a higher price elsewhere, after agreeing the price with a purchaser but before a legally binding contract has been made.

general average loss: the term used in the *marine insurance market whereby it is agreed that the loss or damage of any cargo at sea is shared by all and not just by the owner of that particular cargo, provided the cause of the loss is a risk common to all. If, for example, some cargo had to be thrown overboard to prevent the ship from sinking then the ship's owners and the owners of all the other cargo would contribute towards the cost of the lost cargo. It would then be up to each to claim what they have been obliged to pay from their own insurance companies.

general meeting: a meeting of company members whose decisions can bind the company. Certain *reserved powers*, specified by the Companies Act, can only be exercised by a general meeting.

gilt-edged securities: fixed-interest securities which are issued, or guaranteed, by the British government, and which are, in theory at least, without any financial risk.

gold standard: many countries used to use this monetary system whereby the value of the standard unit of currency was the equivalent of a fixed weight of gold and could be changed for it at any time.

gross profit: the amount of money made on the selling of goods over and above the cost of their manufacture. Gross profit does not take into account such costs as selling the goods, transporting them, office overheads, etc. When these are deducted from the gross profit the amount remaining is the net profit.

government securities: see **gilt-edged securities**.

guarantee: see **indemnity**.

half commission man: the term used on the *Stock Exchange for a person who introduces clients to a *stockbroker in return for a share in the broker's commission.

hammered: when a *stockbroker is hammered it means he cannot meet his debts. It is thus termed because a *Stock Exchange waiter makes three blows with a hammer before the name of the broker is announced.

head lease: when the freeholder of a property grants a lease, this is termed a head lease if the leasor then sub-leases the property or part of it.

hearsay evidence (second-hand evidence): evidence of the oral statements of a person other than the witness who is testifying and statements in documents offered to prove the truth of what was asserted. In general, hearsay evidence is inadmissible, but this principle is subject to numerous exceptions.

hereditament: 1. Real property. *Corporeal hereditaments* are tangible items of property, such as land and buildings. *Incorporeal hereditaments* are intangible rights in land, such as *easements. 2. A unit of land that has been separately assessed for rating purposes.

High Court of Justice: a court created by the Judicature Acts 1873–5, forming part of the Supreme Court of Judicature. It is divided into three divisions: the Queen's Bench Division, Chancery Division, and Family Division.

holding company: see **subsidiary company**.

***in camera*:** (Latin: in the chamber) in private. A court hearing must usually be public, but the public may be barred from the court or the hearing may continue in the judge's private room in certain circumstances.

incorporation: the formation of an association that has *corporate personality*, i.e. a personality distinct from those of its members. A corporation, such as a company, has wide legal capacity: it can own property and incur debts. A company is usually incorporated by registration under the Companies Acts but there are other methods, such as by royal charter or a private Act of Parliament.

indemnity: an agreement by one person (X) to pay another (Y) sums that are owed, or may become owed, to him by a third person (Z). It is not conditional on the third person defaulting on the payment, i.e. Y can sue X without first demanding payment from Z. If it is conditional on the third person's default (i.e. if Z remains the principal debtor and must be sued for the money first) it is not an indemnity but a *guarantee.* Unlike a guarantee, an indemnity need not be evidenced in writing.

indent: the term used to describe an order for materials or goods that are required. In the United States an *indent house* is an import company which has a specialized knowledge of overseas suppliers.

indenture: formerly a *deed, generally one creating or transferring an estate in land (e.g. a conveyance or a lease), but nowadays more often used as a term for a written agreement between an apprentice and his master.

index-linked: the term used to describe the process of adding an appropriate sum of money to capital which pays a regular income or a lump sum at the end of a fixed period. The sum added is dependent on the variations of a given index, normally the retail price index. This is done to maintain the real value of the investment.

index-linked policies: the term used when a *life assurance policy, a pension, etc. is linked to a specific index, usually the retail price index, so that the assured sum maintains its real value.

indictable offence: an offence that may be tried by jury in the Crown Court.

inflation accountancy: the term given to a system of accounting (*see* accounts) which tries to present a company's accounts in such a way that inflation is one of the factors in assessing that company's financial position. It is especially pertinent during times of high inflation which tends to distort profit margins and the true value of assets.

injunction: a remedy in the form of a court *order addressed to a particular person that either prohibits him from doing or continuing to do a certain act (a *prohibitory injunction*) or orders him to carry out a certain act (a *mandatory injunction*).

***in loco parentis*:** (Latin: in place of a parent) used loosely to describe anyone looking after children on behalf of the parents, e.g. foster-parents or relatives. In law, however, only a guardian or custodian stands *in loco parentis*; their rights and duties are determined by statutory provisions.

Inns of Court: ancient legal societies situated in central London to which every *barrister must belong.

inquest: an inquiry into a death the cause of which is unknown. An inquest is conducted by a *coroner and often requires the decision of a jury of 7–11 jurors.

insurance: a contract in which one party (the *insurer*) agrees for payment of a consideration (the *premium*) to make monetary provision for the other (the *insured*) upon the occurrence of some event or against some risk. The term *assurance* has the same meaning as insurance but is generally used in relation to events that will definitely happen at some time or another (*see* life assurance), whereas insurance refers to events that may or may not happen.

interim dividend: an interim dividend is paid as an interim payment on the profits earned by *shares. It will, of course, be only a proportion of the *final dividend*, but the amount paid is often an indication of what the final dividend will be.

intestacy: the state in which a person dies without having made a will disposing of all his property.

issued capital: this is the amount of capital that has been actually issued as shares by a company to its members. *See* authorized capital.

jactitation of marriage: a false assertion that one is married to someone to whom one is not in fact married.

Justice of the Peace (JP): a person holding a commission from the Crown to exercise certain judicial functions for a particular *commission area*. Their principal function is to sit as *magistrates but they may also sit in the Crown Court.

kaffirs: the term used on the *Stock Exchange for a group of *shares, especially gold shares, belonging to South African companies.

knock-for-knock agreement: the term used in motor insurance to describe the agreement amongst insurance companies that each should pay the claims of its own clients, whatever the liability. This saves them the time and expense of trying to find out who is to blame when responsibility for an accident is disputed.

laches: neglect and unreasonable delay in enforcing an equitable right. If a plaintiff with full knowledge of the facts takes an unnecessarily long time to bring an action the court will not assist him. Hence the maxim, 'The law will not help those who sleep on their rights.'

lay days: the number of days specified in a charter-party to enable the charterer to load or discharge cargo.

leading question: a question asked of a witness in a manner that suggests the answer sought by the questioner or that assumes the existence of disputed facts to which the witness is to testify.

lease: a contract under which an owner of property (the landlord or *lessor*) grants another person (the tenant or *lessee*) exclusive possession of the property for an agreed period, usually in return for rent.

letter of credit: a document authorizing a bank, at the request of the customer, to pay money to a third party (the *beneficiary*) on presentation of documents specified in the letter.

letters of administration: authority granted by the court to a specified person to act as an administrator of a deceased person's estate when the deceased dies in a state of *intestacy.

letters patent: once an inventor has obtained a *patent for an invention he is granted letters patent.

libel: a defamatory statement made in permanent form, such as writing, pictures, or film (*see* defamation). Radio and television broadcasts for general reception and public performance of plays are treated as being made in permanent form for the purposes of the law of defamation. A libel is actionable in *tort without proof that its *publication has caused special damage (actual financial or material loss) to the person defamed. Libel can also be a crime (*criminal libel*). Proof of publication of the statement to third parties is not necessary in criminal libel and truth is a defence only if the statement was published for the public benefit.

lien: the right of one person to retain possession of goods owned by another until the possessor's claims against the owner have been satisfied. The lien may be *general*, when the goods are held as security for all outstanding debts of the owner, or *particular*, when only the claims of the possessor in respect of the goods held must be satisfied.

life assurance: *insurance providing for the payment of a sum on the occurrence of an event that is in some way dependent upon a human life. In *endowment assurance* the insurer is liable to pay a fixed sum either at the end of a fixed period or at death if the insured should die in the meantime. *Whole life assurance* provides for the payment of a fixed sum on the death of the insured. *Term* (or *temporary*) *assurance* provides for a fixed sum to be paid in the event of the death of the insured within a specified period.

limitation of actions: statutory rules limiting the time within which civil actions can be brought. Actions in simple contract and tort must be brought within six years of the accrual of the cause of action. If the claim is for damages in respect of personal injuries or death the limit is three years from the accrual of the cause of the action or (if later) the plaintiff's date of knowledge of the relevant circumstances, but the court has discretion to extend this period. In actions in respect of land and of contracts under seal the period is twelve years from the accrual of the cause of action.

limited company: a type of company incorporated by registration under the Companies Acts 1948–81 whose members have a limited liability towards their company. In a company limited by shares members must pay the nominal value (*see* authorized capital) of their shares either upon allotment or subsequently (*see* call). In a company limited by guarantee (a *guarantee company*) members must pay an agreed nominal amount (the guarantee) to their company in the event of *winding-up.

liquid assets: the term used for assets which a company or an individual can immediately turn into cash or which they already hold as cash.

liquidation: see **winding-up**.

liquidator: a person who conducts the *winding-up of a company.

liquidity: the term used to describe the speed with which a company or an individual can realize assets for ready cash.

listed company: a company that has entered a *listing agreement* with the *Stock Exchange and whose shares therefore have a *quotation.

litigant: a person who is a party to a court action.

litigation: 1. The taking of legal action by a *litigant. 2. The field of law that is concerned with all contentious matters.

Lloyd's: a society of individual *underwriters that was incorporated by Act of Parliament in 1871. Originally Lloyd's only provided *marine insurance but they now also provide other kinds. The *insurance is undertaken by syndicates of private underwriters (*names*), each of which is managed by a professional underwriter. Each name underwrites a percentage of the business written by the syndicate and has to deposit a substantial sum with the corporation before being admitted as an underwriter. The public deals with the underwriters only through Lloyd's brokers.

loan capital: money borrowed by a company, corporation, or other organization in the form of *debenture stock, corporation stock, or funded debt.

lock-out: the term used when an employer refuses to allow his employees into his place of business to work until they have agreed on proposals he has put to them.

Lord Chief Justice: the chief judge of the Queen's Bench Division of the High Court. He ranks second only to the Lord Chancellor in the judicial hierarchy.

loss leaders: the term used for goods which are sold at no profit or at a loss in order to attract customers who, by the purchase of other goods, will make the trader a bigger profit than he would otherwise have had.

lump-sum award: the form in which damages in *tort are given.

lump system: the term employed in the construction industry where workers are employed not as employees, with all the taxes, restrictions, and regulations that this implies, but as sub-contractors. Sub-contractors are self-employed and therefore receive not a weekly wage but a lump sum when their work is completed.

magistrate: a person qualified to sit in a *magistrates' court. Most magistrates are lay *Justices of the Peace and have no formal legal qualifications. They receive no payment for their services but give their time voluntarily. There are also, however, *stipendiary magistrates in London and other major cities.

magistrates' court: a court consisting of between two and seven *magistrates or a single *stipendiary magistrate exercising the jurisdiction conferred by the Magistrates' Courts Act 1980 and other statutes. The principal function of magistrates' courts is to provide the forum in which all criminal prosecutions are initiated.

maintenance order: a court order providing for payment of sums for the maintenance of a spouse or child.

managing director: a *director to whom management powers have been delegated, either absolutely or subject to supervision, by the other directors of the company under the terms of the articles of association. Managing directors are agents of the company and have wide authority to act on its behalf.

mandate: 1 (in private law). An authority given by one person (the *mandator*) to another to take some course of action. 2 (in international law). The system by which dependent territories were placed under the supervision of mandatory powers by the League of Nations after World War I.

marine insurance: a form of *insurance in which the insurer undertakes to indemnify the insured against loss of the ship (*hull insurance*), the cargo, or any sums paid in freight (*freight insurance*) occurring during a sea voyage. A marine insurance contract may be extended to losses on inland waters or to risks on land that may be incidental to a sea voyage. The risks listed in marine insurance policies include perils of the seas, fire, war perils, jettisons, and *barratry, and the cover may be for a particular voyage, or for a specified voyage, or for a specified time, or both.

market leader: the term used to describe a firm which is the acknowledged leader in producing and/or selling a certain brand of goods which dominates the section of the market at which it is aimed.

marketing: this term is defined by the Institute of Marketing as 'the management function which organizes and directs all those business activities involved in assessing and converting customer purchasing power into effective demand for a specific product or service to the final consumer or user so as to achieve the profit, target, or other objectives set by a company'.

maturity date: the term given to the date when a debt has to be settled or on which a *life assurance policy is paid up.

McNaghten Rules (M'Naghten Rules): rules setting out the conditions under which a defendant may successfully escape conviction on the grounds of insanity.

memorandum of association: a document that must be drawn up when a *registered company is formed and signed by two or more founder members. It states the company's name and registered office, the purpose for which it was formed, the amount of its *authorized capital (if any), and, if applicable, that it is a *limited company.

***mens rea*:** (Latin: a guilty mind) the state of mind that the prosecution must prove a defendant to have had at the time of committing a crime in order to secure a conviction.

merchant banks: unlike *clearing banks merchant banks do not hold cheque accounts for private individuals. Their main business is raising capital for industrial projects at home and overseas, acting as advisers and go-betweens during company takeovers and mergers, and in the financing of international trade.

misfeasance: the negligent or otherwise improper performance of a lawful act.

mitigation: 1. Reduction in the severity of some penalty. 2. Reduction in the loss or injury resulting from a *tort or a breach of contract.

mock auction: an auction during which (1) any lot is sold to someone at a price lower than his highest bid for it; (2) part of the price is repaid or credited to the bidder; (3) the right to bid is restricted to those who have bought or agreed to buy one or more articles; or (4) articles are given away or offered as gifts. The Mock Auctions Act 1961 restricts what articles may be sold in such an auction.

monopoly: a situation in which a substantial proportion of a particular type of business is transacted by a single enterprise or trader.

mortgage: an interest in property created as a form of security for a loan or payment of a debt and terminated on payment of the loan or debt. The borrower, who offers the security, is the *mortgagor*; the lender, who provides the money, is the *mortgagee*.

net book agreement: the term that covers an agreement between book publishers and the Booksellers' Association which prohibits the sale of books below the price set by the publisher.

net profit: see **gross profit**.

no claims bonus: the term used in motor insurance to describe the percentage deducted from the premium when no claims have been made against the policy during a specified period. The deduction can be as much as 60% of the original premium and was introduced to discourage policy holders from making claims for minor damage.

nominee shareholder: a company member who holds the shares registered in his name for the benefit of another. The identity of the person with the true interest may be subject to disclosure under the Companies Act.

notary (notary, public): a legal practitioner, usually a solicitor, who attests or certifies deeds and other documents.

***obiter dictum*:** (Latin: a remark in passing) something said by a judge while giving judgement that was not essential to the decision in the case.

official receiver: the person appointed by the Department of Trade who acts in *bankruptcy matters as interim receiver and manager of the estate of the debtor.

Ombudsman: see **Parliamentary Commissioner for Administration**.

on stream: the term used to describe a factory, or other organization like an oil rig, when it has become fully functional and therefore at least potentially profitable.

order: 1. A direction or command of a court. In this sense it is often used synonymously with judgement. 2. The document bearing the seal of the court recording its judgement in a case. 3. A subdivision of the Rules of the Supreme Court and the County Court Rules.

paper profit: the term used to describe a profit when it has been made but not yet realized. A *share can rise above the price at which it was bought but this difference is only a paper profit until the share has been sold.

Parliamentary Commissioner for Administration (Ombudsman): an independent official appointed under the Parliamentary Commissioner Act 1967 to investigate complaints by individuals or corporate bodies of injustice arising from maladministration by a government department.

parole (release on licence): the conditional release of a prisoner from prison. Anyone sentenced to more than three years' imprisonment may be considered for parole after he has served one year in prison, including the time spent in custody, or one-third of his sentence.

particular average: see **average**.

partnership: an association of two or more people formed for the purpose of carrying on a business. Partnerships are governed by the Partnership Act 1890. Unlike an incorporated company (*see* incorporation), a partnership does not have a legal personality of its own and therefore partners are liable for the debts of the firm, though *limited partners* are only liable to the extent of their investment.

passing off: conducting one's business in such a way as to mislead the public into thinking that one's goods or services are those of another business.

patent: the grant of an exclusive right to exploit an invention.

perjury: the offence of giving false evidence or evidence that one does not believe to be true (even if it is in fact the truth). The offence may be committed by any witness who has taken the oath or affirmed, by the defendant at any stage of the trial, and by an interpreter. Perjury is only committed, however, in judicial proceedings, which include any proceedings before a court, tribunal, or someone with the power to hear evidence on oath. The evidence given must be relevant to the proceedings and must be given with knowledge that it is false, or recklessly.

petty sessions: a court of summary jurisdiction now known as a *magistrates' court.

piece-work: this is the term used to describe the payment of an employee, not by the hour or by the week but by the amount he produces.

PLC (public limited company): see **limited company; public company**.

precedent: a judgement or decision of a court, used as an authority for reaching the same decision in subsequent cases.

preference share: see **share**.

prerogative orders: orders issued by the High Court for the supervision of inferior courts, tribunals, and other bodies exercising judicial or quasi-judicial functions. Until 1938 they were *prerogative writs* but the only one now remaining is habeas corpus.

***prima facie* case:** a case that has been supported by sufficient evidence for it to be taken as proved in the absence of adequate evidence to the contrary.

private company: a type of registered company that cannot offer its securities to the public.

profit-and-loss account: a document presenting in summary form a true and fair view of the company's profit or loss as at the end of its financial year.

pro forma invoice: the term used for the type of invoice which is sent to a customer to pay before he receives the goods specified on the invoice.

promissory note: an unconditional promise in writing, made by one person to another and signed by the maker, to pay a specified sum of money to a specified person either on demand or at a future date.

proscribed organization: an organization or association declared to be forbidden by the Home Secretary under the Prevention of Terrorism Act 1976, because it appears to be concerned with terrorism.

proxy: a person, not necessarily a company member, appointed by a company member to attend and vote instead of him at a company meeting.

publication: 1 (in the law of *defamation). The communication of defamatory words to a person or persons other than the one defamed. In the English law of *tort, publication to at least one other person must be proved. Communication between husband and wife does not amount to publication, but communication by the defendant to the spouse of the plaintiff does. Dictation of a defamatory statement to a secretary or typist is publication. Publication to persons other than the one defamed is not required in Scottish law or in criminal *libel. 2 (in copyright law). The issuing of reproductions of a work or edition to the public. Protection under the Copyright Act 1956 may depend on whether the work has been published.

public company: a type of registered company that can offer its shares to the public (*compare* private company). Its *memorandum of association must state that it is a public company, that its name ends with the words 'public limited company' (*or* PLC), and that its *authorized capital is at least the authorized minimum (£50 000).

putative father: a man alleged to be the father of an illegitimate child.

quantity surveyor: someone who is qualified in assessing the likely cost of materials and labour for a new building.

quotation: a listing of a share price on the *Stock Exchange, which indicates that the *share can be dealt on the Exchange.

R & D expenditure: see **research and development expenditure**.

rateable value: all rateable land and buildings in a local authority's area are given a rateable value assessed by the Inland Revenue. Each year, the local authority fixes its rate, as an amount per pound of rateable value. For example, if the rate fixed for that year is 75p in the pound the rates payable on a property with a rateable value of £100 will be £75.

recommended retail price: this is the price at which the manufacturer recommends the retailer to sell his goods.

registered company: a company incorporated by *registration under the Companies Acts 1948–81. There are several types of registered company (*see* limited company; private company; public company; unlimited company).

registration of a company: the most usual method of forming an incorporated company. Under the Companies Act the following documents must be delivered with the appropriate fee to the *Companies Registry: the *memorandum of association signed by at least two company members, *articles of association (if any), statements relating to the directors, secretary, and the registered office, and a statutory declaration that the Companies Acts have been complied with. The Registrar will then enter the company's name in the companies register and issue a certificate of incorporation.

reinsurance: the procedure in which an insurer insures himself with another insurer against some or all of his liability for a risk that he has himself underwritten in an earlier *insurance contract.

republication of will: the re-execution of a will that has been revoked, or the execution of a *codicil to it, showing the testator's intention that the will should be effective notwithstanding the earlier revocation.

resale price maintenance: this is the term used for the agreement made between the manufacturers and those who sell his goods that the goods shall not be sold below a certain price.

research and development expenditure: the term used in an industrial context to describe work directed on a large scale towards the innovation, introduction, and improvement of products and processes.

restrictive covenant: an obligation created by *deed that curtails the rights of an owner of land; for example, a covenant not to use the land for the purposes of any business. A covenant imposing a positive obligation on the landowner (the covenantor), for example to repair fences, is not a restrictive covenant.

reverse takeover: the term used when a small company takes over a larger organization, almost invariable with its prior agreement. It is usually done for tax or legal reasons.

rights issue: a method of raising share capital for a company from existing members rather than from the public at large. Members are given a right to acquire further shares, usually in proportion to their existing holding, and at a price below the market value of existing shares.

royalties: the sums payable for the right to use someone else's property for the purpose of gain. An author's royalty is a percentage, normally around 10%, of the publisher's *recommended retail price for his book.

sedition: the speaking or writing of words that are likely to incite ordinary people to public disorder or insurrection.

sequestration: a court order in the form of a writ to usually four commissioners (*sequestrators*), ordering them to seize control of a person's property.

share: one of a large number of titles of ownership of an incorporated company but not of its property. A *shareholder* is a member of the company and his name is recorded on the register of members. Shares provide the means by which the members of a company can share in the profits of the company, vote at general meetings, and share in the distribution of the assets on a member's voluntarily *winding-up while at the same time limiting their liability in the case of any kind of winding-up. If a *limited company is forced into liquidation (*see* winding-up) fully paid-up shareholders are not liable for any company debts, although their shareholding itself may become valueless.

Preference shares are usually fixed-interest securities, the holders of which have a prior claim to dividends and return of capital. *Participating preference shares* carry the right to share in any surplus profits or capital. Preference shares are usually cumulative in that if no dividend is declared in one year, holders are entitled to arrears when eventually one is paid. Preference shareholders usually have voting rights but only where it concerns the rights attached to their shares.

Ordinary shares constitute the risk capital of a company, as they carry no prior rights over dividends and returned capital. The ordinary shareholders, however, have other advantages not shared by preference shareholders: if the company is successful and is able to pay high dividends, the bulk of this (after paying the fixed-interest preference shareholders) will be shared by the ordinary shareholders. Again, if the company is successful, the value of the ordinary shares will rise while the preference shares will be pegged to a value determined by current interest rates. Ordinary shareholders, except those holding non-voting 'A' shares, will have full voting rights at company meetings.

Redeemable shares are issued subject to the proviso that they will or may be bought back (at the option of the company or the company member) by the company. They cannot be bought back unless fully paid up, and then only out of profits or the proceeds of a fresh issue of shares made for the purpose.

share premium: the amount by which the price at which a share was issued exceeds its nominal value (*see* authorized capital).

sheriff: the principal officer of the Crown in a county.

slander: a *defamatory statement made by such means as spoken words or gestures, i.e. not in a permanent form. Generally slander is only actionable on proof that its publication has caused special damage (actual financial or material loss), not merely loss of reputation.

sleeping partner: the term given to someone who invests money in a *partnership business but takes no part in the running of it.

solicitor: a legal practitioner admitted to practice under the provisions of the Solicitors Act 1974.

stag: a speculator who applies for a new issue of securities in a public company with the intention of making a quick profit by reselling them if they increase in value within a few days of issue. This will only occur if the issue is oversubscribed, i.e. if there are more applicants for shares than there are shares available.

statute law: the body of law contained in Acts of Parliament.

statutory companies: a company incorporated by a private Act of Parliament.

stipendiary magistrate: a barrister or solicitor of not less than seven years' standing, appointed by the Lord Chancellor to sit in a magistrates' court on a full-time salaried basis.

stockbroker: see **Stock Exchange**.

Stock Exchange: a market in London in which securities in public companies are bought and sold. Only securities that have been granted a *quotation can be dealt in on the Exchange. The Stock Exchange consists of an association of *stockbrokers* and *stockjobbers*. Typically, a prospective buyer or seller of shares approaches a broker, who will negotiate a deal with a jobber. Jobbers maintain holdings of quoted securities and will price them according to demand and available information bearing on the company's prospects. The Council of the Exchange regulates proceedings in order to safeguard both members and the investing public; it has the power to discipline both brokers and jobbers for misconduct.

stockjobber: see **Stock Exchange**.

subpoena: an order to a person to appear in court on a certain day to give evidence.

subsidiary company: a company controlled by another company, its *holding* (or *parent*) *company*, either through shareholding alone or through shareholding coupled with control of the composition of the subsidiary's board of directors.

summary offence: an offence that can only be tried summarily, i.e. before magistrates. Most minor offences are summary.

surrender value: the term used for the amount of money a *life assurance policy holder will receive if he cashes in the policy before its *maturity date.

suspended sentence: a prison sentence that does not take effect immediately.

takeover bid: a technique for effecting the control of a company or by effecting a merger with it. The bidder makes an offer to the members of the target company to acquire their shares in the hope of receiving sufficient acceptances to obtain voting control of the target company.

tap issue: the term given to securities which have been issued by the Treasury direct to chosen recipients and not placed on the market.

tap stock: a term given to stock, primarily *gilt-edged securities, which are always available.

term assurance: see **life assurance**.

testamentary capacity: the ability to make a legally valid will. Persons under 18 years—apart from members of the armed forces on active service—and mental patients do not have testamentary capacity.

third-party insurance: insurance against risks to people other than those that are parties to the policy.

time charter: see **charter-party**.

title deeds: the documents that prove a person's ownership of land and the terms on which he owns it.

tort: (Old French: harm; wrong, from Latin *tortus*, twisted or crooked) a wrongful act or omission for which *damages can be obtained in a civil court by the person wronged, other than a wrong that is only a breach of contract.

treasure trove: items of gold and silver that have been found in a concealed place, having been hidden by an owner who is untraceable. They belong to the Crown by virtue of the royal prerogative.

underwriter: 1. A member of an

insurance company or a *Lloyd's syndicate who decides whether or not to accept a particular risk for a specified premium. 2. An individual, finance company, or issuing house who undertakes for an agreed remuneration to acquire, at their issue price less a discount, those securities of a company that are not taken up by the public during a *flotation.

undischarged bankrupt: a person who has been made bankrupt and who has not yet received an order of discharge from the court. Such a person is disqualified from holding certain offices. He must not obtain credit for more than £50 without informing the creditor that he is an undischarged bankrupt, and he must not carry on a business without disclosing the name under which he was made bankrupt to those who deal with him.

unfair dismissal: the dismissal of an employee that the employer cannot show to be fair.

unit trust: a trust enabling small investors to buy interests in a diversity of companies and other investments.

unlimited company: a type of *registered company whose members have an unlimited liability. Thus on *winding-up the company can make demands upon its members until it has sufficient funds to meet the creditors' claims.

unreasonable conduct: conduct of a respondent that may be evidence that a marriage has broken down irretrievably, entitling the petitioner to a *divorce. Such conduct may not be unreasonable in itself—the real test is whether it is reasonable to expect the petitioner to continue living with the respondent, taking into account the behaviour of both spouses and their particular personalities and characteristics (*see also* breakdown of marriage).

voluntary winding-up (voluntary liquidation): a *winding-up procedure initiated by a special or extraordinary resolution of the company. In a *members' voluntary winding-up*, the directors must make a statutory *declaration of solvency* within the five weeks preceding the resolution. This declaration states that the directors have investigated the affairs of the company and are of the opinion that the company will be able to pay its debts in full within a specified period, not exceeding 12 months from the date of the resolution. The *liquidator is appointed by the company members. In a *creditors' voluntary winding-up*, the creditors can appoint the liquidator.

voyage charter: see **charter-party**.

waiver: the act of abandoning or refraining from asserting a legal right.

ward of court: 1. A minor under the care of a guardian (appointed by the parents or the court), who exercises rights of custody over the child subject to the general control and discretion of the court. 2. A minor in respect of whom a *wardship order has been made and over whom the court exercises parental rights and duties.

wardship: the jurisdiction of the High Court to make a child a *ward of court and assume responsibility for its welfare.

wasting assets: property forming part of a deceased's estate and having a reducing value, e.g. a leasehold interest in land. Unless the will directs otherwise, the personal representatives have a duty to sell such assets.

whole life assurance: see **life assurance**.

will: a document by which a person (called the *testator*) appoints *executors to administer his estate after his death, and directs the manner in which it is to be distributed to the beneficiaries he specifies. To be valid, the will must comply with the formal requirements of the Wills Act 1837 (*see* execution of will) and the testator must have *testamentary capacity when the will is made.

winding-up (liquidation): a procedure by which a company can be dissolved. It may be instigated by members or creditors of the company (*see* voluntary winding-up) or by order of the court (*see* compulsory winding-up by the court). In both cases the process involves the appointment of a *liquidator to assume control of the company from its directors.

without prejudice: a phrase used to enable parties to negotiate settlement of a claim without implying any admission of liability. Letters and other documents headed 'without prejudice' cannot be adduced as evidence in any court action without the consent of both parties.

writ: an order issued by a court in the sovereign's name directing some act or forbearance.

wrongful dismissal: the termination of an employee's contract of employment in a manner that is not in accordance with that contract.

yield: the term given to the amount earned on an investment.

EVERYDAY COMPUTER TERMS

* indicates a separate entry

abort: (of a process) to terminate abnormally on reaching a point from which it is unable to continue to a successful conclusion.
access: (noun) the action of reading and acting upon data.
access: (verb) to gain entry to filed information.
access time: the time taken by a system to retrieve information from storage.
accumulator: a *register holding data on which the *arithmetic and logic unit can perform operations.
acoustic coupler: a type of *modem converting digital data into audio frequency sound signals for transmission down a telephone line.
ADA: (*Trademark*) a high-level programming language developed for the US Department of Defense for control programs, such as navigation.
adder: a digital electronic device enabling two numbers to be added together.
address: (noun) one or more labelled locations within the memory of a computer.
address: (verb) specify a location.
AI: see **artificial intelligence**.
Algol: (= *algo*rithmic *l*anguage) the generic term for a family of high-level programming languages.
algorithm: a set of defined procedures for carrying out a task in a step-by-step manner.
alphanumeric: (adjective) designating any of a set of characters comprising the 26 letters of the Roman alphabet and the arabic numerals 0 to 9.
alphanumeric: (noun) an *alphanumeric character.
alternate: (adjective) designating a key on many computer keyboards which, when pressed in conjunction with one of the character keys, converts the latter into a *function key.
ALU: see **arithmetic and logic unit**.
analog: (adjective) designating properties (e.g. force, voltage, etc.) which vary continuously over time, rather than in discrete steps.
analog computer: a computer operating at least partly with analog properties.
AND gate: a *logic circuit whose output is logic 1 (true) only when all (two or more) inputs are logic 1, and in all other cases the output is logic 0 (false).
APL: (= *a* *p*rogramming *l*anguage) a high-level programming language having a rich set of powerful operators for handling multi-dimensional *arrays.
application software: *software consisting of one or more *applications programs, as opposed to *systems software.
applications program: a program

that enables a particular computer or computer system to carry out a function for the end-user rather than a system-oriented function.

architecture: the general design features of a computer system or a circuit pattern on a *chip as opposed to their *implementation in a specific computer.

archive: (noun) the repository of data transferred by the process of *archiving.

archive: (verb) to transfer (data, a file, etc.) to a lower level of storage, typically from *disk to *magnetic tape.

arithmetic and logic unit (ALU): a part of the *central processing unit of a computer, performing arithmetical and logical operations on data sent to it.

array: an ordered set of data or collection of elements of the same type, indexed by dimension (one, two, or more).

artificial intelligence: the development of programs enabling computers to carry out tasks for which human beings use their intelligence in ways that appear not to be readily definable in terms of formal decision procedures, such as game playing, the understanding of natural language and speech, and acting on visual and auditory perceptions.

ASCII: (pronounced 'ass-key'; = *A*merican *S*tandard *C*ode for *I*nformation *I*nterchange) a standard way of encoding characters and control instructions into a seven-bit *binary code, used in many computers, allowing 128 characters to be coded.

assembler: (1) a program that translates a program written in *assembly language into *machine code; (2) (colloq.) *assembly language.

assembly language: a low-level programming language using a notation that represents *instructions in *machine code in terms that a programmer can easily read and remember.

asynchronous: (adjective) not controlled by time signals, denoting a way of controlling computer operations by which the completion of an operation is the indication that the next is to begin.

attach: (verb) to make a device available for use by a system.

audit trail: a permanent record of every transaction occurring within a computer system, used especially to detect and/or deter violations of security.

backing store: a memory holding information for reference rather than for direct execution, e.g. a *disk.

backup: (noun) a secondary resource duplicating a primary resource in anticipation of its future failure or *corruption.

back up: (verb) copy (a file, etc.) as a *backup.

Backus normal form or **Backus–Naur form:** see **BNF**.

band printer: an impact line-printer in which the font is etched on a steel band.

base: (of a number system) the factor by which the value of a single digit number increases if that digit is moved to the next column to the left, rendering the first column zero (e.g., two for *binary, ten for decimal, sixteen for *hexadecimal, etc.).

BASIC: (=*B*eginner's *A*ll-purpose *S*ymbolic *I*nstruction *C*ode) a high-level programming language widely used, especially for programming personal computers, because of its simplicity.

batch processing: a method of organizing work for a computer system by grouping together similar jobs before inputting them for processing.

baud: (from the name of J. M. E. Baudot) the unit of signalling speed, usually equal to one *bit per second.

baud rate: the number of times per second a system, especially a data transmission channel, changes state.

belt printer: see **band printer**.

benchmark: a problem designed to evaluate the performance of a system.

benchmark test: a test in which the performance of several systems is compared using the same *benchmark.

binary: a numbering system with a *base of two, using only the digits 0 and 1.

binary chop: see **binary search algorithm**.

binary code: a system of coding using the digits 0 and 1.

binary search algorithm: a searching *algorithm in which a *file is arranged in ascending order, the middle item is examined, and the top or bottom part of the file chosen, depending on whether its items are larger or smaller than that sought, the middle item of that part is then examined, and the process repeated until the sought-after item is found or shown to be absent.

bit: (= *b*inary dig*it*) the smallest possible unit of data, a two-state true/false, yes/no, 1/0 alternative.

bit density: the maximum number of *bits stored per unit length of a magnetic recording medium.

bit mapping: a graphics display technique whereby each *pixel corresponds to one or more *bits in the processor's memory.

bit rate: the number of *bits transmitted per second, usually given as b.p.s., bits per second.

block: a collection of data, such as *words, *characters, or *records, stored in adjacent physical positions in memory or on a peripheral storage device.

BNF: (= *B*ackus *n*ormal *f*orm or *B*ackus–*N*aur *f*orm) a widely used formal notation for describing the *syntax of a programming language.

Boolean algebra: (from George Boole) a type of mathematical logic important in computing and reflected in the design of *logic circuits.

boot: (verb) see **bootstrap**.

bootstrap: (noun) a *bootstrap program.

bootstrap: (verb) to enter the *systems software onto a computer system.

bootstrap program: a program, frequently *hardwired into the computer, that loads a longer program, usually the *operating system, when the power is first turned on.

bottom-up development: a method of program development involving building up primitive routines provided by the programming language and using these to construct new elements, themselves to be used for further elements, that are more powerful in the context of the required program.

browse: (verb) (of an unauthorized user) to search *files for information not specifically known to exist.

bubble memory: see **magnetic bubble memory**.

bubble sort: a method of *sorting in which pairs of items that are out of order are interchanged in a series of passes through the file, until no such pairs exist.

buffer: a temporary data memory for accommodating the difference in the rate at which two devices can handle data during a transfer.

bug: an error in a program or a system.

bulk memory: see **backing store**.

bus: two or more conductors in parallel, carrying information from one part of a computer system to another.

byte: a sequence of adjacent *bits (usually eight) operated on by the *central processor as a whole.

C: a high-level *systems programming language developed for the implementation of the *UNIX *operating system.

CAD: see **computer-aided design**.

CAM: see **computer-aided manufacturing**.

capacity: the amount of information that can be held on a *storage device, measured in *words, *bytes, *bits, or *characters.

card: a card storing data or instructions, originally in the form of holes punched in paper, but now also in magnetic strips on, or in a *chip embedded in, a plastic card.

card reader: a machine sensing and translating data, etc. on a *card for further processing.

carriage return: a control code affecting the format of displayed or printed output, shifting the display or print position to the leftmost margin of a new line.

cartridge: a container for protecting and facilitating the use of various computer-related media such as *magnetic tape, *magnetic disk, or printer ink ribbon.

cassette: a container resembling a *cartridge but conventionally limited to a device resembling or interchangeable with an ordinary audio cassette.

cathode-ray tube: an evacuated glass envelope with a heated negative electrode (the cathode) from which a beam of electrons may be directed onto a phosphorescent screen, under an electric field, producing a visible display.

central processing unit (CPU) or **central processor:** the principal operating part of a computer, comprising the *arithmetic and logic unit and the *control unit, together with some associated storage *registers.

chad: the material removed when holes are punched in card or in continuous form paper to produce the tractor holes.

character: (1) an element of a given *character set; (2) a subdivision of a *word, comprising six, seven, or eight *bits, sometimes called a *byte.

character set: the set of characters (e.g. *ASCII, *EBCDIC) handled by a specified machine, usually including graphics characters, *alphanumeric, special and operations characters (e.g. +, −, *, /), and various control characters.

checksum: a simple error detection method consisting of summing the *bits present in a piece of information, appending to it the units part of the result, and comparing this sum digit at a later time or at a different location.

chip: a piece of a *semiconductor, usually silicon, on which an *integrated circuit is manufactured; the entire circuit so formed.

circuit board: a single rigid insulating board on which an electrical circuit has been built.

clear: an *instruction causing a given *register or counter to be set to zero.

COBOL: (= *Co*mmon *B*usiness-*O*riented *L*anguage) a high-level programming language developed and used for commercial *data processing.

CODASYL: (= *Co*nference *on* *D*ata *Sy*stems *L*anguages) a particular formally-defined *database management system for *network databases.

code: (1) any piece of program text written in the programming language; (2) the particular language in which it is written, e.g. *machine code.

coding: the transformation of a detailed design into an actual program.

comment: a part of a program included for the benefit of the reader and ignored by the computer.

compaction: (1) any of a number of methods for reducing unused or unusable space in memory; (2) the removal of redundant data from a *record.

compatibility: (1) the ability of *hardware from one manufacturer to be used with that from another; (2) the ability of *software written on one computer to be *run on another.

compiler: a program that translates a high-level programming language into a low-level one, usually *machine code.

computer: a device or system capable of carrying out a sequence of operations in a distinctly and explicitly defined manner, able to store and manipulate data, and communicate with other computers, devices, and human beings.

computer-aided design (CAD): the application of computer technology to the process of design or the design of a product.

computer-aided manufacturing (CAM): the use of computer techniques for process control, ordering of materials, scheduling, stock control, etc., in manufacturing.

concurrency: the running of two or more processes or programs at the same time, requiring special features in the programming language.

control key: a key which, when used in conjunction with another, activates one or more pre-programmed operations.

controller: circuitry handling the operation of peripheral devices or communication channels.

control unit: a part of the *central processing unit that contains the *registers and other elements necessary for controlling the movement of information between the memory, the *arithmetic and logic unit, and other parts of the machine.

copy: (verb) to duplicate (some stored information) elsewhere in a store or in a different storage device as a guard against the loss or *corruption of important *records.

corruption: the total or partial loss of characters, etc. in stored or transmitted data.

CP/M: (*Trademark* = *c*ontrol *p*rogram for *m*icros) an *operating system for microprocessor-based single-user systems.

CPU: see **central processing unit**.

crash: (noun) a system failure requiring the intervention of the operator and often some maintenance.

crash: (verb) (of a system) to suffer or be caused to suffer a *crash.

CRT: see **cathode-ray tube**.

cursor: a small luminous often flashing symbol on a display screen indicating where the next input will appear.

cylinder: a method of minimizing access time for *records on a *disk pack in which related records are arranged into a notional cylinder by writing them to the same track on different disk surfaces.

daisywheel: a type of impact printer in which the font is formed on the end of spring fingers that extend radially from a central hub.

DASD: see **direct-access storage device**.

data: information as inputted, outputted, stored, or manipulated by a computer system, often viewed as distinct from text, voice, or image because of its highly formatted nature in traditional data-processing applications.

database: a structured arrangement of data in a computer system for user access or for processing by *applications programs.

database management system (DBMS): an integrated *software system with facilities for defining the logical and physical structure of data in a *database and for accessing, entering and deleting data.

data dictionary: a structured description of the entities in a *database as distinct from the raw data held in one.

data entry: the process of using a keyboard or other device to input data directly into a system.

data processing: a class of computer applications involving the storage and processing of large quantities of data on a routine basis, e.g. payroll and personnel records.

DBMS: see **database management system**.

debug: (verb) to identify and remove *bugs from (a system, program, etc.).

deletion: the removal or obliteration of a *record or item of data.

density: a measure of the amount of information per given dimension of a storage medium, such as information recorded per unit length on *magnetic tape, or, for *disks, a fixed number of *bits per *sector, *sectors per track, and tracks per disk.

diagnostic routine: a procedure within a program that is activated when an error is detected, and which attempts to trace the cause of the error in the *software or *hardware.

dialect: the version of a high-level programming language that *runs on a specific computer.

dictionary: a data structure of a set of elements that can support the insertion and deletion of elements as well as a test for membership.

digital: (adjective) of or pertaining to digits; involving only discrete amounts, units, etc. rather than continuous ones (see *analog).

digital computer: a computer operating with digital data.

digitization: the process of representing a continuous variation in a value by a series of discrete values obtained through sampling the value of the continuous variation at intervals.

direct-access storage device (DASD): any of a class of storage devices (e.g. a *disk) that can *access any storage location in any order.

directory: a means of locating data items, usually *files, by establishing a set of links between them and their locations in a *direct-access storage device.

disk: a flat circular plate acting as a storage medium (*see* magnetic disk, optical disk).

disk cartridge: a data storage medium consisting of a single rigid *magnetic disk permanently housed within a protective plastic cover.

disk drive: a peripheral device that can store and retrieve data from *magnetic disks (singly or in a *disk pack) or *optical disks.

diskette: see **floppy disk**.

disk operating system: see **DOS**.

disk pack: a data storage medium consisting of an assembly of rigid *magnetic disks mounted on the same axis with equal spacing.

display: (noun) a device able to *display information, e.g. a *CRT, television, or *VDU.

display: (verb) to make information visible in a temporary form.

distributed database: a *database in which the data is contained within a number of different subsystems, usually in different physical locations.

documentation: a description of the *hardware or *software of a system, designed to facilitate its use and make it more understandable.

DOS: (= *d*isk *o*perating *s*ystem) a set of computer programs chiefly handling the transfer of data between a computer system and *disk storage.

dot matrix printer: a printer in which each character is formed from an array of dots created by transferring ink on the heads of several electromechanically-operated styli.

downtime: the amount of time or the percentage of time a computer system is unavailable for use.

dumb terminal: a *terminal without the capacity to store and manipulate data.

dump: (noun) (1) a *magnetic tape record of the state of the *disks in a system, made periodically; (2) a *printout of the contents of a system's memory when a *crash has occurred.

dump: (verb) to make a magnetic or printed copy of.

EBCDIC: (= *e*xtended *b*inary

*c*oded *d*ecimal *i*nterchange *c*ode) an eight-*bit *character encoding scheme.

EDP: electronic *data processing.

electronic mail: messages sent from one user to one or more other users, held and transported by the computer system.

embedded computer system: any system whose prime function is not that of a computer, but which uses a computer as a component.

emulation: the exact execution on a given system of a program written for a different one, accepting identical data and producing identical results.

emulator: any system enabling *emulation to be carried out.

enable: (verb) to selectively activate a device or function.

enter: an *instruction on some computer systems, often activated by a key so labelled, causing a line of *code to be inserted into a program.

EPROM: (= *e*rasable *p*rogrammable *r*ead-*o*nly *m*emory) a type of *PROM that can be re-programmed in certain circumstances by the user.

error message or **report:** a message displayed when an error is detected in a program or in system operation, often coded to indicate the particular type of error.

exec.: see **execute**.

execute (noun) a key labelled 'execute' in some systems which, when pressed, causes the system to *execute an *instruction or program.

execute: (verb) to carry out an *instruction or program.

expert system: a computer program using the techniques of *artificial intelligence and data acquired previously from human experts, built to help solve problems in areas such as medical diagnosis and mineral prospecting.

external storage: any storage device connected to and controlled by a computer, but not integrated within it, such as *disk drives, etc.

field: a subdivision of a *record consisting of a number of characters, *bytes, words, or codes treated together, e.g. a name, an address, a date, etc.

fifth generation: the next *generation of computers, being planned and designed to have human-like 'intelligence'.

file: a collection of data stored beyond the time of execution of a single *job, often a set of similar or related *records.

file organization: the way in which *records within a *file are organized on the physical medium (*see* sequential file).

file updating: the incorporation of changes to the data in a *file without alteration of its structure or significance.

firmware: *software held in *ROM circuits.

first generation: the earliest *generation of calculating and computing machines designed between 1945 and 1955 and employing electronic tube circuitry, delay line, rotating, or electrostatic memory.

fixed head: one of usually a series of reading or writing *heads in a *disk drive which cannot move relative to the disk centre and are incorporated into a head assembly so that there is one head per track.

flag: a data storage location in the *arithmetic and logic unit, whose value indicates whether a certain condition exists after an arithmetical or logical operation has been performed, and is used as a basis for conditional branching and similar decision processes in running programs.

flip-flop: an electronic circuit exhibiting either of two states, able to switch between these in a reproducible manner, and forming the basis of one-*bit memory circuits when these states correspond to logic 1 and logic 0.

floppy disk: (also called a *diskette) a magnetic information-storage medium with a small flexible *disk, consisting of a polyester base coated with magnetic oxide, enclosed within a stiff envelope having one or more radial slots through which an appropriate *disk drive can read or write onto the disk.

flow chart: a graphical representation of the structure of a program or *algorithm showing the sequence in which operations are carried out, with arrows between differently shaped boxes containing notation describing the action or decision.

footprint: the area of front panel, desk, or floor space occupied by a peripheral device.

format: (noun) the arrangement of the pattern of information recorded, displayed, or printed by a computer system.

format: (verb) (1) to put (data) into a predetermined structure; (2) to divide (a storage medium) so that it is ready to receive data (e.g. divide a *disk into *sectors).

formatter: the *logic circuits that determine the *format of data recorded on magnetic media; a program accepting text with *format instructions embedded in it, which produces a new version of the document in line with these.

FORTH: a high-level programming language, much in use in microcomputing, in which new user-defined program *statements can be used alongside the existing ones.

FORTRAN: (=*for*mula *tran*slation) a high-level programming language widely used for scientific computation and having a notation strongly reminiscent of algebra.

fourth generation: the *generation of computers designed after 1970 and characterized by the use of integrated circuit technology and very large memories.

function key: a key on a keyboard that initiates or will cause the initiation of an operation.

fuzzy logic: a form of traditional logic introduced to model knowledge and human reasoning more closely, in which propositions may have degrees of uncertainty with such truth values as 'not very false', 'not very true', 'true', 'very true', etc.

garbage: unwanted or invalid information in memory, usually the result of *compaction.

gate: see **logic gate**.

generation: an informal system of classifying computer systems, chiefly according to the electronic technology used in their manufacture.

generator: a program that accepts

the definition of an operation and writes a program to accomplish it.

giga-: (symbol **G**) a prefix indicating a multiple of 10^9, one thousand million, or, loosely, 2^{30} (actually 1 073 741 824).

GIGO: (= *g*arbage *i*n, *g*arbage *o*ut) a computing proverb, a program working on incorrect data produces incorrect results.

global: (adjective) designating a *variable that is accessible from all parts of a program.

hacker: a computer enthusiast, especially one who attempts to break into secure computer systems or a programmer whose obsessive tinkering with *systems software is often badly documented and has unfortunate side-effects.

handshaking: a control procedure making it possible for two devices to transfer data across an *interface.

hands on: (adjective) designating the experience of an operator who has actually operated the computer system in question.

hands on: (noun) a mode of operation of a system in which an operator is in control.

hard copy: a permanent, usually printed, copy of data from a system.

hard disk: a *magnetic disk consisting of an aluminium base coated or plated with a magnetic material.

hardware: the physical portion of a computer system including electrical/electronic, electromechanical, and mechanical components.

hardwired: (adjective) denoting circuits that are permanently interconnected to perform a specific function.

hash function: a mathematical function mapping a *key on to a limited set of integers in a regular fashion.

hashing: a technique for rapid searching and look-up of tabular data whereby all the items have unique *keys which yield, via a *hash function, integers (identifying places in the table) that are evenly distributed and range over the table size.

head: a part of a peripheral device, such as the magnetic head in a *disk drive, that is in direct contact with the storage medium and is responsible for writing onto or reading from it.

hex: see **hexadecimal**.

hexadecimal or **hex:** a number system with a *base of sixteen and digits represented by 0 to 9 and A to F, of particular use because of the ease by which eight-*bit binary numbers and their corresponding two-digit numbers in hexadecimal can be interconverted.

hierarchical database: a *database in which data is arranged hierarchically, each *record being 'owned' by another.

high-level (programming) language: a programming language using *statements and control and data structures closely akin to natural human language, and requiring to be translated into *machine code by a *compiler or *interpreter before it can be understood by a computer.

host or **host computer:** a computer that is attached to a *network and provides services other than simply holding or transporting messages.

housekeeping: (adjective) designating a program or system that maintains the internal orderliness of the program or system rather than any external requirements.

housekeeping: (noun) the actions performed by a housekeeping program or system.

IC: see **integrated circuit**.

icon: a schematic representation of a device or process, displayed, often with other such representations, on a *VDU or *monitor to illustrate the range of activities or choices from which a user can make a selection (usually by means of a *mouse), and which is an important technique in making *software user-friendly for the total computer novice.

illegal character: any character not in the *character set of a given machine or programming language.

impact printer: any printer using mechanical impact to print characters on to paper.

implementation: the activity of proceeding from a given design to a working model, or the specific way in which some part of a system fulfils its function.

index: an ordered list containing not the desired value associated with a data item, but a location at which further searching should continue.

information: collections of symbols that may be communicated.

information system: a computer-based system with the capacity to provide *information to users in one or more organizations, for example, an *expert system.

information technology (IT): the modern electronic technology for handling *information, incorporating the whole of computing and telecommunications technology, major parts of consumer electronics, and broadcasting, with applications in industry, commerce, administration, education, medicine, science, the professions, and the home.

input: (noun) the process of putting data into any part of a computer system; (an item of) this data.

input: (verb) to put (data) into a system.

input device: any device transferring data, programs, etc., into a system, most usually by means of a *keyboard.

input/output (I/O): the part of a computer system concerned with the movement of information into or out of the *central processing unit, often involving the translation of this information from one form (e.g. *machine code) into another (e.g. English).

instruction: a description of an operation to be performed by a computer or the word standing for this in a programming language, usually divided into arithmetic-, logic-, or *input/output-related functions, and often distinguished from a *statement, the latter referring to high-level languages only.

integrated circuit (IC): a circuit in which all the components are formed upon a single *chip of *semiconductor, usually silicon, allowing the miniaturization of very complex circuitry.

integrity: the resistance of data to alteration by system errors, usually ensured by frequently copying the *files, which lessens their privacy and security.

intelligent terminal: a *terminal having some processing capability by means of which information may be transferred to and from a larger processing system.

interactive: (adjective) designating a system or mode of working in which there is a direct response to operator instructions as they are *input.

interface: (noun) (1) a boundary between two systems, devices, programs, etc.; (2) the physical connection between devices, usually involving some control circuitry.

interface: (verb) (1) to provide an *interface; (2) to interact.

interpreter: a *processor in many *micros which translates each line of *code into *machine code for immediate execution rather than producing a machine code version of the whole program first (like a *compiler).

I/O: see **input/output**.

IT: see **information technology**.

iteration: the repetition of a process, where the results from one stage form the *input for the next, continued until some preset bound or condition is achieved, which is of particular use in many numerical methods.

job: a set of programs and the data to be manipulated by them; the execution of a set of programs.

joystick: a computer input device consisting of a unit with a small stick which can be used to control the movements of the *cursor on a *VDU.

jump: a point in a program, often conditional on some value, at which the flow of the program shifts to another part of the program; an instance of this.

K or **k:** see **kilo-**.

key: a value used to identify a member of a set, such as *records in a *file; a value used to establish authority to access particular information.

keyboard: an *array of captioned buttons or marked areas on a plane causing the printing of a character on a *VDU etc., or some other action, when depressed.

keypad: a compact, often handheld, version of a *keyboard with only a small number of captioned buttons or pressure-sensitive areas on a plane, which is used in conjunction with data collection equipment or as a means of entering limited information, such as a personal identification number.

key to disk: (designating) a system of data entry in which data entered by a number of keyboard operators is accumulated on *magnetic disk.

key to tape: (designating) a system of data entry in which data entered by a number of keyboard operators is accumulated on *magnetic tape.

keyword: a word or symbol in a programming language having a special meaning for a *compiler or *interpreter of that language (e.g. LET, IF, PRINT, etc. in *BASIC).

kilo-: (symbol **K** or **k**) a prefix indicating a multiple of 10^3 (1000), or, loosely, 2^{10} (actually 1024), often used on its own for kilobytes (e.g. '10k memory', a memory of 10 240 bytes).

label: (1) a short *file on *magnetic tape containing the name and characteristic of the whole tape or the file that follows; (2) a numerical or *alphanumeric identifier associated with a line or *statement in a program.

laser printer: a printer in which the required image is written by a beam of laser light on to a photoconductive drum or band producing charged areas that attract pigment and allowing an image to be formed on paper pressed against the drum or band.

LCD: (= *l*iquid-*c*rystal *d*isplay) a *display used in digital watches, calculators, etc., in which groups of segments containing a normally transparent anisotropic liquid can be selectively made opaque by the application of an electric current, thereby delineating a character.

LED display: (= *l*ight-*e*mitting *d*iode) a *display used in some electronic equipment, consisting of an arrangement of diodes which can be selectively illuminated when an appropriate current is applied, thereby delineating a character.

light pen: a pen-like *input device used with a *VDU or *CRT display, having a photosensitive tip that responds to the peak illumination occurring when the *CRT scanning dot passes its point of focus, and, with some associated *software, can be used to 'draw' shapes, etc. on the display.

line printer: a printer that produces a line of type for every printing cycle rather than one character at a time.

LISP: (= *lis*t *p*rocessing) a high-level programming language employing *list processing and designed for the manipulation of non-numeric data, which is widely used in *artificial intelligence.

list processing: a programming technique for dealing with data structures that consist of similar items which contain the *address or addresses of further items in a list.

load: (verb) (1) to enter (data) into the store of a computer system; (2) to transfer (a program, etc.) from a storage medium to the computer memory.

local: (adjective) designating *variables that are accessible only in a restricted part of a program, such as a *subroutine.

local area network: a communications network consisting of a number of computer systems linked over a small area, such as a single building or site.

location: see **address**.

logic 0, 1: a state in a *logic circuit, high voltage representing true (logic 1) and low voltage false (logic 0).

logical: (adjective) involving or used in the science of reasoning, proof, thinking, or influence; conceptual or virtual, involving conceptual entities, as opposed to physical or actual ones.

logic circuit: an electrical circuit involved in the logical systems of a computer, required to produce specific binary outputs as a result of specific binary inputs, usually accomplished by the use of *logic gates, and which produces what is called the hardware circuitry.

logic gate: a device, usually electronic, which implements an elementary logic function (e.g. *AND, *NOT, *OR gates), having one or two outputs and two to eight inputs, and forming the basis of the *logic circuits of a computer.

log in, log on: (noun) the process by which a user identifies himself to a system.

log in, log on: (verb) to identify oneself to a system, usually by means of a *password.

log off, log out: (noun) the process by which a user ends his use of a computer at one session.

log off, lot out: (verb) to end one's session with a computer.

loop: (1) a sequence of instructions repeated until a required bound or prescribed condition is met, such as agreement with some data element or the completion of a count (*see also* iteration); (2) one configuration of a *local area network, consisting of *terminals or computers connected in a ring.

low-level (programming) language: a programming language directly reflecting the *architecture of the *machine it is used on, having little resemblance to human languages.

M: see **mega-**.

machine: a computer or *processor.

machine code: the *code used in particular *machines for carrying out a set of instructions, which is produced for that machine by a *compiler, *interpreter, or sometimes the operator, working from a high-level programming language.

macro: (= *macro*-instruction) an *instruction in a programming language, usually *assembly language, which is replaced by a sequence of instructions prior to the language being processed by an *assembler or *compiler.

macro-assembler: an *assembler allowing a user to define *macros, specifying their form, arguments, and replacement text, and which, when a *macro is encountered, inserts a particular body of text at various places in a program.

magnetic bubble memory: a type of *non-volatile memory in which data is stored as magnetic bubbles (stable magnetic domains) in, and that can be made to move through, a stationary planar medium, usually a thin layer of complex garnet deposited on a simpler garnet.

magnetic disk: a storage medium in the form of a circular plate coated on one or both sides with a magnetic film, which may be flexible (*see* floppy disk) or rigid (*see* hard disk).

magnetic tape: a storage medium consisting of a magnetic coating on a flexible backing in tape form, which may be wound on reels, sometimes contained within a *cartridge or *cassette.

magtape: see **magnetic tape**.

mailbox: a repository, usually secure, for data transmitted via an *electronic mail system, accessible to the addressee via his own unique identification code.

mainframe: (1) the combination of *central processing unit and primary memory of a computer system; (2) a large computer, originally manufactured in a modular fashion.

main memory: the principal storage associated with the processor of a computer system, from which data can be directly accessed and to which resulting data can be sent and stored prior to transfer to the *backing store or to output.

mass storage: an *on-line *backing store system which is capable of storing larger quantities of data than a conventional backing store, now able to store in the order of several hundred gigabytes.

master–slave system: a system having more than one processor, in which one processor, capable of many different functions, is designated the *master* and all the others the *slaves*.

master tape: a *magnetic tape used unchanged in a data-processing application, containing a primary *file of *records and protected from accidental or deliberate erasure.

matching: the basic mechanism of a *database management system whereby desired *records are identified by comparing the values in the *fields of the records with the data values provided.

matrix: a two-dimensional *array in which each of the elements is indexed by its column and row number.

mega-: (symbol **M**) a prefix indicating a multiple of one million (10^6) or, loosely, a multiple of 2^{20} (actually 1 048 576).

memory: a device or medium that can retain information for subsequent retrieval, most usually held internally in a computer and directly addressed by operating instructions.

memory map: a schematic presentation of the way the *memory of a system is used by a given program, usually indicating what data is stored where.

menu: a displayed list with a single code opposite each item from which a choice can be made by selecting and keying the appropriate code or indicating one's choice by another means, such as a *light pen, *mouse, etc.

menu-driven: (adjective) designating a class of *user-friendly programs presenting the user with a series of options at each stage and usually requiring no more than a simple selection to be made.

micro: a *microcomputer or *microprocessor.

microcircuit: a small *integrated circuit, such as a *microprocessor, generally performing a very complex function.

microcomputer: (1) a computer system using a *microprocessor as its central processing and arithmetic unit; (2) a single *chip containing all the logic elements necessary for a complete computer system, in contrast to a *microprocessor, which requires additional supporting chips.

microprocessor: a *semiconductor *chip or set of chips acting as the *central processing unit of a computer, consisting of at least an *arithmetic and logic unit and a *control unit, and characterized by speed, *word length, *architecture, and its set of *instructions.

minicomputer or **mini:** originally a

computer that could be physically contained within a single cabinet; now a cheap, slow, small-capacity computer, intermediate between a *mainframe and a *micro (the boundary between micros and minis being unclear).

mnemonic (code): *assembly language; an *instruction in assembly language, usually a series of letters, etc. for a particular operation, such as LDA for 'load *accumulator', standing for the binary code actually used by the machine.

mode: the status of the operation and use of a computer system, such as *on-line, *interactive, etc.

modem: (= *mo*dulator–*dem*odulator) a device converting a stream of digital information into an analog signal suitable for transmission down a communication channel, typically a unit allowing the connection of a computer to a telephone line.

modular programming: a style of programming in which a complete program is divided into a set of *modules, each of which is of manageable size, has a well-defined purpose, and a well-defined connection with the outside world.

module: a subdivision of a large program performing a single limited task, such as governing the input or output routines, often called up as a *subroutine by the 'main module' of the program, which chiefly concerns itself with the flow of control between the other modules.

monitor: (1) see *VDU; (2) a set of *systems software concerned with supervising the operation of the computer system.

mouse: a hand-moved device having a transparent panel with a fine cross and several switches, allowing a precise position to be indicated on an appropriately wired tablet; a similar device with wheels generating pulses proportional to the distance moved, often used in conjunction with *menu-driven programs to indicate a particular choice. Its near-hemispherical shape and trailing cable are suggestive of a mouse.

multiplier: a part of the *arithmetic and logic unit used to perform multiplication, often accomplished by repeated use of an *adder.

multitasking: the *concurrent execution of a number of jobs or processes in a computer system.

MVS: (= *m*ultiprogramming with a *v*ariable number of processe*s*) an operating system commonly used on large IBM or IBM-compatible processors.

nested loop: a *loop completely executed during every cycle of another loop within which it is embedded.

nesting: a feature of a programming language in which constructs can be embedded within instances of themselves, e.g. a *nested loop.

network: a communications system consisting of interconnected *terminals, *nodes, etc.

network database: a *database system based on the concept of 'ownership' in which member *records are owned by owner records and each of the latter may have a number of record types.

node: a computer used at the connection points of a communications *network for the purpose of monitoring and/or switching communications.

noise: any signal occurring in an electronic or communications system which may be considered extraneous to the desired signal being propagated.

non-volatile: (adjective) designating a type of memory whose contents are not lost when the power to the memory fails, e.g. *magnetic bubble memory, *PROM, and *ROM.

NOT gate: a *logic circuit outputting logic 1 (true) if the input was logic 0 (false) and vice versa.

number cruncher: (colloq.) a *supercomputer.

OCR: (= *o*ptical *c*haracter *r*ecognition) a process in which a machine scans, recognizes, and encodes information that has been printed or typed in *alphanumeric characters.

off-line: (adjective) not *on-line.

on-line: (adjective) connected to the system and readily usable; directly accessible.

operating system: the *software elements that jointly control the *resources of a computer system and the processes using these.

optical character recognition: see **OCR**.

optical disk: a storage device consisting of a flat circular plate which uses a laser to record and read digital data on its surface in the form of microscopic marks in concentric or spiral tracks.

OR gate: a *logic circuit whose output is logic 0 (false) only when all (two or more) inputs are logic 0, and logic 1 (true) in all other circumstances.

output: (noun) (1) the result of any computer activity when it is presented external to the system; the process of so presenting results; (2) a signal obtained from an electronic device or circuit.

output: (verb) to produce an *output.

output device: any device converting information held within a computer into a form that can be used by human beings, such as a printer or a *VDU.

overwrite: to destroy data, information, etc. in a memory location by replacing it with new information, etc.

package: (1) a set of programs sold together and directed to a particular application; (2) the text of a program and its supporting documentation, possibly including training manuals.

packet: a grouping of *bits, having a fixed maximum size and defined *format, transmitted as a whole through a *packet switching network.

packet switching: a technique for the dynamic allocation of communication resources to multiple communicating entities in which *packets are passed through a *network until they reach their destination.

parallel processing: the running of more than one computing activity at any given instant; loosely, the running of one process at any one instant while many other processes are potentially able to be run.

parameter: (1) an item of information passed to a *subroutine, *procedure, or function; (2) a quantity selected or estimated according to the circumstances, and to be distinguished from *variables and constants.

parity check: a simple transmission error detection method akin to a *checksum, in which an extra digit is added to every binary group, 0 if the number of 1s in the original group was even and 1 if it was odd, and allowing any errors to be quickly spotted by comparing the 'parity bit' before and after transmission.

parse: (verb) to determine whether a string of input symbols is a 'sentence' or defined structure of a given 'language' or schema, and if so to determine the syntactic structure or role of the string as defined by a 'grammar' or the rules of the schema.

Pascal: a common high-level programming language designed as a tool to assist in the teaching of systematic programming, to which end it incorporates the structures of *structured programming and the data forms of *arrays, *records, *files, etc., and user-defined types.

password: a common means of authentication and identification, most usually requested when a user attempts to *log in, when its value is compared with that held by the system, and the user allowed to log in only if the values agree.

patch: (noun) (colloq.) a change to a program, usually correcting an error, which is introduced for convenience and speed as a temporary alteration or correction.

patch: (verb) (1) to make a temporary change to a program; (2) to connect by means of a *patch board.

patch board or **panel:** a matrix of sockets that can be interconnected by means of cables with plugs at each end, used to make temporary connections between devices.

pattern recognition: the process of detecting the presence of a specified pattern in information (visual or otherwise) and assigning a probability to its presence, which forms an important area of research in *artificial intelligence.

PC: see **personal computer**.

peek: (noun) a function enabling an address to be *peeked for its contents.

peek: (verb) to examine the contents of an absolute memory location from a high-level language, usually by means of a function that operates on the address in question.

peripheral: any *hardware device that can be connected to, and used with, a computer system.

personal computer: a general-purpose single-user *microcomputer designed to be operated by one person at a time and ranging from cheap hobby machines with limited memory, program storage on cassette tape, and a domestic television as the *display, to sophisticated machines with *disk drives and high-resolution *monitors.

pixel: (from picture element) one of the elements of a large *array holding data representing the brightness and possibly the colour, etc. of a small region of the image displayed on a *VDU or *monitor.

plasma display: a form of small-scale *display provided by electrical discharge through cells containing a gas which then glows with an orange or red light.

PL/I: (= *p*rogramming *l*anguage *I*) an IBM-developed high-level programming language intended to replace all pre-existing languages, incorporating features from *COBOL, *FORTRAN, and *Algol, but not taken up by manufacturers other than IBM.

plotter: an *output device for translating information from a computer into pictorial or graphical form on paper, etc.

poke: (noun) the function allowing the contents of an *address to be *poked.

poke: (verb) to alter the contents of an absolute memory location from a high-level language, usually by means of a function operating on the *address and the value to be placed there.

port: a connection point and its associated circuitry allowing an *I/O device to be connected to a *microprocessor; loosely, an interconnection in a communications *network.

portable: (adjective) designating *software that can be readily transferred to other machines, although not actually independent of a machine.

postprocessor: a program that performs operations on the output of another, such as *formatting the output of some device.

preprocessor: a program that performs modifications on data so that it conforms to the input requirements of a standard program, such as a *compiler.

print: (noun) an instruction causing a computer system and its associated printer to *print.

print: (verb) to output data by printing it on paper or on a *VDU screen.

printer: an *output device converting the coded information of the *processor into readable form on paper.

printout: the output of a *printer.

procedure: a section of a program identified by name, which can be called up from any part of a high-level language program, usually carrying out a well-defined operation on data specified by *parameters.

process: a stream of activity defined by an ordered set of machine instructions, specifying the actions it is to take, and the data it can summon, output, and manipulate.

processor: a computer; the *central processing unit; a *microprocessor.

profile: a histogram or another type of representation of an aspect of a system, such as the proportion of time spent in each of the individual *procedures during the *running of the program.

profiling: the production of *profiles.

program: a set of instructions submitted to a computer system as a single unit, which is used to direct the behaviour of that system.

programming language: a notation for the precise description of a program or algorithm, in which the *syntax and meaning are strictly defined.

PROLOG: (= *pro*gramming *log*ic) a logic programming language widely used in *artificial intelligence, and selected as the basis for the *fifth-generation computers.

PROM: (= *p*rogrammable *r*ead-*o*nly *m*emory) a form of *semiconductor *ROM whose contents are added by a separate process, after the manufacture of the device, that is irreversible so that the memory cannot be altered.

prompt: a message sent from a process to a user telling the user that the process now expects the user either to present fresh data or to respond in some defined manner.

protocol: (an agreement governing) the procedures used to exchange information between entities, covering such things as how much and how often information is to be sent, how to recover from transmission errors, and who is to receive the information.

pseudocode: an informal notation resembling a programming language but containing natural-language text, which is used to describe the functioning of a *procedure or a program, chiefly as an aid to the design of that program or procedure.

query language: a programming language for interrogating a *database and forming part of a *database management system.

queue: a linear list where all insertions are made at one end and all removals at the other, used in *hardware, like a *stack, as a specialized form of addressless memory.

RAM: (= *r*andom-*a*ccess *m*emory) a *semiconductor *read–write memory, each cell of which is available via *random access, constituting the *volatile memory of a system, and used for the storage of data and programs.

random access: a type of memory *access for which the time to access any item in the memory is independent of its *address or the address of any previous item.

raster: the pattern of successive horizontal parallel traces that an electron beam makes in producing a *CRT picture on a television, *monitor, or *VDU.

raw data: data in the form in which it reaches a computer system from the outside world.

read: (verb) to sense and retrieve or interpret data from storage or from an *input device.

read-only memory: see **ROM**.

read/write head: a magnetic *head which can *read, *write, and erase data encoded on *magnetic disk, tape, or drum.

read–write memory: a type of memory allowing the user to *read from or *write to an individual location within the device, such as *RAM.

real-time system: any computer system in which the time of output is significant, particularly control systems such as those used in navigation, in which the *response time of the system must correlate with the velocity of the thing being controlled.

record: (noun) a collection of data relating to one subject or handled together in transfers to and from peripheral devices, but especially a data structure relating a number of named elements, not necessarily of the same type, called *fields.

record: (verb) to *write.

recovery: the process of restoring normal operation after the occurrence of a fault.

recursion: the process of defining or expressing a function, *procedure, etc. in terms of itself.

recursive: (adjective) designating a function, *procedure, etc. described or defined by, or operating upon itself.

refresh: (verb) to repeat the *display of information on a *CRT, *monitor, or television screen at sufficient intervals for the display to appear continuous.

register: a group of temporary storage locations for digital information, handled as one unit, and usually found in the *central processing unit, where it enables arithmetic and logic operations to be carried out.

relational database: a type of *database based upon the mathematical concept of a relation, in which the data may be regarded as arrayed in a series of 'tables' each expressing one particular relation between items of the database, which allows the database to be structured at the time a query is made by combining the existing relevant 'tables' until the desired relation that can answer the query is obtained.

reliability: the ability of any element of a system to perform its function correctly for a given period of time; for a computer this may be expressed as the percentage of *uptime.

remote: (adjective) designating any process or system requiring a communications link, such as a *terminal located some distance from the computer it is being used with.

repair time: the (mean) time needed to diagnose and repair any hardware or software failure.

report: a message produced by a system or piece of software when some prescribed condition is reached or detected, such as the remarks produced by the *systems software when an error is detected (*see* error message).

reset: (verb) to set a *register to an all-zero state.

resident: (adjective) designating what is permanently present in the *main memory as opposed to that which is loaded as required.

resolution: the amount of graphical information that can be clearly displayed on a *monitor, *VDU, etc., often defined by the number of *pixels that can be displayed in the vertical and horizontal directions.

resource: any of the parts of a computer system and the facilities that it offers.

response time: the time that elapses between some action by the user of a system and some response from the system.

robustness: a measure of the ability of a system to recover from externally or internally generated error conditions.

ROM: (= *r*ead-*o*nly *m*emory) a *non-volatile *semiconductor memory used to store data that will never require to be modified, whose contents are built into it during manufacture and may be read in a *random access fashion.

run: (verb) to execute (a program).

running: (adjective) (of a program or process) currently being executed.

save: (noun) the command or key causing a program, etc. to be *saved.

save: (verb) to make a copy of (a program, data held in a system's main memory) on a *non-volatile storage medium such as *magnetic disk, tape, etc.

scroll: (verb) to move the information displayed on a screen or panel towards the top or bottom of the *display allowing new information to appear at the bottom or top edge respectively (it may also be possible to make the system scroll from side to side).

searching: the process of finding information in a table or *file by using a special *field of each *record, called a *key, to locate the record (if any) possessing that key.

secondary memory, storage, etc.: any *hardware device that can store information in a *non-volatile fashion, such as *magnetic disk, *magnetic tape, etc.

second generation: a *generation of computers designed between about 1955 and 1960 and characterized by the use of vacuum tubes and discrete transistors.

sector: a subdivision of a track on a *magnetic disk, representing the smallest portion of data that can be modified by *writing and that has a unique *address.

security: protection against unauthorized alteration of stored data, often achieved by using a *password.

semiconductor: a material (such as silicon or germanium) having a conductivity which is intermediate between metals and insulators and may be increased by increasing temperature or by the addition of specific element impurities (such as phosphorus or arsenic).

sequential file: a *file whose organization is sequential, each *record only being accessible as it appears in sequence in the file.

service routines: a collection of programs and *subroutines forming part of every computer system and providing a variety of functions, such as *file copying or deleting, text preparation, and program cross-referencing.

sign off: see **log off**.

sign on: see **log on**.

single-step operation or **single-stepping:** going through the execution of a program by single instructions or single steps within an instruction (either manually or on the system), used as a method of program or *hardware debugging.

smart card: a credit-card-sized plastic *card having a *chip embedded in it, proposed for use in financial transactions because of its greater security from fraud than ordinary credit or cash cards.

SNOBOL: (= *s*tri*n*g-*o*riented sym*bol*ic language, after *COBOL) a high-level programming language for the manipulation of character strings, incorporating powerful string-searching and pattern-matching operations.

soft-sectored: (adjective) designating a *disk in which the size and position of the *sectors is determined by the control electronics and the *software.

software: those components of a computer system that are non-physical, usually the programs that may be executed by a system as distinct from its physical *hardware, which may be divided into *application software and *systems software.

software house: a company primarily producing or assisting in the production of *software.

software life-cycle: the complete lifetime of a software system from conception and design to final obsolescence, traditionally modelled as a successive number of phases, typically, identification of *hardware and *software requirements, overall and detailed design, production, testing, release, operation, and maintenance.

sort: (noun) a method of *sorting.

sort: (verb) to apply a method of *sorting to (information) so as to arrange it into some predetermined order.

sorting: the process of arranging information into ascending or descending order by means of *sortkeys, used to identify and count all items with the same identification, to compare two *files, and to assist in *searching.

sortkey: the information associated with a *record, which must be capable of being ordered, and which is compared during *sorting.

spaghetti programming: an unstructured (and deprecated) way of writing programs in which extensive and ill-considered use of *jumps results in such a tangled flow of control that interpreting it and trying to correct errors proves extremely difficult.

split screen: a *VDU screen in which different areas of the screen face may be treated as separate screens for the purposes of data manipulation; for example, one part could be used for entering data from a keyboard while another displays instructions or *prompts.

spool: (noun) the reel upon which *magnetic tape, etc. is wound.

spool: (verb) to transfer (data intended for a peripheral device) to an intermediate store either so that it can be transferred to a peripheral at a more convenient time or so that separately generated data can be transferred in bulk.

stack: a linear 'list' (actually, a set of data locations in storage) where accesses, insertions, and removals are made at one or both ends; strictly, such a 'list' allowing these operations at one end only, the most recently inserted item being the first to be removed.

stand-alone: (denoting) a computer system capable of operation without being connected to any other computer system or subsystem.

standard interface: an *interface between two devices at which all the physical, electrical, and logical *parameters are in accordance with a set of predetermined values collectively used in other instances, such as the RS232C interface which is used to connect slow *peripherals to *processors or *modems.

statement: one of the sequence of units from which a high-level language program is constructed, often distinguished from an *instruction by restricting the latter to *machine code operations.

storage: a device or medium that can retain data for subsequent retrieval.

storage device: a device that can receive and retain data for subsequent retrieval, such as the *main memory of a *processor or a *backing store.

store: (noun) see **storage**.

store: (verb) to enter or retain for subsequent retrieval.

string: a one-dimensional *array consisting of characters handled as a single unit by a computer.

string manipulation: the action of any of the fundamental operations that can be performed on *strings, such as their creation, the union of two or more strings into a single string consisting of all the separate strings' characters in sequence, the extraction of segments of a string, *string matching, comparison, discovering their length, replacing *substrings by other strings, storage, input, and output.

string matching: searching within a *string for a given *substring.

structured programming: a method of writing programs using an analysis that breaks down the problem into 'sub-problems' for which *modules can be written, and in which only three types of control structure, sequential (one *statement follows another), conditional (when some condition is met *jump to a specified statement), and iterative (repeat a statement until a condition or count number is reached), are allowed, arbitrary transfer of control by *jumps being expressly forbidden.

subroutine: a part of a program that is located out of sequence and is called up from the main flow of the program, executed, and control returned to the main program after the call-up *statement or *instruction, and used as a method of saving space and simplifying the control flow, since it can be summoned many times by a single statement or instruction.

substring: a *string formed by any number of characters taken in an unbroken sequence from a larger string.

suite: a group of programs or *modules designed to meet some overall requirement, each member of which meets some part of the requirement.

supercomputer: any of a class of extremely large and powerful computers.

support program: a program serving to assist in the operation of a system rather than actually performing its prime function.

synchronous: (adjective) controlled by common timing signals; involving or requiring a form of computer control operation in which sequential events occur at fixed times.

syntax: the rules defining the sequence of elements in a language which are allowed, e.g. most high-level languages require variables to be declared and defined before they can be used.

system: a *network of devices or activities, whose overall behaviour is determined by the pattern of the network; a computer and all its peripheral devices working together.

system design: the process of proceeding from a set of requirements for a *system to a design meeting those requirements.

systems analysis: the analysis of the role of a proposed system and the identification of a set of requirements it should meet, the starting point for *system design.

systems programming: the production of *systems software.

systems software: software concerned with the operation of the system rather than the performance of applications.

tab: (noun) (abbrev.) a tabulation character, a control character for positioning the print or display position in laying out data.

tab: (verb) (abbrev.) to tabulate or lay out data.

table look-up: a rapid method of interconverting two sets of data values, in which the target data is stored in a table or *array and the source data is used to search the table.

tag: (noun) a *field used to discriminate between variants of the same type.

tag: (verb) to mark any point in a data structure that has been traversed.

tape format: the *format of information recorded on *magnetic tape, allowing a system to recognize, control, and verify data.

tape library: (1) an area in which reels of *magnetic tape are stored when not actually in use; (2) a peripheral device storing *cartridges or reels of magnetic tape and automatically transferring any chosen one to the tape transport where it can be used.

task: a *process; a *job.

teleconferencing: a computer-based system enabling several users to participate and interact with each other in some activity, such as the management of a complex project, while remaining separated in space or time.

teletex: a method of medium- to high-speed text transmission using public data *networks.

teletext: a one-way information-broadcasting system, primarily in text but with some primitive graphics capability, using spare television channel capacity and adapted domestic television receivers.

terminal: an input and/or output device that is connected to a controlling *processor to which it is usually remote and subservient.

testing: any activity that checks by means of actual execution whether a system or component is behaving in the desired and designed manner, frequently achieved by supplying the system with test data for which the correct responses are known, and comparing the actual results with the expected ones.

text editor: a program specifically designed to enter and modify textual data, whether this is written in a high-level programming language or in a natural language such as English.

text processing: see **word processing**.

thermal printer: a type of printer in which the image is produced by the localized heating of a thermo-sensitively-coated paper allowing two colourless, previously separate, dyes to mix and make visible marks corresponding to the heated area.

third generation: a *generation of computers designed between about 1960 and 1970, characterized by various technologies but using discrete transistors and having the first comprehensive *operating systems.

timeout: a condition occurring when a process which is waiting for the expiry of a preset time interval, and possibly an external event, reaches the end of the time interval, the possible external event not having been detected.

time sharing: a technique allowing the apparent *concurrent running of several *jobs, the computer switching between them so rapidly that each job appears to have the whole computer system entirely to itself.

toggle: see **flip-flop**.

top-down development: an approach to program development beginning with the general requirements of the program, dividing these into even more basic elements, and continuing this process until the level of the *implementation language is reached where these elements can be defined directly in the language.

trace program: a program monitoring the *execution of some *software system and providing information about the dynamic behaviour of that system by producing a *trace*, that is, a report, of the sequence of actions carried out.

trailer record: a *record following a group of related records and containing data relevant to them, for example, one at the end of a *file containing the total of its monetary fields as a security check.

transaction: a single coherent action on a *file or *database; the data generated by this; a single *record arising from any operation.

translator: a program such as a *compiler, converting a program written in one programming language into an equivalent program in another programming language.

transmission rate: the rate at which *information may be transferred from one device to another, usually expressed in units relating to the amount of information transferred per second, such as *characters or *bits (*see* baud rate).

truth table: a tabular description of a *logic circuit or *logic gate, listing all the possible input states and their corresponding output states.

Turing machine: an imaginary computing machine developed by Alan Turing in 1936 in order to clarify precisely the notion of an effective procedure or algorithm.

turnkey operation: the delivery and installation of a complete computer system, including *systems software and *applications software, so that the system may be placed into immediate use by the purchaser or user.

ULA: see *uncommitted logic array.

uncommitted logic array: an

uncompleted logic *chip which can be 'programmed' by the user with a final circuit pattern.

UNIX: (*Trademark*) an *operating system introduced by Bell Laboratories in 1971 with the aim of providing a simple uniform environment in which a relatively small number of users, with substantial co-operation, could collaborate on a single system.

updating: the amending, addition, and deletion of *records in a *file so that the file reflects the latest situation, which can be *random-access fashion (in which case only the items that have changed need be dealt with), or serially (in which case the whole file has to be re-created), depending upon the organization of the file.

uptime: the amount of time or the percentage of the time during which a computer system is actually operating correctly.

user: any individual or group exercising control over or using a particular *resource, or ultimately making use of the output of a computer system.

user area: the part of the *main memory of a computer that can be used for the programs of the *user rather than those regions reserved for the *operating system and its facilities.

user-friendly: (adjective) denoting any part of a computer system, *hardware, *software, *documentation, *peripherals, etc., that is easy for non-professional programmers, users unfamiliar with that particular item, or novice computer users to operate.

utility program: a *systems software program, often part of the *operating system, that facilitates the *running and *testing of *applications programs by providing a variety of generally useful functions, such as file copying or deleting, input/output routines, text preparation, etc.

validity check: a test that an entity respects the restraint that is required of that entity, such as, when a data item is input, checking that its value is within the range of values that might be expected for such an item.

variable: a character *string denoting some value stored within the computer, which may be altered during the execution of a program; a location in the memory that can contain a value that may alter; the value contained in such a location.

VDU: (= *v*isual *d*isplay *u*nit) an output device that can temporarily display both *alphanumeric and graphical information, usually employing a *cathode-ray tube (*CRT) although other technologies are used, and having a selection of display attributes to emphasize or differentiate items, such as flashing, enhancing brilliance, displaying characters in reverse (i.e. white character on a black background), underlining, and colours.

vector: a one-dimensional *array, in physics and mathematics describing entities that have both direction and magnitude, although the 'direction' may be abstractly visualized rather than really occurring in three dimensions.

verification: the process of checking the accuracy of transcribed information, usually applied to data encoded by keyboard operators reading from documents, in which case the same document is entered by two operators and compared by the computer, which signals any differences.

verification and validation: the complete range of checks performed on a system in order to increase confidence in its suitability for its intended purpose.

version control: the control of the creation and usage of the various versions of a given entity, such as a piece of *software, which may have undergone several changes either because errors were corrected in the earlier versions or because an alternative approach is being employed to meet the same requirements.

video terminal: a *VDU displaying information on a *cathode-ray tube and generally having an associated keyboard.

videotex: a system enabling a keyboard to be used in conjunction with an ordinary television and telephone to form a *terminal providing *interactive access to one or more remote information services.

virtual machine: a collection of *resources emulating the behaviour of an actual machine, so that, for example, a process cannot determine whether its output is passed directly to a printer or whether it is sent via a *spooling system.

virtual memory: a system in which the working memory of a *process is held partly in a high-speed memory and partly on a slower, cheaper *backing store, so that when the process refers to a location held in the slower backing store, the system *hardware detects this, interrupts the process, and informs the user, system supervisor, etc., that the relevant part of the memory is held on the backing store and that this must be transferred to the main memory for the process to continue.

visual display unit: see **VDU**.

VM/CMS: (*Trademark*, = *v*irtual *m*achine, *c*onversational (originally *C*ambridge from Cambridge, Mass., where first developed) *m*onitor *s*ystem) the first *operating system to use the *virtual machine concept rather than the *virtual memory, based on a supervisory level that creates a number of virtual machines in each of which a user can run a program.

volatile: (adjective) designating a type of memory whose contents are destroyed on the removal of the power to the memory, for example, semiconductor *RAMs in *micros.

von Neumann machine: (from John von Neumann) any computer (the vast majority of the current computers) characterized by having a *control unit, *arithmetic and logic unit, *memory, *input and *output facilities, programs and data sharing the same memory, and control and arithmetic units combined into a *central processing unit which determines the actions to be carried out by *reading the instructions from memory.

Winchester disk: (from IBM's Winchester laboratories) a complete assembly of *hard disk, *read/write head, and carriage assembly contained in a hermetically sealed enclosure which when mounted in the drive unit is coupled to a system that supplies it with filtered cooling air, and is capable of holding data in capacities from a few to several hundred megabytes.

window: a rectangular area on a display screen within which part of a *file or an image can be displayed.

windowing: the process of displaying data, etc. through one or more *windows on a display screen.

word: a group of *bits handled as a single unit by a computer and usually stored in locations designated by a single *address.

word length: the number of *bits a computer can handle in one unit, now usually 16 or 32, and usually long enough to contain an *instruction or an integer.

word processing: an office automation facility enabling users to write documents using a computer, with editing, re-formatting, storing, and printing facilities, and in particular the ability to insert, delete, copy, and move text around in a document, include text from other *files, and search for and replace words or phrases in the document.

Wordstar: (*Trademark*) a common *word processing package for use with *microcomputers using the *CP/M *operating system.

workspace: a block of locations within the *main memory used for the temporary storage of data during processing.

workstation: a place for a user of a system that is equipped with all the facilities required for a particular task, which in *data processing, for example, would include a *VDU and a keyboard.

wrap-around: a display facility allowing a *VDU to display lines that would otherwise be too long to be displayed completely, the line appearing on the screen as two or more smaller lines.

write: (verb) to cause data to be recorded on some form of storage.

WYSIWYG: (= *w*hat *y*ou *s*ee *i*s *w*hat *y*ou *g*et) a form of display in *word processing and other text processing applications in which what appears on the display screen is exactly what is printed on outputting to a printer.

EVERYDAY SCIENTIFIC AND MEDICAL TERMS

* indicates a separate entry

abductor: any muscle that, when it contracts, moves one part of the body away from another or from the midline of the body.

ablation: surgical removal of tissue, a part of the body, or an abnormal growth, usually by cutting.

abreaction: the release of strong emotion associated with a buried memory. Abreaction may be induced as a treatment for hysteria, anxiety state, and other neurotic conditions.

Achilles tendon: the *tendon of the muscles of the calf of the leg (the gastrocnemius and soleus muscles), situated at the back of the ankle and attached to the calcaneus (heel bone).

acupuncture: traditional Chinese system of healing in which thin metal needles are inserted into selected points beneath the skin to relieve pain or induce anaesthesia.

adaptive radiation (divergent evolution): the evolution from one species of animals or plants of a number of different forms.

adenoids (pharyngeal tonsils): the collection of lymphatic tissue at the rear of the nose. Enlargement of the adenoids may cause obstruction to breathing through the nose.

adipose tissue: a body tissue comprising cells containing fat and oil.

adrenal glands: a pair of *endocrine glands situated immediately above the kidneys.

adrenalin: a *hormone produced by the inner portion of the *adrenal glands, called the *medulla*, which increases heart and breathing activity, and improves muscle activity, to prepare the body for 'fright, flight, or fight'.

aerobic respiration: a type of cellular respiration in which foodstuffs (*carbohydrates) are completely oxidized by atmospheric oxygen, with the maximum chemical energy from the foodstuffs.

aestivation: 1 (in zoology). A state of inactivity occurring in some animals, notably lungfish, during prolonged periods of drought or heat. Feeding, respiration, movement, and other bodily activities are considerably slowed down. 2 (in botany). The arrangement of the parts of a flower-bud, especially of the sepals and petals.

afferent: carrying (nerve impulses, blood, etc.) from the outer regions of a body or organ towards its centre. The term is usually applied to types of nerve fibres or blood vessels.

agoraphobia: a morbid fear of public places and/or open spaces.

AIDS (acquired immune deficiency

syndrome): a syndrome, caused by a virus, in which the body's natural resistance to disease is destroyed leaving it vulnerable to fatal infections and cancers.

albinism: the inherited absence of pigmentation in the skin, hair, and eyes. An *albino* is an individual that lacks this. Albinos have white hair and pink skin and eyes.

algae: a large and diverse group of simple plants that contain *chlorophyll, and can therefore carry out *photosynthesis, and live in aquatic habitats and in moist situations on land.

alimentary canal: the long passage, extending from the mouth to the anus, through which food passes to be digested and absorbed.

alkaloid: one of a group of nitrogenous organic compounds derived from plants and having diverse pharmacological properties, which include morphine, cocaine, atropine, quinine, and caffeine.

allergy: a disorder in which the body becomes hyper-sensitive to particular *antigens (called *allergens*), which provoke characteristic symptoms whenever they are subsequently encountered. Different allergies afflict different tissues and may have either local or general effects, varying from *asthma and *hay fever to severe *dermatitis or gastroenteritis or extremely serious shock.

allopathy: (in homoeopathic medicine) the orthodox system of medicine. Compare *homoeopathy.

allopatric: describing or relating to groups of similar organisms that could interbreed but do not because they are geographically separated.

alternating current (a.c.): an electric current that reverses its direction with a constant frequency.

amino acid: an organic compound containing an amino group and a carboxyl group. Amino acids are fundamental constituents of all *proteins. Some can be synthesized by the body, others must be obtained from protein in the diet.

ammonite: an extinct aquatic mollusc of the class *Cephalopoda. Ammonites were abundant in the *Mesozoic era (225–65 million years ago) and are commonly found as fossils in rock strata of that time.

amniocentesis: withdrawal of a sample of amniotic fluid surrounding an *embryo in the womb, by means of a syringe inserted through the abdominal wall.

amoeba: any single-celled microscopic animal of jelly-like consistency and irregular and constantly changing shape. Some amoebae cause disease in man.

ampere: the *SI unit of electric current. The constant current that, maintained in two straight parallel infinite conductors of negligible cross-section placed one metre apart in a vacuum, would produce a force between the conductors of $2 \times 10^{-7}\,\mathrm{N\,m^{-1}}$.

amphetamine: a drug that has a marked stimulant action on the central nervous system.

Amphibia: the class of vertebrates that contain the frogs, toads, newts, and salamanders.

amylase: any of a group of closely

related *enzymes that degrade *starch, *glycogen, and other *polysaccharides.

anabolic: promoting tissue growth by increasing the metabolic process involved in protein synthesis. Anabolic agents are usually synthetic male sex hormones.

anaemia: a reduction in the quantity of the oxygen-carrying pigment *haemoglobin in the blood.

anaerobic respiration: type of cellular respiration in which foodstuffs (*carbohydrates) are never completely oxidized because molecular oxygen is not used.

analeptic: a drug that restores consciousness to a patient in a coma or faint.

analgesic: a drug that relieves pain.

angina: a sense of suffocation or suffocating pain. *Angina pectoris:* pain in the centre of the chest. It occurs when the demand for blood by the heart exceeds the supply of the coronary arteries.

angle of incidence: 1. The angle between a ray falling on a surface and the perpendicular (normal) to the surface at the point at which the ray strikes the surface. 2. The angle between a wavefront and a surface that it strikes.

angle of reflection: 1. The angle between a ray leaving a reflecting surface and the perpendicular (normal) to the surface at the point at which the ray leaves the surface. 2. The angle between a wavefront and a surface that it leaves.

angle of refraction: 1. The angle between a ray that is refracted at a surface between two different media and the perpendicular (normal) to the surface at the point of refraction. 2. The angle between a wavefront and a surface at which it has been refracted.

annual: a plant that completes its life cycle in one year, during which time it germinates, flowers, produces seeds, and dies.

anode: a positive electrode.

anodizing: a method of coating objects made of aluminium with a protective oxide film.

anorexia: loss of appetite. *Anorexia nervosa*: a psychological illness, most common in female adolescents, in which the patient has an aversion to eating.

anthrax: an acute infectious disease of farm animals. In man it attacks either the lungs, causing pneumonia, or the skin, producing severe ulceration.

antibody: a special kind of blood protein that is synthesized in *lymphoid tissue in response to the presence of a particular *antigen and circulates in the *plasma to attack the antigen and render it harmless.

anticyclone (high): an area of the atmosphere that is at a higher pressure than the surrounding air.

anti D: the *rhesus-factor antibody, formed by rhesus-negative individuals following exposure to rhesus-positive blood.

antigen: any substance that the body regards as foreign or potentially dangerous and against which it produces an *antibody.

antrum: a cavity, especially one in a bone.

aorta: the main artery of the body, from which all others derive.

aphasia: a disorder of speech and its understanding, caused by disease in the left half of the brain (for a right-handed person).

apogee: the point in the orbit of the moon, or an artificial earth satellite, at which it is furthest from the earth.

appendix (vermiform appendix): the short thin blind-ended tube, 7–10 cm long, that is attached to the end of the *caecum. It has no known function in man and is liable to become infected and inflamed.

aquifer: a deposit of rock that yields economic supplies of water to wells or springs as a result of porosity or permeability.

Arachnida: a class of terrestrial *arthropods comprising about 65 000 species and including spiders, scorpions, ticks, and mites.

Archimedes' principle: the weight of the liquid displaced by a floating body is equal to the weight of the body. The principle was not in fact stated by the Greek mathematician Archimedes (287–212 BC), though it has some connection with his discoveries.

arteriosclerosis: any of several conditions affecting the arteries.

artery: a blood vessel that carries blood away from the heart towards the other body tissues.

artesian basin: a structural basin in the earth's crust in which a zone of water-bearing rock, or *aquifer, is confined between impermeable beds. Water enters the aquifer where it reaches the surface and becomes trapped. As the point of intake of the water is above the level of the ground surface, a well sunk into the aquifer through the overlying impermeable rock will result in water being forced up to the surface by hydrostatic pressure.

arthritis: inflammation of one or more joints.

Arthropoda: a phylum of invertebrate animals comprising over one million species—the largest in the animal kingdom. Arthropods inhabit marine, freshwater, and terrestrial habitats world-wide.

asbestosis: a lung disease caused by fibres of asbestos inhaled by those who are exposed to large amounts of the mineral.

asphyxia: suffocation.

asteroids: a number of small bodies that orbit the sun, mostly between the orbits of Mars and Jupiter.

asthma: a condition characterized by paroxysmal attacks of bronchospasm, causing difficulty in breathing.

astigmatism: a lens defect in which when rays in one plane are in focus those in another plane are not. The eye can also suffer from astigmatism, usually when the *cornea is not spherical.

astrophysics: the branch of astronomy concerned with the physical processes associated with the celestial bodies and the intervening regions of space. It deals principally with the energy of stellar systems and the relation between this energy and the evolution of the system.

atavism: the phenomenon in which an individual has a character or disease known to have occurred in a remote ancestor but not in his/her parents.

ataxia: the shaky movements and unsteady gait that result from the brain's failure to regulate the body's posture and the strength and direction of limb movements.

atmospheric pressure: the pressure exerted by the weight of the air above it at any point on the earth's surface. At sea level the atmosphere will support a column of mercury about 760 mm high.

atom: the smallest part of an element that can exist chemically. Atoms consist of a small dense nucleus of *protons and *neutrons surrounded by moving *electrons.

atomic number (proton number): the number of *protons in the *nucleus of an atom. The atomic number is equal to the number of *electrons orbiting the nucleus in a neutral atom.

atrium: 1. Either of the two upper chambers of the heart. The left atrium receives arterial blood from the lungs via the pulmonary artery; the right atrium receives venous blood from the *venae cavae. 2. Any of various anatomical chambers into which one or more cavities open.

atrophy: the wasting away of a normally developed organ or tissue due to degeneration of cells.

atropine: a drug extracted from belladonna that inhibits the action of certain nerves of the *autonomic nervous system.

audiofrequency: a frequency that is audible to the human ear.

aurora: the luminous phenomena seen in the night sky in high latitudes, occurring most frequently near the earth's geomagnetic poles. The displays of aurora appear as coloured arcs, rays, bands, streamers, and curtains, usually green or red. The aurora is caused by the interaction of the atoms (mainly atomic oxygen) and molecules in the upper atmosphere (above about 100 km) with charged particles streaming from the sun, attracted to the auroral regions by the earth's magnetic field. The aurora is known as the *aurora borealis* (or northern lights) in the northern hemisphere and as the *aurora australis* (or southern lights) in the southern hemisphere.

***Australopithecus*:** a *genus of fossil primates that lived 1.3–4 million years ago.

autonomic nervous system: the part of the vertebrate *peripheral nervous system that supplies stimulation via motor nerves to the smooth and cardiac muscles (the involuntary muscles) and to the *glands of the body.

autotomy: the shedding by an animal of part of its body followed by the regeneration of the lost part.

aversion therapy: a form of behaviour therapy that is used to reduce the occurrence of undesirable behaviour. The patient is conditioned by repeated pairing of some unpleasant stimulus with a stimulus related to the undesirable behaviour.

Aves: the birds: a class of bipedal vertebrates with feathers, wings, and a beak. They evolved from reptilian ancestors and modern birds still have scaly legs, like reptiles.

axon: the long thread-like part of a nerve cell.

bacteria: a group of micro-organisms all of which lack a distinct nuclear membrane and have a cell wall of unique composition. They live in soil, water, or air or as parasites of man, animals, and plants. Some parasitic bacteria cause diseases by producing poisons.

barbiturate: any of a group of drugs derived from barbituric acid that depress activity of the *central nervous system.

basal metabolic rate: the rate of energy metabolism required to maintain an animal at rest. BMR is measured in terms of heat production per unit time: it indicates the energy consumed in order to sustain such vital functions as heartbeat, breathing, nervous activity, active transport, and *secretion. Different tissues have different metabolic rates (e.g. the BMR of brain tissue is much greater than that of bone tissue) and therefore the tissue composition of an animal determines its overall BMR.

basalt: a fine-grained basic *igneous rock.

basilar artery: an artery in the base of the brain, formed by the union of the two vertebral arteries.

basilic vein: a large vein in the arm, extending from the hand along the back of the forearm, then passing forward to the inner side of the arm at the elbow.

BCG (bacille Calmette–Guérin): a strain of tubercle bacillus that has lost the power to cause tuberculosis but retains its *antigenic activity. It is therefore used to prepare a *vaccine against the disease.

Beaufort wind scale: a scale of wind speed that was devised in the early 19th c. Originally based on observations of the effect of various wind speeds on the sails of a full-rigged frigate, it has since been modified and is now based on observations of the sea surface or, on land, such easily observable indicators as smoke and tree movement. The scale ranges from 0 (calm) to 12 (hurricane).

biennial: a plant that requires two growing seasons to complete its life cycle. During the first year it builds up food reserves, which are used during the second year in the production of flowers and seeds.

big-bang theory (superdense theory): the cosmological theory that all the matter and energy in the universe originated in a superdense agglomeration that exploded at a finite moment in the past. This theory successfully explains the expansion of the universe, the galaxies flying apart like fragments from an exploding bomb. It is now considered to be more satisfactory than the rival *steady-state theory.

bile: a thick alkaline fluid that is *secreted by the liver and stored in the gall bladder.

bile pigments: coloured compounds—breakdown products of the blood pigment haemoglobin—that are excreted in bile. The two most important bile pigments are *bilirubin*, which is orange or yellow, and its oxidized form *biliverdin*, which is green.

bilirubin: see **bile pigments**.

biliverdin: see **bile pigments**.

binary stars: a pair of stars revolving about a common centre of mass. In a *visual binary* the stars are far enough apart to be seen separately using an optical telescope. In an *astrometric binary* one component is too faint to be seen and its presence is inferred from the perturbations in the motion of the other. In a *spectroscopic binary* the stars cannot usually be resolved by a telescope, but motions can be detected by different *Doppler shifts in the spectrum at each side of the binary, according to whether the components are approaching or receding from the observer.

biological clock: the mechanisms, presumed to exist within many animals and plants, that produce regular periodic changes in behaviour or physiology.

biopsy: the removal of a small piece of living tissue from an organ or part of the body for microscopic examination.

biorhythm: a roughly periodic change in the behaviour or physiology of an organism that is generated and maintained by a *biological clock.

black body: a hypothetical body that absorbs all the radiation falling on it. *Black-body radiation* is the *electromagnetic radiation emitted by a black body.

black hole: an object in space that has collapsed under its own gravitational forces to such an extent that its *escape velocity is equal to or greater than the *speed of light. Black holes are thought to originate from *supernovae explosions in which the core of matter left after the explosion is very large (several solar masses). The core of matter then continues to contract and a very strong gravitational field is produced. Eventually it reaches a point at which the field is sufficiently large to prevent *electromagnetic radiation leaving—the object has then become a black hole.

blastocyst: an early stage of embryonic development that consists of a hollow ball of cells with a localized thickening (the *inner cell mass*) that will develop into the actual embryo.

blood group: any one of the many types into which a person's blood may be classified, based on the presence or absence of certain inherited *antigens on the surface of the red blood cells.

blood pressure: the pressure of blood against the walls of the main arteries. Pressure is highest during systole, when the ventricles are contracting, and lowest during diastole, when the ventricles are relaxing and refilling. Blood pressure is measured—in millimetres of mercury—by means of a sphygmomanometer at the brachial artery of the arm. A young adult would be expected to have a systolic pressure of around 120 mm and a diastolic pressure of 80 mm. These are recorded as 120/80.

blue baby: an infant suffering from congenital malformation of the heart as a result of which some or all of the blue (deoxygenated) blood is pumped around the body instead of passing through the lungs to be oxygenated.

botulism: a serious form of food poisoning from foods containing the toxin produced by the bacterium *Clostridium botulinum*, which thrives in improperly preserved foods.

Boyle's law: the volume of a given mass of gas at a constant temperature is inversely proportional to its pressure.

brachial artery: an artery that extends from the axillary artery at the armpit, down the side and inner surface of the upper arm to the elbow, where it divides into the radial and ulnar arteries.

brainstem: the enlarged extension upwards within the skull of the spinal cord, consisting of the *medulla oblongata, *pons, and *midbrain.

brucellosis: a chronic disease of farm animals caused by the bacteria of the *genus *Brucella*, which can be transmitted to man either by contact with an infected animal or by drinking non-pasteurized contaminated milk.

caecum: a pouch in the alimentary canal of vertebrates between the *small intestine and *colon. The caecum (and its *appendix) is large and highly developed in herbivorous animals (e.g. rabbits and cows), in which it contains a large population of bacteria essential for the breakdown of cellulose. In humans the caecum is a vestigial organ and is poorly developed.

Caesarean section: a surgical operation for delivering a baby through the abdominal wall.

Cainozoic: the geological era that began about 65 million years ago and extends to the present.

calorie: the quantity of heat required to raise the temperature of 1 gram of water by 1 degree C (1 K). The calorie, a c.g.s. unit, is now largely replaced by the *joule, an *SI unit. 1 calorie = 4.1868 joules.

Calorie (kilogram calorie; kilocalorie): 1000 calories. This unit is still in limited use in estimating the energy value of foods, but is obsolescent.

calorific value: the heat per unit mass produced by complete combustion of a given substance. Calorific values are used to express the energy values of fuels. These are usually expressed in megajoules per kilogram. They are also used to measure the energy content of foodstuffs; i.e. the energy produced when the food is oxidized in the body. The units used in this case are kilojoules per gram, although *calories (kilocalories) are often still used in non-technical contexts.

Cambrian: the earliest geological period of the *Palaeozoic era. It is estimated to have begun about 570 million years ago and lasted for some 100 million years. During this period marine animals with mineralized shells made their first appearance and Cambrian rocks are the first to contain an abundance of fossils.

cancer: any malignant tumour, including *carcinoma and *sarcoma. It arises from the abnormal and uncontrolled division of cells that then invade and destroy the surrounding tissues.

capillary: an extremely narrow blood vessel.

carapace: 1. The dorsal part of the *exoskeleton of some *crustaceans, which spreads like a shield over several segments of the head and *thorax. 2. The domed dorsal part of the shell of tortoises and turtles, formed of bony plates fused with the ribs and vertebrae and covered by a horny epidermal layer.

carbohydrate: one of a group of organic compounds. The simplest carbohydrates are the sugars (saccharides). *Polysaccharides are carbohydrates of much greater molecular weight and complexity.

carbon dating: a method of estimating the ages of archaeological specimens of biological origin. As a result of *cosmic radiation a small number of atmospheric nitrogen nuclei are continuously being transformed by neutron bombardment into radioactive nuclei of carbon-14. Some of these radiocarbon atoms find their way into living trees and other plants in the form of carbon dioxide, as a result of *photosynthesis. When the tree is cut down photosynthesis stops and the ratio of radiocarbon atoms to stable carbon atoms begins to fall as the radiocarbon decays. The ratio in the specimen can be measured and enables the time that has elapsed since the tree was cut down to be calculated. The method has been shown to give consistent results for specimens up to some 40 000 years old.

Carboniferous: a geological period in the *Palaeozoic era. It began about 345 million years ago and ended about 280 million years ago.

carbuncle: a collection of boils with multiple drainage channels.

carcinogen: any agent, like tobacco smoke, that produces *cancer.

carcinoma: any cancer that arises in epithelium, the tissue that lines the skin and internal organs of the body.

cardiac arrest: the cessation of effective pumping action of the heart.

caries: decay and crumbling of the substance of a tooth or a bone.

Carnivora: an order of mainly flesh-eating mammals that includes the dogs, wolves, bears, badgers, weasels, and cats.

carotid artery: the major artery that supplies blood to the head.

carpal: 1. Relating to the wrist. 2. Any of the bones forming the eight bones of the wrist, called the carpus.

carpel: the female reproductive organ of a flower.

cartilage: a dense connective tissue, consisting chiefly of chondroitin sulphate, that is capable of withstanding considerable pressure. In the foetus and infant cartilage occurs in many parts of the body, but most disappears during development.

catalyst: a substance that increases the rate of a chemical reaction without itself undergoing any permanent chemical change.

cataract: any opacity in the lens of the eye, resulting in blurred vision.

catheter: a tube for insertion into a

narrow opening so that fluids may be introduced or removed.

cathode: a negative *electrode.

caul: (in obstetrics) a *membrane, part of the amnion, that may cover an infant's head at birth.

cell: 1 (in physical chemistry). A system in which two *electrodes are in contact with an *electrolyte. 2 (in biology). The structural and functional unit of all living organisms.

Celsius scale: a temperature scale in which the fixed points are the temperatures at standard pressure of ice in equilibrium with water (0 degrees C) and water in equilibrium with steam (100 degrees C). This scale was formerly known as the *centigrade scale*.

central nervous system: the part of the nervous system that co-ordinates all neural functions.

centre of gravity: see **centre of mass**.

centre of mass: the point at which the whole mass of a body may be considered to be concentrated.

centrifugal force: apparent outward force on a body moving in a circular path, balancing the *centripetal force.

centripetal force: a force acting on a body causing it to move in a circular path.

cephalic version: a procedure for turning a foetus that is lying in a breech or transverse position so that its head will enter the birth passage first.

Cephalopoda: the most advanced class of molluscs, containing the squids, cuttlefishes, octopuses, and the extinct *ammonites.

cerebellum: the largest part of the *hindbrain.

cerebral cortex: the intricately folded outer layer of the *cerebrum, making up some 40% of the brain by weight. It is directly responsible for consciousness, with essential roles in perception, memory, thought, mental ability, and intellect, and it is responsible for initiating voluntary activity.

cerebral palsy: a developmental abnormality of the brain resulting in weakness and incoordination of the limbs and often caused by injury during birth.

cerebrum: the largest and most highly developed part of the brain.

cervix: a neck-like part. *Cervix uteri:* the narrow passage at the lower end of the *uterus (womb), which connects with the *vagina.

Cestoda: a class of flatworms comprising the tapeworms—ribbon-like parasites within the gut of vertebrates.

Cetacea: an order of marine mammals comprising the whales, which includes what is probably the largest known animal—the blue whale (*Balaenoptera musculus*), over 30 m long and over 150 tonnes in weight.

chemotherapy: the prevention or treatment of disease by the use of chemical substances.

Cheynes–Stokes respiration: striking form of breathing in which there is a cyclical variation in the rate, which becomes slower until breathing stops for several seconds before speeding up to a peak and then slowing again. It occurs particularly in states of coma.

chimaera: an organism composed of

tissues that are genetically different. Chimaeras can develop if a *mutation occurs in a cell of a developing embryo.

chiropractic: a system of treating diseases by manipulation, mainly of the vertebrae of the backbone.

Chiroptera: an order of flying mammals comprising the bats.

chlorophyll: one of a group of green pigments, found in all green plants and some bacteria, that absorb light to provide energy for the synthesis of *carbohydrates from carbon dioxide and water. *See also* photosynthesis.

cholesterol: a fat-like material present in the blood and most tissues, especially nervous tissue. Elevated blood concentration of cholesterol is often associated with the degeneration of the walls of the arteries (atheroma) in human beings.

chorea: a jerky involuntary movement particularly affecting the shoulders, hips, and face. *Huntingdon's chorea:* an inherited form in which the involuntary movements are accompanied by a progressive dementia.

choroid: the layer of the eyeball between the *retina and the sclera (*see* sclerotic). It contains blood vessels and a pigment that absorbs excess light and so prevents blurring of vision.

chromatography: a technique for analysing or separating mixtures of gases, liquids, or dissolved substances.

chromosome: one of the thread-like structures in a cell *nucleus that carry the genetic information in the form of genes. It is composed of a long double filament of *DNA coiled into a helix together with associated *proteins.

circadian rhythm (diurnal rhythm): any 24-hour periodicity in the behaviour or physiology of animals or plants. Circadian rhythms are generally controlled by *biological clocks.

cirrhosis: a condition in which the liver responds to injury or death of some of its cells by producing interlacing strands of fibrous tissue between which are nodules of regenerating cells.

clavicle: a collar-bone.

cleft palate: a fissure in the midline of the palate due to failure of the two sides to fuse in embryonic development.

clitoris: the female counterpart of the penis, which contains erectile tissue but is unconnected with the urethra.

coaxial cable: a cable consisting of a central conductor surrounded by an insulator, which is in turn contained in an earthed sheath of another conductor.

coccyx: the lowermost element of the backbone: the vestigial human tail.

cochlea: the spiral organ of the labyrinth of the ear, which is concerned with the reception and analysis of sound.

cocoon: a protective covering for eggs and/or larvae produced by many invertebrates.

coelacanth: a bony fish that was believed to have been extinct until 1938 when the first specimen of modern times was discovered.

coeliac disease: a condition in which the small intestine fails to digest and absorb food. It is due to sensitivity of the intestinal lining to the protein gliadin, which is contained in *gluten in the germ of wheat and rye and causes atrophy of the digestive and absorptive cells of the intestine.

colectomy: surgical removal of the *colon.

Coleoptera: an order of insects comprising the beetles and weevils and containing about 330 000 known species—the largest order in the animal kingdom.

colon: the main part of the large intestine.

colostomy: a surgical operation in which a part of the *colon is brought through the abdominal wall and opened in order to drain or decompress the intestine.

comet: a small body that travels around the sun in a highly eccentric orbit.

conductivity: 1 (thermal conductivity). A measure of the ability of a substance to conduct heat. 2 (electrical conductivity). The reciprocal of the *resistivity of a material.

conductor: a substance that has a high thermal or electrical *conductivity.

conjunctivitis: inflammation of the delicate *mucous membrane that covers the front of the eye and lines the inside of the eyelids.

contagious disease: originally a disease transmitted only by direct physical contact, but now usually taken to mean any communicable disease.

continental drift: the theory that the earth's continents once formed a single mass and have since moved relative to each other.

convergent evolution: the development of superficially similar structure in unrelated organisms, usually because the organisms live in the same kind of environment.

corm: an underground organ formed by certain plants, e.g. crocus and gladiolus, that enables them to survive from one growing season to the next.

cornea: the transparent circular part of the front of the eyeball.

corolla: the petals of a flower, collectively, forming the inner whorl of the *perianth.

corona: 1. The outer part of the sun's atmosphere. 2. A glowing region of the air surrounding a *conductor when the potential gradient near it exceeds a critical value.

coronary thrombosis: the formation of a blood clot (thrombus) in the coronary artery, which obstructs the flow of blood to the heart.

corpus: any mass of tissue that can be distinguished from its surroundings. *Corpus luteum:* the glandular tissue in the ovary that forms at the site of a ruptured *Graafian follicle after *ovulation.

cortex: 1 (in botany). The tissue between the *epidermis and the vascular system in plant stems and roots. 2 (in zoology). The outermost layer of tissue of various organs.

corticosteroid: any of several hormones produced by the cortex of the *adrenal glands.

cortisol: a *hormone produced by the *adrenal glands which promotes the synthesis and storage of *glucose and is therefore important in the normal response to stress, suppresses or prevents inflammation, and regulates the deposition of fat in the body.

cortisone: a *hormone produced by the *adrenal glands that is closely related to, and has a similar reaction to, *cortisol. It is also the name for a synthetic version of cortisol.

cosmic radiation: high-energy particles that fall on the earth from space.

crepitation: a soft fine crackling sound heard in the lungs through the stethoscope—not normally heard in healthy lungs.

Cretaceous: the final geological period of the *Mesozoic era. It extended from about 136 million years ago to about 65 million years ago. The name is derived from *creta* (Latin: chalk) and the Cretaceous was characterized by the deposition of large amounts of chalk in western Europe.

critical mass: the minimum mass of fissile material that will sustain a nuclear chain reaction.

Cro-Magnon man: the earliest form of modern man (*Homo sapiens*), which is believed to have appeared in Europe about 35 000 years ago and possibly earlier in Africa and Asia.

crustacea: a class of *arthropods containing over 35 000 species distributed world-wide, mainly in freshwater and marine habitats, where they constitute a major component of *plankton.

cryogenics: the study of very low temperatures and the techniques for producing them.

cryosurgery: the use of extreme cold in a localized part of the body to freeze and destroy unwanted tissues.

curettage: the scraping of the internal surface of an organ or body cavity by means of a spoon-shaped instrument (*curette*).

cyanosis: a bluish discoloration of the skin and *mucous membranes resulting from an inadequate amount of oxygen in the blood.

cyst: 1. An abnormal sac or closed cavity lined with *epithelium and filled with liquid or semi-solid matter. There are many varieties of cysts occurring in different parts of the body. 2. A dormant stage produced during the life cycle of certain protozoan parasites of the *alimentary canal. 3. A structure formed by and surrounding the *larvae of certain parasitic worms.

cystic fibrosis: a hereditary disease affecting the *exocrine glands.

cystitis: inflammation of the urinary bladder, often caused by infection.

cytology: the study of the structure and function of cells.

cytoplasm: the jelly-like material surrounding the *nucleus of a cell.

Dalton's law: the total pressure of a mixture of gases or vapours is equal to the sum of the partial pressures of its components.

dance of the bees: a celebrated example of communication in animals. Honey-bee workers on returning to the hive after a successful foraging expedition perform a 'dance' on the comb that contains coded information about the distance and direction of the food source. Other workers, sensing vibrations from the dance, follow the instructions to find the food source.

Darwinism: the theory of evolution proposed by Charles Darwin (1809–82) which postulated that present-day species have evolved from simpler ancestral types by the process of *natural selection acting on the variability found within populations.

Decapoda: an order of crustaceans distributed world-wide, mainly in marine habitats. Decapods comprise swimming forms (shrimps and prawns) and crawling forms (crabs, lobsters, and crayfish). All are characterized by five pairs of walking legs.

decibel: a unit used to compare two power levels, usually applied to sound or electrical signals.

deltoid: a thick triangular muscle that covers the shoulder joint.

dengue: a viral disease that occurs throughout the tropics and sub-tropics.

depression (low; disturbance): an area of low atmospheric pressure in the mid and high latitudes that is surrounded by several closed *isobars.

dermatitis: inflammation of the skin caused by an outside agent.

detached retina: separation of the *retina from the *choroid, causing loss of vision in the affected part of the retina.

Devonian: a geological period in the *Palaeozoic era that extended from about 395 million years ago to about 345 million years ago.

dew-point: the temperature at which the water vapour in the air is saturated. As the temperature falls the dew-point is the point at which the vapour begins to condense as droplets of water.

diabetes: any disorder of metabolism causing excessive thirst and the production of large volumes of urine.

dialysis: a method of separating particles of different dimensions in a liquid mixture, using a thin semi-permeable *membrane. A solution of the mixture is separated from distilled water by the membrane; the solutes pass through the membrane into the water while the proteins, etc. are retained. The principle of dialysis is used in the artificial kidney.

diastole: the period between two contractions of the heart, when the muscle of the heart relaxes and allows the chambers to fill with blood.

Dictyoptera: an order of insects comprising the cockroaches and the mantids, occurring mainly in tropical regions.

digitalis: an extract from the dried leaves of foxgloves which contains substances that stimulate the heart muscle.

dilatation and curettage (D and C): an operation in which the neck of the womb is expanded and the lining of the womb is peeled off.

dimorphism: (in biology) the existence of two distinctly different types of individual within a species.

diode: an electronic device with two *electrodes.

dipsomania: a morbid and insatiable craving for alcohol, occurring in *paroxysms.

Diptera: an order of insects comprising the true, or two-winged, flies.

direct current (d.c.): an electric current in which the net flow of charge is in one direction only.

display behaviour: stereotyped movement or posture that serves to influence the behaviour of another animal.

diuresis: increased secretion of urine by the kidneys.

diurnal: daily.

divergent evolution: see **adaptive radiation**.

diverticulitis: inflammation of a diverticulum, a sac or pouch formed at weak points in the walls of the alimentary tract, most commonly of one or more colonic diverticula.

DNA (deoxyribonucleic acid): the genetic material of nearly all living organisms, which is a major constituent of the *chromosomes within the cell nucleus. It plays a central role in the determination of hereditary characteristics by controlling *protein synthesis in cells. *See also* genetic code.

Doppler effect: the apparent change in the observed frequency of a wave as a result of relative motion between the source and the observer. For example, the sound made by a low-flying aircraft as it approaches appears to fall in pitch as it passes and flies away.

Down's syndrome: a form of mental subnormality due to a *chromosome defect. The main physical features include a slightly oblique slant to the eyes, a round head, flat nasal bridge, and short stature.

dropsy: see **oedema**.

duodenal ulcer: an ulcer in the *duodenum.

duodenum: the first of the three parts of the *small intestine.

dwarf star: a small star that lies on the main sequence in a *Hertzsprung–Russell diagram. *See also* white dwarf.

dyslexia: a developmental disorder selectively affecting a child's ability to learn to read and write.

earth's atmosphere: the gas that surrounds the earth. The composition of dry air at sea level is: nitrogen 78.08%, oxygen 20.95%, argon 0.93%, carbon dioxide 0.03%, neon 0.0018%, helium 0.0005%, krypton 0.0001%, and xenon 0.00001%. In addition to water vapour, air in some localities contains sulphur compounds, hydrogen peroxide, hydrocarbons, and dust particles. The lowest level of the atmosphere, in which most of the weather occurs, is called the *troposphere*. Its thickness varies from about 7 km at the poles to 28 km at the equator and in this layer temperature falls with increasing height. The next layer is the *stratosphere*, which goes up to about 50 km. Here the temperature remains approximately constant. Above this is the *ionosphere*, which extends to about 1000 km, with the temperature rising and composition changing substantially. At about 100 km and above, most of the oxygen has dissociated into atoms; at above 150 km the percentage of nitrogen has dropped to nil. In the ionosphere the gases are ionized by the absorption of solar radiation. This enables radio transmissions to be made round the curved surface of the earth, as the ionized gas acts as a reflector for certain wavelengths.

echolalia: pathological repetition of the words spoken by another person.

echopraxia (echokinesis): pathological imitation of the actions of another person.

ectomorphic: describing a body type that is relatively thin, with a large skin surface in comparison to weight.

ectopic pregnancy: the development of a foetus at a site other than in the womb.

efferent: 1. Designating nerves or neurones that convey impulses from the brain or spinal cord to muscles, glands, and other effectors. 2. Designating vessels or ducts that drain fluid from an organ or part.

electrode: a conductor that emits or collects electrons in a cell. The *anode* is the positive electrode and the *cathode* is the negative electrode.

electrolysis: the production of a chemical reaction by passing an electric current through an *electrolyte. In electrolysis, positive *ions migrate to the cathode and negative ions to the anode.

electrolyte: a liquid that conducts electricity as a result of the presence of positive or negative ions.

electromagnetic radiation: energy resulting from the acceleration of electric charge and the associated electric fields and magnetic fields.

electromagnetic spectrum: the range of wavelengths over which *electromagnetic radiation extends.

electromotive force (e.m.f.): the greatest potential difference that can be generated by a particular source of electric current.

electron: an *elementary particle. Electrons are present in all *atoms in groupings called shells around the nucleus.

elementary particles: the fundamental constituents of all the matter in the universe. Until the discovery of the *electron it was assumed that *atoms were the fundamental constituents of matter. This discovery and the discovery of the atomic nucleus and the *proton made it apparent that atoms were not themselves elementary, in the sense that they have an internal structure. The discovery of the *neutron completed the atomic model based on an atomic nucleus consisting of protons and neutrons surrounded by sufficient *electrons to balance the nuclear charge.

elephantiasis: gross enlargement of the skin and underlying connective tissues caused by obstruction of the lymph vessels.

embryo: an animal at the earliest stage of development.

e.m.f.: see **electromotive force**.

encephalitis: inflammation of the brain.

endocrine gland: a *gland that manufactures one or more hormones and secretes them directly into the bloodstream and not through a duct to the exterior.

endogenous: arising within or derived from the body.

endomorphic: describing a body type that is relatively fat, with highly developed *viscera and weak muscular and skeletal development.

endoskeleton: a supporting framework that lies entirely within the body of an animal.

endosperm: a nutritive tissue, characteristic of flowering plants, that surrounds the developing embryo in a seed.

entropy: a measure of the unavailability of a system's energy to do work: an increase in entropy is accompanied by a decrease in energy availability.

enzyme: a *protein that acts as a *catalyst in biochemical reactions.

Eocene: the second geological epoch of the *Tertiary period. It extended from about 54 million years ago to about 38 million years ago.

epicentre: the point on the surface of the earth directly above the focus of an earthquake or directly above or below a nuclear explosion.

epidermis: 1 (in zoology). The outermost layer of cells of the body of an animal. 2 (in botany). The outermost layer of cells covering a plant.

epidural: see **spinal anaesthesia**.

epiglottis: a thin leaf-shaped flap of cartilage, covered with *mucous membrane, situated immediately behind the root of the tongue.

epilepsy: any one of a group of disorders of brain function characterized by recurrent attacks that have a sudden onset.

epithelium: a tissue in vertebrates consisting of closely packed cells in a sheet with little intercellular material. It forms a *membrane over the outer surfaces of the body and walls of the internal cavities.

ergonomics: the study of man in relation to his work and working surroundings.

ergotism: poisoning caused by eating rye infected with the *fungus ergot.

erogenous: describing certain parts of the body, the physical stimulation of which leads to sexual arousal.

escape velocity: the minimum speed needed by a space vehicle, rocket, etc., to escape from the gravitational field of the earth, moon, or other celestial body.

Eustachian tube: the tube that connects the middle ear to the *pharynx. It allows the pressure on the inner side of the ear-drum to remain equal to the external pressure.

euthanasia: the act of taking life to relieve suffering.

exocrine gland: a *gland that discharges its *secretion into a body cavity, such as the gut, or on to the body surface.

exogenous: originating outside the body.

exoskeleton: a rigid external covering for the body in certain animals.

Fallopian tube: either of a pair of tubes that conduct ova from the ovary to the womb.

Faraday's laws: two laws describing electrolysis. In the modern form they are: 1. The amount of chemical change during electrolysis is proportional to the charge passed. 2. The charge required to deposit or liberate a mass m is given by $Q = Fmz/M$, where F is the Faraday constant, z the charge of the ion, and M the relative ionic mass.

farinaceous: starchy; describing foods rich in starch (e.g. flour, bread, cereals) or diets based on these foods.

feedback: the use of part of the output of a system to control its performance. In *positive feedback* the output is used to enhance the input, and in *negative feedback* it is used to reduce the input.

femoral: of or relating to the thigh or to the *femur. *Femoral artery:* an artery arising from the external *iliac artery.

femur: the thigh-bone, a long bone between the hip and the knee.

fibrillation: a rapid and chaotic beating of the many individual muscle fibres of the heart, which is consequently unable to maintain effective synchronous contraction.

fibula: the long thin outer bone of the lower leg.

field: a region in which a body experiences a *force as the result of the presence of some other body or bodies.

fistula: an abnormal communication between two hollow organs or between a hollow organ and the exterior.

follicle: a small secretory cavity, sac, or *gland.

fontanelle: an opening in the skull of a foetus or young infant due to incomplete *ossification of the cranial bones and the resulting incomplete closure of the *sutures.

force: the agency that tends to change the momentum of a massive body, defined as being proportional to the rate of increase of momentum.

forebrain (prosencephalon): one of the three sections of the brain of a vertebrate embryo. The forebrain develops to form the *cerebrum, *hypothalamus, and *thalamus in the adult.

fossil: the remains or traces of any organism that lived in the geological past. In general only the hard parts of organisms become fossilized (e.g. bones, teeth, shells, and wood) but under certain circumstances the entire organism is preserved. For example, virtually unaltered fossils of extinct mammals, such as the woolly mammoth and woolly rhinoceros, have been found preserved in ice in the Arctic. Small organisms or parts of organisms (e.g. insects, leaves, flowers) have been preserved in amber.

front: (in meteorology) the sloping interface between two air masses of different temperature and humidity. When the air masses come together the warm air, being lighter, rises and slopes over the colder air. Distinctive weather phenomena are associated with fronts. At a *warm front* (the boundary zone at the front of the warm sector of a *depression), warm air is overtaking cold air and rising above it with a slope of about 1:150. At a *cold front*, which is usually found to the rear of a depression, warm air is forced to rise by an advancing under-cutting wedge of cold air. This is accompanied by a sudden veering of the wind, a fall in temperature, and heavy rainfall. An *occluded front* (or *occlusion*) occurs when a cold front overtakes a warm front in an atmospheric depression.

fructose: a simple sugar found in honey and in such fruit as figs. Fructose is one of the two sugars in sucrose.

fungi: a group of simple plants lacking chlorophyll.

galactose: a simple sugar and a constituent of the milk sugar lactose. Galactose is converted to glucose in the liver.

galaxy: a vast collection of stars, dust, and gas held together by the gravitational attraction between its components.

gallstone: a hard mass composed of bile pigments, *cholesterol, and calcium salts, in varying proportions, that can form in the gall bladder.

gamete: a mature sex cell: the ovum of the female or the spermatozoon of the male. Gametes are haploid, containing half the normal number of chromosomes.

gamma rays: electromagnetic radiation of wavelengths shorter than *X-rays, given off by certain radioactive substances.

ganglion: 1 (in neurology). Any structure containing a collection of nerve cell bodies and often also numbers of *synapses. Ganglia are found in the *sympathetic and parasympathetic nervous systems. Within the *central nervous system certain well-defined masses of nerve cells are called ganglia. 2. An abnormal but harmless swelling (*cyst) that sometimes forms in *tendon sheafs, especially at the wrist.

gangrene: death and decay of part of the body due to deficiency or cessation of blood supply.

gene: the basic unit of genetic material, which is carried at a particular place on a *chromosome. Originally it was regarded as the unit of inheritance and mutation but is now usually defined as a piece of *DNA or *RNA that acts as the unit controlling the formation of a single *polypeptide chain.

genetic code: the means by which genetic information in *DNA controls the manufacture of specific proteins by the cell.

genetic engineering: the techniques involved in altering the characters of an organism by inserting *genes from another organism into its *DNA.

genetics: the science of inheritance.

genus: a category used in the classification of organisms that consists of a number of similar or closely related *species.

geriatrics: the branch of medicine concerned with the diagnosis and treatment of disorders that occur in old age and with the care of the aged.

gestation: the period in animals bearing live young (especially mammals) from the fertilization of the egg to birth of the young. In man gestation is known as *pregnancy*.

giant star: a very large, highly luminous star, no longer on the main sequence of the Hertzsprung–Russell diagram.

gingivitis: inflammation of the gums.

glabella: the smooth rounded surface of the frontal bone in the middle of the forehead, between the two eyebrows.

gland: a group of cells or a single cell in animals or plants that is specialized to secrete a specific substance. In animals there are two types of glands, the *endocrine and the *exocrine.

glaucoma: a condition in which loss of vision occurs because of an abnormally high pressure in the eye.

glottis: the space between the two vocal cords. The term is often applied to the vocal cords themselves or to that part of the *larynx associated with the production of sound.

glucose: a white crystalline sugar which occurs widely in nature.

gluten: a mixture of two proteins, gliadin and glutenin, occurring in the *endosperm of wheat grain.

glycogen (animal starch): a *polysaccharide consisting of a highly branched *polymer of *glucose occurring in animal tissues, especially in liver and muscle cells.

gneiss: a coarse-grained rock that is characterized by compositional banding of *metamorphic origin.

goitre: a swelling of the neck due to enlargement of the *thyroid gland.

gonad: male or female reproductive organ, which produces the *gametes.

gonorrhoea: a *venereal disease, caused by the bacterium *Neisseria gonorrhoeae*, that affects the genital *mucous membranes of either sex.

gout: a disease in which a defect in *uric acid metabolism causes an excess of the acid and its salts to accumulate in the bloodstream and the joints.

Graafian follicle: a mature *follicle in the *ovary prior to *ovulation, containing a large fluid-filled cavity that distends the surface of the ovary.

gravitational field: the region of space surrounding a body that has the property of *mass. In this region any other body that has mass will experience a force of attraction. The ratio of the force to the mass of the second body is the *gravitational field strength*.

gravity: the phenomenon associated with the gravitational force acting on any object that has mass and is situated within the earth's *gravitational field. The weight of the body (*see* mass) is equal to the force of the gravity acting on the body.

hadron: any of a class of subatomic particles. The class includes *protons, *neutrons, and pions.

haematoma: an accumulation of blood within the tissues that clots to form a solid swelling.

haemoglobin: one of a group of globular proteins occurring widely in animals as oxygen carriers in blood.

haemophilia: a hereditary disorder in which the blood clots very slowly.

haemorrhoids (piles): enlarged (*varicose) veins in the wall of the anus.

halitosis: bad breath.

Halley's comet: a bright *comet with a period of 76 years. Visible early spring 1986.

hallucinogen: a drug that produces hallucinations.

harelip: the congenital deformity of

a cleft in the upper lip, on one or both sides of the midline. It is often associated with a *cleft palate.

hay fever: a form of allergy due to pollen.

heavy water (deuterium oxide): water in which hydrogen atoms are replaced by the heavier *isotope deuterium.

heliotropism: see **phototropism**.

Hemiptera: an order of insects comprising the true bugs.

hepatitis: inflammation of the liver due to a virus infection or such diseases as amoebic dysentery and *lupus.

herbaceous: describing a plant that contains little permanent woody tissue. The aerial parts of the plant die back after the growing season. In *annuals the whole plant dies; in *biennials and herbaceous *perennials the plant has organs (e.g. bulbs or corms) that are modified to survive beneath the soil in unfavourable conditions.

herbivore: an animal that eats vegetation, especially any of the plant-eating mammals, such as ungulates (cows, horses, etc.).

hernia: the protrusion of an organ or tissue out of the body cavity in which it normally lies.

herpes: inflammation of the skin caused by viruses and characterized by collections of small blisters.

Hertzsprung–Russell diagram (H–R diagram): a graphical representation of the absolute magnitude of stars plotted against the spectral class or colour index. One axis represents the energy output of the star and the other its surface temperature. The majority of stars on such a diagram fall on a band running from the top left to the bottom right of the graph. These are called *main-sequence stars* (the sun falls into this class). The few stars falling in the lower left portion are called *white dwarfs. The *giants fall in a cluster above the main sequence and the *supergiants above them.

heterophoria: a tendency to squint.

hindbrain: the part of the brain comprising the *cerebellum, *pons, and *medulla oblongata.

histology: the study of the structure of tissues by means of special staining techniques combined with light and electron microscopy.

Hodgkin's disease: a malignant disease of lymphatic tissues, usually characterized by painless enlargement of one or more groups of *lymph nodes in the body.

holistic: describing an approach to patient care in which the physical, mental, and social factors in the patient's condition are taken into account, rather than just the diagnosed disease.

Holocene (Recent): the most recent geological epoch of the *Quaternary period, comprising roughly the past 10 000 years.

homoeopathy: a system of medicine based on the theory that 'like cures like'. The patient is treated with extremely small quantities of drugs that are themselves capable of producing symptoms of his particular disease.

homoeostasis: the physiological process by which the internal systems of the body are maintained at equilibrium, despite variations in the external conditions.

hormone: a substance that is produced by an *endocrine gland in one part of the body, passes into the bloodstream, and is carried to other organs or tissues, where it acts to modify their structure or function.

humerus: the bone of the upper arm.

hydrocephalus: an abnormal increase in the amount of cerebrospinal fluid within the ventricles of the brain.

hydrophyte: any plant that lives either in very wet soil or completely or partially submerged in water.

hydrosphere: the water on the surface of the earth. Some 74% of the earth's surface is covered with water, 97% of which is in the oceans.

hymen: the membrane that covers the opening of the *vagina at birth but usually perforates spontaneously before puberty.

Hymenoptera: an order of insects that includes the ants, bees, and certain types of flies.

hyperglycaemia: an excess of *glucose in the bloodstream.

hyperkinesia (hyperactivity): a state of over-active restlessness in children.

hypertension: high blood pressure.

hypochondria: preoccupation with the physical functioning of the body and with fancied ill health.

hypothalamus: the region of the *forebrain in the floor of the third ventricle, linked with the *thalamus above and the *pituitary gland below. It contains several important centres controlling body temperature, thirst, hunger, eating, water balance, and sexual function.

hypothermia: 1. Accidental reduction of body temperature below the normal range. 2. Deliberate lowering of body temperature for therapeutic purposes.

hysterectomy: the surgical removal of the womb.

ice age: a period in the earth's history during which ice advanced towards the equator and a general lowering of temperatures occurred. The last major ice age ended about 10 000 years ago.

igneous rocks: a group of rocks formed from the crystallization of *magma (molten silicate liquid).

ileostomy: a surgical operation in which the ileum, the lowest of the three portions of the small intestine, is brought through the abdominal wall to create an artificial opening through which the intestinal contents can discharge, thus bypassing the *colon.

iliac arteries: the arteries that supply most of the blood to the lower limbs and pelvic region.

impetigo: bacterial skin infection usually caused by staphylococci.

induction: (in obstetrics) the artificial starting of childbirth.

inertia: the property of matter that causes it to resist any change in its motion.

infarction: the death of part or the whole of an organ that occurs when the artery carrying its blood supply is obstructed by a blood clot (thrombus) or an embolus.

inner ear: the structure in vertebrates, surrounded by the temporal bone of the skull, that contains the organs of balance and hearing.

Insecta (Hexapoda): a class of arthropods comprising some 700 000 known species, but many more are thought to exist. Ranging in length from 0.5 to over 300 mm, an insect's body consists of a head, a thorax of three segments and usually bearing three pairs of legs and one or two pairs of wings, and an abdomen of eleven segments.

Insectivora: an order of small, mainly nocturnal, mammals that includes the hedgehogs, moles, and shrews.

insulator: a substance that is a poor conductor of heat and electricity.

insulin: a hormone that promotes the uptake of *glucose by body cells and thereby controls its concentration in the blood. Underproduction of insulin results in the accumulation of large amounts of glucose in the blood and its subsequent excretion in the urine. This condition, known as *diabetes mellitus*, can be treated successfully by insulin injections.

integrated circuit: a miniature electronic circuit produced within a single crystal of a *semiconductor.

interstellar space: the space between the stars. The *interstellar matter* that occupies this space constitutes several per cent of the Galaxy's total mass and it is from this matter that new stars are formed.

intravenous: into or within a vein.

ion: an atom or group of atoms that has either lost one or more electrons, making it positively charged (an anion), or gained one or more electrons, making it negatively charged (a cation).

ionization: the process of producing *ions.

ionosphere: see **earth's atmosphere**.

iris: the part of the eye that regulates the amount of light that enters. It forms a coloured muscular diaphragm across the front of the lens.

isobar: 1. A line on a map or chart that joins points or places that have the same atmospheric pressure. 2. A curve on a graph representing readings taken at constant pressure. 3. One of two or more nuclides that have the same number of nucleons but different *atomic numbers.

isotherm: 1. A line on a map or chart joining points or places of equal temperature. 2. A curve on a graph representing readings taken at constant temperature.

isotope: one of two or more atoms of the same element that have the same number of *protons in their *nucleus but different numbers of *neutrons.

IUD (intra-uterine device): a plastic or metal coil, spiral, or other shape, about 25 mm long, that is inserted into the cavity of the womb to prevent conception.

jactitation: restless tossing and turning of a person suffering from a severe disease, frequently one with a high fever.

jaundice: yellowing of the skin or whites of the eyes, indicating excess *bilirubin in the blood.

joule: the *SI unit of work and energy equal to the work done when the point of application of a force of one *newton moves, in the direction of the force, a distance of one metre.

jugular: relating to or supplying the neck or throat.

Jurassic: the second geological period of the *Mesozoic era. It began about 190 million years ago and ended about 139 million years ago.

kelp: any large brown seaweed.

keratin: fibrous protein that forms the body's horny tissues, such as fingernails.

kineplasty: a method of amputation in which the muscles and tendons of the affected limb are arranged so that they can be integrated with a specially made artificial replacement.

kinetic effect: a chemical effect that depends on reaction rate rather than on *thermodynamics.

kleptomania: a pathologically strong impulse to steal, often in the absence of any desire for the stolen object(s).

labile: unstable.

lactase: an *enzyme, secreted by the glands of the small intestine, that converts lactose (milk sugar) into *glucose and *galactose during digestion.

lactation: the secretion of milk by the mammary glands of the breasts, which usually begins at the end of pregnancy.

lallation: 1. Unintelligible speech-like babbling, as heard from infants. 2. The immature substitution of one consonant for another (e.g. *l* for *r*).

Lamarckism: one of the earliest superficially plausible theories of evolution, proposed by the French biologist Jean-Baptiste de Lamarck (1744–1829) in 1809. He suggested that changes in an individual are acquired during its lifetime, chiefly by increased use or disuse of organs in response to 'a need that continues to make itself felt', and that these changes are inherited by its offspring.

larva: the juvenile stage in the life cycle of most invertebrates, amphibians, and fish, which hatches from the egg, is unlike the adult in form, and is usually incapable of sexual reproduction.

larynx: the organ responsible for the production of vocal sounds, also serving as an air passage conveying air from the *pharynx to the lungs.

laser: (*l*ight *a*mplification by *s*timulated *e*mission of *r*adiation) a light amplifier, also called an *optical laser*, usually used to produce monochromatic coherent radiation in the infra-red, visible, and ultraviolet regions of the *electromagnetic spectrum.

Lassa fever: a serious virus disease confined to Central West Africa.

legionnaires' disease: a bacterial infection of the lungs.

Lepidoptera: an order of insects comprising the butterflies and moths, found mainly in tropical regions.

leresis: rambling speech, immature both in syntax and pronunciation. It is a feature of dementia.

lesion: a zone of tissue with impaired function as a result of damage by disease or wounding.

leucocyte (white blood cell): any blood cell that contains a *nucleus.

leucotomy: the surgical operation of interrupting the pathways of white nerve fibres within the brain. *Prefrontal lobotomy:* the original form of the operation, which involved cutting through the nerve fibres connecting the frontal lobe with the *thalamus and the associated fibres of the frontal lobe.

leukaemia: any of a group of malignant diseases in which increased numbers of certain immature or abnormal *leucocytes are produced.

libido: the sexual drive.

Lichenes (lichens): a group consisting of organisms that are symbiotic associations (*see* symbiosis) between certain types of *fungi and certain types of *algae. The fungus usually makes up most of the plant body and the cells of the alga are distributed within it.

ligament: a tough band of white fibrous connective tissue that links two bones together at a joint.

ligature: any material that is tied firmly round a blood vessel or duct to prevent bleeding, the passage of materials, etc.

lightning: a high-energy luminous electrical discharge that passes between a charged cloud and a point on the surface of the earth, between two charged clouds, or between oppositely charged layers of the same cloud. In general, the upper parts of the clouds are positively charged and the lower parts are negatively charged.

light year: a unit of distance used in astronomy; the distance travelled by light in a vacuum during one year.

lipase: an *enzyme secreted by the *pancreas and the glands of the *small intestine of vertebrates that catalyses the breakdown of fats into fatty acids and glycerol.

littoral: designating or occurring in the marginal shallow-water zone of a sea or lake, especially (in the sea) between high and low tide lines. In this zone enough light penetrates to the bottom to support rooted aquatic plants.

lobotomy: see **leucotomy**.

lockjaw: see **tetanus**.

LSD: see **lysergic acid diethylamide**.

lumbar: relating to the loin. *Lumbar puncture* is a procedure in which cerebrospinal fluid is withdrawn for diagnostic purposes by means of a hollow needle inserted into the subarachnoid space in the region of the lower back (usually between the third and fourth lumbar vertebrae).

lupus: any of several chronic skin diseases.

lymph: the fluid present within the vessels of the *lymphatic system, which is derived from the fluid that bathes the tissues.

lymphatic system: the network of vessel that conveys electrolytes, water, proteins, etc.—in the form of *lymph—from the tissue fluids to the bloodstream.

lymph node: a mass of *lymphoid tissue, many of which occur at intervals along the *lymphatic system. *Lymph in the lymphatic vessels flows through the lymph nodes, which filter out bacteria and other foreign particles, so preventing them from entering the bloodstream and causing infection.

lymphocyte: a variety of white blood cell (leucocyte), present also in the *lymph nodes, *spleen, *thymus gland, gut wall, and bone marrow.

lymphoid tissue: a tissue responsible for the production of *lymphocytes and antibodies. It occurs in the form of the *lymph nodes, *tonsils, *thymus and *spleen, and also as diffuse groups of cells.

lysergic acid diethylamide (LSD): a *psychedelic drug that is also a *hallucinogen.

Mach number: the ratio of the relative speed of a fluid and a rigid body to the speed of sound in that fluid under the same conditions of temperature and pressure. If the Mach number exceeds 1 the fluid or body is moving at a *supersonic speed*. If the Mach number exceeds 5 it is said to be *hypersonic*.

macrophage: a large scavenger cell (*see* phagocyte) present in connective tissue and many major organs and tissues.

magma: hot molten material that originates within the earth's crust or mantle and when cooled and solidified forms *igneous rock.

magnetic field: a *field of force that exists around a magnetic body (*see* magnetism) or a current-carrying conductor.

magnetism: a group of phenomena associated with *magnetic fields. Whenever an electric current flows a magnetic field is produced.

magnitude: a measure of the relative brightness of a star or other celestial object.

malignant: 1. Describing a *tumour that invades and destroys the tissue in which it originates and can spread to other sites in the body. 2. Describing any disorder that becomes progressively worse if untreated.

maltase: an *enzyme, present in saliva and *pancreatic juice, that converts *maltose into *glucose during digestion.

maltose: sugar consisting of a compound of two *molecules of *glucose.

Mammalia: a class of vertebrates containing some 4250 species. Mammals are warm-blooded animals, typically having sweat *glands whose secretion cools the skin and an insulating body covering of hair. All mammals have mammary glands, which secrete milk to nourish the young.

mandible: one of a pair of horny *mouthparts in insects, *crustaceans, centipedes, and millepedes.

map projections: the methods used to represent the spherical surface of the earth on a plane surface.

mass: a measure of a body's *inertia, i.e. its resistance to acceleration.

mastectomy: surgical removal of a breast.

mastitis: inflammation of the breast.

mastoid: relating to the *mastoid process*, a nipple-shaped process (thin prominence or protuberance) on the temporal bone that extends downward and forward behind the ear canal. The *mastoid antrum* is an air-filled channel connecting the mastoid process to the cavity of the middle ear. *Mastoid cells* are air spaces in the mastoid process.

mastoidectomy: an operation to remove some or all of the mastoid cells when they have become infected.

maxilla: 1. One of a pair of *mouthparts in insects, *crustaceans, centipedes, and millepedes. 2. One of a pair of large tooth-bearing bones in the upper jaw of vertebrates.

mechanics: the study of the interaction between matter and the forces acting on it.

medulla oblongata: part of the vertebrate *brainstem, derived from the *hindbrain, that is continuous with the spinal cord. Its function is to regulate the reflex responses controlling respiration, heartbeat, blood pressure, and other involuntary processes.

membrane: a sheet-like tissue that covers, connects, or lines biological cells and their structures.

Mendelism: the theory of heredity that forms the basis of classical genetics.

meninges: the three connective tissue *membranes that line the skull and vertebral canal and enclose the brain and spinal cord: the dura mater, arachnoid mater, and pia mater.

meningitis: an inflammation of the *meninges due to viral or bacterial infection.

meniscus: a concave or convex upper surface that forms on a liquid in a tube as a result of *surface tension.

menopause (climacteric): the time in a woman's life when *ovulation and menstruation (*see* menstrual cycle) cease and the woman is no longer able to bear children. The menopause can occur at any age between the middle thirties and the late fifties.

menstrual cycle: the periodic sequence of events in sexually mature non-pregnant women by which an egg cell (ovum) is released from a *follicle in the *ovary at four-weekly intervals until the *menopause. The secretion of *progesterone in the ruptured follicle causes the lining of the womb to become thicker and richly supplied with blood in preparation for pregnancy. If the ovum is not fertilized the womb lining is shed at menstruation.

Mesozoic: the geological era that extended from the end of the *Palaeozoic era, about 225 million years ago, to the beginning of the *Cainozoic era, about 65 million years ago.

metabolism: the sum of the chemical reactions that occur within a living organism and enable its continuing growth and functioning.

metacarpus: the five bones of the hand that connect the carpus (wrist) to the phalanges (digits).

metamorphic rocks: one of the three major rock categories, which is formed when existing rock is subjected to either chemical or physical alteration by heat, pressure, or chemically active fluids.

metamorphosis: the rapid transformation from the *larval to the adult form that occurs in the life cycle of many invertebrates and amphibians.

metastasis: the distant spread of disease, especially a malignant tumour, from its site of origin.

metatarsus: the five bones of the

foot that connect the tarsus (ankle) to the phalanges (toes).

meteor: a streak of light observable in the sky when a particle of matter enters the earth's atmosphere and becomes incandescent as a result of friction with atmospheric *atoms and *molecules.

microbe: see **micro-organism**.

micro-organism: any organism that can be observed only with the aid of a microscope.

midbrain: the small portion of the *brainstem, excluding the *pons and the *medulla oblongata, that joins the *hindbrain to the *forebrain.

middle ear (tympanic cavity): the air-filled cavity within the skull of vertebrates that lies between the *outer ear and the *inner ear. It is linked to the *pharynx, and therefore to outside air, via the *Eustachian tube.

migraine: a recurrent throbbing headache that characteristically affects one side of the head and is often accompanied by prostration and vomiting.

Milky Way: The sun belongs to a spiral galaxy known as the *Galaxy* (with a capital G) or the *Milky Way system*. There are some 10^{11} stars in the system, which is about 30 000 *parsecs across with a maximum thickness at the centre of about 4000 parsecs. The sun is about 10 000 parsecs from the centre of the Galaxy.

mimicry: the resemblance of one animal to another, which has evolved as a means of protection.

molecular weight: see **relative molecular weight**.

molecule: a particle consisting of two or more *atoms held together by chemical bonds. It is the smallest unit of an element of compound capable of existing independently.

Mollusca: a *phylum of soft-bodied invertebrates characterized by an unsegmented body differentiated into a *head*, a ventral muscular *foot* used in locomotion, and a dorsal *visceral hump* covered by a fold of skin which secretes a protective shell in many species.

monosaccharide (simple sugar): a *carbohydrate that cannot be split into smaller units by the action of dilute acids.

monotremes: see **Prototheria**.

mouthparts: modified paired appendages on the head segments of *arthropods, used for feeding.

mucous membrane: the moist *membrane lining many tubular structures and cavities.

multiple sclerosis: a chronic disease of the nervous system affecting young and middle-aged adults.

muscular dystrophy: any one of a group of muscle diseases in which there is a recognizable pattern of inheritance.

mutation: a sudden random change in the genetic material of a cell that may cause it and all cells derived from it to differ in appearance or behaviour from the normal type.

myopathy: any disease of the muscles.

myopia: short-sightedness.

natural selection: the process that, according to *Darwinism, brings about the evolution of new species of animals and plants.

nautical mile: a measure of distance used at sea. In the UK it is defined as 6080 feet, but the international definition is 1852 metres.

Neanderthal man: a form of fossil man that appeared in Europe and Western Asia about 100 000 years ago. He was thought to be a different species (*Homo neanderthalensis*) from modern man but is now generally regarded as a subspecies of *Homo sapiens*.

nebula: originally a fixed, extended, and somewhat fuzzy white haze observed in the sky with a telescope. Many of these objects can now be resolved into clouds of individual stars and have been identified as *galaxies. They are still sometimes referred to as *extragalactic nebulae*. The *gaseous nebulae*, however, cannot be resolved into individual stars and consist, for the most part, of interstellar dust and gas.

negative feedback: see **feedback**.

neo-Darwinism (modern synthesis): the current theory of the process of evolution, formulated between about 1920 and 1950, that combines evidence from classical genetics with the Darwinian theory of evolution by *natural selection (*see* Darwinism). It makes use of modern knowledge of *genes and *chromosomes to explain the source of the genetic variation upon which selection works. This aspect was unexplained by traditional Darwinism.

neolithic: (relating to) the New Stone Age, beginning in the Middle East approximately 9000 BC and lasting until 6000 BC, during which man first developed agriculture.

nephritis (Bright's disease): inflammation of the kidney.

nephrology: the branch of medicine concerned with the study, investigation, and management of diseases of the kidney.

nerve: a strand of tissue comprising many *nerve fibres plus supporting tissues, enclosed in a connective-tissue sheath. Nerves connect the *central nervous system with the organs and tissues of the body.

nerve ending: the final part of one of the branches of a *nerve fibre, where a *neurone makes contact either with another neurone or with a muscle or *gland cell.

nerve fibre: the axon of a *neurone together with the tissues associated with it.

nervous system: the vast network of *cells specialized to carry information (in the form of nerve impulses) to and from all parts of the body in order to bring about bodily activity.

neuralgia: a severe burning or stabbing pain often following the course of a nerve.

neurone (nerve cell): an elongated branched cell that is the fundamental unit of the *nervous system.

neurosis: a mental illness in which insight is retained but there is a maladaptive way of behaving or thinking that causes suffering.

neutron: a neutral *hadron that is stable in the atomic nucleus but decays into a *proton, an *electron, and an antineutrino with a mean life of 12 minutes outside the *nucleus.

neutron star: a star that has reached the end of its evolutionary life and runs out of nuclear fuel.

newton: the *SI unit of force, being the force required to give a mass of one kilogram an acceleration of $1\,m\,s^{-2}$.

Newtonian mechanics: the system of *mechanics that relies on *Newton's laws of motion. Newtonian mechanics is applicable to bodies moving at speeds relative to the observer that are small compared to the speed of light. Bodies moving near to the speed of light require an approach based on *relativistic mechanics, in which the mass of the body changes with its speed.

Newton's laws of motion: the three laws of motion on which *Newtonian mechanics is based. 1. A body continues in a state of rest or uniform motion in a straight line unless it is acted upon by external forces. 2. The rate of change of momentum of a moving body is proportional to and in the same direction as the force acting on it. 3. If one body exerts a force on another, there is an equal and opposite force, called a *reaction*, exerted on the first body by the second.

nexus: (in anatomy) a connection or link.

nictitating membrane: a clear *membrane forming a third eyelid in amphibians, reptiles, birds, and some mammals, but not man. It can be drawn across the *cornea independently of the other eyelids, thus clearing the eye surface and giving added protection without interrupting the continuity of vision.

nova: a star that, over a period of only a few days, becomes very much brighter than it was, subsequently fading to its original brightness.

nucleus (of atom): the central core of an *atom that contains most of its mass.

nucleus (of cell): the large body embedded in the *cytoplasm of all plant and animal *cells (but not the cells of bacteria or blue-green algae) that contains the genetic material *DNA.

nystagmus: rapid involuntary movements of the eyes that may be from side to side, up and down, or rotatory.

occipital bone: a saucer-shaped bone of the skull that forms the back and part of the base of the cranium.

occluded front: see **front**.

Odonata: an order of insects containing the dragonflies and damselflies, most of which occur in tropical regions.

oedema: excessive accumulation of fluid in the body tissues: popularly known as *dropsy*. The resultant swelling may be local, as with an injury or inflammation, or more general.

Oedipus complex: repressed sexual feelings of a child for its opposite-sexed parent, combined with rivalry towards the same-sexed parent: a normal stage of development. Arrest of development at the Oedipal stage is said to be responsible for sexual deviations and other neurotic behaviour.

oesophagus: the gullet. A muscular tube that extends from the *pharynx to the stomach.

oestrogen: one of a group of female

sex *hormones, produced principally by the ovaries, that control female sexual development.

ohm: the derived *SI unit of electrical resistance, being the resistance between two points on a *conductor when a constant potential difference of one *volt, applied between these points, produces a current of one *ampere in the conductor.

Oligocene: the third geological epoch of the *Tertiary period. It began about 38 million years ago and finished about 12 million years ago.

Ordovician: the second geological period of the *Palaeozoic era. It began about 500 million years ago and lasted for about 60 million years.

omentum (epiploon): a double layer of *peritoneum attached to the stomach and linking it with other abdominal organs.

omnivore: an animal that eats both animal and vegetable matter.

open cluster: a diffuse group of between 20 and a few hundred stars that move through the *Milky Way together.

origin of life: the process by which living organisms developed from inanimate matter, which is generally thought to have occurred on earth between 3500 and 4000 million years ago. It is supposed that the primordial atmosphere was like a chemical soup containing all the basic constituents of organic matter: ammonia, methane, hydrogen, and water vapour. These underwent a process of chemical evolution using energy from the sun and electric storms to combine into ever more complex molecules, such as amino acids, proteins, and vitamins. Eventually self-replicating nucleic acids, the basis of all life, could have developed. The very first organisms may have consisted of such molecules bounded by a simple membrane.

orogenesis: the process by which major mountain chains are formed.

orthopaedics: the science or practice of correcting deformities caused by disease of or damage to the bones and joints of the skeleton.

osmosis: the passage of a solvent through a *semi-permeable membrane* separating two solutions of different concentrations.

ossification: the process of bone formation. It is brought about by the action of special cells called *osteoblasts*, which deposit layers of bone in connective tissue.

osteomyelitis: inflammation of the bone marrow due to infection.

osteopathy: a system of healing based on the theory that most diseases are caused by displacement of bones from their correct position.

osteosclerosis: an abnormal increase in the density of bone.

outer ear (external ear): the part of the ear external to the tympanum (ear-drum).

ovary: 1. The reproductive organ in female animals in which eggs (ova) are produced. 2. The hollow base of the *carpel of a flower.

oviparity: reproduction in which fertilized eggs are laid or spawned by the mother and hatch outside her body.

ovoviviparity: reproduction in which fertilized eggs develop and hatch in the oviduct of the mother.

ovulation: the release of an egg cell from the *ovary.

ozone layer (ozonosphere): a layer of the earth's atmosphere in which most of the atmosphere's ozone is concentrated. It occurs 15–20 km above the earth's surface and is virtually synonymous with the stratosphere.

paediatrics: the general medicine of childhood.

Palaeocene: the earliest geological epoch of the *Tertiary period. It began about 65 million years ago and lasted for about 11.5 million years.

palaeolithic: (relating to) the Old Stone Age, lasting in Europe from about 2.5 million to 9000 years ago, during which man used primitive stone tools made by chipping stones and flints.

palaeontology: the study of extinct organisms, including the structure, environment, evolution, and distribution, as revealed by their *fossil remains.

Palaeozoic: the first era of *Phanerozoic time.

pancreas: a *gland in vertebrates lying between the *duodenum and the *spleen.

pancreatic juice: the mixture of digestive *enzymes *secreted by the *pancreas. Its production is stimulated by *hormones secreted by the *duodenum.

pantropic: describing a *virus that can invade and affect many different tissues of the body without showing a special affinity for any one of them.

paranoid: describing a mental state characterized by fixed and logically elaborated delusions.

paraplegia: paralysis of both legs, usually due to disease or injury of the spinal cord.

parkinsonism: a disorder of middle-aged and elderly people characterized by tremor, rigidity, and a poverty of spontaneous movements.

paroxysm: 1. A sudden violent attack, especially a spasm or convulsion. 2. The abrupt worsening of symptoms or recurrence of disease.

parsec: a unit of length used to express astronomical distance. The distance at which the mean radius of the earth's orbit subtends an angle of one second of arc. One parsec is equal to 3.0857×10^{16} metres or 3.2616 light years.

parthenogenesis: the development of an organism from an unfertilized egg. This occurs sporadically in many plants and in a few animals, but in some species it is the main and sometimes only method of reproduction; for example, in some species of aphid.

particle: 1 (in physics). One of the fundamental components of matter. *See* elementary particles. 2 (in mechanics). A hypothetical body that has mass but no physical extension.

parturition: the act of giving birth to young at the end of the *gestation period. *Hormones probably cause the process to start but the mechanism is not fully understood.

patella: a small rounded movable bone that is situated in a *tendon in front of the knee joint in most mammals, including humans. Its function is to protect the knee.

pectoral: relating to the chest or breast.

pedicel: the stalk attaching a flower to the main floral axis (*see* peduncle). Some flowers, described as **sessile*, do not have a pedicel and arise directly from the peduncle.

peduncle: the main stalk of a plant that bears the flowers, which may be solitary or grouped.

pelagic: describing organisms that swim or drift in a sea or a lake, as distinct from those that live on the bottom.

pellicle: a thin layer of skin, *membrane, or any other substance.

pelvic girdle (hip girdle): the bony structure to which the bones of the lower limbs are attached. It consists of the right and left hip bones.

pelvis: 1. The bony structure formed by the hip bones, *sacrum, and *coccyx. 2. The cavity within the bony pelvis. 3. Any structure shaped like a basin.

pepsin: an *enzyme in the stomach that begins the digestion of *proteins by splitting them into *peptones (*see* peptidase).

peptide: any of a group of organic compounds comprising two or more *amino acids linked by *peptide bonds*. These bonds are formed by the reaction between adjacent carboxyl and amino groups with the elimination of water.

peptidase: one of a group of a digestive *enzymes that split *proteins in the stomach and intestine into their constituent *amino acids.

peptone: a large *protein fragment produced by the action of *enzymes on proteins in the first stages of protein digestion.

perennial: a plant that lives for a number of years.

perianth: the part of a flower situated outside the *stamens and *carpels.

pericardium: the *membrane surrounding the heart.

perinatal: relating to the period from about three months before to one month after birth.

peripheral nervous system: all parts of the nervous system excluding the *central nervous system.

peristalsis: waves of involuntary muscular contraction and relaxation that pass along the *alimentary canal, forcing food contents along.

peritoneum: the *serous membrane of the abdominal cavity.

peritonitis: inflammation of the *peritoneum.

Permian: the last geological period in the *Palaeozoic era. It extended from about 280 million years ago to about 225 million years ago.

phagocyte: a cell that is able to engulf and digest *bacteria, *protozoa, cells and cell debris, and other small particles. Phagocytes include many white blood cells and *macrophages, which play a major role in the body's defence mechanism.

Phanerozoic: geological time since the end of the *Precambrian, represented by rock strata containing clearly recognizable *fossils. It comprises the *Palaeozoic, *Mesozoic, and *Cainozoic eras and has extended for about 570 million years from the beginning of the *Cambrian period. Fossils are extremely rare in Precambrian rocks.

pharyngeal tonsils: see **adenoids**.

pharynx: a muscular tube, lined with *mucous membrane, that extends from the beginning of the *oesophagus (gullet) up to the base of the skull.

phenobarbitone: a *barbiturate drug.

phlebitis: inflammation of the wall of a vein.

photic zone: the upper layer of a sea or a lake, in which there is sufficient light for *photosynthesis. The limit of the photic zone varies from less than a metre to more than 200 metres, depending on the turbidity of the water.

photon: a particle with zero *rest mass consisting of a *quantum of *electromagnetic radiation.

photosphere: the visible surface of the sun or other star and the source of its absorption spectrum.

photosynthesis: the chemical process by which green plants synthesize organic compounds from carbon dioxide and water in the presence of sunlight.

phototropism (heliotropism): the growth of plant organs in response to light.

phylum: a category used in the classification of animals that consists of one or several similar or closely related classes. Phyla are grouped into the kingdom Animalia. In plant classification, the division is usually used instead of the phylum.

Piltdown man: fossil remains, purported to have been found by Charles Dawson at Piltdown, Sussex, in 1912. In 1953 dating techniques showed the specimen to be a fraud.

pineal gland: an outgrowth of the *forebrain. In man its functions are obscure, but in other vertebrates it acts as an *endocrine gland, secreting *hormones that affect reproductive function and behaviour.

pink disease: a severe illness of children of the teething age.

pistil: female part of a flower.

pituitary gland: a pea-sized *endocrine gland attached by a thin stalk to the *hypothalamus at the base of the brain.

placebo: a medicine that is ineffective but may help to relieve a condition because the patient has faith in its powers.

placenta: the organ in mammals and other viviparous animals by means of which the embryo is attached to the wall of the uterus.

plankton: minute *pelagic organisms that drift or float passively with the current in a sea or lake. Plankton includes many microscopic animals and plants, such as *algae, *protozoans, various animal *larvae, and some worms.

plasma: the straw-coloured fluid in which the blood cells are suspended.

Pleistocene: the earlier period of the *Quaternary period. It extended from the end of the *Pliocene, about 2 million years ago, to the beginning of the *Holocene, about 10 000 years ago.

pleura: the covering of the lungs,

and of the inner surface of the chest wall.

pleurisy: inflammation of the *pleura.

Pliocene: the fifth and final epoch of the *Tertiary period. It began about 7 million years ago and lasted for about 5 million years.

pneumoconiosis: a lung disease caused by inhaling dust.

polygon: a plane figure with a number of sides. In a *regular polygon* all the sides and internal angles are equal.

polyhedron: a solid bounded by polygonal faces. The cube is one of five possible regular polyhedrons. The others are the *tetrahedron* (four faces), the *octahedron* (eight faces), the *dodecahedron* (twelve faces), and the *icosahedron* (twenty faces).

polymer: a substance formed by the linkage of a large number of smaller molecules known as *monomers*.

polyp: a growth, usually benign, protruding from a *mucous membrane.

polypeptide: a *peptide comprising ten or more *amino acids.

polysaccharide: any of a group of *carbohydrates comprising long chains of *monosaccharide (simple sugar) molecules.

pons (pons Varolii): a thick tract of nerve fibres in the brain that links the *medulla oblongata to the *midbrain.

portal vein: a vein that conveys blood from the stomach, intestines, *spleen, and *pancreas to the liver.

Precambrian: the division of geological time from the formation of the earth, believed to be about 4600 million years ago, to the beginning of the *Cambrian period, some 570 million years ago.

premenstrual tension: a condition of nervousness, irritability, emotional disturbance, headache, and/or depression affecting some women for up to 10 days before menstruation.

printed circuit: an electronic circuit consisting of a conducting material deposited (printed) on to the surface of an insulating sheet.

prism: 1 (in mathematics). A *polyhedron with two parallel congruent polygons as bases and parallelograms for all other faces. A *triangular prism* has triangular bases. 2 (in optics). A block of glass or other transparent material, usually having triangular bases.

Proboscidea: the order of mammals that comprises the elephants.

progesterone: a *hormone, produced primarily by the *corpus luteum of the ovary, but also by the *placenta, that prepares the inner lining of the *uterus for implantation of a fertilized egg cell.

progestogen: one of a group of naturally occurring or synthetic *steroid hormones, including *progesterone, that maintain the normal course of pregnancy.

prognosis: an assessment of the future course and outcome of a patient's disease.

prolapse: downward displacement of an organ or a part from its normal position.

prostate gland: a male accessory sex *gland that opens into the *urethra. During ejaculation it secretes an alkaline fluid that forms part of the semen.

protein: any of a large group of organic compounds found in all living organisms. Proteins comprise carbon, hydrogen, oxygen, and nitrogen, and most also contain sulphur.

protein synthesis: the process by which living cells manufacture proteins from their constituent *amino acids, in accordance with the genetic information carried in the *DNA of the *chromosomes.

proton: an *elementary particle that is stable, bears a positive charge equal in magnitude to that of the *electron, and has a mass that is 1836.12 times that of the electron. The proton is a hydrogen *ion and occurs in all atomic nuclei.

protoplasm: the granular material comprising the living contents of a *cell, i.e. all the substances in a cell except large *vacuoles and material recently ingested or to be excreted. It consists of a *nucleus embedded in a jelly-like *cytoplasm.

Prototheria: a subclass of mammals—the monotremes—that lay large yolky eggs. It contains only the duckbilled platypus and the spiny ant-eater. After hatching, the young feed on milk from simple mammary glands inside a maternal abdominal pouch.

Protozoa: a *phylum comprising unicellular or acellular, usually microscopic, organisms. They are very widely distributed in marine, freshwater, and moist terrestrial habitats.

psoriasis: a chronic skin disease in which itchy scaly red patches form on the elbows, forearms, knees, legs, scalp, and other parts of the body.

psychedelic: describing drugs, such as cannabis and *LSD, that can induce changes in the level of consciousness of the mind.

psychoanalysis: a school of psychology and a method of treating mental disorders based upon the teachings of Sigmund Freud (1856–1939).

psychopath: a person who behaves in an antisocial way and shows little or no guilt for antisocial acts and little capacity for forming emotional relationships with others.

psychosomatic: relating to or involving both the mind and body. It usually applies to illnesses that are caused by the interaction of mental and physical factors.

puberty: the time at which the onset of sexual maturity occurs and the reproductive organs become functional.

pudendum: the external genital organs, especially those of the female.

puerperal (puerperous): relating to childbirth or the period that immediately follows it. *Puerperal fever:* blood poisoning in a mother shortly after childbirth resulting from infection of the lining of the womb or the *vagina.

pulsar: a celestial source of radiation emitted in brief regular pulses. First discovered in 1968, a pulsar is believed to be a rotating *neutron star.

pupa: the third stage of development in the life cycle of some insects. During the pupal stage locomotion and feeding cease and *metamorphosis from the larva to the adult form takes place.

quadriplegia (tetraplegia): paralysis affecting all four limbs.

quantum: the minimum amount by which certain properties, such as energy or angular momentum, of a system can change. Such properties do not, therefore, vary continuously, but in integral multiples of the relevant quantum. This concept forms the basis of the *quantum theory. In waves and fields the quantum can be regarded as an excitation, giving a particle-like interpretation to the wave or field. Thus, the quantum of the electromagnetic field is the *photon.

quantum mechanics: a system of *mechanics that was developed from *quantum theory and is used to explain the properties of *atoms and *molecules.

quantum theory: the theory devised by Max Planck (1858–1947) in 1900 to account for the emission of the *black-body radiation from hot bodies.

quasars: a class of astronomical objects that appear on optical photographs as star-like but have large *red-shifts quite unlike those of stars. They were first observed in 1961 when it was found that strong radio emission was emanating from many of these star-like bodies.

Quaternary: the second period of the *Cainozoic era, which began about 2 million years ago, following the *Tertiary period, and includes the present. It is subdivided into two epochs—the *Pleistocene and *Holocene.

quinine: a drug formerly used to prevent and treat malaria, now largely replaced by more effective less toxic drugs.

quinsy: a pus-filled swelling in the soft palate around the *tonsil: a complication of tonsillitis.

radiation: 1. Energy travelling in the form of electromagnetic waves or *photons. 2. A stream of particles, especially alpha- or beta-particles from a radioactive source or neutrons from a nuclear reactor.

Ramapithecus: a genus of extinct primates that lived between 8 and 14 million years ago.

Ratitae: a group comprising the flightless birds, including the ostrich, kiwi, and emu.

red-shift: 1 (Doppler red-shift). A displacement of the lines in the spectra of certain galaxies towards the red end of the visible spectrum (i.e. towards longer wavelengths). It is usually interpreted as a *Doppler effect resulting from the recession of the galaxies along the line of sight. 2 (gravitational *or* Einstein red-shift). A similar displacement of spectral lines towards the red caused not by a Doppler effect but by a high gravitational field. This type of red-shift was predicted by Einstein, and some astronomers believe that this is the cause of the large red-shifts of *quasars.

referred pain (synalgia): pain felt in a part of the body other than where it might be expected.

refraction: the change of direction suffered by a wavefront as it passes obliquely from one medium to another in which its speed of propagation is altered. The phenomenon occurs with all types of wave, but is most familiar with light waves.

relative density: the ratio of the density of a substance at a specified temperature to the density of a reference substance. It was formerly known as *specific gravity*.

relative molecular mass (molecular weight): the ratio of the average mass per molecule of the naturally occurring form of an element or compound to $\frac{1}{12}$ of the mass of a carbon-12 atom. It is equal to the sum of the relative atomic masses of all the atoms that comprise a molecule.

relativity: one of several theories concerning motion, designed to account for departures from *Newtonian mechanics that occur with very high-speed relative motion. The theory implied is now usually one of two proposed by Albert Einstein (1879–1955).

REM (rapid eye movement): describing a stage of sleep during which the muscles of the eyeballs are in constant motion behind the eyelids. REM sleep usually coincides with dreaming.

renal: relating to or affecting the kidneys.

renin: a substance released into the body by the kidney in response to stress.

rennin: an *enzyme produced in the stomach that coagulates milk. This ensures that the milk remains in the stomach, exposed to protein-digesting *enzymes, for as long as possible.

Reptilia: the class that contains the first entirely terrestrial vertebrates, which can live in dry terrestrial habitats as their skin is covered by a layer of horny scales, preventing water loss.

resistivity: a measure of a material's ability to oppose the flow of an electric current.

respiratory distress syndrome (hyaline membrane disease): the condition of a new-born infant in which the lungs are imperfectly expanded.

rest mass: the mass of a body at rest when measured by an observer who is at rest in the same frame of reference.

reticuloendothelial system (RES): a community of *phagocytes that is spread throughout the body. The RES is concerned with defence against microbial infection and with the removal of worn-out blood cells from the bloodstream.

retina: the light-sensitive layer that lines the interior of the eye.

rhesus factor: a group of *antigens that may or may not be present on the surface of the red blood cells. It forms the basis of the rhesus blood group system. Most people have the rhesus factor, i.e. they are *Rh-positive*. People who lack the factor are termed *Rh-negative*.

rheumatic fever: a disease affecting mainly children and young adults that arises as a delayed complication of infection of the upper respiratory tract.

rhombus: a parallelogram in which all the sides are of equal length.

ribonucleic acid: see **RNA**.

Richter scale: a logarithmic scale

devised in 1935 by C. F. Richter to compare the magnitude of earthquakes. The scale ranges from 0 to 10 and the Richter scale value is related to the logarithm of the amplitude of the ground motion divided by the period of the dominant wave.

rickets: a disease of children in which the bones do not harden and are malformed due to a deficiency of vitamin D.

RNA (ribonucleic acid): a complex organic compound (a nucleic acid) in living cells that is concerned with *protein synthesis. In some viruses, RNA is also the hereditary material. Most RNA is synthesized in the *nucleus and then distributed to various parts of the *cytoplasm.

Rodentia: an order of mammals characterized by a single pair of long curved incisors in each jaw. These teeth are specialized for gnawing.

Rorschach test: a test to measure aspects of personality, consisting of ten inkblots in colour and black and white.

rubella: German measles.

rupture: see **hernia**.

sacrum: a curved triangular element of the backbone consisting of five fused vertebrae.

saliva: the alkaline liquid secreted by the *salivary glands and the *mucous membrane of the mouth. Its principal constituents are water and mucus, which keep the mouth moist and lubricate food, and *enzymes that begin the digestion of starch.

salivary gland: a gland that produces *saliva. There are three pairs: the parotid glands, sublingual glands, and submandibular glands.

Salk vaccine: a *vaccine against poliomyelitis.

salmonella: a *bacterium that inhabits the intestines of animals and man. Certain species cause such diseases as food poisoning, gastroenteritis, and *septicaemia.

sarcoma: any *cancer of connective tissue.

scabies: a skin infection caused by the itch mite, *Sarcoptes scabiei*.

scapula: the shoulder-blade.

scarlet fever: a highly contagious disease, mainly of childhood, caused by bacteria of the genus *Streptococcus*.

schizophrenia: a severe mental disorder (or group of disorders) characterized by a disintegration of the process of thinking, of contact with reality, and of emotional responsiveness.

sciatica: pain felt down the back and outer side of the thigh, leg, and foot.

sciatic nerve: the major nerve of the leg and the nerve with the largest diameter. It runs down behind the thigh from the lower end of the spine.

sclerosis: hardening of tissue, usually due to scarring (fibrosis) after inflammation.

sclerotic (sclera): the tough external layer of the vertebrate eye. At the front of the eye, the sclera is modified to form the *cornea.

scrofula: tuberculosis of *lymph nodes, usually those in the neck, causing the formation of abscesses.

scurvy: a disease that is caused by a deficiency of vitamin C and results from the consumption of a diet devoid of fresh fruit and vegetables.

secretion: 1. The process by which a *gland isolates constituents of the blood or tissue fluid and chemically alters them to produce a substance that it discharges for use by the body or excretes. 2. The substance that is produced by a gland.

sedimentary rocks: a group of rocks formed as a result of the accumulation and consolidation of sediments. Sedimentary rocks are one of the three major rock groups forming the earth's crust.

sedimentation: the settling of the solid particles through a liquid either to produce a concentrated slurry from a dilute suspension or to clarify a liquid containing solid particles.

semiconductor: a crystalline solid, such as silicon, with an electrical conductivity intermediate between that of a *conductor and an *insulator.

senescence: the changes that occur in an organism (or part of an organism) between maturity and death, i.e. ageing.

senile dementia: loss of intellectual faculties, beginning for the first time in old age.

senility: the state of physical and mental deterioration that is associated with the ageing process.

septicaemia: widespread destruction of tissues due to absorption of disease-causing *bacteria or their toxins from the bloodstream.

septum: any dividing wall in a plant or animal. Examples are the septa that separate the chambers of the heart.

serous: 1. Relating to or containing *scrum. 2. Resembling serum or producing a fluid resembling serum.

serum: the fluid that separates from clotted blood or blood *plasma that is allowed to stand.

sessile: 1. Describing animals that live permanently attached to a surface, i.e. sedentary animals. 2. Describing any organ that does not possess a stalk where one might be expected.

sex chromosome: a *chromosome that is involved in the determination of the sex of the individual. Women have two X chromosomes; men have one X chromosome and one Y chromosome.

Siamese twins: identical twins that are physically joined together at birth.

sibling: one of a number of children of the same parents.

side-effect: an unwanted effect produced by a drug in addition to its desired therapeutic effects.

sidereal period: the time taken for a planet or satellite to complete one revolution of its orbit measured with reference to the background of the stars.

silicon chip: a single crystal of a semiconducting silicon material, typically having micrometre dimensions, fabricated in such a way that it can perform a large number of independent electronic functions (*see* integrated circuit).

silicosis: a lung disease—a form of *pneumoconiosis—produced by inhaling silica dust particles.

Silurian: a geological period of the

*Palaeozoic era that began about 440 million years ago and lasted for about 45 million years.

sinus: 1. An air cavity within a bone, especially any of the cavities within the bones of the face or skull. 2. Any wide channel containing blood, usually venous blood. 3. A pocket or bulge in a tubular organ, especially a blood vessel. 4. An infected tract leading from a focus of infection to the surface of the skin or a hollow organ.

sinusitis: inflammation of one or more of the paranasal sinuses.

Siphonaptera: an order of wingless insects comprising the fleas.

SI units: Système International d'Unités: the international system of units now recommended for all scientific purposes.

sleeping sickness: a disease of tropical Africa caused by the presence in the blood of parasitic protozoans which are transmitted to man through the bite of tsetse flies.

small intestine: the portion of the *alimentary canal between the stomach and the large intestine.

smallpox: an acute infectious *virus disease causing high fever and a rash that scars the skin.

solar energy: the electromagnetic energy radiated from the sun.

solar system: the sun, the nine major planets (Mercury, Venus, Earth, Mars, Jupiter, Saturn, Uranus, Neptune, and Pluto) and their natural satellites, the *asteroids, the *comets, and the meteoroids (*see* meteors).

solar wind: a continuous outward flow of charged particles, mostly *protons and *electrons, from the sun's *corona into interplanetary space. The particles are controlled by the sun's *magnetic field and are able to escape from the sun's *gravitational field because of their high thermal energy.

solenoid: a coil of wire wound on a cylindrical former in which the length of the former is greater than its diameter. When a current is passed through the coil a *magnetic field is produced inside the coil parallel to its axis. This field can be made to operate a plunger inside the former so that the solenoid can be used to operate a circuit breaker, valve, or other electromechanical device.

species: 1 (in biology). A category used in the classification of organisms that consists of a group of similar individuals that can usually breed among themselves and produce fertile offspring. Similar or related species are grouped into a *genus. Within a species groups of individuals may become reproductively isolated because of geographical or behavioural factors. Such populations may, because of different selection pressures, develop different characteristics from the main population and so form a distinct subspecies. 2 (in chemistry). A chemical entity, such as a particular *atom, *ion, or *molecule.

specific: 1 (in physics). *a.* Denoting that an extensive physical quantity so described is expressed per unit mass. *b.* In some older physical quantities the adjective 'specific' was added for other reasons (e.g. specific gravity, specific resistance). These names are now no longer used. 2 (in biology). Relating to a *species.

specific gravity: see **relative density**.

specific volume: the volume of a substance per unit mass.

speed of light: the speed at which electromagnetic radiation travels; usually means the speed of light in a vacuum: $c = 2.997 \times 10^8 \mathrm{m\,s^{-1}}$.

speed of sound: the speed at which sound waves are propagated through a material medium.

spermatozoa (sperm): mature male sex cells. The tail of a sperm enables it to swim, which is important as a means for reaching and fertilizing the ovum.

spinal anaesthesia: 1. Suppression of sensation in part of the body by the injection of a local anaesthetic into the space surrounding the spinal cord. In *epidural spinal anaesthesia* the anaesthetic is injected into the outer lining of the spinal cord. 2. Loss of sensation in part of the body as a result of injury or disease to the spinal cord.

spirochaete: any one of a group of spiral-shaped *bacteria that lack a rigid cell wall and move by means of muscular flexions of the cell.

spleen: a large dark-red ovoid organ situated on the left side of the body below and behind the stomach. The spongy interior (*pulp*) of the spleen consists of *lymphoid tissue within a meshwork of reticular fibres. The spleen is a major component of the *reticuloendothelial system.

spontaneous combustion: combustion in which a substance produces sufficient heat within itself, usually by a slow oxidation process, for ignition to take place without the need for an external high-temperature energy source.

spore: a reproductive cell that can develop into an individual without first fusing with another reproductive cell.

stalactites and stalagmites: accretions of calcium carbonate in limestone caves. Stalactites are tapering cones or pendants that hang down; stalagmites are upward projections from the floor.

stamen: one of the male reproductive parts of a flower.

starch: the form in which *carbohydrates are stored in many plants and a major constituent of the diet.

steady-state theory: the cosmological theory that the universe has always existed in a steady state, that it had no beginning, will have no end, and has a constant mean density. *See also* big-bang theory.

sternum: the breastbone.

steroid: one of a group of organic compounds that include the male and female sex hormones (androgens and *oestrogens), the *hormones of the adrenal cortex, *progesterone, bile salts, and sterols. Synthetic steroids have been produced for therapeutic purposes.

stratosphere: see **earth's atmosphere**.

streptococcus: a *genus of Gram-positive non-motile spherical *bacteria occurring in chains.

streptomycin: an antibiotic that is effective against a wide range of bacterial infections.

subclavian artery: either of two arteries supplying blood to the neck and arms.

subcutaneous: beneath the skin.

sucrose: a *carbohydrate consisting of *glucose and *fructose.

sulphonamide (sulpha drug): one of a group of drugs, derived from sulphanilamide (a red dye), that prevent the growth of *bacteria.

sunspot: a relatively dark patch in the sun's *photosphere resulting from a localized fall in temperature.

superdense theory: see **big-bang theory**.

supergiant: the largest and most luminous type of star.

supernova: an explosive brightening of a star which increases the energy radiated. It takes several years to fade and while it lasts dominates the whole galaxy in which it lies.

suppository: a medicinal preparation in solid form suitable for insertion into a body cavity.

surface tension: the property of a liquid that makes it behave as if its surface is enclosed in an elastic skin.

suture: 1 (in anatomy). A type of immovable joint, found particularly in the skull, characterized by a minimal amount of connective tissue between the two bones. 2. (in surgery). The closure of a wound or incision with material such as silk or catgut to facilitate the healing process. 3. The material used to sew up a wound.

symbiosis: a mutually advantageous interaction between individuals of different *species.

sympathetic nervous system: one of the two divisions of the *autonomic nervous system.

synalgia: see **referred pain**.

synapse: the junction between two adjacent *neurones (nerve cells).

syndrome: a combination of signs and/or symptoms that forms a distinct clinical picture indicative of a particular disorder.

synovia (synovial fluid): the thick colourless lubricating fluid that surrounds a joint and fills a *tendon sheaf.

synovial membrane: the *membrane that lines the *ligament surrounding a freely movable joint.

syphilis: a chronic *venereal disease caused by the bacterium *Treponema pallidum*.

systemic: relating to or affecting the body as a whole, rather than individual parts and organs.

tachycardia: an increase in the heart rate above normal.

tarsal: relating to the bones of the ankle and foot. The *tarsus* is the seven bones of the ankle and proximal part of the foot.

taste bud: a small sense organ in most vertebrates, specialized for the detection of taste.

taxis: (in surgery) the returning to a normal position of displaced bones, organs, or other parts by manipulation only.

taxonomy: the study of the theory, practice, and rules of classification of living and extinct organisms.

tendon: a tough whitish cord, consisting of numerous parallel bundles of collagen fibres, that serves to attach a muscle to a bone.

tennis elbow: a painful inflammation of the *tendon at the outer border of the elbow, caused by over-use of the forearm muscles.

Tertiary: the older geological period of the *Cainozoic era. It began about 65 million years ago and lasted till about 2 million years ago. It is subdivided into the *Palaeocene, *Eocene, *Oligocene, Miocene, and *Pliocene epochs in ascending order.

testosterone: the principal male sex *hormone.

test-tube baby: a baby born to a woman as a result of fertilization of one of her ova by her husband's sperm outside her body.

tetanus (lockjaw): an acute infectious disease, affecting the nervous system, caused by the bacterium *Clostridium tetani*.

tetracycline: one of a group of antibiotic compounds.

thalamus: part of the vertebrate *forebrain that lies above the *hypothalamus.

thalidomide: a drug that was formerly used as a sedative. If taken during the first three months of pregnancy, it was found to cause foetal abnormalities.

thermodynamics: the study of the laws that govern the conversion of energy from one form to another, the direction in which heat will flow, and the availability of energy to do work.

thorax: the anterior region of the body trunk of animals.

thrombosis: a condition in which the blood changes from a liquid to a solid state and produces a blood clot (*thrombus*).

thymus: an organ, present only in vertebrates, that is concerned with development of *lymphoid tissue and hence the antibody-producing white blood cells (*lymphocytes) and the immune response.

thyroid: a large *endocrine gland situated in the base of the neck.

tibia: 1. The larger of the two bones of the lower hindlimb of terrestrial vertebrates, which articulates with the *femur at the knee and the *tarsus at the ankle. 2. The fourth segment of an insect's leg, which is attached to the femur.

tinnitus: any noise (buzzing, ringing, etc.) in the ear.

tonsil: a mass of *lymphoid tissue, several of which are situated at the back of the mouth and throat in higher vertebrates. In humans there are the *palatine tonsils* at the back of the mouth, *lingual tonsils* below the tongue, and *pharyngeal tonsils* (or **adenoids*) in the *pharynx.

tourniquet: a device to press upon an artery and prevent flow of blood through it, usually a cord, rubber tube, or tight bandage. Tourniquets are no longer recommended as a first-aid measure to stop bleeding from a wound; direct pressure on the wound itself is considered less harmful.

toxaemia: blood poisoning that is caused by toxins formed by *bacteria growing in a local site of infection.

toxic: having a poisonous effect; potentially lethal.

trachea: 1. The windpipe in air-breathing vertebrates. 2. An air channel in insects and most other terrestrial *arthropods.

trachoma: a chronic contagious eye

disease that is common in tropical regions.

traction: the application of a pulling force as a means of counteracting the natural tension in the tissues surrounding a broken bone.

tranquillizer: a drug that produces a calming effect, relieving anxiety and tension.

trauma: 1. A physical wound or injury. 2 (in psychology). An emotionally painful and harmful event, which may lead to *neurosis.

trench foot: blackening of the toes and the skin of the foot due to death of the superficial tissues and caused by prolonged immersion in cold water.

trichosis: any abnormal growth or disease of the hair.

trilobite: an extinct marine *arthropod belonging to the class Trilobita (some 4000 species), *fossils of which are found in deposits dating from the *Precambrian to the *Permian period (590–280 million years ago).

troposphere: see **earth's atmosphere**.

tuber: a swollen underground stem or root in certain plants.

tuberculosis: an infectious disease caused by the bacillus *Mycobacterium tuberculosis* and characterized by the formation of nodular lesions (tubercles) in the tissues.

tumour: any abnormal swelling in or on a part of the body. The term is usually applied to an abnormal growth of tissue, which may be benign or malignant.

tweeter: a small loudspeaker capable of reproducing sounds of relatively high frequency.

tympanic cavity: see **middle ear**.

typhoid fever: an infection of the digestive system.

ulcer: a break in the skin or in the *mucous membrane lining the *alimentary tract that fails to heal and is often accompanied by inflammation.

ulna: the inner and longer bone of the forearm.

umbilical cord: the strand of tissue connecting the foetus to the *placenta.

upper atmosphere: the upper part of the *earth's atmosphere above about 300 km. This is the part of the atmosphere that cannot be reached by balloons.

urethra: the tube that conducts urine from the bladder to the exterior.

uric acid: the end product of purine breakdown in most primates, birds, terrestrial reptiles, and insects and also (except in primates) the major form in which metabolic nitrogen is excreted. Being fairly insoluble, uric acid can be expelled in solid form, which conserves valuable water in arid environments. The accumulation of uric acid in the synovial fluid (*synovia) of joints causes *gout.

uterus (womb): the organ of female mammals in which the embryo develops.

vaccination: a means of producing immunity to a disease by using a *vaccine.

vaccine: a special preparation of antigenic materials that can be used to stimulate the development of *antibodies and thus confer active immunity against a specific disease or number of diseases.

vacuole: a space within the *cytoplasm of a living *cell that is filled with air, water or other liquid, sap, or food particles.

vagina: the lower part of the female reproductive tract.

Van Allen belts (radiation belts): regions of intense radiation surrounding the earth, consisting of high-energy charged particles trapped in the earth's *magnetic field, within which they follow roughly helical paths.

varicose veins: veins that are distended, lengthened, and tortuous. The superficial veins of the legs are most commonly affected.

vas deferens: either of a pair of ducts that conduct *spermatozoa from the epididymis to the *urethra on ejaculation.

vasectomy: the surgical operation of cutting the *vas deferens. Bilateral vasectomy causes sterility and is an increasingly popular means of birth control.

vein: a blood vessel conveying blood towards the heart.

vena cava: either of the two main veins, conveying blood from the other veins to the right *atrium of the heart.

venereal disease: any infectious disease transmitted by sexual intercourse.

ventricle: 1. Either of the two lower chambers of the heart. The left ventricle receives blood from the pulmonary vein and pumps it into the *aorta. The right ventricle pumps blood from the *venae cavae into the pulmonary artery. 2. One of the four fluid-filled cavities within the brain.

vertebra: one of the 33 bones of which the backbone is composed.

vertigo: a disabling sensation in which the affected individual feels that either he or his surroundings are in a state of constant movement.

villus: a microscopic outgrowth from the surface of some tissues and organs, which serves to increase the surface area of the organ.

virus: a particle that is too small to be seen with a light microscope or to be trapped by filters but is capable of independent metabolism and reproduction within a living cell.

viscera: the organs within the body cavities, especially the organs of the abdominal cavities.

viscosity: a measure of the resistance to flow that a fluid offers when it is subjected to shear stress.

vitamin: one of a number of organic compounds required by living organisms in relatively small amounts to maintain normal health.

viviparity: 1 (in zoology). A form of reproduction in animals in which the developing embryo obtains its nourishment directly from the mother via the *placenta or by other means. 2 (in botany). *a.* A form of asexual reproduction in certain plants. *b.* The development of young plants on the inflorescence of the parent plant.

volcano: a vent in the earth's crust through which *magma, associated gases, and ash are extruded on to the surface.

volt: the *SI unit of electricity potential, potential difference, or *e.m.f. defined as the difference of potential between two points on a conductor carrying a constant current of one *ampere when the power dissipated between the points is one *watt.

watt: the *SI unit of power, defined as a power of one *joule per second.

whiplash injury: damage to the ligaments, vertebrae, spinal cord, or nerve roots in the neck region, caused by sudden jerking back of the head and neck.

white dwarf: a star of low mass in its final phase of stellar evolution, resulting from its gravitational collapse after its thermonuclear fuel has been exhausted. *See also* Hertzsprung–Russell diagram.

whitlow: an abscess affecting the pulp of the fingertip.

X-rays: *electromagnetic radiation of shorter wavelength than ultraviolet radiation and longer wavelength than gamma radiation.

yaws: a tropical infectious disease caused by the presence of the *spirochaete *Treponema pertenue* in the skin and its underlying tissues.

zooplankton: the animal component of *plankton.

WEIGHTS AND MEASURES

Note. The conversion factors are not exact unless so marked. They are given only to the accuracy likely to be needed in everyday calculations.

1. British and American, with metric equivalents

Linear Measure

1 inch	= 25.4 millimetres exactly
1 foot = 12 inches	= 0.3048 metre exactly
1 yard = 3 feet	= 0.9144 metre exactly
1 (statute) mile = 1,760 yards	= 1.609 kilometres

Square Measure

1 square inch	= 6.45 sq. centimetres
1 square foot = 144 sq. in.	= 9.29 sq. decimetres
1 square yard = 9 sq. ft.	= 0.836 sq. metre
1 acre = 4,840 sq. yd.	= 0.405 hectare
1 square mile = 640 acres	= 259 hectares

Cubic Measure

1 cubic inch	= 16.4 cu. centimetres
1 cubic foot = 1,728 cu. in.	= 0.0283 cu. metre
1 cubic yard = 27 cu. ft.	= 0.765 cu. metre

Capacity Measure

British

1 pint = 20 fluid oz.	= 0.568 litre
= 34.68 cu. in.	
1 quart = 2 pints	= 1.136 litres
1 gallon = 4 quarts	= 4.546 litres
1 peck = 2 gallons	= 9.092 litres
1 bushel = 4 pecks	= 36.4 litres
1 quarter = 8 bushels	= 2.91 hectolitres

American dry

1 pint = 33.60 cu. in.	= 0.550 litre
1 quart = 2 pints	= 1.101 litres
1 peck = 8 quarts	= 8.81 litres
1 bushel = 4 pecks	= 35.3 litres

American liquid

1 pint = 16 fluid oz.	= 0.473 litre
= 28.88 cu. in.	
1 quart = 2 pints	= 0.946 litre
1 gallon = 4 quarts	= 3.785 litres

Avoirdupois Weight

1 grain	= 0.065 gram
1 dram	= 1.772 grams
1 ounce = 16 drams	= 28.35 grams
1 pound = 16 ounces	= 0.4536 kilogram
= 7,000 grains	(0.45359237 exactly)
1 stone = 14 pounds	= 6.35 kilograms
1 quarter = 2 stones	= 12.70 kilograms
1 hundredweight = 4 quarters	= 50.80 kilograms
1 (long) ton = 20 hundredweight	= 1.016 tonnes
1 short ton = 2,000 pounds	= 0.907 tonne

2. Metric, with British equivalents

Linear Measure

1 millimetre	= 0.039 inch
1 centimetre = 10 mm	= 0.394 inch
1 decimetre = 10 cm	= 3.94 inches
1 metre = 10 dm	= 1.094 yards
1 decametre = 10 m	= 10.94 yards
1 hectometre = 100 m	= 109.4 yards
1 kilometre = 1,000 m	= 0.6214 mile

Square Measure

1 square centimetre	= 0.155 sq. inch
1 square metre	= 1.196 sq. yards
1 are = 100 sq. metres	= 119.6 sq. yards
1 hectare = 100 ares	= 2.471 acres
1 square kilometre	= 0.386 sq. mile

Cubic Measure

1 cubic centimetre	= 0.061 cu. inch
1 cubic metre	= 1.308 cu. yards

Capacity Measure

1 millilitre	= 0.002 pint (British)
1 centilitre = 10 ml	= 0.018 pint
1 decilitre = 10 cl	= 0.176 pint
1 litre = 10 dl	= 1.76 pints
1 decalitre = 10 l	= 2.20 gallons
1 hectolitre = 100 l	= 2.75 bushels
1 kilolitre = 1,000 l	= 3.44 quarters

Weight

1 milligram	= 0.015 grain
1 centigram = 10 mg	= 0.154 grain
1 decigram = 10 cg	= 1.543 grains
1 gram = 10 dg	= 15.43 grains
1 decagram = 10 g	= 5.64 drams
1 hectogram = 100 g	= 3.527 ounces
1 kilogram = 1,000 g	= 2.205 pounds
1 tonne (metric ton) = 1,000 kg	= 0.984 (long) ton

3. Temperature

Fahrenheit: water boils (under standard conditions) at 212° and freezes at 32°.
Celsius or Centigrade: water boils at 100° and freezes at 0°.
Kelvin: water boils at 375.15 K and freezes at 273.15 K.
$F = 9C/5 + 32$ or $F + 40 = 9(C + 40)/5$.
$C = 5(F - 32)/9$ or $C + 40 = 5(F + 40)/9$.
$K = C + 273.15$.

4. The power notation

This expresses concisely any power of ten (any number that is composed of factors 10), and is sometimes used in the dictionary. 10^2 or ten squared $= 10 \times 10 = 100$; 10^3 or ten cubed $= 10 \times 10 \times 10 = 1{,}000$. Similarly, $10^4 = 10{,}000$, and $10^{10} = 1$ followed by ten noughts $= 10{,}000{,}000{,}000$. Proceeding in the opposite direction, dividing by ten and subtracting one from the index, we have $10^2 = 100$, $10^1 = 10$, $10^0 = 1$, $10^{-1} = \frac{1}{10}$, $10^{-2} = \frac{1}{100}$, and so on; $10^{-10} = 1/10^{10} = 1/10{,}000{,}000{,}000$.

5. The Metric Prefixes

	Abbreviations	*Factors*
deca	da	10
hecto	h	10^2
kilo	k	10^3

mega	M	10^{6}
giga	G	10^{9}
tera	T	10^{12}
peta	P	10^{15}
exa	E	10^{18}
deci	d	10^{-1}
centi	c	10^{-2}
milli	m	10^{-3}
micro	μ	10^{-6}
nano	n	10^{-9}
pico	p	10^{12-}
femto	f	10^{-15}
atto	a	10^{-18}

Pronunciations and derivations of these are given at their alphabetical places in the dictionary. They may be applied to any units of the metric system: hectogram (abbr. hg) = 100 grams; kilowatt (abr.kW) = 1,000 watts; megahertz (MHz) = 1 million hertz; centimetre (cm) = $\frac{1}{100}$ metre; microvolt (μV) = one millionth of a volt; picofarad (pF) = 10^{-12} farad, and are sometimes applied to other units (megabit, microinch).

6. Chemical Notation

The symbol for a molecule (such as H_2O, CH_4, H_2SO_4) shows the symbols for the elements contained in it (C = carbon, H = hydrogen, etc.), followed by a subscript numeral denoting the number of atoms of each element in the molecule where this number is more than one. For example, the water molecule (H_2O) contains two atoms of hydrogen and one of oxygen.

THE CHEMICAL ELEMENTS

Element	*Symbol*	*Atomic Number*
actinium	Ac	89
aluminium	Al	13
americium	Am	95
antimony	Sb	51
argon	Ar	18
arsenic	As	33
astatine	At	85
barium	Ba	56
berkelium	Bk	97
beryllium	Be	4
bismuth	Bi	83
boron	B	5
bromine	Br	35
cadmium	Cd	48
caesium	Cs	55
calcium	Ca	20
californium	Cf	98
carbon	C	6
cerium	Ce	58
chlorine	Cl	17
chromium	Cr	24
cobalt	Co	27
copper	Cu	29
curium	Cm	96
dysprosium	Dy	66
eisteinium	Es	99
erbium	Er	68
europium	Eu	63
fermium	Fm	100
fluorine	F	9
francium	Fr	87
gadolinium	Gd	64
gallium	Ga	31
germanium	Ge	32
gold	Au	79
hafnium	Hf	72
helium	He	2
holmium	Ho	67
hydrogen	H	1
indium	In	49
iodine	I	53
iridium	Ir	77
iron	Fe	26
krypton	Kr	36
lanthanum	La	57
lawrencium	Lr	103
lead	Pb	82
lithium	Li	3
lutetium	Lu	71
magnesium	Mg	12
manganese	Mn	25
mendelevium	Md	101
mercury	Hg	80
molybdenum	Mo	42
neodymium	Nd	60
neon	Ne	10
neptunium	Np	93
nickel	Ni	28
niobium	Nb	41
nitrogen	N	7
nobelium	No	102
osmium	Os	76
oxygen	O	8
palladium	Pd	46
phosphorus	P	15
platinum	Pt	78
plutonium	Pu	94
polonium	Po	84
potassium	K	19
praseodymium	Pr	59
promethium	Pm	61
protactinium	Pa	91
radium	Ra	88
radon	Rn	86
rhenium	Re	75
rhodium	Rh	45

Element	*Symbol*	*Atomic Number*
rubidium	Rb	37
ruthenium	Ru	44
samarium	Sm	62
scandium	Sc	21
selenium	Sc	34
silicon	Se	14
silver	Ag	47
sodium	Na	11
strontium	Sr	38
sulphur	S	16
tantalum	Ta	73
technetium	Tc	43
tellurium	Te	52
terbium	Tb	65
thallium	Tl	81
thorium	Th	90
thulium	Tm	69
tin	Sn	50
titanium	Ti	22
tungsten	W	74
uranium	U	92
vanadium	V	23
xenon	Xe	54
ytterbium	Yb	70
yttrium	Y	39
zinc	Zn	30
zirconium	Zr	40

LOGIC SYMBOLS

and	$\wedge$
belongs to	$\in$
does not belong to	$\notin$
is equivalent to	$\leftrightarrow$
there exists	$\exists$
for all	$\forall$
implies	$\rightarrow$
is included in	$\subset$
is not included in	$\not\subset$
includes	$\supset$
does not include	$\not\supset$
intersection	$\cap$
or	$\vee$
union	$\cup$

PROOF-CORRECTION MARKS

(Where appropriate, the marks should also be used by copy-editors in marking up copy)

Instruction to Printer	*Textual mark*	*Marginal mark*
Correction made in error. Leave unchanged	----- under character(s) to remain	⊘
Remove extraneous marks or replace damaged character(s)	Encircle marks to be removed or character(s) to be changed	×
(Wrong fount) Replace by character(s) of correct fount	Encircle character(s) to be changed	⊗
Insert in text the matter indicated in the margin	⋏	New matter followed by ⋏
Delete	Stroke through character(s) to be deleted	∂
Substitute character or substitute part of one or more word(s)	/ through character or ⊢—⊣ through word(s)	New character or New word(s)
Set in or change to italic type	—— under character(s) to be set or changed	⊔⊔
Change italic to roman type	Encircle character(s) to be changed	⊔⊔ (struck through)
Set in or change to capital letter(s)	≡ under character(s) to be set or changed	≡
Change capital letter(s) to lower-case letter(s)	Encircle character(s) to be changed	≡ (struck through)
Set in or change to small capital letter(s)	= under character(s) to be set or changed	=
Change small capital letter(s) to lower-case letter(s)	Encircle character(s) to be changed	= (struck through)
Set in or change to bold type	∿∿ under character(s) to be changed	∿∿
Set in or change to bold italic type	—— / ∿∿ under character(s) to be changed	⊔⊔ / ∿∿
Invert type	Encircle character to be inverted	∩
Substitute or insert character in 'superior' position	/ through character or ⋏ where required	ץ under character (e.g. ³ץ)
Substitute or insert character in 'inferior' position	/ through character or ⋏ where required	⋏ over character (e.g. ⋏₈)
Insert full point or decimal point	⋏ where required	⊙
Insert colon, semi-colon, comma, etc.	⋏ where required	⊙/;/,/(/)/[/]/ ’ ’ “ ”
Rearrange to make a new paragraph here	⌐ before first word of new paragraph	⌐
Run on (no new paragraph)	⊂⊃ between paragraphs	⊂⊃
Transpose characters or words	⊔⊓ between characters or words to be transposed, numbered where necessary	⊔⊓
Insert hyphen	⋏ where required	⊢-⊣
Insert rule	⋏ where required	⊢1em⊣ ⊢4mm⊣ (i.e. give the size of the rule in the marginal mark)
Insert oblique	⋏ where required	⊘
Insert space between characters	| between characters	Y
Insert space between words	Y between words	Y
Reduce space between characters	| between characters	⊤
Reduce space between words	⊤ between words	⊤
Equalize space between characters or words	| between characters or words	X

WORD INDEX

For 'Word Formation', 'Vocabulary', 'Grammar', 'Principles of Punctuation', 'Words Commonly Misspelt', 'Clichés and Modish and Inflated Diction', 'Pronunciation', and 'English Overseas'

Words and phrases are entered in strict alphabetical order, ignoring spaces between two or more words forming a compound or phrase (hence *as for* follows *ascendant* and *court martial* follows *courtesy*).

An asterisk is placed in front of forms or spellings that are not recommended; reference to the page(s) indicated will show the reason for this ruling in each case.

A

C

D

E

F

H

I

J

K

L

M

O

P

Q

R

T

U

V

W

X

Y

Z

SUBJECT INDEX